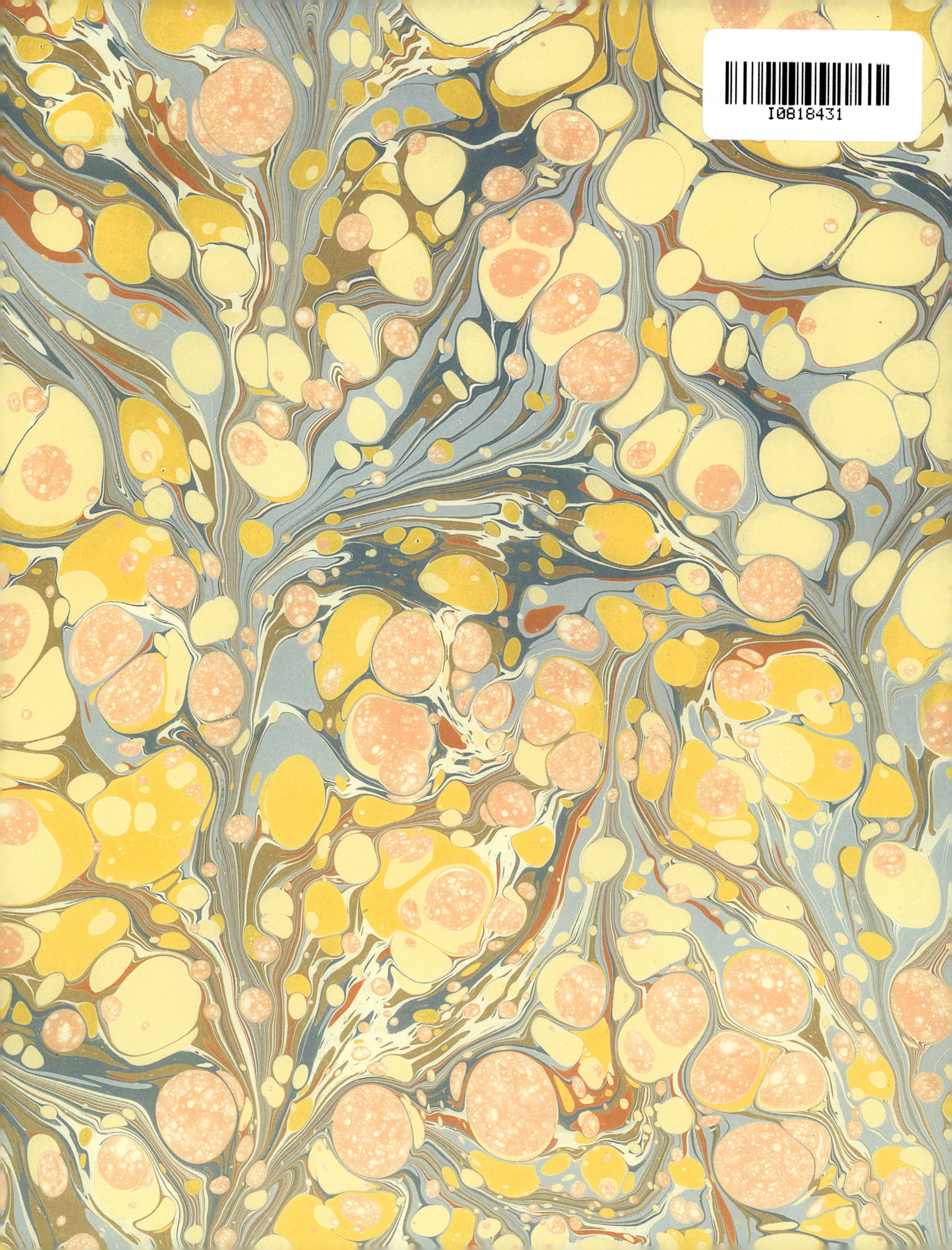
I0818431

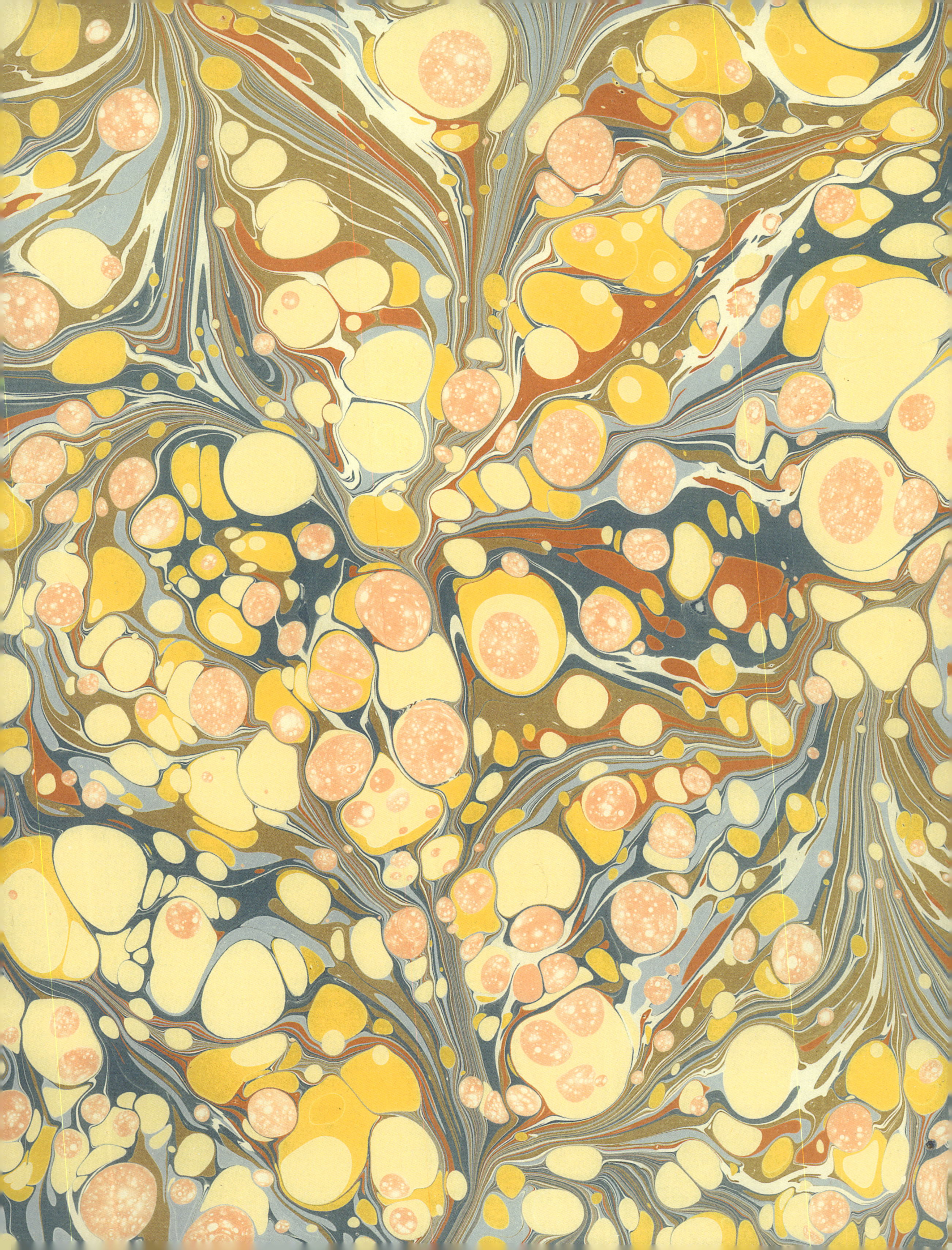

TURNER & CONSTABLE

Turner & Constable

Rivals and Originals

Edited by Amy Concannon

With contributions by Thomas Ardill, Frank Bowling, Nicole Cochrane, Sarah Gould, Richard Johns, Katharine Martin, Nicola Moorby, Bridget Riley, Nicholas Robbins, Emma Roodhouse, George Shaw, Emma Stibbon and Joyce H. Townsend

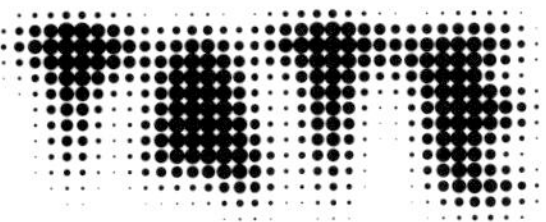

Amy Concannon is Manton Senior Curator, Historic British Art at Tate.
Thomas Ardill is Curator of Paintings, Prints and Drawings at the London Museum.
Nicole Cochrane is Assistant Curator, Historic British Art (1790–1850) at Tate.
Sarah Gould is Assistant Professor in History of Art at the Université Paris 1- Panthéon Sorbonne.
Richard Johns is Senior Lecturer in History of Art at the University of York.
Katharine Martin is a curator and PhD researcher at the Victoria and Albert Museum / University of Sussex.
Nicola Moorby is Curator, Historic British Art (1790–1850) at Tate.
Nicholas Robbins is Lecturer in British Art 1700–1900 at University College London.
Emma Roodhouse is Collections and Learning Curator: Art at Colchester and Ipswich Museums.
Joyce H. Townsend is Senior Conservation Scientist at Tate.

First published 2025 by order of the Tate Trustees by Tate Publishing, a division of Tate Enterprises Ltd, Millbank, London SW1P 4RG
www.tate.org.uk/publishing

on the occasion of the exhibition *Turner and Constable*

Tate Britain, London
27 November 2025 – 12 April 2026

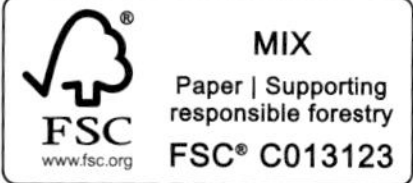

Turner and Constable is in partnership with LVMH.

LVMH

Supported by

the
HUO FAMILY
FOUNDATION

JAMES BARTOS

With additional support from the Turner and Constable Exhibition Supporters Circle:
Asbjorn Lunde Foundation, Inc.
Robert Lehman Foundation

Tate Americas Foundation and Tate Members

Research supported by the Manton Historic British Art Scholarship Fund.

A catalogue record for this book is available from the British Library

ISBN 978 1 84976 984 6 (hardback)
ISBN 978 1 84976 985 3 (paperback)

Distributed in the United States and Canada by ABRAMS, New York

Library of Congress Control Number: applied for

Designed by Joe Hales studio
Colour reproduction by DL Imaging, London
Printed and bound in Italy by Graphicom

Hardback front cover and paperback back cover: J.M.W. Turner, *The Burning of the Houses of Lords and Commons, October 16, 1834* exhibited 1835 (see no.162, pp.198–9)
Hardback back cover and paperback front cover: John Constable, *The White Horse* 1819 (see no.127, p.160)
Endpapers: Courtesy Jemma Lewis 2025

Measurements of artworks are given in centimetres, height before width, before depth.

CONTENTS

SUPPORTER'S FOREWORD

The 75 Maisons of the LVMH Group represent a unique heritage, often centuries old, deeply rooted in French and Western culture. LVMH Maisons are resolutely future-facing and continually reinvent themselves, drawing on their rich legacy or heritage and savoir-faire. Intimately engaged with French culture, arts and creative talents, LVMH has for over 30 years been an active partner to the world of culture, with an emphasis on access for the widest possible audience. The Group pursues corporate philanthropy initiatives in support of artistic, intellectual and scientific endeavours in France and around the world.

Tate has long played a vital role in supporting artists and inspiring creativity around the world. LVMH is proud to continue our enduring relationship with Tate by partnering on the landmark *Turner and Constable* exhibition at Tate Britain. We are honoured to support this major exhibition and contribute to the worldwide celebrations of the 250th birthday of J.M.W. Turner in 2025 and John Constable in 2026 – marking the legacy of two of Britain's most influential artists.

Jean-Paul Claverie
Advisor to Bernard Arnault, Chairman and
Chief Executive of LVMH

LVMH

DIRECTOR'S FOREWORD

This exhibition is organised to mark the 250th anniversary of the births of J.M.W. Turner and John Constable, born in 1775 and 1776, respectively. While they have often been compared, in their own time and to this day, this is the first major exhibition to look in tandem at Britain's two most famous and beloved landscape artists. As such it will allow visitors to appreciate afresh, and to compare, the evolution of their practices as true originals. Between them, they reinvented and elevated the field of landscape painting, laying the foundations for a rich posthumous legacy, from Impressionism and other aspects of modern art into the twentieth century. Turner and Constable were contemporaries, colleagues and rivals. The exhibition aims to reveal both the similarities and significant differences of their aims, experiences and extraordinary bodies of work.

Turner, a trades-class Londoner, was fast out of the gates, while Constable, born into an affluent and genteel Suffolk family, had his first taste of success a good decade later. When considering their contributions, it should also be remembered that Turner outlived Constable by fourteen years, his career stretching into the Victorian age, but by challenging the artistic norms of their day, both were subject to criticism for the innovations they brought to landscape painting. Their posthumous reputations have been consistently equal but for most of his lifetime Constable felt overshadowed by Turner. For all that, there were moments when they went head-to-head in the competitive arena of the Royal Academy's annual exhibition, and this exhibition re-stages one of those occasions by bringing together Constable's *Salisbury Cathedral from the Meadows* with Turner's *Caligula's Palace and Bridge* – the clash of 'fire and water', as one critic put it.

Turner's habit as an inveterate traveller across Europe fuelled his work. Though Constable made work in a much more varied array of places than is commonly known – including the Lake District, Dorset, London, and Sussex – we associate him with his native 'Constable Country', a square mile or so on the River Stour, the Suffolk/Essex border. Constable's intense and persistent focus on his native landscape catalysed his innovative and relentless pursuit of a naturalistic representation of landscape, while Turner adopted a far more stylised approach to his geographically and historically expansive subjects, one of drama, amplification and maximum effect. His works often tran scend the day-to-day, whether his motif was factual or imaginary.

The enormous influence Constable and Turner have had on subsequent art, and culture generally, is reflected in the international dispersal of their work. We are enormously grateful to all the lenders who have parted with their works for this special exhibition. These include paintings that have not been seen in London in many years, such as Turner's *The Burning of the Houses of Lords and Commons* 1835 (Cleveland Museum of Art) which has not been seen in a public exhibition in the UK since 1883; Turner's *Juliet and her Nurse* (private collection) has not been exhibited in the UK since Turner showed it at the Royal Academy in 1836. Constable's oil sketch, *The Opening of Waterloo Bridge, seen from Whitehall Stairs*, recently rediscovered and lent from a private collection, has no record of being exhibited at all. A number of other works have not been seen in London since the 1970s, including Turner's *Fifth Plague of Egypt* (Indianapolis Museum at Newfields) and *Ancient Italy – Ovid Banished From Rome* (lent in honour of Richard Feigen by his children and grandchildren, in memoriam).

Many loans to the exhibition are star works in museum collections. We thank our colleagues at the Victoria and Albert Museum and the Royal Academy in London, the Clark Art Institute, Williamstown, and the Yale Center for British Art, New Haven, for lending significant quantities of works. The Frick Collection, New York, the National Gallery of Art, Washington, Art Institute of Chicago, the Huntington Art

Collection, California, Philadelphia Museum of Art, and National Galleries of Scotland have also loaned key works. Indeed we are very grateful to all the institutional lenders to the exhibition. It is also a special privilege to be able to share so many works from private collections, and it is a mark of the passion for these artists that individuals have been so enthusiastic and kind in the lending of works. Without their generosity this exhibition would be much the poorer.

We at Tate have the honour of being custodians of the Turner Bequest, a remarkable group of nearly 300 oil paintings and around 37,000 sketches and watercolours left by the artist to the nation and housed in the Clore Gallery at Tate Britain. This legacy has not only served to perpetuate the memory of Turner's achievements but has also given rise to an abundance of scholarship. So vast is Turner's output and so many the thematic avenues through it that Turner's work has spawned innumerable monographic exhibitions. To only a slightly lesser degree the same can be said of Constable, whose work, thanks to the bequest in 1888 from his daughter, Isabel, is held in greatest number by the Victoria and Albert Museum. We thank the V&A for the seventeen loans they have contributed to the exhibition.

Turner and Constable: Rivals and Originals is curated by Amy Concannon, Manton Senior Curator of Historic British Art at Tate, who has brought fresh insight to this project and led it with extraordinary determination and vision. She was joined by Professor Mark Hallett, then at the Paul Mellon Centre, in the early stages of the project before he became Märit Rausing Director of the Courtauld Institute of Art; we are grateful to Mark for his scholarly input. Especial thanks are due to David Thomson for his valuable advice at various stages of the project, and his generous support of Emmeline Hallmark's crucial role in fostering links with private collections. In its latter stages the project has benefitted from the enthusiasm and drive of Assistant Curator Nicole Cochrane and Exhibitions Assistant Bethany Husband. This exhibition builds on a wealth of scholarship on both artists, much of it generated by former Tate curators; we are fortunate that this project has been enriched by the advice of two of these, Anne Lyles and Ian Warrell. I also wish to thank all Tate colleagues who have contributed their knowledge and skills, including Carolyn Kerr, Kiko Noda, Nicola Moorby, Bella Probyn, Ella Baker, Jude Comyn and Jen Collingwood.

This book includes perspectives from a range of voices, and we are grateful to Thomas Ardill, Sarah Gould, Richard Johns, Katharine Martin, Nicholas Robbins, Emma Roodhouse, and colleagues Nicola Moorby, Joyce Townsend and Nicole Cochrane. Alice Chasey has skilfully managed the editorial production of this book. Turner's and Constable's lasting resonance is captured within a section of this book, and a film made for the exhibition, in which living artists reflect on what Turner and Constable mean to them, and we are grateful to Frank Bowling, Bridget Riley, George Shaw and Emma Stibbon for sharing their insights and reflections.

Turner and Constable is produced in partnership with LVMH. It is supported by the Huo Family Foundation and James Bartos, with additional support from the Turner and Constable Exhibition Supporters Circle: Asbjorn Lunde Foundation, Inc.; Robert Lehman Foundation, and from Tate Americas Foundation and Tate Members. Research for the exhibition has been supported by the Manton Historic British Art Scholarship Fund. This exhibition has been made possible by the provision of insurance through the Government Indemnity Scheme. Tate would like to thank HM Government for providing Government Indemnity and the Department for Digital, Culture, Media and Sport and Arts Council England for arranging the indemnity.

Alex Farquharson OBE
Director, Tate Britain

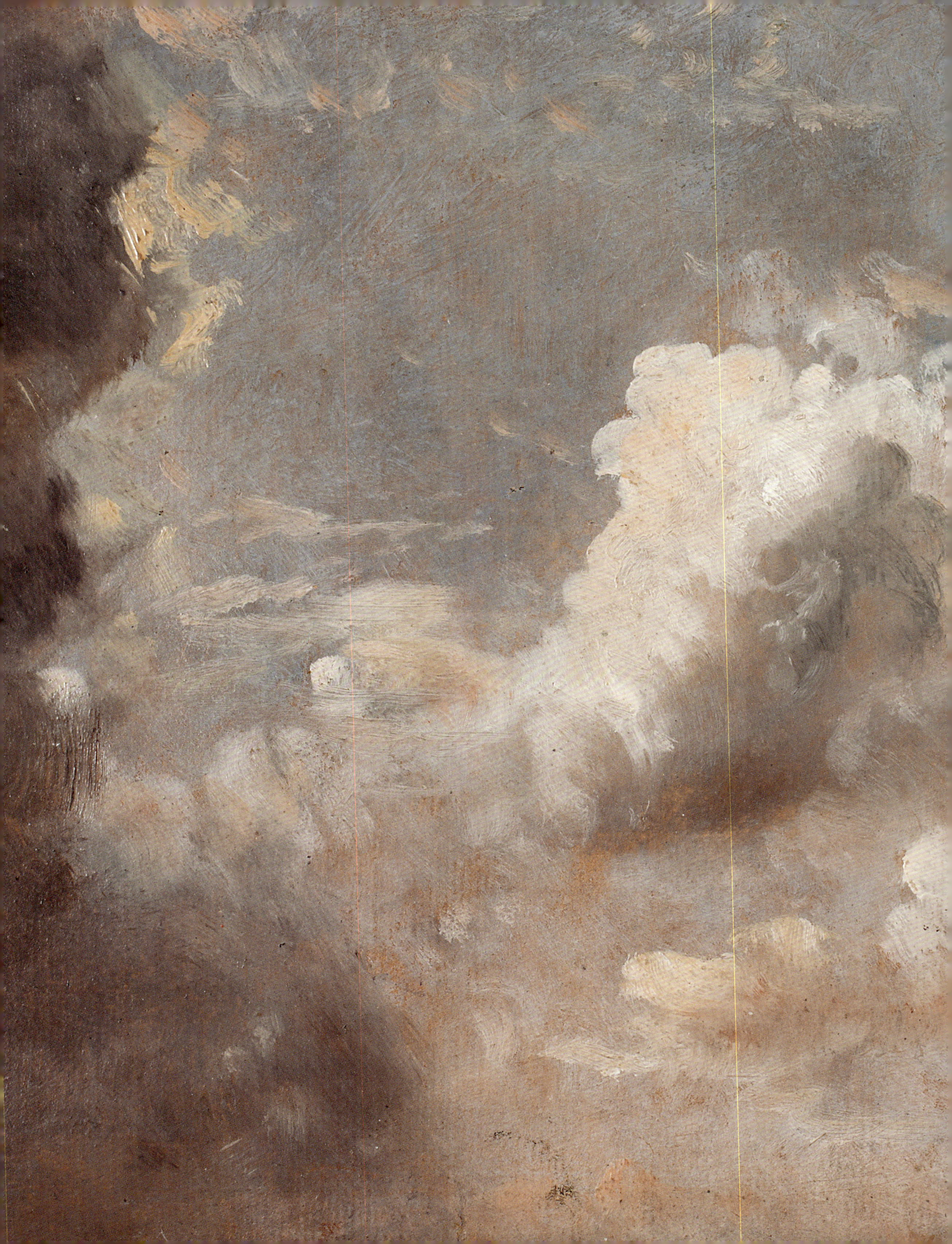

CURATOR'S ACKNOWLEDGEMENTS

This project owes to the expertise, enthusiasm, patience and kindness of so many people.

Nicholas Alfrey's University of Nottingham undergraduate module 'Romantic British Art' gave me my first brush with Turner and Constable. My subsequent immersion in their world has been enriched by scholars too numerous to mention, whose perspectives on these artists have shaped my own. I have been fortunate to call many of them colleagues and friends: Nicholas Alfrey, David Blayney Brown, Stephen Daniels, Richard Johns, Anne Lyles, Nicola Moorby, Martin Myrone, Cecilia and Nicholas Powell, Emma Roodhouse, Sam Smiles and Ian Warrell.

Mark Hallett became co-curator of the exhibition in its early stages, and I am very grateful to him for his insights. The exhibition has also been shaped by conversations with David Thomson, whose knowledge, advice and generosity were a vital catalyst. Emmeline Hallmark, Anne Lyles and Ian Warrell have played important roles, too, providing warm-hearted encouragement and valuable guidance as the exhibition evolved. It is stronger thanks to all their input.

Learning about Turner and Constable from the viewpoint of artists has been an immense privilege. Frank Bowling, George Shaw, Emma Stibbon and Bridget Riley have written personal reflections for this book. Each has been so welcoming, generously giving their time to talk and appear in a film for the exhibition. Along with the authors of this book's essays, their rich contributions show how alive the legacy of Turner and Constable is. I am extremely grateful to them all.

Fellow museum professionals have given much support along the way, be it through advocacy of loans or otherwise, and I would like to thank: Patricia Allerston, Laurie Bassam, Esther Bell, Antonia Boström, Emma Boyd, Emerson Bowyer, Xavier Bray, Caroline Campbell, John Chu, Jay A. Clark, Nicola Coleby, Tara Contractor, Martina Droth, Rebecca England, Kaywin Feldman, James Finch, Jenny Gaschke, Ketty Gottardo, Melissa Gustin, Grace Hailstone, Hannah Higham, Niall Hodson, Imogen Holmes-Roe, Frederick Ilchman, Elizabeth Jacklin, Franklin Kelly, Cory Korkow, Lucinda Lax, Heather Lemonedes Brown, Elenor Ling, Melinda McCurdy, Sarah Moulden, Aimee Ng, Victoria Partridge, Lucy Peltz, Christine Riding, Xavier F. Salomon, Robert Schindler, Karen Serres, Xa Sturgis, Hedley Swain, Jennifer A. Thompson, Charlotte Topsfield, Edward Town, Francesca Vanke and Clarrie Wallis.

I am also grateful for the belief in the project by the private lenders who have generously shared works for display.

Support of all kinds has come from many directions. I am very grateful to: Gill Adam, Amalia Amoedo, Tim Barringer, James Bartos, Ben Bowling, Sacha Bowling, Sara Chan, Adam Chen, Leo Costello, Anthony Crichton-Stuart, Elena Crippa, Margaret Dalivalle, Tom Davies, Philippa Feigen Malkin, Gillian Forrester, Julian Gascoigne, James Hamilton, Wyn Hughes, Daniel Katz, Andrew Loukes, Ailbhe Murphy, Jonathan Payn, Michael Rosenthal, Spencer Richards, Jacqueline Riding, Clementine Sinclair, Susan Sloman, Bob and Roberta Smith, Sarah Victoria Turner, Pieter van der Merwe and Andrew Wilton.

Colleagues past and present at Tate have gone the extra mile to ensure this project's success. Maria Balshaw, Alex Farquharson, Carolyn Kerr, Roland Rudd and Andrea Schlieker are owed especial thanks for their advice, enthusiasm and support throughout. Ella Baker, Jen Collingwood, Duncan Holden and Sarah Monteath have been excellent cheerleaders. Thanks also go to: Eleanor Appleby, Tabitha Barber, Bethan Bowers, Catherine Carver Dunn, Jude Comyn, Liam Darbon, David Dibosa, Arantza Dobbels Busto, Susan Doyon, Hilary Floe, Lauren Greenwood, Claire Gylphé, Dominique Heyse-Moore, Alice Insley, Carol Jacobi, Sam Jones, Christine Kurpiel, Margot Lombaert, Caroline McCarthy, Celeste McEvoy, Kirsteen McSwein, Chiedza Mhondoro, Bella Probyn, Charlotte Sanguinetti, Sophie Sardokie, Minnie Scott, Hamid Shabir, Andy Shiel, Gates Sofer, Perry Stewart, Liam Tebbs, David Wilson and Dale Wilson.

Nicole Cochrane, Bethany Husband and Kiko Noda have been patient and attentive colleagues, expertly handling the project's delivery. I am grateful to Alice Chasey, Aki Gurung, Joe Hales and Felicity Maunder for their commitment to and deft production of this book and to Sofia Contino, Scott Morris, and Reece Straw for their brilliant work on the film for the exhibition.

I am always in debt to my lovely parents, Joyce and Vincent. 'Thank you' does not do justice to the day in, day out roles played by Chris, and our young son, Rory, who, with unwitting diplomacy, alternated his choice of favourite artist between Turner and Constable with each passing month.

Amy Concannon
Manton Senior Curator, Historic British Art, Tate

John Constable *Cloud Study* (detail) 1822 (p.142)

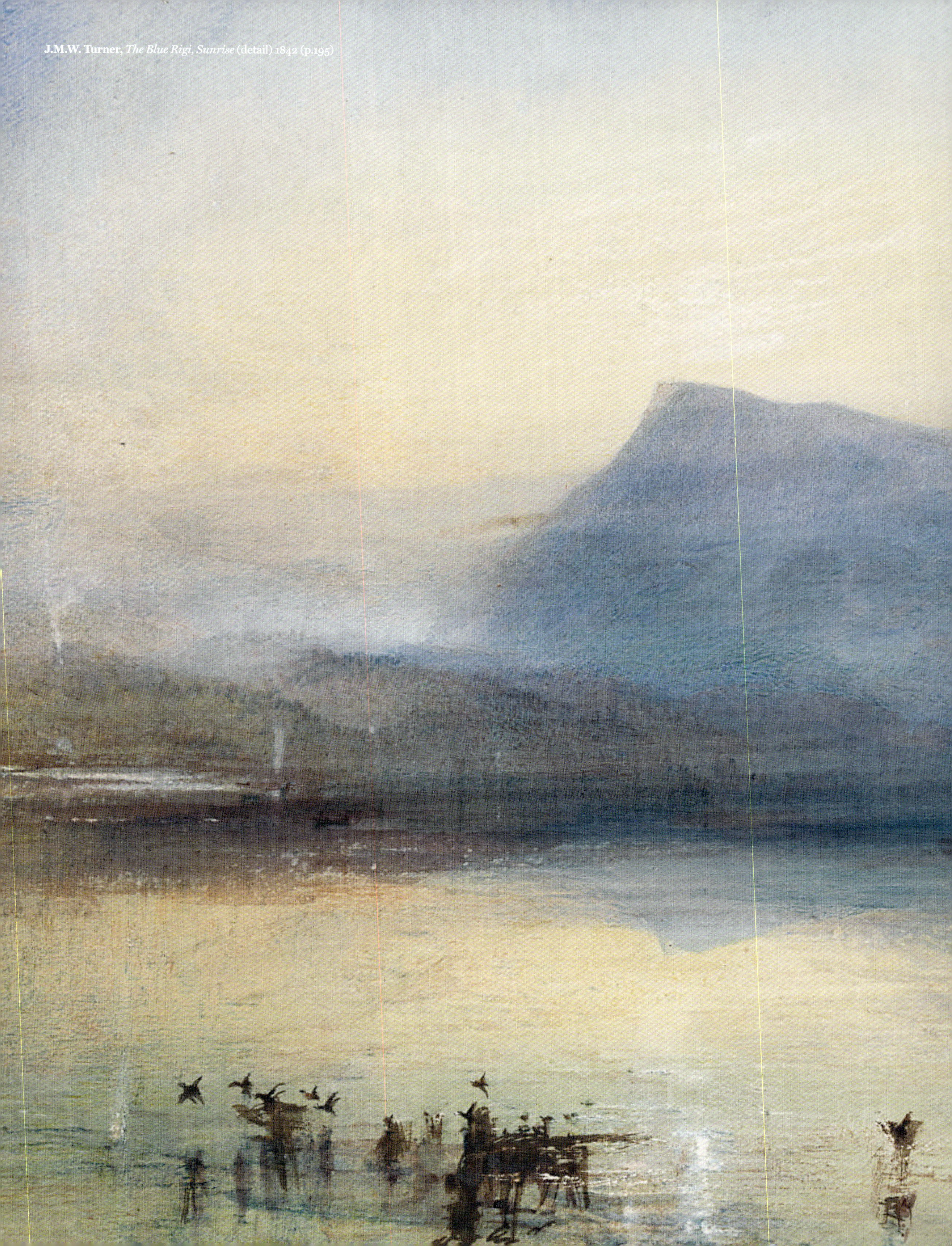
J.M.W. Turner, *The Blue Rigi, Sunrise* (detail) 1842 (p.195)

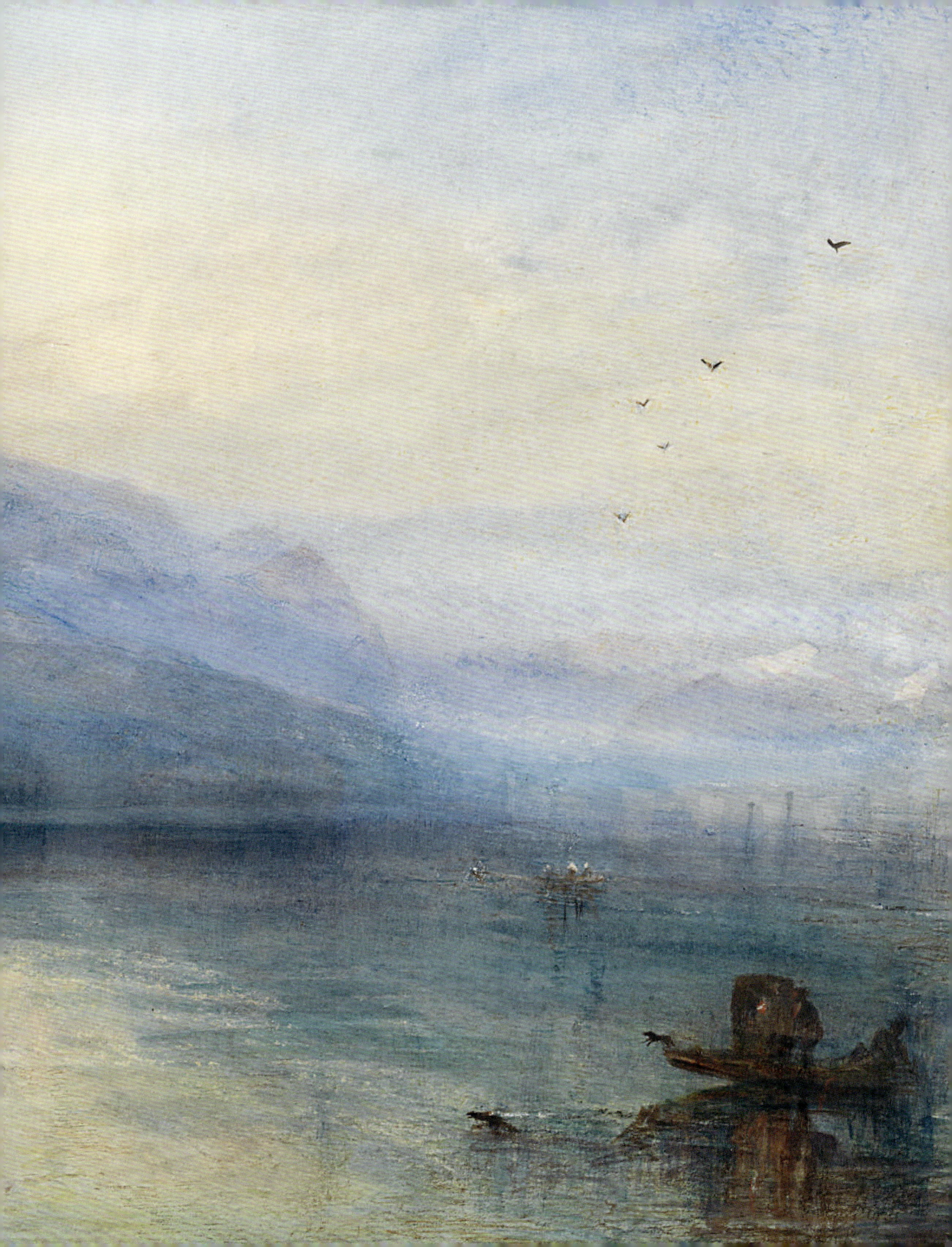

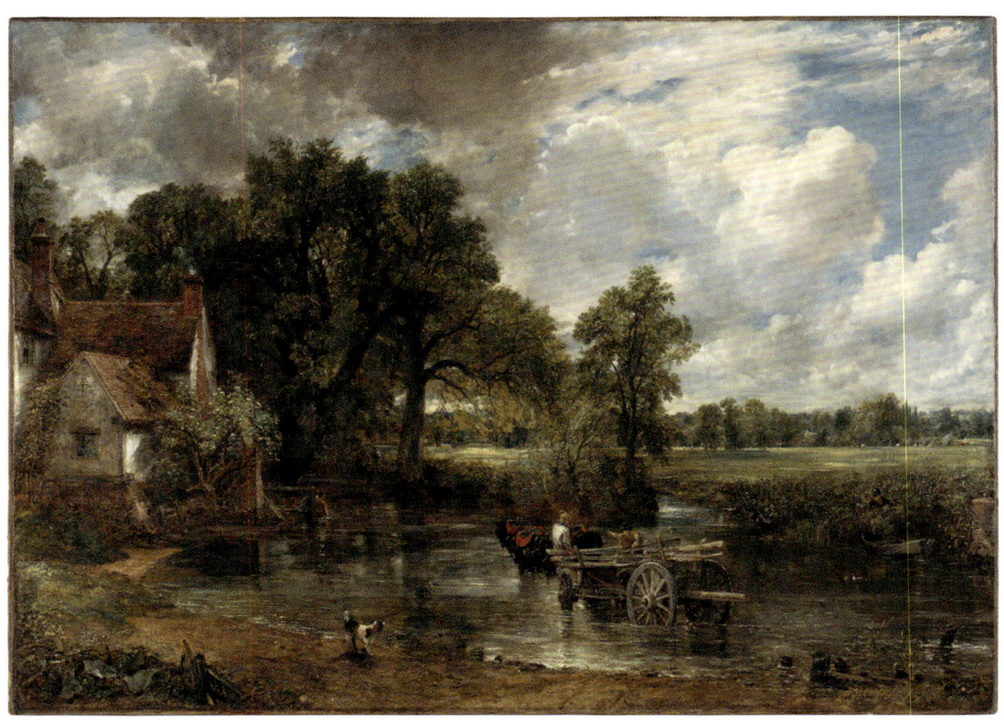

FIG. 1 **John Constable** *The Hay Wain* 1821
Oil paint on canvas, 130·2 × 185·4
The National Gallery, London. Presented by Henry Vaughan, 1886

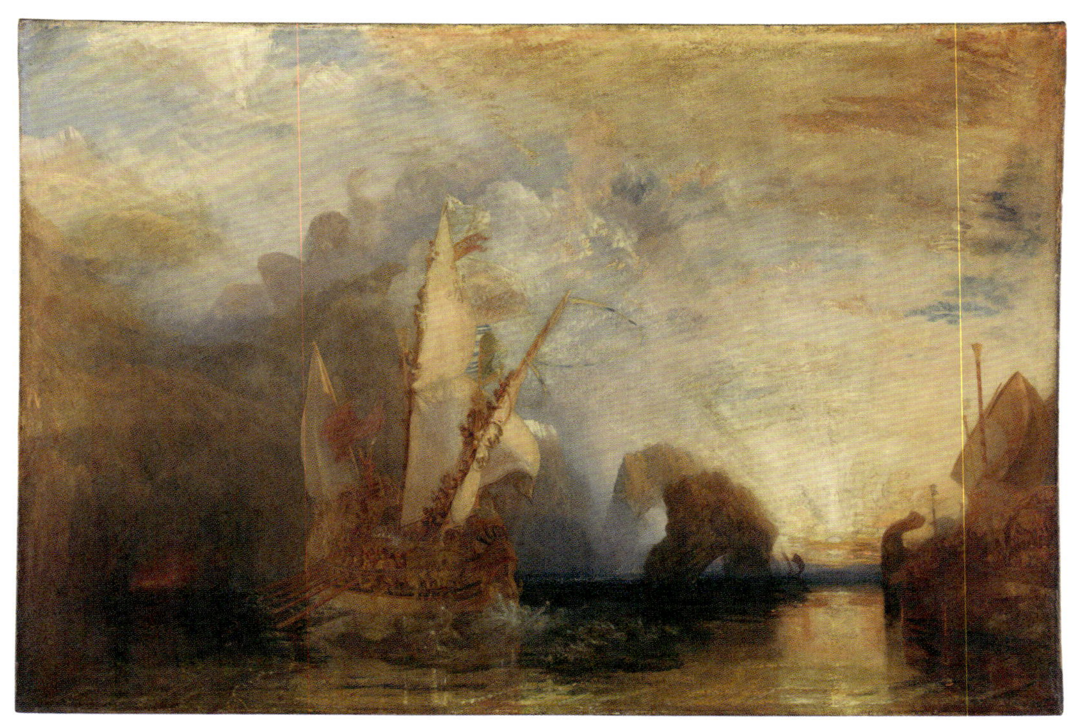

FIG. 2 **J.M.W. Turner** *Ulysses deriding Polyphemus – Homer's Odyssey* 1829
Oil paint on canvas, 132·5 × 203
The National Gallery, London. Turner Bequest, 1856

TURNER AND CONSTABLE: RIVALS AND ORIGINALS

AMY CONCANNON

'Fire and water' was how one critic summed up an arrangement of work by J.M.W. Turner and John Constable at the 1831 Royal Academy Summer Exhibition.[1] The works were *Caligula's Palace and Bridge* and *Salisbury Cathedral from the Meadows* respectively, a pairing that gave rise to a more lively, direct and sustained comparison of the two painters' work than ever seen before (nos.136 and 135). The art critics delighted in a raft of metaphors that cast Turner and Constable as sparring titans in command of opposing natural forces: *Caligula's Palace* was 'all heat' to *Salisbury Cathedral*'s 'humidity', the pairing a show of 'Turner's fire and Constable's rain'.[2] It was perhaps all part of Constable's plan. As a member of the hanging committee for the Royal Academy exhibition that year he was responsible for placing *Salisbury Cathedral* in dialogue with Turner's work. This juxtaposition of paintings played into an evolving idea of the two painters as opposites. Their work was directly compared in the press as early as 1819, when it was deemed 'equally successful', though Constable was said to have 'none of the poetry of Nature like Mr Turner, but ... more of her portraiture'.[3]

There could be 'no stronger contrast' to Turner than Constable, wrote one art critic in 1829. That year Constable's main exhibit was *Hadleigh Castle: The Mouth of the Thames, Morning after a Stormy Night* (no.132) and among Turner's was *Ulysses deriding Polyphemus* (fig.2). Constable was 'all truth' and Turner was 'all poetry: the one is silver, the other gold'.[4] If such comparisons were made even when their work hung in separate rooms, as was the case in 1829, Constable's arrangement of *Salisbury Cathedral* next to *Caligula's Palace* in 1831 was surely an outright invitation for all to continue the compare-and-contrast exercise between him and Turner. Indeed, this hang sparked something new in the dynamic between the two artists and their public image, becoming a prelude to the more famous incident of 1832, when Turner escalated the competition by adding a small daub of red paint to his pastel-coloured seascape *Helvoetsluys* (Fuji Art Museum, Tokyo) (fig.41, p.187). With elegant but savage simplicity, Turner's act detracted from the scattered red accents in Constable's *The Opening of Waterloo Bridge* (no.150). Constable reportedly said, 'He has been here ... and fired a gun'.[5] Arguably, in pairing his and Turner's works in 1831, Constable had fired the first shot.

Art history loves a rivalry: Leonardo da Vinci and Michelangelo, Reynolds and Gainsborough, Manet and Degas, Picasso and Matisse – the list goes on.[6] In the first history of art text to be written, Giorgio Vasari posited competition as a necessary ingredient in artistic progress; envy was deemed its unproductive counterpart. Peppered with references to Renaissance rivalries, Vasari's narrative draws heavily, however, on gossip and second-hand anecdotes, such that the text is perhaps a more colourful account than if its subjects had spoken for themselves.[7] In the case of Turner and Constable there is certainly plenty of fuel to spin a narrative of bitter rivalry between men who were poles apart in all but their choice of occupation. Take their domestic circumstances, for example. Constable was father to seven children and sole parent to them after the loss of his wife Maria, aged forty-one, in 1828. Turner fathered (but did not parent) two daughters and supposedly once said, 'I hate married men ... they never make any sacrifice to the Arts, but are always thinking of their duty to their wives and families, or some rubbish of that sort'.[8] While there is scant evidence to support one biographer's claim that Turner 'did not much like Constable', there is plenty of evidence – in part owing to the comparative abundance of his extant correspondence – of Constable's frustration at Turner's dominance.[9] He wrote:

> I feel deeply the honour of having found an original style & independent of him who would be Lord over all – I mean Turner.[10]

Pride that his art was distinct from Turner's could also slide into pettiness, as seen in his reference to Turner's print project and manifesto for landscape art *Liber Studiorum* (1807–19) as the 'liber stupidorum'.[11]

The only evidence we have of Turner's thoughts on Constable's art is unreliable. Critics had long been troubled by Constable's application of white highlights, which he believed added 'sparkle' to his paintings. Like 'splashing from a white-washing ceiling' was how Turner supposedly described the effect in 1829, presumably in relation to *Hadleigh Castle* (no.132). [12] That the remark was repeatedly attributed to Turner points to the enduring journalistic appetite for rivalry-stoking gossip. True or not, it may have got under Constable's skin; later that summer he relayed a remarkably similar comment about Turner's work, which he said he had heard compared to a 'spitting box at a hospital'. [13] Anyone would be forgiven for thinking that never the twain shall meet.

As their childhood homes show (figs.3 and 4), they certainly were from different worlds. Turner was a city boy, born in 1775 and raised in his father's barbershop in Covent Garden, the beating heart of commercial London. Constable was born a year later in the East Anglian countryside. His father's business wealth apparently allowed him to live in a 'very elegant house' like 'a country squire'. [14] Identified as a rising star, Turner's landscapes brought him fame extremely quickly. Constable took longer to reach the same professional milestones. When he was just beginning his studies at the Royal Academy Schools, Turner was being endorsed by senior artists and was elected an Associate Member of this all-important professional body. At twenty-seven and with a list of commissions he could hardly keep up with, Turner became a full Academician, a title that eluded Constable – who sold far less work than Turner – until he was fifty-three. Today, some 250 years after their birth, there are those who think of their work as being so different as to originate in different times altogether; indeed, many are surprised that they were born only a year apart. It might even come as a surprise that Constable was thought to rival Turner. Their obvious oppositional qualities continue to be invoked in order to say what the other's work is *not*. [15] But were they really so different? This project emerged from a wish to take stock, and to explore what happens when we put Turner and Constable together. It considers the divergent paths they took to become distinctive, original landscape painters as much as their fundamental similarities and their shared goal for landscape painting.

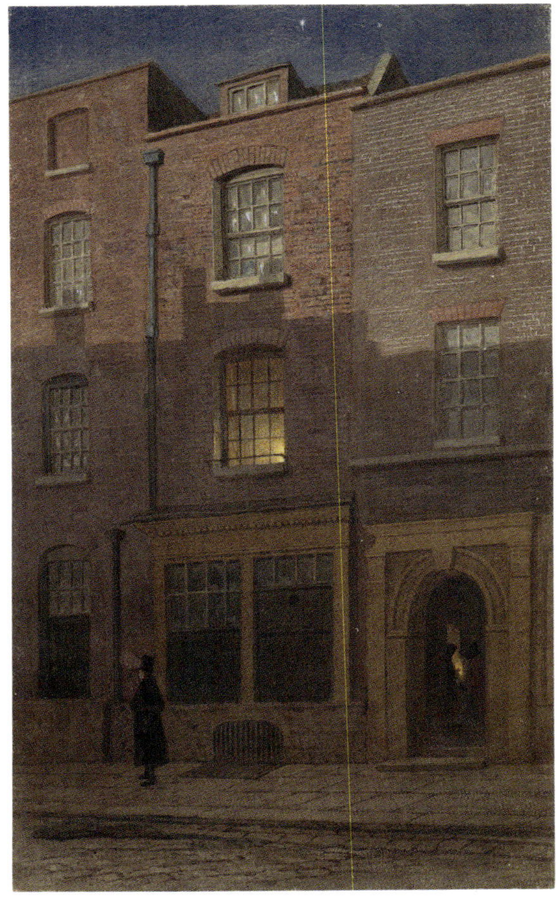

FIG. 3 **John Wykeham Archer**
J.M.W. Turner's birthplace in Maiden Lane, Covent Garden 1852
Watercolour, 35·5 × 22·2
The British Museum, London

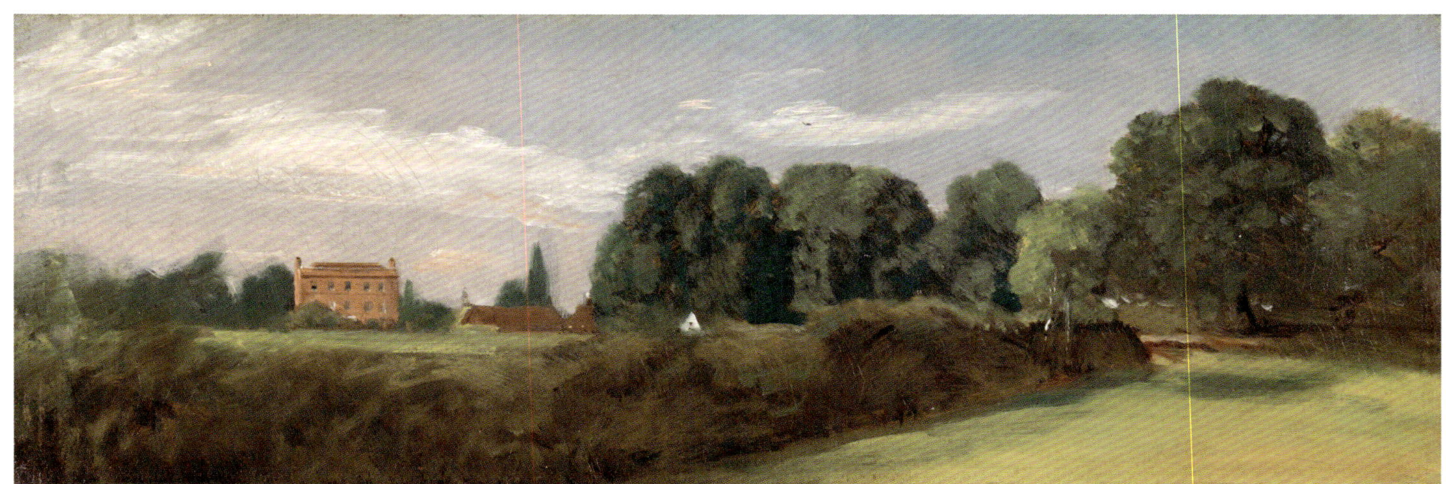

FIG. 4 **John Constable** *East Bergholt House* c.1809
Oil paint on canvas, 22·5 × 68·6
Tate. Presented by Miss Isabel Constable 1887

Two paths into landscape

The root of their innovative contribution to British art lies in their early dedication to the genre of landscape. As Royal Academy students they received no training in landscape nor in oil painting, the medium most exalted by the Academy. While they could look to the landscapes of recently deceased Academicians Richard Wilson and Thomas Gainsborough, their scholastic training centred on life drawing, a skill needed to produce what the Academy prized most: large, figural history paintings with morally edifying narratives (fig.6). Yet when it came to the art market, landscape was where the buzz was. [16] In its many formats – from popular entertainments like gigantic panoramas to maps, guidebooks and regional histories – this was a dynamic area of opportunity. Beyond its appeal to armchair tourists and souvenir seekers, landscape reflected war, colonisation, urbanisation, industrialisation and political upheaval, changes that quite literally shaped the world in which Turner and Constable lived. Landscape also accounted for a growing quota of exhibits at the Royal Academy Summer Exhibition. Here, in 1790 and 1802, when they were fifteen and twenty-six respectively, Turner and Constable made their exhibiting debut with landscapes of their own: Turner an architectural watercolour (no.4) and Constable an unknown work entitled simply 'Landscape' but which is believed to be an oil painting, possibly akin to the similarly dated *A Wood* (fig.5).

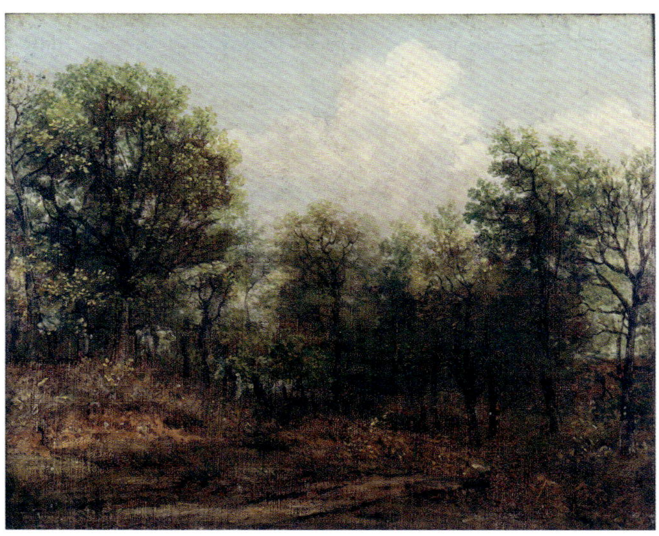

FIG. 5 **John Constable** *A Wood* c.1798 Oil paint on canvas, 76·5 × 98·4
Victoria and Albert Museum, London

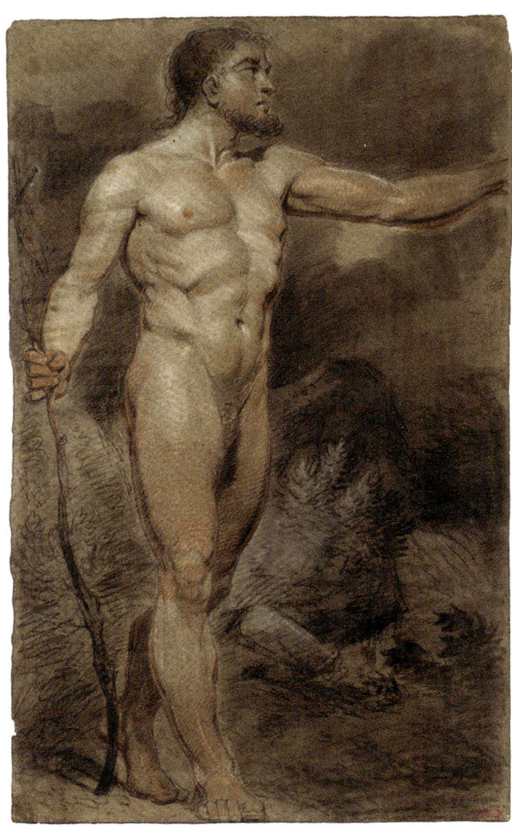

FIG. 6 **J.M.W. Turner** *A Standing Male Nude, holding a Staff and with Left Arm outstretched, in a Landscape Setting* c.1794–5
Black, white and red chalks with stump on laid buff-grey paper, 46·7 × 29·8
Tate. Accepted by the nation as part of the Turner Bequest 1856

Beyond the discrepancy in age at which they reached this milestone, these works say much about their different routes and the networks they cultivated as emerging artists. Turner received training to make topographically specific and carefully drawn watercolours by architectural draughtsman and engraver Thomas Malton (c.1751–1804). This was one of a number of positions during Turner's teens and early twenties that furnished him with skills, income or both. It was said of him that he 'had the passion for art ... but he had the far commoner passion for accumulating money'. [17] Who could blame him? While the Academy provided free tuition, there were no bursaries for materials or living costs. Living with his father in Covent Garden Turner would have been expected to earn his keep. Thus, alongside his studies at the Royal Academy, Turner seized opportunities – most of them centred around landscape – to sharpen and cash in on his talent. He coloured prints for top mezzotint engraver John Raphael Smith, whose studio was two streets away from the Turner barbershop; he sold watercolours of skies for use as the backdrop to amateur artists' drawings, and at physician Dr Thomas Monro's night school for young artists he copied landscape watercolours by established artists like John Robert Cozens and Edward Dayes. [18] These odd jobs were valuable beyond payment and networking. From them Turner learned the ingredients of a successful landscape, be it subject, composition or technique. Soon his own watercolours marked him out as a fast-rising star and from 1793 – as borne out by the recent rediscovery of *The Rising Squall* (no.7) – he was exhibiting oils. *Fishermen at Sea* exh. 1796 struck a winning balance between tradition and innovation (see no.12).

As a topographically specific scene that demonstrated skills easily monetised in the print trade, Turner's exhibition debut represented a commercial aspect of landscape art. Constable's early work of some twelve years later, on the other hand, more emphatically reflected academic ideals. In works like *A Wood*, a landscape in oil paint that revealed knowledge of celebrated precedents – a Gainsborough-esque woodland scene with the cool colouring of the Dutch school – Constable was trading in notions of 'high art', particularly those promoted by all-powerful and opinionated tastemaker Sir George Beaumont. Dedicated to landscape and Old Master connoisseurship, and disparaging of the rising prominence of watercolour (one of the very waves that Turner rode to fame), Beaumont was also a catalyst in Constable's entry into the London art world. At nineteen, Constable's mother arranged for him to meet Sir George, who was visiting family at Dedham; at twenty, during work experience at his uncle's brewery in north London, Constable met other antiquarians and artists who further inspired his earnest study of academic texts on painting and the Old Masters. [19] In 1799, after years of parental reticence, Constable moved to London to pursue his passion. He went there with a head full of ideas, a letter of introduction to the very well-networked landscapist (and Beaumont associate) Joseph Farington RA and, crucially, a bursary from his father. While not entirely insulated from the need to earn money, as a sideline in portraiture attests, Constable's entry into the art world was far more detached from the gritty business of making landscape pay. [20] Surrounded by his network of gentlemen connoisseurs he focused more than Turner could at the same stage in his career on his landscapes' intellectual qualities, rather than their market appeal.

Another patent difference is the geographical range of their subject matter. While much has been made of Constable's declaration 'I should paint my own places best', his motivation to depict the Stour went beyond his own familiarity and fondness for place, for such paintings of working landscapes chimed with a wider, patriotic visual culture of Britain's waterways as sites of productivity and improvement. [21] Constable's innovation was his assertion of the Stour's place in this narrative, and indeed his escalation of ambition for such scenes. No one before him had depicted them on such a grand scale or rendered them in such a bold style that prized the articulation of atmosphere – of breeziness, freshness and light – over finesse. [22] It is important too to remember that Constable is about much more than 'Constable country'. He went on a sketching tour to the Peak District in 1801 and exhibited paintings of the highly popular Lake District after touring there, just as Turner did, and included urban places in his six-foot repertoire. Indeed, while *Chain Pier, Brighton* was Turnerian in subject, his *Waterloo Bridge* may have reciprocally motivated Turner to see what he could do with Constable's vantage point (nos.142, 150 and 160). Even when enjoying success in France – of the kind Turner never achieved abroad despite his attempts to court it – Constable remained in Britain. Conversely, Turner would leave London late every summer and see as much of his chosen destination as possible, using winter to work up material either for print publishers or exhibition the following spring. Until Turner was forty the Napoleonic Wars rendered Europe out of bounds, but wherever he went he sought out the most resonant subjects. These might be of contemporary or historical importance, popular tourist destinations or places with impressive natural scenery, anywhere that allowed Turner to demonstrate his ability to tell the story of a place through dynamic compositions, intriguing detail and atmosphere.

Their processes for recording what they saw also reveal their different priorities. Never without a sketchbook, Turner favoured pencil drawings that became increasingly spare as his confidence grew. This allowed him to be fleet of foot – he was reported to have said that 'he could make 15 or 16 pencil sketches to one coloured'. [23] His occasional use of colour in the field is evidenced by a rain-spattered sketchbook (no.10) and atmospheric watercolours made later in life in favoured places like Venice and Margate. Constable's concern for authenticity of light effect and colour led him to sketch in oils outdoors, sometimes working on larger canvases outside too, as in *Flatford Mill* (no.102). Oil sketching outdoors had an art historical prestige, and while Constable was by no means the only artist to adopt the habit, he applied an unprecedented rigour and near obsession to the practice that has – for example in his cloud studies – resulted in some of the most celebrated examples of landscape in British art. [24] Turner, starting out with what might be termed a 'time is money' attitude, can be contrasted to Constable here, whose lack of overt commercial engagement made possible his idealistic focus on authenticity and more protracted process. While of course Constable would have preferred not to have to rely on portraiture for income, when it came to the making of landscape he could at least afford to be principled and make it as he wished to make it, at his own pace.

Yet despite his comparatively modest upbringing, Turner possessed two major advantages over Constable: first, geographical, for native Londoners were more likely to attend the Royal Academy and, second, parental support. [25] Constable's parents repeatedly urged him to settle for a role in the family business. Even ten years after their son had moved to London to pursue art, they were (understandably, with the little he was earning) unable to see how his chosen path would allow him to live a respectable, gentlemanly life. His father's 'earnest wish', his mother wrote to him, 'is to have you ... *earn money*', [26] while family members offered unsolicited advice on how he might 'finish' his landscapes to help them sell. In the end it was the death of his father in 1816 that brought about a firmer financial footing and allowed him to marry Maria Bicknell after a seven-year courtship. The Constables were a hard-working family, but not one exposed to the realm of career possibilities that life in London had given the Turners. Men connected with the Royal Academy, then at Somerset House, may have frequented the Turner barbershop, providing Turner's father with tangible role models for his son's future. He embraced Turner's talents with enterprising spirit, hanging his teenage drawings in his shop window and arranging tuition to help his admission to the Royal Academy Schools; he would later become his son's studio and gallery assistant. His early interventions and their location in commercial Covent Garden no doubt helped create the foundation for art making as the primary basis for Turner's eventual financial freedom. That Turner understood both the value of this help, but also the risks attached, is evident in his later response to a father who had written seeking advice on how to support his son, an aspiring artist. Writing at the height of his fame, Turner cautioned the parent about the 'difficulties' of making it as an artist, writing, 'you alone can judge how far you are inclined to support him during a period of long expense', and that even tuition would not ensure success 'in a profession which requires more care, assiduity and perseverance than any person can guarantee'.[27]

Each artist left a substantial paper trail that has shaped how we discuss them and their work. Turner's sketchbooks reflect his lifelong compulsion to sketch. Around three hundred in number, carefully labelled and kept by the artist, they are private 'storehouses of memory' that register his movements on tour and interest in topics ranging from chemistry to opera.[28] Other documents include manuscripts for lectures he gave as the Royal Academy's Professor of Perspective and snippets of poetry, collectively named *The Fallacies of Hope*.[29] Still, Turner remains more of an enigma than Constable. He too left behind lecture notes, his being on landscape painting, and, by contrast to Turner's purely image-based print series *Liber Studiorum*, wrote a text for his *English Landscape Scenery* (in which he took pains to avoid 'pompous' explanations) (see nos.177–80).[30] We can get closer to Constable – his love of family life, his anxieties, his politics and his wicked sense of humour – via the vast extant body of his correspondence. There is a risk, however, that we take what is there at face value, reading his art solely through the prism of his own words. While ostensibly private, letter-writing was a social performance and Constable would have been aware that his pen was contributing as much as his brush to his persona.[31] Extant letters from Turner show him driving hard bargains with print publishers, keeping up with friends and discussing business with Thomas Griffiths, the dealer he employed late in his career. Their comparative scarcity is not, as John Gage has pointed out, because Turner disavowed the polite culture of letter-writing or because he was antisocial, but rather simply down to caches of letters having been destroyed, such as those to his Leeds-based patron, landowner and MP Walter Fawkes.[32]

Gage's point bears emphasis given how easy it is to characterise Turner as a fish out of water in the elite world of the fine arts. Constable's first impression that Turner was 'uncouth' but had 'a wonderfull [*sic*] range of mind' plays to this.[33] Certainly Turner was from a background that became increasingly rare among Academy students, but the fact that he never lost his Cockney accent, a twang deemed especially jarring, perhaps shows he was never particularly concerned with concealing his roots.[34] Constable's accent may have also given away *his* background. Nonetheless, his dedication to painting his native region reveals a pride in his rural roots, and perhaps a sense of pride in his status as a geographical outsider – indeed, he professed amusement that his move to London put him in the category of artist Vasari termed 'the Itinerants'.[35] Perhaps Cockney Turner and country boy Constable were equally determined to preserve, at least when it suited, mannerisms that marked them out as different from their peers or which helped them craft their professional identities.

'Fire and water'

Let us return to the moment in 1831 when, hung side by side, Turner's *Caligula's Palace* and Constable's *Salisbury Cathedral* (nos.136 and 135) prompted a spate of metaphorical hot versus cold comparisons. These paintings play to type: Turner gives us the heat and haze of Italian sun while Constable, true to his cloud studies, conjures a complex cloudscape and appears to visualise the 'four seasons in one day' trope of the British weather. Turner combines some of his favourite subjects in *Caligula's Palace* – a blend of classical history and myth, architecture and the hubris of man – and bathes it in his favourite colour, chrome yellow.[36] Despite intolerance towards Turner's predilection for this colour, critics praised *Caligula's Palace*'s 'magical' atmosphere. On Constable's part, *Salisbury Cathedral* was his most ambitious painting to date and it too emblemised his brand of landscape. He had exhibited paintings of Salisbury Cathedral before (no.116) but this time he enveloped the nationally recognisable icon within a scene that has clear echoes of his Stour Valley paintings; indeed, the dog is taken directly from *The Cornfield* (fig.35, p. 56), while the cart is reminiscent of that in *The Hay Wain* (fig.1).[37]

Patent aesthetic differences aside, these works have much in common. Each painter underlined the emotive and cerebral significance of their work by appending poetry to its entry in the Royal Academy's exhibition catalogue, Constable citing eighteenth-century poet James Thomson's *Seasons* (also a favourite of Turner's) and Turner his own verse. The large size of their paintings would ensure visibility in the crowded exhibition hang, but, more profoundly, upheld that landscape was a genre fit for the grandeur of a large canvas. Sizeable landscapes by Old Masters were the pride of notable collections when Turner and Constable were starting their careers, and though they might have disagreed as mature artists on the best way to pay homage to their heroes (see nos.29–32), they had both absorbed as young men the advice of the Royal Academy's first President, Sir Joshua Reynolds:

> Study nature attentively, but always with those masters in your company; consider them as models which you are to imitate, and at the same time as rivals with whom you are to contend. [38]

Turner performed the latter part of this dictum with aplomb, but both artists took the message to heart. Indeed, Turner was dubbed the 'modern Claude', and Constable was compared to the seventeenth-century Dutch artists he so admired, such as Jacob van Ruisdael. [39]

As much as they looked back to illustrious precedents, however, their technique propelled painting forward. They each evolved distinctive and innovative ways to apply paint and use colour, making paintings of the like never seen before, risking sales and reputation. In the 1830s Constable wrote of setting down his palette knife, which gave his painted surfaces their choppy, textural surface, commenting that other artists had taken it up at the point he had 'cut [his] throat with it'. When critics complained he used too much yellow, Turner quipped he had indeed 'taken it *all*' but was shocked to learn that even loyal buyers were unsure about the 'new' aesthetic of 1840s watercolours like *The Blue Rigi* (no.158). [40] Between Turner's vivid colouring and Constable's agitated surface, critics dramatically deduced in 1831 that 'productions more strongly bespeaking the hand of genius, betraying more glaring defects, or fraught with more redeeming beauties, will not easily be found'. [41]

This encapsulates the tension often found in descriptions of their work. 'Genius', in particular, was a loaded term; a risky attribute, it required keeping in check by other qualities like 'truth' or 'harmony'. [42] Constable's works were 'monsters', showing 'singular originality' and failure to 'harmonize with the works of other men'; Turner's obituary in the *Athenaeum*, meanwhile, referred to the 'eccentricities of great genius'. [43] Turner and Constable were collectively termed 'extravagant painters': showing off was not acceptable. While criticism did not always run like water off a duck's back, neither artist pandered too much to public taste (liberated, as they were, by relative financial freedom). [44] They displayed their 'genius' with abandon, forging distinctive visions and names for themselves in the history of British art in the process.

Their core mission was the same: to make highly affective and original paintings rooted in the study of nature. Constable's bugbear was artifice, be it through minute replication of nature's forms or what he perceived as unnatural colouring. His goal was authenticity. From this stemmed his use of vivid greens – a cause he took up in defiance of even Sir George Beaumont – and his radical handling of paint, which saw his increasing eschewal of smooth, polished surfaces. Constable wanted his viewers to appreciate how he had used his medium to evoke nature's textures, its atmosphere and quality of light – to sense, as you might when you look at *The Leaping Horse* (no.130), that a breeze has enlivened the trees or, as he put it,

> to give 'to one brief moment caught from fleeting time', a lasting and sober existence, and to render permanent many of those splendid but evanescent Exhibitions, which are ever occurring in the changes of external nature. [45]

This was not unlike Turner's vision. When one of his most daring late paintings, *Snow Storm – Steam-Boat off a Harbour's Mouth* (no.166), was ridiculed as 'a domestic joke on a washing day ... a mass of whirling soapsuds', he is reported to have bristled, '[s]oapsuds and whitewash! ... I wonder what they think the sea's like? I wish they'd been in it.' [46] Claiming his research had seen him tied to a mast in a storm, he said, 'I did not paint it to be understood, but I wished to show what such a scene was like.' [47] Whether Turner was actually tied to a mast is a moot point, but the story nevertheless shows that he shared Constable's concern for authenticity, however much his subject matter might differ. It is important to remember, however, that authenticity to them was often more about feeling than fact. Notwithstanding a rootedness in observation and Constable's early, idiosyncratic determination to make finished paintings outdoors (see no.94, *Boat-Building*), ultimately both their finished paintings were studio concoctions. Composing their landscapes, often with reference to Old Master blueprints, they moved features around (as Constable did in *The Leaping Horse*) or compressed lateral space (as seen in *Salisbury Cathedral* and Turner's *Brighton*, nos.135 and 121), concealing and revealing elements that helped them tell their story and capture the spirit of a place.

Conceptually, *Salisbury Cathedral* and *Caligula's Palace* have much in common. By reference to the past – in Turner's case the hubris of Roman Emperor Caligula and in Constable's the longevity of Christianity in Britain – both paintings speak to a present in the grip of uncertainty and on the brink of major change. The political landscape of 1831, when these paintings were exhibited, was very much in flux: revolution was again coursing its way through Europe and pressure for political reform in Britain was mounting. *Salisbury Cathedral* depicts the metaphor – the 'Church under a cloud' – used to describe the threat posed by reform to the Anglican Church's political authority; it is thus in part an emotive protest by a politically conservative, staunch Anglican artist who was troubled by threats to the status quo. [48] Where Turner's world-view can be gleaned, it is more liberal-leaning, seen most notably in his indictment of the slave trade, *Slavers Throwing Overboard the Dead and Dying, Typhon Coming On* (fig.37, p.58). [49] Both use atmospheric effects to echo their narratives, from Turner's metaphorical use of the sun to signify the rise and fall of empire (nos.125 and 126) to Constable's insertion of the rainbow to *Salisbury Cathedral* years later, after the political storm had passed. [50]

Both artists' polymathic interests – in science, literature, history and current affairs – and the signs of the times in which they lived are woven into their work. It was not just the 'brief moment' of a storm or a scudding cloud that they captured, but a sense of their era, its changes and its concerns. Even when Constable's Stour paintings have been taken by later viewers as 'timeless', we cannot escape that the time in which they were painted – one of immense change and tumult in agrarian society – gives them an urgency and a contemporary relevance that is easily overlooked. These narratives multiply the ways in which a painting might communicate with its viewer, if that viewer only had the same range of references at their disposal. While Constable understood that most wouldn't (therefore writing careful descriptions of his work for his print series, *English Landscape Scenery*), Turner's penchant for elaborate and, at times, obscure narratives frustrated his critics and has provided endless grounds for scholarly speculation ever since. Indeed, their critics, so preoccupied with their technical execution, often ignored the narratives of their paintings. It is in this realm that the efforts of both artists marked them out most prominently from their peers.

In February 1829 Constable was finally elected a Royal Academician. Turner visited him to relay congratulations and they whiled away the evening in the company of another artist, George Jones, parting at one in the morning 'mutually pleased with one another' according to Constable. [51] Becoming an Academician mattered. The Royal Academy had been the backbone of both artists' professional lives since their time as teenage students in the 1790s, when landscape was not yet the dynamic genre they had made it. Constable's new status as an 'RA' was a win for landscape in the competition between genres; it also unlocked new potential for the creative dialogue between him and Turner. For just as Vasari had believed that competition propelled art forwards, so too did Turner. Thus we can read his application of the red daub to his *Helvoetsluys* in 1832 not as a slight to Constable but in fact as an invitation to become a player in his game of ideas and technical showmanship. Perhaps it was a riposte to Constable's placing of *Salisbury Cathedral* in the prime position in the 1831 exhibition. Perhaps Constable felt validated and wished to draw attention to his treatment as an insider – fair game in a competition he had set going a year earlier – when he referred to Turner having 'fired a gun'. [52] Either way, Turner's red daub might just have been the biggest compliment and expression of acceptance Constable could have received. For all the critics' sensationalist commentary, this kinship mattered: they could be rivals, but they also recognised one another as originals.

Turner and Constable Today

Since their deaths in 1837 (Constable) and 1851 (Turner), the ebb and flow of taste and academic enquiry has amplified different aspects of their work and thus shaped and reshaped their significance. John Ruskin, self-appointed defender against Turner's critics in the artist's lifetime, became ever more vocal and influential after his death, lauding Turner's earlier work as his greatest and panning later work as 'inferior' or evidencing 'mental disease'. [53] Ruskin had described Constable, uncharitably, as giving 'countenance to the blotting and blundering of Modernism', but an alternative, more celebratory angle on this took hold, one that saw *The Hay Wain*'s success at the 1824 Paris Salon as laying the foundation for the quintessentially 'English' artist to become the father of modern French landscape painting. [54] Turner was drawn into this lineage by Renoir, Monet and Pissarro themselves, who co-signed a letter stating they inherited Turner's quest for light and colour. [55] As the twentieth century dawned Turner and Constable were proclaimed modern painters, celebrated not so much for *what* they painted, but *how*, stimulated by displays of unfinished, preparatory work, of the kind neither would have shown in public. *Norham Castle* (no.181) and other late unfinished works were shown at the Tate Gallery in 1906, paving the way for Turner to be cast as the artist of light, colour and modernism *avant la lettre* in an exhibition at New York's Museum of Modern Art in 1966. The exhibition was mounted, they said, '[b]ecause we know a modern painter when we see one', [56] prompting abstract expressionist Mark Rothko to quip '[t]hat chap Turner learned a lot from me!' [57] In 1892 a reviewer of Constable's work found that '[t]he sketches were better'; decades on, it was in oil sketches that Bloomsbury Group painter and critic Roger Fry said we would find 'the real Constable'. [58] More recently it was deemed that in Turner's late work we see the 'Turner who matters'. [59]

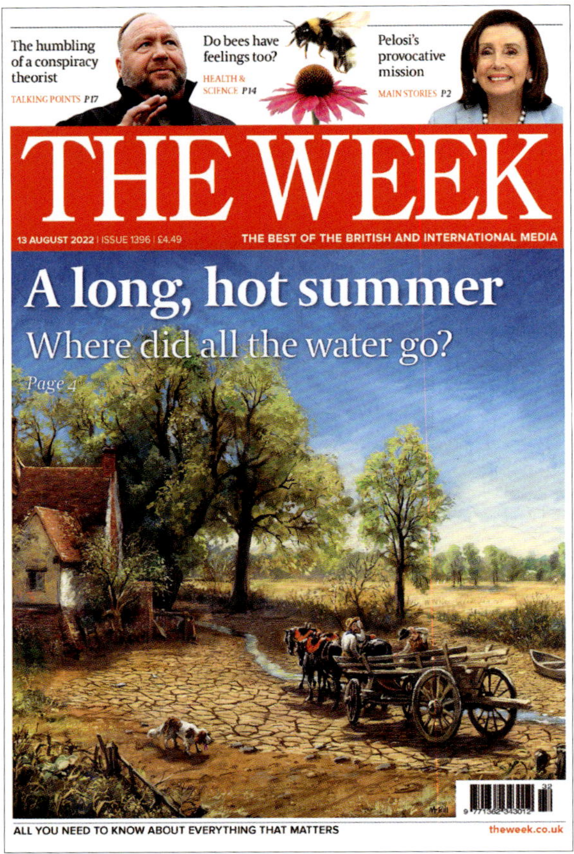

FIG. 7 Cover, *The Week*, 13 August 2022

Today these artists have taken on divergent identities in the popular imagination: Turner the adventurous painter of profound and dazzling works, Constable the 'completely English' painter of places now preserved by the National Trust in his name. These identities have crystallised thanks to, and sometimes in spite of, attempts by successive generations to reframe or reinvent their work. Thus, a wave of scholarship in the 1980s and 90s that sought to complicate perceptions of Constable's work as solely 'green and pleasant' coincided with a trend in interior decoration that celebrated his paintings as just that, seeing them installed in homes as icons of nostalgia and tradition (chiming with values promoted by Conservative politics at the time).[60] In this way 'Constable Country', as it came to be known even in Constable's lifetime, has been taken as a proxy depiction of Britain and his images invoked as such in protests and coverage on environmental threats (fig.7).[61] Turner wished to secure himself a prominent legacy in British cultural life, as expressed in the Turner Bequest of works he gifted to the nation and his wish to have a gallery dedicated to its showing. His name still connotes innovation in today's contemporary culture thanks to the eponymous Turner Prize and the opening in 2011 of Margate's Turner Contemporary, a gallery that regularly hosts artists in dialogue with Turner in a place in which he found much inspiration. The UK government's deployment of both his and Constable's legacies – with Turner appearing on the twenty-pound note since 2020 (fig.8) and Constable in the 2015–20 'Creative United Kingdom' UK passport design – brings them into currency, in Turner's case quite literally, in a way that neither artist could have predicted.

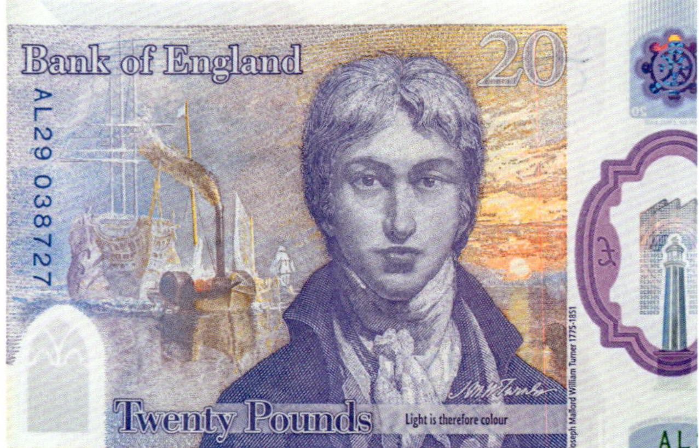

FIG. 8 £20 note (detail), first issued by the Bank of England 20 Feburary 2020, printed polymer with purple and silver foil patches, 13·9 × 7·3

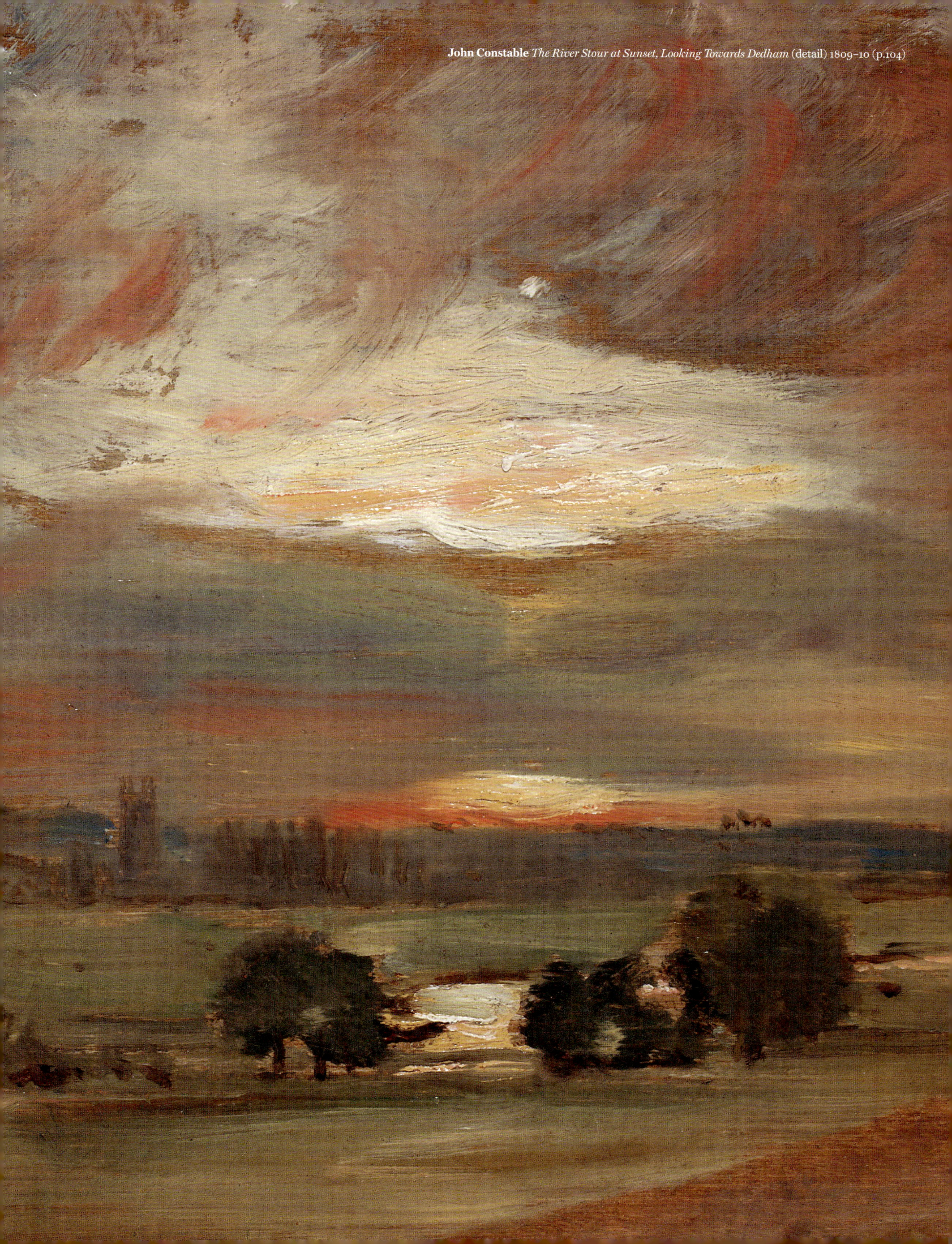

John Constable *The River Stour at Sunset, Looking Towards Dedham* (detail) 1809–10 (p.104)

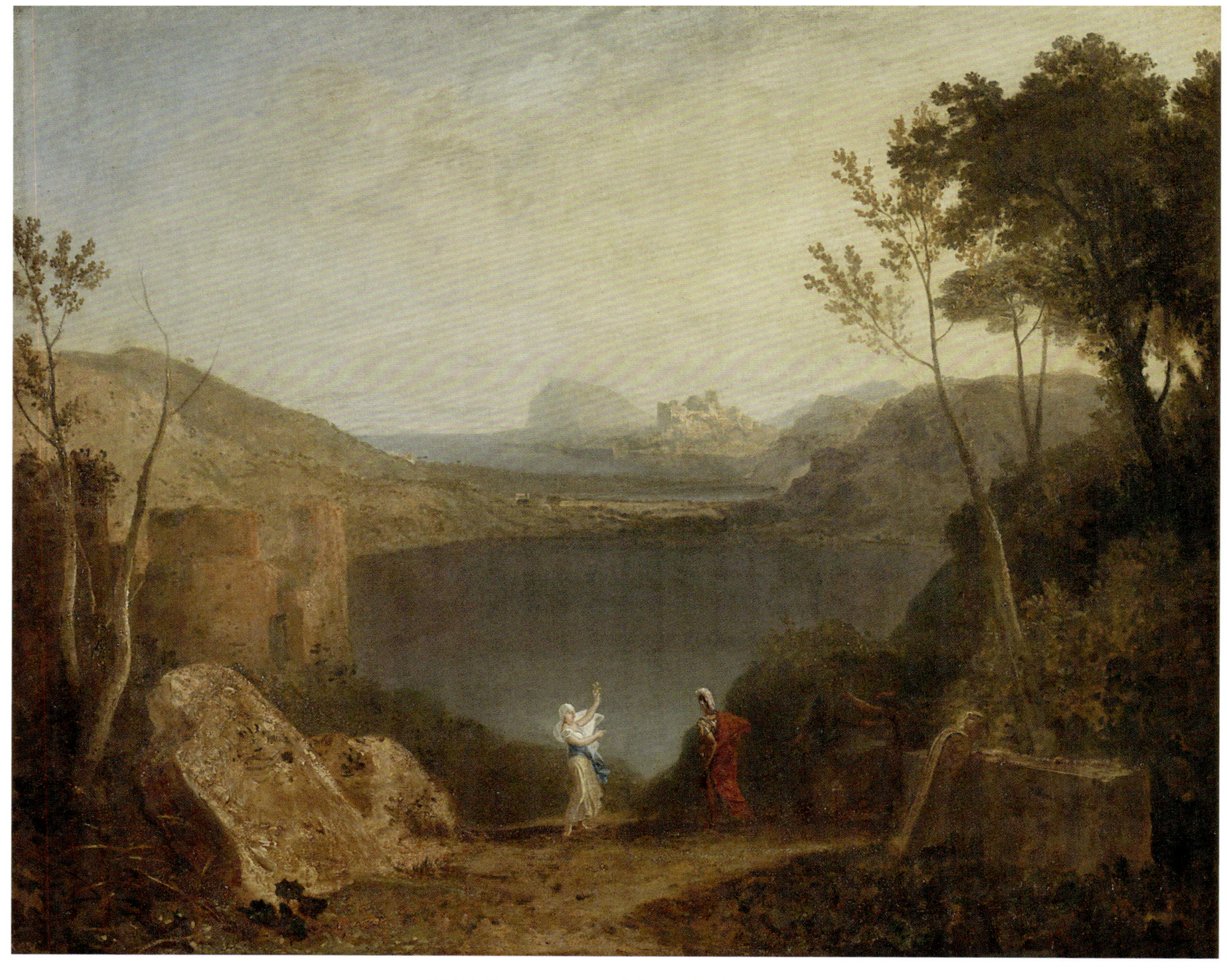

FIG. 9 **J.M.W. Turner** *Aeneas and the Sibyl, Lake Avernus* c.1798
Oil paint on canvas, 76·5 × 98·4
Tate. Accepted by the nation as part of the Turner Bequest 1856

TURNER'S ANCIENT WORLDS: MYTH AND REALITY

NICOLE COCHRANE

In 1850 Turner showed work at the Royal Academy for the last time. The four paintings he exhibited follow the story of Dido and Aeneas, the doomed love affair between the Queen of Carthage and the future founder of Rome as told by the ancient poet Virgil. The critics were divided. Some praised the 'colours of a most dazzling hue', while others were confused by the apparent slide into abstraction. [1] This series was the artist's final engagement with a lifelong source of inspiration, the *Aeneid*, a text that had already given rise to at least six previous paintings. [2] The stories of the ancient world, both mythical and historical, fascinated him. Classical landscapes offered fertile ground for experimentation and interpretation: tales of magic and mysticism, epic heroes and courageous battles, love and despair, ambition and hubris, transformation and the turning wheels of fate.

As a student at the Royal Academy Schools in the early 1790s, Turner's first interaction with the classical world would have been through the casts of ancient statuary he was required to study. [3] In the hierarchies of art taught at the Academy the most prized genre was history painting, the term broadly used to describe scenes from ancient history, classical mythology and the Bible; landscape painting (along with still life and portraiture) was considered less prestigious. [4]

Despite this, Turner was able to follow the example of artists who were believed to have elevated the landscape genre, none more so than Claude Lorrain (c.1600–1682). The French painter often filled his scenes with classical myth and history, enriching them with narrative interest and thereby augmenting their intellectual appeal. Not only were these landscapes highly regarded, they were also visible, with many located in British collections by the end of the eighteenth century, ready for a young artist of ambition to view them and be inspired. [5] They would likely have appealed to Turner as an opportunity to align himself with his predecessor. [6] As David Solkin notes, Turner 'never tired of matching his talents against those forerunners whom he most admired'. [7]

Aeneas and the Sibyl, Lake Avernus c.1798 (fig.9) was Turner's first attempt at a classical narrative landscape painting in the model of Claude, and his first depiction of a scene from Virgil's *Aeneid*. [8] Showing the moment Aeneas seeks divine guidance on his destiny, the work was commissioned by Sir Richard Colt Hoare for his classically influenced country seat Stourhead in Wiltshire. Hoare, who recognised the promise in the young artist, likely intended the work as a companion to Richard Wilson's *The Lake of Nemi, or Speculum Dianae* c.1758, which he also owned (fig.10). An amateur artist himself, Hoare provided Turner (who had yet to visit Italy) with sketches made of Lake Avernus during his own Grand Tour. [9] Turner later reworked the painting into a second version in 1815, which Hoare likely exchanged for the first (no.81). [10] Turner drew upon the traditions of Claude's harbour scenes, particularly *Seaport with the Embarkation of the Queen of Sheba* 1648 (fig.11), for two of the most significant paintings of his career (nos.125 and 126). *Dido Building Carthage, or The Rise of the Carthaginian Empire*, exhibited in 1815, also adapted Virgil's epic poem. Set just before Aeneas's trip to Lake Avernus, it depicts Dido, in resplendent robes, observing the building of a tomb for her deceased husband Sychaeus. Warm sun bathes the harbour in light. In the foreground young boys float toy boats in water illuminated by a sunrise: a metaphor for the seafaring power that Carthage would become.

The work's companion piece, *The Decline of the Carthaginian Empire*, was exhibited two years later and shifts from the realms of myth to history, to the first century BC, at the end of the Third Punic War. [11] It directly addresses the first picture: the children who floated their toy boats in the harbour are now being taken as prisoners of war, while the hopeful sunrise has become a languid sunset. Painted in the immediate aftermath of the Napoleonic Wars, together the pair provide a thoughtful allegory on the rise and fall of empires from the perspective of a country recovering from the hardships of conflict. [12]

It was travel that would provide the inspiration for the biggest shift in Turner's classical landscapes. Hostilities between Britain and France had prevented travel to continental Europe for much of his early career. However, the Peace of Amiens in 1802 temporarily halted the Napoleonic Wars and allowed Turner to visit France and Switzerland, an experience that immediately fed into his interest in classical myth and history. In 1812 he exhibited *Snow Storm: Hannibal Crossing the Alps* (no.80), a painting that fused the elemental sublime with an episode from history. Returning once again to the Punic Wars between Carthage and Rome, Turner paints

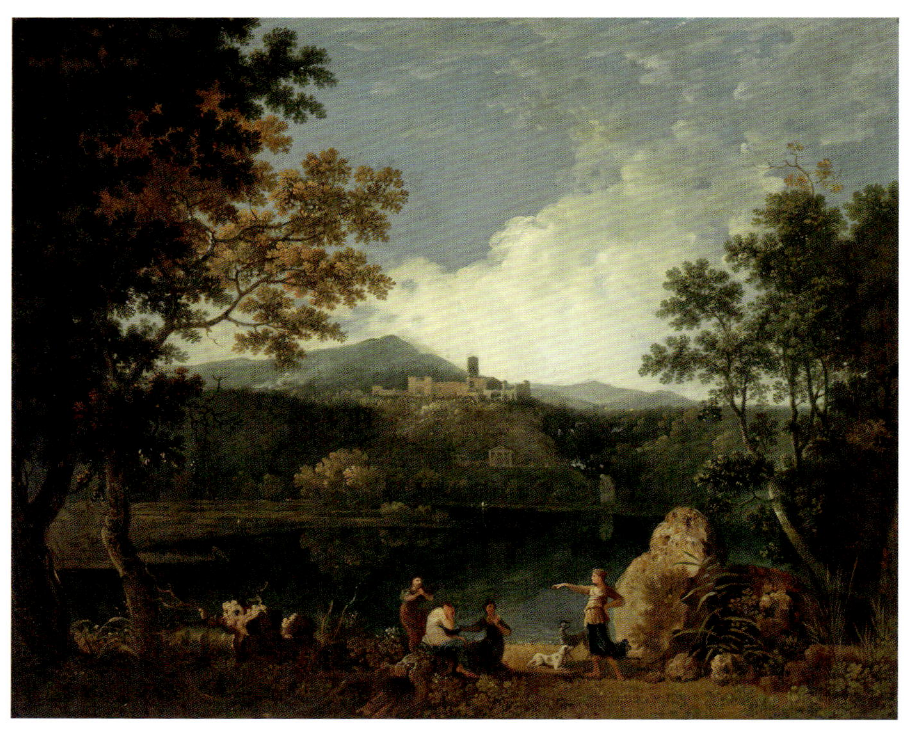

FIG. 10 **Richard Wilson** *The Lake of Nemi or Speculum Dianae* c.1758
Oil paint on canvas, 76·5 × 98·4
Stourhead, Wiltshire, National Trust, on loan to the National Trust from the Trustees of Constance Sarah Hoare Discretionary Settlement

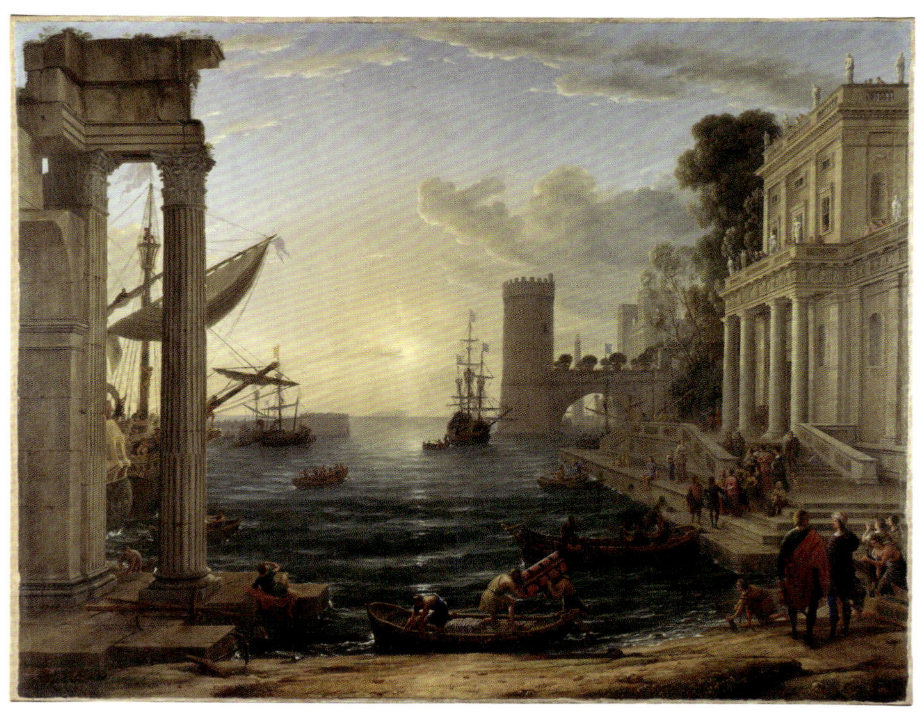

FIG. 11 **Claude** *Seaport with the Embarkation of the Queen of Sheba* 1648
Oil paint on canvas, 149·1 × 196·7
The National Gallery, London. Bought, 1824

the notorious attempt by Carthaginian general Hannibal Barca to invade Rome via the Alps atop elephants. Unusually, Hannibal is not readily identifiable in the composition; rather the overwhelming force of the snowstorm, depicted as a swirling vortex of cloud, rain and snow, is the narrative's chief protagonist – so much so that Turner wished for the work to be hung below the line, so that viewers would feel as if they were being pulled into nature's power.[13]

Turner was forty-four when he finally visited Italy in 1819. Only then was he able to experience at first hand the light and landscape that had inspired so many artists before him. Following his Italian travels, he bathed his paintings with light and colour, and his classical landscapes from this time possess an otherworldly quality, as if trying to capture the wonder of Italy and its antiquities. In *Bay of Baiae, with Apollo and the Sibyl*, exhibited in 1823 (no.91), the vivid blue of the sky contrasted with the yellow and orange of the buildings and scenery gives the painting an almost dreamlike hue.

Bay of Baiae tells the story from Ovid's *Metamorphoses* of the Cumaean Sibyl, who asked the god Apollo to live as long as there were grains of sand in her palm. Exhibited with the lines 'Waft me to sunny Baiae's shores', taken from Horace's *Ode to Calliope*, it speaks of Turner's wistful reminiscences of his time in Italy. Audiences were unsure of the 'unnatural' use of colour, with a critic for the *Spectator* writing that it has 'only an allowable heightening of the hues of nature, to suit the colouring of poetic fancy'.[14]

On Turner's second visit to Italy in 1828 he focused his attention on Rome, taking up a studio there and exhibiting his works. Completed in the city but later reworked, *Regulus* saw Turner return again to the theme of ancient Carthage and Claude's harbours. Marcus Attius Regulus was a Roman statesman and general. His capture and subsequent torture during the First Punic War, reportedly by having his eyelids removed so he would be blinded by the sun, became a legendary symbol of patriotism. As in *Hannibal*, Regulus as a protagonist is almost imperceptible; instead, Turner highlights the bright sun that blinded him. When reworking *Regulus* (fig.12) for exhibition in 1837, an episode immortalised by Charles West Cope (no.159), Turner was seen applying thick white paint in ruled lines. The resulting effect was described by one critic: 'all is glare, turbulence and uneasiness'.[15]

Caligula's Palace and Bridge 1831 returned to the folly and hubris of those in power, depicting the fabled bridge of pontoon boats that Emperor Caligula ordered to be constructed across the Bay of Baiae. Turner reimagined the wooden bridge as a crumbling, overgrown stone ruin. Here again, hazy Neapolitan afternoon light highlights the decaying remains of a former empire, now populated with labourers who work and relax in the bay.[16] Placed next to John Constable's *Salisbury Cathedral from the Meadows* (no.135) at the Royal Academy Exhibition of 1831 (a landscape largely based on observation), the arrangement loudly pronounced Turner's imaginative prowess and interest in the classical landscape during a time when classicism was declining in popularity.[17] The juxtaposition of these two conflicting styles would cause one critic to compare them as 'Fire and water'.[18]

Rome as a symbol for the cycles of history and the rise and fall of empires would serve as a frequent inspiration for Turner's late works. *Ancient Italy – Ovid Banished from Rome*, exhibited in 1838 (no.165), focused on Ovid's exile from Rome to the island of Tomis, now Constanta in Romania. While historians have debated the exact cause of the poet's banishment, Turner was likely alluding to the suggestion that it was related to indecent or politically provocative poetry written against the emperor Augustus. The intense yellow of the composition and the looming classical architecture, melting into the setting sun, create an aura of decline, equating the disavowal of artistic talent with the inevitable end of empire.

Despite not being hung together, Turner's final four exhibited paintings revisited the story of Dido and Aeneas as a narrative sequence. They charted their meeting in *Aeneas Relating his Adventures to Dido* (now lost) and *Visit to the Tomb* (Tate, N00555), the divine intervention of the gods in *Mercury Sent to Admonish Aeneas* (no.184), as Aeneas is reminded of his divine purpose, and finally *Departure of the Fleet* (Tate, N00554), sparking the centuries-long feud between Carthage and Rome, Turner's enduring inspiration.[19] Fittingly, for an artist whose own life was lived during tumultuous times, Turner's classical paintings stand as a perfect vessel to explore humanity's place in the changing tides of history and the rise and fall of empires.

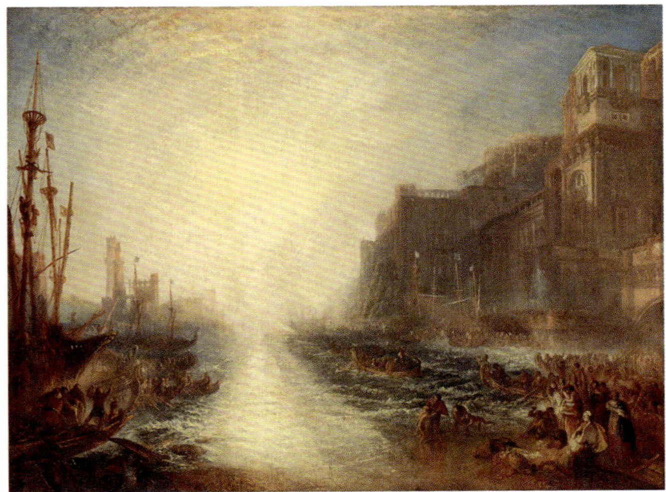

FIG. 12 **J.M.W. Turner** *Regulus* 1828, reworked 1837
Oil paint on canvas, 89·5 × 123·8
Tate. Accepted by the nation as part of the Turner Bequest 1856

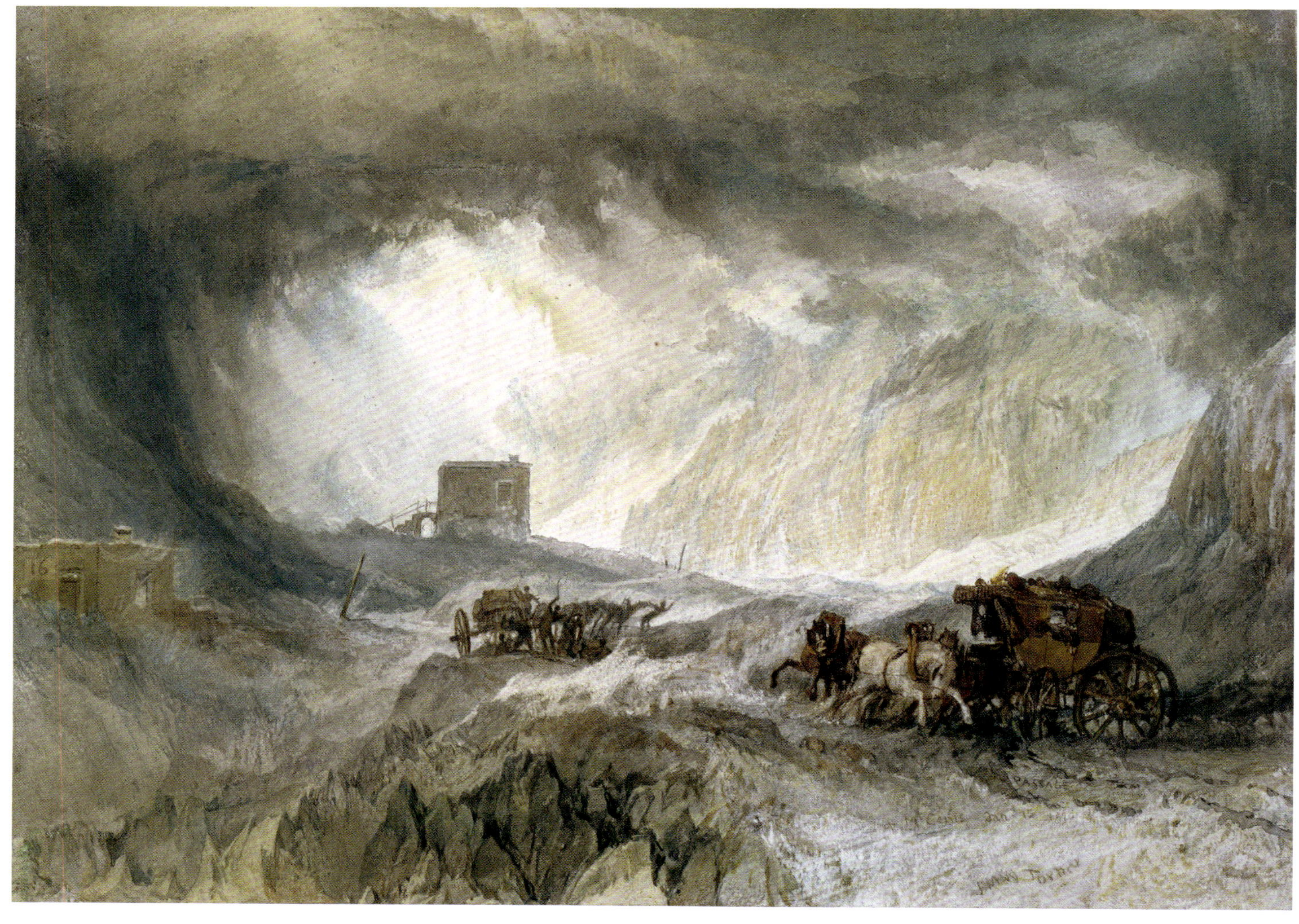

FIG. 13 **J.M.W. Turner** *Snowstorm, Mont Cenis* 1820
Watercolour, 29·2 × 40
Birmingham Museum & Art Gallery. Presented by J Leslie Wright 1953, received on his death, 1954

'WORN-OUT BOOTS': TURNER AND TRAVEL

NICOLA MOORBY

'A man must travel and turmoil,' wrote Lord Byron from Italy in 1820, 'or there is no existence.' [1] An inveterate traveller himself, between 1812 and 1818 the famous (or infamous) writer had published his long narrative poem *Childe Harold's Pilgrimage*, a semi-autobiographical ode to wandering and the intellectual benefits of visiting new places. Travel, Byron believed, served as a crucial stimulant to romantic aesthetics; the notion of creativity responding to the intensity of direct experience. Actively placing oneself within an alien environment was a vital strategy for accumulating source material.

Such a sentiment would have been complete anathema to John Constable. Neither a fan of Byron's (he openly criticised 'the deadly slime' of his influence) nor of travel for the sake of it, Constable was a man whose movements were driven by practicality. [2] He went from place to place for personal reasons: to Dorset or Salisbury when visiting his friend John Fisher; to Brighton when his wife's illness made sea air a necessity; and, of course, back and forth between his childhood home in Suffolk and his professional base in London. Travel as an aid to painting did not come into it. Instead, Constable made a virtue of being what he called a 'stay-at-home' artist. [3] Like the seventeenth-century Dutch masters he so admired, Constable engaged most productively and profoundly with his home turf, local landscapes that accrued meaning through the measured motions of everyday familiarity. 'I was born to paint ... my own dear England', he wrote. [4] Even then, *his* England was largely the one he could see without stirring too far from his doorstep. The finest view in Europe, he claimed, was that looking towards central London from his own drawing room in Hampstead. [5]

'How on earth would *you* know?', Turner might well have retorted had such an opinion ever been aired in his presence. Unlike Constable, who never went abroad once, Turner was one of the most widely travelled artist-tourists of his generation. This, therefore, is one of the easiest comparisons to draw between their respective landscape practices. If to understand a man we should first walk a mile in his shoes, then a quiet afternoon sitting beside the River Stour in Suffolk is a good way to get close to Constable. By contrast, one of the best ways of getting inside Turner's head is to literally follow in his footsteps, hitting the road with a sketchbook and racking up the mileage on a journey of discovery.

Turner's liking for travel emerged early, perhaps as a result of being intermittently sent away as a child when family life was difficult at home. The act of leaving London came to represent a sense of release so that, as early as 1791 and as late as 1845, it became his custom to head off on a research trip at least once during his working year. The moment of departure was usually late summer or early autumn, after the rush of the exhibition season was over. Sometimes in company but more often on his own, he utilised whatever routes and modes of transportation were available to him: horseback, horse-drawn carriage, sailing boats, ferries, often his own two feet. Latterly, he took advantage of more modern modes of transport, steam-powered boats and trains that whisked him forth with greater speed and noise and which provided their own form of visual stimulus. Whether by road, river or sea, he likened the act to the soaring freedom of a bird in flight. 'I'm on the wing', he frequently wrote to friends, before setting out on yet another expedition. [6]

Turner's itinerant habits go a long way towards explaining the substantial number of sketchbooks he used during his lifetime (nearly three hundred, compared with an estimated forty-five used by the more sedentary Constable). [7] On tour was when he sketched most prolifically, filling page after page with swift, reactive records of unfamiliar sights. Sometimes in watercolour (courtesy of a homemade set of portable paints, no.35), but more often in graphite, much of what he saw eventually proved to be incidental. Forming a veritable reference library, the travel material was consigned to a shelf in the studio, where only a fraction ever made its way directly into his painted work. For Turner, though, this was beside the point. En masse the sketchbooks were an essential data-gathering, data-filtering tool and they speak to their owner's wide-ranging intellectual curiosity. What is more, in the present day they provide important evidence about his biography. The geographical labels Turner gave to his sketchbooks and their near-continuous visualisation of his travels have helped to sequence his life story, filling in gaps within his chronology as a series of annual journeys.

Liberating as he found them, Turner's travels were not holidays. They were business trips, executed with all the precision of a military campaign. Employing maps, guidebooks and published itineraries, he planned his routes and destinations according to varying professional objectives (nos. 53 and 82). His trip to the Alps in 1802, for example, was a quest for the sublime mountainous scenery that could nourish impactful pictures for the Royal Academy Exhibition. Other work was commercial: sets of watercolours commissioned by a private patron, for example, or most commonly illustrations catering to the market in picturesque topography. In 1811, for instance, Turner was tasked with creating contemporary coastal views of southern England for a print publication. To fulfil the brief, he had to do the legwork and set off on a round trip of sites throughout Dorset, Devon and Cornwall. These kinds of jobs saw Turner repeatedly criss-cross the length and breadth of Britain. From Land's End to the Scottish Highlands, and from Welsh Snowdonia to East Anglia and the Yorkshire Dales, he recorded all manner of terrain, including coastlines, moorland, hills and valleys, rural villages and rapidly changing urban centres. Wherever he went he was alert both to landscape and to the life found therein: the past and present histories of a place and the complexity of man's relationship with nature.

Europe, too, drew him forth. Notwithstanding the travelling he continued to do within Britain, with peace restored abroad in the second half of his career, Turner made at least twenty-two separate European journeys. This represented a huge commitment of his time and energy. With each tour lasting anywhere from a week to several months, at a conservative estimate he cumulatively spent well over a thousand days on the continent. Braving hazards such as poor roads, bandits and extreme weather, he resourcefully navigated himself around multiple kingdoms or states. At least once he was nearly shipwrecked, and twice he was in a carriage that overturned in snow (fig.13). No wonder he was described as regularly losing more than half his luggage. Nor did he have the advantage of languages to assist him. A contemporary later described him as speaking 'but a few words of Italian, about as much of French, which two languages he jumbles together most amusingly'.[8] He was forced to rely on the most basic of tourist phrases, some of which we find jotted down within his sketchbooks: in Italian, 'Dove è l'Accademia di Belle Arti?' (Where is the art gallery?),[9] and in German, 'Was is die weg' (Which is the way?), or 'Wie weit ist es' (How far is it?) (no.56).

The benefits of travel far outweighed the challenges, however, and remained a yearly prompt for the artist to rejuvenate his repertoire. During the 1820s, while Constable was making a name for himself as the chronicler of the River Stour, Turner was actively exploring the great waterways of Europe: the Seine, the Rhine and its tributaries. During the 1830s he revisited the Alps, and by the 1840s it was Venice, Switzerland and Germany that newly fired his imagination. Byron's reference to travelling and turmoil comes to mind when we read an account of Turner's last major European tour. 'I went … to Lucerne and Switzerland', he told a friend in 1844, 'little thinking or supposing such a cauldron of squabbling, political or religious, I was walking over.'[10] He went on: 'The rains came on early so I could not cross the Alps, twice I tried, was set back with a wet jacket and worn-out boots and after getting them heel-tapped I marched up some of the small valleys of the Rhine and found them more interesting than I expected.' Even as old age began to catch up with him, he remained eager for the wonder only travel could bring him, indefatigable in mind, body and spirit.

TURNER AND HIS ECO-CRITICS: TRACING ENVIRONMENTAL CONCERNS IN THE ARTIST'S WORK

THOMAS ARDILL

In the poetic lines Turner wrote to accompany his only exhibited oil painting of London's metropolitan centre, he described a 'world of care' shrouded in a 'murky veil' of 'doubtful air'.[1] London's pollution was frequently commented on in this period but not universally condemned. Artist Benjamin Robert Haydon remarked that 'far from the smoke of London being offensive to me, it has always been to my imagination the sublime canopy that shrouds the City of the World'.[2] Lord Byron mocked this attitude with his character Don Juan, who regarded 'each wreath of smoke / [...] as a magic vapour / Of some alchymic furnace, from whence broke / The wealth of worlds'.[3] In all three accounts, air pollution was a powerful symbol – of labour and anxiety, the glories of empire, or commercial success – but not an environmental problem. By the 1830s, however, when Turner painted *The Thames above Waterloo Bridge* (no.160), urban smoke pollution was recognised as a growing concern to society.[4]

Turner left no written accounts of his attitudes towards polluted skies and water, landscapes scarred by industry and urbanisation or denuded of trees, though we see these represented throughout his work.[5] Indeed, there was little understanding of long-term environmental pollution in the early nineteenth century, and only a very theoretical conception of the potential for human activity to affect the climate. It was not until after Turner's death that John Ruskin, an early environmentalist with an increasing dread of industrialisation, first raised the idea that Turner's works might offer a demonstration, or foreshadowing, of humanity's destructive effects on the environment. He described the watercolour *Dudley, Worcestershire* c.1830–3 (no.151), in which the town's medieval castle and church are surrounded by smoking chimneys and glaring forges, as '[o]ne of Turner's first expressions of his full understanding of what England was to become'.[6] Ruskin has offered a point of entry for many modern scholars to approach environmental issues in Turner's work.[7]

Over the last fifty years, as knowledge of the climate and nature crises has grown, scholars have taken an eco-critical approach to exploring a range of environmental topics in Turner's work. These studies have revealed new insights into how the artist responded to and was entangled in his changing world. Sarah Gould has traced the origins of the modern 'Ecological Turn(er)' to 1972, with publications by John Berger and John Gage on Turner's response to steam power. While they offered different interpretations (Gage seeing *Rain, Steam, and Speed* 1844 as a celebration of technical innovation, and Berger arguing that Turner's response to the Industrial Revolution was coloured by his social class), they nevertheless converged in challenging the modernist narrative that the artist was principally concerned with form and effect.[8]

Following Berger and Gage, a key interest of eco-scholarship has been Turner's response to the Industrial Revolution. Writers have debated whether his attitude towards the industrialising world was positive, negative, or both.[9] In the words of Frédéric Ogée, 'Turner's awareness of the profound changes affecting the world he experienced with such intensity is evidenced in several of his pictures, on a wide spectrum of registers, from blinding fascination to darkest anguish.'[10] It is no coincidence, Ogée argues, that the 'triumph of landscape as the highest pictorial genre in the English school of art' coincided with industrialisation, borrowing the phrase 'anthroposcenic' from David Matless to demonstrate how artists responded to the new era (the Anthropocene) in which human activity became the dominant influence on the environment.[11]

Air pollution, the consequence of industrialisation that perhaps had the most profound effect on Turner's development of his late, dematerialised style, has received much scholarly attention, giving new meaning to John Constable's 1836 comment that 'he seems to paint with tinted steam, so evanescent and so airy'.[12] William H. Rodner argued that steam power and its visual effects were appealing for the artist as the vaporous and smoky byproducts of this technology suited his increasing interest in the dissolution of form, generating new subjects in an increasingly atmospheric style.[13] Michel Serres, James Nisbet and Sarah Gould have further explored the relationship between pollution and the painterly effects Turner developed to represent it, respectively considering his 'thermodynamic' handling of form, his proto 'environmental abstraction', and his use of surface texture.[14] Alongside these art historical accounts, scientific studies claim that stylistic and colour developments in Turner's work correspond with optical changes in the atmosphere created by increased levels of pollution. Airborne particles cause sunlight passing through them to appear redder and reduce the contrast and increase the white tint of objects. Turner made these characteristics prominent in his depictions of urban and industrial scenes, and in the works he painted shortly after volcanic eruptions threw particles into the atmosphere across Europe. These studies propose that, through his careful observation of nature, Turner responded profoundly, though perhaps unwittingly, to the effects of air pollution.[15]

David Trotter is so far alone in examining another form of pollution: everyday litter. Taking as a starting point Ruskin's observation that Turner grew up around and frequently depicted dirt and detritus, Trotter argues that Turner used litter as a way of admitting the forces of chance into his pictures of human purpose. While Trotter is not concerned with ecology, we might nevertheless conclude that the artist's apparent disinterest in the 'system which produced' the rubbish and waste strewn across the landscape and floating in the sea still reveals something about the attitudes of a society that (to use Ruskin's phrase) 'endured' it.[16]

Turner's representation of the extraction and exploitation of finite natural resources has been explored in several studies. David Stacey, for example, while not framing his research in ecological terms, has nevertheless shown that the effects of mining, quarrying and industrial and urban development on natural land forms led Turner to explore new subjects from the 1790s to the 1810s.[17] Similarly, James Hamilton demonstrated how Turner addressed widespread deforestation in his work. In *The Vale of Ashburnham* 1816 (fig.14), he argues, 'the subtext of the watercolour – trees and the shrinking of woodland – infuses every detail'. The area had previously provided wood fuel for ironworks and lumber for ship building, but over-felling led to the decline of both industries.[18] This had a very unequal effect on society as, while the labouring classes suffered, the owner of this landscape, John Fuller MP, was economically insulated by his investments in Jamaican sugar plantations worked by enslaved people, of which Turner, through Fuller's patronage, was also an indirect beneficiary. Turner's *Slave Ship (Slavers Throwing Overboard the Dead and Dying, Typhoon Coming On)* (fig.37, p.58) has also inspired recent thinking on the relationship between colonial and environmental violence by Malcom Ferdinand, who has used the painting as a starting point for his theory of decolonial ecology.[19] Closer to home, the entanglement of extractive capitalism and labour exploitation has been explored by Caterina Franciosi, who examines shifting power relations in *Dudley, Worcestershire* and another watercolour, *Shields, on the River Tyne* 1823 (fig.15).[20] These studies raise the issue of climate injustice by highlighting the global scale and unequally distributed effects of environmental and human exploitation involved in the extractivist economies that Turner painted and relied on professionally.

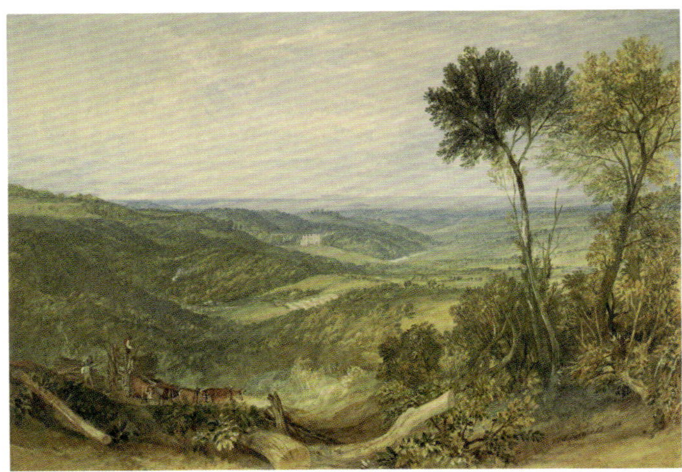

FIG. 14 **J.M.W. Turner** *The Vale of Ashburnham* 1816
Watercolour on paper, 38 × 56·4
The British Museum, London

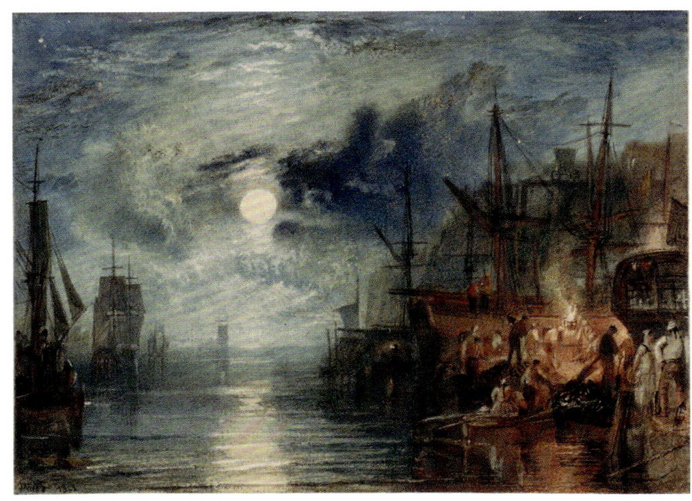

FIG. 15 **J.M.W. Turner** *Shields, on the River Tyne* 1823
Watercolour on paper, 15·4 × 21·6
Tate. Accepted by the nation as part of the Turner Bequest 1856

Turner's use of industrially extracted art materials has been a particular focus of recent scholarship, combining the disciplines of art history and conservation science to explore the artist's own role in ecological breakdown. Tobah Aukland-Peck has looked at carbon as an artistic medium, pointing out the 'central contradiction, [that] the landscape [of Cumbria] could be made legible on paper only by the despoilation of that same landscape' through mining for the graphite with which Turner drew it.[21] Amy Concannon similarly argues for 'the profound relationship between [...] material composition and [...] iconography and narratives' in Turner's *Whalers* sketchbook, c.1845 (fig.16). Here the artist

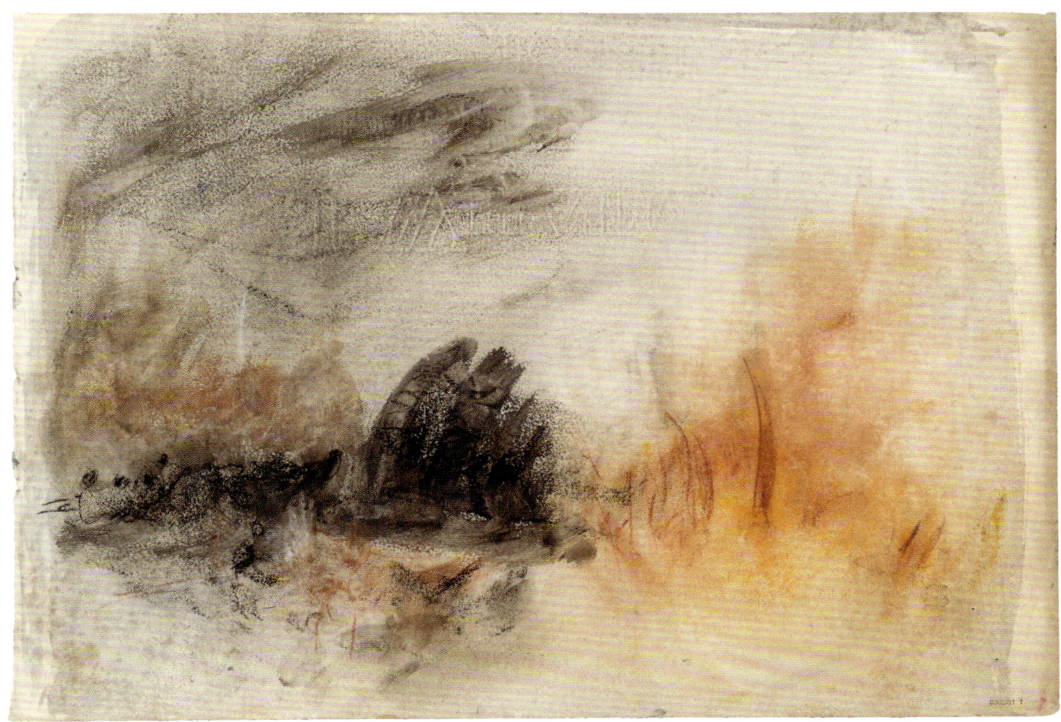

FIG. 16 **J.M.W. Turner** *Burning Blubber* c.1844–5
Watercolour and pastel on paper, 21·8 × 33
Tate. Accepted by the nation as part of the Turner Bequest 1856

made extensive use of coloured chalks, especially those made of the pigment lamp black, derived from the soot of oil lamps, which usually burned whale oil.[22] Others have pointed to Turner's reliance on the exploitative trade in artists' materials, such as his use of Indian Yellow, derived from the urine of cows fed on a diet of mango leaves in rural India, and ultramarine, powdered by enslaved people, along with his eagerness to use new chemical pigments, the extraction and processing of which involved environmentally harmful processes across the globe. According to Nathan Hensley, 'Turner's canvases embody, therefore, the regime of extraction and capture they depict as theme and form.'[23]

Connections between Turner's subject matter, style and biography, interdisciplinary approaches to research, and increased attention to questions of climate justice point the way for future studies of Turner and the environment. These should be mindful that the objectives of eco-criticism are not just to interpret cultural production in light of environmental issues, but also to raise awareness and encourage sustainability and activism. By exploring Turner's depiction of the environment, and revealing how he was inevitably implicated in its declining health, we should reflect on our own position in relation to the Earth's fragile ecology and our capacity to accelerate or mitigate environmental harm.[24]

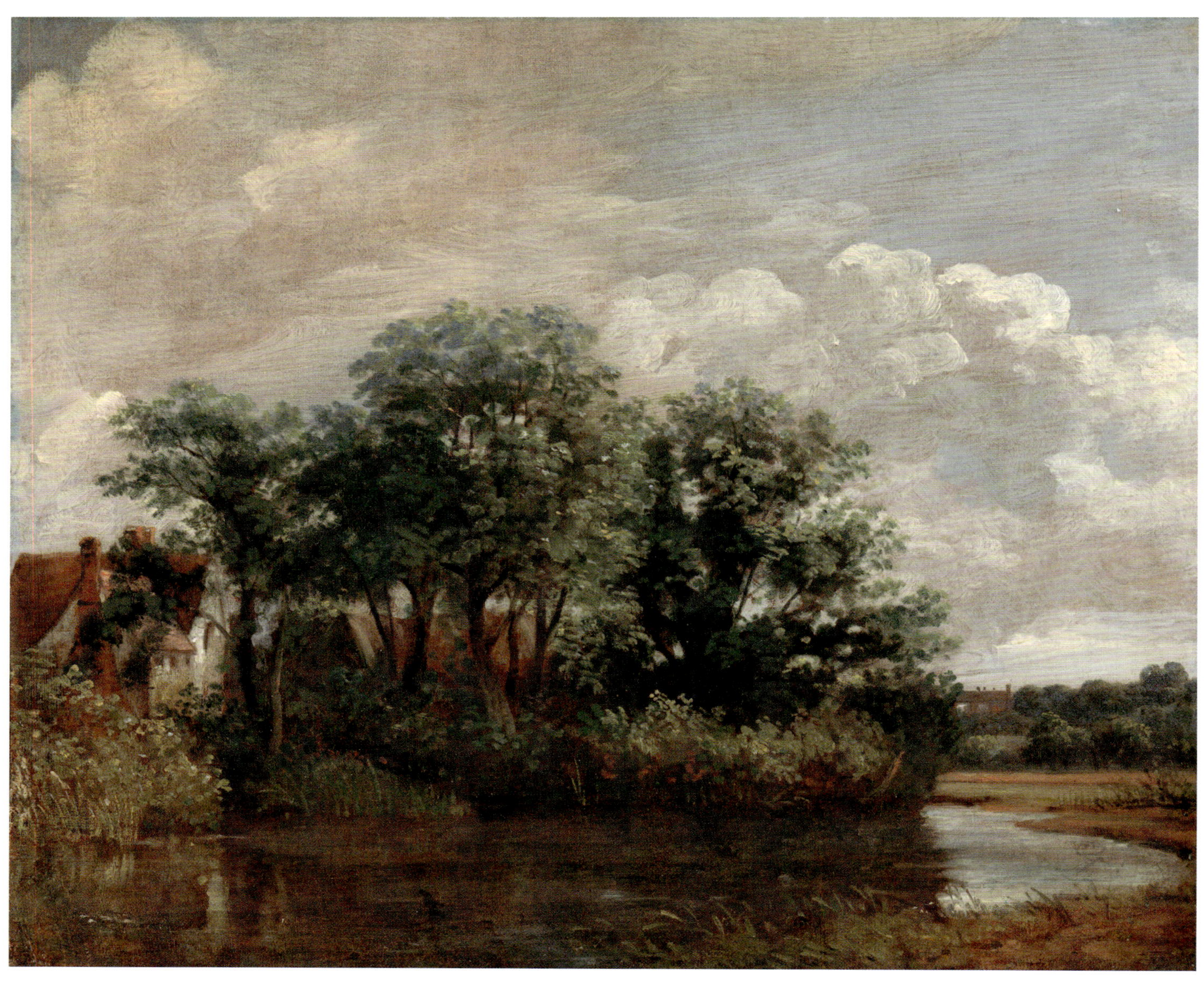

FIG. 17 **John Constable** *Willy Lott's House* 1802
Oil paint on canvas, 33·7 × 42·5
The National Gallery, London. Turner Bequest, 1856

EARLY IMPRESSIONS OF CONSTABLE COUNTRY

EMMA ROODHOUSE

Late one afternoon in October 1803, the Ipswich artist George Frost and his young companion John Constable sat down by the banks of the River Orwell to sketch and paint the warehouses and docks of Ipswich, and the ships moored there. [1] Frost had guided them that day for miles along the river, past shipyards, mills, army barracks, cottages and churches, the pair stopping occasionally to draw whatever caught their attention.

Frost was a self-taught, working-class artist thirty years Constable's senior, who amassed a collection of artwork by Suffolk-born Thomas Gainsborough and spent his life drawing the local landscape. He wrote to Constable:

> You know I am extravagantly fond of Gainsbro' perhaps foolishly so ... For my own part my prospect is so limited that I do nothing nor mean to do nothing but hunt after small scraps of Nature which one or other take off as fast as I do them. [2]

He encouraged Constable's outdoor sketching, introducing him to the places Gainsborough had 'often sat to sketch'. [3] Over twelve miles away in Dedham, Constable's family friend Lucy Hurlock wrote letters praising his 'progress of an early genius'. [4] Constable's associations with Frost and Hurlock are only two among several East Anglian friendships that helped to nurture and support the young artist, a cast of characters that has often been overshadowed by the intense scrutiny of Constable Country as a place. [5]

Born as the son of a wealthy merchant and farmer, with family values rooted in the traditional social order and loyalty to Church and king, Constable's status eased his ability to form relationships with people who would further his career. Indeed, his entry into the London art world was ultimately facilitated by this Suffolk network. Elizabeth Cobbold (1767–1824), a well-known local writer and pioneering palaeontologist, was a central figure in the region's cultural scene, routinely welcoming artists, poets and scientists to her home in Ipswich. While staying with the Cobbolds in 1799, Constable met the writer, philanthropist and Quaker Priscilla Wakefield (1750–1832). Impressed by him, Wakefield wrote a letter of introduction for Constable to the prominent Royal Academician Joseph Farington, who later assisted his entry into the Royal Academy Schools. [6]

Once in London and enrolled in art school, Constable kept in regular contact with his Suffolk circle. His letters to John Dunthorne Snr (1770–1844), another of his earliest supporters, reveal a relationship in which Constable felt free to express his ambitions – catalysed by his time in London – with impassioned conviction. It was to him that Constable wrote the often-quoted line, 'there is room enough for a natural painture [type of painting]'. [7] Dunthorne had arrived in East Bergholt just a year after the sixteen-year-old Constable had carved an outline of a mill and his name into a timber beam at Pitt's Mill (no.18). [8] Dunthorne was a painter of inn signs and church hatchments, a skilled carpenter and instrument maker with an interest in art and science. As a restless local teenager, passionate about being an artist, Constable was naturally interested in Dunthorne's experience and knowledge. He became a companion with whom Constable could wander the lanes and fields, sharing ideas along the way. Back in London, Constable reflected to Dunthorne his memories of their sketching jaunts:

> The fine weather almost makes me melancholy; it recalls so forcibly every scene we have visited and drawn together. I even love every stile and stump, and every lane in the village, so deep rooted are early impressions. [9]

In later years Dunthorne's lack of social standing and 'religious principle' challenged this pivotal friendship, which would eventually be reconciled by the older man's son, John Dunthorne Jnr, who became Constable's only studio assistant. [10]

To provide a more socially privileged cultural mentor than Frost or Dunthorne, Constable's mother, Ann, drew upon her acquaintance with Lady Rachel Beaumont, whose son Sir George Beaumont was a keen amateur painter and influential patron of the arts. Through Beaumont, Constable had the opportunity to study an extensive private art collection containing the work of numerous influential landscape artists, including Claude Lorrain (1604/5?–1682), Richard Wilson (1714–1782) and watercolourist – and friend of Turner – Thomas Girtin (1775–1802).

Despite the encouragement and advances these relationships brought, Constable's parents remained concerned about their son's financial prospects. They insisted he focus on securing paid work, particularly portraiture, and used their own contacts to obtain commissions. The painting of *Christ Blessing the Elements* 1810 in St James's church, Nayland, was encouraged by his mother and aunt Martha (Patty) Smith (1739–1820):[11]

> You will now I hope find time and inclination to begin the Altar Piece for Nayland Church ... We hear with pleasure glad tidings of your Pictures at the Exhibition ... and pray it may lead to your profit.[12]

Between 1800 and 1816 Constable maintained a steady work pattern, splitting his time between London and East Bergholt, creating a great body of outdoor oil sketches. Summers in Suffolk were spent painting sunrises and sunsets, while an early view of Willy Lott's House from 1802 (fig.17) would later become source material for *The Hay Wain*. Constable mentioned to Dunthorne Snr his intention to 'finish a small picture on the spot for everyone I intend to make in future'.[13] He went even further in 1813 by starting a small sketchbook noting distances of walks and inserting pieces of ferns and other plants as a way of preserving the physical memory of places, a practice Turner had participated in when placing leaves into his sketchbooks to act as a reference for the foliage of a particular location.[14]

Towards the end of this fruitful period, on 11 June 1815 Golding Constable made a proud birthday toast to his son John, to 'the painter and his pictures', in recognition and acceptance of his son's career.[15] The pictures Constable would show that year included *Stour Valley and Dedham Church* (no.95) and *Boat-Building near Flatford Mill* (no.94), both focused on an industrious landscape and river. However, only weeks after this milestone of family acceptance, Constable's father was taken ill and the artist was back in East Bergholt helping to care for him; his mother had passed away earlier in the year. This was an unsettled time for the Constable family and for the country at large after years of war with France, high taxes, rising unemployment and the impending removal of common land through the Enclosures Act, which would ultimately lead to riots and unrest. Constable took to his paints and captured in oil two intensely personal views from the family home, overlooking the house's flower and kitchen gardens (figs.18 and 19). This pair of small-scale pictures encapsulates the Constable world-view on the cusp of change: Ann's orderly planted flowers, Golding's prosperous farmland, a working mill in the distance, and the rectory where the artist's future wife, Maria, would visit her grandfather. Constable never parted with this pair of deeply personal paintings.

Golding passed away the following year and the family sold East Bergholt House. After Constable's marriage in 1816, his family and artistic life became settled in London, and the long Suffolk summers making studies in the fields became impossible to sustain. Yet he remained closely connected to his East Anglian friends and would take his young family on trips to visit their country relatives.

It was against this backdrop that Constable's artistic commitment to the area found its most forceful expression: the series of 'six-footers' made between 1819 and 1825, which immortalised the landscape as 'Constable Country'. The term first appeared in 1832, during the artist's lifetime, and has since become synonymous with the location immediately around Flatford.[16] Towards the end of the nineteenth century, with the advent of the railways, interest in travelling to Constable Country grew enormously. The area's increasing fame coincided with the historic opportunity to establish a collection of Constable's work in Ipswich and the campaign to preserve Willy Lott's House.[17] Dedham Vale and Stour Valley (a designated National Landscape since 1970) continue to inspire artists and writers. However, were we to follow Constable's early journeys more closely, our travels would take us much farther, beyond what has come to be defined as 'Constable Country'. We would, like him, follow George Frost along the banks of the Orwell, meander through East Bergholt after John Dunthorne, and seek out the church of St James at Nayland, where Constable's altarpiece *Christ Blesses the Elements* still hangs. More remains than we might think of John Constable's early impressions.

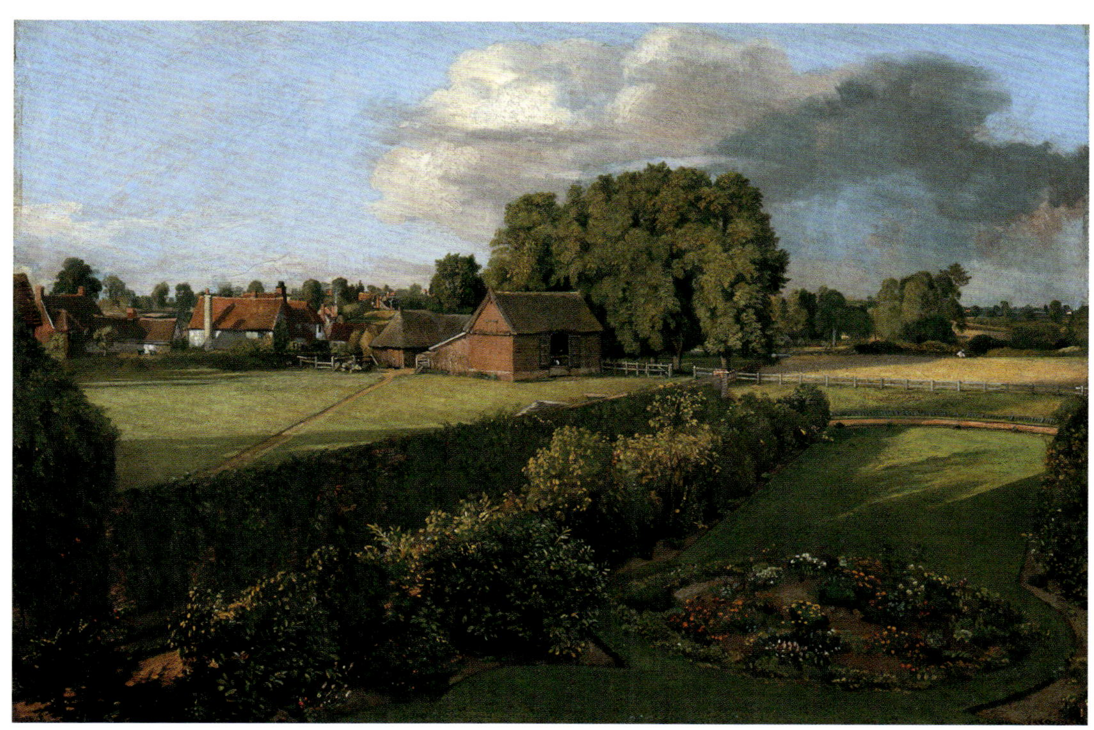

FIG. 18 **John Constable** *Golding Constable's Flower Garden* August 1815
Oil paint on canvas, 33 × 50·8
Colchester and Ipswich Museums Service: Ipswich Borough Council Collection

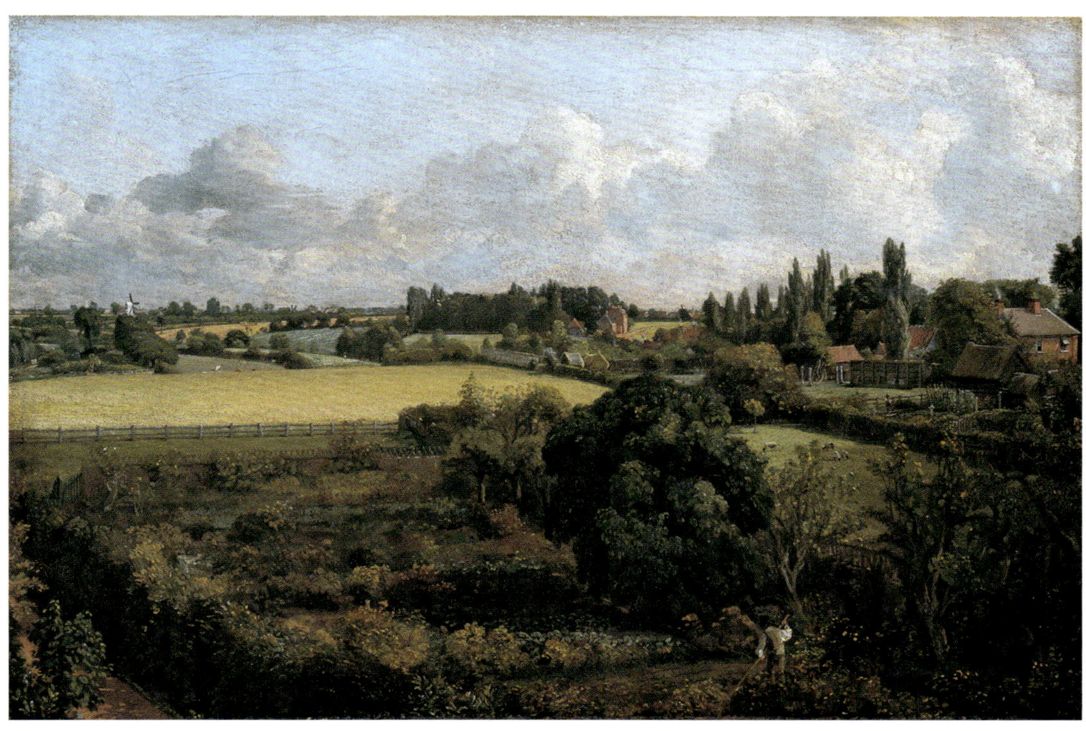

FIG. 19 **John Constable** *Golding Constable's Kitchen Garden* July 1815
Oil paint on canvas, 33 × 50·8
Colchester and Ipswich Museums Service: Ipswich Borough Council Collection

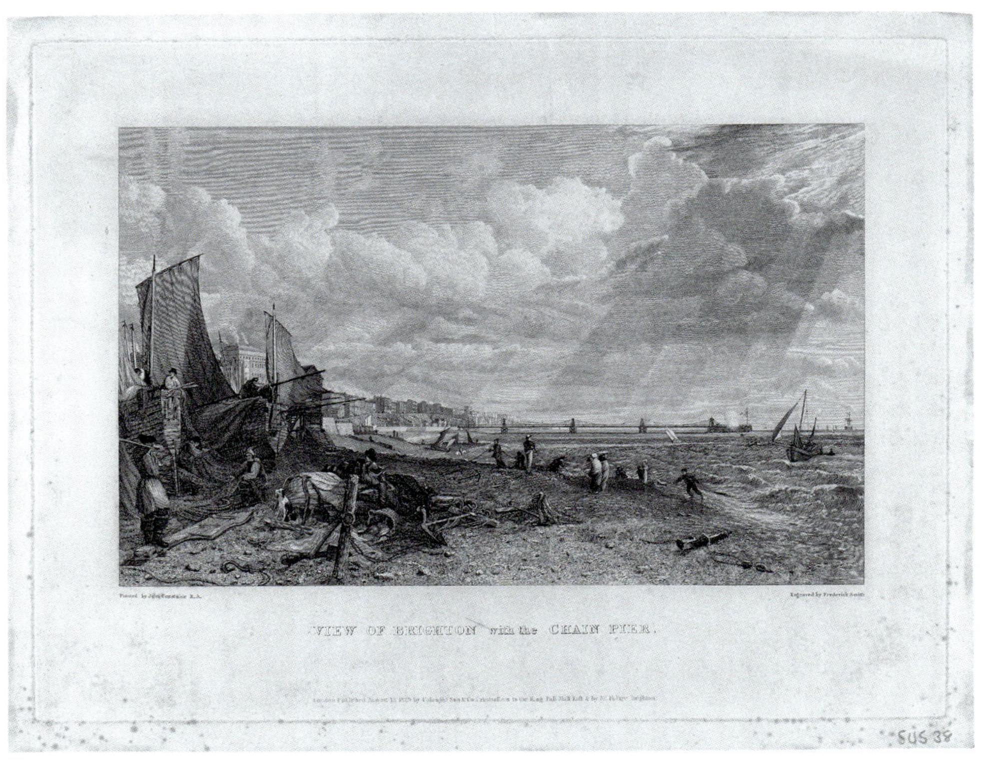

FIG. 20 **Frederick Smith after John Constable**
View of Brighton with the Chain Pier
Engraving published 12 August 1829, 27·8 × 37·8
Royal Collection Trust, London

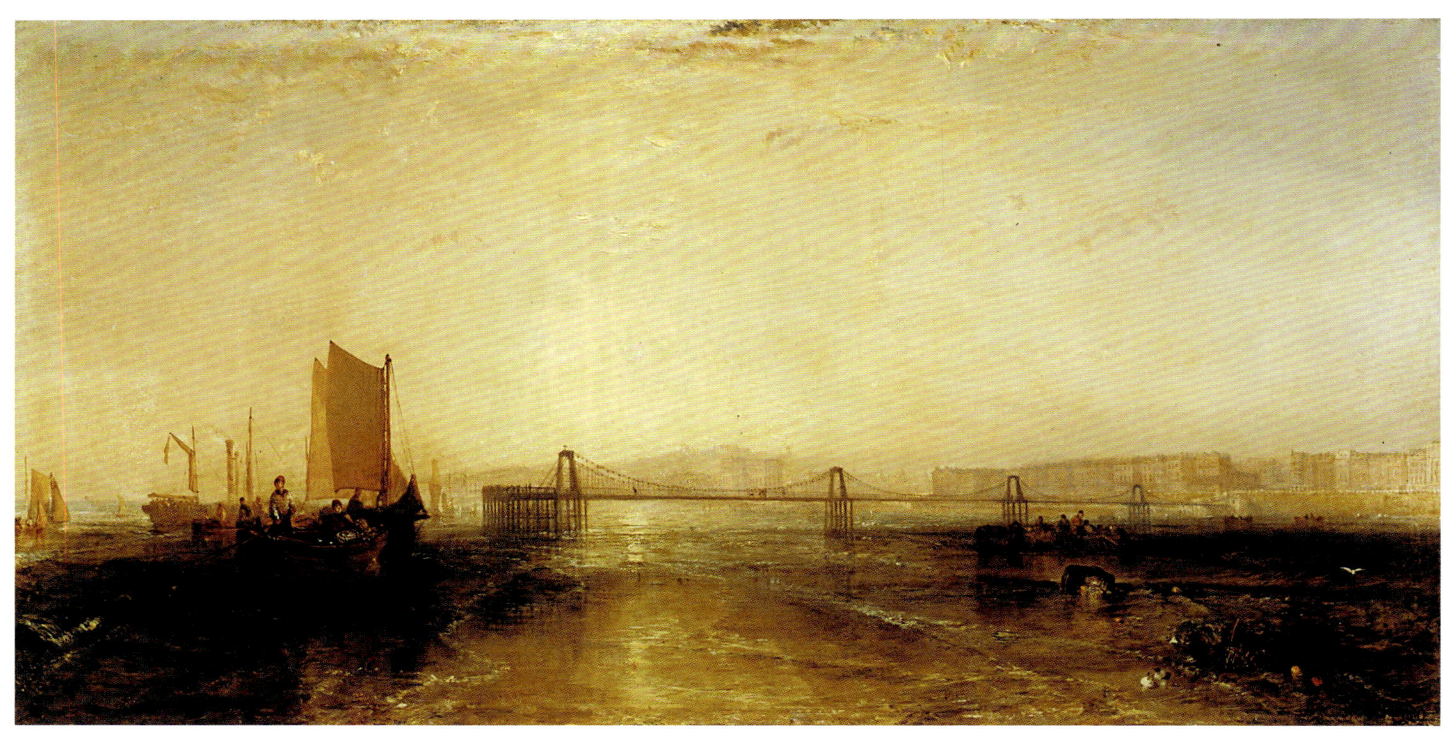

FIG. 21 **J.M.W. Turner** *Brighton from the Sea* 1829–30
Oil paint on canvas, 63·5 × 132
Tate. Accepted by HM Government in lieu of tax and allocated to the Tate Gallery 1984. In situ at Petworth House

'NOTHING HERE FOR THE PAINTER'? CONSTABLE'S URBAN LANDSCAPES

AMY CONCANNON

We do not tend to think of Constable as a painter of the city or the town, yet three of his major 'six-footers' depict the urban locales of Brighton, Salisbury and London. If Constable's art was, as his friend Charles Robert Leslie described it, a 'history of his affections', how do we explain these paintings by an artist who saw London's 'brick walls and dirty streets' as no match for the 'endearing scenes of Suffolk', and reported from Brighton that there was 'nothing here for the painter but the breakers – & the sky'? [1] The answer is that while Constable certainly did paint places he was fond of, he knew that the key to furthering his status lay in demonstrating versatility. Studying Constable's urban pictures closely reveals not just a different side to the artist but also his vision for landscape painting at its most sophisticated and daring. These were places of national renown where change was in the air; committing them to canvas demanded new levels of pictorial ingenuity.

The setting for *Chain Pier, Brighton* (no.142) was Britain's most fashionable and fastest growing town. [2] The former fishing village was transformed first by health tourism, as convalescents followed new advice on the benefits of sea-bathing, and further still by its association with the pleasure-seeking, scandal-ridden King George IV (former Prince Regent). [3] Constable spent several summers in Brighton, hoping that sea air would improve his wife Maria's health. The family arrived for their first stay in May 1824, just in time for the much-anticipated launch of the cross-channel steamship *Rapid* from the newly built Chain Pier, which, along with rows of new houses, hotels and the onion-domed Royal Pavilion, came to symbolise Brighton's boom. Compared to Turner's watercolour of 1824 (no.121), comparatively little of Brighton can be seen in Constable's painting. [4] Yet signs of its modernity – its pier and glistening seafront – *are* there. They are key to the painting's message, and their very inclusion signifies Constable's ingenuity. Mainstays of topographical prints and tourist souvenirs, these features were seldom seen in oil paintings, a format laden with expectations of adherence to traditional iconography and aesthetic conventions. And yet, by foregrounding Brighton's traditional identity as a fishing village, amplifying the windswept atmospherics of sea and sky and rendering the scene in the cool tones of the Dutch marine tradition, Constable carefully assimilates Brighton's modern seafront into an image befitting the elevated medium of oil paint. He perhaps hoped the picture would appeal to the tastes of collector and Chain Pier investor Lord Egremont, who had visited his Brighton studio, yet in the end Egremont commissioned Turner, who gave the Chain Pier his best honey-toned tranquil sunset treatment (fig.21).

Naming his painting *Chain Pier, Brighton*, but placing the town's traditional maritime economy in the foreground, Constable plays on the contrast between old and new. We effectively travel forwards in time as our eye follows the shoreline from the old – signified by the fishing equipment – to the new chain pier in the distance. The print made after it, the first to be made after one of Constable's six-footers, enhances this contrast, featuring a cloud of cannon smoke signalling the imminent arrival of the steam-packet on the far distant horizon (fig.20). Change – be it the 'ever-varying' surface of the sea or the town's transformation from 'a fishing village of so little importance' to 'one of the largest, most splendid' places – was also the theme of the text Constable wrote to accompany a seaward-facing image of Brighton in his print portfolio *English Landscape Scenery* (1830). [5] Describing Brighton as a place so 'connected ... with the Metropolis' as to be 'the marine side of London', Constable gave his own reasoning, one not found in any other text about Brighton from the time, for the town's change. '[N]atural local causes ... have secretly wrought this change', he wrote, describing how, in contriving to make Brighton so appealing and habitable, its rivers, hills and temperature were agents of urban change. [6] In preparation for a lecture he gave in 1836, Constable professed his belief that the act of landscape painting could function as 'experiments' in 'Natural Philosophy'. [7] Read as a narrative on the evolution of Brighton's landscape, predicated on man's ability to harness – and to tame – nature, *Chain Pier, Brighton* might be said to express a 'Natural Philosophy' of Brighton's evolution, and therefore a positivistic reflection on the town's identity, as a place founded on a harmonious synergy between man and nature.

Constable's acute geographical sensibility is also evident in *Salisbury Cathedral from the Meadows* 1831 (no.135). If

Brighton was a popular subject, Salisbury was a potent one. Together with the nearby 'rotten borough' of Old Sarum, the cathedral was a symbol of a broken parliamentary system in which the church held too much political authority, and an unpopulated mound – Old Sarum being the former site of Salisbury Cathedral – could still return two Members of Parliament. Like Brighton, as an architectural subject the cathedral was most often seen in watercolour and print; indeed a view by Turner of Old Sarum, with the cathedral rising prominently in the background (fig.22), was exhibited in London just a month before Constable departed for the visit to Salisbury that would generate the idea for his six-footer. Newly emboldened by his election as a Royal Academician, the expressive potential of this highly resonant subject – a place that he knew better than Turner or any other artist thanks to visits dating back to 1811 – was surely irresistible.

He would have known from his own explorations of Salisbury – often along its rivers – and from the book he owned on the city's history by 'cathedral man' John Britton, that the key to Salisbury's story was water. Situated on a fertile plain fed by three rivers, this was the 'English Venice', the 'well watered' city, founded here when access to water became an issue at Old Sarum. [8] In the late 1820s Constable was actively defining himself in opposition to established pictorial tropes, as evidenced by his wish to depict Stonehenge (no.172) as something more than a 'Stone Quarry', which had 'so often been done', he said. [9] Departing from precedent in its format, composition and painterly execution, *Salisbury Cathedral* works between extremes of distance and proximity, between detail and breadth, to create a highly novel representation of Salisbury. Constable uses the watercourse to draw together the city, the cathedral and, seen at far right, the surrounding downs. He thus combines all the signature elements in Salisbury's topography through a deft manipulation of space: first by compressing lateral space, bringing these features closer together, and also by bringing the cathedral forward. This makes for an unusually intimate and comprehensive description of the Salisbury landscape, one that emphasises Constable's personal outlook: to him Salisbury was a microcosm of the ideal society, in which city, countryside, church and God were closely aligned and functioned in symbiotic harmony. Reflective of both Constable's belief that the sky should be the 'key note' in any landscape, and illustrative of the refrain 'the church under a cloud', *Salisbury Cathedral* registers the reformers' challenge to this status quo in the sky, from the brooding clouds to the bolt of lightning hitting the cathedral's roof (assuming here that the rainbow was added later). [10] This metaphorical statement on current affairs was exhibited between two major and contentious political reform milestones: the 1829 Catholic Emancipation Act, which increased civil rights for Catholics in Britain, and the 1832 Representation of the People Act. Referencing this most divisive political scenario in his depiction of Salisbury, Constable was demonstrating his ability to register even the most controversial contemporary resonance of a place steeped in history.

There could be no more potent icon of modernity and change than the metropolis, the subject of the last of Constable's exhibited six-footers. *Whitehall Stairs, June 18th, 1817*, as the artist called the work we now refer to as *The Opening of Waterloo Bridge*, is a painting in which present and past are juxtaposed (no.150). Considering this work's long gestation period, spanning thirteen years between conception and exhibition, time was an issue in its very production, yet it is the presence of time *in* the picture that will be discussed here. Constable specifies the time of his painting through its title, 18 June 1817, but also through the smoke on the bridge: at 3 o'clock that day battle veterans fired a French cannon taken at Waterloo.

Yet, as has often been pointed out, the tall white tower on the right of the painting was not there that day: it was erected nine years later. Constable's initial sketch of 1819 includes a number of other towers. Rather than exclude these from the frame, as other artists chose to do, Constable in fact amplified this industrial element as his composition developed, as if to mirror industry's growing presence in Lambeth, on the Thames's southern shore. In early versions of Constable's painting these towers emit only thin, wispy trails of smoke, or none at all (no.149). In the resulting six-footer this area is shrouded in a prominent cloud of black emissions. It would not have been difficult for Constable to find out when the 1826 shot-tower was erected, so rather than viewing it as a slip in topographical veracity, might we see its inclusion as a deliberate way for Constable to endow his painting with a more sophisticated narrative, one that goes further than the illustration of a singular event?

It was daring of Constable to include this industrial element so prominently in his oil painting. While *Waterloo Bridge* clearly emulates the Thames scenes of Venetian painter Canaletto (1697–1768), as with Brighton and Salisbury, imagery of London was predominantly paper-based. Even in the less prestigious realm of prints, however, the inclusion of industrial towers was a source of contention. Some saw them as admirable signs of Britain's technological ingenuity and wealth, but others railed against their presence. One reviewer of an 1827 print series featuring the industrial south bank found it 'horrifying', bemoaning 'gawky chimnies [*sic*], and clouds of annoying smoke' as 'the most complete specimen of the anti-picturesque'. [11] The arguments against these towers were not just aesthetic. Over the years that Constable had *Waterloo Bridge* in his studio, concerns mounted about the environmental impact of smoke, particularly in Lambeth. [12]

Indeed, a principal advocate of the 1821 Steam Engines and Furnaces Act, which aimed to reduce smoke emissions, Tory-turned-Whig MP Michael Angelo Taylor lived in one of the houses above Whitehall Stairs, on the left-hand side of Constable's painting. Amid these concerns about the adverse impact of industrialisation and urbanisation, Constable's emphatic depiction of the smoke cloud transforms what was by 1832 an untimely depiction of an event that had taken place seventeen years earlier into a painting of contemporary affairs that reflects on the evolution of the Thames landscape.

Possibly inspired by Constable, Turner took up the subject of smoke clouds encroaching the view of Waterloo Bridge in a painting he left unfinished (no.160). By 1839, two years after Constable's death, Constable's painting was in the ownership of Birmingham-based coal-mine owner and ironmaster Charles Birch (fl.1825–70). For a man whose fortune rested on the means of producing that very smoke cloud, Constable's vision of London – melding monumental neoclassicism with the raw modernity of industry – was no doubt an auspicious encapsulation of the centrality of industry to modern Britain.

Rather than considering Constable's urban six-footers alien to his Stour Valley scenes, we might see them as extensions of his vision to articulate not just the spirit but the workings of place. Through them he shares with us his interest in the history of urban locales and crafts narratives that highlight the tensions within modern society as well as the productivity of man's use of natural resources. As such, these works are powerful and bold meditations on landscape and change in modern Britain, as well as on the relationship between time – present, past and future – and place.

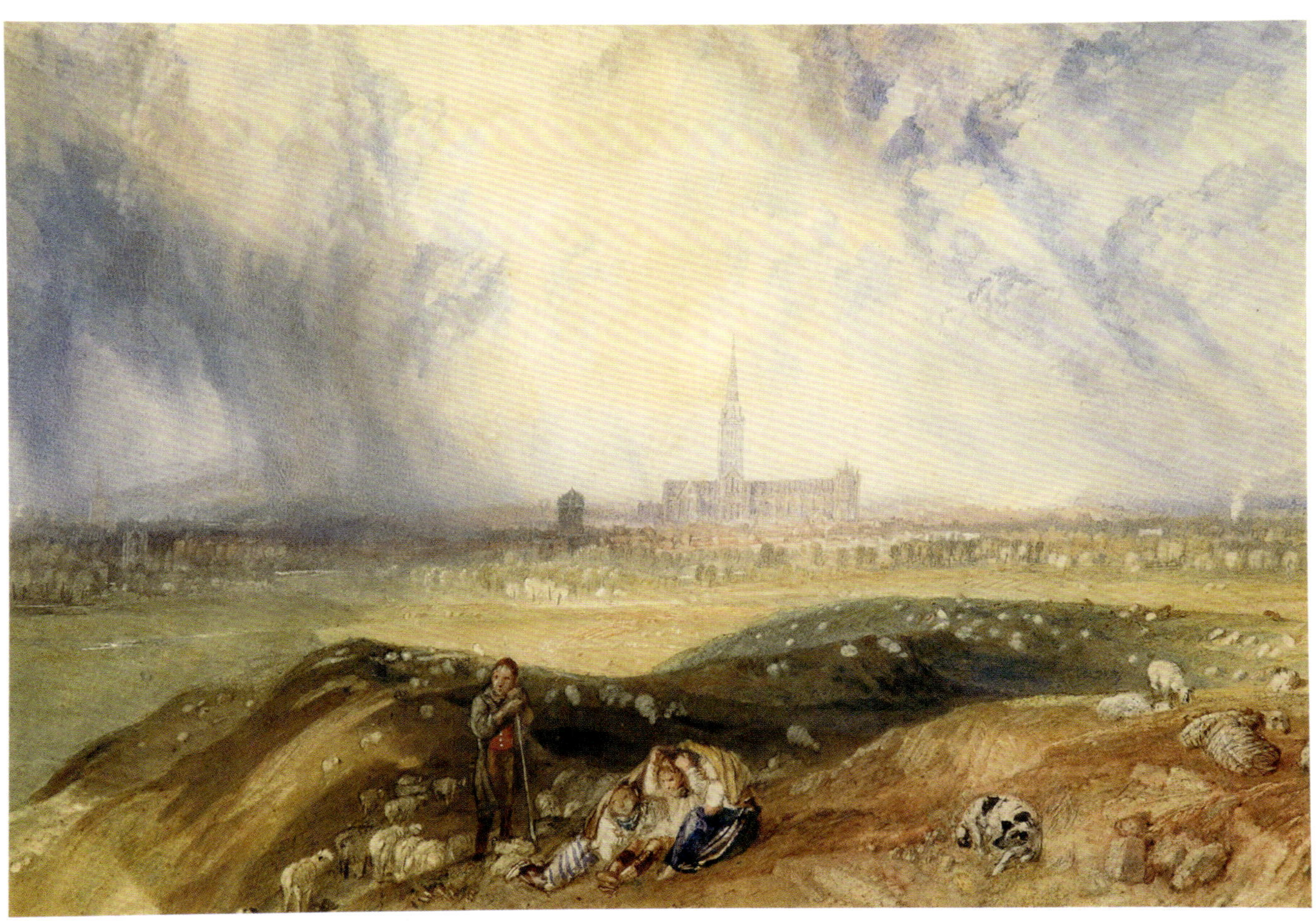

FIG. 22 **J.M.W. Turner** *Distant View from Old Sarum* c.1827
Watercolour on paper, 27·2 × 39·5
The Salisbury Museum. Acquired through Acceptance in Lieu from Dept of National Heritage

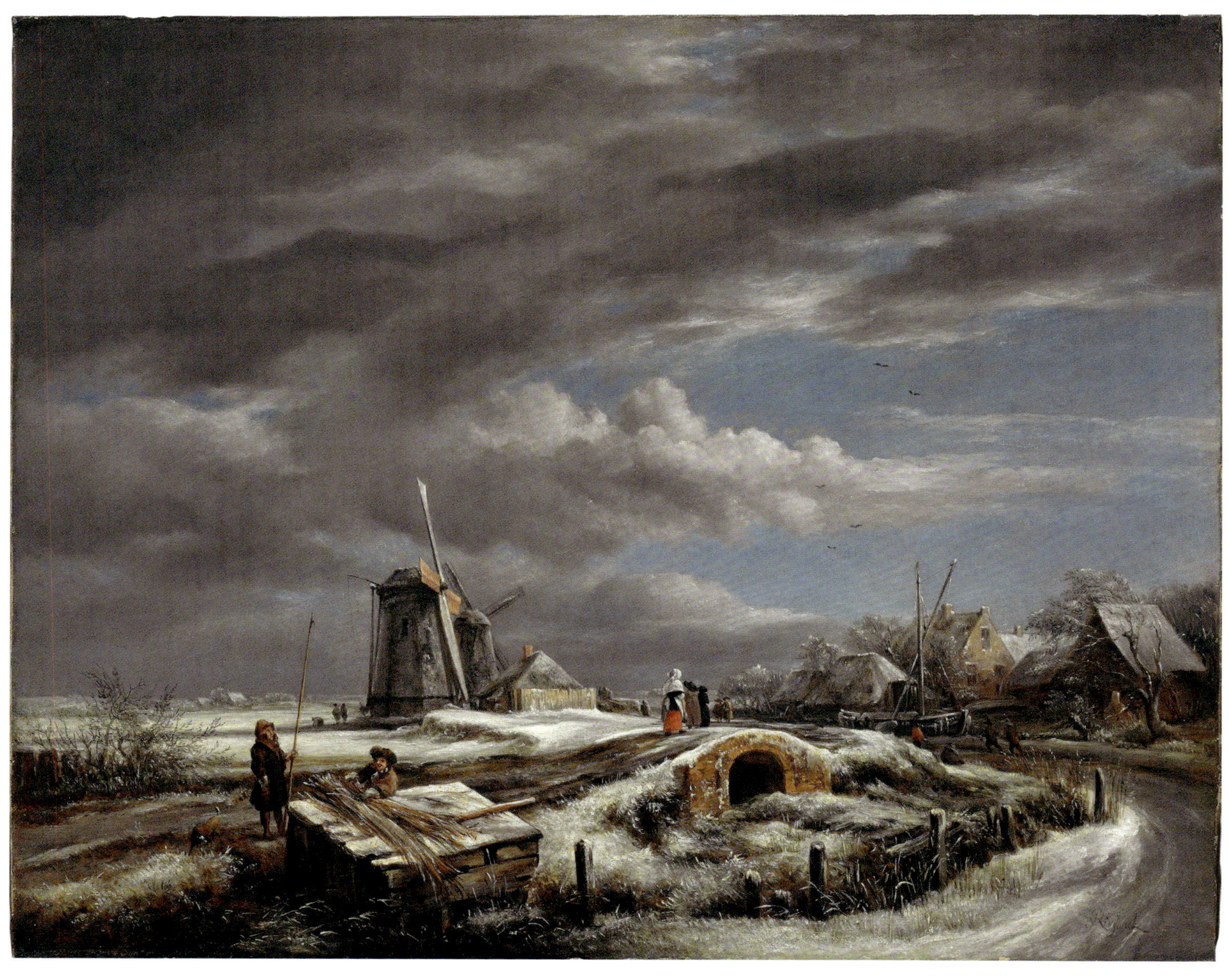

FIG. 23 **John Constable** after Jacob van Ruisdael
Winter Landscape with Figures on a Path, a Footbridge and Windmills Beyond 1832. Oil paint on canvas, 55·8 × 71·4
Private Collection

THE ORGAN OF SENTIMENT

NICHOLAS ROBBINS

In the last few years of his life, John Constable gave a series of lectures about the art of landscape. Walking his audience through landscape's gradual emergence as a serious subject for painting, he paused to discuss a copy he had made of a wintry scene by the seventeenth-century Dutch painter Jacob van Ruisdael (fig.23).

> The picture represents an approaching thaw. The ground is covered with snow, and the trees are still white; but there are two windmills near the centre; the one has the sails furled, and is turned in the position from which the wind blew when the mill left off work; the other has the canvas on the poles, and is turned another way, which indicates a change in the wind. The clouds are opening in that direction, which appears by the glow in the sky to be the south (the sun's winter habitation in our hemisphere), and this change will produce a thaw before the morning. The concurrence of these circumstances shows that [Ruisdael] *understood* what he was painting. [1]

This is a curious way to read a painting. Constable's interest is not in composition or colour, or in the specific associations of Ruisdael's depiction of rural life. Instead, via the movements of windmills and clouds in the painting, he begins to imagine an unfolding of atmospheric conditions that takes us far beyond the moment the painting depicts. He draws here on the knowledge from his childhood in East Bergholt, where he observed the mills owned and operated by his father, and from his lifetime spent watching the weather closely. [2] Ruisdael's picture, he says, 'told a story', but this story is about the movement of air and the thawing of ice, about the path travelled by the sun in the northern hemisphere, about the whole set of 'circumstances' that make up the feeling of the painting. [3] This, Constable believed, was the kind of knowledge and experimentation painting should embody.

Constable made dozens of oil sketches of clouds and skies over the course of his career. [4] The most famous of these were painted on Hampstead Heath between 1820 and 1823, which Constable (as one writer puts it) experienced as a kind of natural '"observatory" for meteorological phenomena'. [5] While many of the artist's predecessors and contemporaries had painted outside, directly in front of their motifs, Constable took this practice further, focusing intently on perhaps the most fugitive subject possible. He built up an entire archive of cloud forms – a kind of 'natural history...of the skies', as he put it – that served both professional and, it seems, private purposes. [6] Each of the studies is different; we might say each has its own personality. Some linger on a sense of mobility and breeziness or on the silvery illumination in seemingly edgeless clouds (no.114); in some the atmospheric world is populated by hastily notated figures, as at sunset near the ocean (no.145), or in others by birds as they glide through the air (no.109). The repetition of subject matter results not in narrowness but in a gradual attunement to difference and variety.

Constable's deeper interest in painting clouds began around 1820 at a moment when he was being criticised for the inaccuracy or obtrusiveness of the skies in his landscape paintings exhibited at the Royal Academy. The cloud studies could, in this way, be seen as a straightforward way of responding to his public. But in a letter he wrote to his close friend John Fisher, we see that the aims of this self-improvement ran deeper. In landscape painting, Constable wrote, the sky is the '"*key note*", the *standard of* "*Scale*", and the chief "*Organ of sentiment*"...The sky is the "*source of light*" in nature – and governs every thing.' [7] To paint the sky was to try to get at the very origin of landscape and the source of its unity and significance. 'Sentiment', here, is a complex word. It concerns not just an emotional response but also knowledge obtained through physical experience and through the senses. The images that emerge from the cloud studies are complemented by inscriptions on the back, recording the time and day of their making, the weather when they were made and (sometimes) the weather that followed. The sky yielded a combination of emotional and empirical effects.

Near the conclusion of his 'Lectures on Landscape', Constable made what might have seemed a startling claim about his profession: 'Painting is a science, and should be pursued as a branch of natural philosophy, of which pictures are but the experiments.' [8] The empirical bent of Constable's painting is perhaps most evident in his cloud studies. They evidence the kind of slow, patient, repetitive acts of looking and recording that were at the heart of natural history, both popular works like Gilbert White's *Natural History of Selborne* (1789) and the more specialist publications that Constable consulted.[9] For Constable the 'experiment' was experience itself: the translation of his sensations into the recalcitrant but alchemical medium of paint, particularly in the rapid, provisional responses recorded in the brushwork of his oil-on-paper sketches. To give form and substance to clouds, to understand their motion and interrelation, was in itself the work of natural history.

Constable pursued this painterly experiment in parallel with the developing science of meteorology. The nomenclature we now use for clouds – cumulus, cirrus, stratus, nimbus – was proposed in 1802 by the chemist Luke Howard, as part of his own lifelong pursuit to study and enumerate Britain's climate.[10] Howard, an avid sketcher, included in his essay on clouds a set of images of these newly named cloud-forms to aid other weather record-keepers in their efforts to read the sky (fig.24). Howard's cloud classifications have often been claimed as a key source for Constable's cloud studies.[11] They are perhaps more productively viewed in parallel, as related but different efforts to give form to the atmosphere and to understand the laws of climate that, like light, were imagined to 'gover[n] every thing'.

Over the course of Constable's lifetime, meteorological record-keeping in Britain went from being a private pursuit to a matter of state and imperial concern.[12] His exhibition landscapes were understood by critics to convey a particularly 'English' atmosphere, a sense of 'English' weather, freshness, bloom and vitality. This was important in a moment when climate was understood to shape the politics and culture of nations. England's damp and changeable climate, formerly considered inhospitable to the making of art, was refashioned in Constable's paintings as a generative environment for artists and for the refinement of aesthetic taste. The cloud studies were also made at a moment of acceleration in the use of fossil fuels, urbanisation and industrialisation, and intensive extraction of resources in Britain and the British empire. These changes, too, were being recorded in the atmosphere, though the artist would not have been able to sense this. For Constable, the momentary changeability of the cloud was balanced by his belief in climate's stability, in England's climate as some kind of permanent sign of belonging and identity.[13]

In *The Englishness of English Art*, Nikolaus Pevsner wrote that Constable took an 'atmospheric view of the world'.[14] In this stance we can also sense a different way of understanding what appears to be Constable's intensely local understanding of landscape. In his description of Ruisdael's painting, all the motions and changes of the world are filtered through the sensitive arms of these two windmills. The air, then, was understood as a medium of communication from far-away places; clouds could be read as portents of past and future.[15] Constable's oil sketches model a kind of responsiveness to these changes, a windmill-like sensitivity to small shifts in wind, light and air, to effects both near and far.

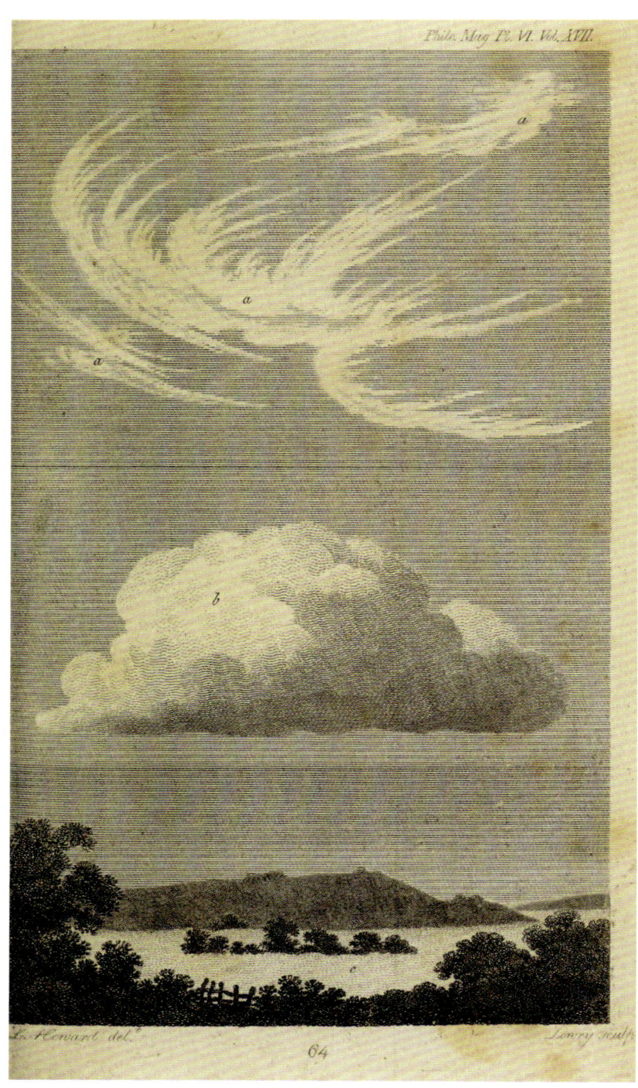

FIG. 24 **Wilson Lowry after Luke Howard**, illustration for 'On the Modifications of Clouds' in *Philosophical Magazine* 17 (1803), line engraving

'MORE MATTER WITH LESS ART': CONSTABLE'S TEXTURAL AESTHETIC

SARAH GOULD

In an 1802 letter to his mentor and childhood friend John Dunthorne, John Constable, then twenty-six and far from the public recognition he would later achieve, famously declared his fundamental commitment to naturalism: 'there is room enough for a natural painture [a type of painting]'. In the same letter he also made a lesser-known but critical observation: 'The great vice of the present day is bravura, an attempt at something beyond the truth.' [1] Constable's invocation of 'bravura' – which connotes visible brushwork – highlights what he saw as a prevailing tendency towards over-painting as opposed to a serious quest for veracity. Yet, paradoxically, it is these very qualities – painterly boldness combined with a commitment to truth – that would profoundly shape the character of his work.

The relationship between English painters and oil paint is 'almost always dangerous', wrote the French essayist Elie Faure, in his early 1920s *History of Art*; these artists 'triturate it, they thicken it'. Constable did not escape his criticism, indulging in the 'heavy cookery in which Reynolds left almost all his gifts'. [2] Faure's depiction not only reflects a critical ambivalence towards Constable's technique – accused in his time of spoiling and muddling the surfaces of his works – but also encapsulates a broader narrative. While we often associate the material relief of painting with a break from conventions and norms (think of the Impressionists in late nineteenth-century France), [3] British art narrates an alternate tale, one in which both Constable and Turner gained official recognition thanks to and despite their painterly innovations, but also one in which the next generation of artists, the Pre-Raphaelites, aligned meticulously slick surfaces with aesthetic radicalism.

Constable's approach to painting challenged the precepts of classicism, which implied that the less visible the traces of production, the more the painting resembled nature. Yet his technique was not simply one of 'bravura', a form of virtuosic execution that points to the creative process, [4] but rather, as the Queen in *Hamlet* demands, one of 'more matter with less art'. [5] This request correlates the conceptual hierarchy between mind and matter, suggesting that art, like mind, stands in opposition to matter. For Hamlet's mother, art is deception whereas matter is truth. This philosophical stance is central to understanding Constable's art. How, then, can we situate Constable's painterliness within the narrative of British art? What made the textures of his works so radical at a time when the very fabric and substance of the industrial world he inhabited and breathed was undergoing profound changes?

The reception of Constable's flaunted textures was marked by bafflement and perplexity, echoing that of Turner, whose brushwork, a matter of taste, provoked grotesque speculation about the materials he used: 'eggs', 'mustard', 'curry' or 'spinach'. [6] For Constable the ridicule was similarly textured, though expressed through meteorological metaphors; critics sneeringly asked whether his paintings depicted 'rain' or 'snow', as if the weather itself had fallen out of his canvases.

By 1821 critics were routinely commenting on the 'coarseness' or 'spottiness' of his work, but in 1823 one critic, commenting on the 'handling' of *Salisbury Cathedral*, said that Constable had given 'to all his trees and herbage the appearance of sleet or snow having fallen'. [7] This was the first occurrence of the reference to 'snow', which would reappear in 1831 and become a standard running joke among critics with the coining of the term 'Constable's snow', used to describe his use of white flecks of paint scattered across the canvas. [8]

Henri Fuseli once quipped that he needed protection to see Constables: 'bring me my umbrella! I'm go-oing to looke at Meester Cone-stable's pictur.' [9] This joke captures the essence of Constable's fascination with atmospheric conditions so vividly rendered that viewers joked about getting soaked. Mark Hallett has noted this obsession with 'freshness', around the year 1825, both in the critical voice and in Constable's letters.[10] He points out that the terminology reflects the embodied experience the artist's work created, particularly in crowded exhibition spaces where it had to attract considerable attention. This vocabulary also indicates the direct hold on nature that a new relationship with the observed matter introduces.

Central to the artistic debates of the period was the notion that landscape painters should go beyond the mere depiction of nature – a task traditionally assigned to topographers – and instead aim to create embodied representations. A skilled landscape painter was one who not only depicted nature but also captured the sensory experience of being in it. Critics often found Constable's work puzzling, dismissing his style, what they called his 'mannerism'.[11] Yet in their criticisms they inadvertently highlighted what we now recognise as the 'agency' of his works. In Constable's paintings one encounters the stuff of nature: vividly rendered clouds (*Cloud Study* 1822,, no.114), moist leaves (*Dedham Vale* 1828, no.32) and bark (fig.25), all materialised in paint. We are confronted with what anthropologist Alfred Gell has described as the 'enchantment of technology'; here, technique is not merely a tool but what activates the work.[12] Through his shaggy textures and rough brushstrokes, natural elements become animated and tangible.

Constable's white spots, also characterised as 'whitewashed' by the critics,[13] intriguingly play with the notion of cleanliness – spotted, yet immaculately white. Again, these were not purely formal choices. Nicholas Robbins notes Constable's ambivalent, almost 'phobic relationship to London', citing what he perceived as his reaction to 'the coal-smoked atmosphere of the city, from which his thickly deposited white "dew" aimed to protect the interior volume of light and air'.[14] In a sense, Constable's works are a verso to Turner's depictions of steamships and industrial cityscapes, which remain out of frame in Constable's works (except in the cityscape *The Opening of Waterloo Bridge* 1832).[15] According to conservator Sarah Cove, Constable deliberately brightened his canvases to counteract the darkening effects of pollution.[16] We're invited to reflect not only on the impact of polluted atmospheres on Constable's works, but to understand how their substances are intrinsically woven into the fabric of their world.

What critics pointed out was that Constable represented what the art historian Jennifer Roberts calls 'unbounded matter', a phrase she uses in her discussion of the 'material turn' in art history to describe the new scholarly attention to intangible elements such as clouds, rain, snow and air.[17] Constable painted at a moment when the elements themselves were undergoing dramatic changes, changes that demanded a new kind of artistic engagement. His works somehow empathise texturally with their subjects. Throughout his career he sought not only to depict nature, but also to recreate textures, to create works that were analogous to it, to provide a painterly equivalent of the world.

As Faure noted, Constable and Gainsborough share a painterly lineage, yet they differ significantly in their approaches. Gainsborough's 'odd scratches and marks', to quote Reynolds's backhanded compliment, captured the materiality of objects like fabric and leaves, while Constable and Turner shifted to depicting elemental materiality: clouds, air, steam, rain.[18] They were the first generation to bridge the gap between the representation and materialisation of solid textures and more unbounded, fluid ones. Yet what about the generations that followed?

Constable's legacy is immense. The radicality of his brushwork was a significant source of influence for whole generations of artists. When the Grand Palais in Paris embarked on the project of a Constable exhibition in 2003, they called on the expertise of Lucian Freud. Towards the end of the 1970s Freud began to use the lead-based paint Cremnitz White, the sculptural density of which he found ideal for depicting the solidity of flesh. But what about another London School painter? In Frank Auerbach's works, thickly laid-on, pigmented matter is slashed across the canvas: it soars, bulges and threatens to fall. The paint is sometimes squeezed out directly from the tube; it creates what I call a ready-made texture, pulsating with substance and revealing an alternative version of the modernist dictate of 'truth to the medium'. R.B. Kitaj discussed this in terms of the 'human clay'.[19] There is a palpable tension between the mundane reality Freud or Auerbach paint and the reality of the paint itself. Like Constable's, their works confront viewers with a surplus of material presence, but here it's a testament to the flesh, the human body.

This lineage invites us to consider Constable's impastos not merely as technical showmanship, but as deeply contextual – aesthetically and environmentally. By exhibiting blatant factures and leaving brushstrokes visible on the surface, Constable – and Turner as well – sought to transcend the two-dimensional fate of painting, giving a tangibility that, in turn, lent their landscapes both literal and symbolic density and solidity. While it is often said that they elevated landscape to the genre of history painting, they also imbued the elements themselves with historical significance.

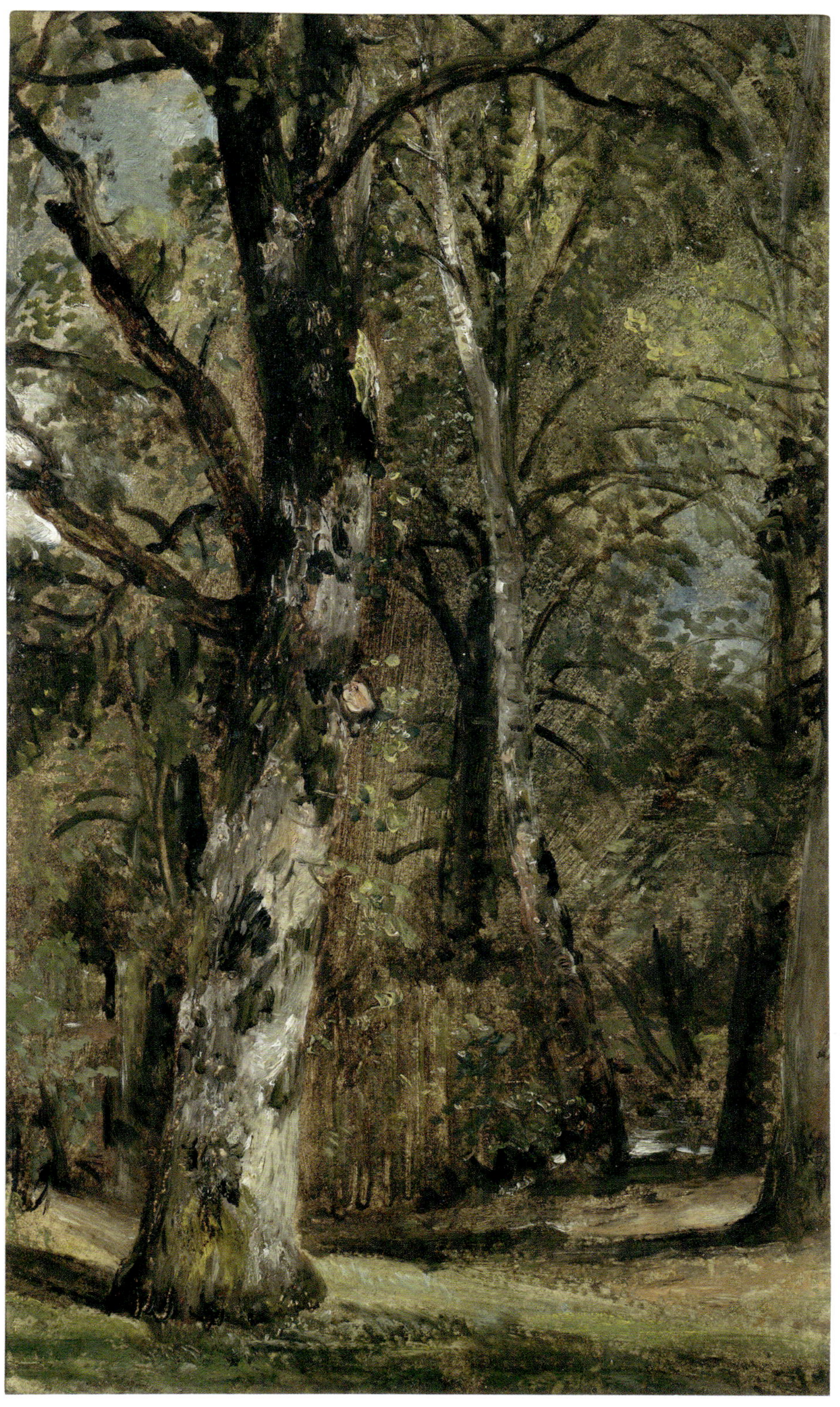

FIG. 25 **John Constable** *Avenue of Trees* c.1820
Oil paint on canvas, 52 × 36
Colchester and Ipswich Museums. Purchased from the Barratt Collection

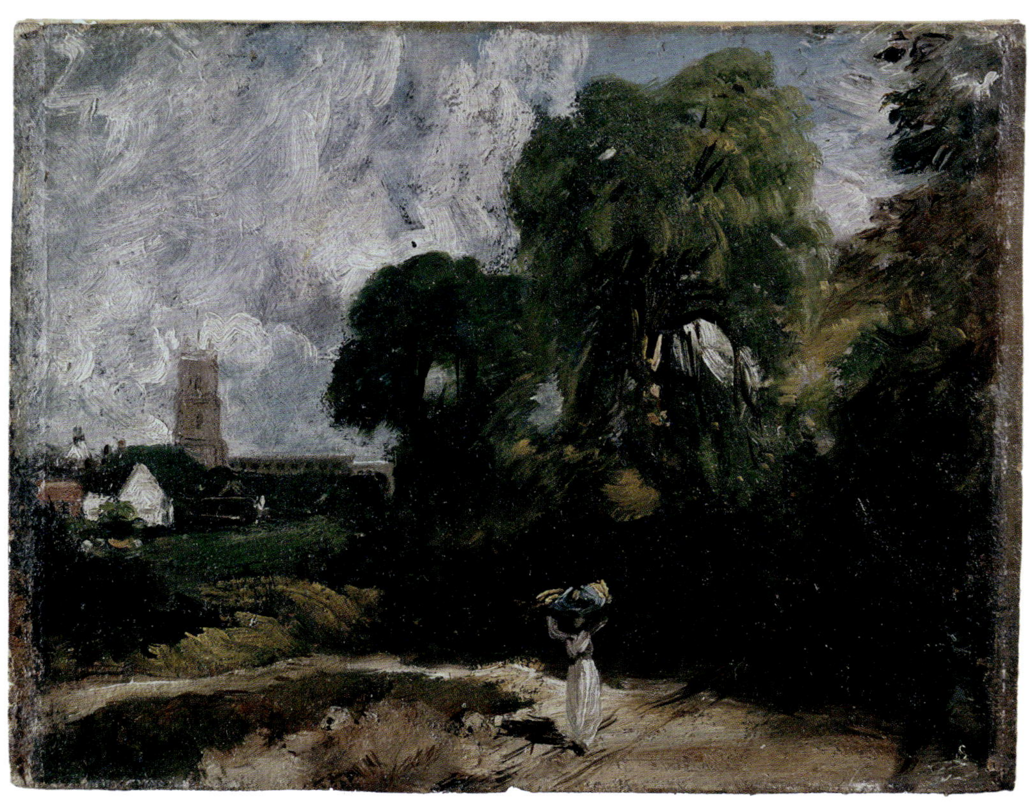

FIG. 26 **John Constable** *Stoke-by-Nayland* c.1830
Oil paint on canvas, 33 × 45·3
Victoria and Albert Museum, London

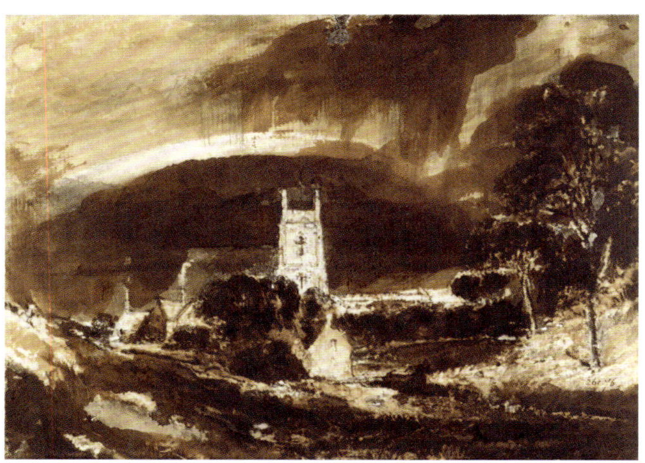

FIG. 27 **John Constable** *Stoke-by-Nayland* c.1830
Sepia and paper, 12·7 × 18·3
Victoria and Albert Museum, London

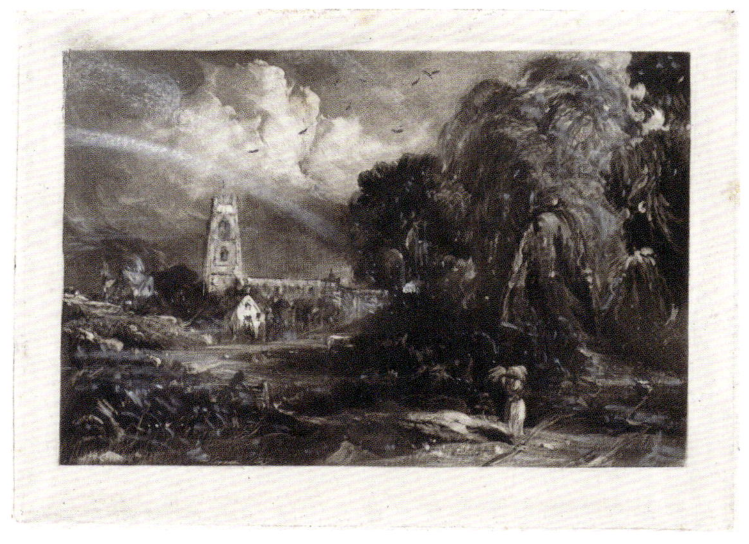

FIG. 28 **John Constable and David Lucas** *Stoke-by-Neyland* 1829
Mezzotint touched with white chalk and black ink; proof before published state, 17·8 × 25·1
The Metropolitan Museum of Art, New York. Harris Brisbane Dick Fund, 1927

'UT UMBRA SIC VITA': LIFE IS BUT A SHADOW

KATHARINE MARTIN

'Ut Umbra sic Vita' – Life is but a Shadow. John Constable chose these words to accompany the last plate (fig.29) of *English Landscape Scenery*, a series of mezzotint prints engraved under his close supervision by printmaker David Lucas (1802–1881).[1] The phrase points towards the essence of mezzotint, a monochromatic print technique that Constable chose for its ability to convey deep shadow, bright light and a vast range of tones in between. Yet it also says something of the centrality of light to Constable's artistic vision, and of the periods of both darkness and light in his own life's journey. Although the image depicts Hampstead Heath in London, the artist's home from 1828, 'Ut Umbra sic Vita' directs us back to Constable's native landscape, and to his Christianity, for the phrase is borrowed from the sundial of the church he attended as a boy, St Mary's in the village of East Bergholt on the Suffolk–Essex border. The phrase also reflects Constable's stoicism in the face of difficulty, and his hope that greater truths may lie beyond mortal being. Finally, 'Ut Umbra sic Vita' speaks to Constable's legacy and the landscape series as a testament to his life's work and stated aim to study and depict nature accurately, in particular exploring light and shadow.[2]

In 1828, though recently widowed and father to seven children, Constable nevertheless embarked on a new printmaking venture with his usual indomitable spirit. The outcome was *Various Subjects of Landscape, Characteristic of English Scenery* (commonly referred to simply as *English Landscape*), a series of twenty-two mezzotint prints of landscape views based on Constable's paintings and drawings. These mezzotints were issued in instalments between 1830 and 1832: the first four instalments consisted of four prints each and the final one had six. Constable published a second edition of *English Landscape* in 1833 with one landscape view re-engraved and the prints rearranged. This also allowed him to write text for the series, including an introduction and commentaries on six landscape views, drawing upon subjects that interested him such as meteorology and English history. Constable hoped that the series would bring his work before a wider audience, as a print series could be much more broadly circulated and seen than the original artworks.

In developing his print series with Lucas, Constable was clearly influenced by the 1807–19 *Liber Studiorum* by Turner, whose grandiose vision for his series led Constable to ridicule it as the 'liber stupidorum'.[3] However, in format, style and content, *English Landscape* is closer than Turner's to topographical print series of the period, even though recent research shows that it remains distinct due to its eclectic views and their personal significance.[4] The majority of the prints depict places within a five-mile radius of Constable's birthplace, such as Dedham and Stoke-by-Nayland. Others feature places like Hampstead, Brighton and Salisbury in the south of England with which Constable had developed close connections through visiting family and friends. No one could argue that this mix represents anything like a summary of the landscape of England; it should be read more as *Constable's* English landscape.[5]

What makes *English Landscape* unique is its production quality. To translate Constable's vision and original works of varied sizes into smaller prints was an exceptional challenge. Constable's paintings also relied on minute juxtapositions of light and shadow, thick and expressive brushwork and fresh hues, making them all the harder to map into monochrome. Fortunately, in Lucas Constable found a recently qualified and talented mezzotinter who quickly became a master of the medium.

In mezzotint it is areas of graduated tone that form the image, rather than lines. The printmaker works from a metal plate whose surface has been pitted with a serrated, curved blade called a rocker. Using scrapers and burnishers, the printmaker gradually removes parts of the roughened surface to create the design. This medium was suited to Constable's passion for depicting light effects and for creating a range of light and dark tones called chiaroscuro. Indeed, in his second edition he stated this vision clearly by adding 'the Phenomena of the Chiar'oscuro of Nature' to the title.

For each mezzotint Constable sent one or several of his works to Lucas, who created an initial 'proof' version for Constable to review. Painter and printmaker then worked, often side by side, to 'touch' or correct the proof, Constable also writing additional sets of instructions to Lucas on what he wanted. Lucas implemented the desired changes before printing the next proof for inspection. Sometimes up to thirty proofs were produced to prepare a plate before Constable decided it was fit for publication, a laborious and time-consuming endeavour. The results, however, show why Constable was committed to this process and technique of printmaking.[6] Lucas was capable of capturing extensive tonal variation, texture and 'colour' in an extraordinary way, giving the viewer a true feeling of Constable's art. Furthermore, trial proofs show evidence of where Constable drew directly onto the proof and worked with Lucas to develop the next version, often going beyond the original painting. Undoubtedly, we need to consider these mezzotints as works of art in their own right.

The magnificent view of the fifteenth-century church of St Mary surmounting a hilltop at Stoke-by-Nayland was a favourite of Constable's and he sketched it throughout his career from multiple angles. Constable lent Lucas numerous works to refer to in engraving a plate of the church (no.178).[7] These included an oil sketch (fig.26) and sepia drawing (fig.27) that Constable may have made specifically to illustrate changes he wished Lucas to implement early in the plate's development. The oil sketch depicts the landscaping of the scene and a female figure carrying faggots, while the drawing shows the repositioning of the church tower in relation to the white gabled cottage, all of which Lucas introduced into the plate. In addition, the drawing appears to have inspired the inclusion of a rainbow. To demonstrate the heightened white tonality he was after, Constable also drew the rainbow on a proof with white body colour, scratching into the bow to create the illusion of its fluorescence (fig.28).[8] In addition, he used ink to draw birds in the sky and a man at the gate, which Lucas also engraved into the plate, the latter suggesting potential for interaction between the male and female figures.

Constable and Lucas worked with impressive focus and pace to produce *English Landscape*. Lucas engraved on steel plates, producing roughly one plate per month at his home in Paddington, London. Friends and relatives supported the endeavour, for instance with the painter C.R. Leslie, Constable's close friend and later biographer, occasionally advising Constable on which of his works to turn into mezzotint. Mrs Jane Lucas sourced the blue ribbon requested by Constable to bind the batches of prints together with paper wrappers, purchasers later choosing bindings to replace the original wrappers (which explains why so few survive).[9]

Constable was the commissioner of the work and the 'master' in charge of the project. However, the process was one of reciprocal learning between him and Lucas; Lucas, as the expert in mezzotinting, often advised Constable on how to develop the plates. Letters show that Constable was forever anxious about his financial outlay for the series and became frustrated with Lucas's delays in delivering proofs and his periods of silence. At times he berated Lucas for being 'hopeless' and producing work that 'ever will be as rotten as cow dung'.[10] Nevertheless, he celebrated his work in equal measure, praising its perfection and writing warmly of their 'bond of friendship'.[11] Their collaboration endured until Constable's death in 1837.

Like many contemporary landscape series, *English Landscape* was not a commercial success and sold few copies. It garnered little praise at the time, although one reviewer in the *Athenaeum* wrote enthusiastically that:

> The painter's object, which has evidently been to give the varied effects of chiaroscuro, has been well seconded by the engraver ... To the admirer – but that is a cold word – to the lover of nature, these, which are faithful miniatures of his mistress, will be treasures indeed.[12]

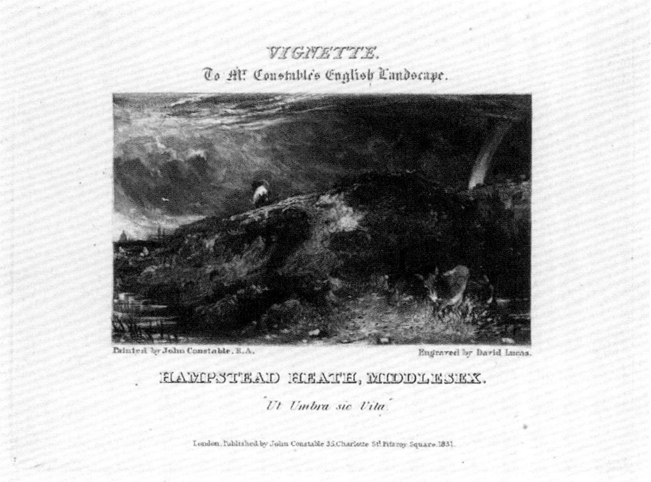

FIG. 29 **John Constable** *Vignette: Hampstead Heath, Middlesex*
Mezzotint on paper, 9·1 × 15·3
Tate. Purchased 1985

TURNER AND CONSTABLE: COLOUR

JOYCE H. TOWNSEND

Turner's keen interest in colour and unusual lighting effects is apparent in his earliest work. He was an early adopter of new materials from a young age. Sir Joshua Reynolds's portraits, some of which lost colour from the flesh tones or developed disfiguring cracks not long after his death in 1792, exemplified the hazards of not sticking to tried and tested materials and processes. Reynolds had cared more for immediate impact in a painting than for its longevity, and Turner maintained the same attitude throughout his life. Both Turner and Constable were born in the early part of the Industrial Revolution, during which new artists' colours were invented. [1] Understanding of their chemistry, their stability to light or any incompatibility with other colours would not develop until after their lifetimes. It is notable that it was artists' colourmen (suppliers) and later 'men of science', as they were styled at the time, who were more concerned about the durability of artists' materials than artists. Constable was the more cautious in material selection, as he was in life generally, but he too would experiment with several of the exciting new colours, mostly later than Turner did. The first studies into the stability of coloured pigments that echo the work of conservation scientists today would be carried out in 1888, partly in response to colour loss in Turner's watercolours, which had been much displayed after his death. [2]

Turner and Constable's paintboxes have survived, along with a large selection of the materials in Turner's studio when he died. [3] This is unusual for their era. Turner's paintbox (no. 33) is capacious enough to hold multiple stiff brushes for oil painting, over a dozen small containers of oil paint in different colours (bladders, the round brown objects placed in their own compartments because they tended to leak once opened), glass medicine bottles and other repurposed containers for dry pigments, bottles of now-discoloured oil, oil medium modifiers and/or watercolour medium, shorter brushes and quill brush heads for painting in watercolour. It could have accommodated stubs of graphite pencil, bottles of ink for sketching, or paintbrushes too. It has a cavity in the base, with grooves for slotting in still-wet sketches made outdoors, so that three could be carried home without risk of them sticking together and spoiling the day's work. The large jars of pigment for topping up the small bottles survive too, in a well-made wooden case that holds sixteen bottles, a majority containing different shades of crimson lakes and the others yellows and blues (fig.31). He owned a smaller, well-padded wooden medicine chest that held four larger bottles (fig.30) containing turpentine for thinning paint, two types of resin in turpentine for use as a medium modifier, and acetate of morphia (good for toothache or bad stomach upsets when abroad or making an extended stay in a friend's house). [4] Some of Turner's palettes survive too; Tate has three wooden ones for oil painting although only one has paint on (fig.33), and he used smaller white ceramic ones – a better background colour when working on off-white paper – for watercolour paint (no.34). He also created pocket-sized pouches with a selection of watercolour blocks stuck down, with covers to prevent spills of wet paint after use (no.35). Watercolour paint could also be rapidly prepared from dry pigment and gum water on a ground glass plate using a flat-bottomed glass muller with a small handle, which accounts for the bottles of dry pigment in the paintbox. Constable's paintbox (fig.32) is smaller than Turner's and the contents are mostly bladders of paint, but he had another large enough to rest on his knees while he made a sketch on millboard that fitted snugly into its lid, then slotted into its base for transport home. Tube paints were just becoming available by the end of Turner's life and his paintbox contains one (chrome yellow), among at least seventy distinct materials.

Turner would soon develop ways to depict in colour what he sketched on his travels. Throughout his life he would expand his range of coloured pigments from traditional ones to new products, such as a bright orange synthetic earth pigment that he sourced in his teens and would employ all his life in both watercolour and oil. The new patent yellow features in early works of Turner's such as *Fishermen at Sea* 1797 (no.12), in moonlight reflected off the water, where he could have used the more traditional pale Naples yellow. [5] Warm yellow and cool blue washes would become characteristic of his unfinished watercolours, such as *Study for Landscape Composition of Tivoli* c.1817 (no.43) or *Sunset Study* c.1820–30 (fig.34). [6] In more finished watercolours these are augmented with greater varieties of yellow and blue tones and telling spots of other colours, as in *Norham Castle on the Tweed* c.1822–3 (no.118) and *The Blue Rigi* 1842 (no.158). Using a wide and non-traditional range of colours in his watercolours,

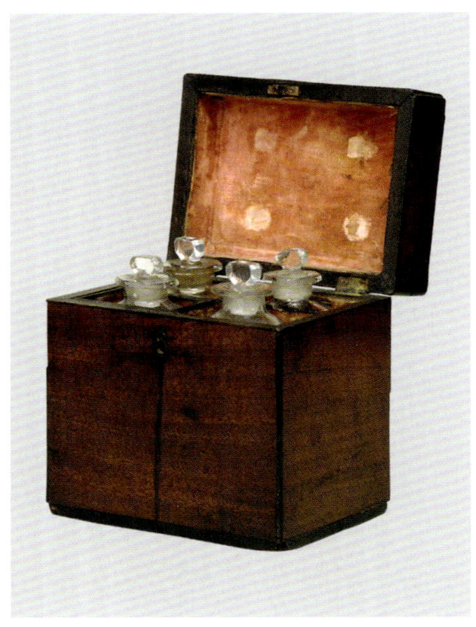

FIG. 30 Small wooden case with silk-lined lid containing four small bottles with glass stoppers which once contained Turpentine, Dammar solution of Turpentine, Acetate of Morphia and a resinous Solution of Turpentine.
Tate Archive, TGA 7315/8

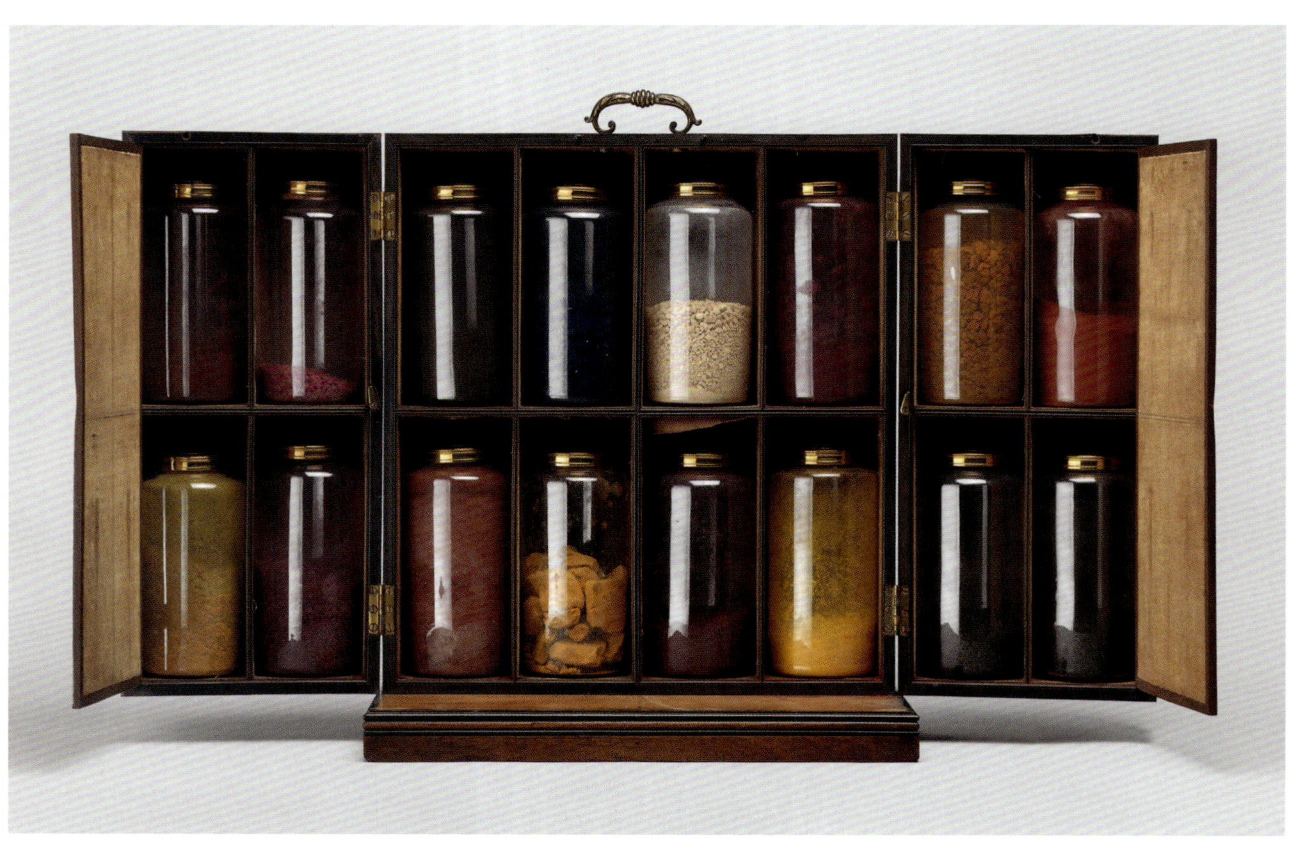

FIG. 31 Turner's pigment cabinet
Large wooden double-doored cabinet with carrying handle incorporating shelves containing sixteen bottles of various chemicals and agents for mixing paints, 52·3 × 47·2 × 22·9 (closed dimensions)
Tate Archive, TGA 7315/7

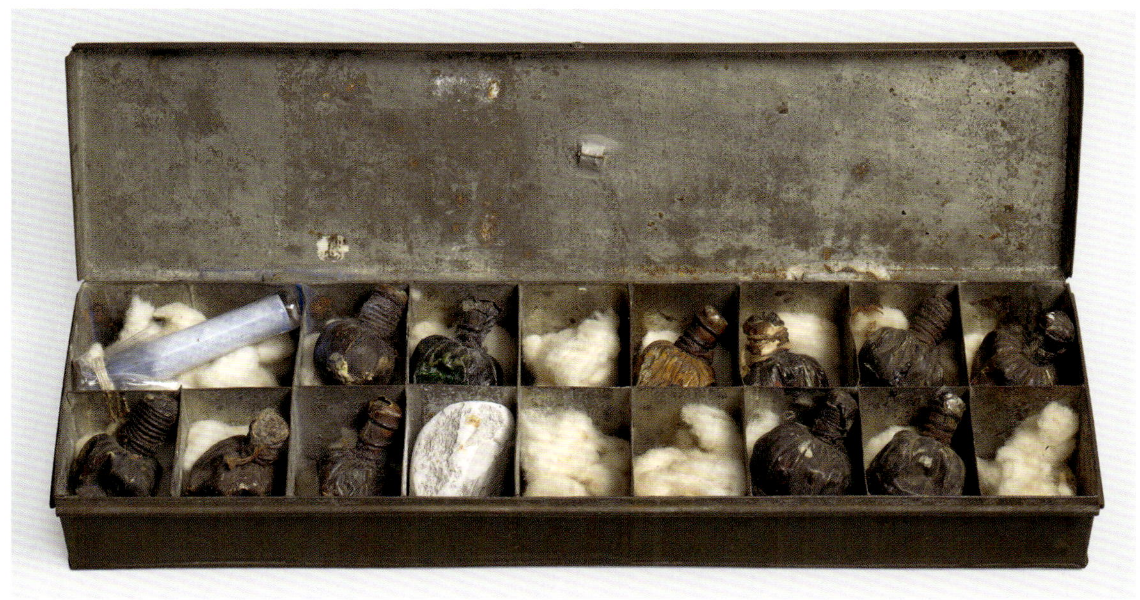

FIG. 32 Constable's metal paint box c.1837
Clark Art Institute, gift of the Manton Art Foundation in memory of Sir Edwin and Lady Manton, 2007.8.57

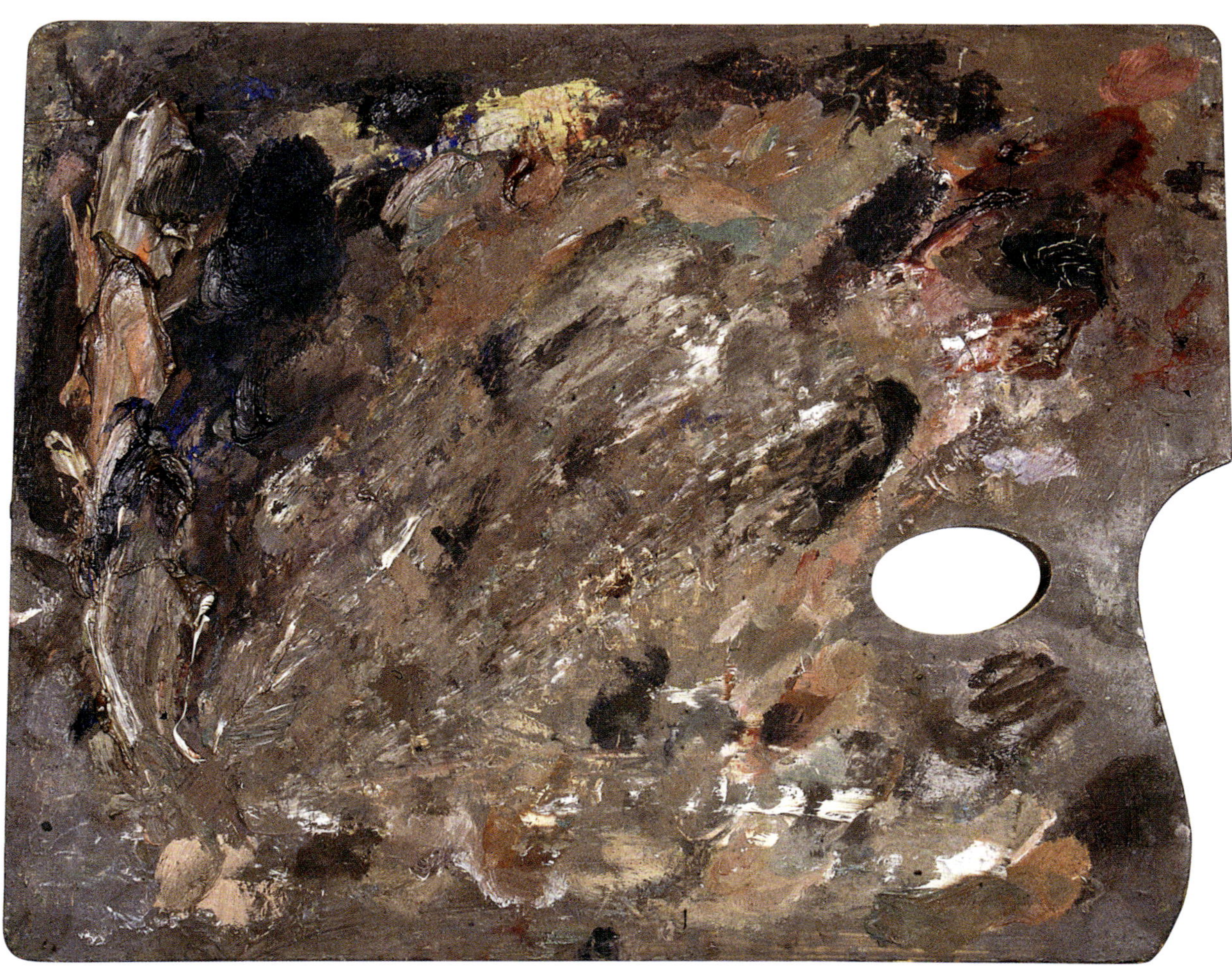

FIG. 33 Turner's 'Chelsea' oil palette
Wooden palette with paint on its surface, 33·6 × 43
Tate Archive, TGA 871/15

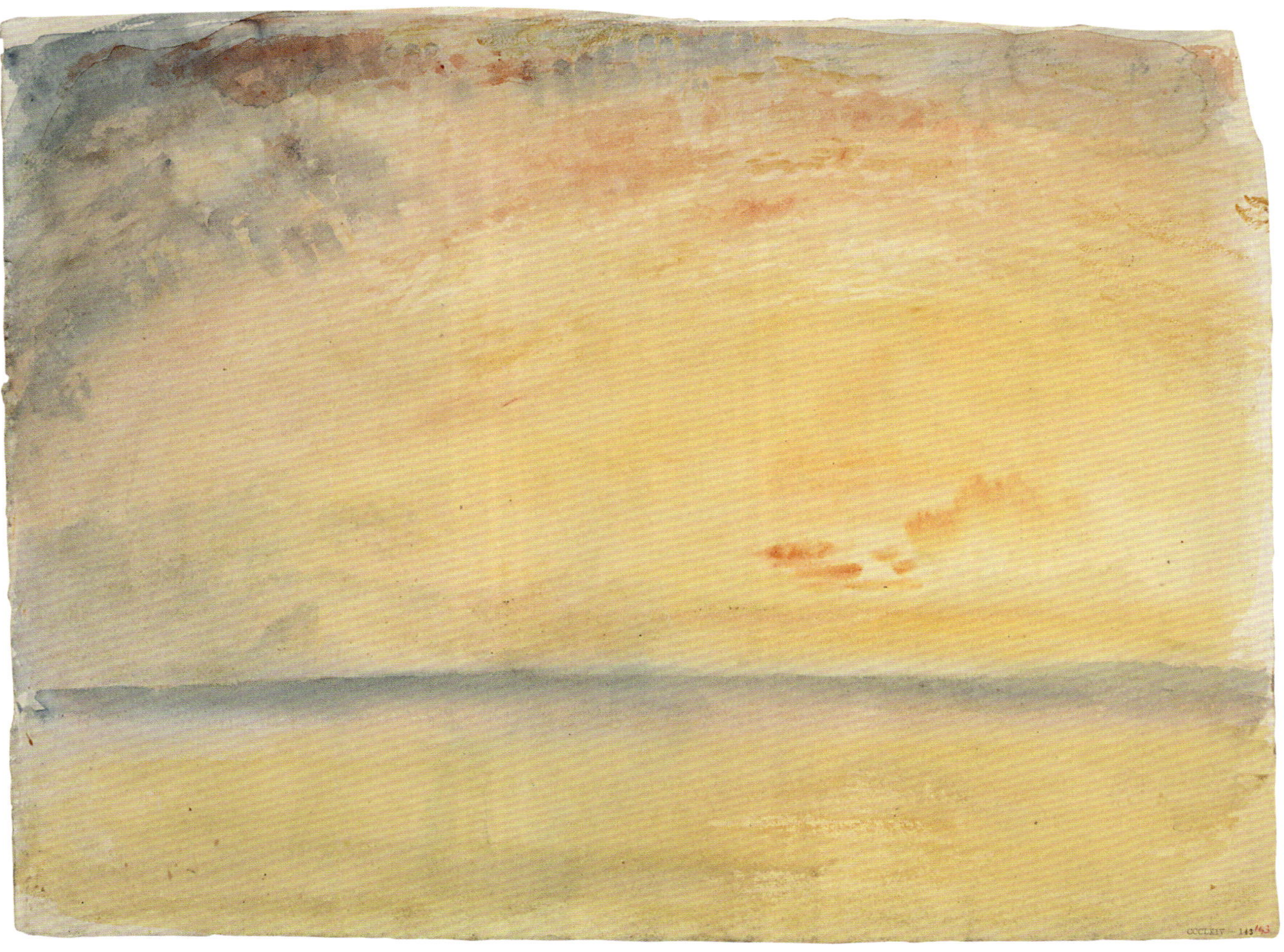

FIG. 34 **J.M.W. Turner** *Sunset Study, Probably for Flint Castle* c.1820–30
Watercolour on paper, 27·4 × 37·5
Tate. Accepted by the nation as part of the Turner Bequest 1856

the same ones as in his oils, gave him a competitive edge and inspired other artists to do so too: John Ruskin (1819–1900) would follow his example in his lifetime, and in the 1850s so did John Frederick Lewis (1804–1876) and Dante Gabriel Rossetti (1828–1882) and his circle.

To be eligible for Royal Academy membership, Turner began to exhibit oil paintings. He introduced small areas of intense colour into his earliest oils: the rainbow in *Buttermere Lake, with Part of Cromackwater, Cumberland, a Shower* 1798 (no.14) gave reason to introduce red vermilion, a crimson lake pigment and intense Prussian blue in an otherwise dark and stormy scene, while in *Morning amongst the Coniston Fells, Cumberland* 1798 (no.15) and *Dolbadern Castle, North Wales* 1800 (no.1) spots of bright yellow created by the strategic use of yellow ochre gleam within the brooding sublime Welsh landscape. These were traditional pigments used by all other artists but deployed to dramatic effect.

Crossing the Brook 1815 (no.30) includes not only vermilion, red lake, yellow ochre, Naples yellow and Prussian blue, which he had used earlier with the very traditional yellow orpiment, but also strontium yellow and cobalt blue, which had just become available. In the same decade he adopted opaque chrome yellow (patented 1814 and used by him in the same year), which he obtained initially in a mid tone and in the next few years in pale, deep and orange tones too. By the 1820s different shades of chrome yellow can be identified in watercolours on off-white and blue papers, and in every oil painting. *Norham Castle* c.1845 (no.181) is a study in pale chrome yellow, ultramarine and cobalt blue, used to great effect on a canvas with a white ground, which was Turner's preferred colour of support for oil painting.

Bright, opaque yellows also appealed to Constable. In 1816 he began to use chrome yellow, and by 1820 he was mixing it with Prussian blue to create a series of brilliant greens for tiny highlights in sunlit landscapes.[7] The blues he used for skies included ultramarine at all periods of his life, plus cobalt blue after about 1820. Throughout his life Constable would mix greens from blue and brown pigments for duller ones and blue and yellow for the brighter ones, giving a vast range of tones augmented further with mixtures of black and a bright yellow. This holds for both oils and watercolours, and for Turner's earlier watercolours of English landscapes as well. Constable's universal use of mixtures of the same blues and yellows used pure elsewhere on the canvas kept the landscape harmonious, so that bright red and blue used for garments worn by relatively small figures within the largest landscapes would stand out dramatically. While Constable's technique garnered much criticism (as Sarah Gould discusses in this volume, see pp.45–7), his use of colour circumvented criticism frequently levelled against Turner for disharmony. From the 1830s Turner unleashed his appetite for bold and brilliant colour, with the intensity of works like *Light and Colour (Goethe's Theory)*, exhibited 1845 (no.167), coming from expanses of chrome yellow and the newly invented emerald green or the bluer-toned viridian green used instead of mixed greens.

Obtaining the newest colours became a constant preoccupation for both artists, and both were friends of the foremost artists' colourman and paint technologist of the age, their contemporary George Field (1777–1854).[8] He supplied both artists with new pigments as well as established ones in newer and more brilliant tones.

The more Turner oils are examined, the earlier the dates seem when the artist first used a new pigment. By the later 1820s he was using emerald green in most paintings, and often for telling spots of intense colours in watercolours on blue paper, for subjects both at home and abroad. He used barium yellow, an opaque pale pigment resembling the earlier patent yellow in *Light and Colour (Goethe's Theory)* and indeed from the end of the 1820s. Iodine scarlet has been found on little-restored Turner oils such as *The Fighting Temeraire*.[9] It is found more regularly in Constable's paintings, which mostly remain in better condition today than Turner's (and therefore have had fewer conservation treatments), due to Turner's habit of applying numerous layers of modified oil media without waiting for the optimum drying of earlier layers.

Both Turner and Constable were experimental and opportunistic in their attitude to colour compared to their peers. Both ignored the concerns expressed by colourmen and critics about the permanence of their colours, Turner to a greater degree. More justified criticism of the permanence of Turner's varied techniques of paint application and his use of additives to his oil paints fell on equally deaf ears. Constable's innovation was in brushwork more than paint modification, and his works are often closer to their original appearance than are many of Turner's.

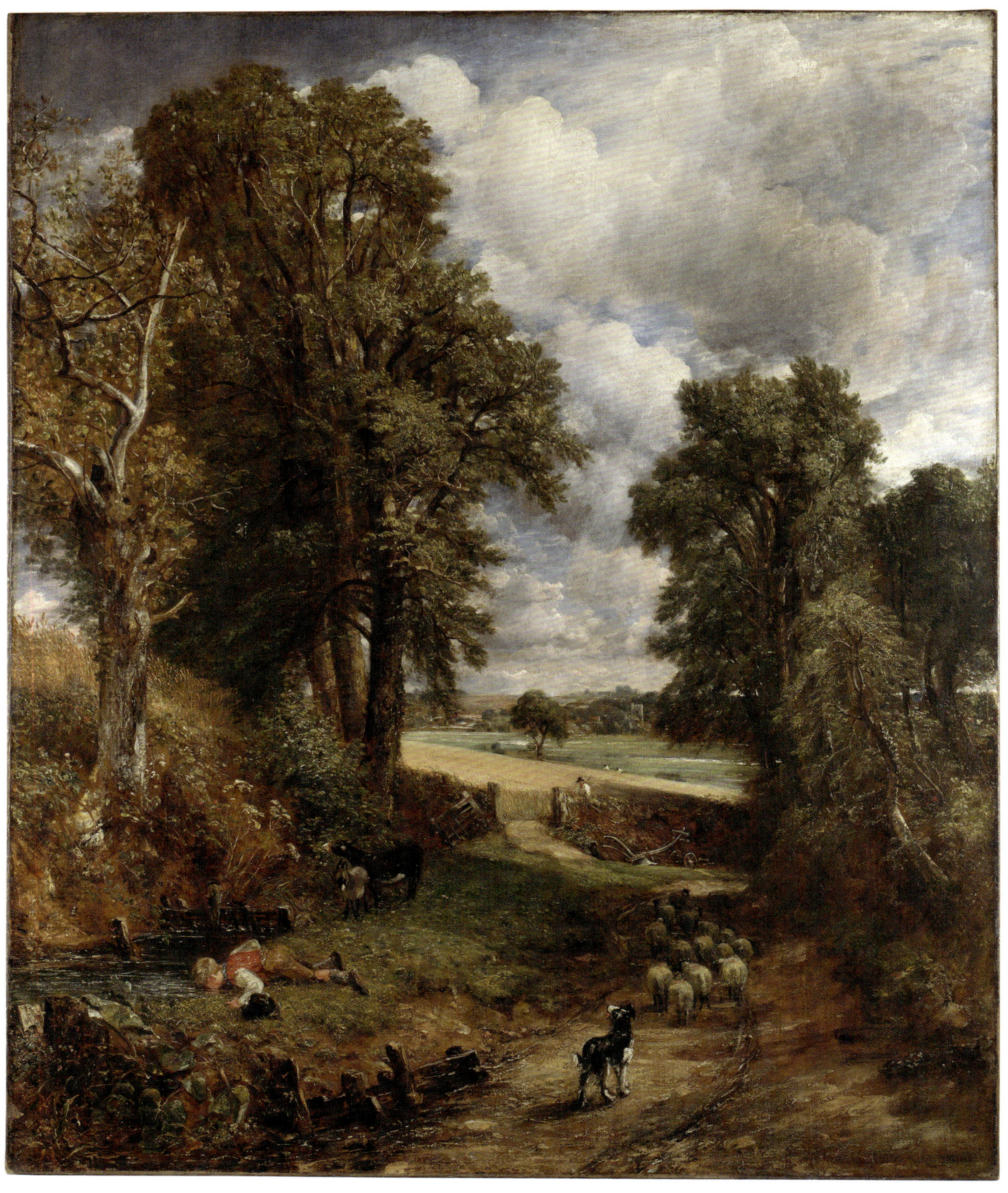

FIG. 35 **John Constable** *The Cornfield* 1826
Oil on canvas, 143 × 122
The National Gallery, London. Presented by subscribers, including Wordsworth, Faraday and Sir William Beechey, 1837

CONSTABLE AND TURNER REMADE

RICHARD JOHNS

> I like the picture not so much for what you *can* see, as for what you can't. I'm always wondering what's going on just round the bend – behind the trees. [1]

Thirty years ago the artist and teacher Colin Painter placed an advertisement in a south London free newspaper with an appeal: 'Do you have this picture in your home, or something with this picture on it?' [2] The picture in question, illustrated but not identified on the page, was *The Cornfield* by John Constable (fig.35), a painting distinguished by being the first from the artist to enter the national collection, shortly after his death in 1837. The testimony of readers who had recognised the painting and taken the trouble to reply formed the basis of an innovative exhibition at London's National Gallery in 1996, in which Constable's celebrated work was displayed alongside dozens of household objects, from ceramic plates to soft furnishings, each bearing a likeness of Constable's creation.

The juxtaposition of a priceless work of art with so many inexpensive copies – some mechanically reproduced, others lovingly handcrafted – brought home the extent to which Constable's vision of rural England had found a place, and meaning, in the everyday experience of a wide cross-section of society. For some contributors to the exhibition, the value placed on their *Cornfield* owed little to the reputation of the artist or to the cultural prestige of the National Gallery (some were unaware of either). For many, *The Cornfield* held memories of a more personal and unpredictable kind: of time spent with family or friends who shared an appreciation of the image, or of a younger self. For others, the sun-dappled country lane and ready harvest represented an imagined alternative to a largely urban existence, away from the polluted air and rivers of the modern city.

It would be easy to dismiss souvenir Constable as little more than a romantic attachment to a mythical Old England, reducing the artist's pictorial innovation to what one critic has called a 'perpetually sentimentalised glow'. [3] By the end of the twentieth century, the rural idyll exemplified by *The Cornfield* had been roundly challenged by a generation of art historians determined to foreground the persistent inequities of the English countryside, including the systemic rural poverty that remains out of the picture whenever the pastoral of Constable country is invoked. [4] In whose interests, came the question, has Constable's art been working so hard for so long? That even the premise of this question continues to provoke an impassioned response, and occasional newspaper headlines, suggests that Constable country remains, as it has always been, a contested field. [5]

The writer Sam Johnson-Schlee reclaims the biscuit-tin appeal of Constable's Suffolk landscapes as an unconscious act of resistance against the displacement of modern capitalism. Making room for Constable country in the home, Johnson-Schlee suggests, can be understood as a creative gesture that brings the possibility of a radical reimagining of the country at large: 'first we will inherit the landscape paintings through cheap reproductions, and next we will take our part of the land.' [6] Or, as one contributor to *At Home with Constable's Cornfield* put it in 1996: 'Being a descendant from a family who "worked the land", I have a great love of pictures depicting rural scenes.' [7] This Land is Your Land.

When Peter Kennard restyled the eponymous hay wain of Constable's other best-known painting into a launch vehicle for three Tomahawk cruise missiles (complete with gas-masked waggoners), he likewise recognised the radical potential of Constable's homeliness (fig.36). [8] Created in 1980 in response to a decision by the UK government to open the English countryside to US-controlled nuclear weapons, Kennard's Cold

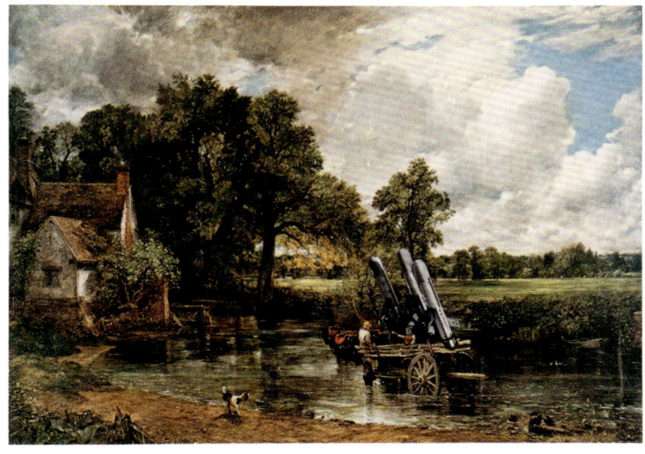

FIG. 36 **Peter Kennard** *Haywain with Cruise Missiles* 1980
Chromolithograph on paper and photographs on paper, 26 × 37·5
Tate. Purchased from the artist 2007

War souvenir found its way into thousands of homes as poster and postcard. The technologies of war may have moved since the 1980s, but as a landscape of resistance Kennard's reworking of *The Hay Wain* has lost little of its original power. For this, the often-imitated *Haywain with Cruise Missiles* owes as much to the familiarity of the cheap reproduction as it does to the avant-garde brio of photomontage.

With the possible exception of *The Fighting Temeraire*, with its changing-of-the-guard nostalgia, Turner has never enjoyed the home life of his great rival. His modern legacy continues to play out in a wider frame, across oceans and between continents. This is thanks, in part, to the deep well of the Turner Bequest, the seemingly inexhaustible repository of the artist's creative life, ranging from exquisitely complete paintings of startling variety to the most elusive experiments on paper and canvas. Since the 1960s, at least, the riches of the Bequest have served a constant schedule of international exhibitions that reframe Turner for new audiences, as an artist out of time – or for all time.

We find Turner the tireless traveller, equally responsive to the deep time of mountains and valleys and to the more recent scars of a continent dogged by war. Constable's landscapes, by contrast, can seem wholly absorbed in the hour (the original title for *The Hay Wain* was *Landscape: Noon*). There is Turner the visionary painter, whose unconventional methods presaged a century or more of modern art; and Turner the harbinger of a perilous, carbon-fuelled future. No need for dissenting photomontage when the artist has already punctured the landscape with an incendiary steam engine.

In other ways, and away from the Bequest, Turner continues to demand attention as an artist whose work foregrounds the colonial violence of modernity. Few works of British art have been the focus of such critical and creative attention in recent years as *Slave Ship (Slavers Throwing Overboard the*

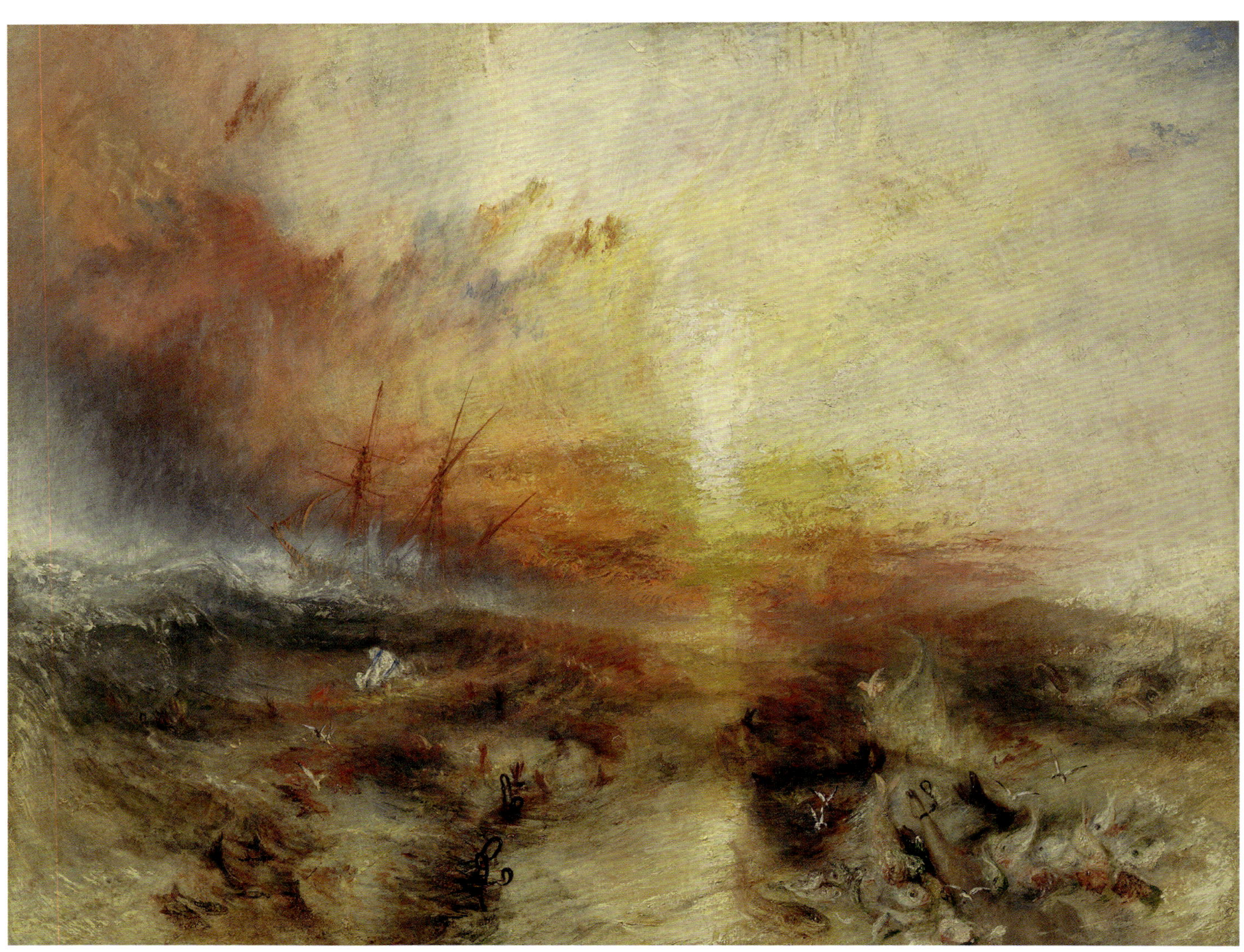

FIG. 37 **J.M.W. Turner** *Slave Ship (Slavers Throwing Overboard the Dead and Dying, Typhoon Coming On)* 1840
Oil paint on canvas, 90·8 × 122·6
Museum of Fine Arts, Boston. Henry Lillie Pierce Fund

Dead and Dying, Typhoon Coming On) 1840 (fig. 37), a painting that teeters provocatively between the highest aesthetic aspirations of European art (pushed to the edge of coherence by Turner) and the spectacle of racialised murder.

In an early account of the painting, Turner's greatest champion John Ruskin attempted (and by most accounts failed) to reconcile the 'intense and lurid splendour' of Turner's canvas with the extreme violence of its subject.[9] In our own time, art historians and critics have sought to understand the painting's violent contradiction by correlating what may be surmised of the artist's motives (always elusive) with adjacent historical events – most prominently, the murder at sea of more than 130 enslaved Africans by the crew of the slave ship *Zong* in 1781, an atrocity unique only in the extent to which it is documented.[10] This archival approach to Turner's painting has resulted in an ever more sophisticated understanding of the *Slave Ship* and its maker in the context of nineteenth-century debates on slavery and abolition. Still, the question remains: what does it mean today to count such a graphic depiction of colonial terror among Turner's 'most celebrated paintings'?[11]

Where art historians have looked to the archive to anchor the *Slave Ship* within a historical frame (often, it seems, in an effort to reassure us of the painting's abolitionist credentials), others have adopted a more liberatory strategy towards the 'intense and lurid' surface of Turner's canvas. In a 1994 poem inspired by the *Slave Ship*, David Dabydeen deploys the duosyllabic 'Turner' in discomforting ways: as the poem's title, and as a name assigned both to the ship's murderous, paedophile captain and to a stillborn child 'tossed overboard from a future ship'.[12] Written from the perspective of the shackled and submerged African that has 'drowned in Turner's (and other artists') sea for centuries', Dabydeen's iconoclastic poem has become a touchstone for creative writers and contemporary artists on both sides of the Atlantic whose work reckons with the aesthetic violence of transatlantic slavery.

In 2010 the artist collective Otolith Group incorporated pixelated fragments of Turner's blood-red sea into *Hydra Decapita*, a film essay on the fugitive effects of light on water.[13] Ruskin's troubled infatuation with Turner's drowning sea provides a narrative of sorts, intercut with the Afrofuturist myth of Drexciya, an undersea world populated by the descendants of pregnant African women murdered during the Middle Passage.[14] In 2018 Sondra Perry digitally rendered and animated Turner's boiling sea for *Typhoon coming on*, an immersive installation for London's Serpentine Galleries (fig.38).[15] Working in a sculptural mode, Kara Walker took a reference from the 'guilty ship' (Ruskin again) in Turner's painting for her *Fons Americanus*, a monumental allegory of the Black Atlantic that towered above visitors to Tate Modern in 2019. Describing her role in the creation of *Fons Americanus* as that of an 'unreliable narrator', Walker conveys the creative potential of remaking as an alternative to the partial truths of the colonial archive.[16] By channelling the *Slave Ship* through the technologies and spaces of contemporary art, these artists – and others who have taken a measure of Turner's painting – challenge their audiences to see the opaque surface of the *Slave Ship* as a threshold to Black futures created and denied by the Middle Passage.[17]

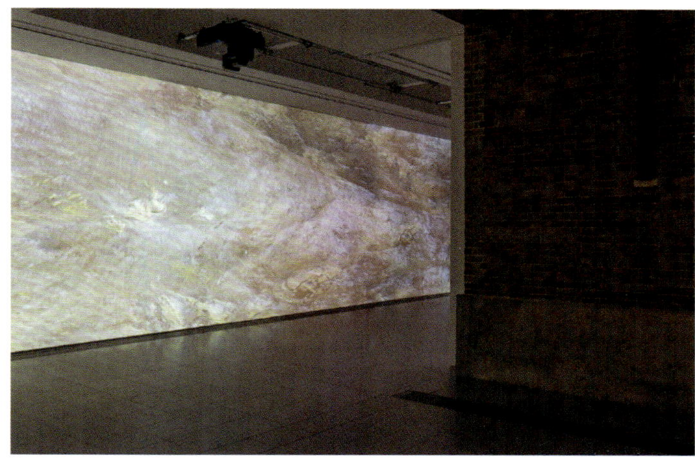

FIG. 38 **Sondra Perry** Installation view, *Typhoon coming on*, Serpentine North Gallery, London (6 March – 20 May 2018)

Turner and Constable are always subject to change. That the work of both artists continues to be reimagined and remade after more than two centuries – that it can still make trouble when trouble is needed – is a testament to the urgency and unpredictability of their art. Bringing that art into dialogue 250 years after their births is also an opportunity to ask where their legacies may intersect: to think, for example, about the ways in which Constable's local landscapes also find meaning within a global perspective. We might begin by following the navigable waterways of the Stour Valley that the artist pictures with such care, and which connect the productive fields of Constable country to Turner's turbulent seas.

DIPLOMA WORKS

AMY CONCANNON

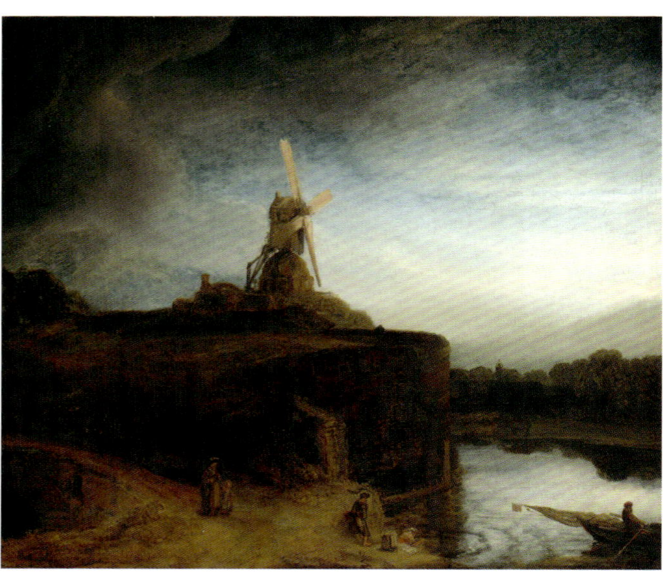

FIG. 39 **Rembrandt van Rijn** *The Mill* 1645/1648
Oil paint on canvas, 87·6 × 105·6
National Gallery of Art, Washington, Widener Collection, 1942.9.62

It was the custom that new members of the Royal Academy should donate a work representative of their talent to its collection. These were known as 'diploma works'. The paintings submitted by Turner and Constable, though reflective of different life stages, signal some of the most profound differences in their vision for landscape (nos.1 and 2).[1]

Turner's *Dolbadern Castle, North Wales* exh. 1800 was painted at a time when the artist was skilfully aligning himself with an all-star cast of artistic predecessors. Its Welsh setting was a nod to British landscape pioneer Richard Wilson (1713–1782), who had unlocked the artistic potential of his native Wales. Italian rebel Salvator Rosa (1615–1673) had provided a model for the original characteristics of landscape described as 'sublime' – vertiginous and rocky mountains, darkness and foreboding. Silhouetting Dolbadern's tower against the most luminous area of sky was a trick borrowed from a much revered composition by Dutch master Rembrandt van Rijn (1606–1669), *The Mill* (fig.39).[2] It draws our attention to the tower just as the contrast of pale skin against dark landscape draws our eye to the picture's protagonist. This, Turner tells us in a verse he appended to the picture (possibly self-penned), is 'hopeless Owen', purportedly imprisoned in 1255 at Dolbadern for having joined a rebellion against his brother Llewellyn, who would be the last Prince of Wales before King Edward I's conquest annexed Wales to England. Tapping into a wider trend across the literary and visual arts that romanticised Wales's struggle for liberty, this theme also rang true for some in the 1790s as the British government, fearful that revolution would spread from France, tried to stave the spread of radical ideas and protest with the so-called Gagging Acts.[3]

Whether this layer of meaning was intended or not, the drawing of allusions between past and present would become a mainstay of Turner's work (for example in his Carthage paintings, nos.125 and 126). The ambition and atmospheric power of *Dolbadern Castle* is therefore founded on what would become a lifelong project for Turner, the symbiosis between landscape and narrative, one reinforcing the other, neither subservient.

When Turner was elected an Academician he was a young man and his direction, though signalled strongly in *Dolbadern Castle*, had yet to be determined. By contrast, Constable was middle-aged and had already painted most of his 'six-footers', the most ambitious works of his career. The painting he chose to represent him in the Royal Academy's collection, *A Boat Passing a Lock*, was a horizontal variation on a larger canvas he had shown in 1824 and goes to the heart of his identity as an artist. [4] One of his motivations for choosing it, as Anne Lyles has suggested, may have indeed been its divergence from Turner's diploma piece. [5] Its subject, the River Stour on the Suffolk–Essex border and its verdant surroundings, was Constable's touchstone. It visualises elements the artist had described in a letter:

> the sound of water escaping from Mill dams ... Willows, Old rotten Banks, slimy posts, & brickwork. I love such things ... As long as I do paint I shall never cease to paint such Places. [6]

Yet rather than portraying these characteristics for the sheer love of them alone, *A Boat Passing a Lock* shows Constable using his subject as a vehicle to rehearse trends in landscape imagery and demonstrate his intellectual rigour, much as Turner did in *Dolbadern Castle*. Rivers, a key strand of both Turner and Constable's iconography, were a staple of topographical landscape culture, their courses the perfect vehicle for exploring the historical, cultural, contemporary and aesthetic qualities of any given place. Crucial to Constable, however, was a more general principle of the harmonious dialogues between people, nature and God, the latter represented in *Boat Passing* by the steeple of Dedham Church on the horizon, in the centre of the painting. Its low viewpoint encourages us to think of these features in dialogue, but also draws our attention upwards to a lively, dynamic sky that evidences his honed skill in the wake of his Hampstead 'skying' campaign, 'as well as his belief that the sky should be the 'keynote' of a picture. [7] In its cool colouring and composition, the painting references seventeenth-century Dutch painter Jacob van Ruisdael (see, for example, *Landscape with Sluice Gate*, Toledo Museum of Art). If Turner was dealing in the sublime, *Boat Passing* and Constable's description of 'rotten Banks, slimy posts' sees him practising its theoretical opponent, the picturesque. Similarly, Constable once referred to the Devil's Dyke, a deep valley in Sussex, as 'grand & affecting' and therefore 'unfit for a picture', believing it was the painter's job to make 'something out of nothing'; in *Dolbadern Castle* we see how Turner made 'grand & affecting' a hallmark of his vision for landscape. [8]

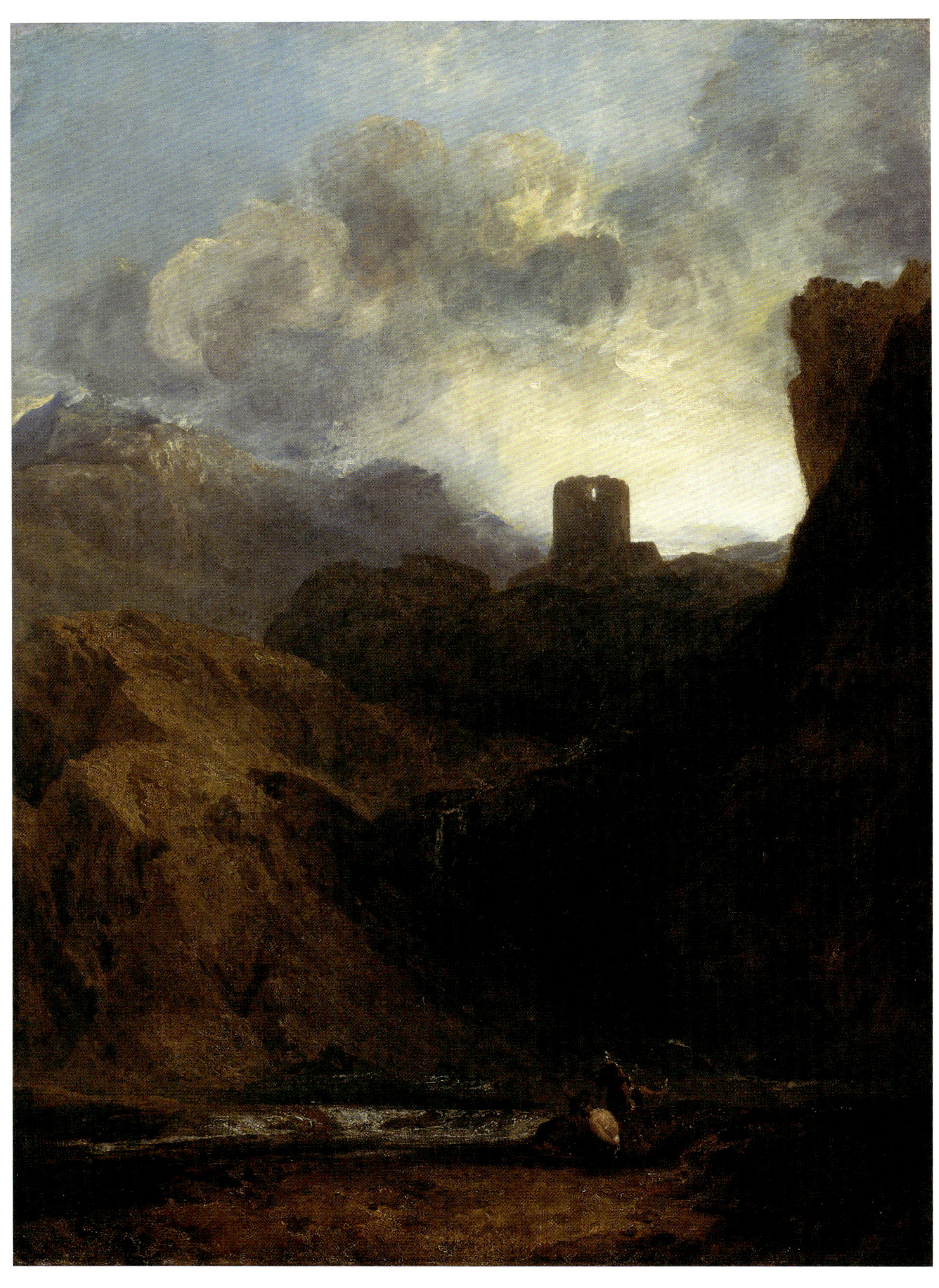

NO. 1 **J.M.W. Turner** *Dolbadern Castle, North Wales* 1800
Oil paint on canvas, 119·4 × 90·2
Lent by the Royal Academy of Arts, London

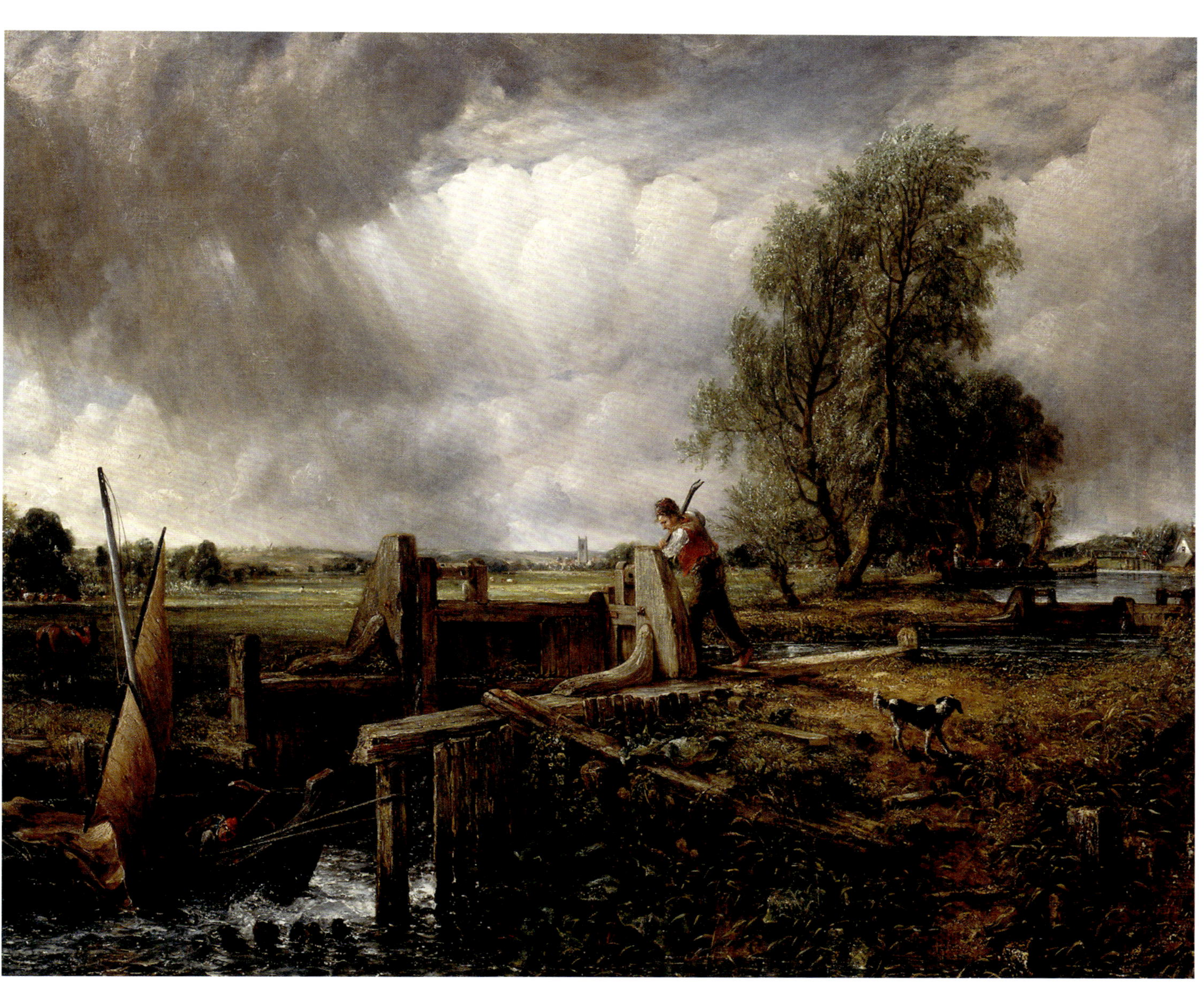

NO. 2 **John Constable** *A Boat Passing a Lock* 1826
Oil paint on canvas, 101·6 × 127
Lent by the Royal Academy of Arts, London

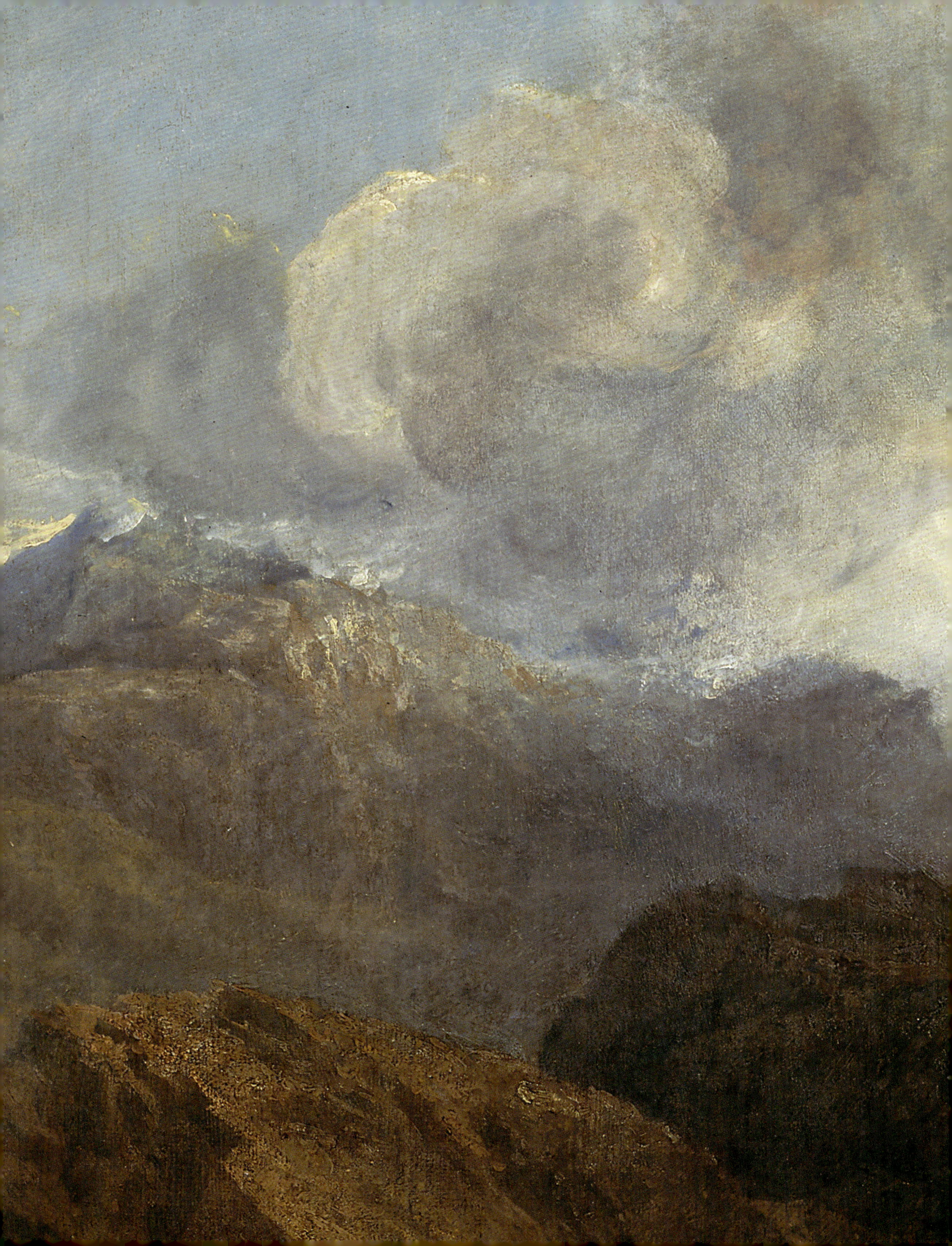

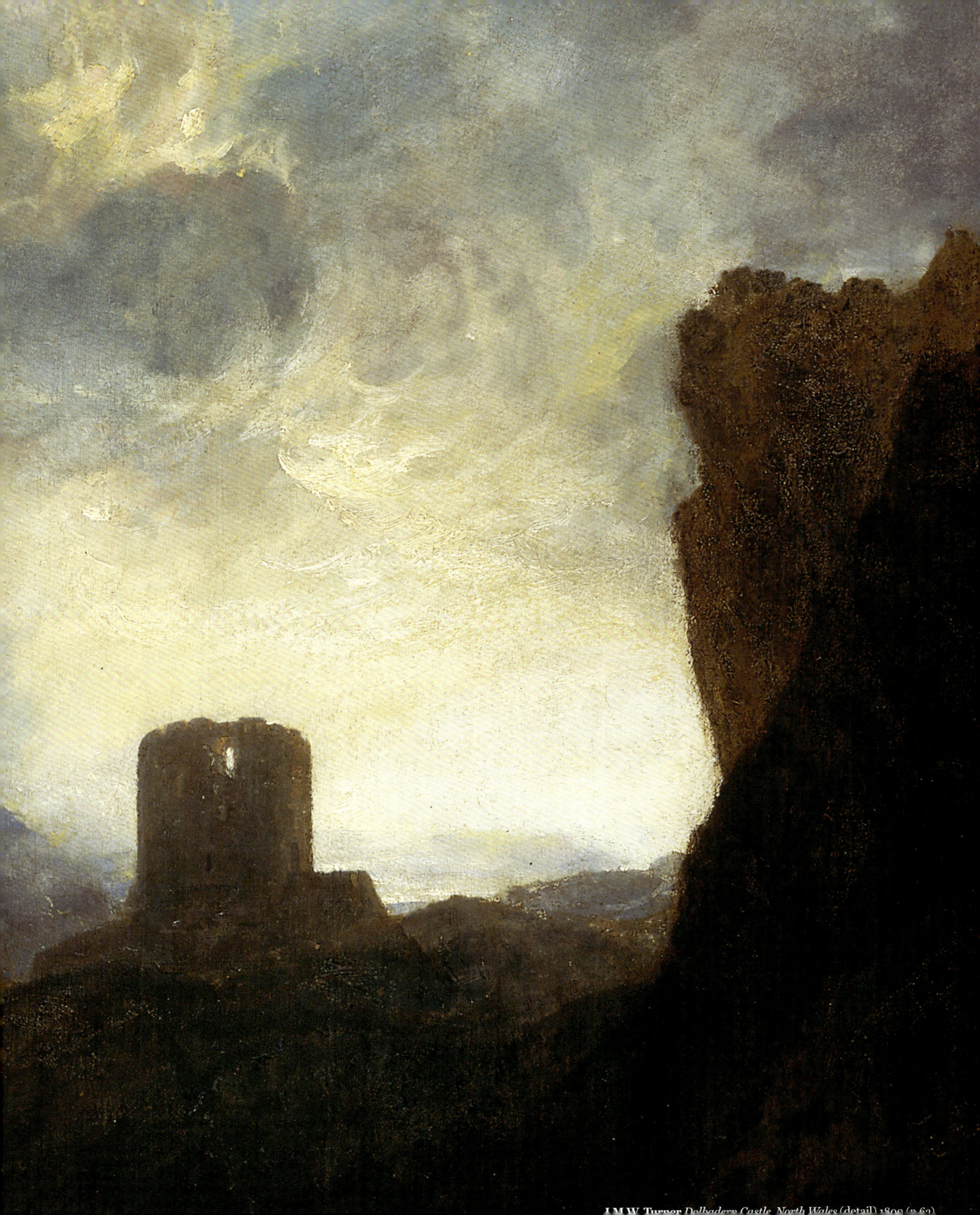

J.M.W. Turner *Dolbadern Castle, North Wales* (detail) 1800 (p.63)

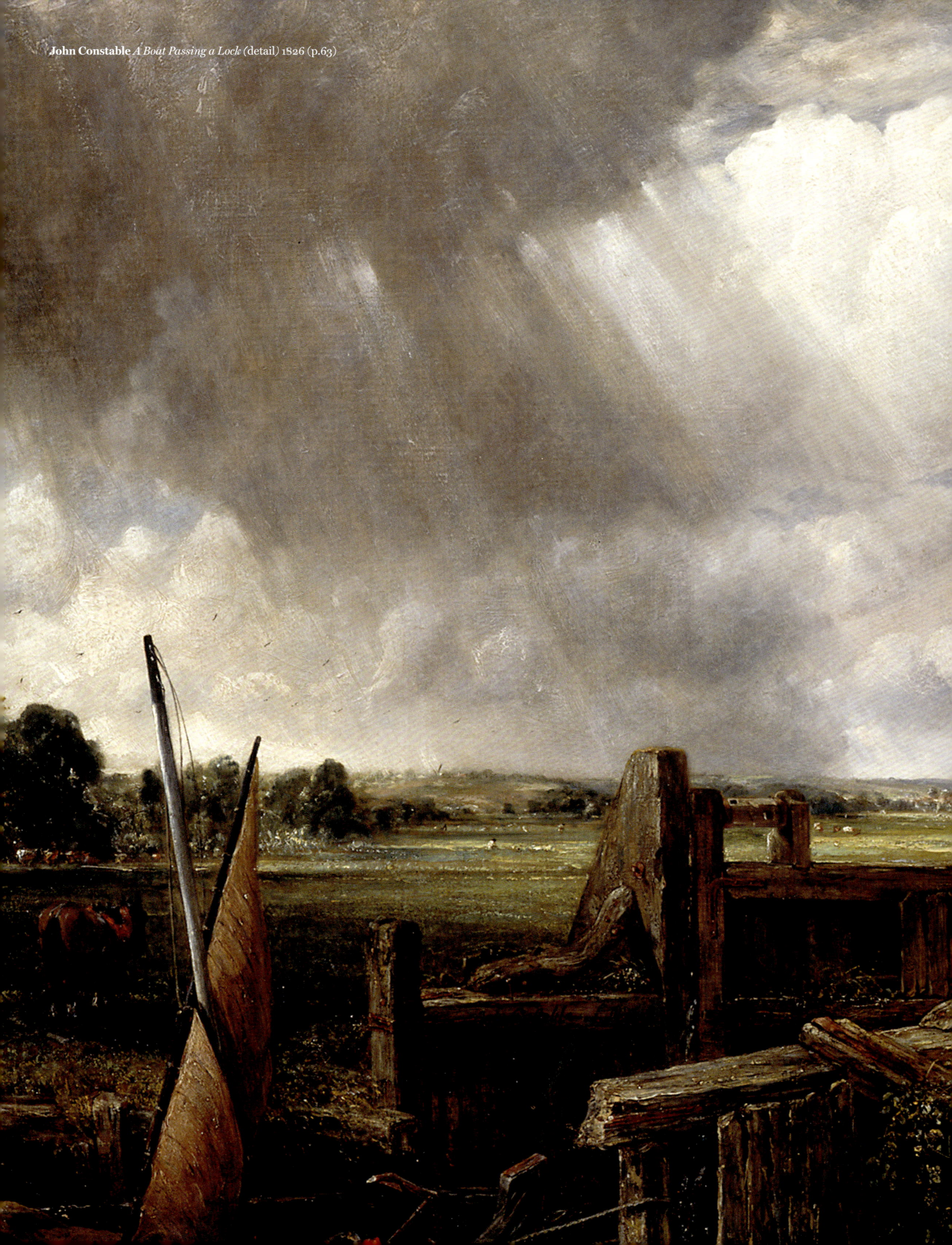

John Constable *A Boat Passing a Lock* (detail) 1826 (p.63)

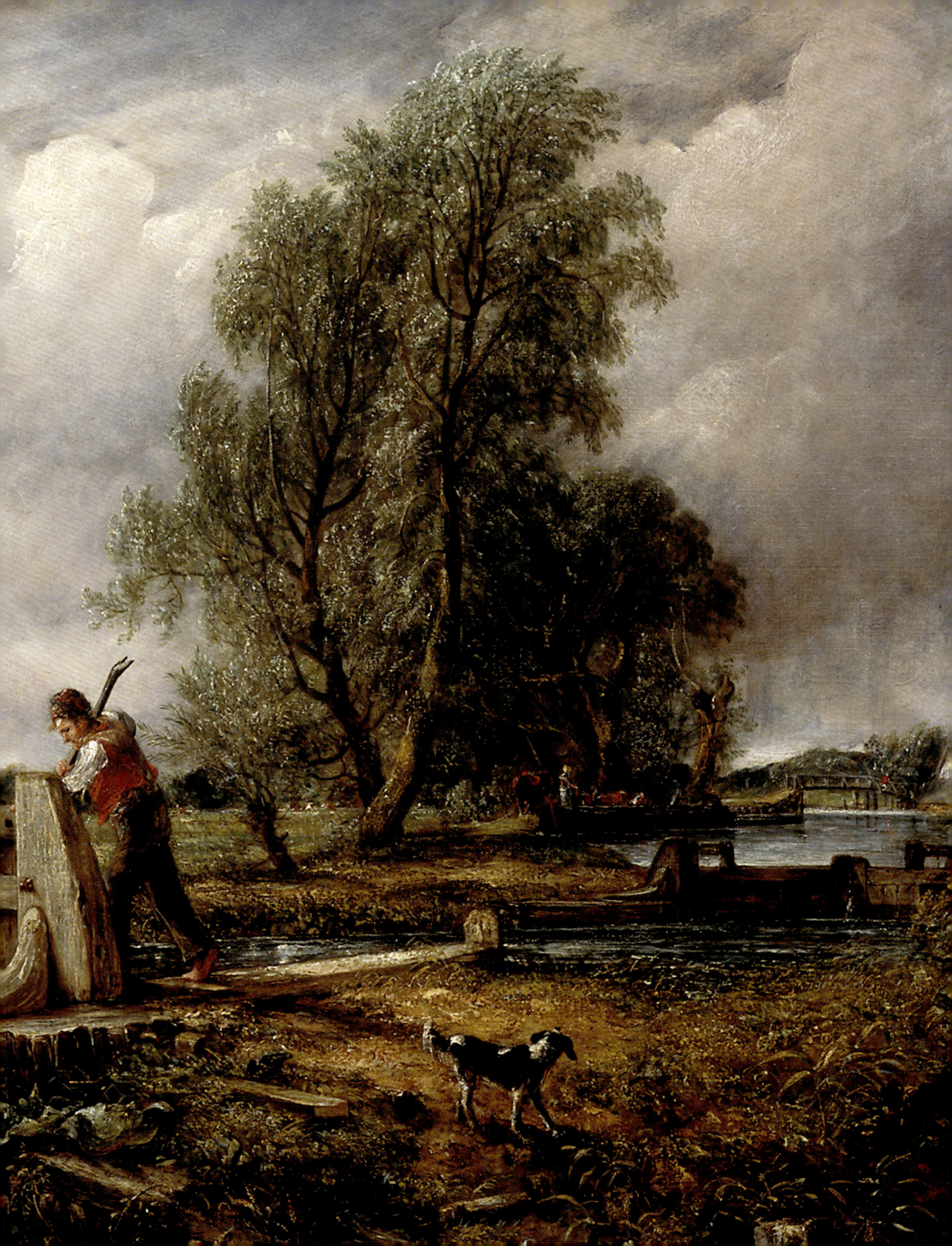

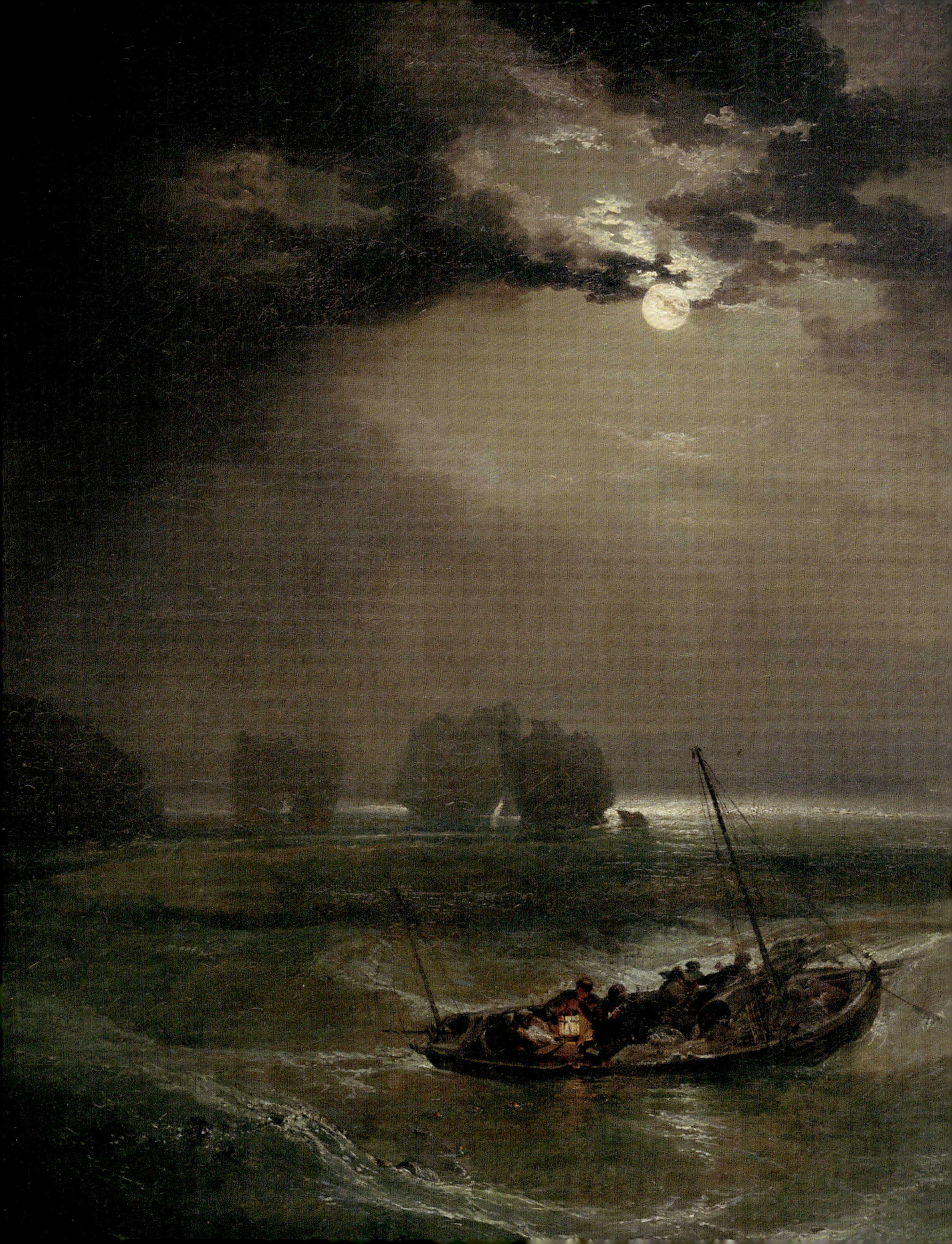

FOUNDATIONS

In 1799 the young Turner and Constable each received a seal of approval from the Royal Academy. Constable had been awarded a place to study there, precipitating his move to London from Suffolk, while Turner, having already passed through the Academy's Schools, was elected an Associate Member. At twenty-four years old, Turner was one of the youngest artists to achieve this status, reflecting his reputation as a fresh new talent with original ideas and impressive technical skill. Portraits capture this moment in their lives (nos. 16 and 17). Turner paints himself with a direct, confident stare, and depicts his clothes – particularly the loose, dangling ends of his cravat – in such a way as to suggest he would rather spend time painting than preening. He had come a long way since the small portrait he made of himself at around fifteen years old (no.3). Constable was painted by his then-housemate Ramsay Richard Reinagle. His contemplative, downcast gaze and more polished presentation exude intellectualism and gentlemanliness, fitting for a portrait that hung in his parents' house. In his self-portrait he looks out at us with a more determined expression (no.22).

The jobs Turner carried out as a teenager – as an architectural draughtsman's assistant and copyist of landscape watercolours – exposed him to a broad range of topographical art. Watercolours produced in his teens and early twenties see him capture the character of places through detailed drawing, novel compositions and enlivening atmosphere. His propensity to experiment and his fascination with light began at this time too, seen here in his 'transparency', a work made to be illuminated from behind (no.8).

It is no surprise that we find Turner, with his lifelong wanderlust and business sense, in Scotland, the Lake District and Wales: these were popular places with tourists and therefore saleable subjects for art. More surprising is Constable's seven-week tour to the Lakes in 1806, which gave rise to three years' worth of material and ten Royal Academy exhibits, including the first to call the artist to the attention of the critics (nos.23–8).[1]

Turner and Constable forged their careers in an art world dominated by enthusiasm for European Old Masters. Foundational to their practice was the study of both Continental antecedents and British landscape trailblazers, who themselves had been inspired by the Old Masters. Into this second category came Suffolk-born Thomas Gainsborough (1727–1788), whose Dutch-inspired woodland scenes were never far from Constable's mind, and Welshman Richard Wilson (1714–1782), whose application of a Claudean filter to the British landscape inspired both Turner and Constable. Constable's enduring appreciation for the Dutch landscape tradition began even before he moved to London to pursue art professionally. He admired prints of Jacob van Ruisdael's depictions of windmills, which he felt showed the artist had understood their workings, while an early windmill drawing (no.21) echoes the composition of a much-lauded work that Turner also admired, Rembrandt's *The Mill* (fig.39, p.60).

Turner's early flair for emulation of the Old Masters' example gave him a degree of notoriety among connoisseurs. *Crossing the Brook* is one of his most overt homages to Claude Lorrain (no.30). It particularly outraged Constable's mentor Sir George Beaumont, who owned and revered Claude's *Hagar and the Angel* (fig.40), an obvious reference point. This painting became the blueprint for Constable's *Dedham Vale* (no.32). Exhibited in 1828, a year after Beaumont's death, Constable no doubt envisioned it as a tribute to his mentor, but it could also have been a provocation to Turner, a lesson in how a homage to Claude *should* be done. While Constable renders Suffolk in the cool colouring he had admired in Dutch painting, and which was viewed by many as apt for Britain's climate, Turner drenches Devon's Tamar Valley in an Italianate warmth.

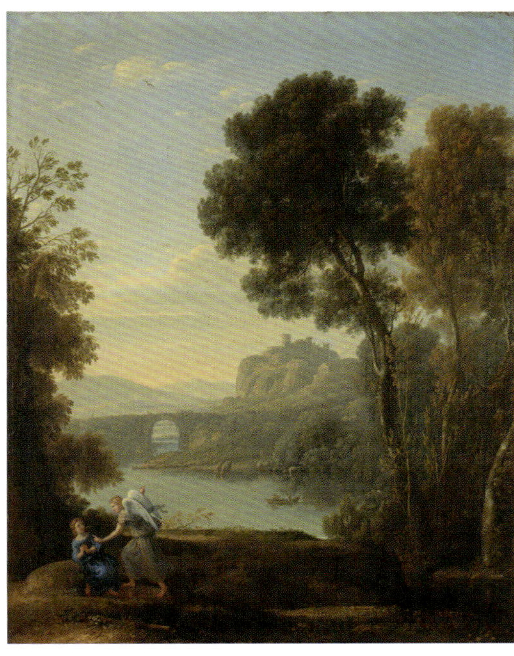

FIG. 40 **Claude** *Landscape with Hagar and the Angel* 1646
Oil on canvas, mounted on wood, 52·2 × 42·3
National Gallery, London. Presented by Sir George Beaumont, 1828

J.M.W. Turner *Fishermen at Sea* (detail) exhibited 1796 (p.74)

NO. 3 **J.M.W. Turner** *J.M.W. Turner* c.1790
Miniature, watercolour on paper, 9·5 × 7
Lent by the National Portrait Gallery, London

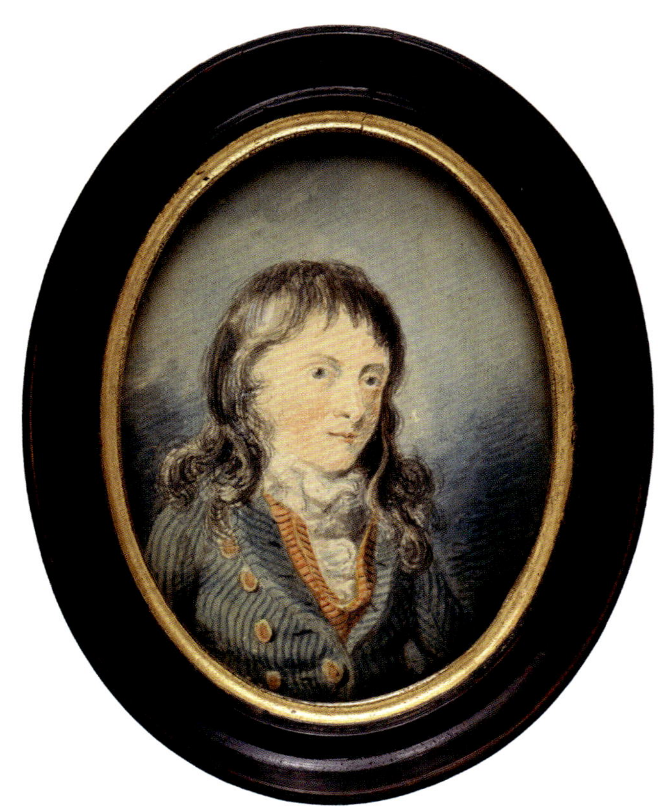

Turner is around fifteen years old in this self-portrait. Having been accepted at fourteen as a student at the Royal Academy Schools, we see him here a teenager testing and proving his skills, perhaps to satisfy family members who might have encouraged him to attempt it. Whatever the circumstances of its production it shows us a young man who could only imagine what he would later go on to achieve.

NO. 4 **J.M.W. Turner** *View of Archbishops Palace, Lambeth* 1790
Watercolour on paper, 26·6 × 38·1
Indianapolis Museum of Art at Newfields, Gift in memory of Dr. and Mrs. Hugo O. Pantzer by their children, 72.166

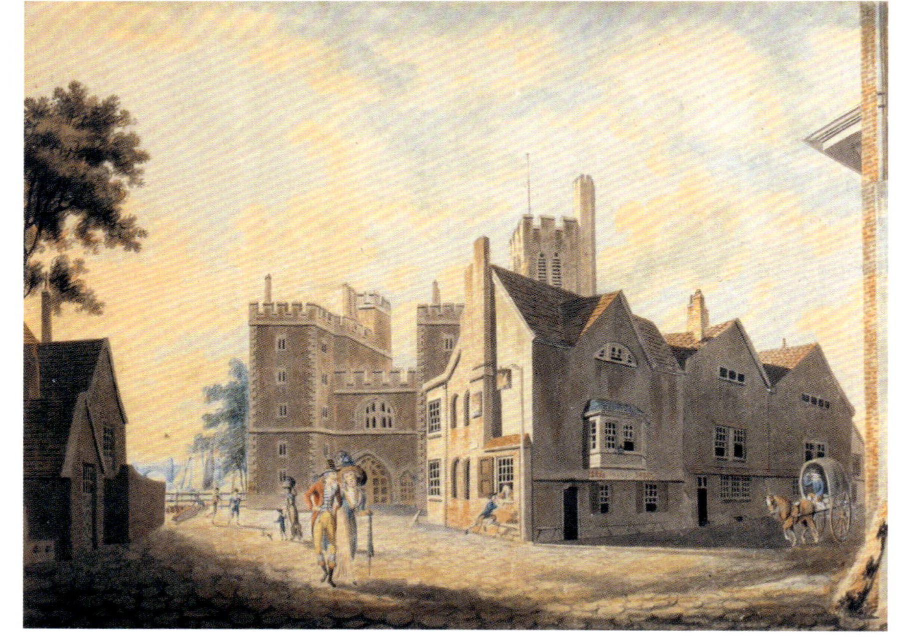

While to most viewers this watercolour would have appeared entirely unremarkable amid a display of similarly fashionable views of historic buildings, it represents a milestone in Turner's career – this was the first work he had accepted for display at the annual Royal Academy Summer Exhibition. Turner would maintain his presence in this exhibition every year, bar only a few exceptions, for the rest of his life. With its low vantage point that dramatises the height of the buildings, the multiple perspectives, and inclusion of figures to animate the streetscape, this watercolour displays skills Turner learnt between 1789 and 1791 under the tutelage of architectural draughtsman, Thomas Malton (c.1751–1804). Turner later referred to Malton as his 'real master'.

NO. 5 **J.M.W. Turner** *Travellers Passing a Ruined Abbey in Squally Weather* c.1791
Watercolour on paper, 26 × 18·8
Private Collection

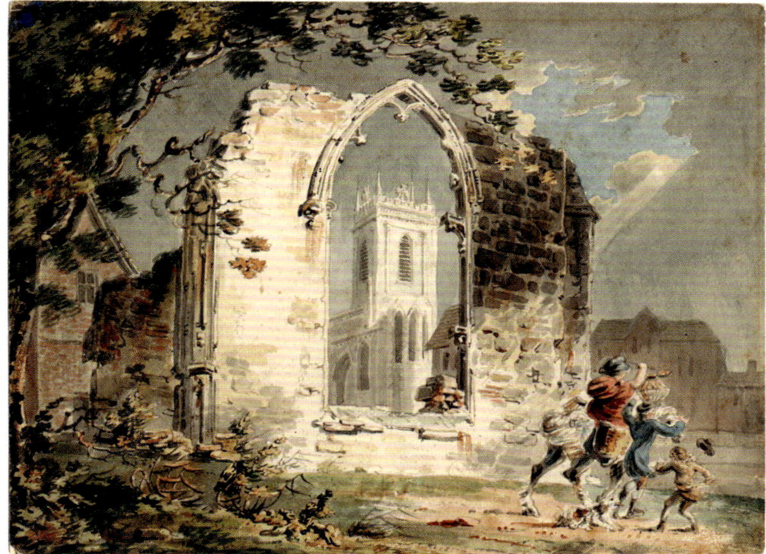

Turner would have been around 16 years old when he painted this watercolour. The subject may be a setting Turner had come across while staying with the Narraway family, friends of his father's, in Bristol in 1791 (see also no.7); it could have also been inspired by his experience of Kent. Stylistically this watercolour bears many similarities with work known to have been made in both these locations around 1791. It may, however, be an early attempt at a *capriccio* – an imaginative composition that combined architectural elements. Turner's early instruction in architectural watercolour drawings is in evidence here, as might be his study of elder watercolourist Michaelangelo Rooker's 'scale practice', which entailed working one colour at a time from light to dark, to produce variations in masonry or foliage. Compositionlly, it shows signs of Turner's inventiveness: a gleaming new church seen through the ruin of another, while the gnarled, looping branches that frame the scene are seen in many of Turner's early watercolours. In 1791, Turner's master, architectural draughtsman Thomas Malton was engaged in reproducing images of artist and caricaturist Thomas Rowlandson. Blown by a gust of wind, the group of figures in this watercolour are highly reminiscent of Rowlandson's, and introduce an element of humour as the dog stubbornly strains against its lead.

NO. 6 **J.M.W. Turner** *South view of Salisbury Cathedral from the Cloisters* 1802
Watercolour on paper, 89·8 × 72·5
Victoria and Albert Museum, London

Both Turner and Constable depicted Salisbury and its surrounding landscape, a locus of historical, religious and political significance. For Constable Salisbury would become particularly important as the home of his closest friend but it was Turner who arrived there first, in 1795. His early depictions of regional cathedrals had attracted the attention of amateur artist, antiquarian and incumbent of the Stourhead estate, Sir Richard Colt Hoare. This watercolour's dynamic composition, in which the cathedral spire is framed by the broken arch of the cloisters, is typical of the lively approach to topographical view-making that marked him out from his contemporaries. It is one of a series of twenty large-format watercolours of Salisbury subjects Hoare commissioned from Turner. Originally intended for a publication which never materialised, the ten sheets depicting Salisbury Cathedral, including this one, were eventually framed and hung at Stourhead – Turner would no doubt have been pleased to have his watercolours installed in this way, as a permanent advert of his skills in one of the country's most prestigious country houses. He has signed his name as if it were etched into the flagstones, in the shadow of the left-hand pillar.

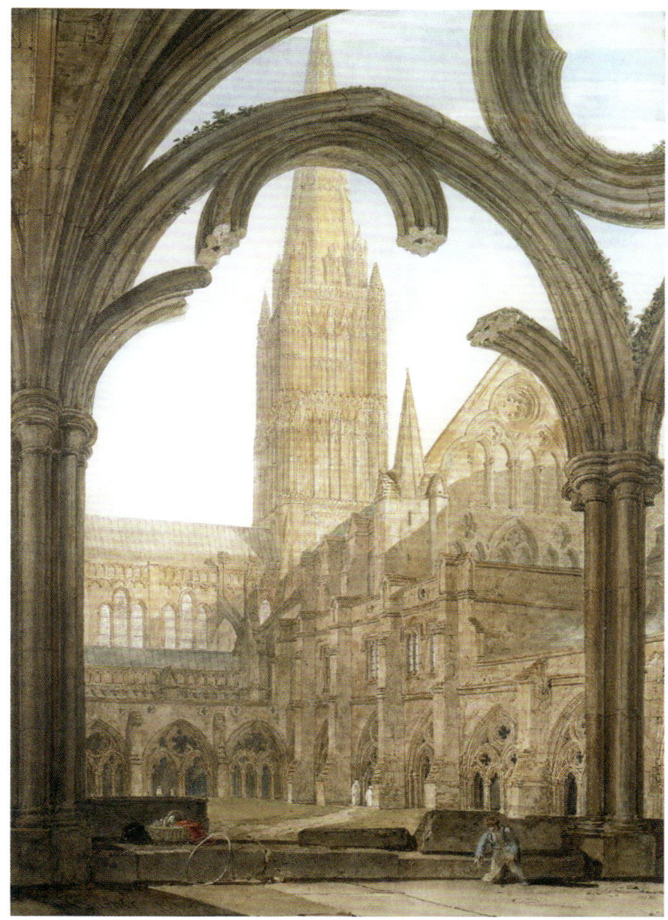

NO. 7 **J.M.W. Turner** *The Rising Squall, Hot Wells, from St Vincent's Rock, Bristol* exhibited 1793
Oil paint on canvas, 58 × 72
Private Collection

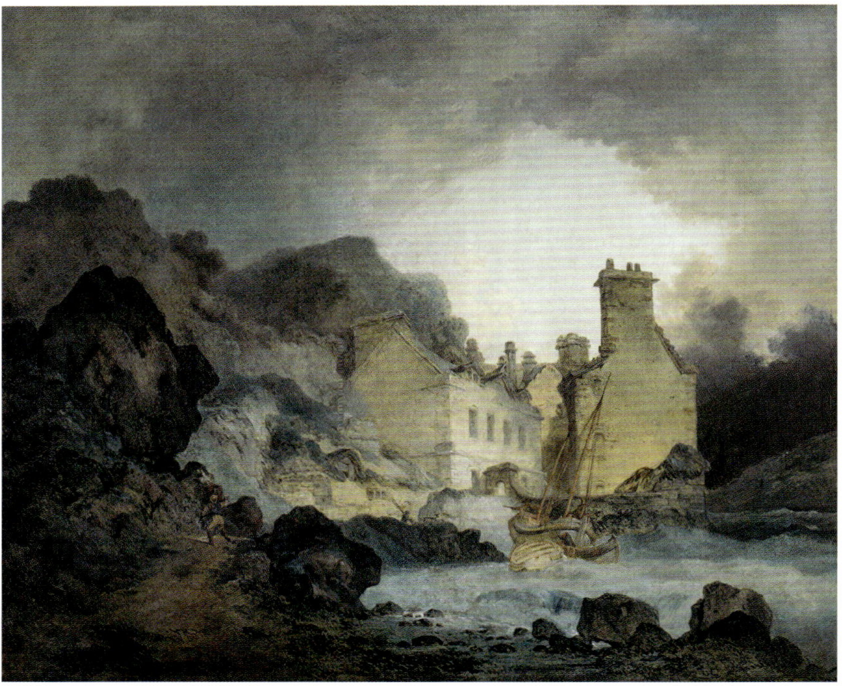

Recently rediscovered after 160 years, this is Turner's first exhibited oil painting. Completed when he was just seventeen years old, it provides us with a new insight into Turner's all-important accomplishment of oil paints, a necessary step for any painter aspiring to membership of the Royal Academy. Compared to the smooth finesse of *Fishermen at Sea* (no.12), previously thought to have been the first oil Turner exhibited, the surface of *The Rising Squall* comprises layers of thin, semi-transparent glazes, much like a watercolour. Indeed, Turner had painted a watercolour study of this scene (Tate, D00389). Compositionally and in its lively atmosphere, *The Rising Squall* closely resembles the work of French émigré artist, Philippe Jacques de Loutherbourg, whose paintings abounded with dramatic effects and dynamic figures. Turner has amplified the drama in *The Rising Squall* by exaggerating the rock formations at this spot on the Avon Gorge where buildings housed a spa and pump system for the hot springs. Turner was clearly impressed by this location. He may have read the Reverend William Gilpin's description of Hotwells as being 'in a great degree picturesque' (*Observations on the River Wye*, 1789, p.143). When staying in Bristol with family friends in 1791 he spent so much time exploring the cliffs of the Avon Gorge that he was nicknamed 'The Prince of the Rocks'. The first owner of *The Rising Squall*, the Reverend Robert Nixon of Foots Cray in Kent, was one of Turner's early supporters. The painting then passed to Nixon's son, who became the Lord Bishop of Tasmania, Australia. Its inclusion here marks the first time it has been seen in a public exhibition since the 1858 'Art Treasures' exhibition in Hobart, Tasmania.

NO. 8 **J.M.W. Turner** *A Transparency: A Moss-Covered Cottage and Shed, with a Man Smoking and a Lantern* (and verso) 1794–5
Gouache, graphite and watercolour on paper, 33·1 × 23·5
Tate. Accepted by the nation as part of the Turner Bequest 1856

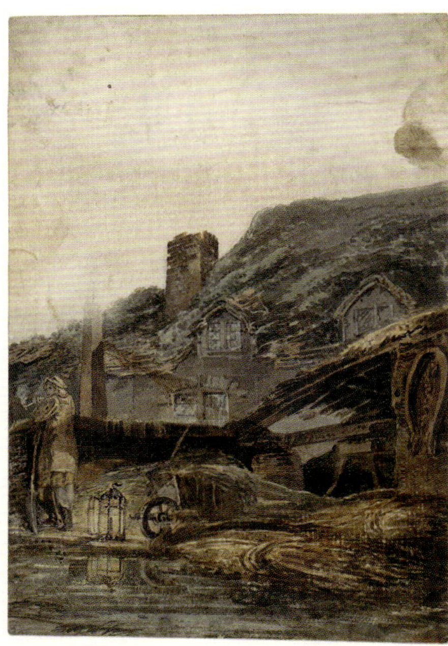

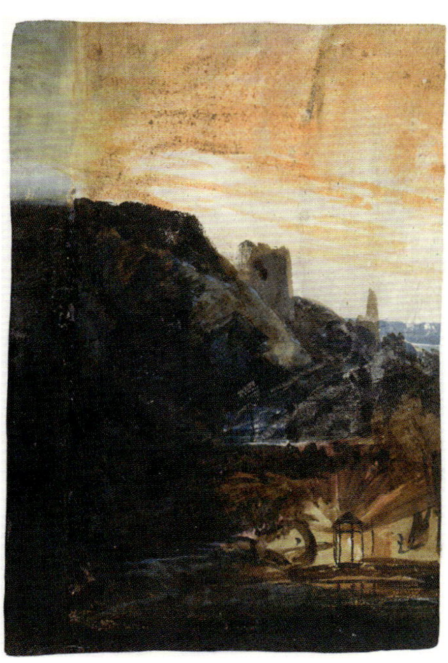

In the 1790s Turner made a series of watercolours intended to be illuminated from behind. Turner was the not the only landscape artist to experiment in this way. His forebear Thomas Gainsborough painted oils on glass and created a 'showbox' to view these in, while de Loutherbourg, whose studio Turner was a frequent visitor to, produced innovations like the 'Eidophusikon', a spectacular three-dimensional theatrical experience that used light effects to animate landscape. Turner reinforced the tonal contrast by applying further washes on the reverse to the area of land. The sky and lantern therefore remain the lightest, most transparent parts of the sheet and glow when lit from behind.

NO. 9 **(?) Thomas Girtin and J.M.W. Turner after John Robert Cozens**
Tivoli, Villa of Maecenas 1794–1797
Graphite and watercolour on paper, 48·9 × 31·8
The Huntington Library, Art Museum, and Botanical Gardens. Gilbert Davis Collection

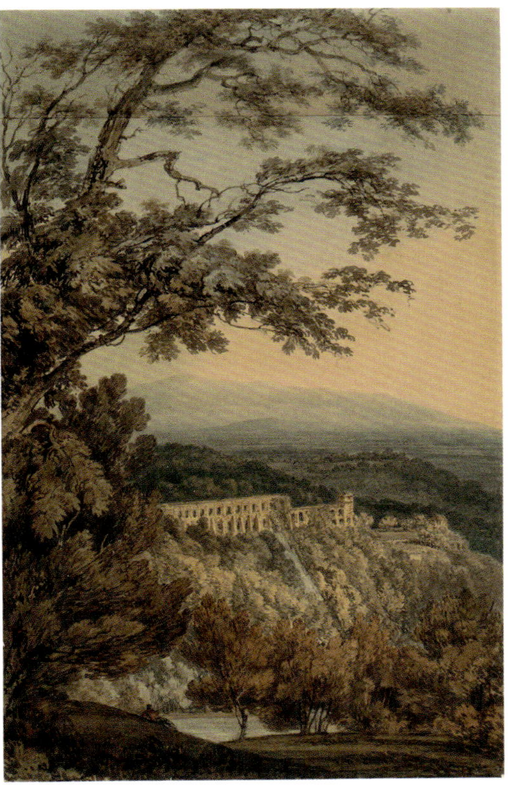

In the winter of 1794, when Turner was nineteen, he started spending Friday nights at the house of amateur artist and keen collector Dr Thomas Monro, who was physician to King George III. At Monro's 'school', as it was called, Turner and other young artists like his close friend Thomas Girtin (1775–1802) would work by candlelight copying watercolours from Monro's collections in return for a small fee and a bowl of oysters. Turner and Girtin worked in tandem, Girtin drawing in the outlines and Turner applying colour washes. Made after a composition by John Robert Cozens (1752–97) this work is likely to be one such joint enterprise, as Greg Smith has recently suggested (see thomasgirtin.com). Evenings at Dr Monro's house provided Turner with chance to study closely the techniques and compositions of his forebears. While war rendered the Continent inaccessible, Cozens's pictures of Italy provided additional exposure to famous and inspiring locations he would later go on to paint himself.

Turner and Girtin were both recognised as rising stars and innovators in watercolour, but Girtin tragically succumbed to consumption at the age of 27. Recognising his friend's genius, Turner later reflected that 'if Tom Girtin had lived, I should have starved' (Thornbury, *Life of J.M.W. Turner*, Volume 1, p.117).

NO. 10 **J.M.W. Turner** *Cader Idris: A Stream among Rocks near the Summit*
from the *Hereford Court* sketchbook 1798
Graphite on paper, 22·9 × 33·2
Tate. Accepted by the nation as part of the Turner Bequest 1856

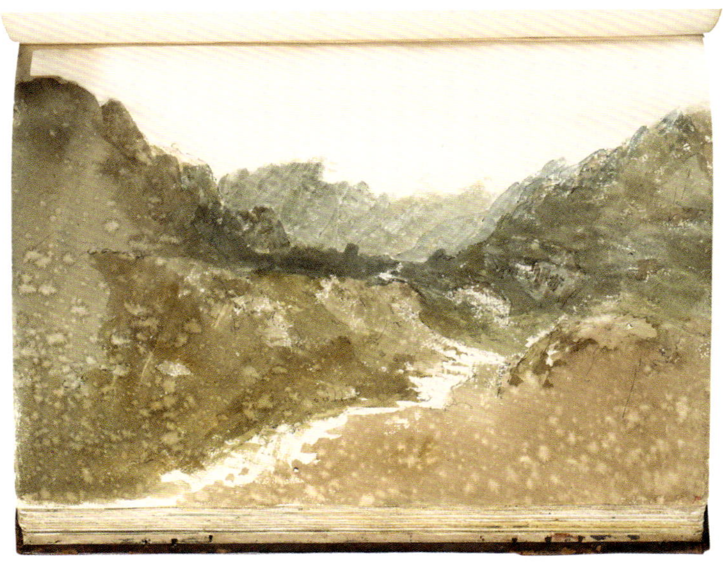

Touring Wales in 1798 Turner was on the trail of Welsh landscape artist Richard Wilson (1713–1782). This view is taken from a point on the southern slopes of Cader Idris, just short of the viewpoint of one of Wilson's most striking paintings of the volcanic lake Lyn Cau (Tate, N005596). In this sketch Turner quickly describes the jagged receding planes of the rocky landscape. As the mottling across the sheet suggests, he was caught in a shower – a reminder of the challenges Turner and Constable both faced when working outdoors.

NO. 11 **J.M.W. Turner** *Sunset over a River* from the *Wilson* sketchbook 1796–7
Watercolour and gouache on blue laid wrapping paper prepared with a red-brown wash, 113 × 93
Tate. Accepted by the nation as part of the Turner Bequest 1856

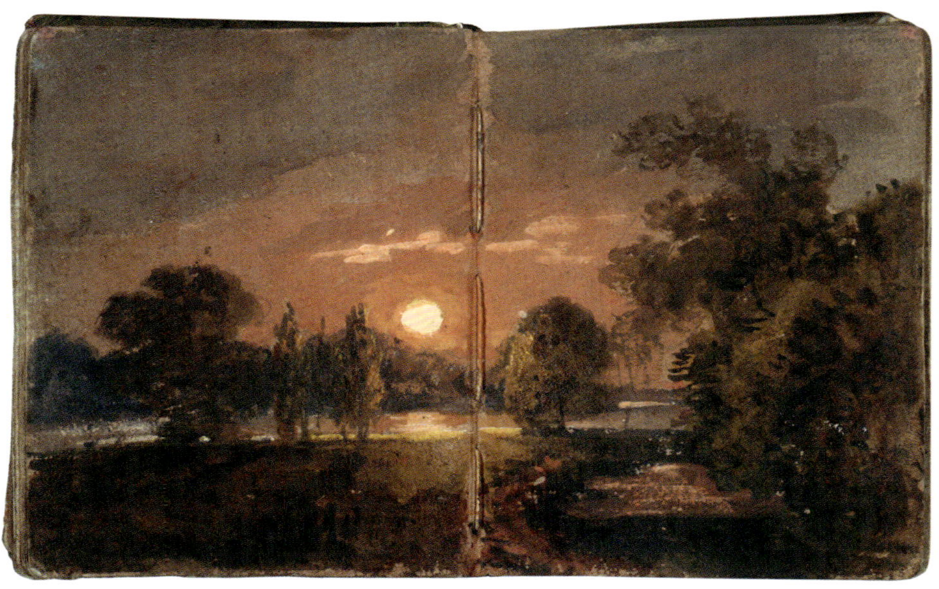

NO. 12 **J.M.W. Turner** *Fishermen at Sea* exhibited 1796
Oil paint on canvas, 91·4 × 122·2
Tate. Purchased 1972

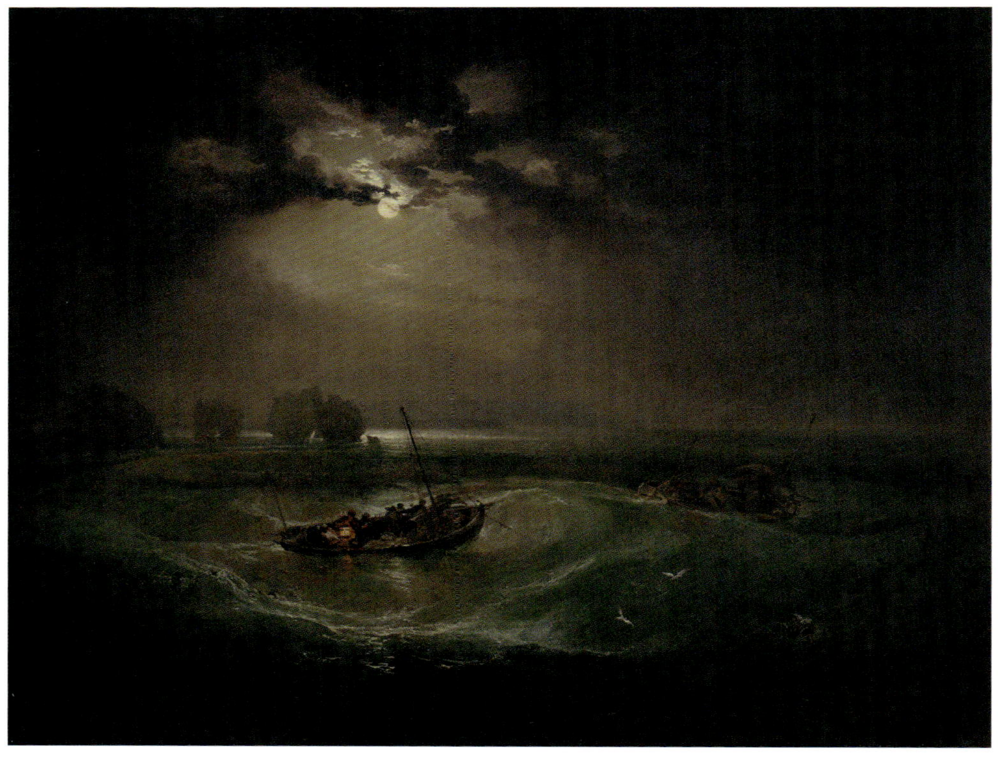

Upon its exhibition in 1796 this powerful painting was deemed by a hard-to-please art critic as 'one of the greatest proofs of an original mind'. It shows the Needles, treacherous rocks off the Isle of Wight. As well as aligning himself with British landscape tradition, which had seen artists like Joseph Wright of Derby and Turner's associate de Loutherbourg fuel the fashion for nocturnal scenes, Turner was surely demonstrating his knowledge of Dutch Old Master Rembrandt here in his skilful depiction of lamplight and moonlight. The subject was also a vehicle for demonstrating that he had now fully mastered oil painting, specifically the technique of working from dark to light and the dramatic contrasts achievable in this medium.

NO. 13 **J.M.W. Turner** *View Across Derwentwater towards Skiddaw from Grange Fell* from the *Tweed and Lakes* sketchbook 1797
Graphite on paper, 27·4 × 37
Tate. Accepted by the nation as part of the Turner Bequest 1856

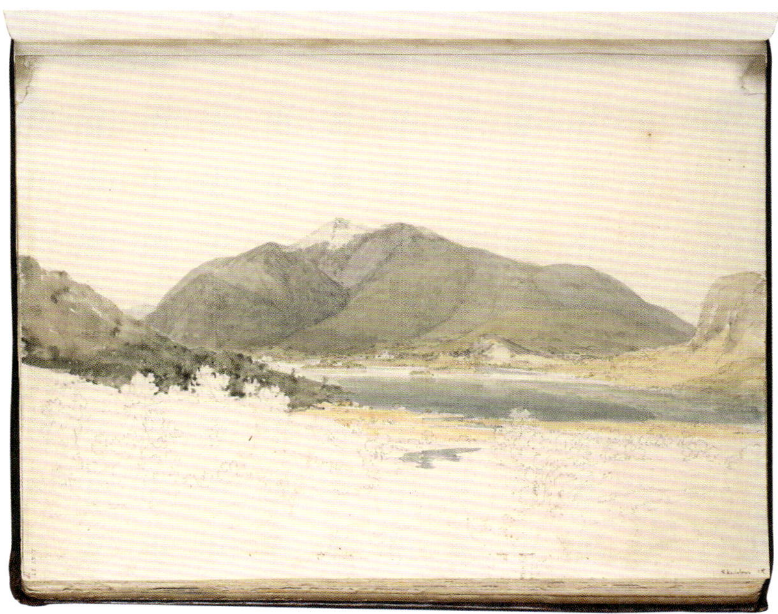

NO. 14 **J.M.W. Turner** *Buttermere Lake, with Part of Cromackwater, Cumberland, a Shower* exhibited 1798
Oil paint on canvas, 88·9 × 119·4
Tate. Accepted by the nation as part of the Turner Bequest 1856

This Lake District scene was shown at the Royal Academy in 1798 following Turner's first tour of the region the previous year. It is based on a sketchbook study (Tate, D01086), which he worked up in watercolour to show stormy conditions, writing 'Black' on the surface of the lake. This was his cue for the mood of this dramatic painting. As for Constable, the rainbow would become a frequent motif. Turner is making a consciously 'Sublime' statement, intended to evoke the viewer's awe at the grandeur of nature. It is not known whether Constable saw Turner's Lake District paintings but he would have known of their existence through others like Joseph Farington and Sir George Beaumont before embarking on his own tour there in 1806 (see nos.23–8).

NO 15 **J.M.W. Turner** *Morning amongst the Coniston Fells, Cumberland*, exhibited 1798
Oil paint on canvas, 122·9 × 89·9
Tate. Accepted by the nation as part of the Turner Bequest 1856

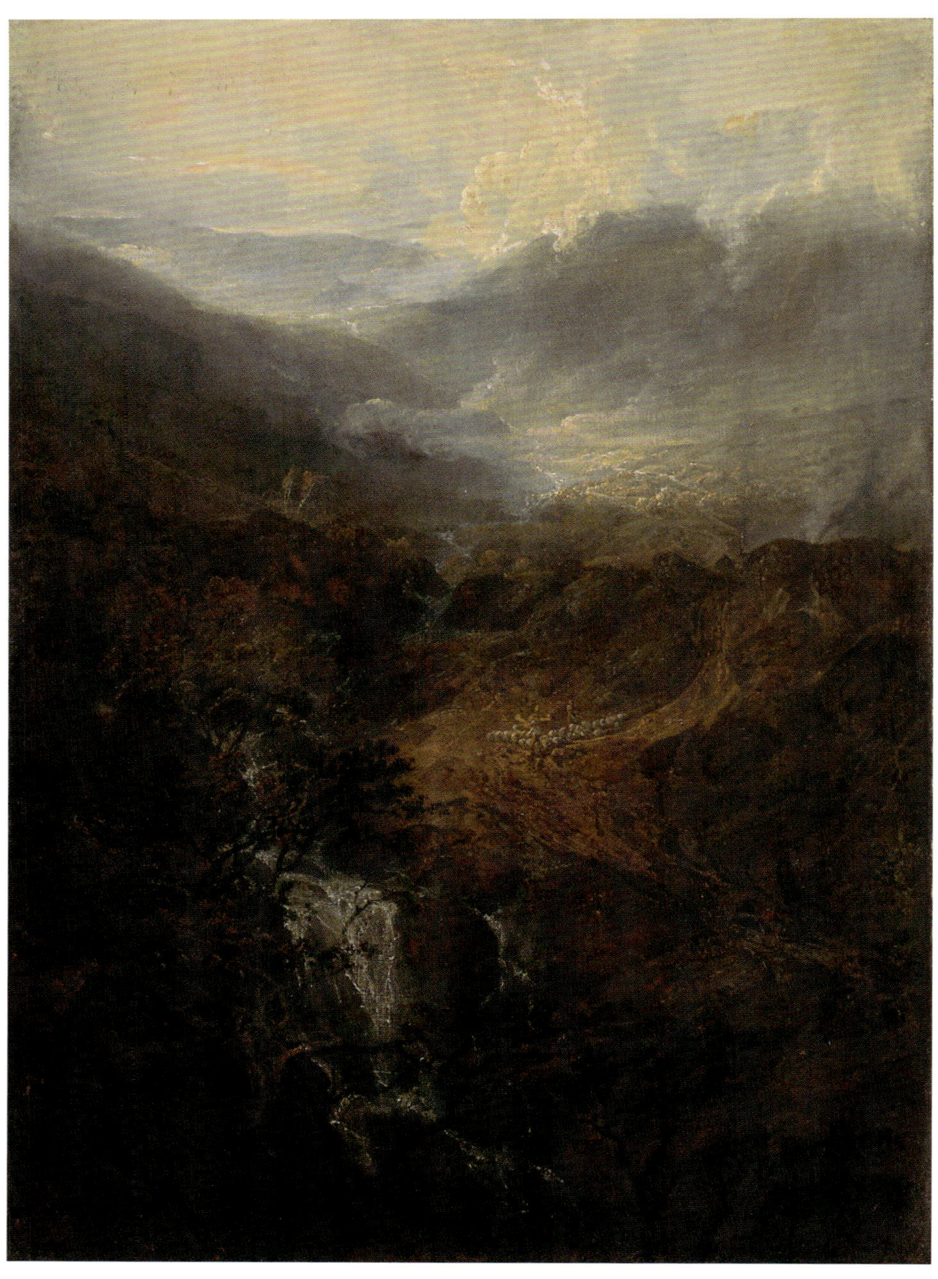

Turner's extensive tour of the north of England in 1797 was an exceptionally productive one. Not only did this tour generate a wealth of work in the years immediately following, but it was still spawning watercolour subjects thirty years later. Turner made the sketch that forms the basis for this painting from a position above the village of Coniston; the lower slopes of the mountain known as the Coniston Old Man rise off to the left while Wetherlam is shrouded in cloud to the right.

Morning amongst the Coniston Fells, Cumberland sees Turner, again, use cerebral references to elevate his depiction of the British landscape. The painting's upright format, its sombre colouring and its focus on falling water would have reminded connoisseurs of French painter Gaspard Dughet (1615–1675) and his celebrated painting *The Falls at Tivoli* (Wallace Collection). For the first time in 1798 exhibitors at the Royal Academy were permitted to append excerpts of poetry to the entries for their paintings in the exhibition catalogue. Turner appended lines from Milton's *Paradise Lost* beginning, 'Ye mists and exhalations that now rise / From hill or streaming [sic – Milton wrote 'steaming'] lake, dusky or gray'. The passage is taken from Milton's 'Morning Hymn' to Adam and Eve; the figures with the flock of sheep in the midground of Turner's painting have been read as allusions to Adam and Eve in a modern-day Paradise. This painting, along with *Buttermere* (no.14), significantly enhanced Turner's reputation. One critic wrote that viewing *Morning amongst the Coniston Fells* felt as if they 'might actually walk into the picture' (*Whitehall Evening Post*, 10–12 May 1798) while another praised its lofty ambition as signalling Turner's 'strength of mind' (*Monthly Magazine*, July 1798).

NO. 16 **J.M.W. Turner** *Self-Portrait* c.1799
Oil paint on canvas, 74·3 × 58·4
Tate. Accepted by the nation as part of the Turner Bequest 1856

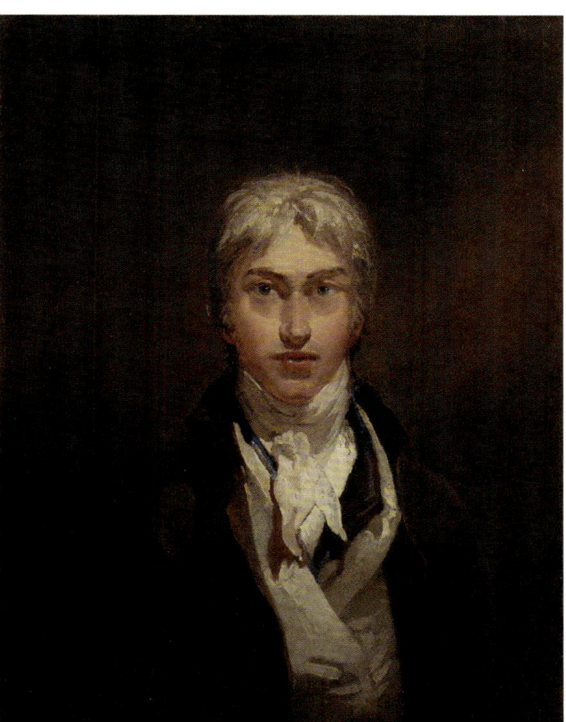

NO. 17 **Ramsay Richard Reinagle** *John Constable* c.1799
Oil paint on canvas, 76·2 × 63·8
Lent by the National Portrait Gallery, London. Given by the Art Fund, 1917

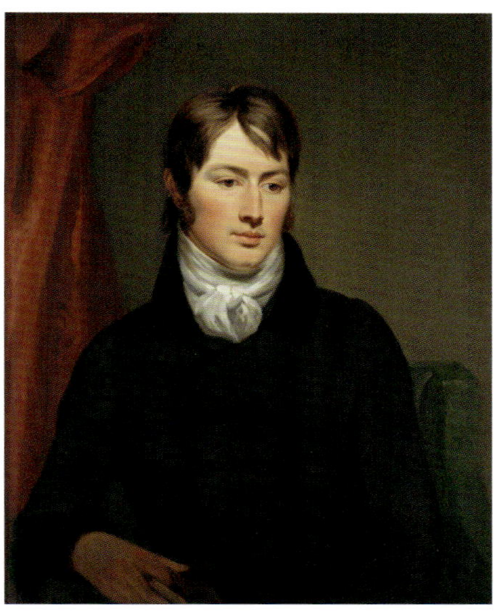

This portrait marks the moment of Constable's move to London in 1799. With his downcast gaze, we see him as a young man of feeling, perhaps deep in contemplation. This is an appropriate look for a student who so earnestly studied his subject, steeping himself in philosophies and theories of art and the work of past masters. It was painted by fellow landscapist, Richard Ramsey Reinagle, with whom Constable lived at this time in Cecil Street, which formerly connected the Strand to the Thames. So pleased were the artist's parents with this image of their son that it hung in the Constable family home at East Bergholt.

NO. 18 **John Constable** *Signed carving of a windmill on two pieces of wood* 1792
Wood, 12·4 × 8·5 & 9·5 × 17
On loan from Colchester Borough Council: Colchester and Ipswich Museum Service

This is one of the first images known to have been created by Constable. It is thought that he carved the image and his signature into the wood of Pitt's Mill, the East Bergholt windmill belonging to his father, during one of his shifts working it (experience which no doubt furnished him with a sophisticated understanding of weather patterns). Its makeshift and rudimentary form embodies the young man's determination to make art in spite of the expectations from his parents that he would take over the family grain milling and shipping business. Fortunately, his younger brother Abram would eventually take the business on. Constable never ceased to be drawn to the depiction of windmills and they became a particularly frequent inclusion in his late work (see no.173).

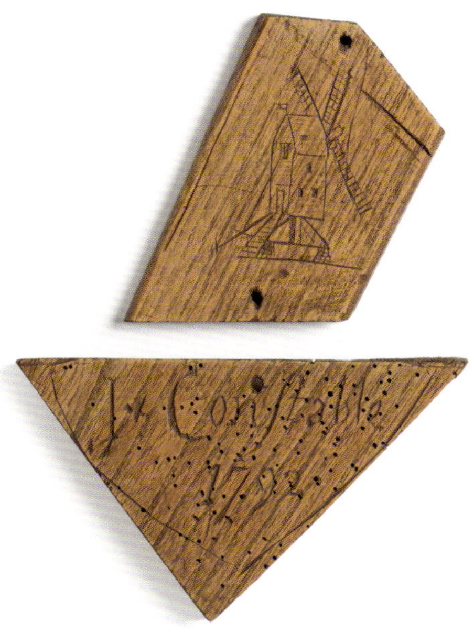

NO. 19 **John Constable** *Helmingham Dell* 1800
Inscribed, bottom right, 'July 23 1800 | Afternoon'.
Graphite and wash on paper, 53·7 × 66·5
Private Collection

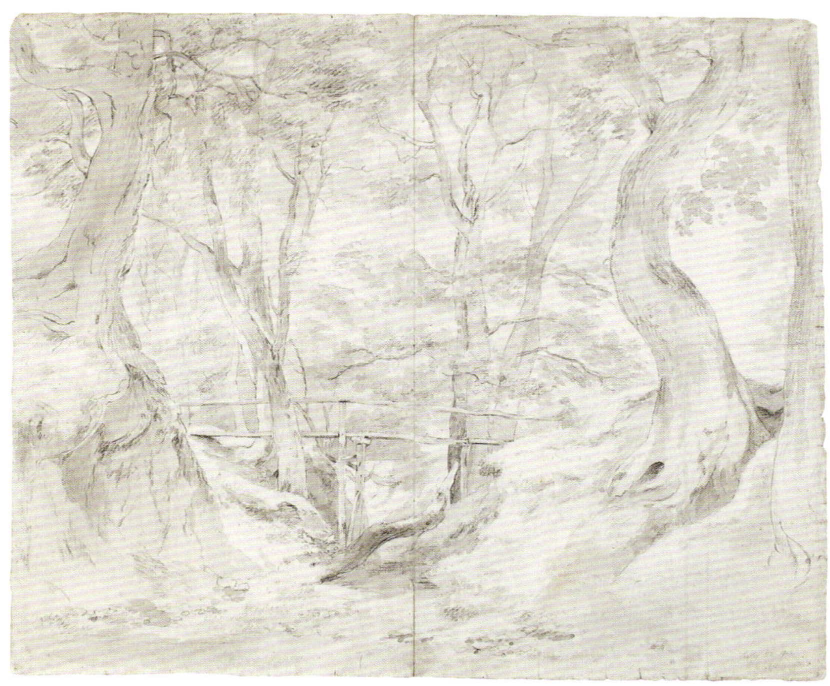

This early drawing shows Constable's ambition and contains several hallmarks of his burgeoning vision for landscape. Made on a large sheet of paper, its composition is bold in its simplicity – there is no grand vista here, but instead Constable asks us to focus our gaze on the sinuous upright forms of the trees, cut through by the horizontal of the bridge. He was inspired at this time by J.T. Smith, whose book, *Remarks on Rural Scenery* (1798), had urged art students to go 'into the inmost recesses of forests...the silent sequestered dell' where they might find 'the richest treasures of picturesque Nature'. Appearing to take this advice to heart, Constable wrote enthusiastically of being 'quite alone amongst the Oaks and solitudes of Helmingham Park'. Trees became a *leitmotif* in Constable's work (see no.169) and he would return to this drawing some thirty years later to make a painting of the same subject (Private Collection).

NO. 20 **John Constable** *The Valley of the Stour, with Langham Church in the Distance* 1800
Watercolour and pen on paper, 34·6 × 53·3
Victoria and Albert Museum, London

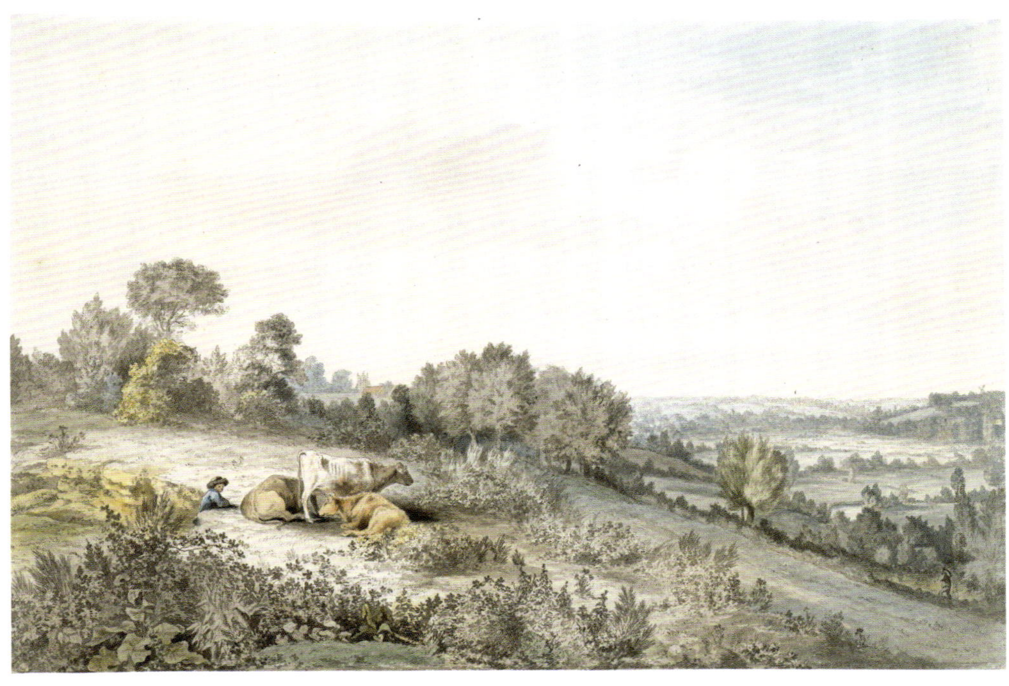

With three others, this detailed watercolour formed a semi-circular panorama across the Stour Valley, from Langham, seen here, in the west, to Dedham in the east. Constable painted the set of watercolours as a gift to his friend Lucy Hurlock, who encouraged his art, upon her marriage in Dedham in 1800. It constitutes his first attempt at a finished work featuring his native scenery.

NO. 21 **John Constable** *A Mill on the Banks of the River Stour* 1802
Black chalk, charcoal and traces of red chalk on paper, 25·8 × 39·7
Victoria and Albert Museum, London

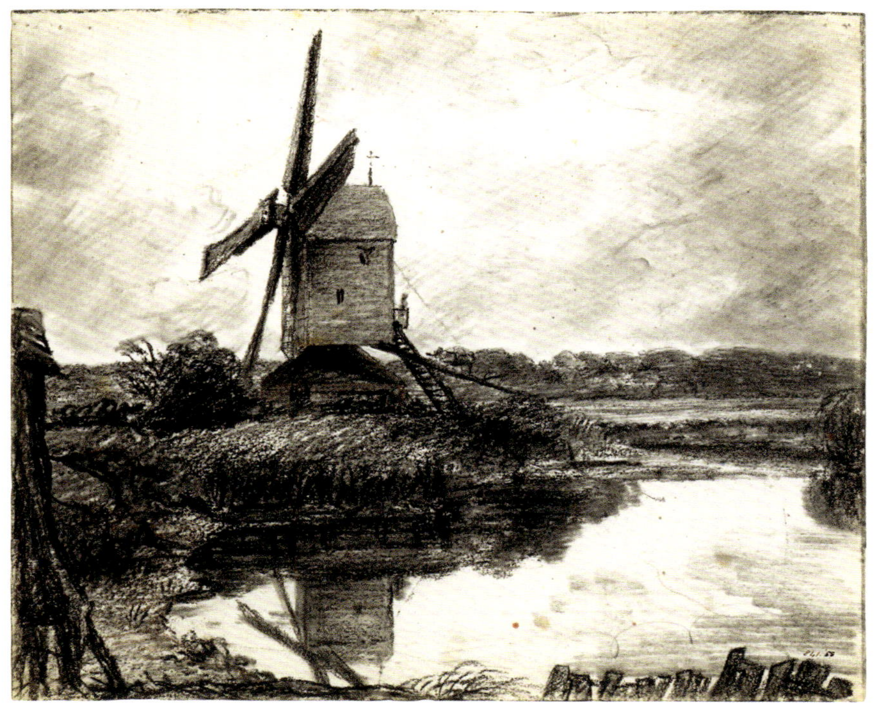

Windmills were an important motif for Constable. While it may have been topographically accurate, this composition is heavily redolent of Rembrandt's painting *The Mill* (fig.39, p.60). Praised for the way in which its dramatic chiaroscuro lent grandeur to the humble windmill, Rembrandt's painting was an important reference point for both Constable and Turner. They would have known it through prints and had the opportunity to see it at exhibitions in London in 1793 and 1806. This drawing was made in 1802, the year Constable exhibited at the Royal Academy for the first time. Executed in chalk and charcoal, it shows him using the media most associated with Old Master drawings, too.

NO. 22 **John Constable** *John Constable* c.1799–1804
Pencil and black chalk heightened with white and red chalk, 24·8 × 19·4
Lent by the National Portrait Gallery, London

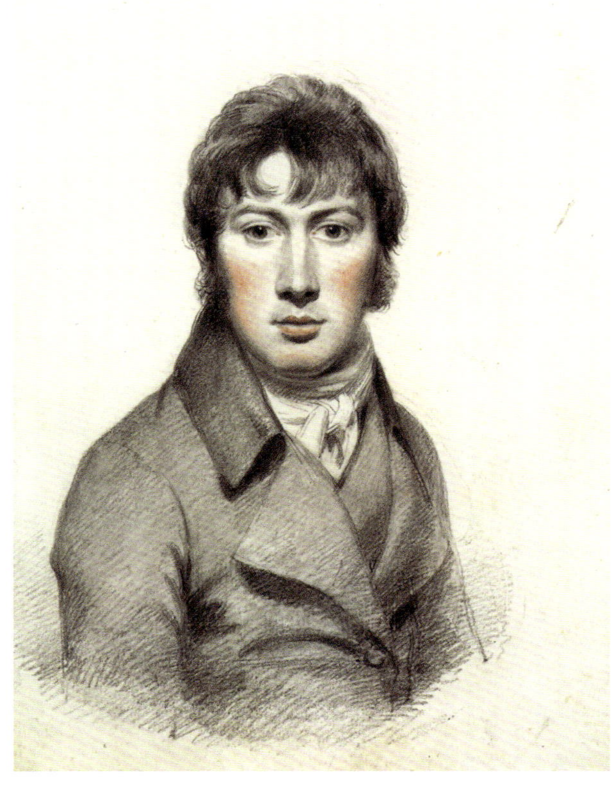

NO. 23 **John Constable** *View along the River Brathay towards Skelwith Bridge* 1806
Inscribed, lower left, '7 [?] Sepr. 1806'
Graphite on paper, 25 × 37·8
Private Collection

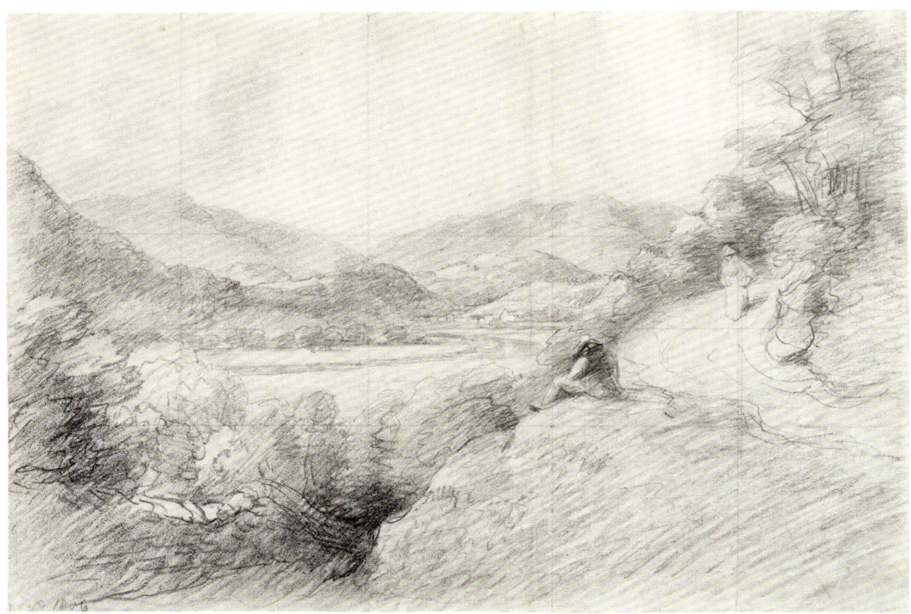

Like Turner, Constable had a keen interest in the science of perspective. The grid in this drawing shows Constable exploring one way to represent space accurately. It is divided into segments that become larger towards the top of the drawing, where objects are further away from view. As Iris Wien has shown, this was a method Constable may have read about in a 1771 treatise on perspective by Edward Noble (Wien, 2020). This drawing is evidence that Constable's Lake District tour was a formative experience, one in which he could rehearse methods of depicting landscape within a new and challenging terrain.

NO. 24 **John Constable** *View of Bowfell (Cumbria) and the Langdale Pikes from near Harry Place* September 1806
Watercolour and graphite on buff wove paper, 16·5 × 30·5
Philadelphia Museum of Art. Purchased with funds contributed by Boies Penrose, 1930-39-59

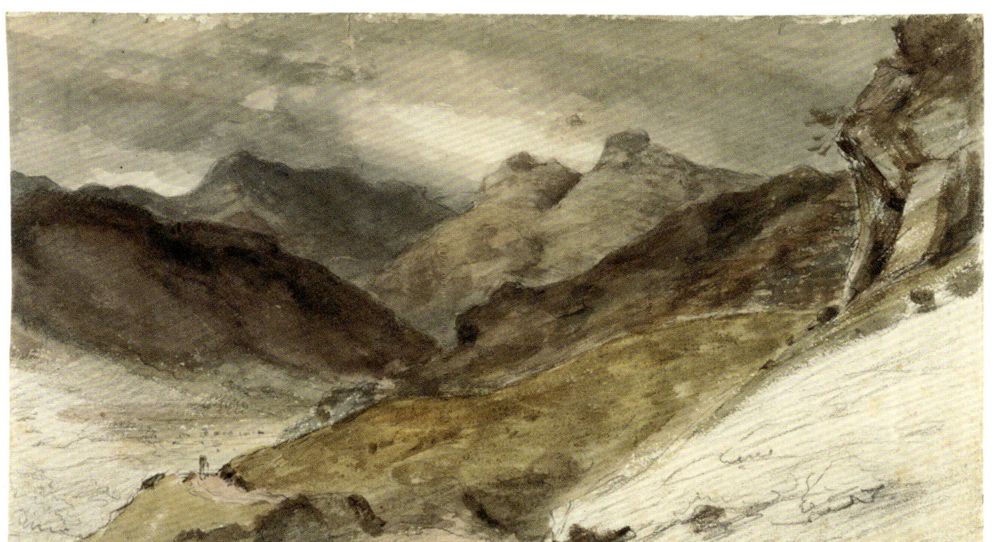

Constable evokes the Lake District on a dark autumnal day in this work, his first attempt at a mountain-top composition. Pencil lines accurately describe the distinctive double-hump of the Langdale Pikes, to the right of centre, and Bow Fell (the subject of no.28), on the left. With only a few layers of sombre colour applied to the upper and central areas he has created a sense of depth while the use of a drier brush suggests the rugged, broken texture of rock in the upper right corner. A mark that may signify a horse, loaded with a pack, draws our eye to an expanse of bronze wash that likely stands in for the yellow-brown tones of bracken.

NO. 25 **John Constable** *Leatheswater (Thirlmere)* 1806
Pencil and grey wash on paper, 12·9 × 38·7
Victoria and Albert Museum, London.
Given by Isabel Constable, daughter of the artist

In May 1815, nine years after his tour of the Lake District, Constable published a print after this drawing. An imminent publication of prints after work by his early mentor Joseph Farrington may have inspired Constable to present his own take on Lakes scenery. Compared to the more picturesque scenes of his contemporaries, Constable's *Leatheswater* shows the Lake District in a more barren guise. With its precise lines and carefully-applied wash, this is likely to have been the drawing worked up to give to the printmaker, Henry Dawe (1790–1848), rather than one made on the spot. Constable had met Henry when helping paint the background of a portrait for his brother, portraitist George Dawe (1781–1829). Mezzotint was Henry Dawe's specialism and the technique Constable would elect fifteen years later for his project *English Landscape*.

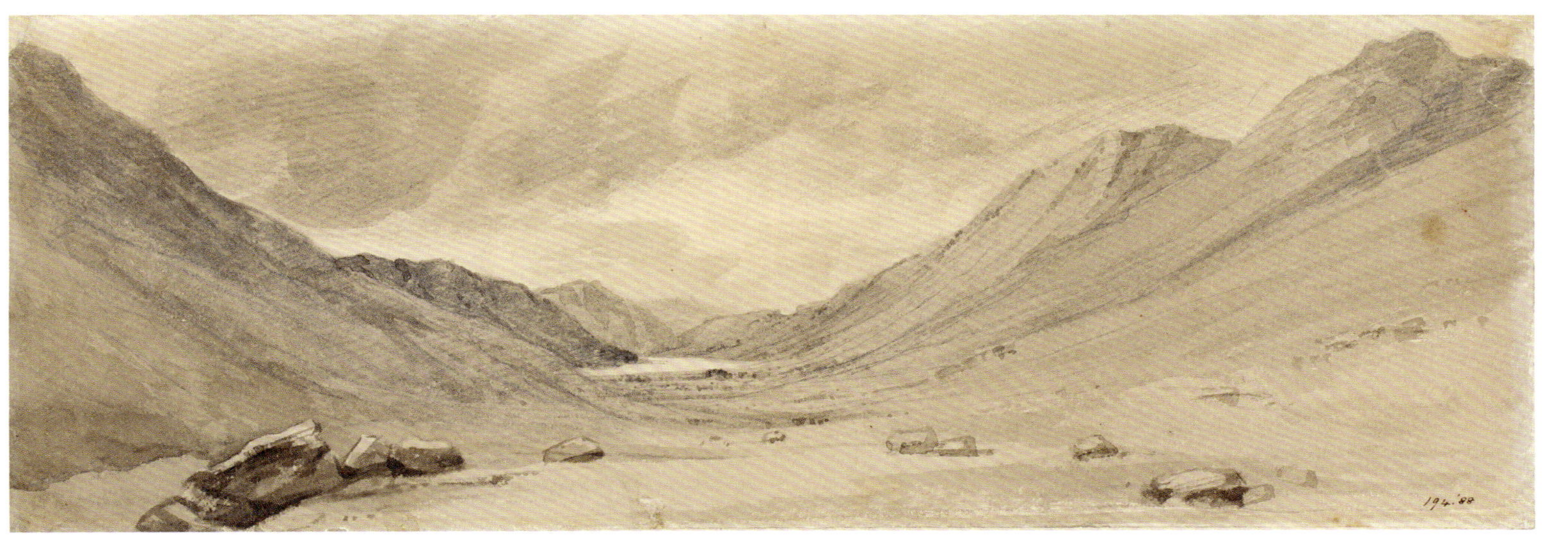

NO. 26 **John Constable** *Saddleback and part of Skiddaw* 1806
Inscribed, verso, '21 Sep. 1806 Stormy Day – noon'
Pencil and watercolour on paper, 7·6 × 29·5
Victoria and Albert Museum, London
Given by Isabel Constable, daughter of the artist

In this drawing and in *Leatheswater (Thirlmere)* Constable employs a panoramic format to frame his view. He had used this format when depicting his native Suffolk landscape. Here, however, it focuses our eye on the dramatic undulating form of the mountains, and gives an immediate sense of their expansiveness – as if the frame must be stretched to accommodate this dramatic scenery. It is inscribed 'Stormy Day – noon'. Even at this early stage in his career observation and the recording of weather was as vital to his process as was the recording of the topography.

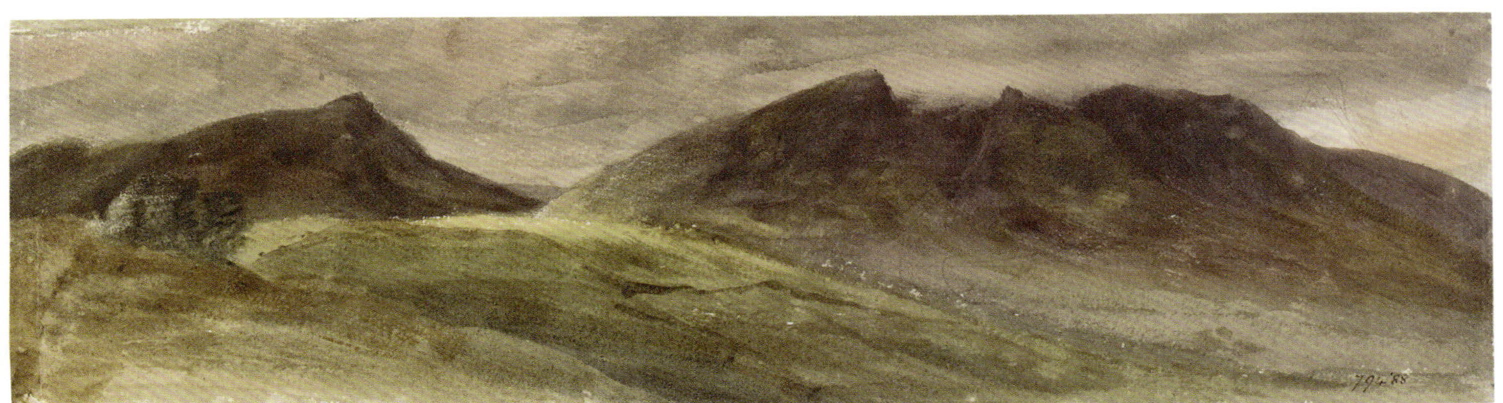

NO. 27 **John Constable** *Folly Bridge, Borrowdale* 1806
Graphite on paper, 28 × 48
Private Collection

By the time of Constable's visit to the Lakes tourist routes were well established. Most paid only a cursory visit to Borrowdale, but Constable spent three of his six touring weeks here (his companion reportedly became bored and returned to Windermere after ten days). In Borrowdale Constable found a lush valley cut through by the winding River Derwent, surrounded by irregular shaped mountains, each view reminiscent of compositions by Gaspard Dughet, the seventeenth-century landscape painter whose work he admired at this time. In *Folly Bridge* Constable uses a variety of tones and strokes to creates depth, mass and texture in what is a more complex composition than others like *Leatheswater*. Probably made towards the end of his stay in Borrowdale, this drawing shows that Constable emerged from his Lakes tour a much more confident and skilled draughtsman.

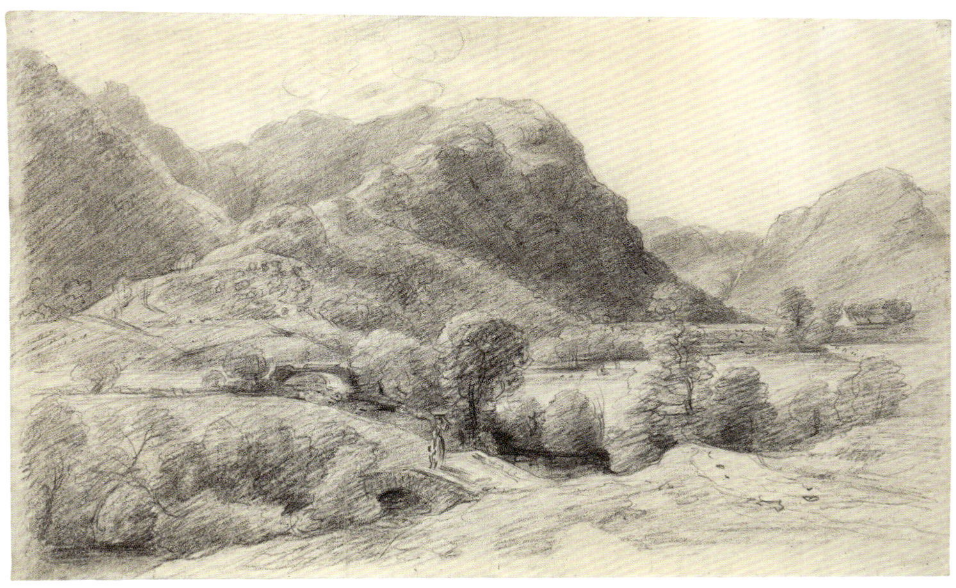

NO. 28 **John Constable** *Bow Fell, Cumberland* 1807
Oil paint on canvas, 20·4 × 25·4
Clark Art Institute, Williamstown, Massachusetts, USA, gift of the Manton Art Foundation in memory of Sir Edwin and Lady Manton

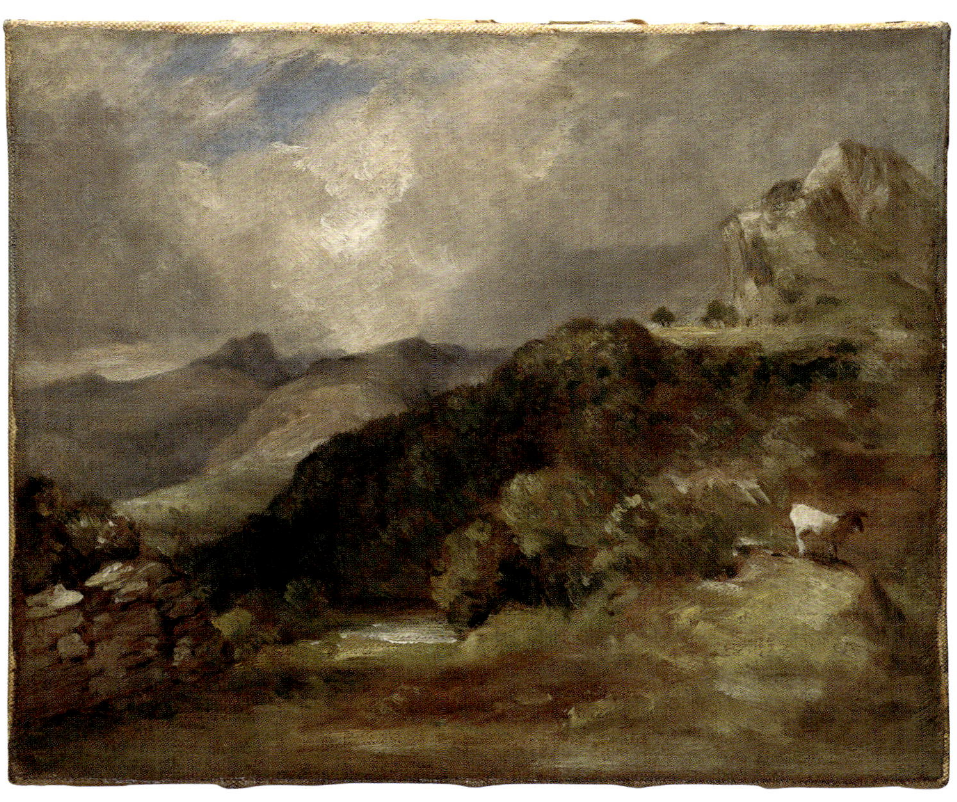

This painting was one of three Lake District subjects that Constable exhibited at the Royal Academy in 1807. It was a breakthrough year for Constable for one of his Lakes oils garnered him his first mention in the press. The Lake District was a popular and marketable subject for landscape artists. Turner's early work featuring the region drew out its Sublime qualities – dark skies, mist and high drama. *Bow Fell* presents a more subtle mood but is nonetheless atmospheric, suggestive of a fast-moving cloudscape and Lakeland's notoriously changeable weather. Its sweeping brush marks are a sign of Constable's study of and admiration for fellow Suffolk-born artist Thomas Gainsborough.

NO. 29 **J.M.W. Turner** *Study for a Picture, Possibly Related to 'Crossing the Brook'* from the *Woodcock Shooting* sketchbook c.1812–13
Ink on paper, 17·8 × 11
Tate. Accepted by the nation as part of the Turner Bequest 1856

NO. 30 **J.M.W. Turner** *Crossing the Brook* exhibited 1815
Oil paint on canvas, 193 × 165·1
Tate. Accepted by the nation as part of the Turner Bequest 1856

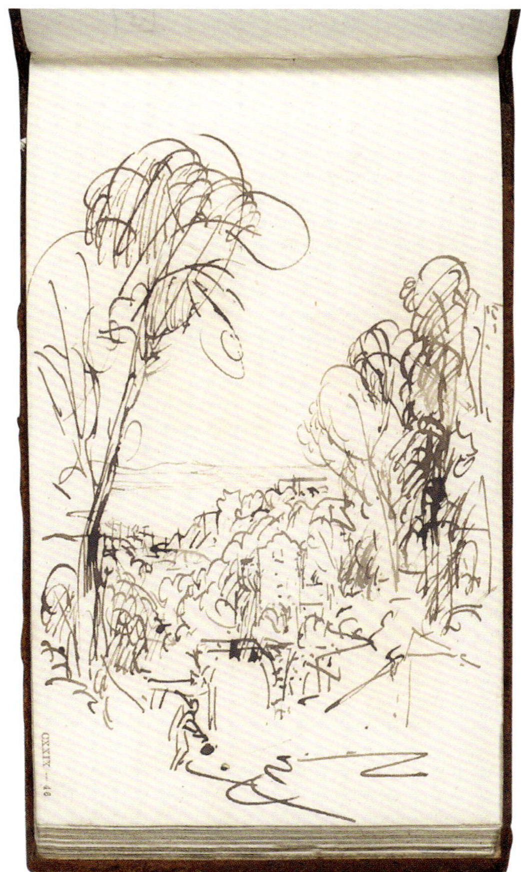

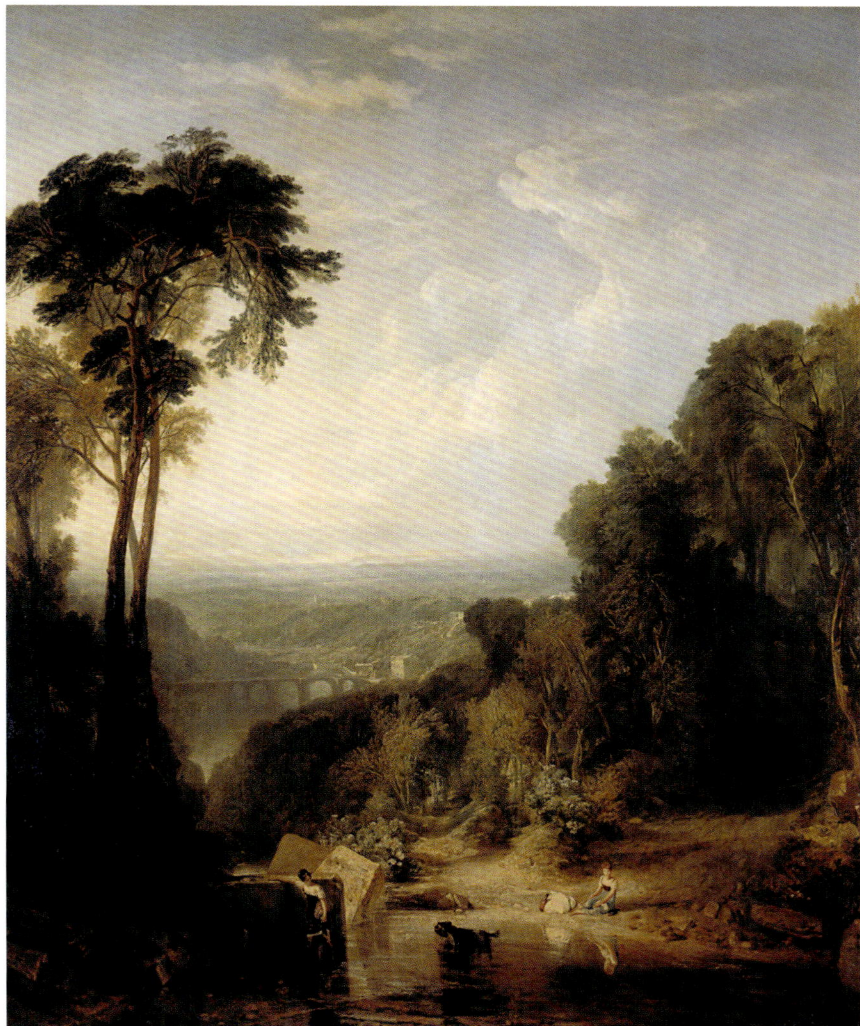

Turner toured Devon in 1813, filling sketchbooks with details that would furnish *Crossing the Brook* (no.30). One of Turner's companions on this tour later recalled how Turner admired the Tamar Valley, and thought Calstock Viaduct to be particularly Italian – though of course Italy was only known then to Turner through the work of other artists. A compositional sketch in pen and ink (no.29) shows the skeleton of the composition – a format which, like Constable's *Dedham Vale*, borrows from Claude (see p.69). It has been suggested that the girls in the foreground are modelled on Turner's daughters, Evelina and Georgiana, who were occasionally seen in his house by visitors. Turner was not the family man Constable was; he never married the girls' mother, Sarah Danby, and does not seem to have played a large role in his daughters' lives.

Despite its clear Claudian references, one rapturous reviewer believed *Crossing the Brook* to be 'purely original' and the most elegant landscape ever seen (*Repository of Arts*, June 1815). Conversely, and perhaps predicably, Turner's long-time detractor, Beaumont (who happened to own the Claude painting that inspired *Crossing the Brook*) said it was full of 'peagreen insipidity', 'like the work of an Old man' who 'no longer saw or felt colour properly' (Farington, *Diary*, 5 June 1815). Turner failed to sell this painting and it remained in his studio; in 1845 Turner described it fondly as 'one of my children' (Gage, *Correspondence*, p.207).

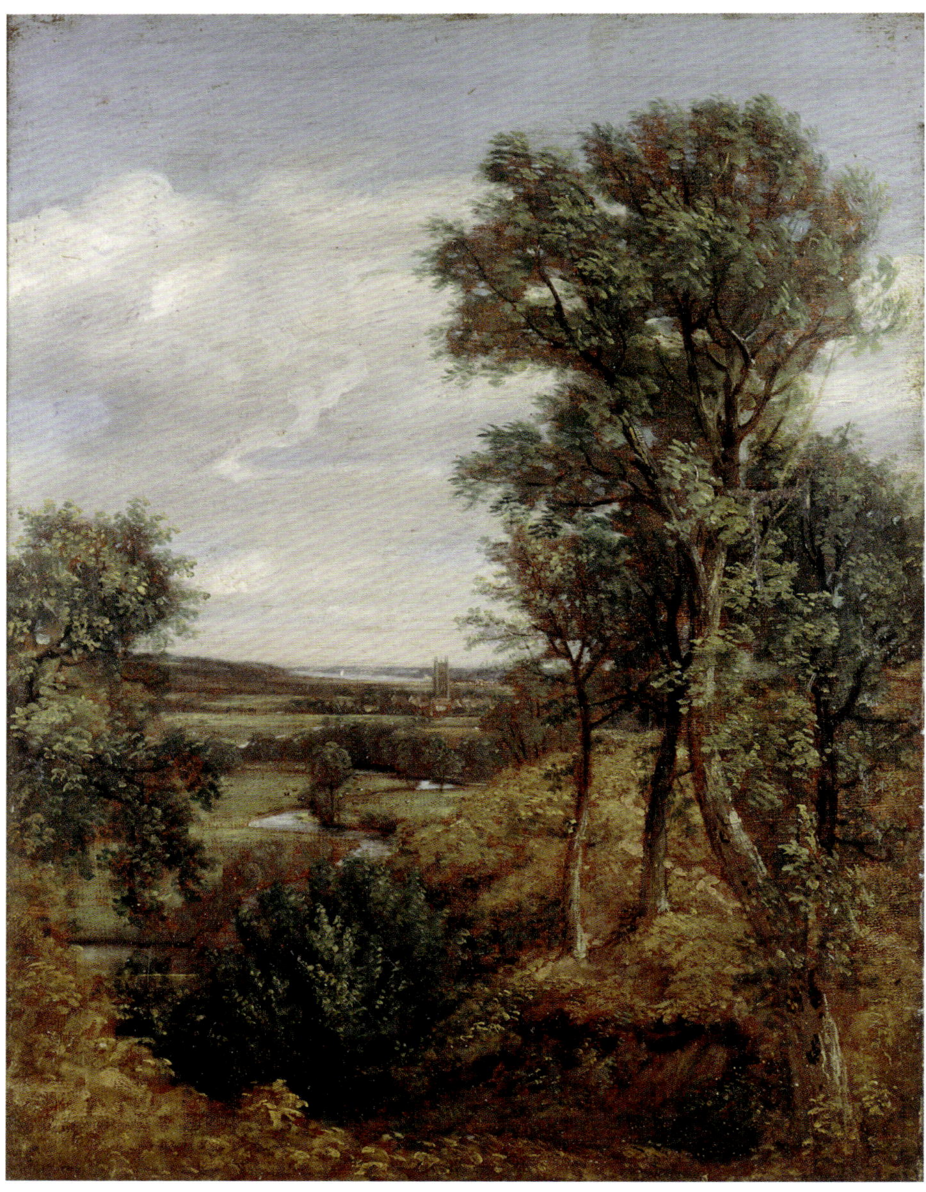

NO. 31 **John Constable** *Dedham Vale from the Coombs* 1802
Oil paint on canvas, 43.5 × 34.4
Victoria and Albert Museum, London

Dedham Vale from the Coombs (no.31) was made at the moment that Constable crystalised his vision for landscape painting and committed to a naturalistic approach based on close observation. It dates from the summer of 1802, when Constable spent time painting outdoors, and depicts the view from near Gun Hill, Langham, with Dedham church and the Stour estuary beyond. Compositionally, however, the work takes inspiration from the same source as Turner's *Crossing the Brook* (no.30). Claude's *Hagar and the Angel* (fig.40, p.69) was the painting his mentor Sir George Beaumont revered most (and reputedly carried with him everywhere). Therefore even as he committed himself to the course of a 'natural peinture', his vision was still subject to the stylised filter of Old Master precedents.

His reasons for taking this composition up again twenty-six years later have been discussed elsewhere (p.69). Showing Constable's confidence in abundance, *Dedham Vale* (no.32) is one of his most celebrated paintings. The recession of space is executed masterfully, from the highlighting of the Stour estuary in the distance to the bent willow trees around Stratford bridge and adjoining buildings in the midground. While this area may draw our eye thanks to its being carefully defined, much of the painting's energy is derived from the loose and highly gestural application of paint and Constable's beloved white highlights, which give the glittering effect of light falling on wet leaves. Reminiscent of Biblical episodes like the Nativity or the Rest on the Flight into Egypt, the figure grouping – a woman and child huddling by a fire – adds gravity to an otherwise idealistic scene.

1828 was not, however, the first time Constable had contemplated making a large painting of a very similar view: when the full-size sketch (National Gallery of Art, Washington) for *The White Horse* (no.127) was x-rayed in 1984, a horizontal version of this view was discovered. Did Constable contemplate it as his first six-footer? In the end his 1828 version of this view proved just as catalytic as *The White Horse*, leading to Constable's election as a member of the Royal Academy the following year.

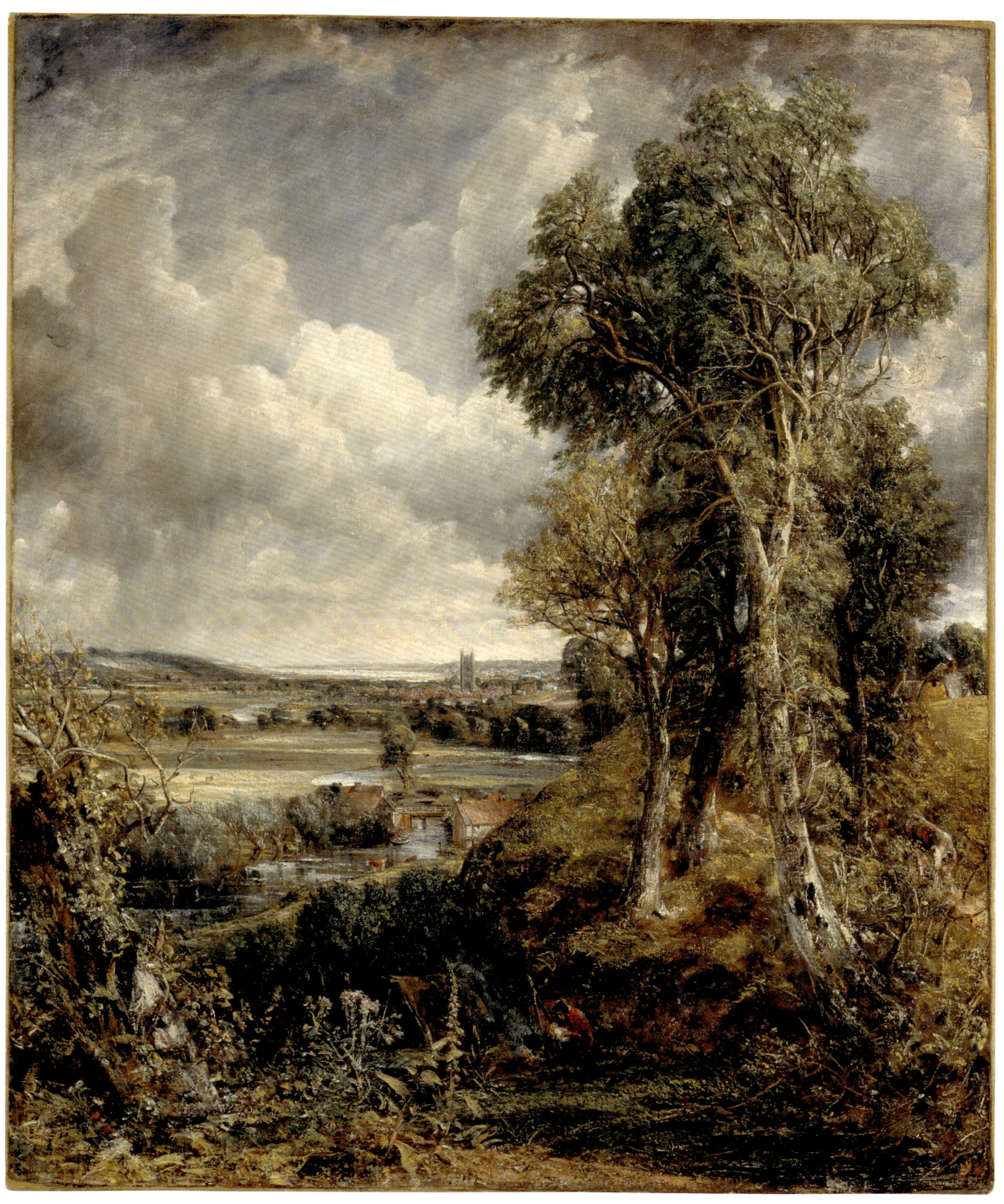

NO. 32 **John Constable** *Dedham Vale* 1828. Oil paint on canvas, 144·5 × 122
National Galleries of Scotland. Purchased with the aid of The Cowan Smith Bequest and Art Fund, 1944

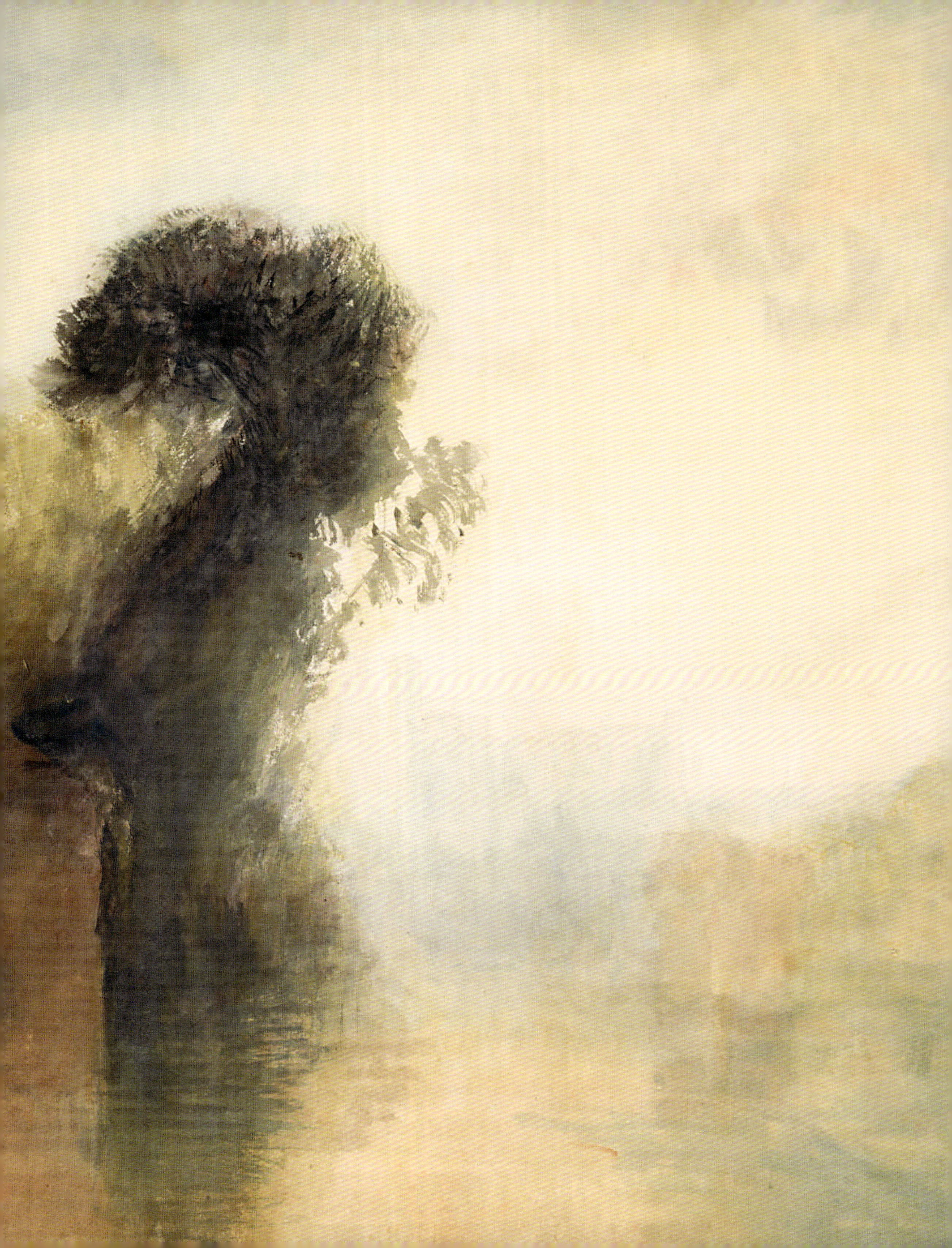

BEHIND CLOSED DOORS: TURNER'S STUDIO

Stacks of a favoured paper, canvases in various stages of completion, a rainbow of pigments in jars, an array of sketchbooks big and small (their labelled spines telling of Turner's travels), and several Manx cats – just some of the things you would have seen if you had been one of the few invited into Turner's studio.[1] This was a place of experimentation where Turner could set his imagination free, fired by real-world experiences and his voracious intellectual curiosity. The objects in this section represent a small glimpse into that world.

From 1799 Turner owned premises at the junction of Queen Anne Street and Harley Street in London; here he had lodgings, a public gallery and a purpose-built studio (Constable established a gallery much further into his career, in 1828). A peephole allowed Turner to spy on visitors to his gallery and to gauge whether he wanted to greet them or not. He was a notoriously private man and his studio a private place. Anecdotes from those who snatched glimpses of him working tell us of sheets hanging on lines to dry, having been submerged in vats of water and drenched in colour.[2]

Despite his guardedness about his own studio, Turner, like Constable, visited those of other artists; early in his career he found himself refused entry by the wife of painter Philippe Jacques de Loutherbourg, since his frequent visits had led her to fear he was trying to steal her husband's secrets.[3]

If the studio was the place for cultivating ideas, it was in the great outdoors that those ideas took root. Just before Constable started his outdoor sketching campaign in earnest, we find Turner in a boat on the western reaches of the Thames, combining his two favourite activities: painting and fishing. In quick, loose oil sketches made on mahogany-veneered panels (perhaps repurposed from old furniture), Turner comes closest to Constable's methods. But by and large his favoured way of translating what he saw and gathering ideas for pictures was with pencil in sketchbooks, which became a visual reference library for his use in the studio; he would often return to a sketch years or decades after first making it.

At the end of Turner's life his studio and gallery were in a lamentable state of repair.[4] One canvas had been cut for a cat flap, another repurposed as tarpaulin under the leaky roof.[5] The way in which we experience the Turner Bequest today – unfinished canvases in frames and even the slightest of sketches framed in mounts – is a far cry from the way the artist left them. Yet each one emerged from the creative chaos of Turner's studio, and it is to our fortune that after his death the contents of this most private space were given to the British public.

J.M.W. Turner *Study for 'Landscape: Composition of Tivoli'* (detail) c.1817 (p.90)

NO. 33 Metal paintbox belonging to J.M.W. Turner n.d.
8·9 × 33·8 × 23·6
Tate Library and Archive

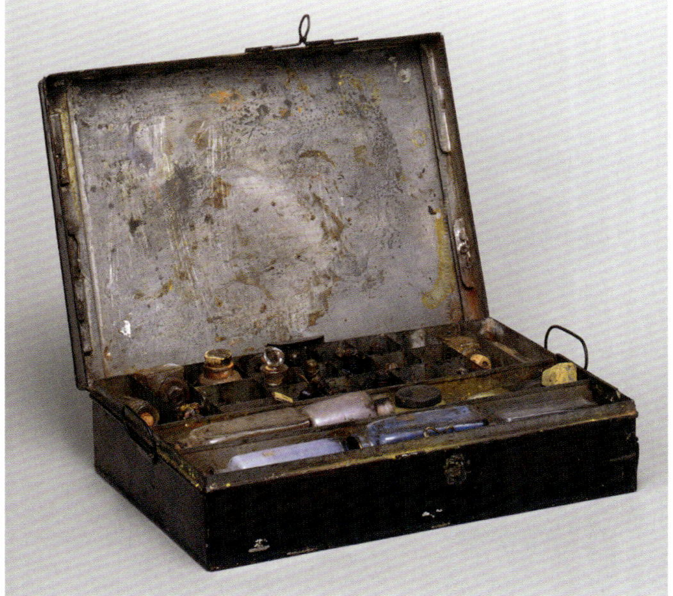

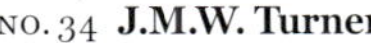

NO. 34 **J.M.W. Turner**
Case Containing Two Pairs of Spectacles, Watercolour Palette and Two Palette Knives n.d.
3·5 × 35·5 × 29·2
Lent by The Ashmolean Museum, University of Oxford

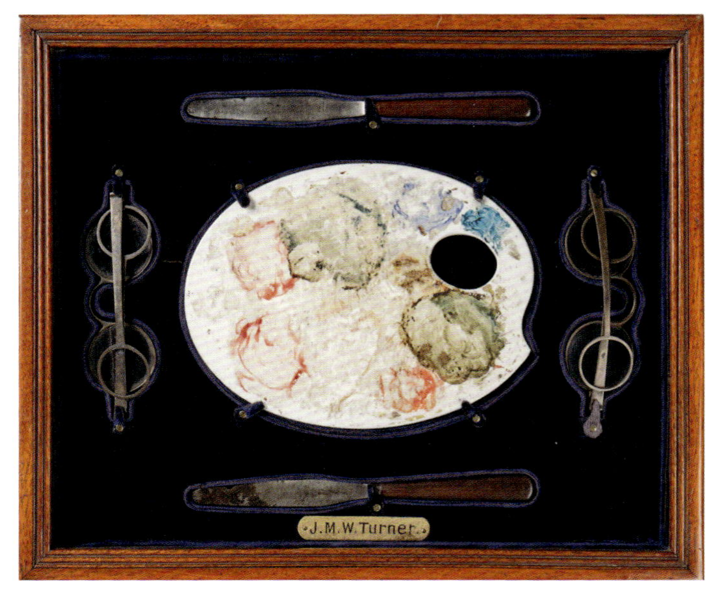

NO. 35 **J.M.W. Turner**
Leather bound travelling watercolour case
11 × 7·5
Private Collection

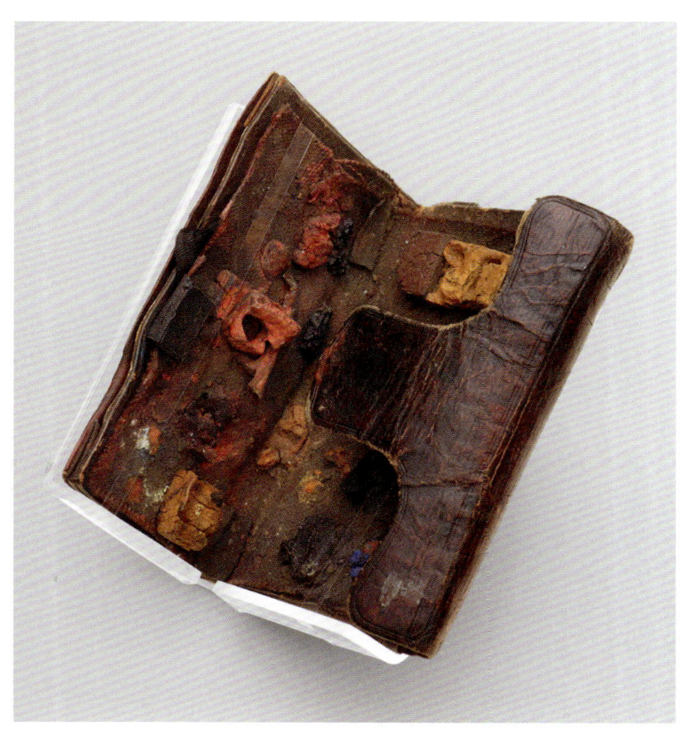

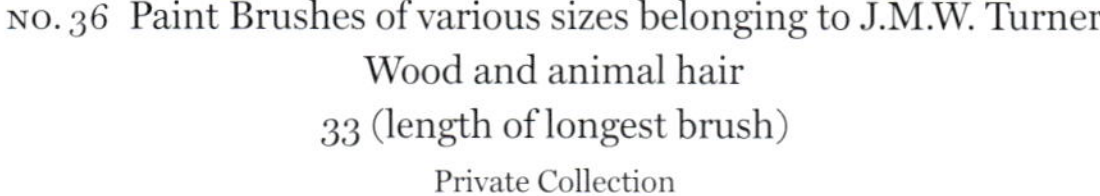

NO. 36 Paint Brushes of various sizes belonging to J.M.W. Turner
Wood and animal hair
33 (length of longest brush)
Private Collection

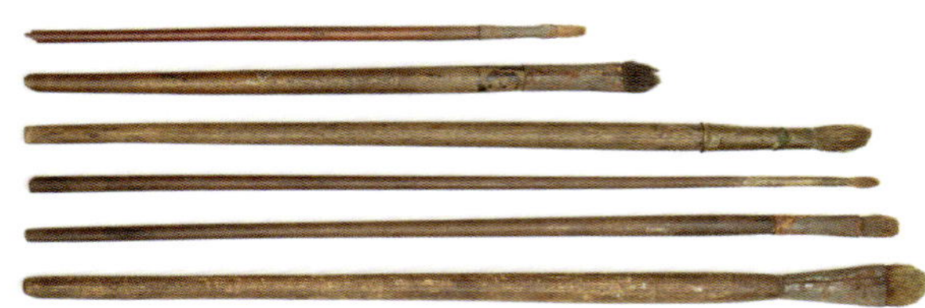

While Turner would often have a sketchbook in his pocket, from the 1830s it became possible to carry a set of watercolours small enough to fit inside a pocket, too. Thanks to new technologies in the production of artists' materials, small cubes of colour (pans) became available. Ingeniously, Turner converted an old leather bookcover into a portable watercolour case featuring these pans of colour.

1804 saw the beginning of a two-year period in which Turner severed his ties with the Royal Academy. Having received complaints from colleagues about his conduct, Turner left the politics of the city behind and headed west to the Thames's leafier stretches. He took homes in Isleworth and Hammersmith before building his own house, Sandycombe Lodge, at St Margaret's, Twickenham (no.49). These riverside locations offered Turner respite and chance to indulge in his favourite hobby, fishing. As well as making a thorough exploration of the river's course, from Oxfordshire down to the estuary, this period also saw him dabble in painting in oils outdoors – much like Constable was doing around the same time in Suffolk. We can surmise, then, that Turner's boat was loaded with equipment for fishing as well as painting. The oil sketches he made are on mahogany-veneered panels (cupboard doors, it has been suggested) prepared with an absorbent ground. This meant Turner's paint would have sunken in quickly, leaving little time to rework or adjust. We therefore see in them fluid paint, quickly applied – in some, paint seems to have been smeared on with a finger. The urge to experiment and loosen up was no doubt a byproduct of living life at a slower pace during Turner's retreat from the city.

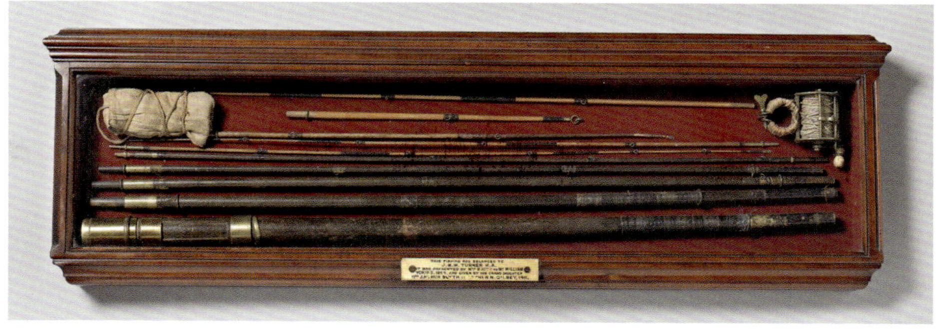

NO. 37 Fishing rod belonging to Turner, made up of five sections, cased, date unknown
27·2 × 89 × 7·2
Lent by the Royal Academy of Arts, London

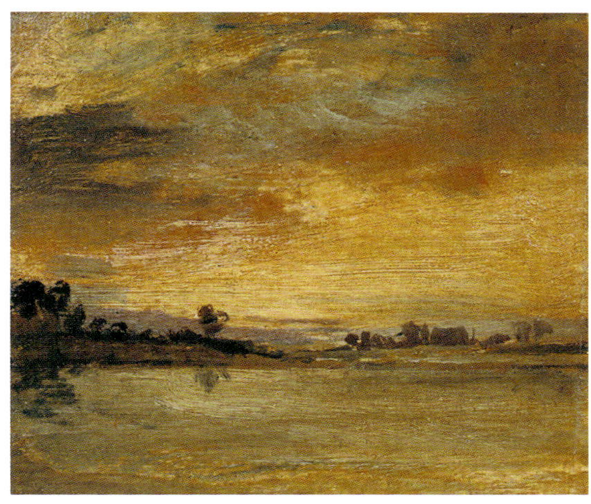

NO. 38 **J.M.W. Turner** *Sunset on the River* 1805
Oil paint on mahogany veneer mounted onto wooden panel, 15·6 × 18·7
Tate. Accepted by the nation as part of the Turner Bequest 1856

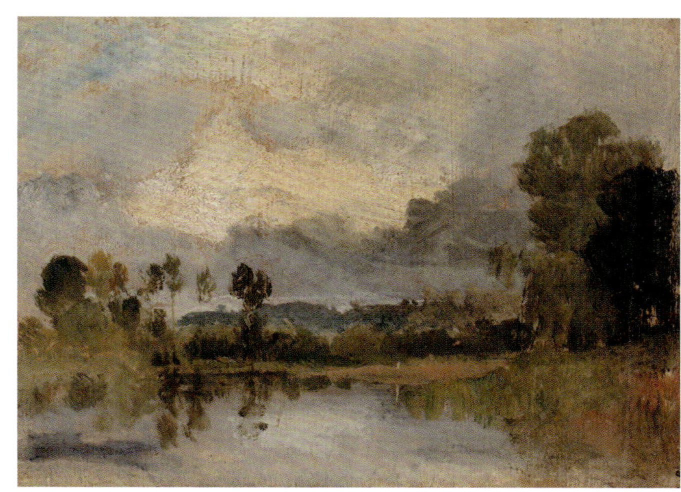

NO. 39 **J.M.W. Turner** *The Thames near Windsor* c.1807
Oil paint on mahogany veneer mounted onto board, 18·7 × 26
Tate. Accepted by the nation as part of the Turner Bequest 1856

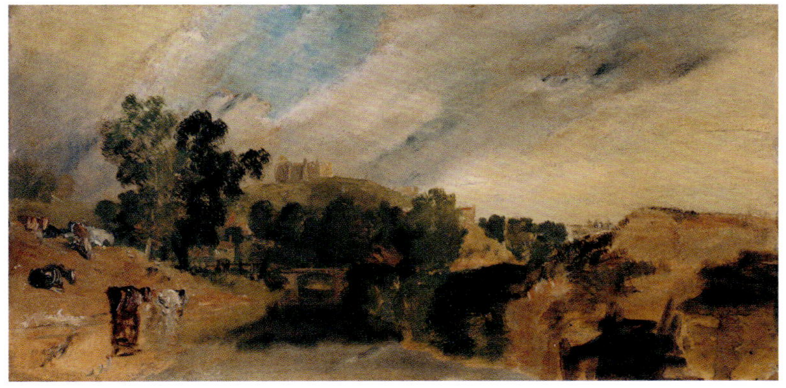

NO. 40 **J.M.W. Turner** *St Catherine's Hill, Guildford* c.1807
Oil paint on mahogany veneer, 36·5 × 73·7
Tate. Accepted by the nation as part of the Turner Bequest 1856

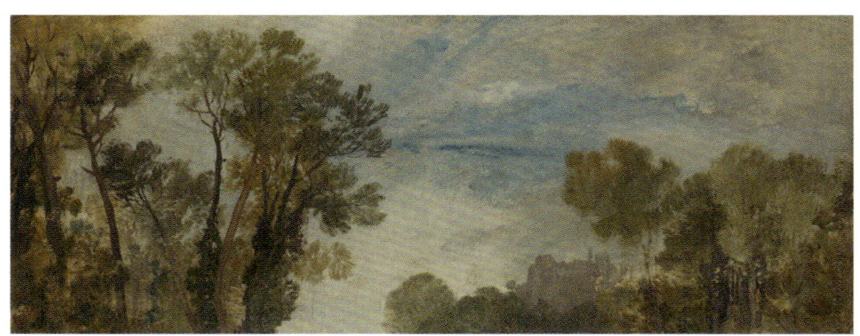

NO. 41 **J.M.W. Turner** *Tree Tops and Sky, Guildford Castle(?), Evening* ?1807
Oil paint on mahogany veneer, 27·6 × 73·7
Tate. Accepted by the nation as part of the Turner Bequest 1856

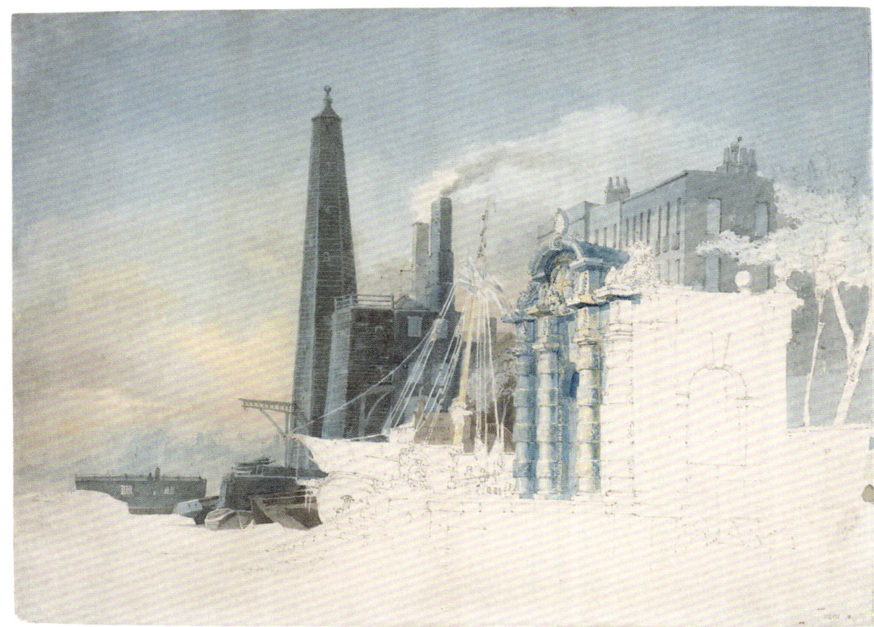

NO. 42 **J.M.W. Turner** *London: York House Water-Gate, Westminster, with York Buildings Waterworks* 1794–5
Graphite and watercolour on paper, 29·8 × 41·9
Tate. Accepted by the nation as part of the Turner Bequest 1856

NO. 43 **J.M.W. Turner** *Study for 'Landscape: Composition of Tivoli'* c.1817
Graphite and watercolour on paper, 66·7 × 100·6
Tate. Accepted by the nation as part of the Turner Bequest 1856

Making watercolours like this was an essential part of Turner's process. Known as 'colour beginnings', they were created as models for colour and light schemes, in this case for a finished watercolour on a similarly large scale, *Landscape: Composition of Tivoli*, which he exhibited at the Royal Academy in 1818 (private collection) and which was engraved in 1827 (Tate impression: T04502). Even in this draft, Turner's evocation of a Claudean formula is in evidence: the sun glows in the centre, reflected in a body of water, while a tree (dark against the light sky) frames the view. The bulk on the right-hand side would become classical architecture in the finished work.

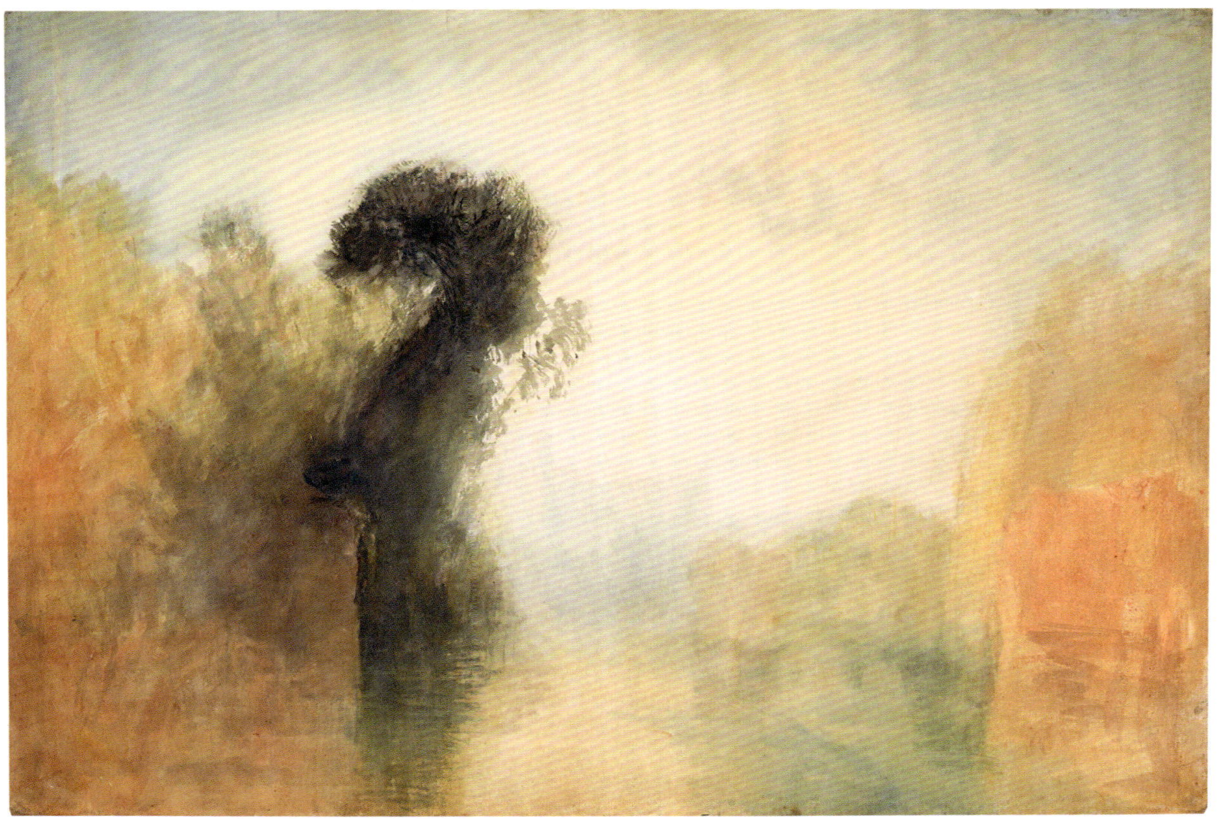

NO. 44 **J.M.W. Turner** *The Scarlet Sunset: A ?French Town on a River* c.1830
Watercolour and gouache on paper, 13·4 × 18·9
Tate. Accepted by the nation as part of the Turner Bequest 1856

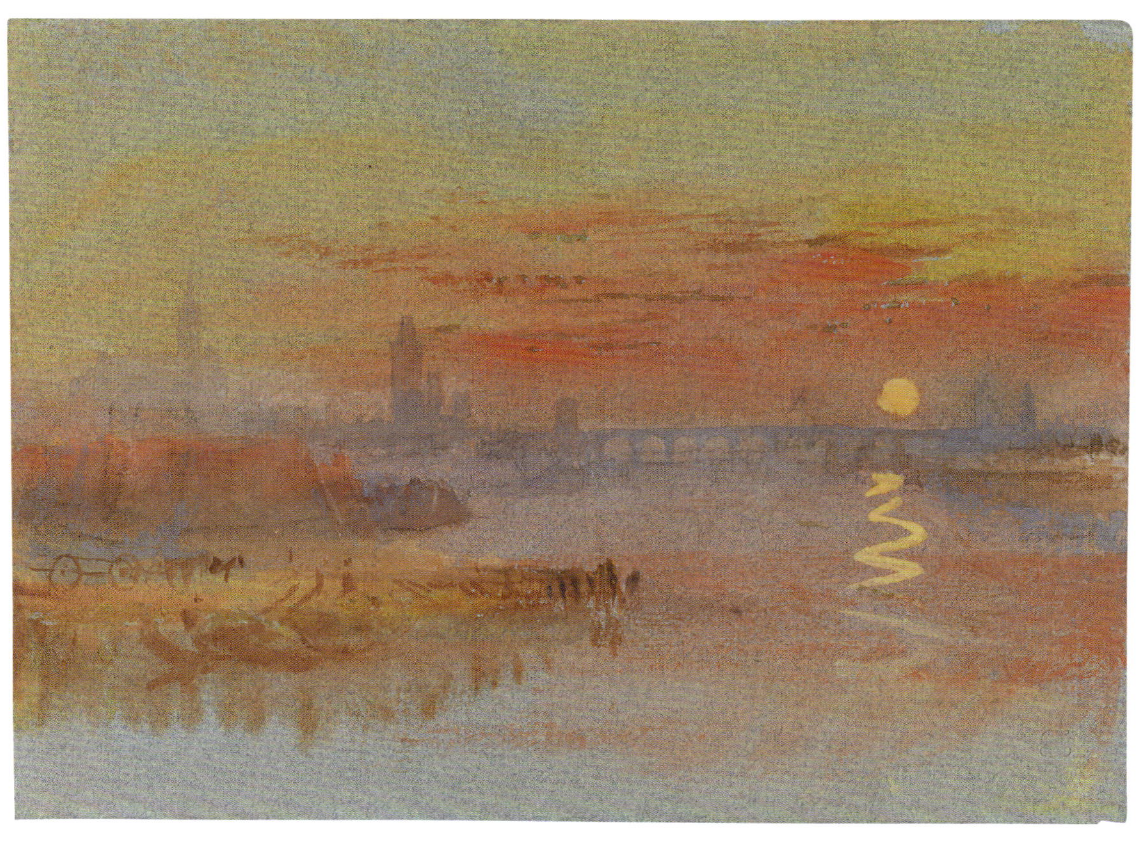

NO. 45 **J.M.W. Turner** *The Sun Rising over Water* c.1825–30
Watercolour on paper, 33·4 × 47·2
Tate. Accepted by the nation as part of the Turner Bequest 1856

NO. 46 **J.M.W. Turner** *Shields Lighthouse* c.1823–6
Watercolour on paper, 23·4 × 28·3
Tate. Accepted by the nation as part of the Turner Bequest 1856

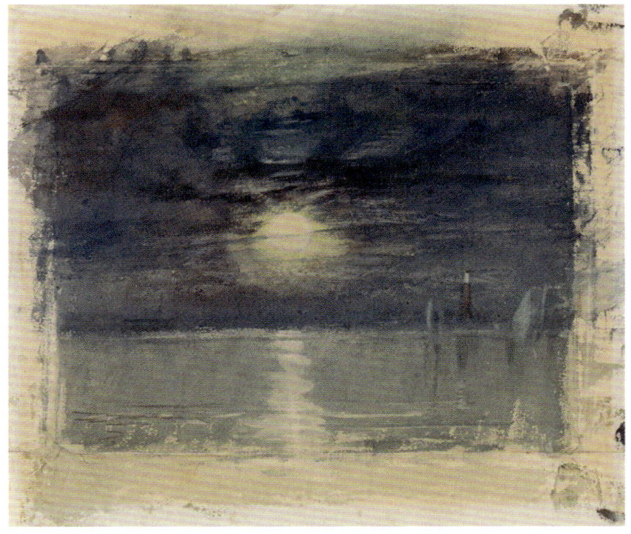

NO. 47 **J.M.W. Turner** *Saint-Germain-en-Laye* c.1829–31
Watercolour on paper, 35·3 × 50·8
Tate. Accepted by the nation as part of the Turner Bequest 1856

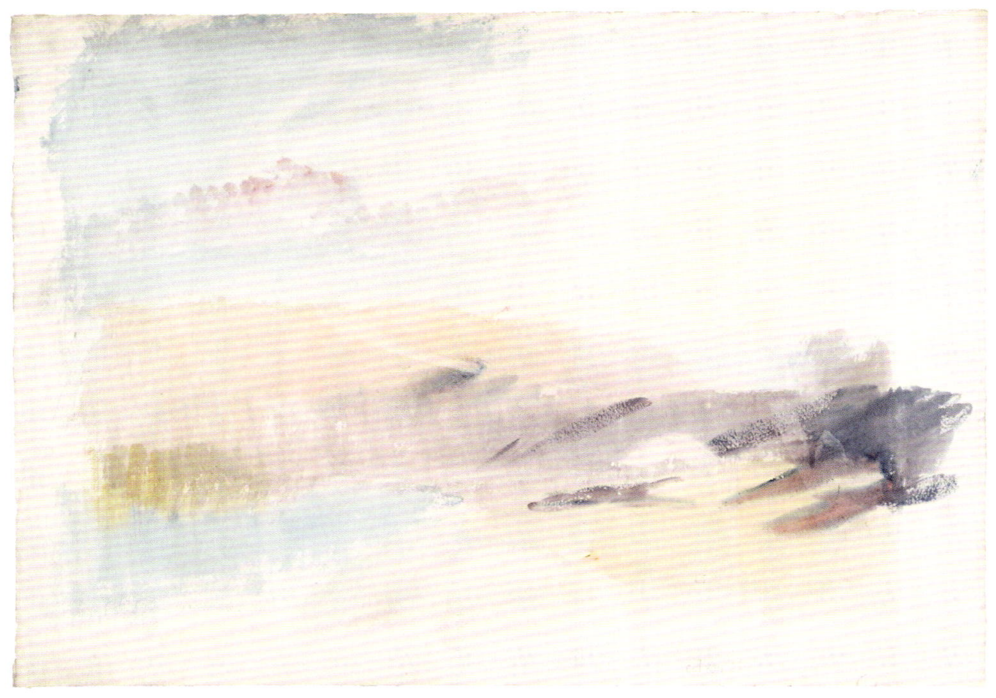

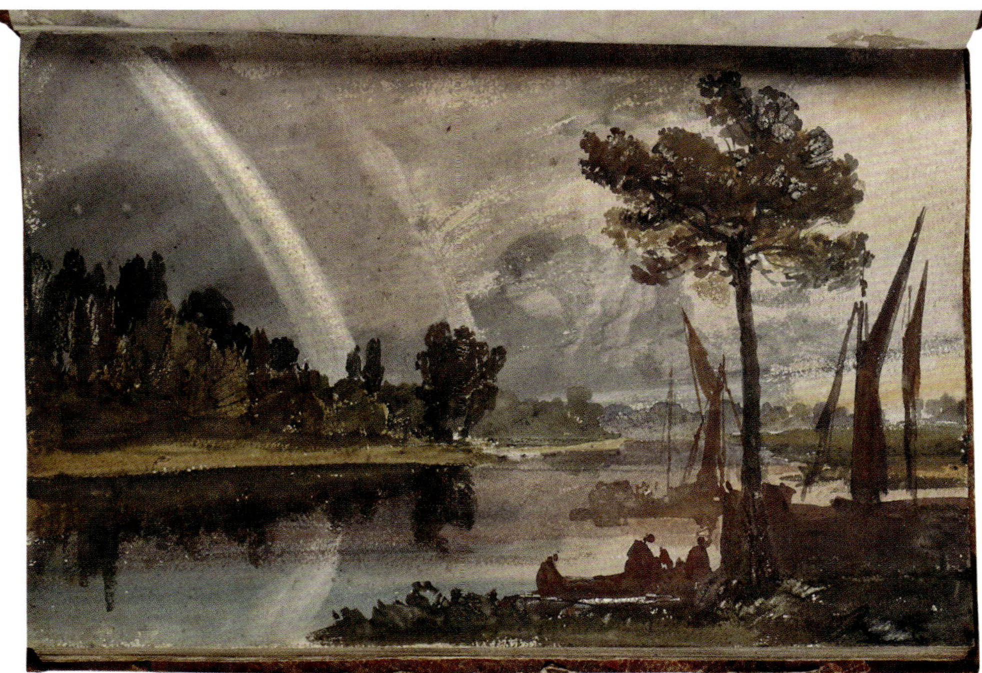

NO. 48 **J.M.W. Turner** *The Thames near Isleworth with a Double Rainbow* from the *Hesperides* sketchbook 1805
Pen and ink on paper, 17·1 × 26·2
Tate. Accepted by the nation as part of the Turner Bequest 1856

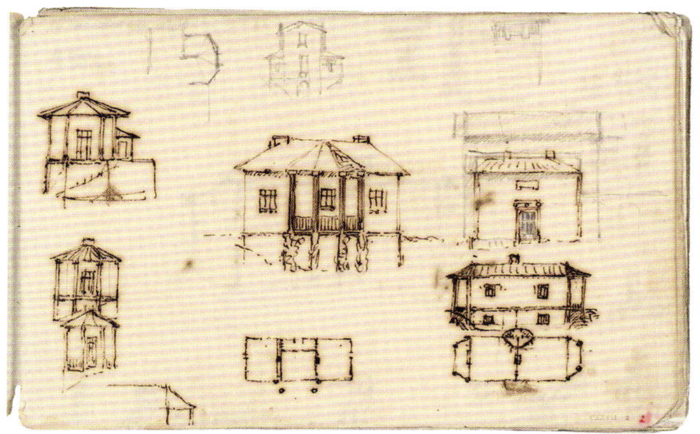

NO. 49 **J.M.W. Turner** *Designs for Sandycombe Lodge, Twickenham* from the *Sandycombe and Yorkshire* sketchbook c.1809–11
Pen and ink and graphite on paper, 12·6 × 20·1
Tate. Accepted by the nation as part of the Turner Bequest 1856

These drawings relate to the Twickenham house, Sandycombe Lodge, that Turner designed with help from his friend and professional architect, Sir John Soane. The small pencil sketch in the centre at the top would be the design that was carried forward, with a tall central block and lower flanking wings. It still stands today.

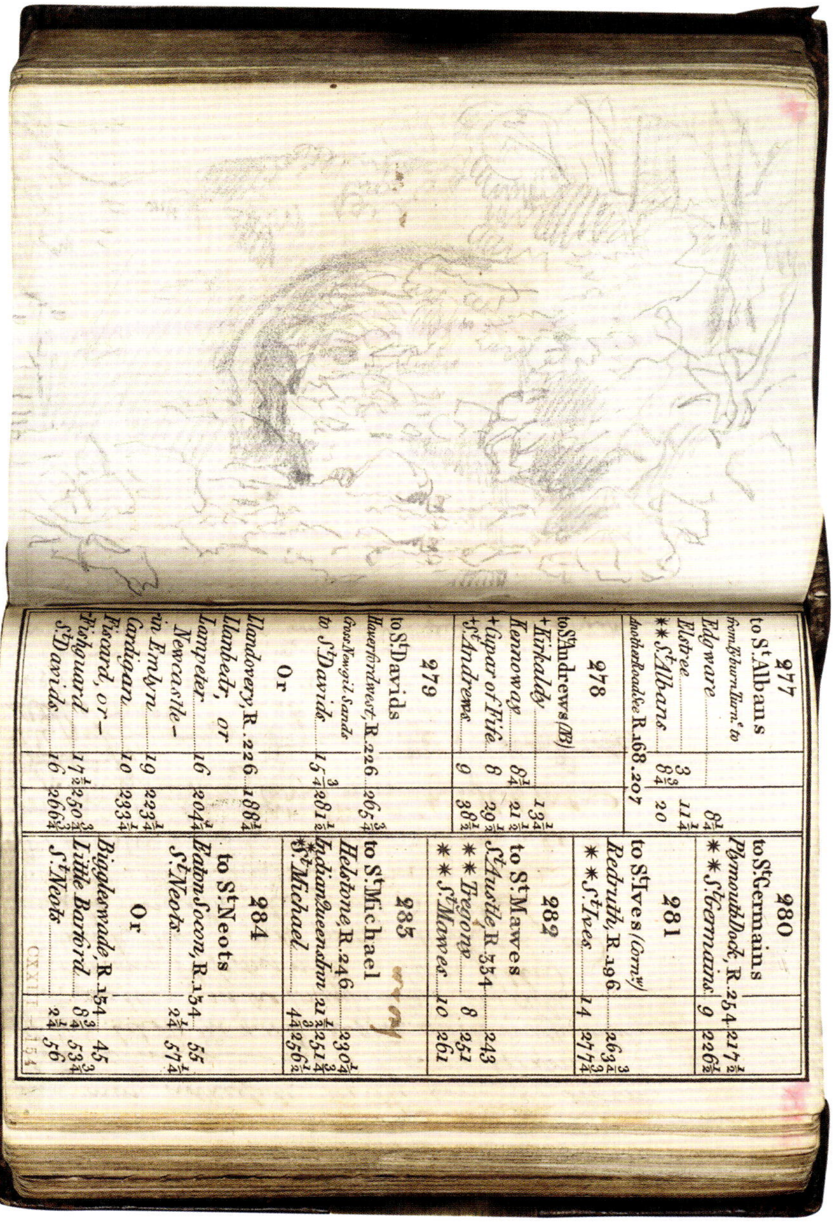

277 to St. Albans		
from Tyburn Turn.e to Edgware		8¼
Elstree	3	11¼
** St. Albans	8¾	20
Another Road see R. 168. 207		
278 to St. Andrews (N.B.)		
+Kirkaldy		13¼
Kennoway	8¼	21½
+Cupar of Fife	8	29½
+St. Andrews	9	38½
279 to St. Davids		
Haverfordwest, R. 226		265¾
Cross Newgil Sands to St. Davids	15¾	281½
Or		
Llandovery, R. 226		188¼
Llanbedr, or Lampeter	16	204¼
Newcastle-in Emlyn	19	223¼
Cardigan	10	233¼
Fiscard, or – Fishguard	17½	250¾
St. Davids	16	266¾
280 to St. Germains		
Plymouth Dock, R. 254		217½
** St. Germains	9	226½
281 to St. Ives (Cornw.)		
Redruth, R. 196		263¾
** St. Ives	14	277¾
282 to St. Mawes		
St. Austle, R. 254		243
** Tregony	8	251
** St. Mawes	10	261
283 to St. Michael		
Helstone, R. 246		230¼
Indian Queens Inn	21½	251¾
** St. Michael	4¾	256½
284 to St. Neots		
Eaton Socon, R. 154		55
St. Neots	2¼	57¼
Or		
Biggleswade, R. 154		45
Little Barford	8¾	53¾
St. Neots	2¼	56

NO. 50 **J.M.W. Turner** *The Ivy Bridge, on the River Erme at Ivybridge* and *Printed Page of Coltman's 'British Itinerary'* from the *Devonshire Coast* sketchbook 1811
Graphite on paper and engraving on paper, each page 7·5 × 11·7
Tate. Accepted by the nation as part of the Turner Bequest 1856

NO. 51 **J.M.W. Turner** *?A Church Spire Reflected in Water, with Storm Clouds* from the *Old London Bridge* sketchbook c.1823–4
Ink wash on paper, 9·8 × 16·2
Tate. Accepted by the nation as part of the Turner Bequest 1856

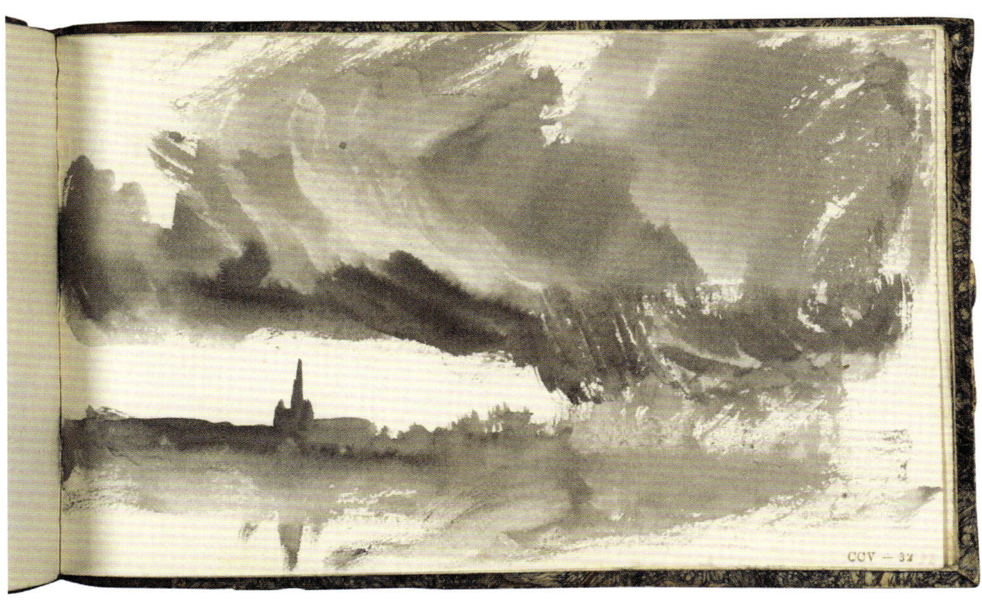

NO. 52 **J.M.W. Turner** *Inscription by Turner: Notes from Nicholson's 'Dictionary of Practical and Theoretical Chemistry'* from the *Chemistry and Apuleia* sketchbook c.1813
Graphite on paper, each page 8·8 × 11·3
Tate. Accepted by the nation as part of the Turner Bequest 1856

Turner's sketchbooks contain much more than drawings. In this instance Turner has written notes on chemistry, relating to colour, copied from William Nicholson's 1808 *Dictionary of Practical and Theoretical Chemistry*. Turner made various notes about yellow in this book, including 'Naples Yellow' but here, as written prominently at the top of the page, the note concerns the method for making 'Golden Yellow'. As transcribed by Matthew Imms, the page reads: 'Antimony 6 parts 2 of Nitre 1 ½ of Salt / one of Charcoal, small portion thrown into a | a crucible.- when fuzed form three mases -the / top spongy when being washed pulverised and dried in / the color / Nitrious Acid acting upon Balsam of Peru / gives by heat a bright yellow mixture this / might be perhaps thrown upon an earth / as alum as a <B...> ground for yellow / [?Mr B]'

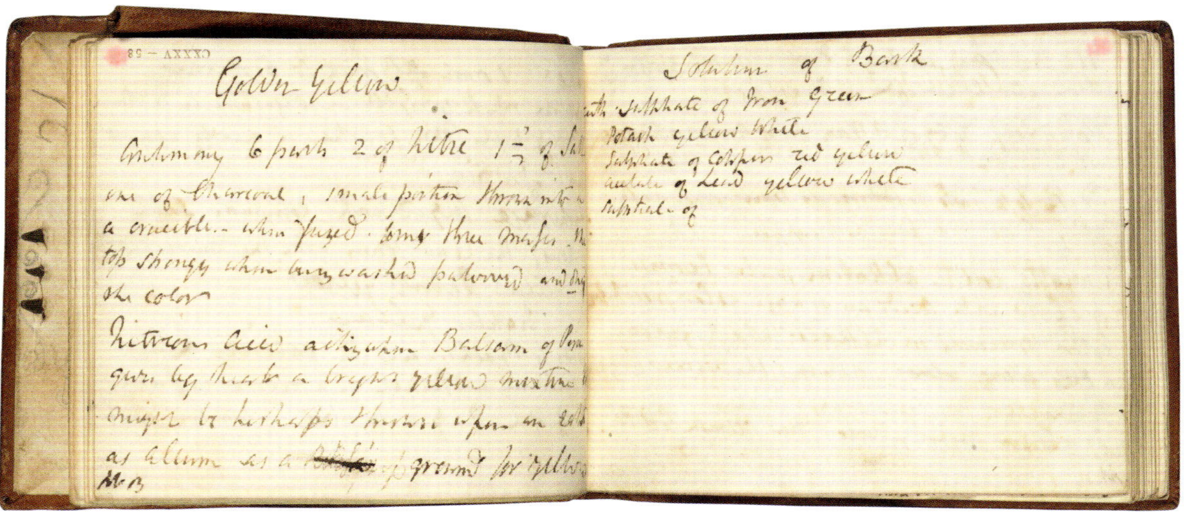

NO. 53 **J.M.W. Turner** *Sketch Map of the Meuse between Verdun and Mouzon; Other Notes and Sketches* and *Sketch Map of the Meuse between Mouzon and Sedan; List of Distances between Northern French and Belgian Towns* from the *Rivers Meuse and Moselle* sketchbook 1824
Graphite on paper, each 7·8 × 11·8
Tate. Accepted by the nation as part of the Turner Bequest 1856

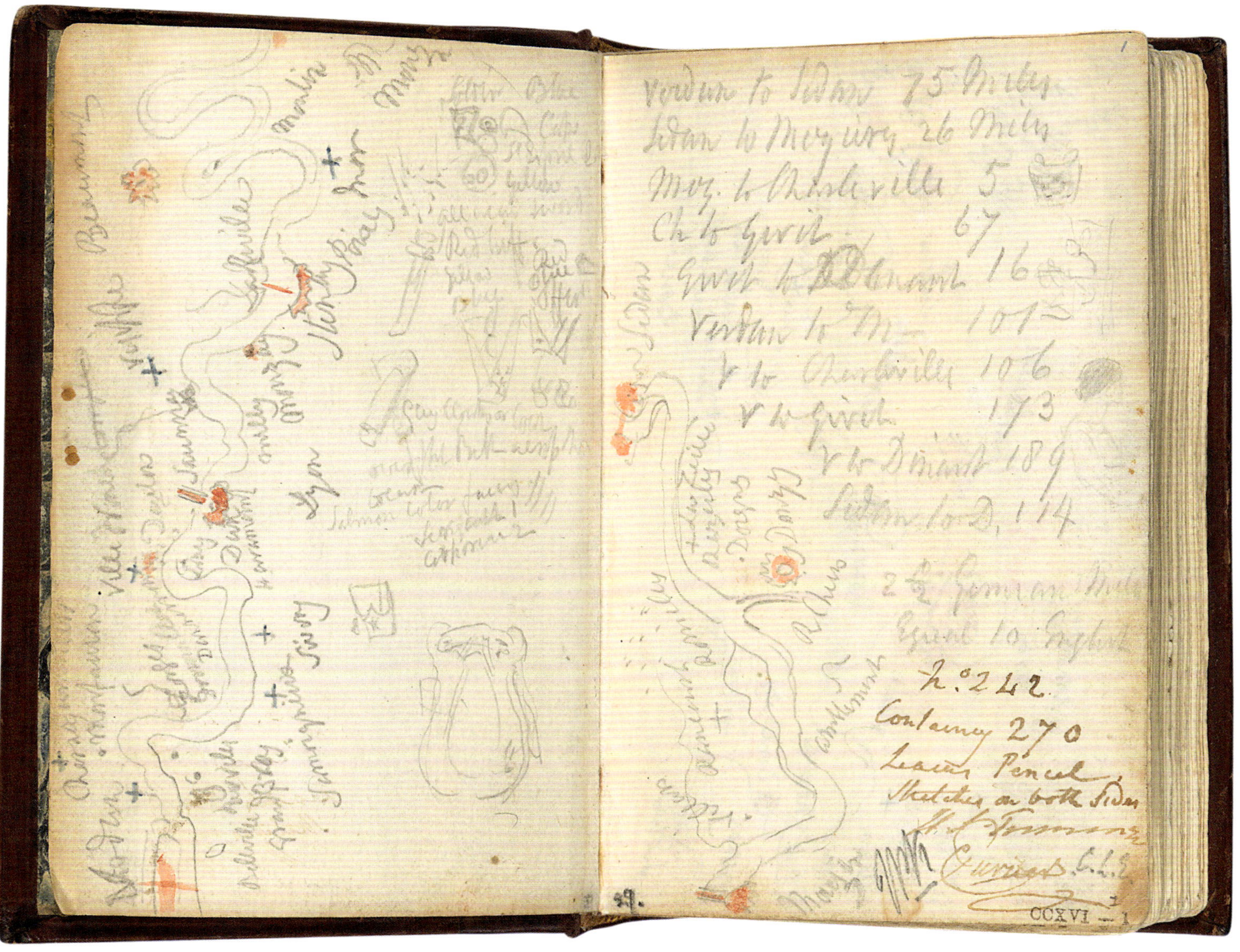

This sketchbook was used by Turner during the five-week tour that took him through France, Belgium, Luxembourg, and Germany along the course of the rivers Meuse, Moselle (known as the Mosel in Germany) and Rhine. To maximise his time abroad, he studied guidebooks and itineraries before setting out. The opening illustrated here is one of several sketched maps that Turner made in preparation for his journey using published maps and a guidebook. The red and blue symbols have been discerned by Cecilia Powell as adopted directly from the guidebook Turner used as code for at-a-glance information – the use of a red circle signifies a walled or open town, for example. Opposite the map he lists the distances between towns on the Meuse.

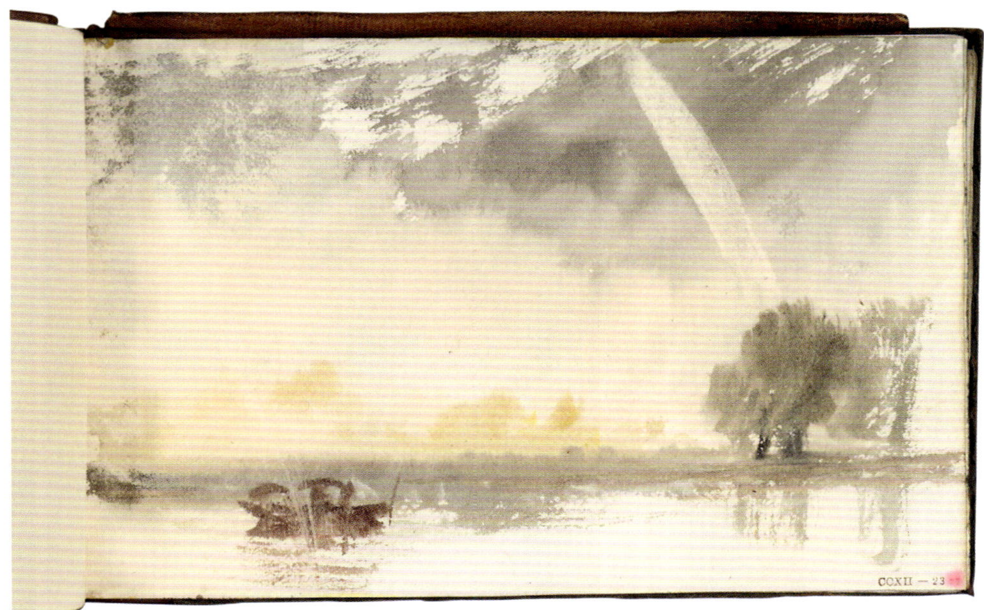

NO. 54 **J.M.W. Turner** *Figures under Umbrellas in a Punt on a River, with a Rainbow* from the *Thames* sketchbook c.1825
Watercolour on paper, 11·4 × 18·8
Tate. Accepted by the nation as part of the Turner Bequest 1856

NO. 55 **J.M.W. Turner** *Sail Boats* and *Sail Boats; Margate, Kent* from the *Gravesend and Margcte* sketchbook c.1832
Graphite on paper, each page 20·6 × 8·6
Tate. Accepted by the nation as part of the Turner Bequest 1856

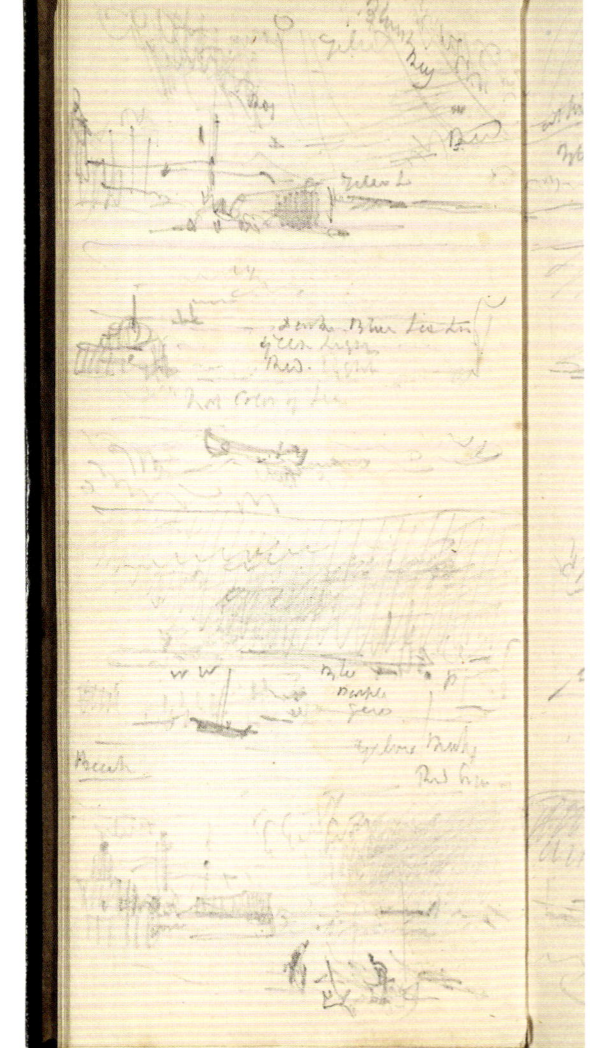

Turner's sketchbooks vary widely in their shapes and sizes. The long, thin format of this book lends itself to the making of panoramic sketches as well as having its pages divided to create the kind of small thumbnail sketches seen here. By design it was also easily stashed in a pocket.

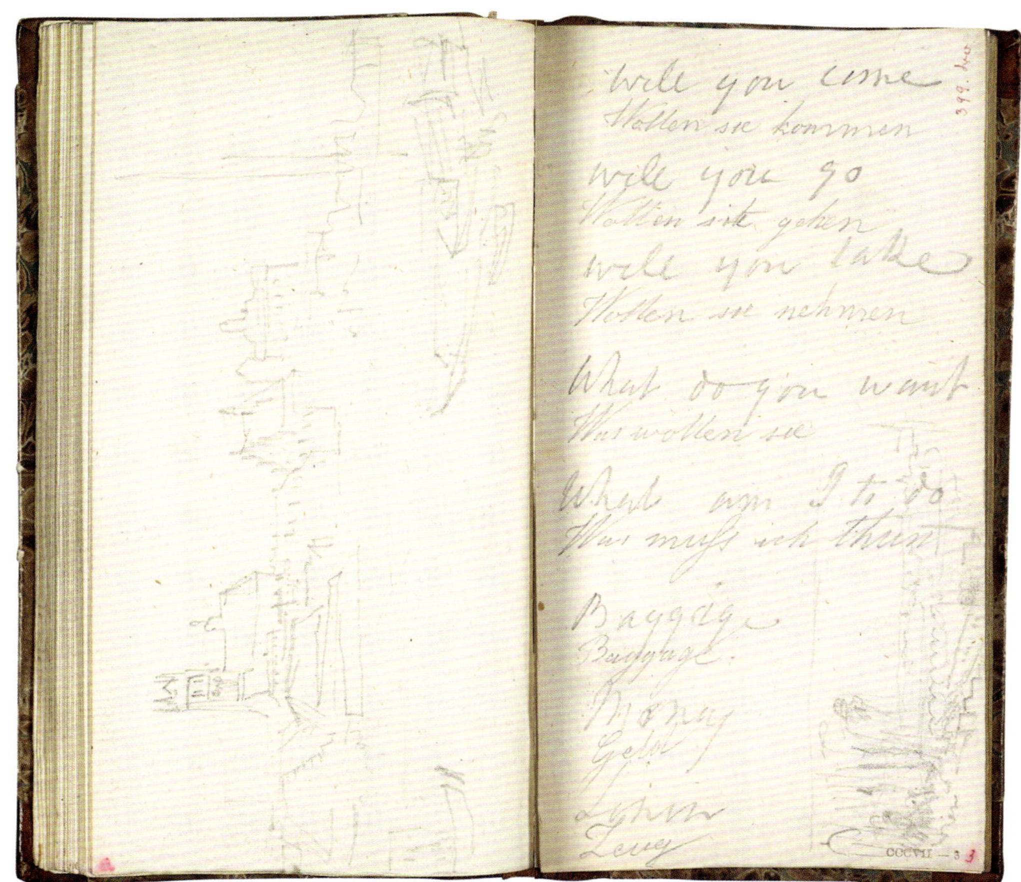

NO. 56 **J.M .W Turner** *Stettin: View across the Oder to St James's and St John's Churches and the Castle* and *Dresden: View on the Bank of the Elbe near the Brühl Terrace, Looking Downstream to the Bridge, with Trees in Background; English and German Phrases* from the *Copenhagen to Dresden* sketchbook 1835
Graphite on paper, each page 8·9 × 16·2
Tate. Accepted by the nation as part of the Turner Bequest 1856

Several of Turner's sketchbooks contain language tips to help ease his way abroad. In this one Turner has had someone write out German translations of phrases like 'Will you come', 'Will you go', 'What do you want', 'What am I to do', and the words for baggage, money and linen.

NO. 57 **J.M.W. Turner** *Two Sketches: St Dizier from the East, Looking along the River Marne; View from a Cross on a High Mountain Pass,?the Col du Bonhomme* and *The West Front of the Cathedral at Reims* from the *Val d'Aosta* sketchbook 1836
Graphite on paper, each page 11·3 × 19
Tate. Accepted by the nation as part of the Turner Bequest 1856

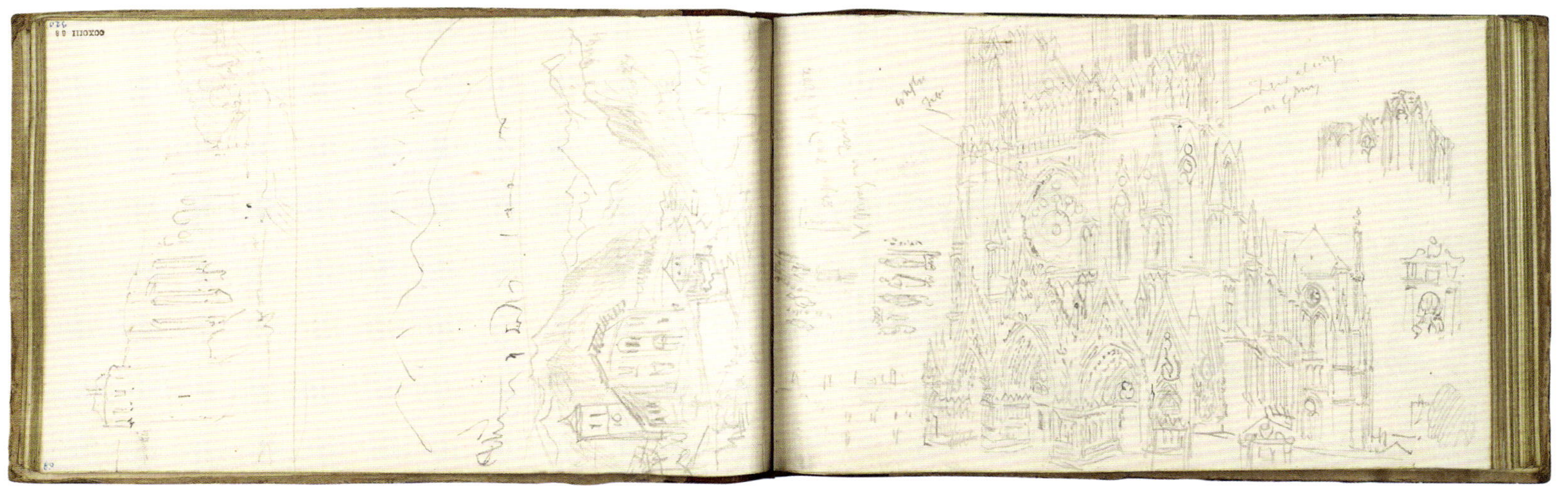

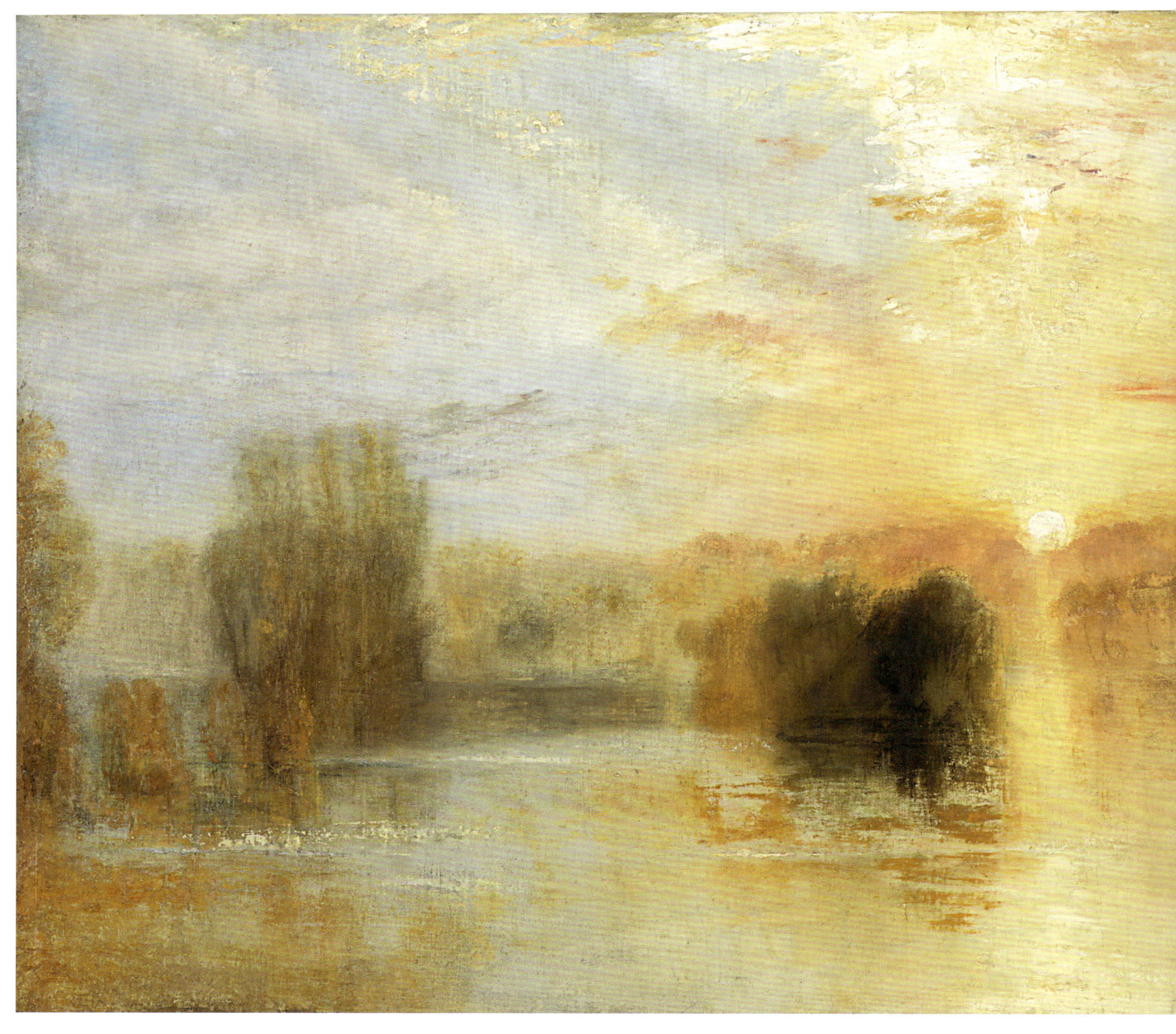

NO. 58 **J.M.W. Turner** *The Lake, Petworth, Sunset; Sample Study* c.1827–8
Oil paint on canvas, 66 × 142·2
Tate. Accepted by the nation as part of the Turner Bequest 1856

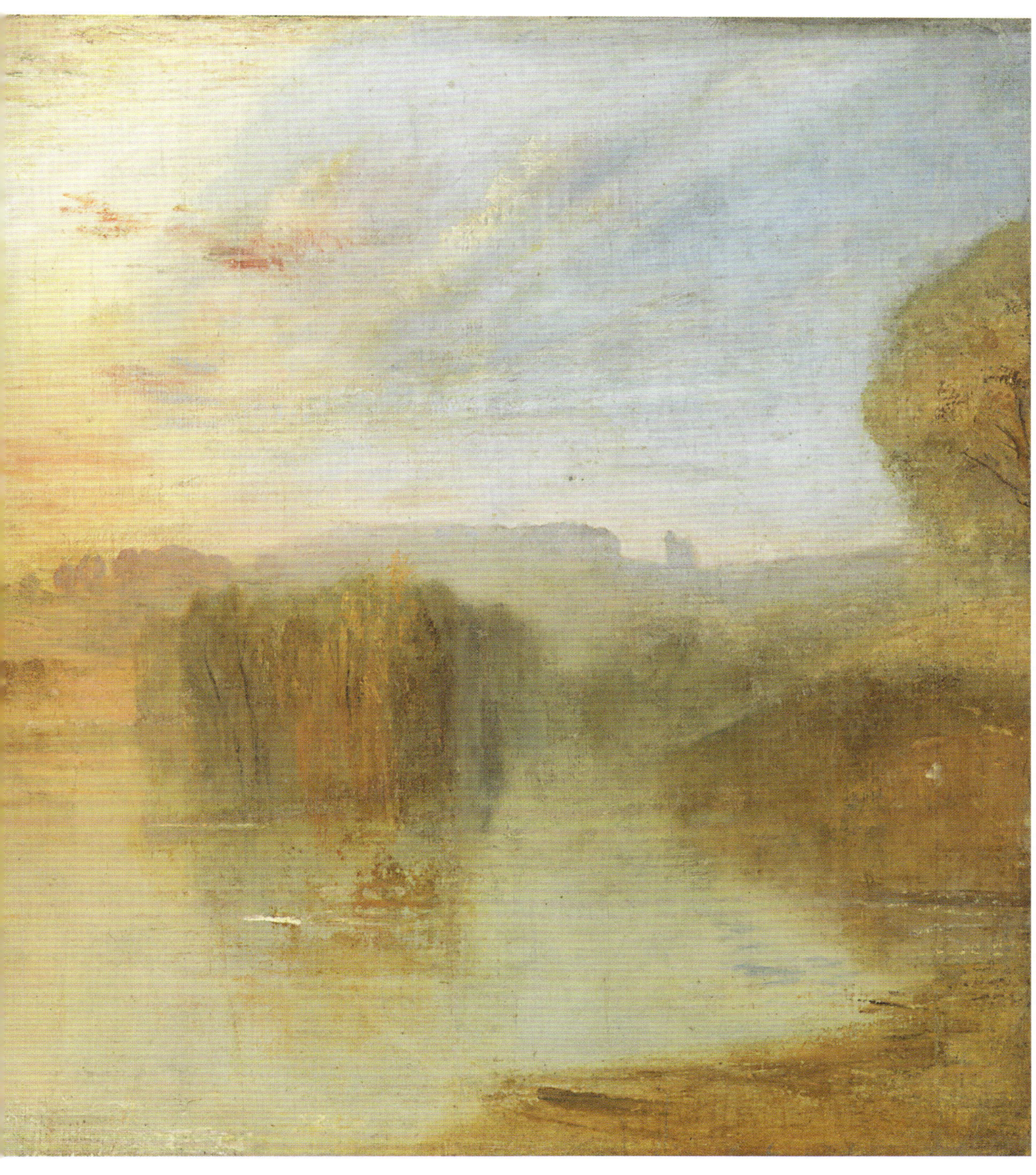

Turner was a frequent visitor to Petworth House in Sussex. Its incumbent, George O'Brien Wyndham, 3rd Earl of Egremont (1751–1837), was an early patron of Turner's and the two became friends. Egremont was a generous patron of contemporary British art and regularly had artists to stay, including Constable, but only Turner seems to have been afforded the special privilege of using the Old Library as a studio. It was here that he is said to have painted a series of four oblong paintings designed for the Earl's dining room. Local landmarks of significance to the Earl featured in Turner's paintings, including Chichester Canal and Brighton's Chain Pier, modern features of the landscape that the Earl had invested in. The present work is, as its title suggests, a study that celebrates the Capability Brown-designed grounds of Petworth House itself. It allowed Turner to indulge in a radiant sunset.

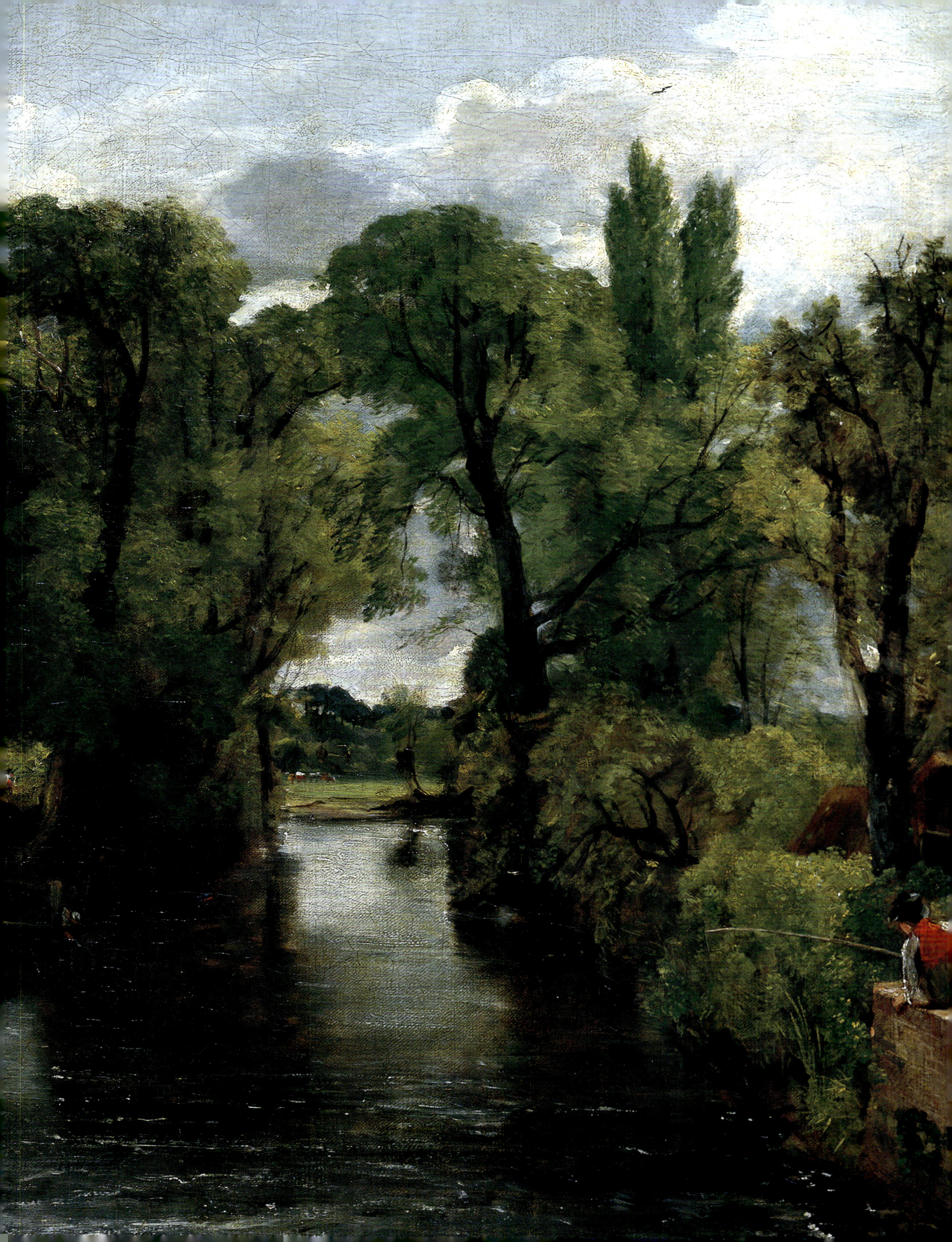

IN THE OUTDOORS: CONSTABLE AND THE OIL SKETCH

By 1810 Constable had mastered the art of the oil sketch and had begun to create the body of work that would not only serve him in the studio for decades to come but would go on to become one of the most defining and celebrated aspects of his output.

He had started to use oils outdoors in 1802 as a means to achieve a 'pure and unaffected representation ... with respect to colour particularly'.[1] It was only around 1808, however, that Constable appears to have taken up the practice in earnest. He described his method for making the sketches: 'in the lid of my [paint] box on my knees'.[2] Like Constable, Turner owned a portable paint box (nos.33 and 60), yet he preferred using pencil in sketchbooks, many of them small enough to be stashed in his pocket. When painting outdoors Constable used pig bladders filled with ready-made oil colours (a relatively recent development in artists' materials) and a folding chair for comfort (no.59).

Painting outside was inherently challenging: gusts of wind, rain showers, insects, passers-by or even curious animals might hamper the process. Under these conditions, rapid brushwork was necessary. Constable's mastery of this skill and his economical application of multiple colours within a single brushstroke are evident in his sketches. He also adopted the same techniques when making sketches in the studio to help him work out his ideas for larger paintings.

Many of the sketches here are notable for their vibrant colouring and atmospheric effects. They reflect Constable's concerted effort to capture different times of day: in *Dedham Vale* (no.64) the valley is still shrouded in early morning mist, while the sunset scenes show Constable's delight in the challenge of capturing this evanescent effect and use of the warm colours that define so many of Turner's skies. Similarly, *Edge of a Heath by Moonlight* (no.67) sees Constable take on the drama of moonlight. Together these sketches signify the power at Constable's hands when his technique perfectly aligned with his vision.

Constable's dedication to sketching outdoors and his evolution of a technique befitting his quest to breathe life into landscape painting led him to create work that was nothing short of daring. By comparison to the tightly finessed surfaces of others' work, Constable's appeared freely and loosely painted. To some, they were 'crude' (this was also a criticism levelled at Turner in exhibits from around the same time).[3] *Flatford Mill from the Lock* (no.72) marks the important moment in Constable's early career when his originality was not only noted but critiqued. This painting gave rise to two conventions that would dominate descriptions of the artist's work for decades to come: that he possessed an 'originality and vigour so peculiar to himself' and that his works required a greater level of finish.[4] A more enthused review gave rise to the quip that other artists might soon find they could not 'outrun the Constable'.[5]

John Constable *The Mill Stream* (detail) c.1810–14 (p.110)

NO. 59 John Constable's Sketching Chair c.1800–15
Wood, cane and brass, 34 × 35 × 65
On loan from the Constable Family courtesy of Gainsborough's House

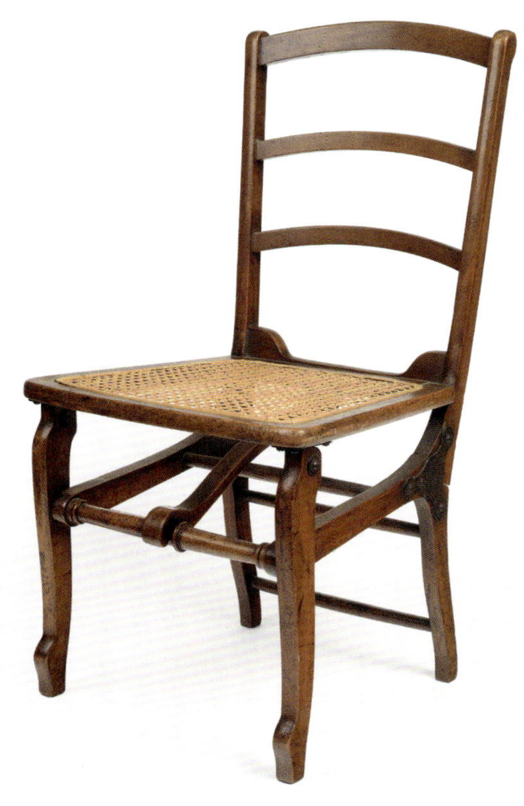

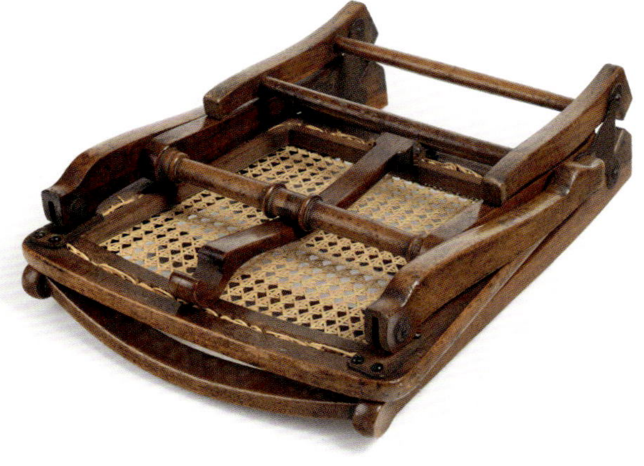

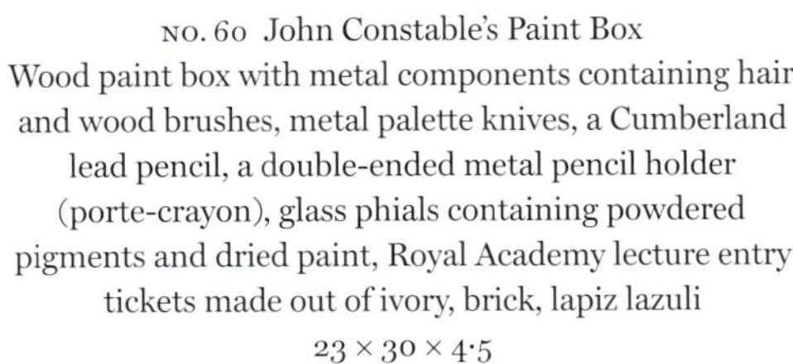

NO. 60 John Constable's Paint Box
Wood paint box with metal components containing hair and wood brushes, metal palette knives, a Cumberland lead pencil, a double-ended metal pencil holder (porte-crayon), glass phials containing powdered pigments and dried paint, Royal Academy lecture entry tickets made out of ivory, brick, lapiz lazuli
23 × 30 × 4·5
On loan from the Constable Family courtesy of Gainsborough's House

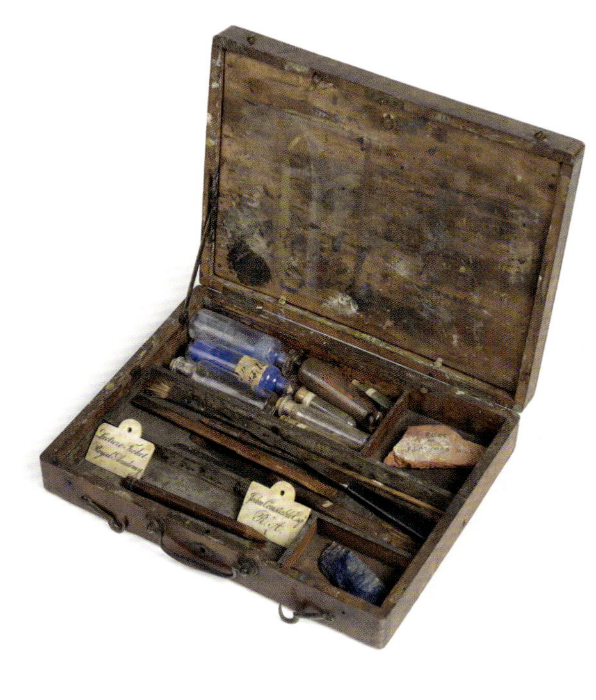

NO. 61 Wooden palette belonging to John Constable
Paint on wood, 40·5 × 24·5
Tate. Presented to the National Gallery in 1887 by Isabel Constable, transferred to Tate Gallery in 1953

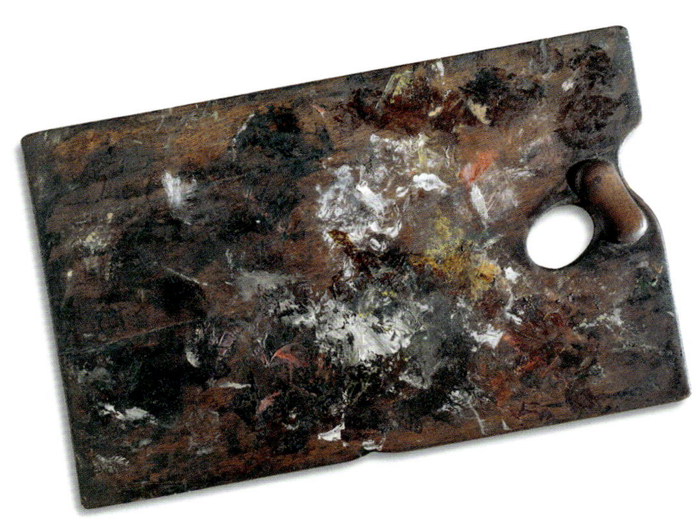

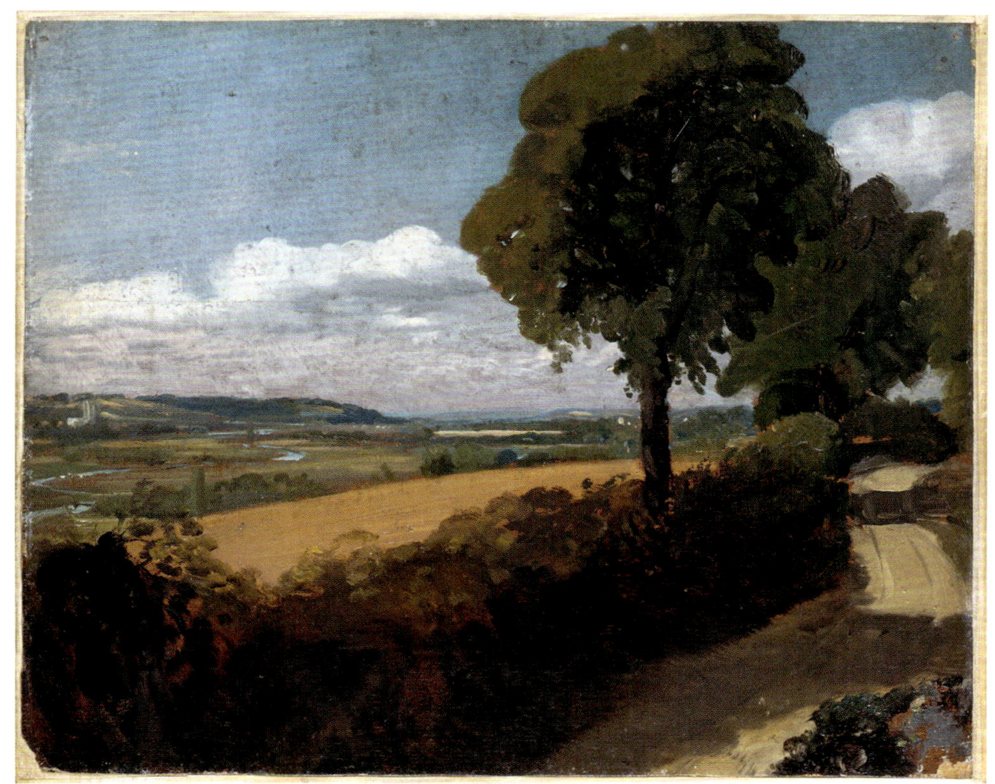

NO. 62 **John Constable** *View of Dedham from the Lane Leading from East Bergholt Church to Flatford* 1809–10
Oil paint on paper, lined onto canvas, 23·9 × 30·2
Victoria and Albert Museum, London

As the pin holes in each corner suggest, Constable made this vibrant sketch in the lid of his portable paintbox (no.60). Divided diagonally by the dark hedge, its composition is as striking as its record of the interplay of light and dark on a bright summer's day. The orange field is aglow with sunlight while dark shadows define the cart tracks and contrast sharply with pools of light on the lane to the right. This lane ran between East Bergholt Church, the Constable family's place of worship, and Flatford, the hub of their family business. From a vantage point slightly above the lane, Constable's sketch takes in Dedham Vale to the left – the bright blue of the River Stour can be seen snaking its course to the estuary, which can be made out in the centre of the horizon. Constable applied his paint more thickly here than in earlier sketches like *Dedham Vale from the Coombs* (no.31) – the large trees are made up of brushstrokes that streak and dab different colours together. This way he could quickly create a sense of depth and varied tone.

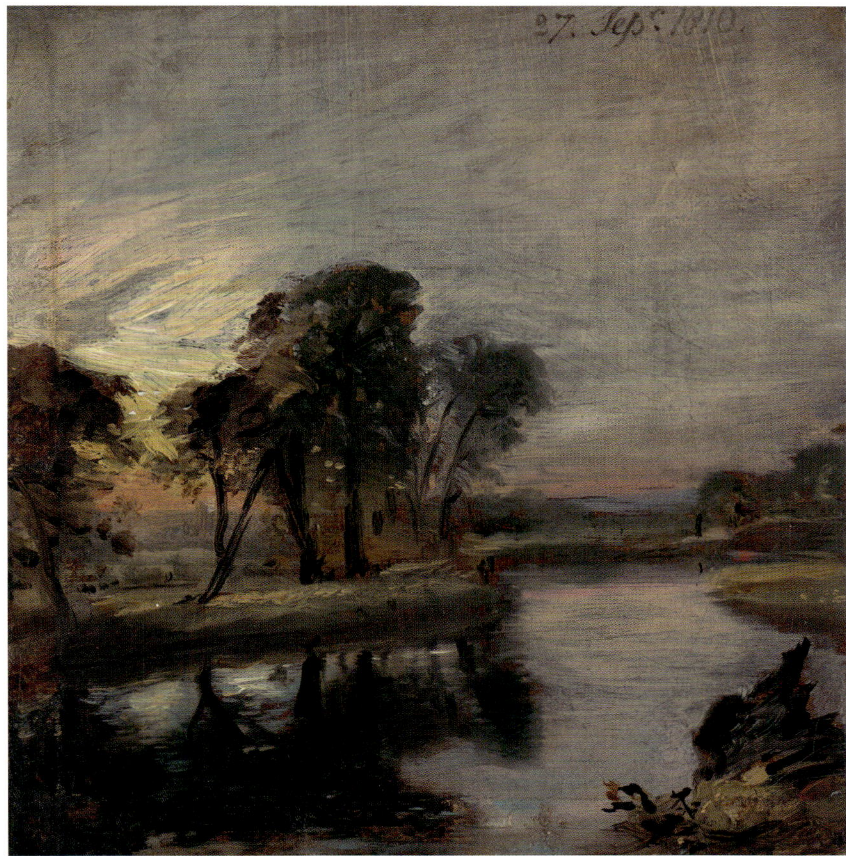

NO. 63 **John Constable** *The Stour* 1810
Inscribed, top right, '27. Sepr. 1810'
Oil paint on canvas, 23·8 × 23·5
John G. Johnson Collection, 1917, cat. 857

Painting the transitory atmosphere of a sunset was a sure way for Constable to test and hone his ability to paint quickly outdoors. With its hurried, sweeping brushwork this sketch demonstrates how Constable rose to the challenge; the reflection of the trees in the water, created by dragging a dry brush through tacky paint, is particularly effective.

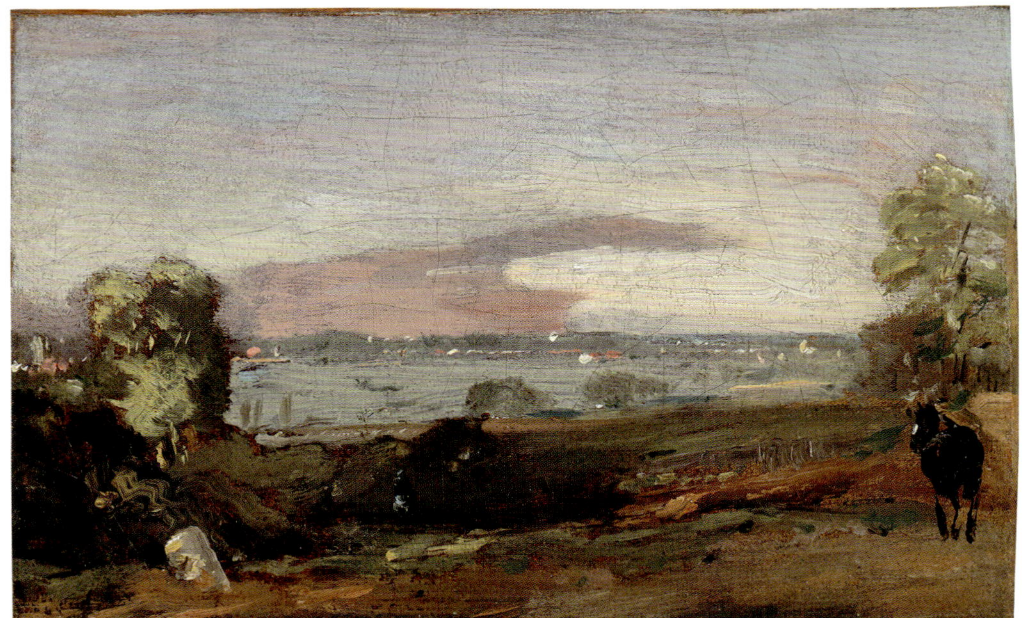

NO. 64 **John Constable** *Dedham Vale* 1810
Oil paint on canvas, 12·7 × 21·5
Private Collection

NO. 65 **John Constable** *The River Stour at Sunset, Looking Towards Dedham*;
(verso, not exhibited) *Golding Constable's House, East Bergholt* 1809–10
Inscribed, vertically at top right edge, '29 Sepr. Evening. 1810
Oil paint on paper, 25 × 19·5
Private Collection

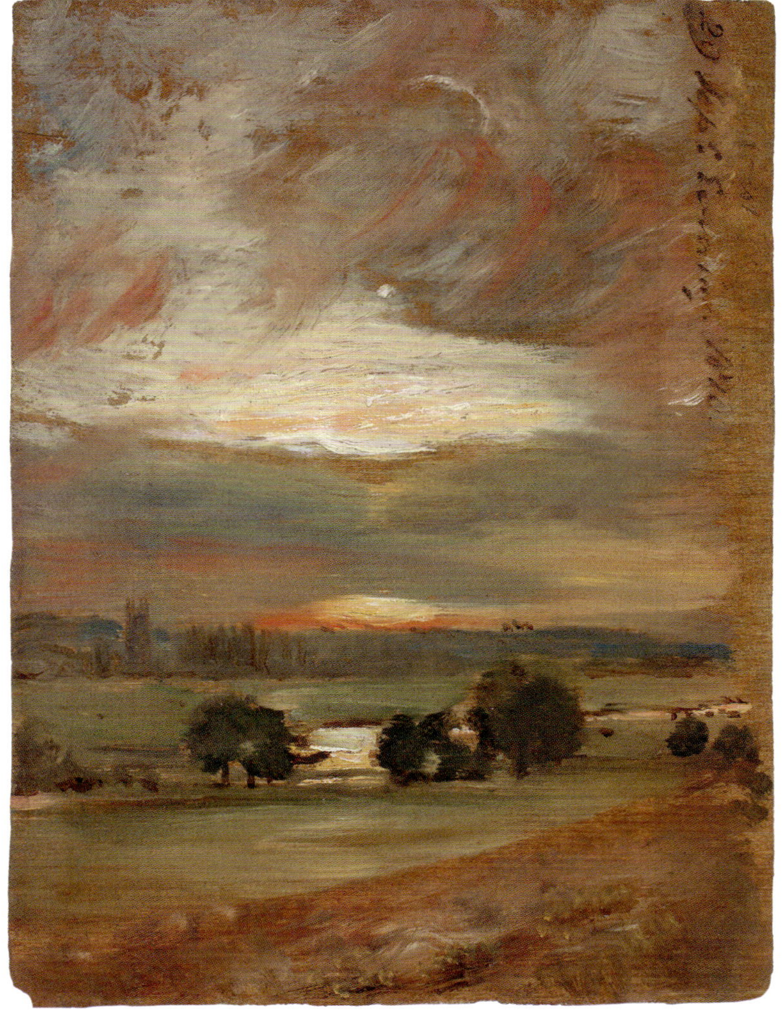

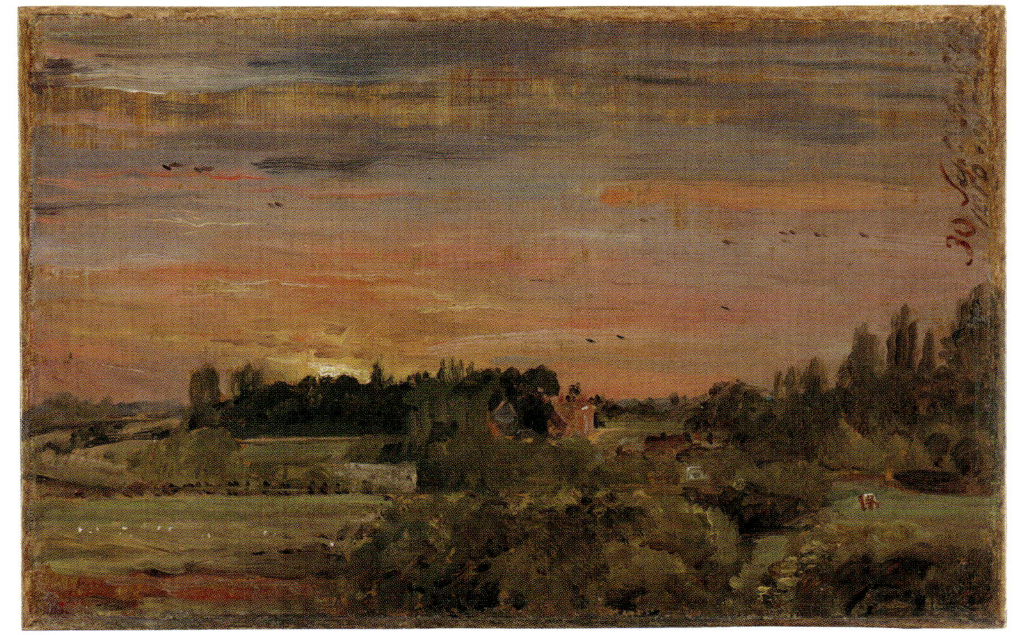

NO. 66 **John Constable** *View toward the Rectory, East Bergholt* 1810
Inscribed, vertically at top right edge, '30 Sep | 1810 | E.Bergholt | Common'
Oil paint on canvas on panel, 15·6 × 24·8
John G. Johnson Collection, 1917, cat. 856

Signified by a squiggle of white paint and a couple of upright strokes suggestive of rays, the setting sun dips behind a clump of trees. This vibrant sketch dates from a time when Constable's oil sketches were becoming bolder – he was painting more freely and exploring a wide-ranging colour palette. While the landscape and sky are characterised by a loose handling of paint, details like the birds in the sky and the grazing cow at bottom right demonstrate the continued importance of observed detail to his oil sketches. This work is not only outstanding for its flashes of hot colouring but also for being the earliest known study painted from a window of Constable's family house. The view is one that Constable would have gazed upon frequently, thinking of his sweetheart, Maria Bicknell, whose grandfather lived in the Rectory, the building seen in the centre. In a letter to Maria he spoke of 'those sweet fields where we have passed so many happy hours together' (Beckett, II, p.78).

NO. 67 **John Constable** *Edge of a Heath by Moonlight* 1810
Oil paint on canvas, 15 × 25·7
Private Collection

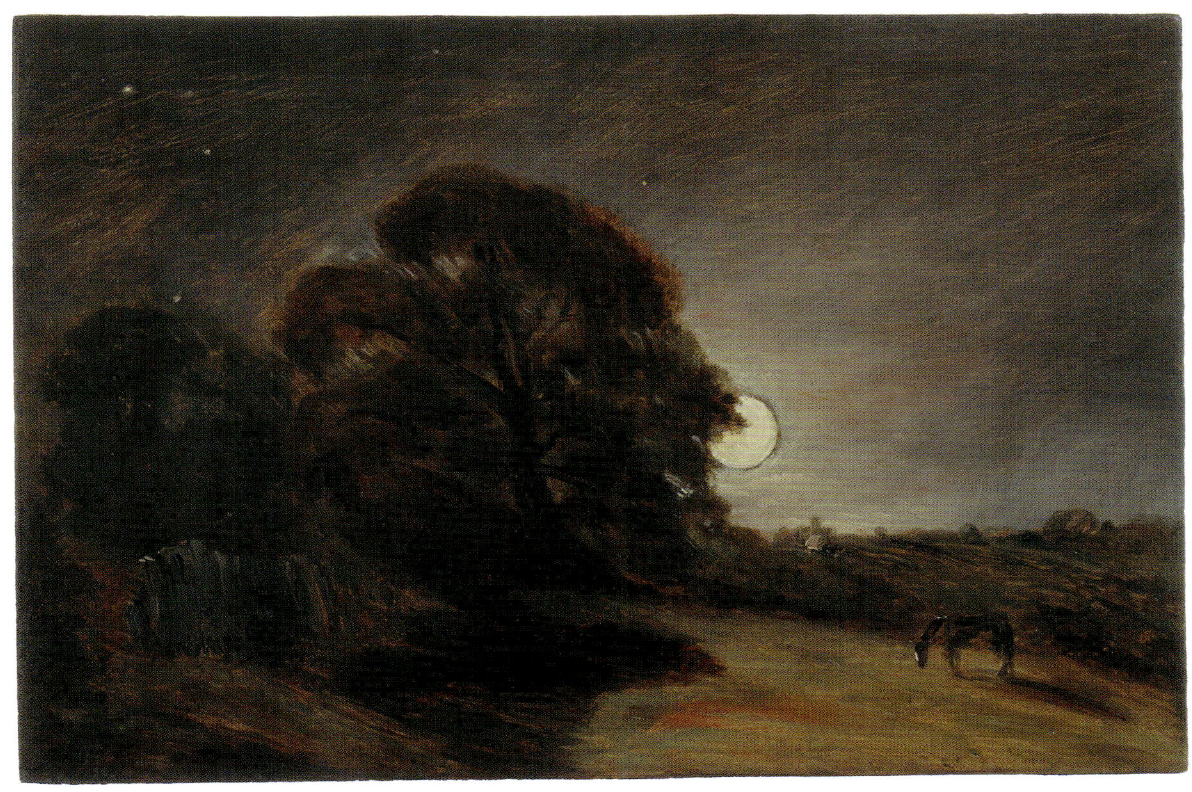

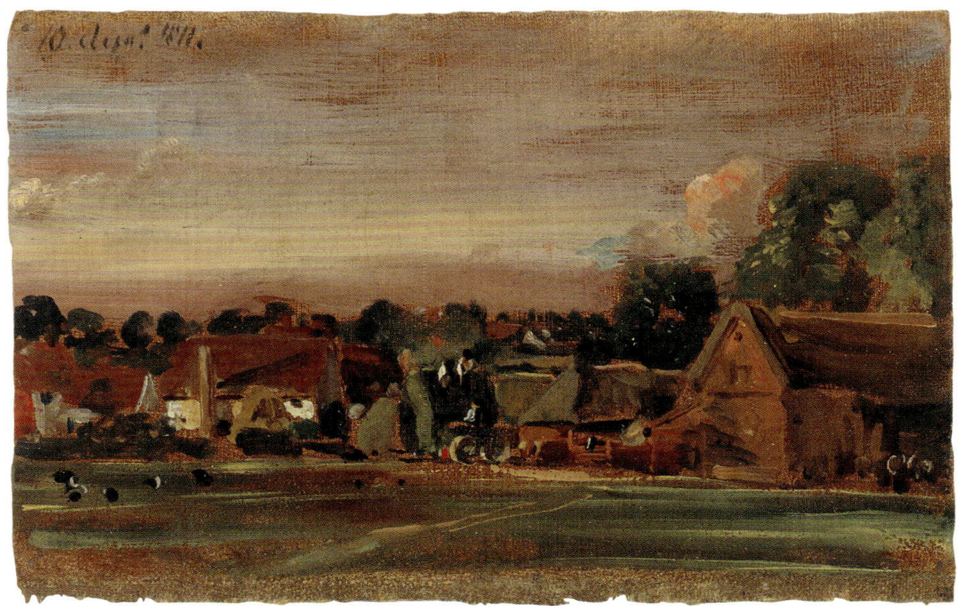

NO. 68 **John Constable** *A sketch of East Bergholt from East Bergholt House* 1811
Inscribed, upper left, '10 Augst 1811'
Oil paint on canvas, 12·5 × 19·3
Private Collection

As in so many of his oil sketches, Constable has used a warm-toned ground here – it can be seen between the gaps of his brushstrokes along the bottom edge and around the trees on the right and serves to carry the glow of sunset throughout the whole scene. Not only did a sunset require him to work quickly, but the array of buildings here presented a challenge for quick brushwork. With a sparing amount of brushstrokes Constable has skilfully modelled them as a tessellation of geometrical shapes, carefully adding highlights and shadows, such as the tall chimney on the white rendered building on the left. This was the view from the back of the Constable family house. Golding Constable's grain store is seen on the right of the composition; three labourers can be made out in the centre and, just to the right of them, the white flash of a horse's nose hanging over a stable door.

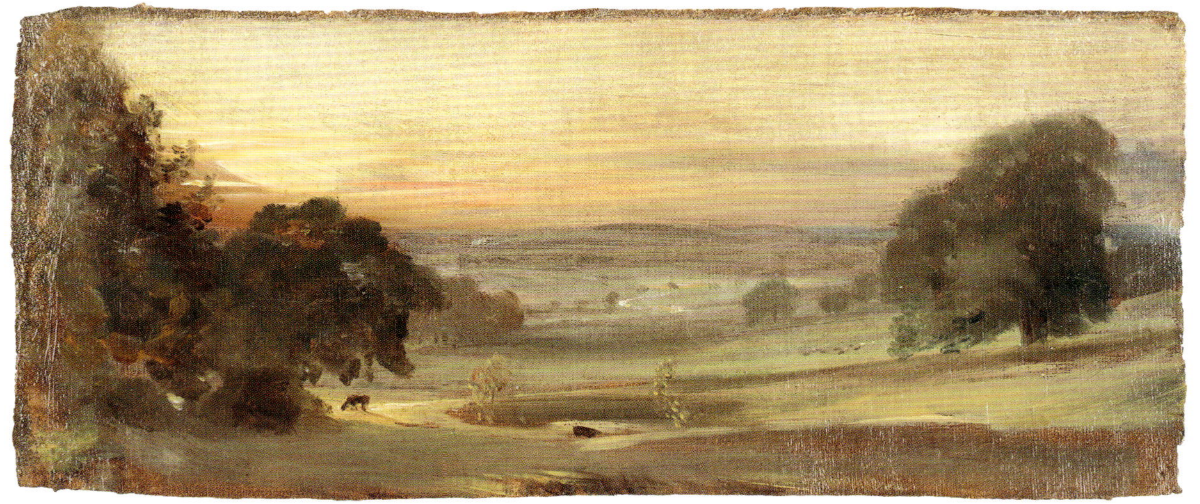

NO. 69 **John Constable** *The Valley of the Stour at Sunset* 1812
Inscribed, reverse, '31. Octr 1812'
Oil paint on canvas, 11·8 × 28
Private Collection

Constable's sketches of sunrise and sunsets were not just motivated by a desire to capture different light effects. In July 1812, months before he painted this work, he wrote to Maria that he had refrained from sketching 'in the middle of these very hot bright days… last year I almost put my eyes out by that pastime' (Beckett, II, p.80). Laid down in sweeping horizontal bands, the pastel hues Constable uses here conjure a hazy, dreamlike atmosphere. Painted on 31 October, this sunset was a significant one for those making a living in rural areas, marking the conclusion of harvest-time and the setting in of winter.

NO. 70 **John Constable** *Flailing Turnip Heads, East Bergholt* 1812–15
Oil paint on canvas, 35·6 × 44·5
Clark Art Institute, Williamstown, Massachusetts, USA, gift of the Manton Art Foundation in memory of Sir Edwin and Lady Manton

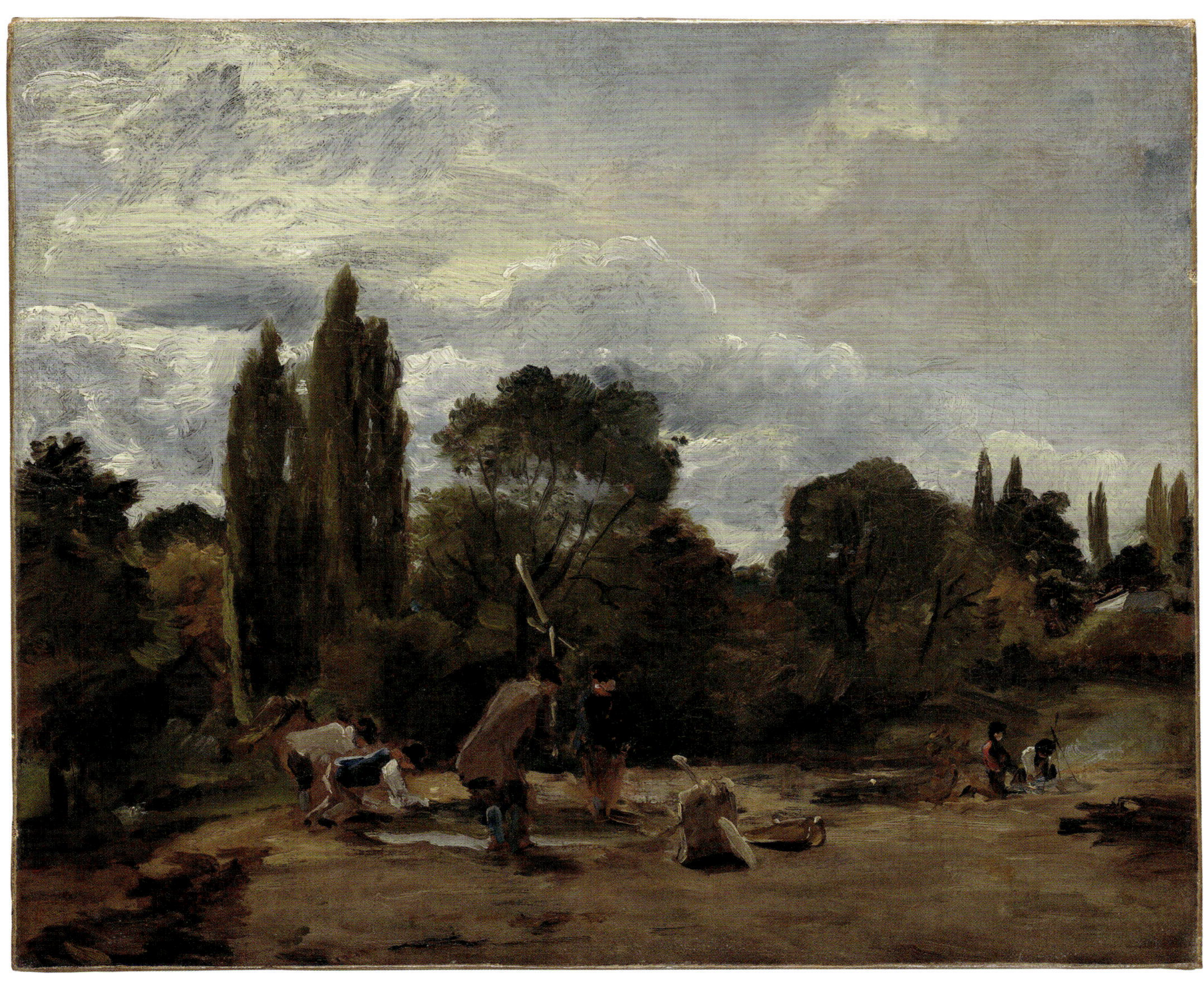

With figures on a larger scale than was usual, Constable seems to have been keen to capture in detail the activity of harvesting seeds from dried turnips. The man in the centre is beating turnip heads to dislodge seeds, those on the left sift the seeds while the boys on the right burn the stems and leaves. Depictions of labour – keying into patriotic symbolism of Britain as a land of plenty – were undergoing a renewed popularity during the Napoleonic Wars, when this sketch was painted. This was also a subject depicted by Turner in *Ploughing Up Turnips, near Slough ('Windsor')*, which he exhibited at his own gallery in 1809. Turnips were a particularly important crop in more capitalistic, large-scale farming of the kind made possible by land enclosures (which placed large swathes of common land under private ownership). Turner's sympathetic depiction of tired labourers carried a hint of critique at the social costs of modern agriculture; as much as Constable was troubled by rural workers' volatile reaction to worsening conditions and reduced employment opportunities, his family's business interests stood to benefit from such changes. While his works, on the whole, celebrate the old ways, his portrayal of turnip flailing shows us the back-breaking reality of the work that went on in the fields he painted.

NO. 71 **John Constable** *Flatford Mill from the Lock* 1810
Oil paint on beige paper mounted on canvas, 19 × 24·1
Clark Art Institute, Williamstown, Massachusetts, USA, gift of the Manton Art Foundation in memory of Sir Edwin and Lady Manton

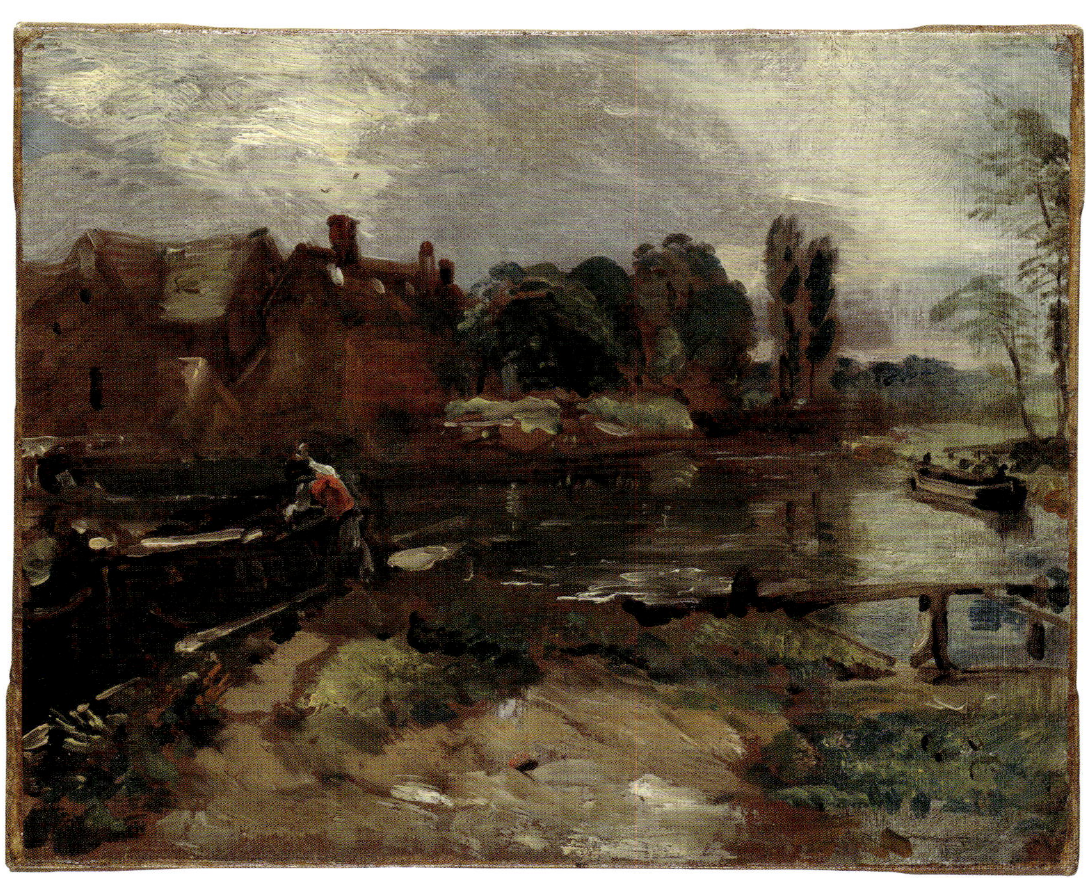

NO. 72 **John Constable** *Flatford Mill from the Lock* 1812
Oil paint on canvas, 66 × 92·7
Private Collection

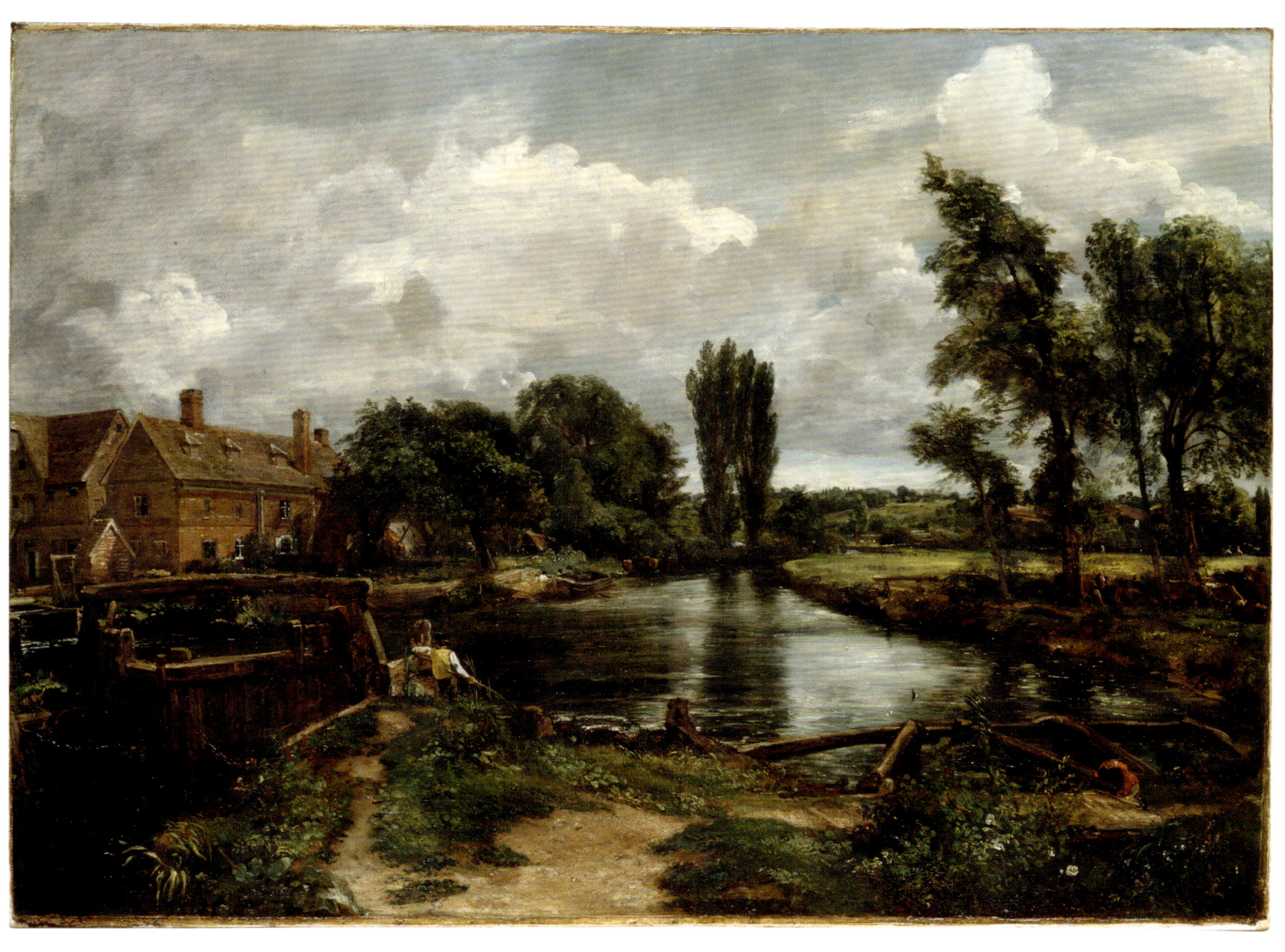

Upon its exhibition in 1812, *Flatford Mill from the Lock* (no.72) garnered Constable more attention than any of his previous exhibits. Critics praised Constable's originality but one sounded a note of caution about the finishing of his work – for already he was flouting expectations of smoothed out brushstrokes and pristine surfaces. Perhaps the most meaningful feedback to Constable was that of Benjamin West, President of the Royal Academy, who reportedly stopped him in the street to convey his admiration. In what would become a favoured practice, Constable based this painting on a sketch made outdoors (no.71).

NO. 73 **John Constable** *The Mill Stream* c.1810
Oil paint on board, 21 × 29·2
Tate. Bequeathed by Henry Vaughan 1900

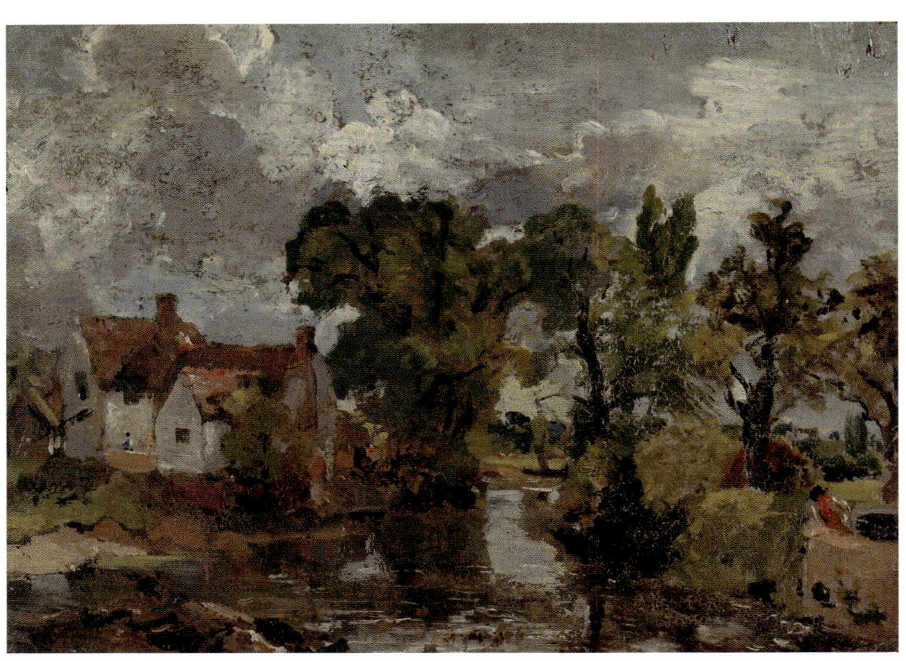

NO. 74 **John Constable** *The Mill Stream* c.1810–14
Oil paint on canvas, 71·1 × 91·5
On loan from Ipswich Borough Council: Colchester and Ipswich Museum Service

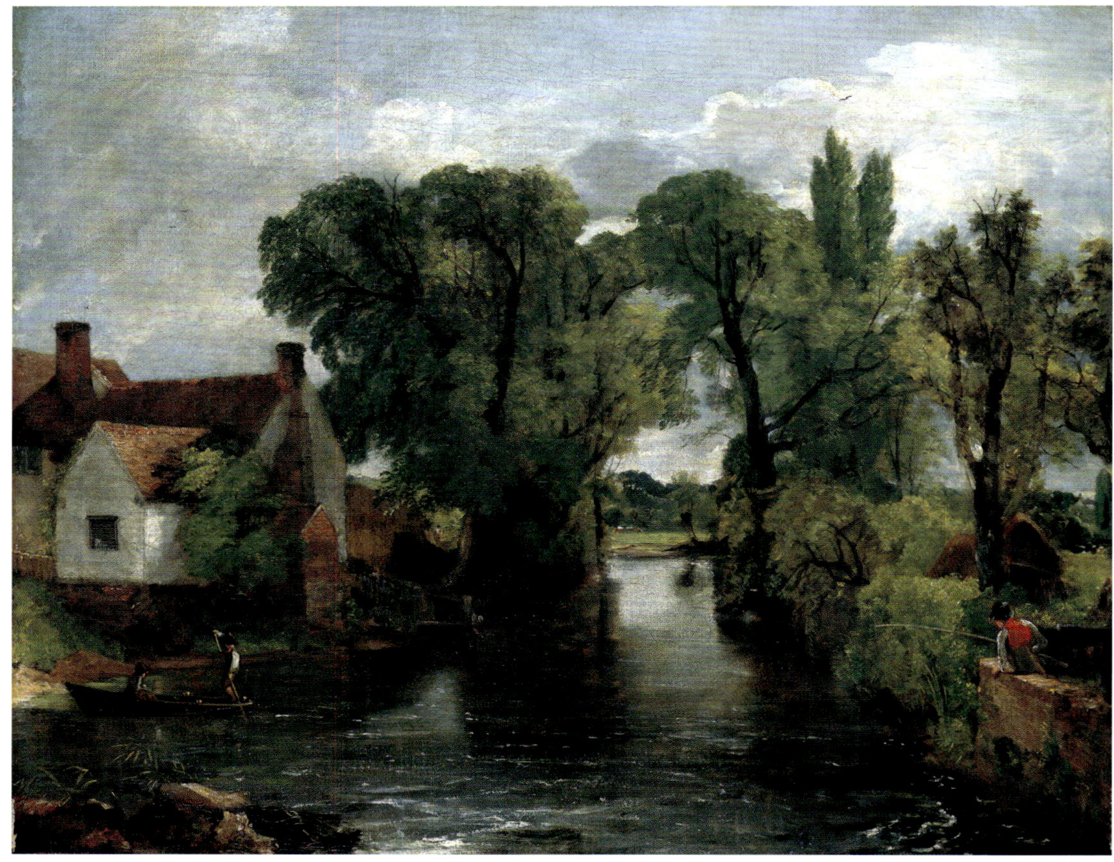

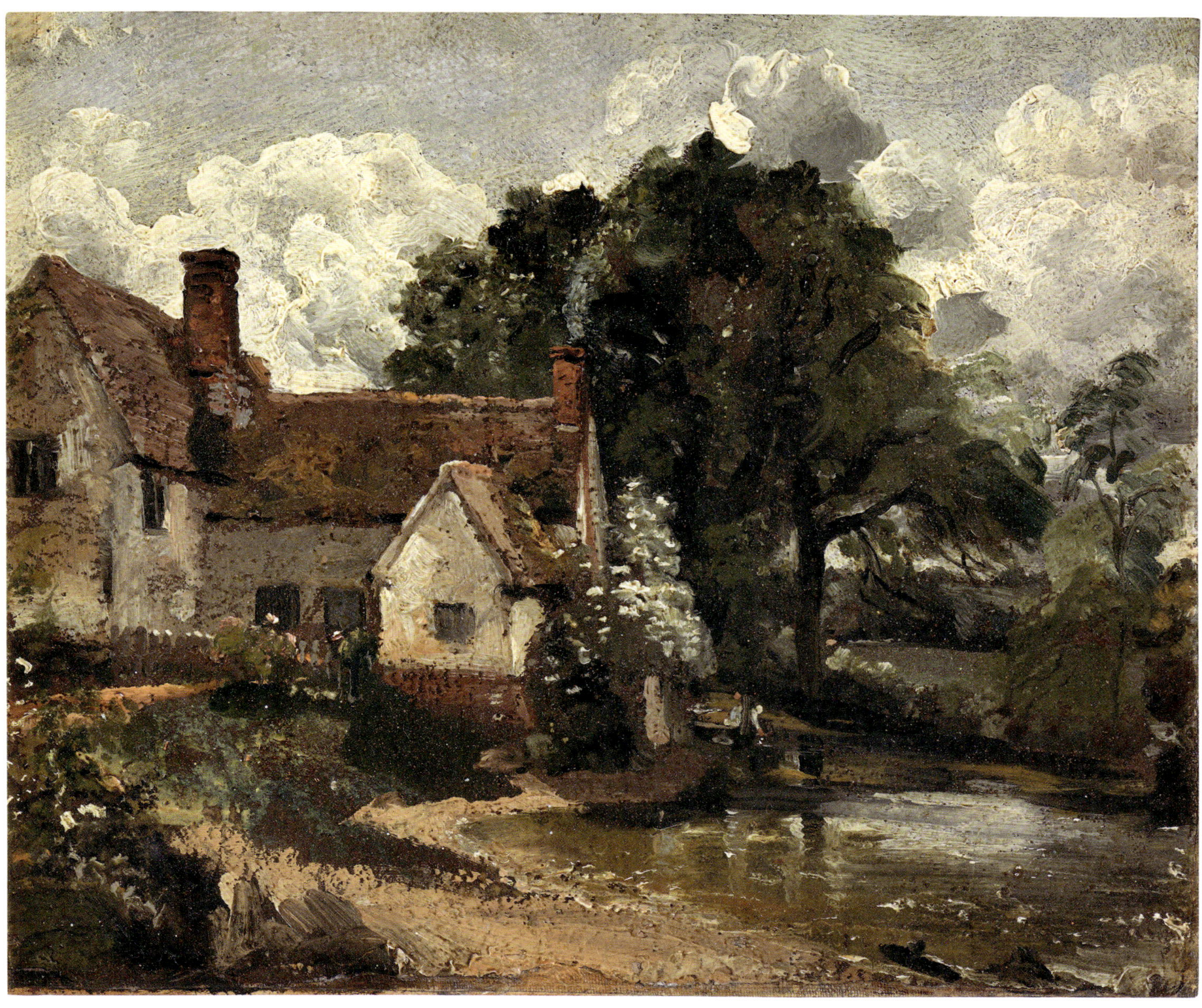

NO. 75 **John Constable** *Willy Lott's House* 1816
Oil paint on paper laid on canvas, 19·4 × 23·8
On loan from Ipswich Borough Council: Colchester and Ipswich Museum Service

As the setting for *The Hay Wain* (National Gallery, London), this is perhaps the most recognisable view in Constable's suite of Stour scenery. The white building is the home of Willy Lott, a tenant farmer who lived there for over 80 years. The earliest of these images, no.73, was painted quickly outdoors on a bright day. Figures include the boy fishing on the right-hand side, and one in the distant field formed by a tiny speck of red and white paint immediately to the right of Lott's house. Constable carried over these details into his finished painting, adding further elements like the ferryman from pencil drawings (no.74). An early commercial success, *The Mill Stream* sold; that Constable deemed this an important composition is signified by his borrowing it back from the owner to have it engraved by David Lucas for *English Landscape*.

Willy Lott's House (no.75) shows how Constable rarely stopped exploring a favoured scene. Details like the white flowering elder bush would find their way from this sketch into *The Hay Wain* (fig.1, p.14).

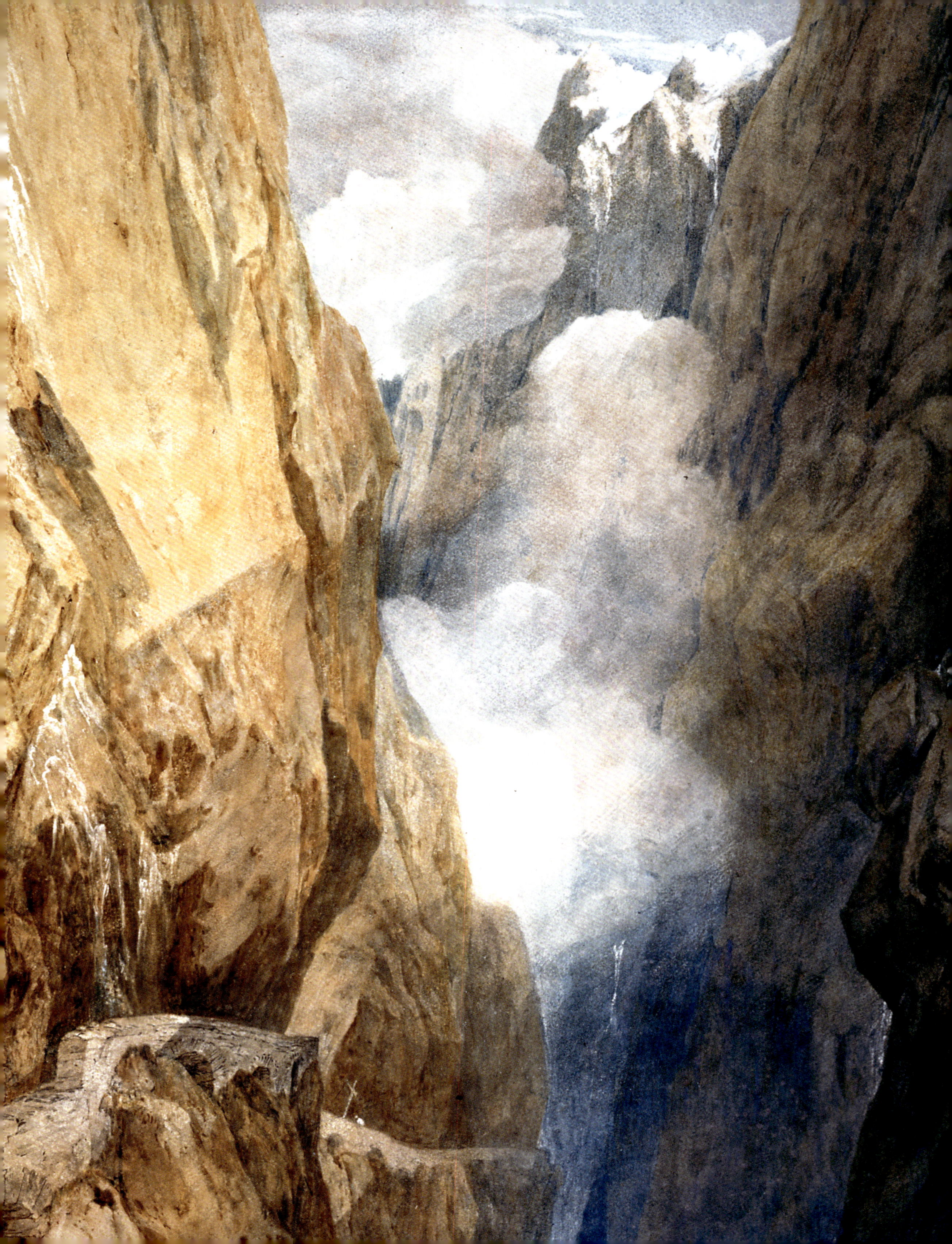

'NO SMALL WONDER': TURNER IN ITALY AND THE ALPS

Travel was the backbone of Turner's art. With sketchbook in hand, he toured extensively across Britain and Europe throughout his life in search of material for his paintings and print projects. There were two locations, however, that particularly sparked Turner's creativity: the Alps and Italy. His experiences of these places were no doubt intensified by a sense of delayed gratification; although he had studied their scenic riches as depicted by other artists, the Revolutionary and Napoleonic Wars largely prevented access to Europe for the first twenty-five years of his career.

A brief cessation of hostilities in 1802 afforded the twenty-seven-year-old Turner his first trip abroad. Alongside thousands of other Brits with pent-up wanderlust, he acquired a passport and crossed the English Channel in mid-July that year, funded by a cohort of aristocratic sponsors. After being 'nearly swampt' in a stormy landing at Calais he journeyed to Paris, where he saw Old Master collections and procured himself a carriage and Swiss guide for his ultimate destination: the Alps.[1] Taking in France, Switzerland and a short excursion to Italy's Val d'Aosta, the region did not disappoint. His revelatory experiences of its magnificent glaciers, peaks and passes took his exploration of the Sublime to new heights and provided him with material for many years to come. He would later describe this tour as 'no small wonder'.[2]

Seventeen years later Turner crossed the Channel again, this time for a deep dive into Italy. Thanks to his many powerful evocations of its landscape and classical literature (for example, no.81) Turner, who was now an established artist of forty-four, had become associated with Italy before he had even seen it with his own eyes. He made extensive preparations for what would be a six-month-long round trip, noting travel advice and making sketches of other artists' views of key sites to visit (no.82). Testament to his hunger for Italy's scenic riches, Turner returned home with twenty-three sketchbooks and a handful of loose sheets that would underpin decades of finished paintings (such as no.91) and future tours to Italy. A view of Venice capturing the crisp light of early morning and a series of dramatic Roman scenes are among the most celebrated of works arising from this tour (nos.85 and 87–90). They reflect Turner's mastery of watercolour at this stage in his career. Indeed, even with only half its sheet coloured, a view of Naples radiates luminosity and warmth (no.84).

J.M.W. Turner *The Passage of Mount St Gothard from the centre of Teufels Broch (Devil's Bridge)* (detail) 1804 (p.115)

NO. 77 **J.M.W. Turner** *The Passage of Mount St Gothard from the centre of Teufels Broch (Devil's Bridge)* 1804
Watercolour with scraping out on paper, 101 × 68
Abbot Hall, Kendal (Lakeland Arts Trust)

When this and other Alpine watercolours deriving from Turner's revelatory 1802 tour went on display in an exhibition in 1819, many visitors thought them the highlight of the show. It is not difficult to see why. On the basis of scale alone, this watercolour is incredibly ambitious – watercolours were not habitually made on such a large scale but to do so was a riposte to those who thought the medium incompatible with intellectual art. Turner is dealing in the Sublime here, the depiction of nature at its most exhilarating. Its scale underscores this – the drama is enlarged – but also makes it easier to appreciate Turner's range of technical tricks, from the removal of wet paint to create the mist, and scraping out to reveal the white of the paper, forming rivulets flowing down the mountainside. The composition has a striking simplicity, enhanced by the vertical contrast of warm and cool colours, a juxtaposition that would become one of Turner's favourite ways to use colour (as also seen, for example, in a watercolour of *Norham Castle*, no.181).

NO. 76 **J.M.W. Turner** *The Source of the Arveyron below the Glacier du Bois and Mer de Glace* 1802
Pencil, watercolour and white gouache with scratching and stopping out on white wove paper prepared with grey wash, 31·3 × 46·8
Tate. Accepted by the nation as part of the Turner Bequest 1856

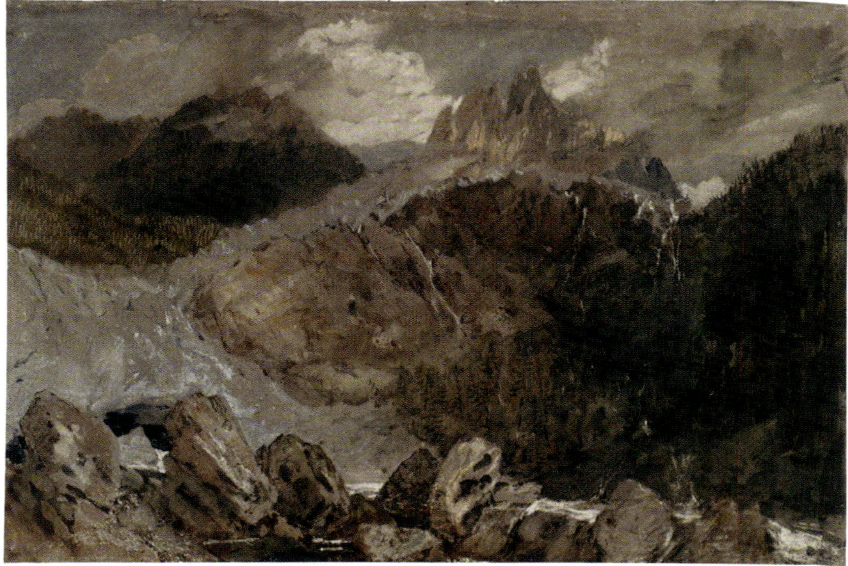

This richly coloured drawing was made in the largest of the sketchbooks Turner took with him to the Alps in 1802, that which he reserved for the most grand vistas he encountered. He used it as the basis for a finished watercolour (Amgueddfa Cymru, National Museums Wales). The River Arveyron is seen in the immediate foreground, flowing down to the right; it records the Glacier du Bois, which no longer exists, and the Mer de Glace above.

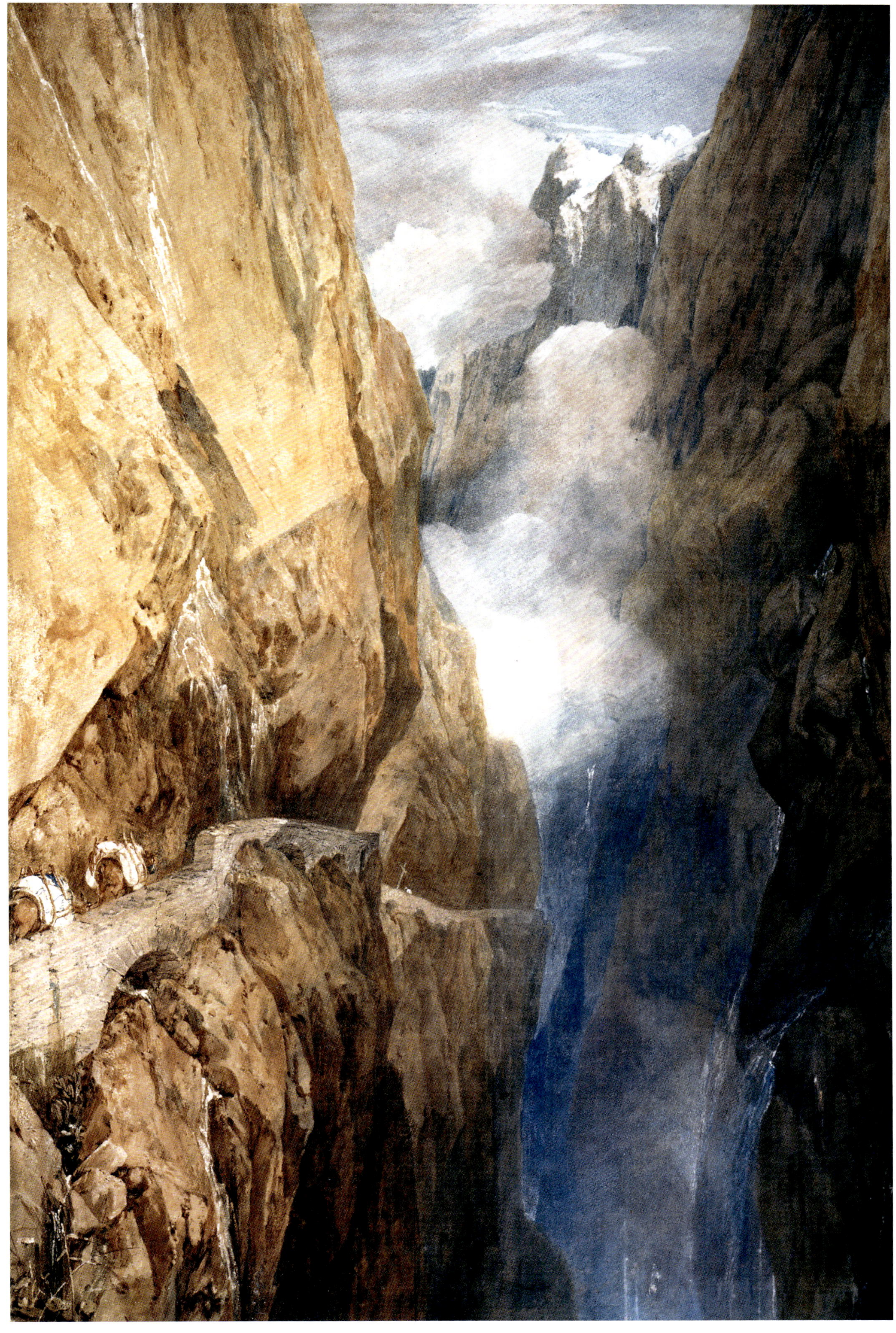

NO. 78 **J.M.W. Turner** *Group of Peasants* from the *Swiss Figures* sketchbook 1802
Graphite and watercolour on paper, each page 19·8 × 16·3
Tate. Accepted by the nation as part of the Turner Bequest 1856

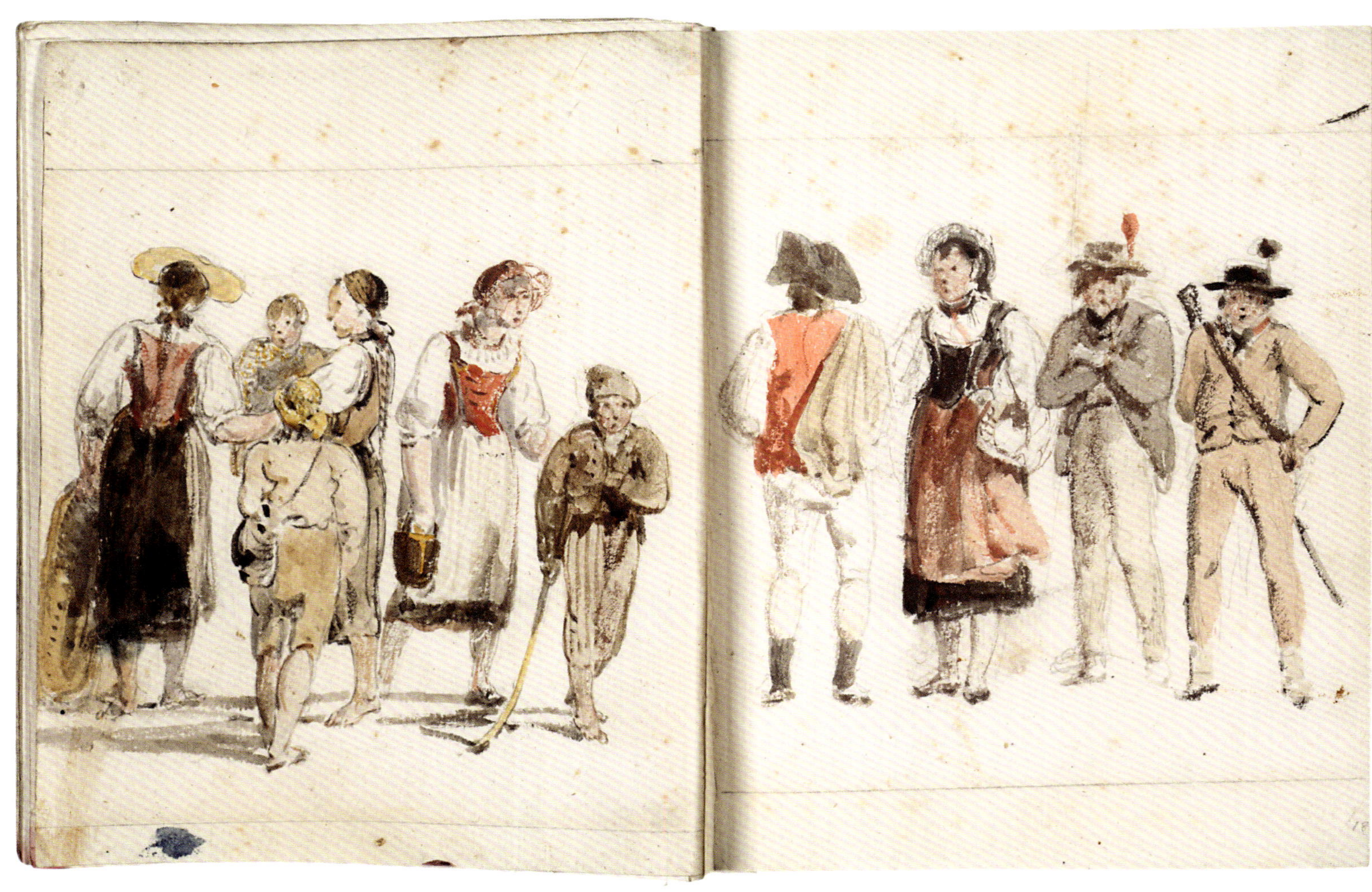

NO. 79 **J.M.W. Turner** *'Entombment of the Dead Christ' After Titian*
and *Commentary on Titian's 'Entombment of the Dead Christ'*
(Inscription by Turner) from the *Studies in the Louvre* sketchbook 1802
Graphite on paper, each page 12·8 × 11·4
Tate. Accepted by the nation as part of the Turner Bequest 1856

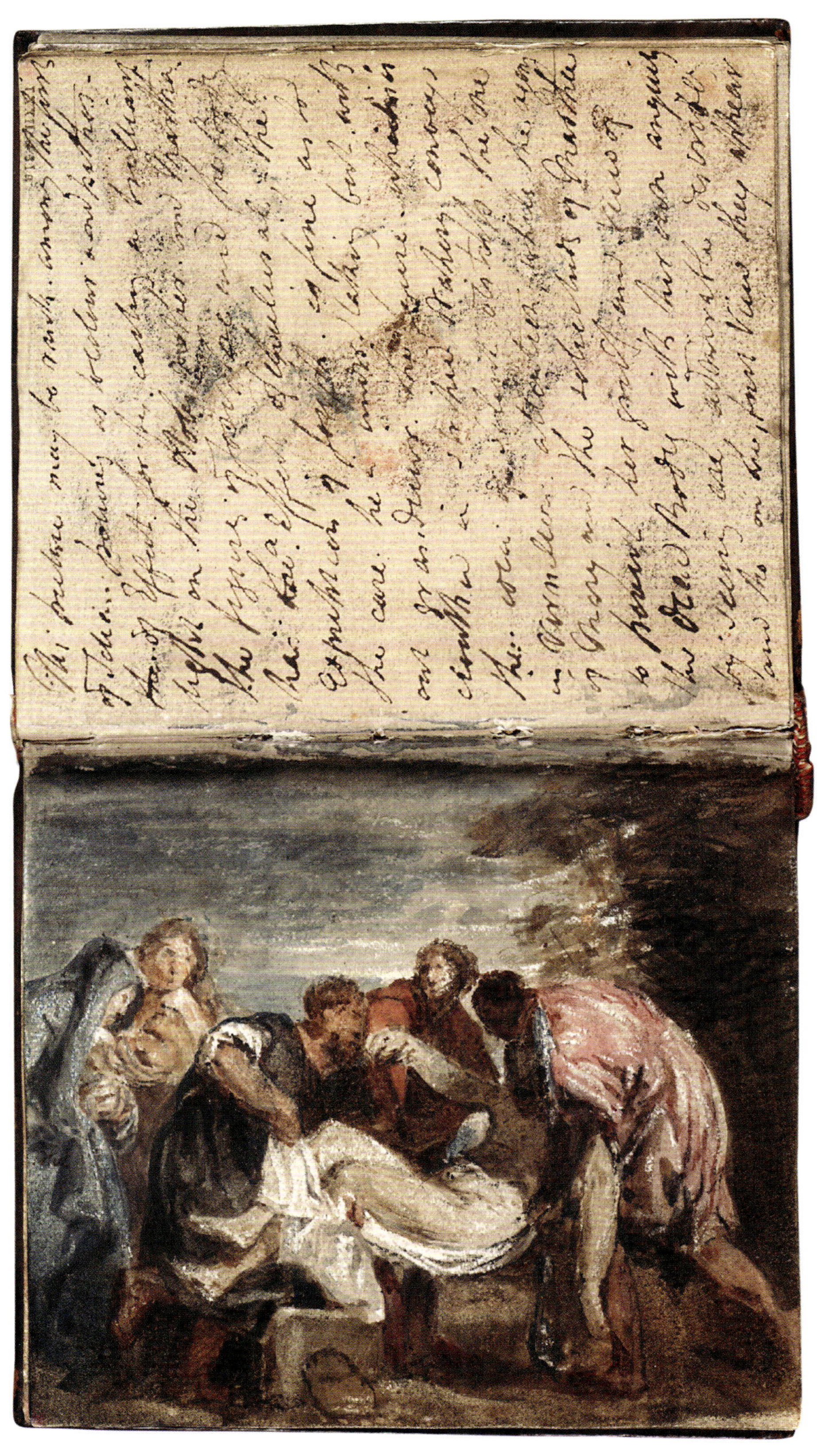

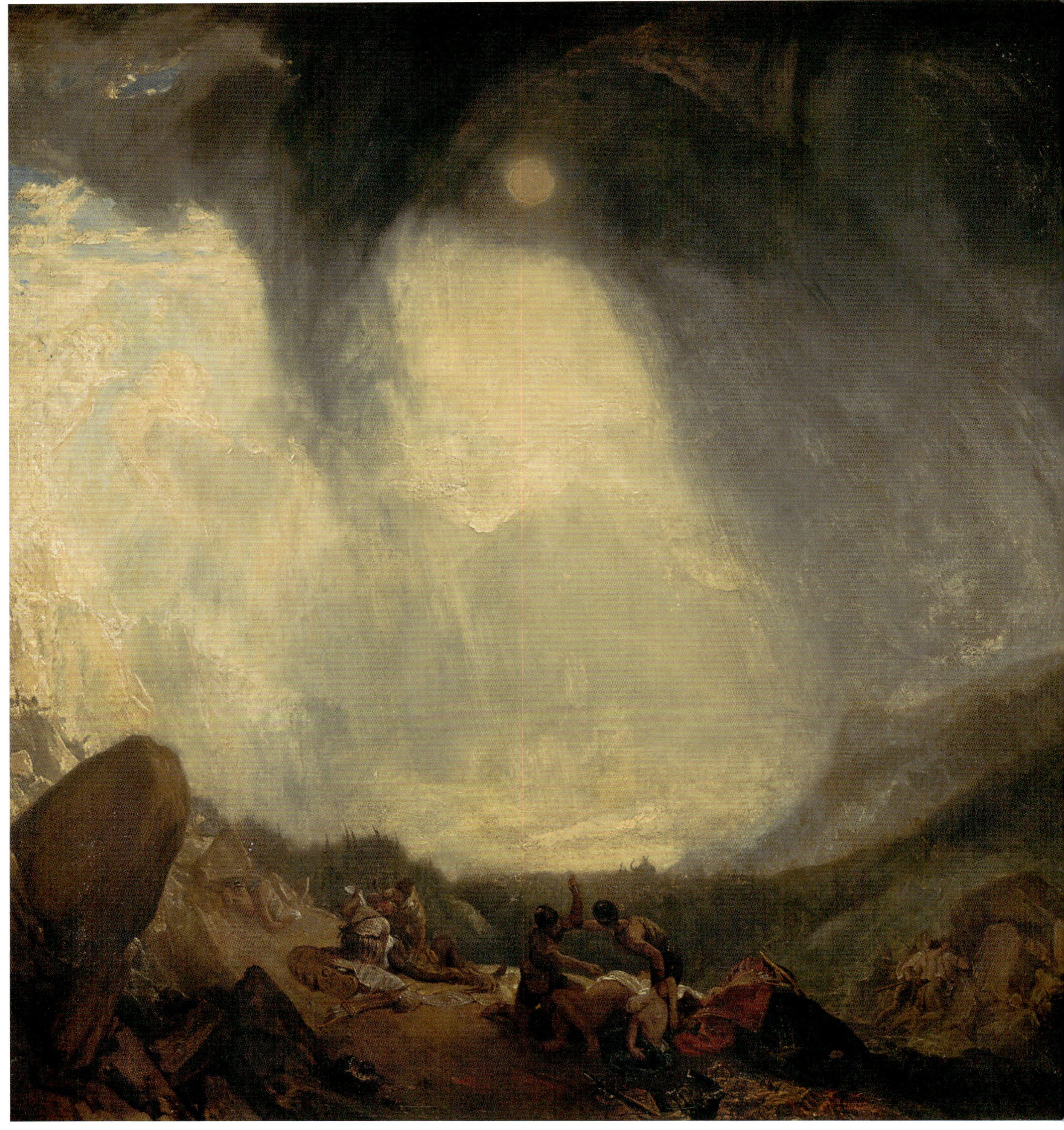

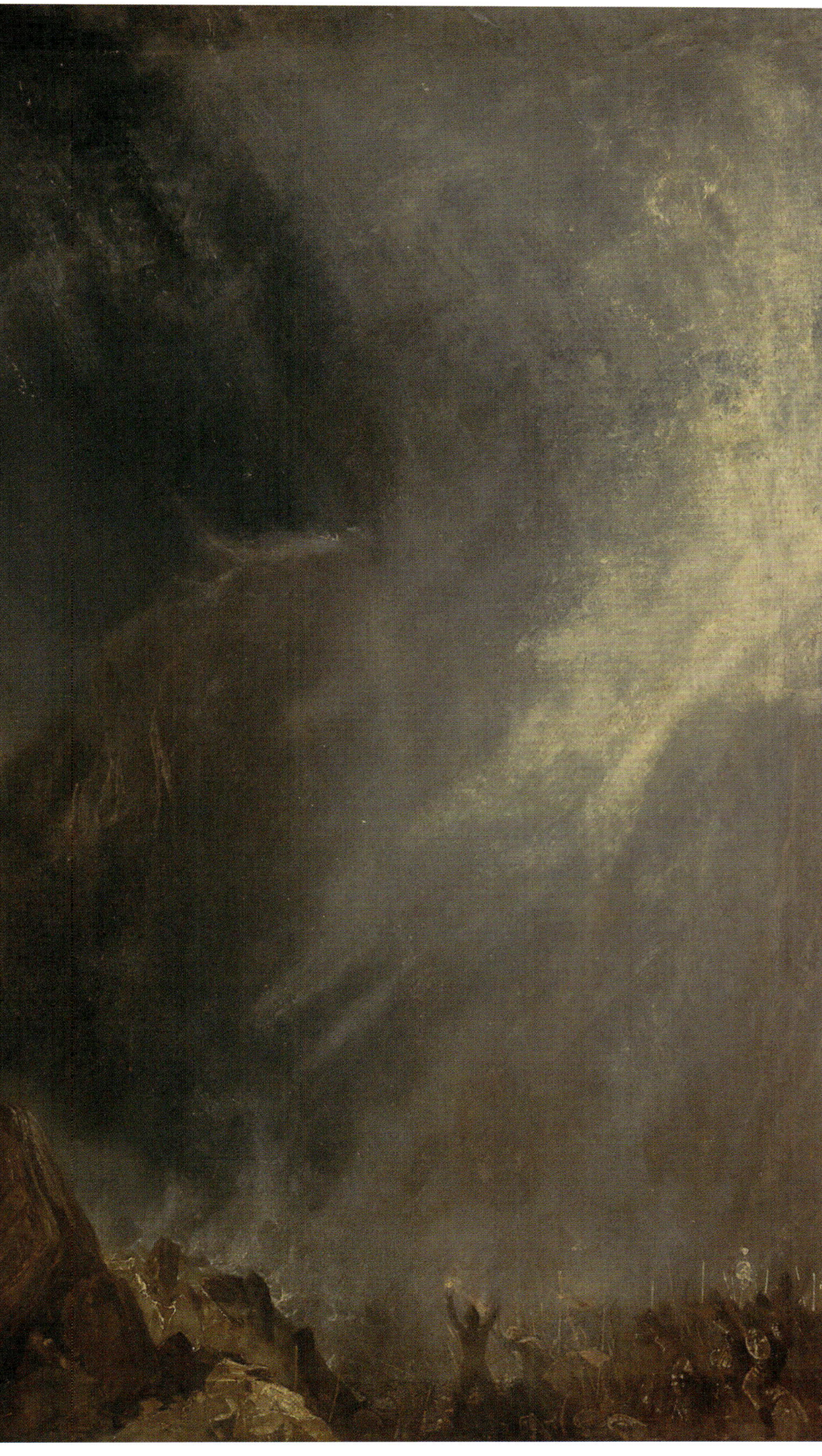

NO. 80 **J.M.W. Turner** *Snow Storm: Hannibal and his Army Crossing the Alps* exhibited 1812
Oil paint on canvas, 146 × 237·5
Tate. Accepted by the nation as part of the Turner Bequest 1856

Turner defied convention by insisting that this work hung at eye level when it was first shown at the Royal Academy exhibition of 1812. Large paintings were usually hung high, particularly if they were paintings by Royal Academicians. Turner had threatened to withdraw all his submissions that year if his colleagues did not respect his wishes. It was surely part of Turner's concept for this painting that viewers felt immersed in it, to be looking down into the valley as if we, too, were in the mountains and close to the chaos. This work would have been understood as a comment on the Napoleonic Wars between Britain and France, which were still raging. French Emperor Napoleon Bonaparte was compared to ancient Carthage's leader, Hannibal, who led his army across the Alps into Italy in 218 BCE. Turner shows Hannibal riding an elephant (seen in silhouette in the distance), overwhelmed by a blizzard and his troops under attack. As in so many of Turner's other paintings, including *Snow Storm: Steam-Boat off a Harbour's Mouth* of thirty years later (no.166), this painting rehearses his favoured theme of nature keeping human ambition in check.

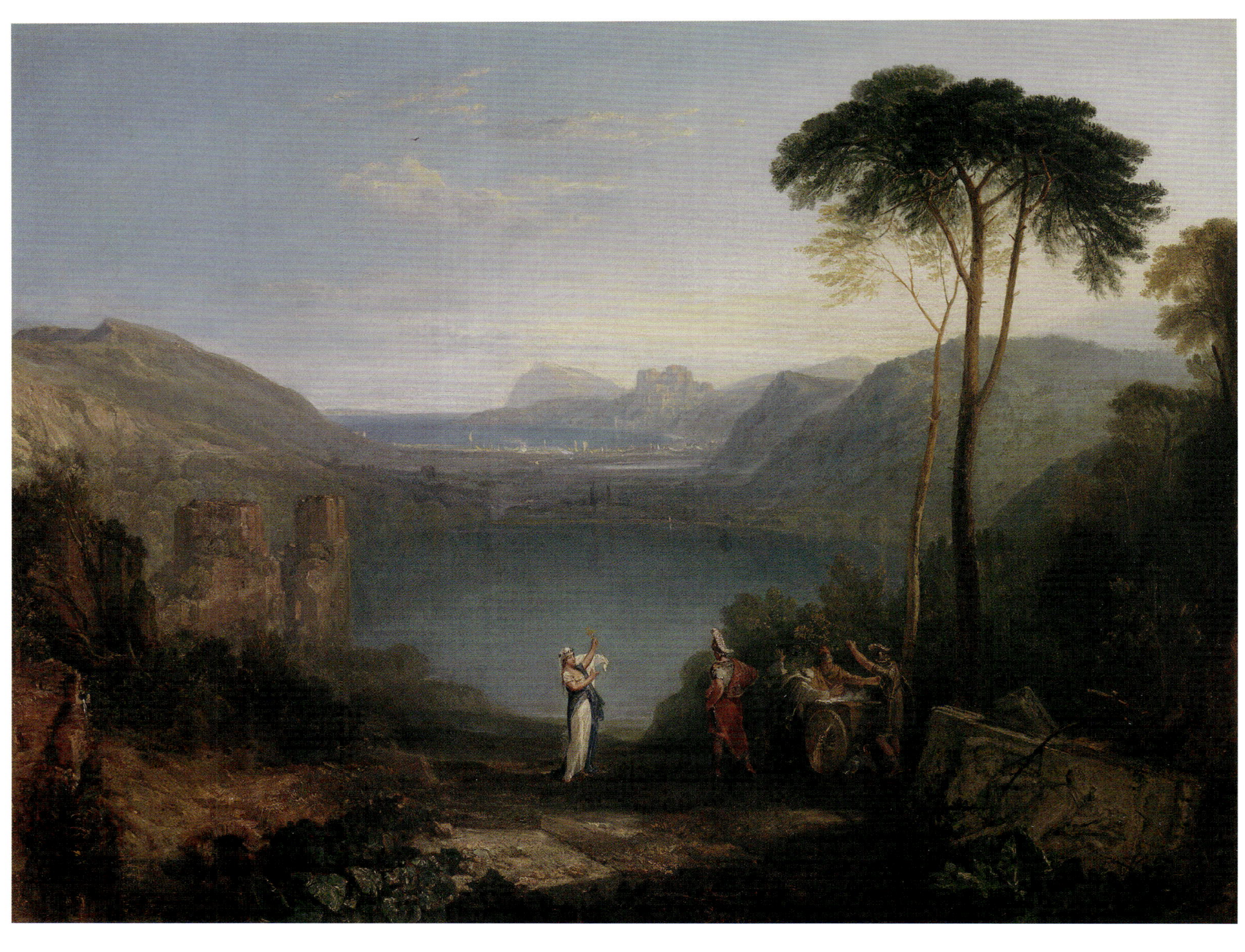

NO. 81 **J.M.W. Turner** *Lake Avernus: Aeneas and the Cumaean Sibyl* 1814
Oil paint on canvas, 71·8 × 97·2
Yale Center for British Art, Paul Mellon Collection

NO. 82 **J.M.W. Turner** *Twelve Copies of Engravings after John 'Warwick' Smith from 'Select Views in Italy'* and *Two Landscapes; one with Ducks and Swans* from the *Italian Guide Book* sketchbook c.1819
Graphite on paper, each page 15·5 × 9·9
Tate. Accepted by the nation as part of the Turner Bequest 1856

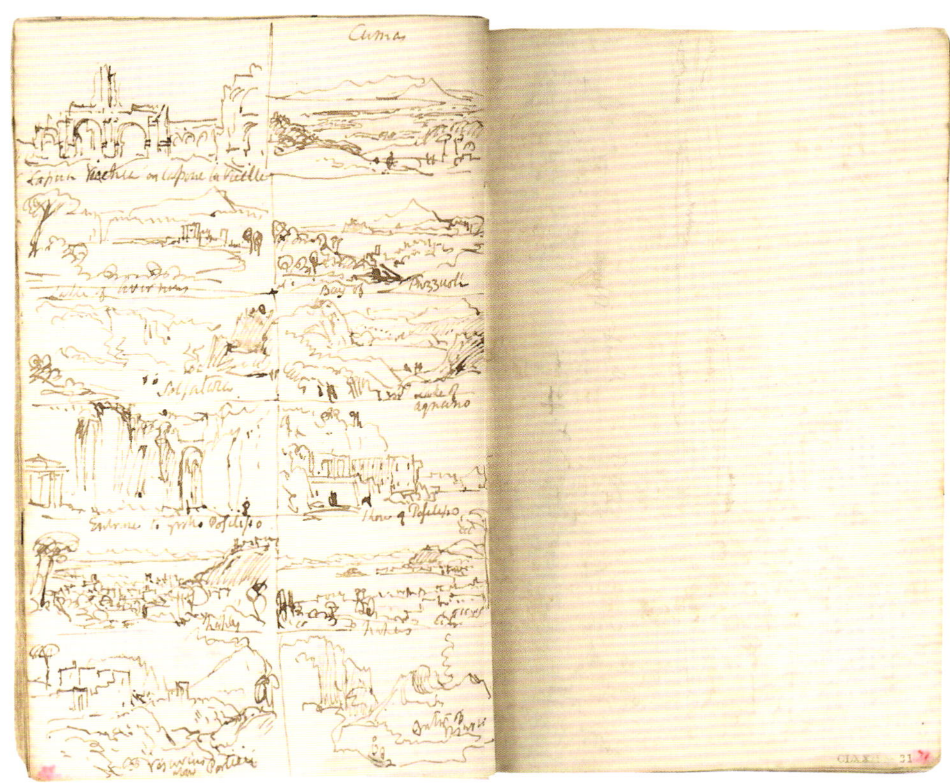

NO. 83 **J.M.W. Turner** *The Grand Canal, Venice, with the Entrance to the Cannaregio Canal beside the Church of San Geremia; Gondolas near a Low Bridge* and *The Grand Canal, Venice, with the Entrance to the Cannaregio Canal beside the Church of San Geremia* from the *Milan to Venice* sketchbook 1819
Graphite on paper, each page 11·2 × 18·5
Tate. Accepted by the nation as part of the Turner Bequest 1856

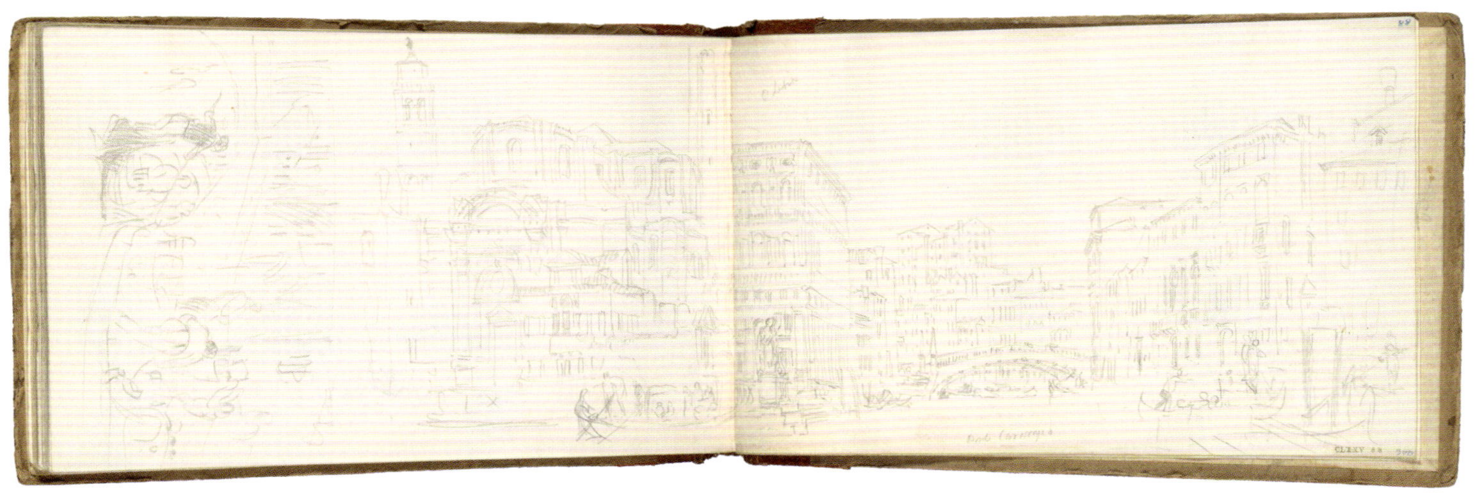

NO. 84 **J.M.W. Turner** *Vesuvius and the Sorrentine Peninsula from Via Posillipo* 1819
Graphite and watercolour on paper, 25·3 × 40·3
Tate. Accepted by the nation as part of the Turner Bequest 1856

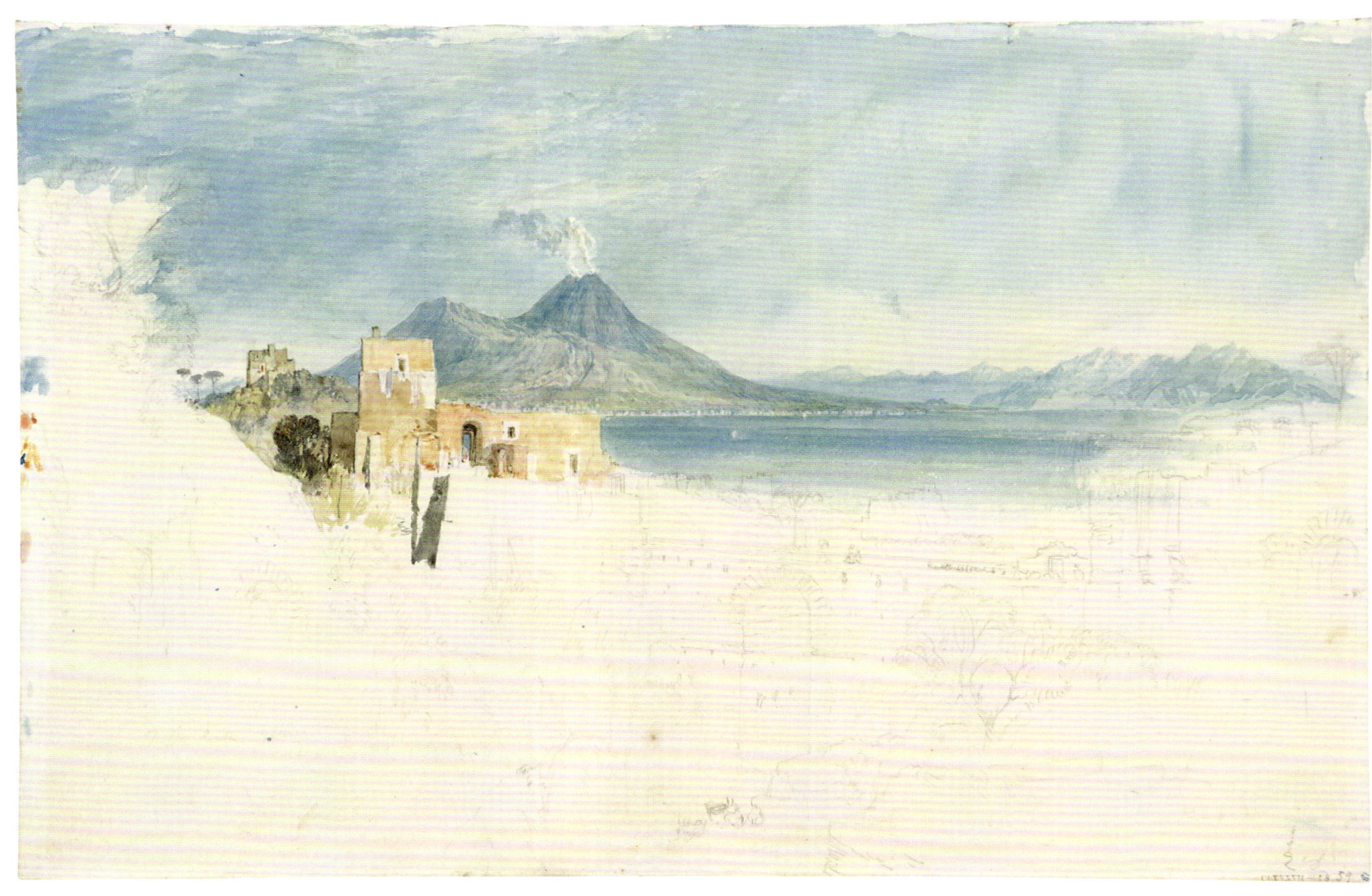

Turner has evoked a sense of brilliant sunlight through his application of watercolour to the upper part of this sheet, leaving the bare bones of his careful pencil drawing visible in the lower part. To capture this view of one of the most famous vistas in Europe, Turner positioned himself on a new road, which was opened in 1812. In the distance sits Vesuvius, its smoking crater a reminder in this otherwise peaceful view of the terror the volcano was capable of inflicting.

NO. 85 **J.M.W. Turner** *Venice: San Giorgio Maggiore – Early Morning* 1819
Watercolour on paper, 22·3 × 28·7
Tate. Accepted by the nation as part of the Turner Bequest 1856

NO. 86 **J.M.W. Turner** *The Forum, Rome, Looking South-East Towards the Arch of Titus* and *The Forum, Rome from the Temple of Saturn, Looking towards the Palatine* from the *Albano, Nemi, Rome* sketchbook 1819
Graphite on paper, each page 11·3 × 18·9
Tate. Accepted by the nation as part of the Turner Bequest 1856

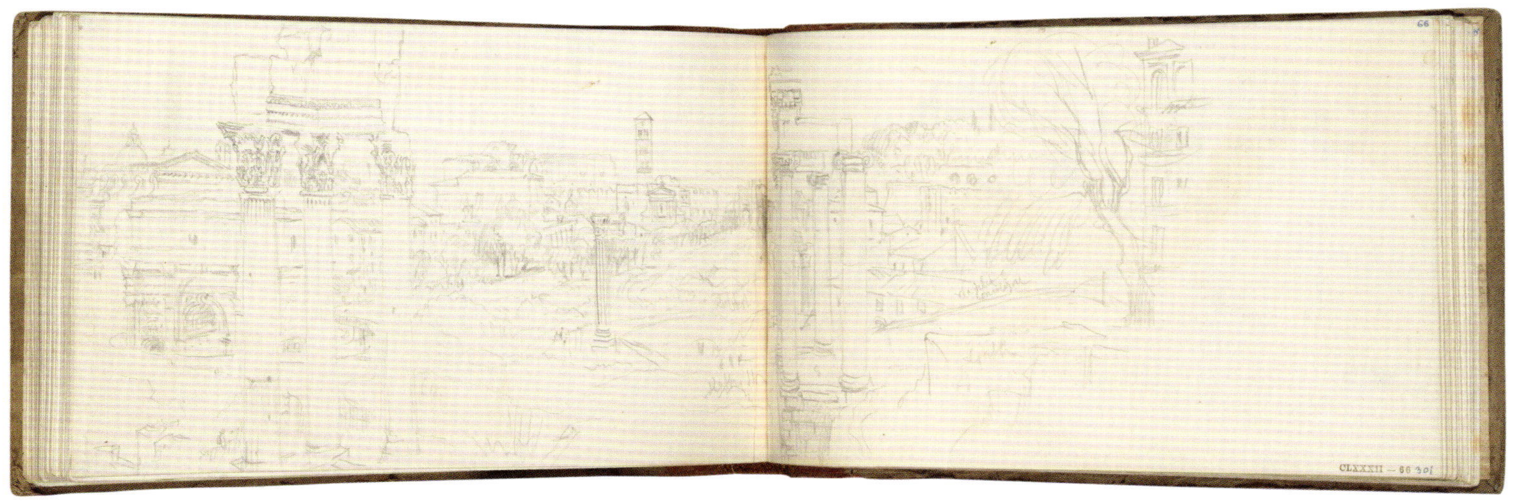

NO. 87 **J.M.W. Turner** *St Peter's and the Vatican from the Gardens of the Villa Barberini, Rome* 1819
Gouache, graphite and watercolour on paper, 23·1 × 37
Tate. Accepted by the nation as part of the Turner Bequest 1856

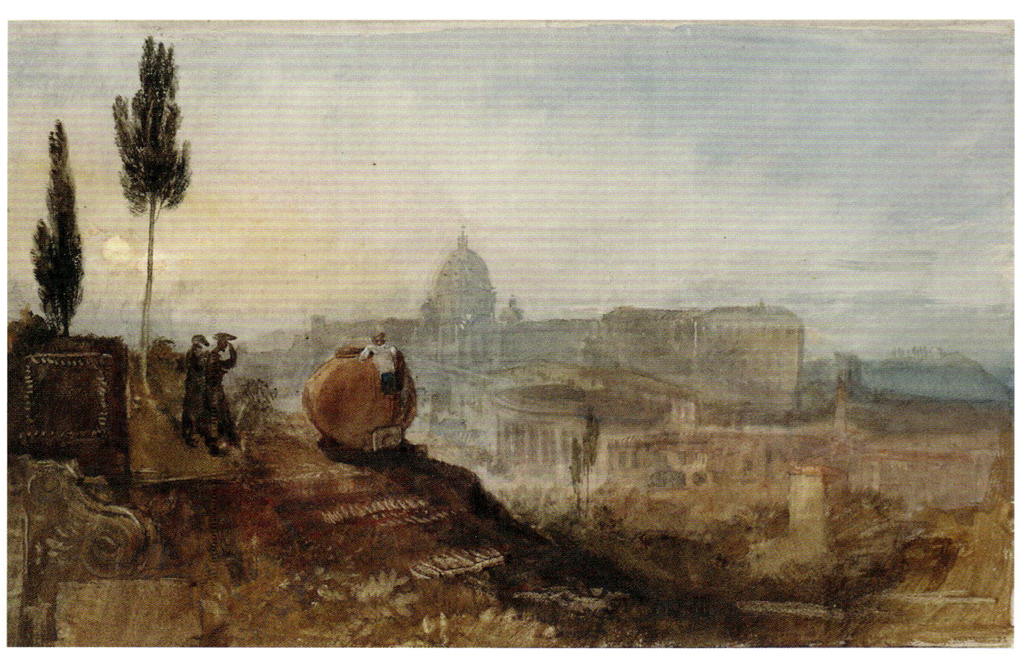

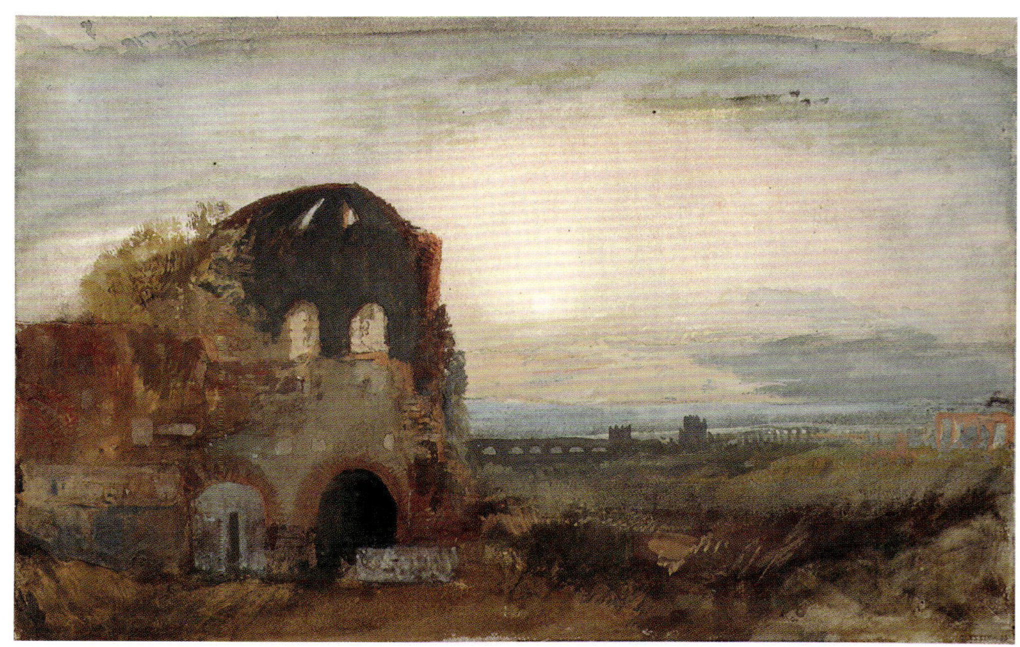

NO. 88 **J.M.W. Turner** *The So-Called Temple of Minerva Medica, Rome, at Sunset* 1819
Gouache on paper, 23 × 36·8
Tate. Accepted by the nation as part of the Turner Bequest 1856

NO. 89 **J.M.W. Turner** *The Colosseum, Rome, from the West* 1819
Gouache, graphite and watercolour on paper, 22·9 × 36·8
Tate. Accepted by the nation as part of the Turner Bequest 1856

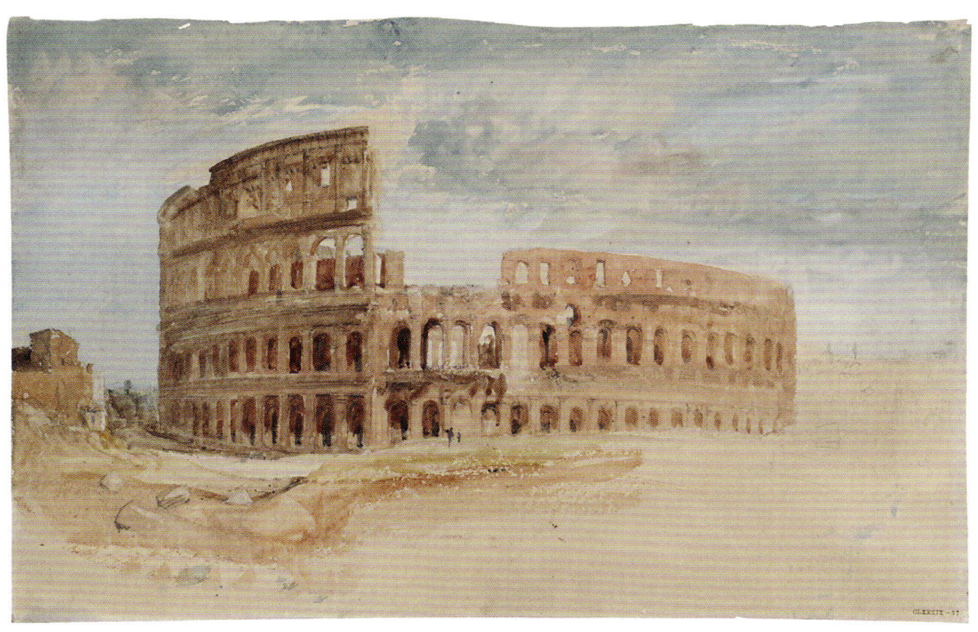

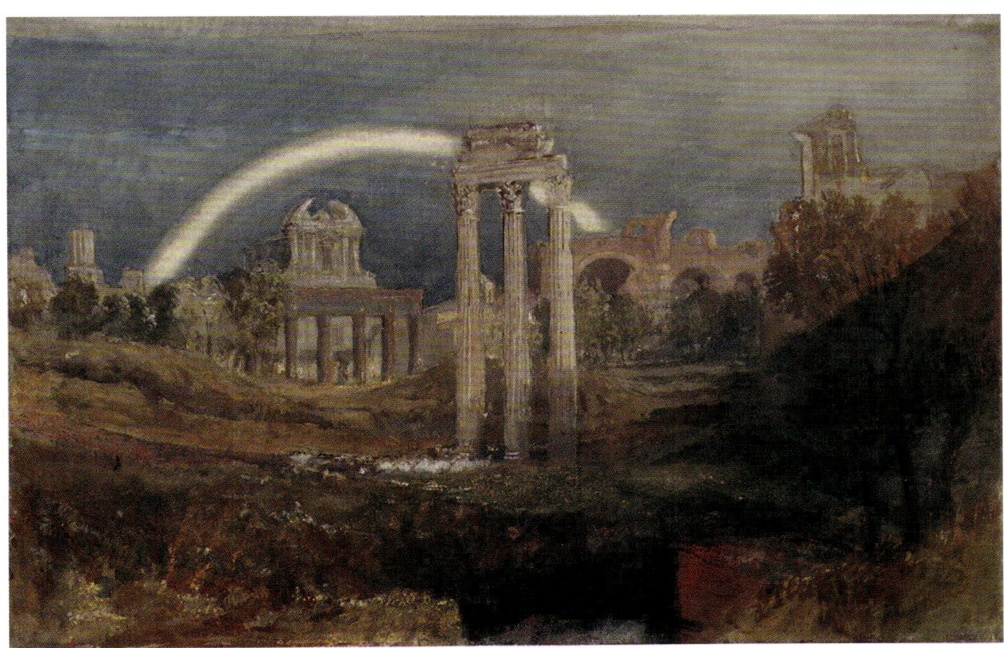

Rome, the 'Eternal City', was not only steeped in history but was also the artistic capital of Europe. Despite having never been there, Turner's imagined visions of Italy were a defining aspect of his reputation. In 1819 the portraitist Thomas Lawrence wrote to landscapist Joseph Farington that 'Turner should come to Rome. His Genius would here be supplied with new Materials and entirely congenial with it.' Indeed, Turner went to Rome that same year, a visit that generated a large body of work. This and other coloured drawings (nos.87, 88 and 89) have been widely admired for their dramatic atmospherics, appropriate to the grandeur of their subject matter.

NO. 90 **J.M.W. Turner** *View of the Forum, Rome, with a Rainbow* 1819
Graphite, watercolour and gouache on paper, 23 × 36·7
Tate. Accepted by the nation as part of the Turner Bequest 1856

NO. 91 **J.M.W. Turner** *The Bay of Baiae, with Apollo and the Sibyl* exhibited 1823
Oil paint on canvas, 145·4 × 237·5
Tate. Accepted by the nation as part of the Turner Bequest 1856

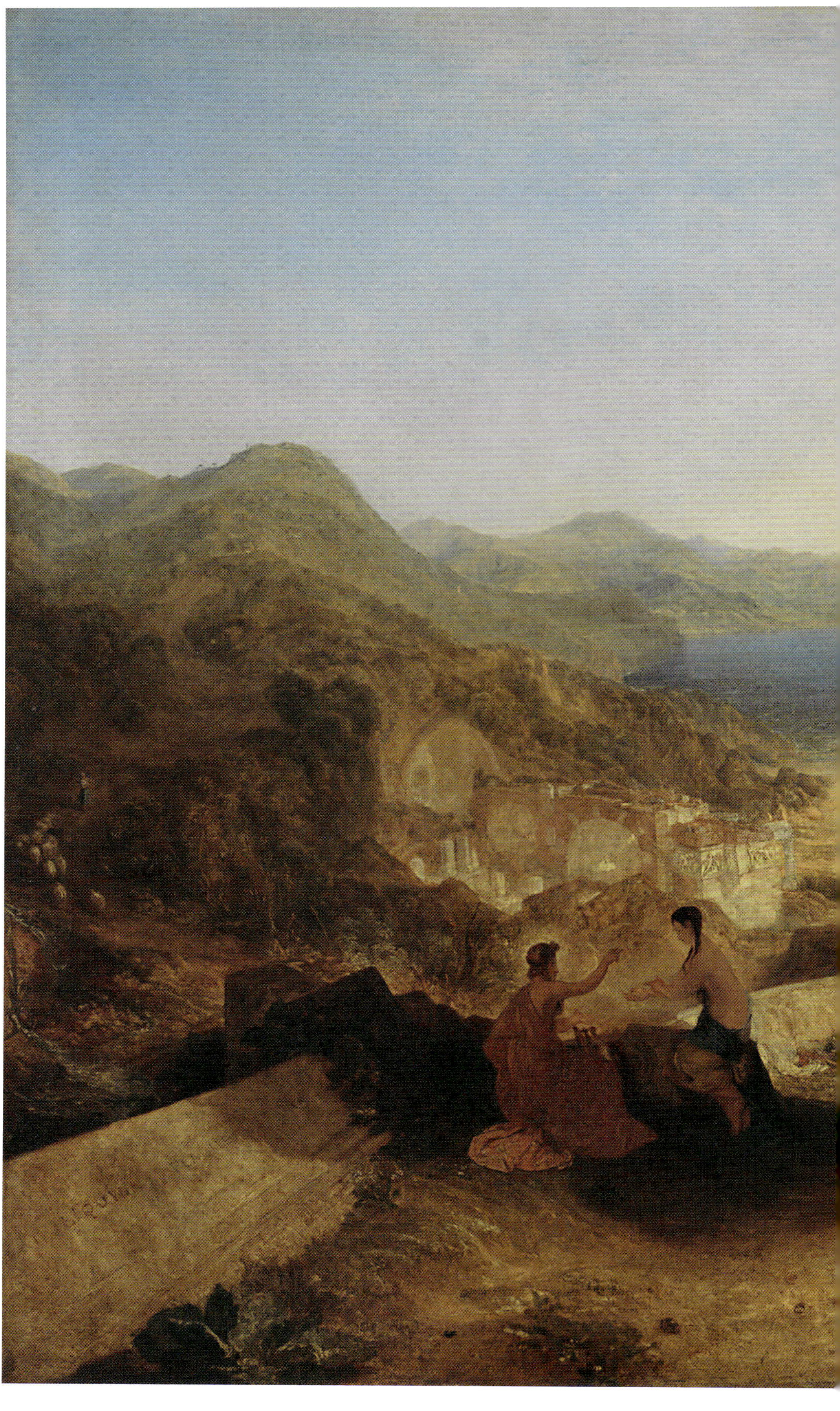

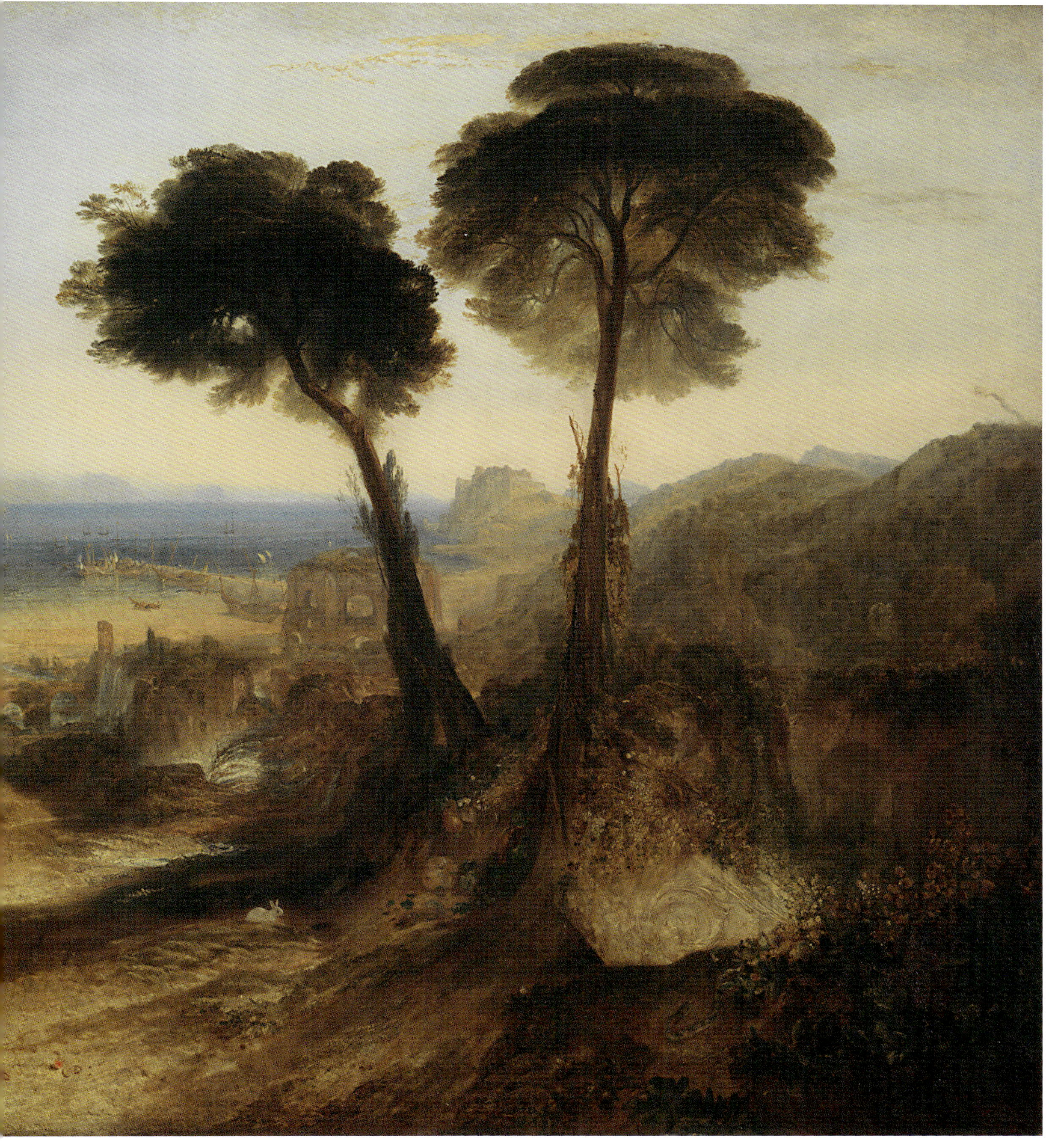

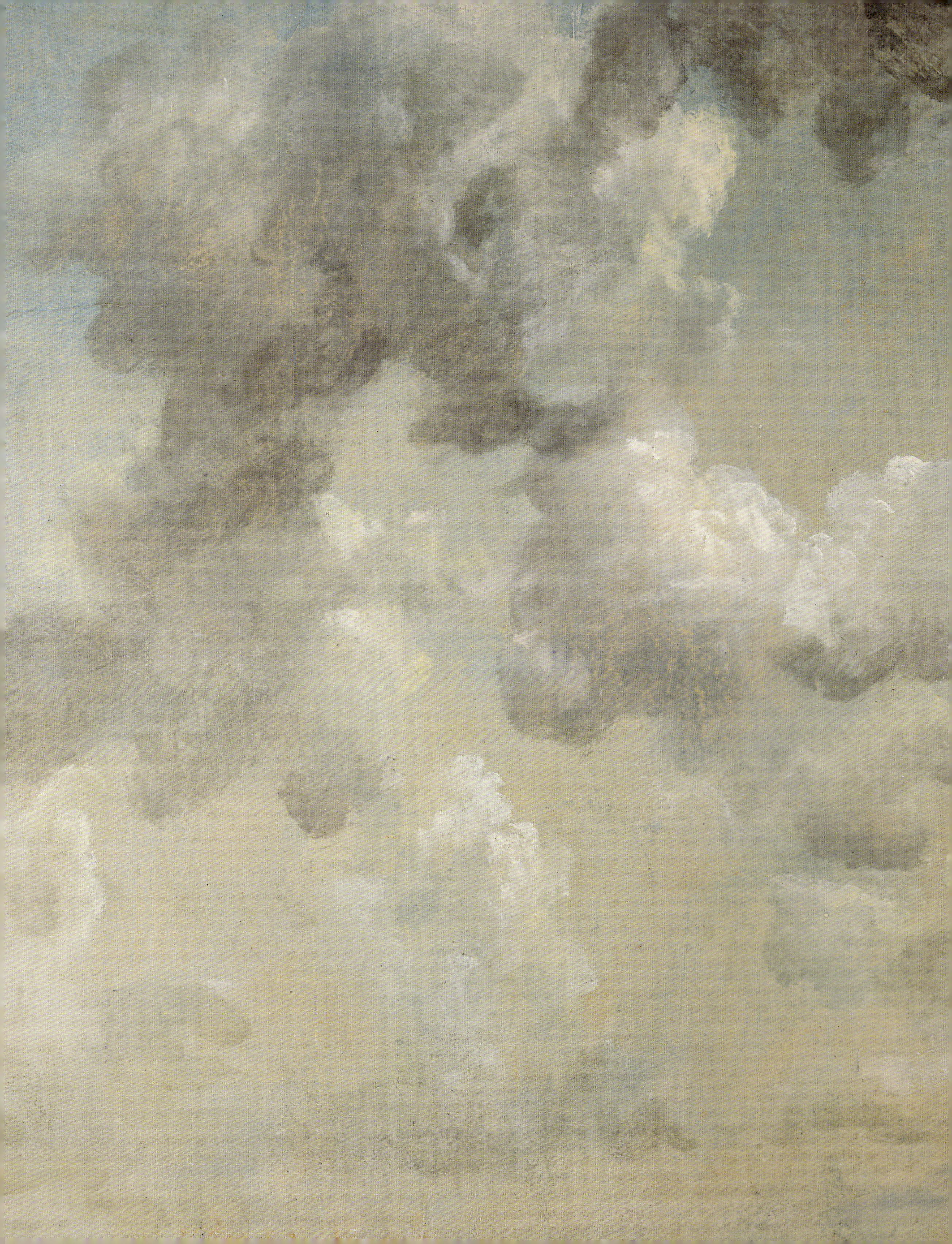

FIELDS AND SKIES: NEW PHASES IN CONSTABLE'S SEARCH FOR 'TRUTH'

'I live wholly in the feilds [*sic*] and see nobody but the harvest men', wrote Constable in late August 1814.[1] His correspondence that summer buzzed with an energy that marked the dawn of a new phase in his life and work. The subsequent years brought much change – marriage, fatherhood and the death of his parents – but also an invigorated and more confident approach to making pictures that would see Constable blaze a radical new trail in landscape.

In the summer of 1814 those fields became Constable's studio. While he continued to make oil sketches outdoors and filled a sketchbook with pencil studies, he took the unprecedented step of making larger, finished paintings outdoors. He was already treading new ground via his compositional choices and subject matter, but in removing the literal distance between painting process and subject, he was taking a more extreme approach to the 'truth' he sought in his work than ever before.

He began this quest with two paintings: *Stour Valley* (no.95), which he painted in the mornings, and *Boat Building*, which occupied his afternoons (no.94). These compositions were not spontaneously derived in the moment Constable sat down to paint but rather honed through preparatory work, much of it made in pencil (no.93). Furthermore, Constable's recent study of Claude's seaports can be seen in *Boat Building*.[2] On its exhibition in 1815 its 'sparkling sun-light', 'freshness' and 'character of truth' was noted.[3] Thus, while they did not know his means and still thought his finish 'crude', the critics understood Constable's quest as part of a wider trend towards an outwardly more relaxed kind of landscape that, though carefully composed, depicted real places in more naturalistic guises and embraced a wider range of atmospheric conditions.

Another innovation laid the groundwork for the idiosyncratic process behind Constable's later 'six-foot' landscapes. *Dedham Lock and Mill* (no.103) is based on a sketch of an equivalent size, likely made outdoors (Tate, N02661). This seemingly simple change to his process became integral to the realisation of his 'six-footers', with *The White Horse* (no.127) of 1819 demonstrating Constable's serious ambition and accelerating his renown.

That same year Constable rented a house in Hampstead, hoping the cleaner air there would alleviate his wife Maria's tuberculosis. The move spawned another unprecedented habit: 'skying' (as he called it), making rapid oil sketches of the skies above Hampstead (nos.104–16). Sometimes he anchored these with a glimpse of treetops or land, but in many the view is unmoored and firmly skywards. Reflecting his knowledge of new meteorological research on cloud classifications, but also the climatic sensitivity that work in his father's windmill instilled in him, he would often annotate these sketches with the prevailing weather conditions.

Throughout this pivotal period Constable grew increasingly familiar with the city of Salisbury and its surrounding landscape. His first visit there in 1811 had been at the invitation of the Bishop of Salisbury. Having encouraged Constable to paint him a view of the cathedral (no.116), the bishop objected to the 'dark cloud' in the sky. Little did Constable know then that the concept of the 'church under a cloud' would take his work to new heights less than a decade later (no.135).

John Constable *Study of Clouds* (detail) 30 September 1822 (p.142)

NO. 92 **John Constable** *Willy Lott's House seen over the Stour by moonlight* and *Two Drawings on One Page: two cows; Stratford Hall and Stratford St Mary Church* 1813–15
Graphite on paper in bound sketchbook
Victoria and Albert Museum, London. Given by Isabel Constable, daughter of the artist

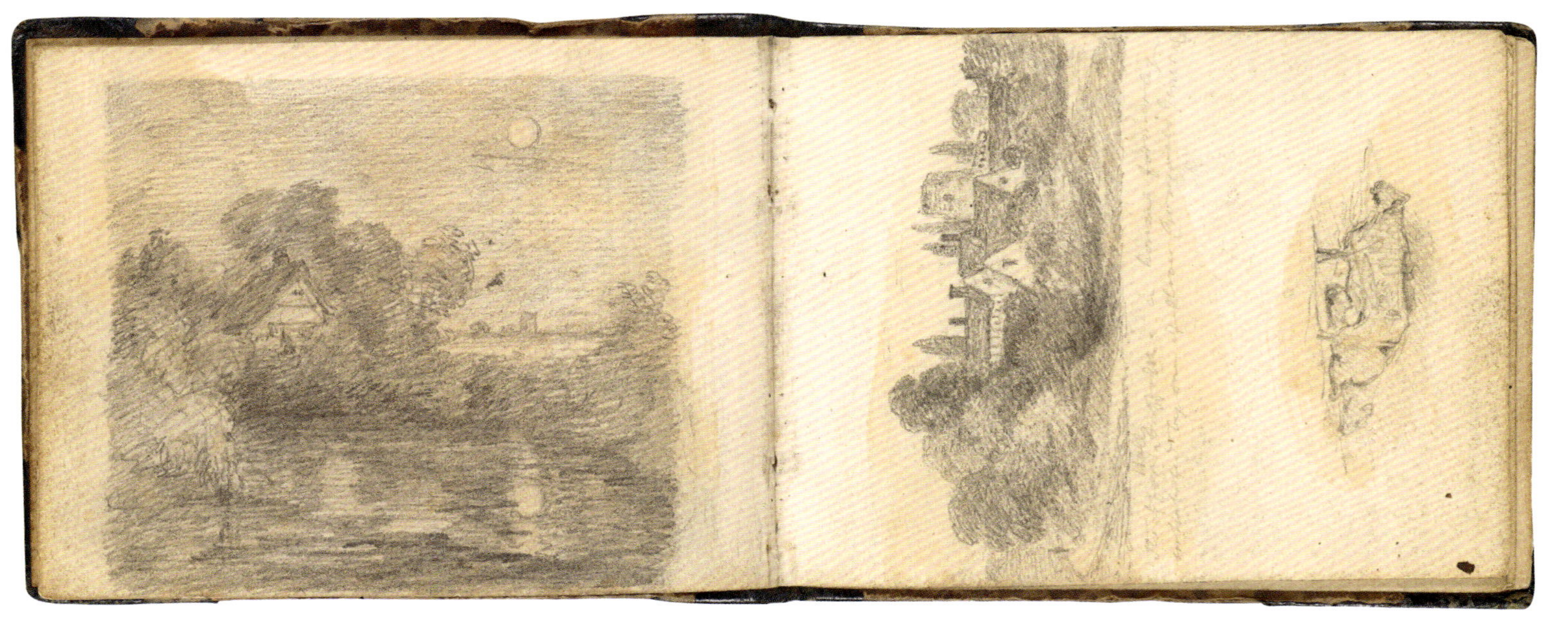

NO. 93 **John Constable** *Barge-building*, and *Drawings of Boat Builders* from the *1814 Sketchbook*
July to October 1814
Graphite on paper in bound leather sketchbook
Victoria and Albert Museum, London. Given by Isabel Constable, daughter of the artist

This sketchbook was used by Constable in Essex and Suffolk between July and October 1814. It contains observed scenes and isolated details as well as thumbnail sketches of compositions. Inscribed with the date, 7 September 1814, this sketch shows a busier version of the scene seen in *Boat-Building* (no.94).

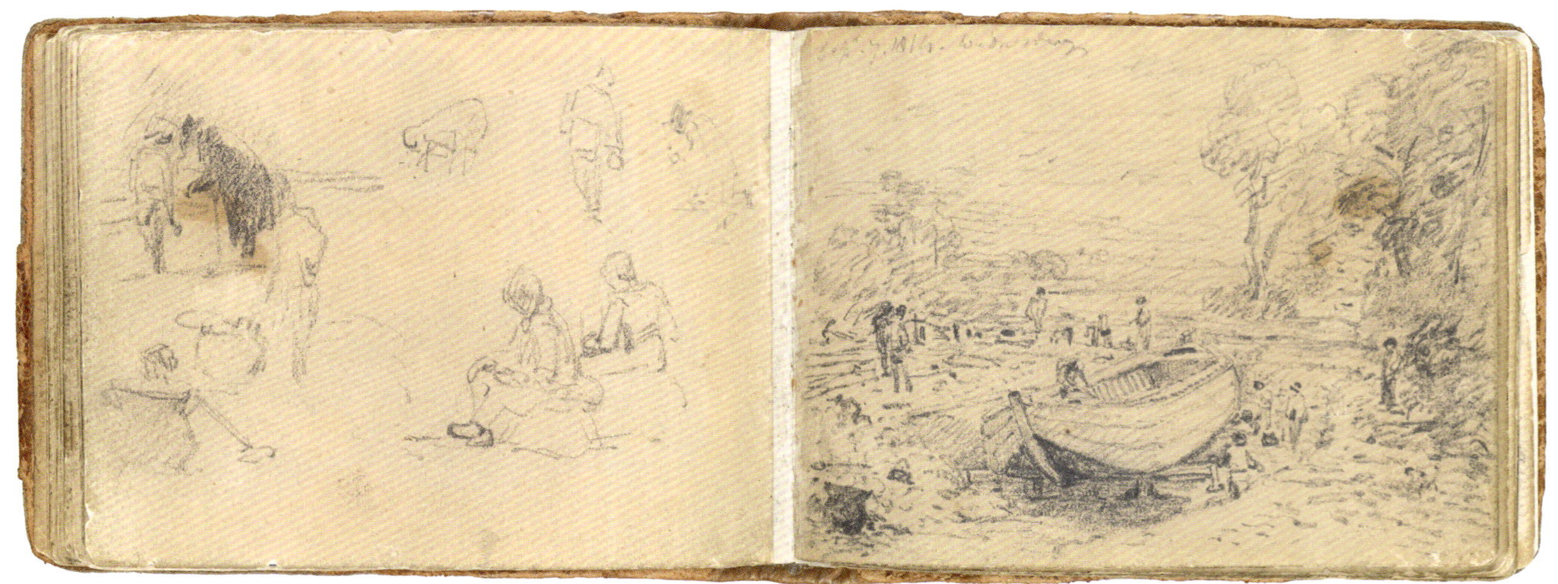

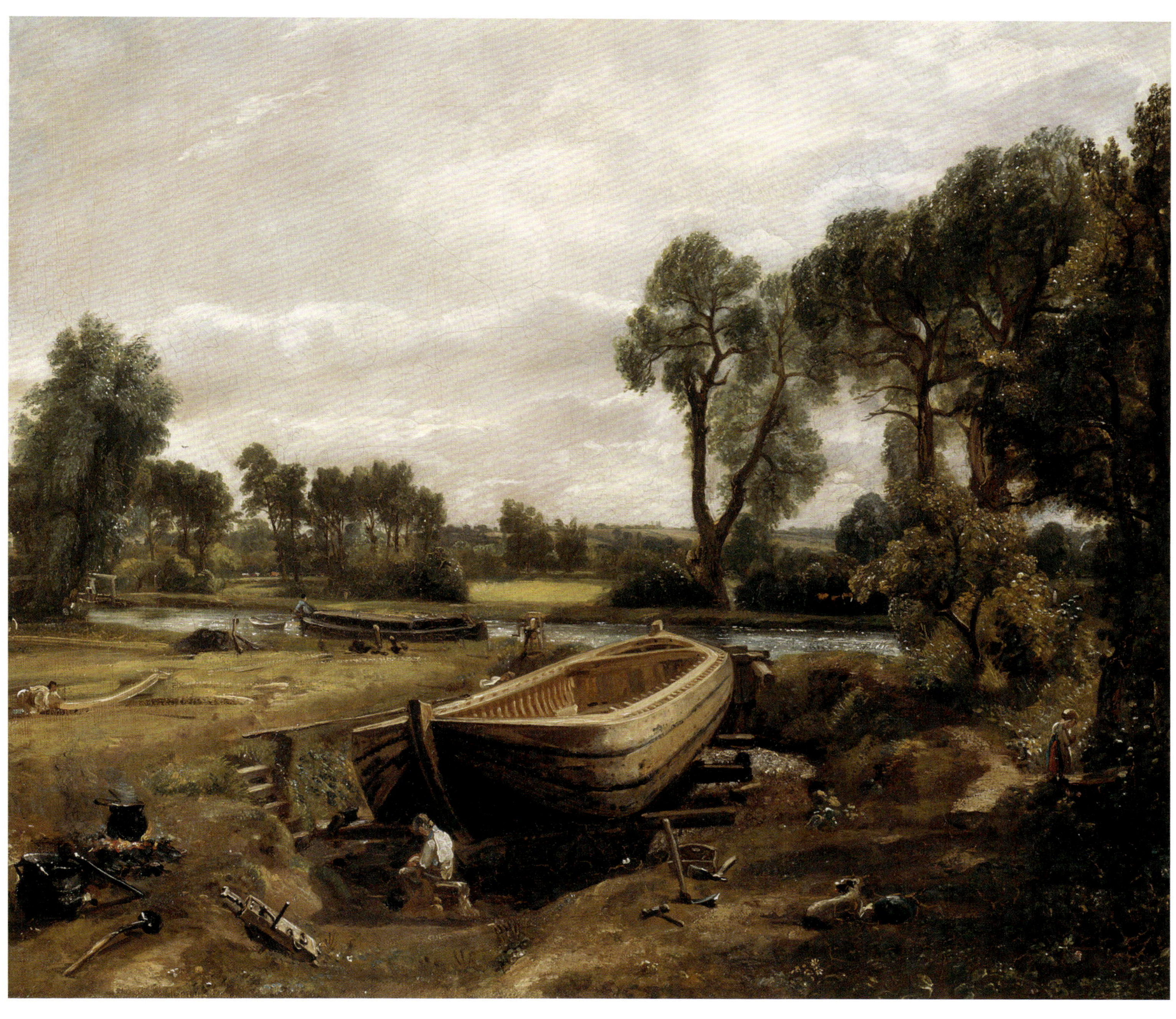

NO. 94 **John Constable** *Boat-Building near Flatford Mill* 1815
Oil paint on canvas, 50·8 × 61·6
Victoria and Albert Museum, London. Given by John Sheepshanks, 1857

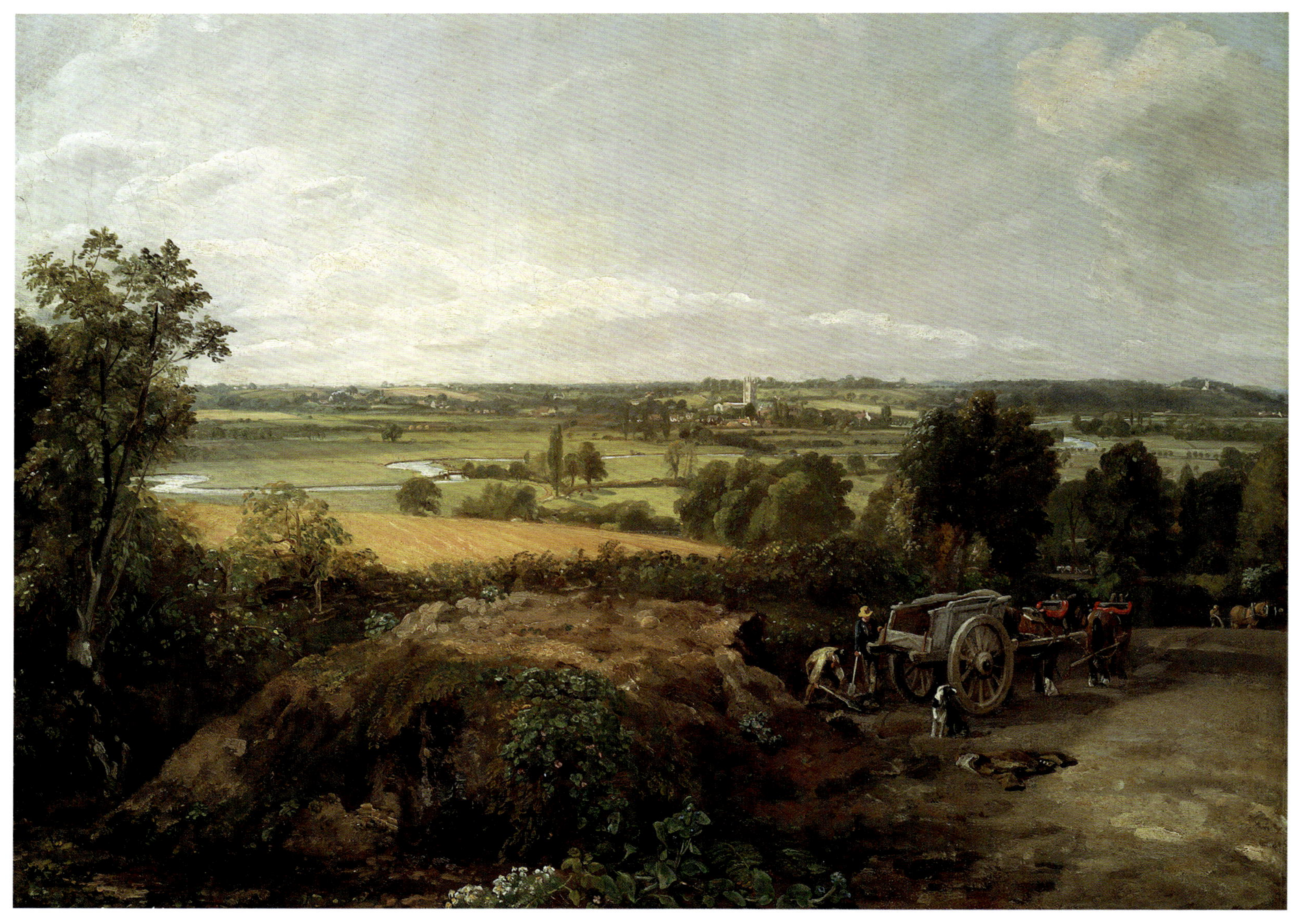

NO. 95 **John Constable** *Stour Valley and Dedham Church* c.1815
Oil paint on canvas, 55·6 × 77·8
Museum of Fine Arts, Boston. Warren Collection—William Wilkins Warren Fund

A dung heap might not be the obvious subject for painting commissioned as a wedding gift. Constable was commissioned to paint it by Thomas FitzHugh, as a gift for his bride, Philadelphia Godfrey. The Godfrey family had been neighbours of Constable's in East Bergholt; the viewpoint is from their estate and features men loading a cart with dung, ready to fertilise the field. Ostensibly a reminder of Philadelphia's childhood home, the painting has also been interpreted as a metaphor for the fertility of the bride herself and hopes of raising a family. The setting is the same field, seen from a slightly different angle, as appears in *The Wheatfield* (no.96); the dung heap, now overgrown, is seen in the left-hand corner. Constable has also painted the same dog, in the same pose, in both. He did the same in two later paintings, *Salisbury Cathedral from the Meadows* (no.135) and *The Cornfield* (fig.35, p.56).

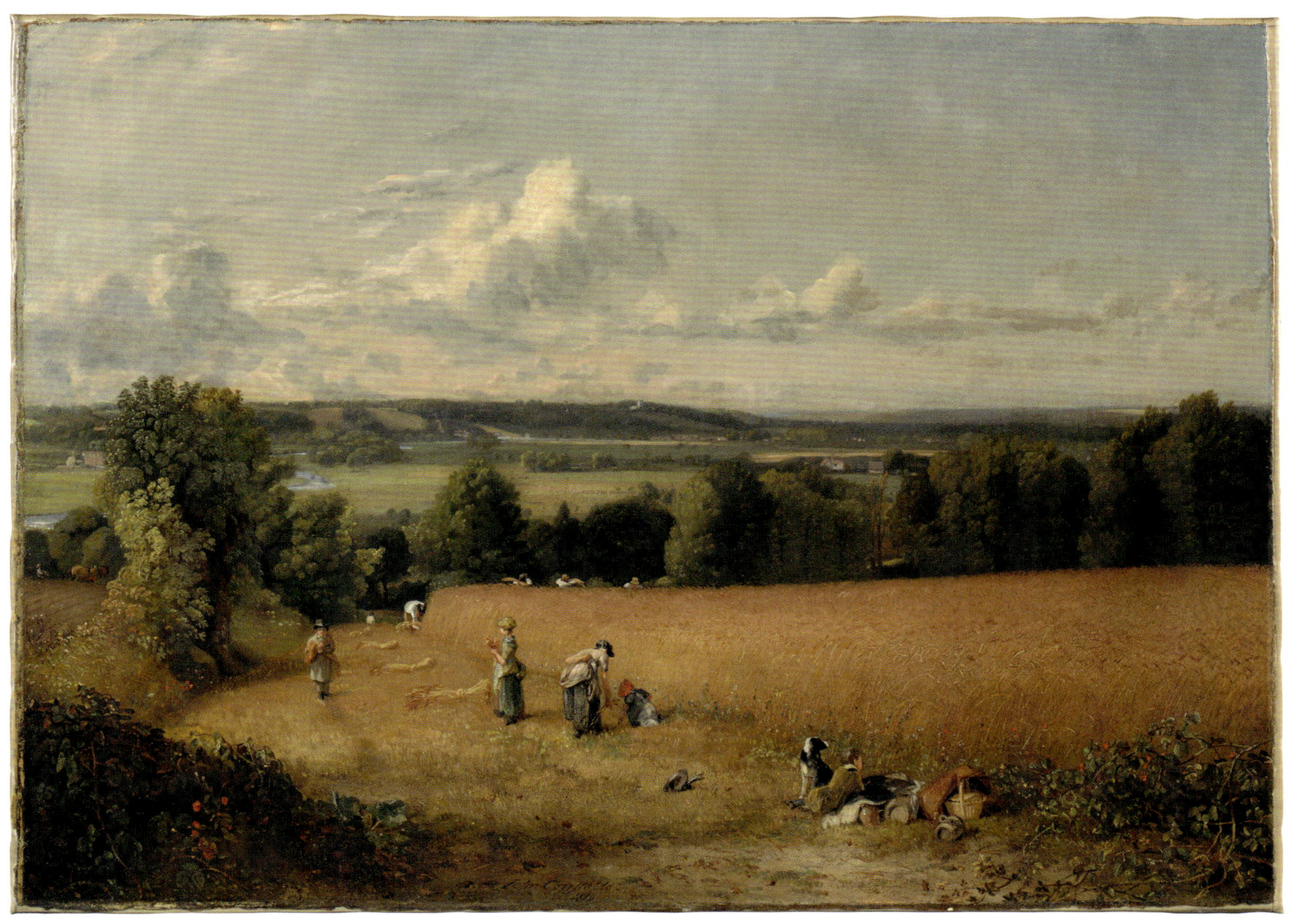

NO. 96 **John Constable** *The Wheatfield* 1816
Oil paint on canvas, 54·6 × 78·1
Clark Art Institute, Williamstown, Massachusetts, USA, gift of the Manton Art Foundation in memory of Sir Edwin and Lady Manton

Against a backdrop of the Stour valley, Constable pictures a shimmering wheatfield attended by men reaping (their heads and arms glimpsed above the wheat in the middle ground) while women and a child glean leftover ears. When Constable exhibited this painting for a second time, in 1817, he appended its entry in the exhibition catalogue with lines from a popular poem by contemporary poet Robert Bloomfield, *The Farmer's Boy* (1800): 'No rake takes here what heaven to all bestows / Children of want, for you the bounty flows!' This reference underlines Constable's idealistic view of the harvest as an uncomplicated time of plenty. Yet Constable was acutely aware that life in the countryside was not as bounteous or as idyllic as it seems here. This period was gripped by agricultural unrest and uncertainty in the wake of economic depression, new farming methods and the Enclosure Acts, which dispossessed many of the right to self-sufficiency. Thought to have been painted largely out in field itself, this canvas might be read as a rose-tinted tribute to the old ways of the countryside in a fast-changing world. In this sense it provides a parallel with Turner's later painting, *Keelmen Heaving in Coals by Moonlight* (no.163).

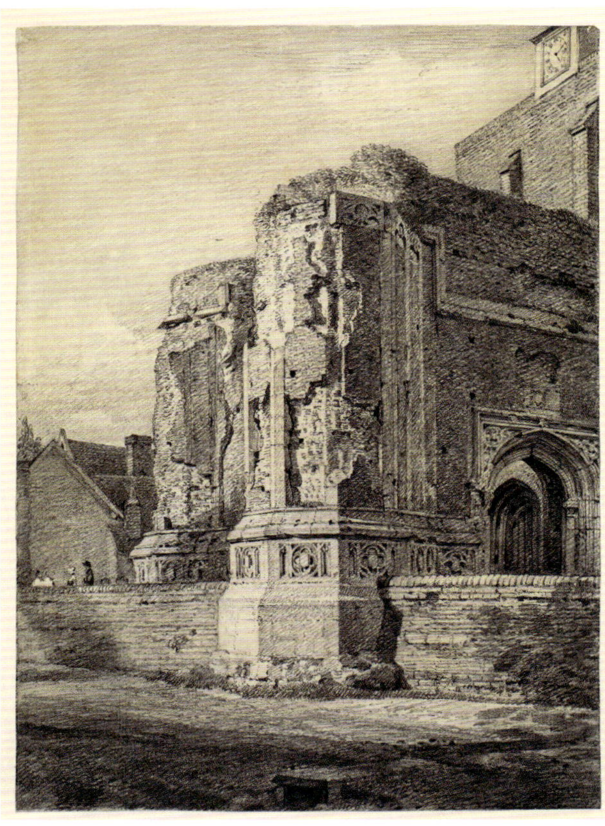

NO. 97 **John Constable** *East Bergholt Church, from the southwest* 1815–17
Graphite on wove paper, 31·8 × 24
The Courtauld, London (Samuel Courtauld Trust)

Unlike Turner, who did not make detailed, worked-up drawings beyond the early years of his career, Constable made highly finished drawings throughout his life (see no.169). Given the importance of chiaroscuro (light and shade) to his thinking, drawing was perhaps a useful test of his ability to represent it using the linear means of graphite only. Here he achieves subtle gradations of tone and texture through different techniques such as varying his pressure on the pencil and the use of hatching and cross-hatching to darken shadows. The building itself is in part drawn with use of a ruler. Likely to have been drawn on the spot, it reveals his study of picturesque drawings by the likes of Turner and Turner's friend Thomas Girtin, whose drawing of Guisborough Priory (V&A) Constable had copied. Constable's subject is very fitting of the picturesque, an aesthetic which privileged time-worn buildings with crumbling textures. Rather than a ruin, however, the base of the church tower at East Bergholt was simply left unfinished. That Constable had grown up attending this church, where his father – who had died a year before he made this work – had been a warden since 1804, makes it an especially meaningful subject.

NO. 98 **John Constable** *Path Towards Stratford St Mary* 1816
Oil paint on paper laid on canvas, 26·7 × 19·1
Private Collection

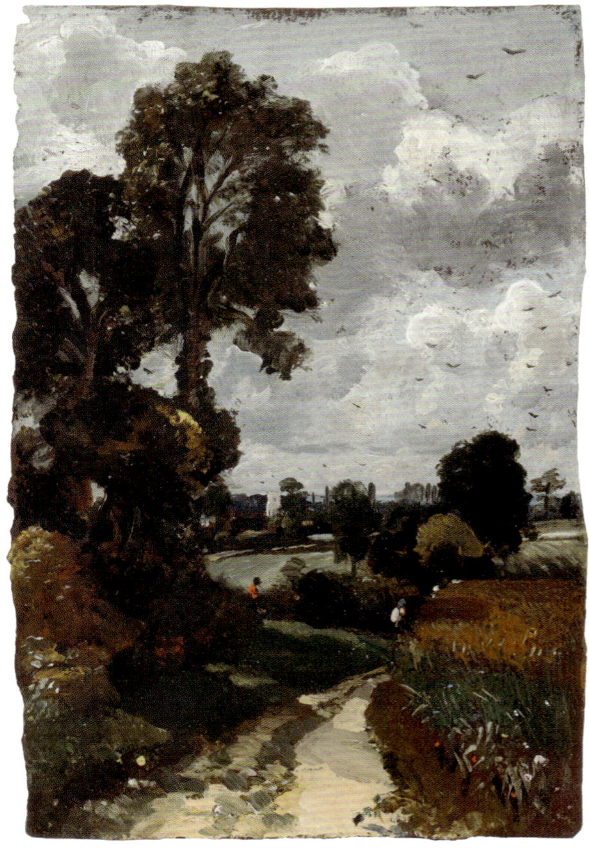

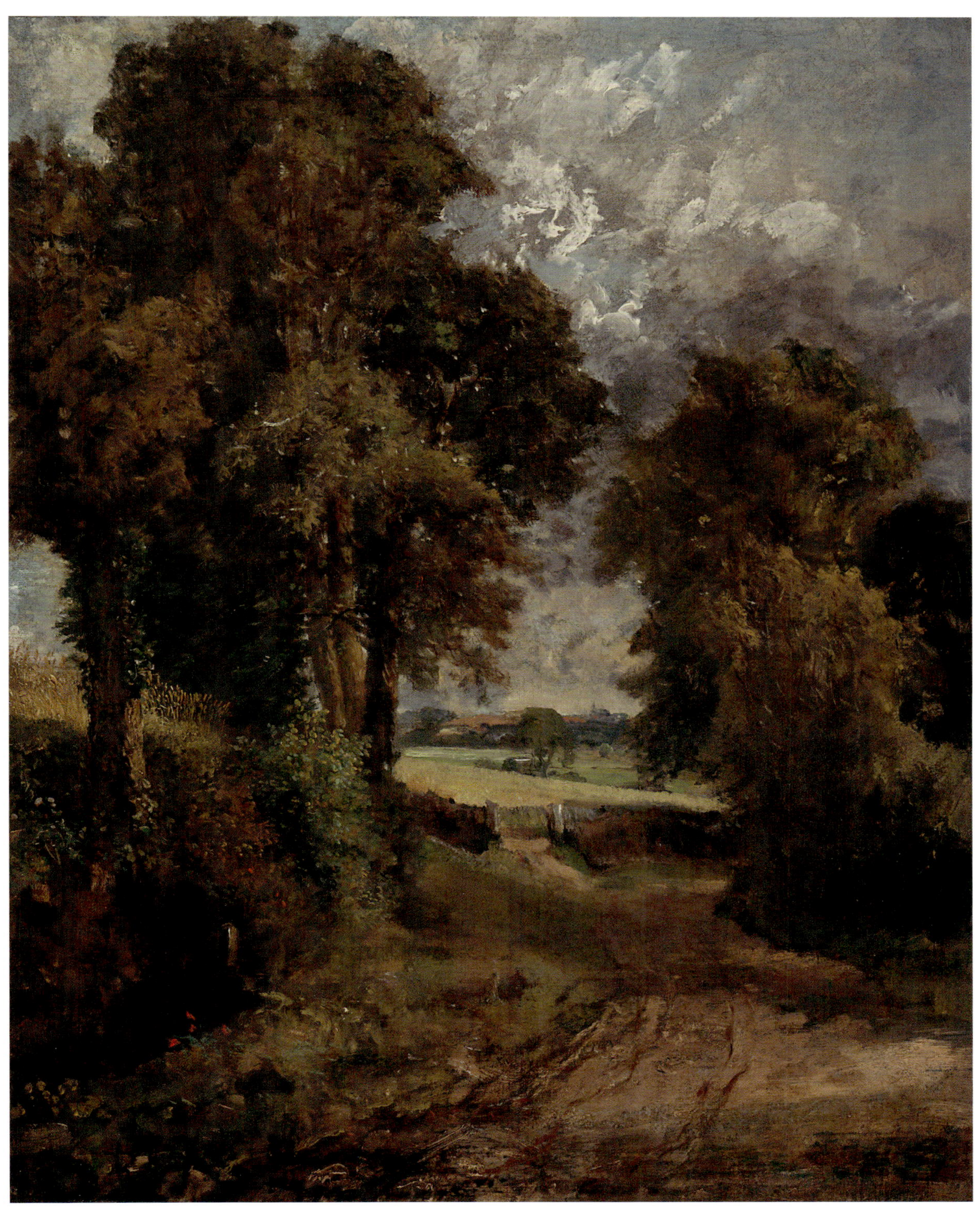

NO. 99 **John Constable** *A Cornfield* 1817
Oil paint on canvas, 61·3 × 51
Tate. Accepted by HM Government in lieu of inheritance tax and allocated to Tate 2004

NO. 100 **John Constable** *Study for 'Flatford Mill'* c.1816
Pencil tracing on paper, 25·5 × 31·2
Tate. Purchased 1988

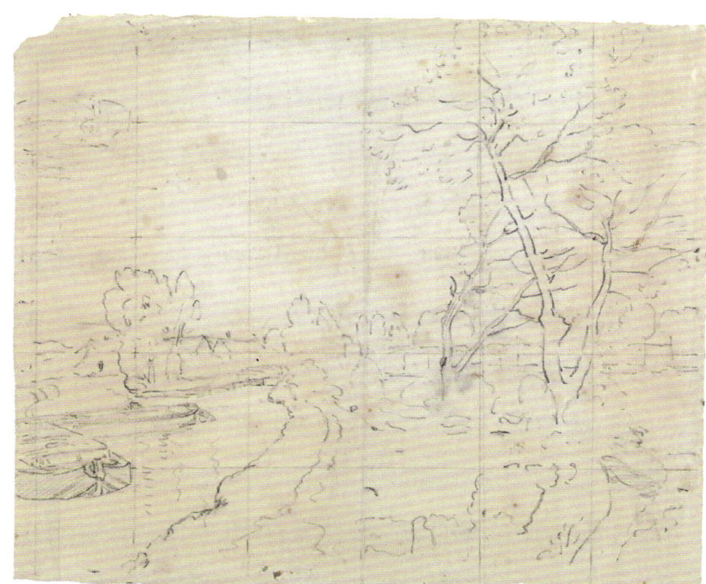

NO. 101 **John Constable** *Scene of Flatford Mill* 1814
Oil paint on canvas, 34·3 × 40·6
Private Collection

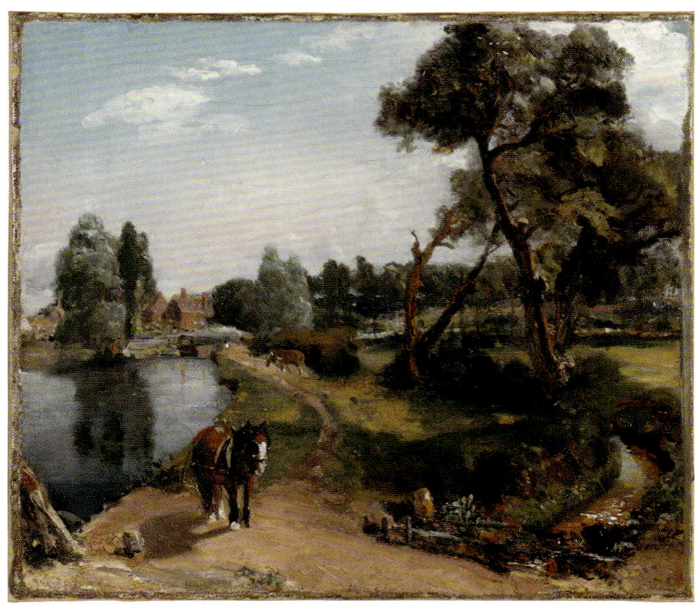

NO. 102 **John Constable** *Flatford Mill ('Scene on a Navigable River')* exhibited 1817
Oil paint on canvas, 101·6 × 127
Tate. Bequeathed by Miss Isabel Constable as the gift of Maria Louisa, Isabel and Lionel Bicknell Constable 1888

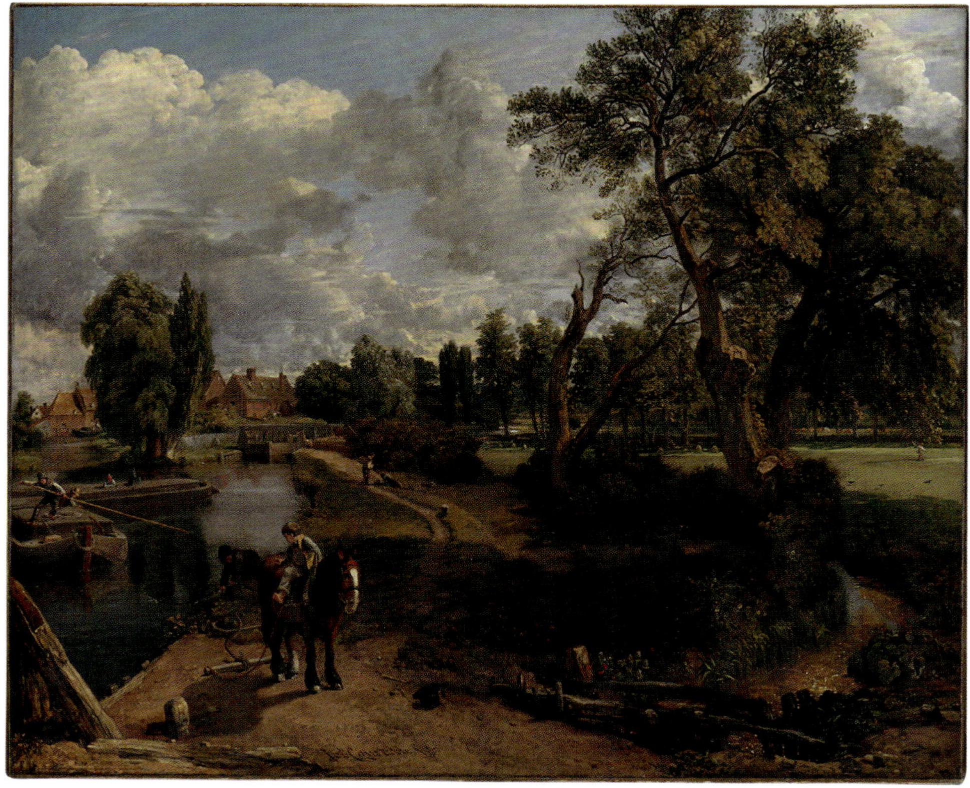

Thought to be the largest painting Constable worked on outdoors, *Flatford Mill* depicts the hub of the Constable family grain milling and shipping business. In the foreground a tow horse has been separated from two barges so that they may pass under the bridge, the support for which can be seen in the bottom right corner. It is shown in this exhibition for the first time with its associated oil sketch (no.101). The related drawing was produced according to a method seemingly inspired by one described by Leonardo da Vinci. It involved placing a glass sheet on an easel, viewing the scene through it and outlining its forms directly on to the glass. Constable then made this drawing by tracing over the outline captured on the glass. The grid is an aide for transfer on to the canvas. We therefore have evidence of the extraordinarily rigorous and time-consuming means Constable adopted in order to paint his scenes as accurately as possible.

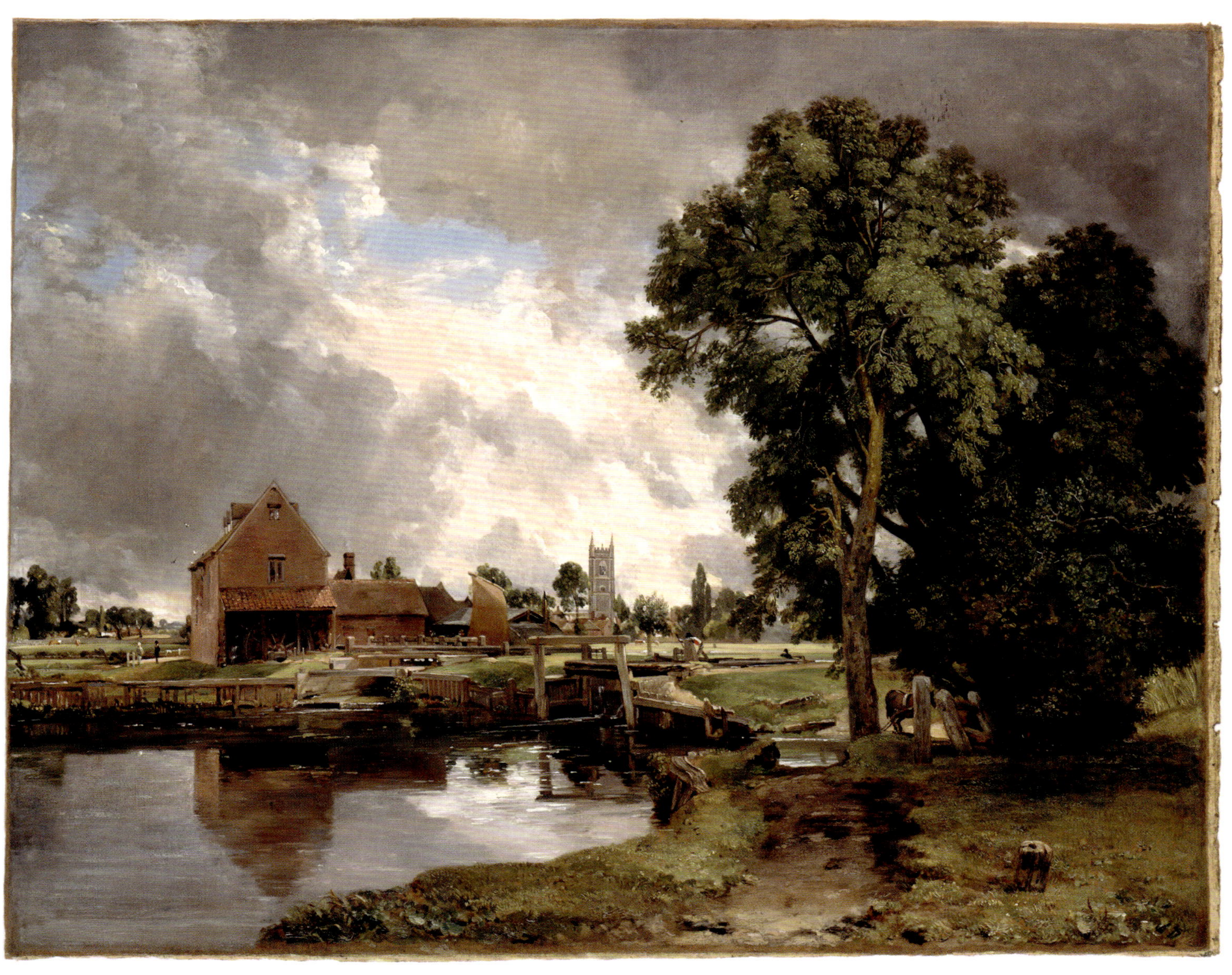

NO. 103 **John Constable** *Dedham Lock and Mill* ?exhibited 1818
Oil paint on canvas, 70 × 90·5
Private Collection

This scene might be read as a microcosm of Constable family values: hard work and devout faith. Dedham Mill was, like Flatford, owned and run by Golding Constable, the artist's father. As has been suggested by Anne Lyles (*Great Landscapes*, 2006, p.118), it may have been the death of Constable's father in May 1816 that prompted him to take up this scene and *Flatford Mill* (no.102), both of which centre on his father's business premises. From the men in white and black on the left of the mill to the donkey beneath the tree on the right (and partly obscured by a post) *Dedham Lock and Mill* is replete with details the artist took evident delight in painting. Its complex interplay of light and dark, meanwhile, reveals a new confidence and facility in the rendering of fleeting effects.
It certainly reflects the wet weather conditions Constable reported as hampering his progress on the composition in the summer of 1816. Constable made several versions of this composition; this is likely to be the version Constable exhibited under the title *Landscape: Breaking up of a shower*, a work which was praised for by critics for its authenticity.

NO. 104 **John Constable** *Cloud Study* c.1821–2
Oil paint on board, 11 × 16
Private Collection

NO. 105 **John Constable** *Study of Clouds over a Landscape* c.1821–2
Oil paint on laminate cardboard mounted on canvas, 24·4 × 29·5
Clark Art Institute, Williamstown, Massachusetts, USA, gift of the Manton Art Foundation in memory of Sir Edwin and Lady Manton

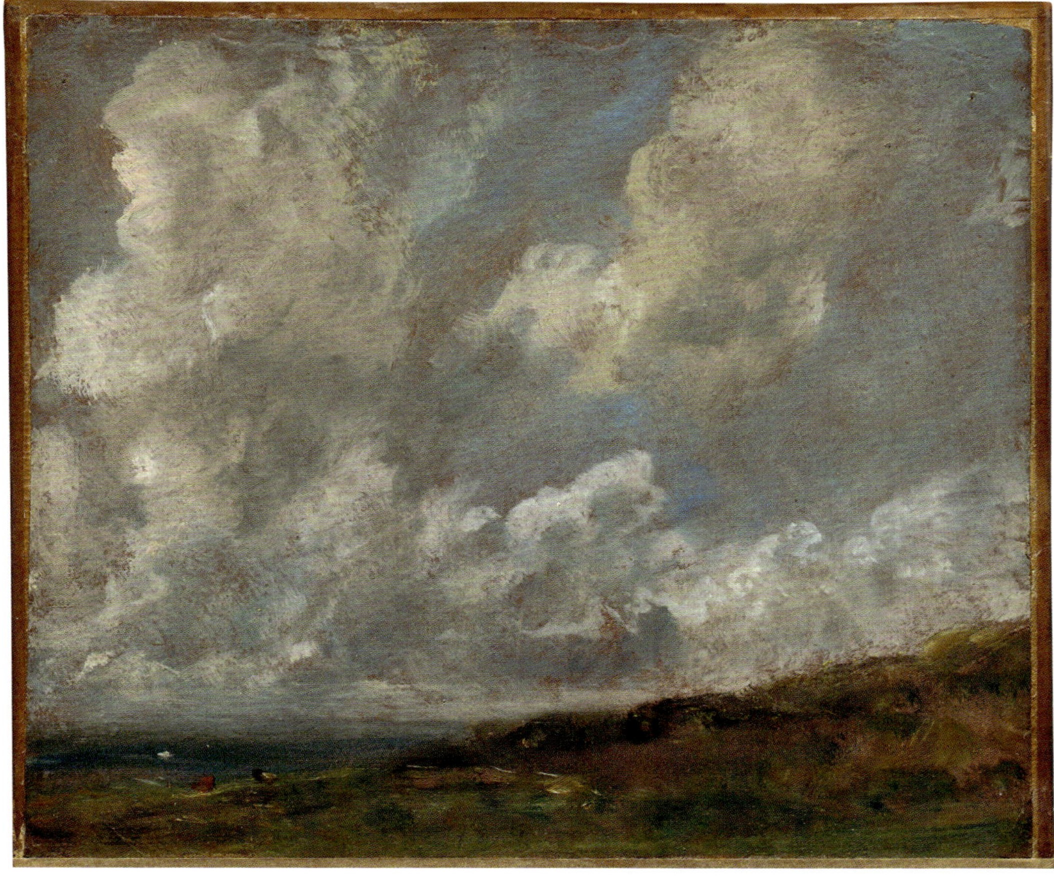

NO. 106 **John Constable** *A Vivid Sunset* 1820
Oil paint on paper laid onto panel, 8·9 × 17·3
Private Collection

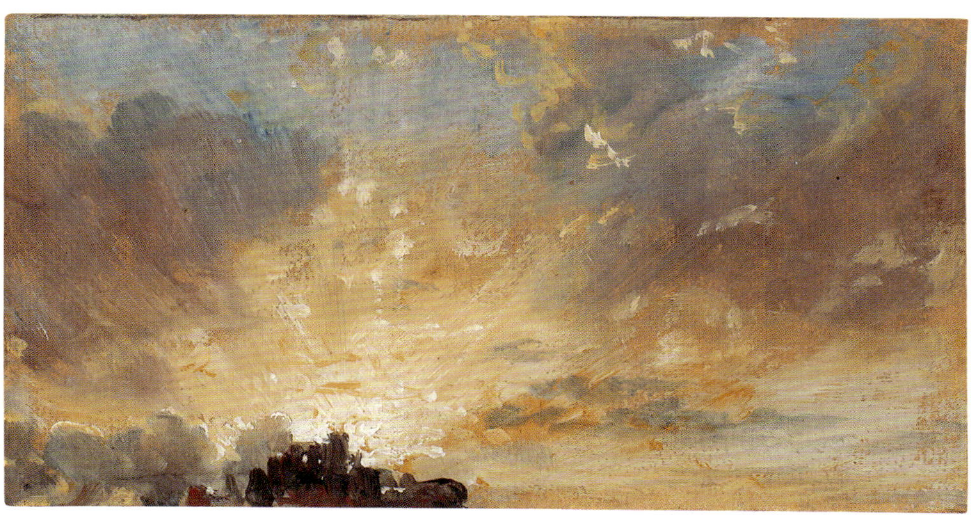

NO. 107 **John Constable** *Cloud Study, Hampstead, Tree at Right* 1821
Oil paint on paper laid on board, red ground, 24·1 × 29·9
Lent by the Royal Academy of Arts, London

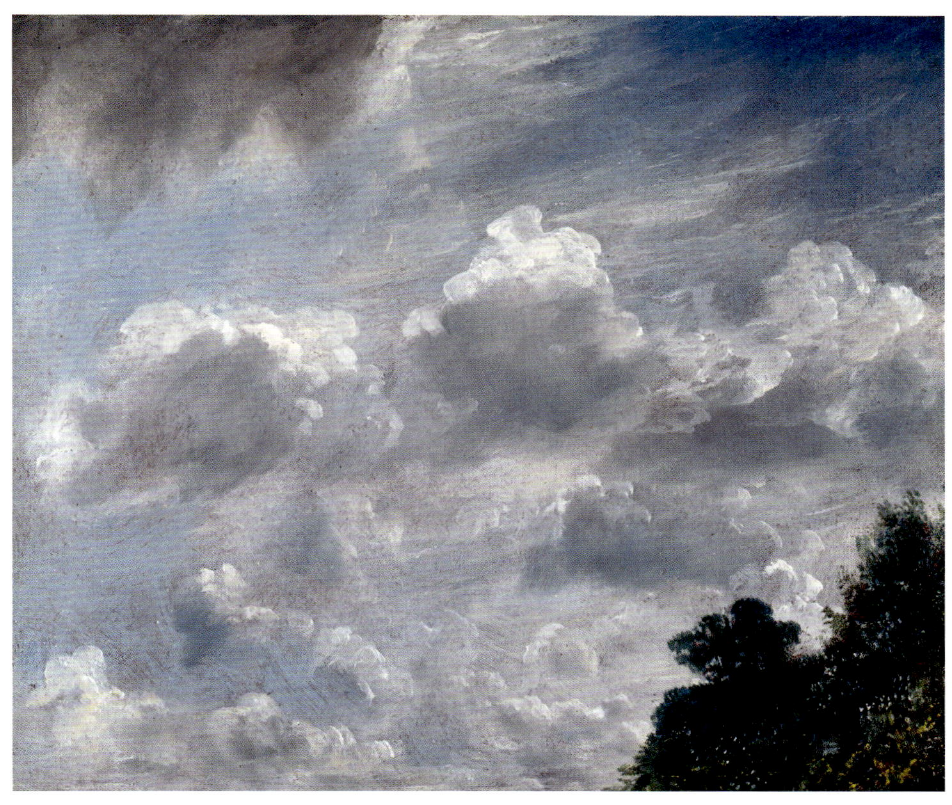

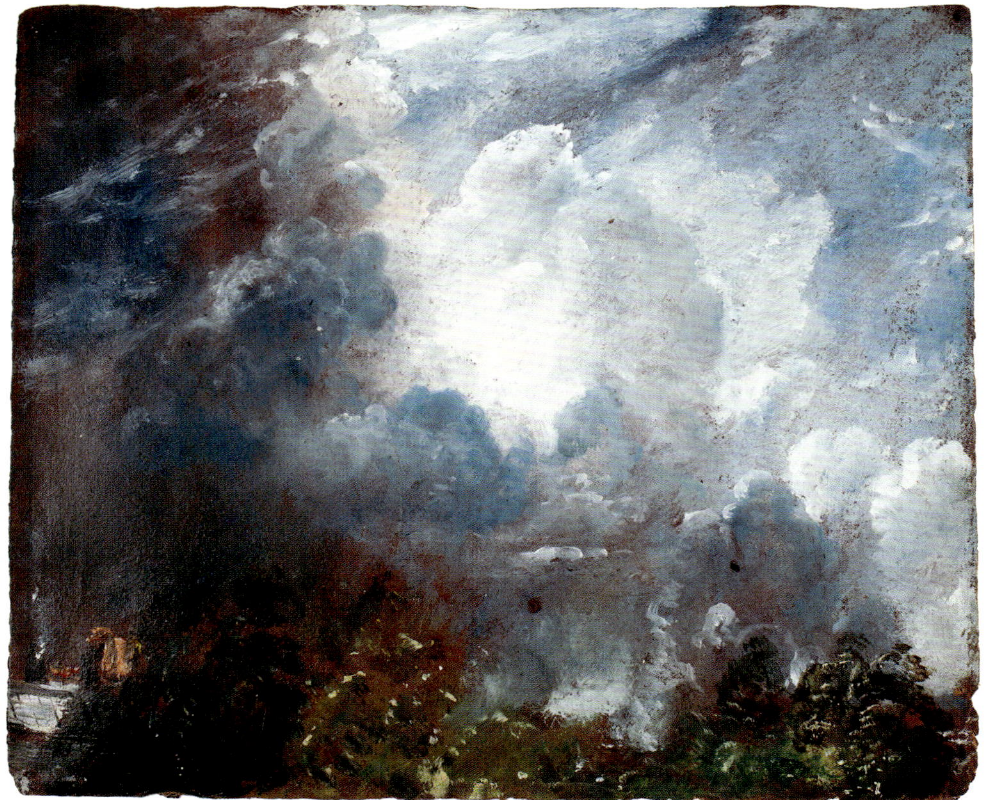

NO. 108 **John Constable** *Cloud Study* 10 September 1821
Oil paint on paper laid on board, 25·5 × 30
Private Collection

NO. 109 **John Constable** *Cloud Study* 1821
Oil paint on paper laid on board, 24·8 × 30·2
Yale Center for British Art, Paul Mellon Collection

NO. 110 **John Constable** *A Study of High Clouds* 1821
Oil paint on paper, 24·1 × 29·2
Private Collection

NO. 111 **John Constable** *Cloud Study* 1821
Oil paint on paper laid on panel, 21·3 × 29·2
Yale Center for British Art, Paul Mellon Collection

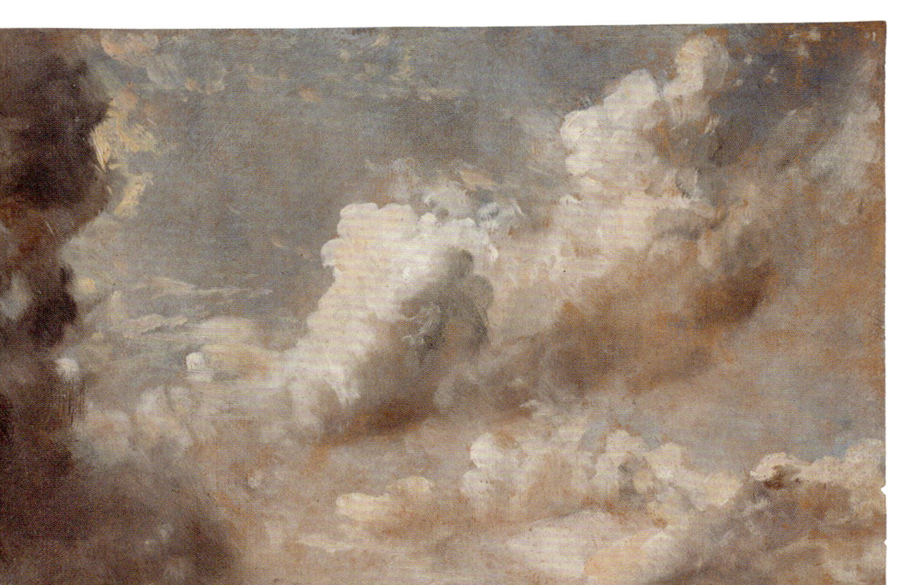

NO. 112 **John Constable** *Cloud Study* 1822
Oil paint on paper, 19·8 × 32
Private Collection

NO. 113 **John Constable** *Study of Clouds* 30 September 1822
Oil paint on paper, 48·7 × 59
Lent by The Ashmolean Museum, University of Oxford.
Presented by Sir E. Farquhar

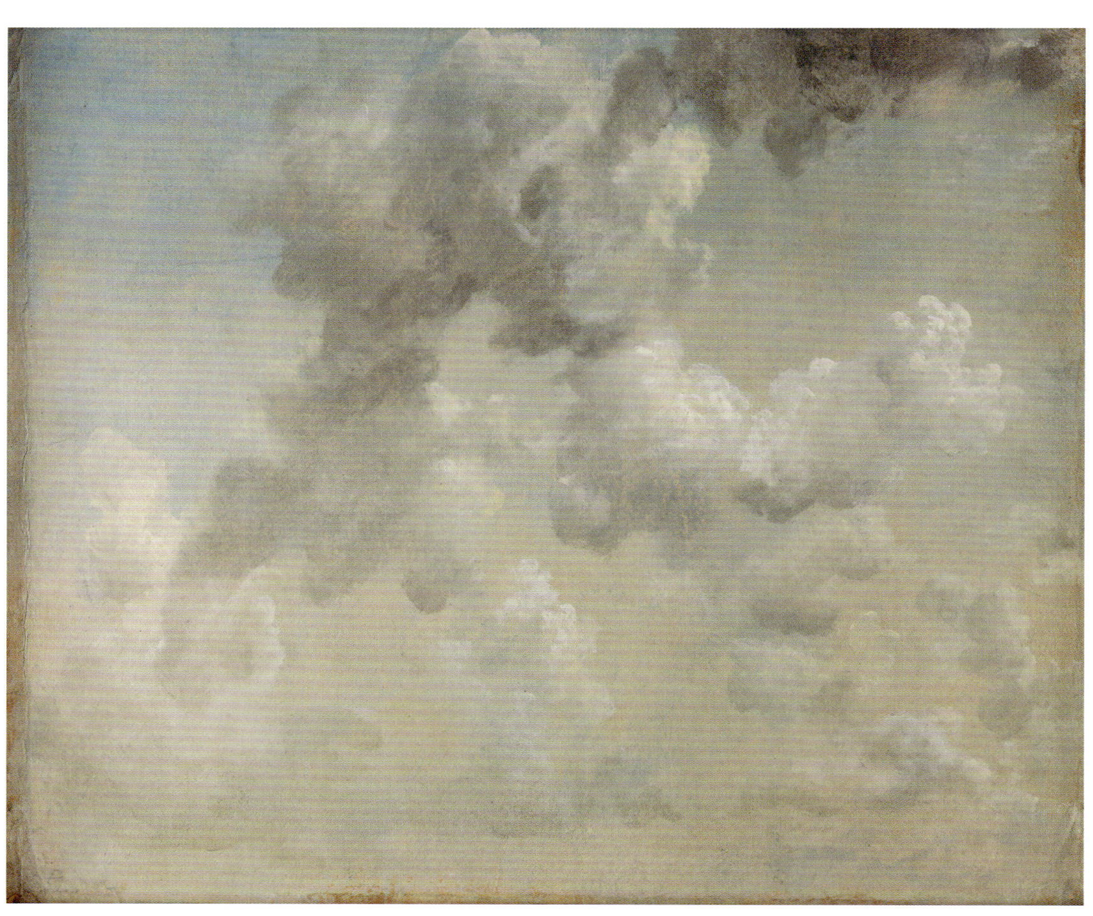

NO. 114 **John Constable** *Cloud Study* 1822
Oil paint on paper on board, 47·6 × 57·5
Tate. Presented anonymously 1952

NO. 115 **John Constable** *Cloud Study* 1822
Oil paint on two superimposed sheets of wove paper laid down on a third sheet, 30·5 × 49
The Courtauld, London (Samuel Courtauld Trust)

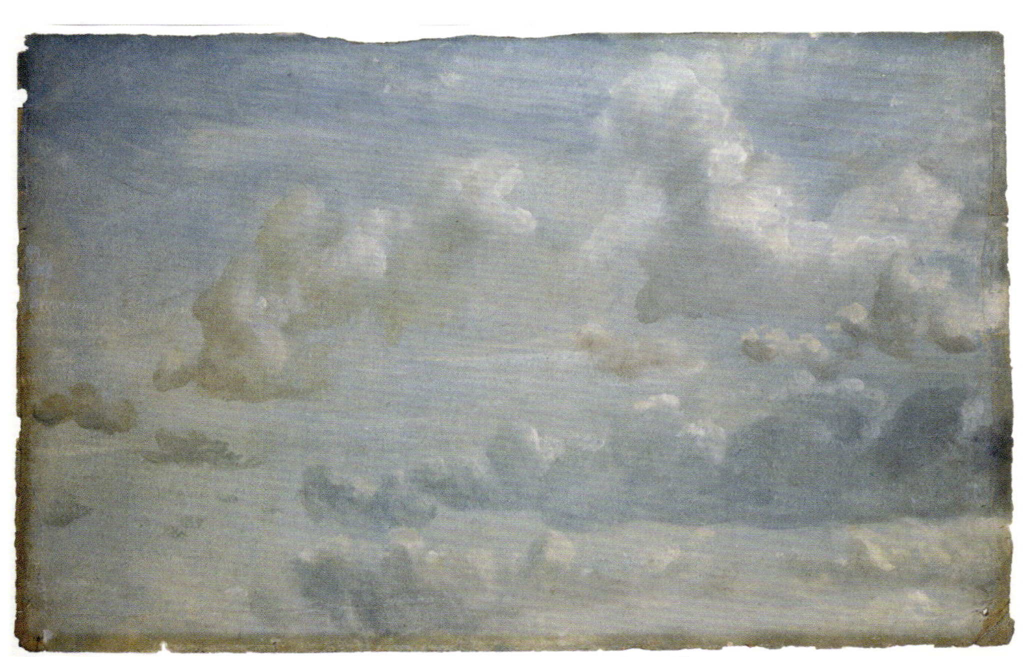

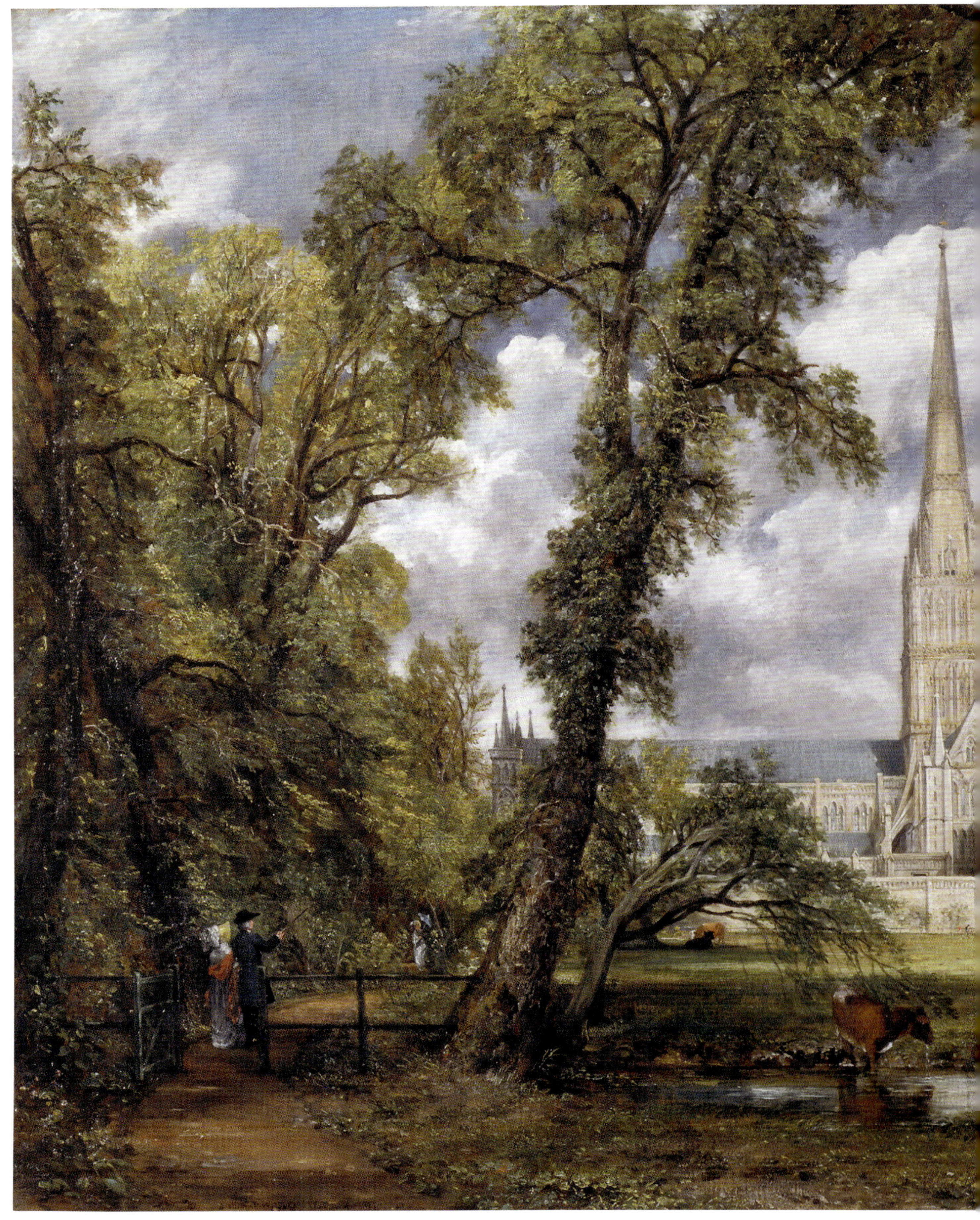

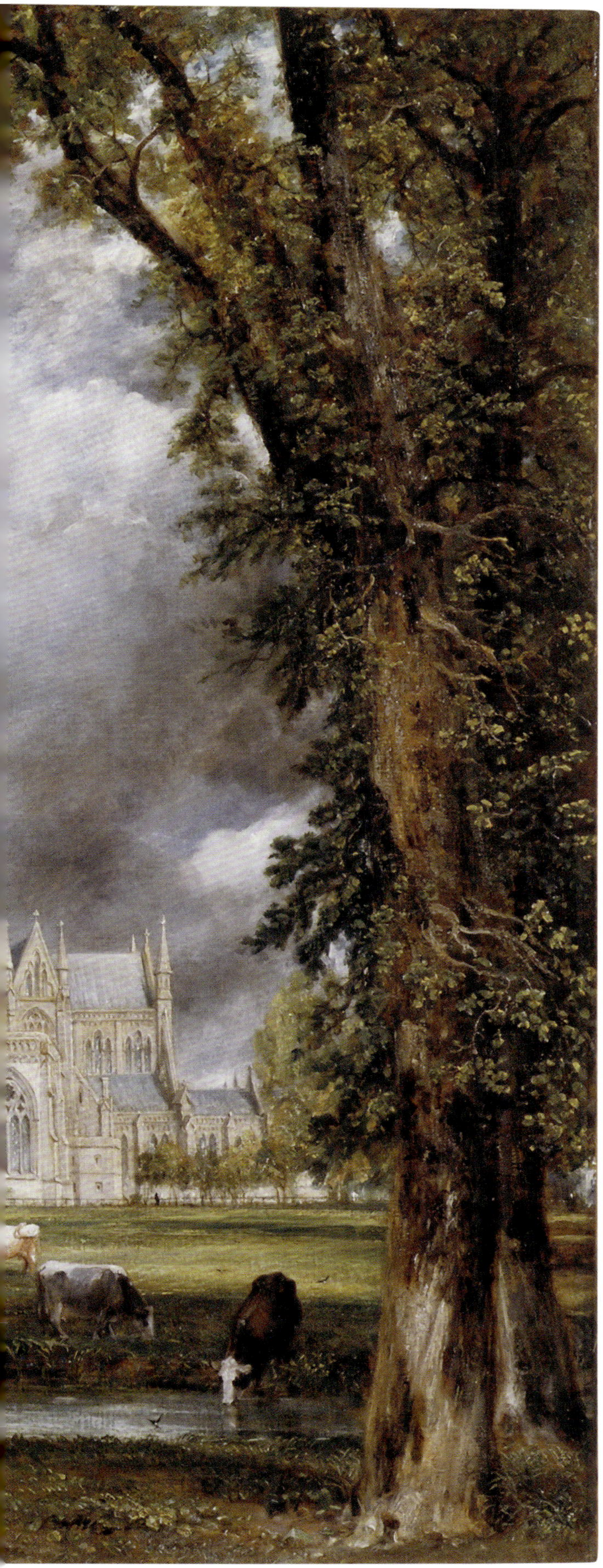

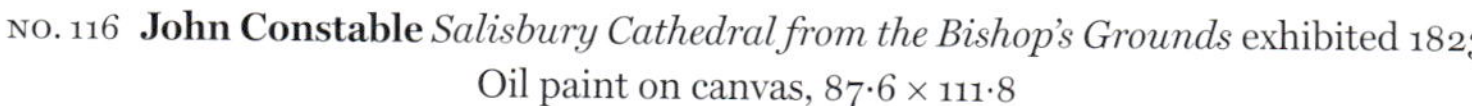

NO. 116 **John Constable** *Salisbury Cathedral from the Bishop's Grounds* exhibited 1823
Oil paint on canvas, 87·6 × 111·8
Victoria and Albert Museum, London. Given by John Sheepshanks, 1857

As flattering as it was to have been commissioned by the Bishop of Salisbury to paint this work, it presented Constable with a series of challenges. He told his friend John Fisher, the Bishop's nephew, that he had been 'dreading' working on it and that it was 'the most difficult subject...[he] had ever had upon [his] easil' (Beckett, VI, p.115). Upon receipt of the finished work, the bishop (who appears at lower left with his wife) expressed his distaste at its dark clouds, prompting Constable to paint a sunnier version (Huntington Collection, San Marino). This attests to the void that had begun to open up between Constable's personal vision for an expressive, animated landscape, and the expectations of his patron.

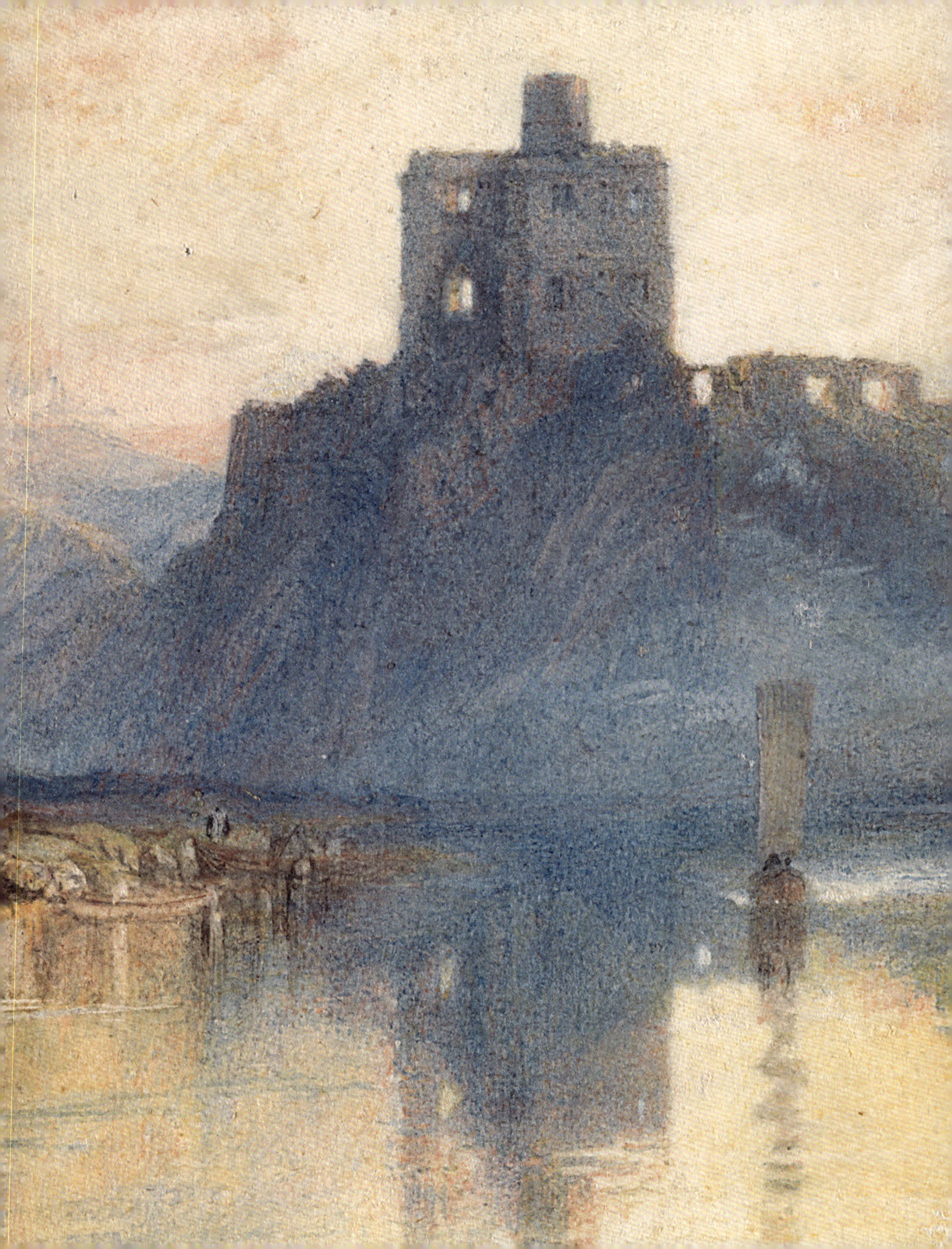

MAGIC ARRANGEMENTS: TURNER'S WATERCOLOURS

Watercolour is a vital part of Turner's story. From the moment he received a set of watercolours as a boy this medium remained a key element of his artistic practice. His early exhibited watercolours were the works that first alerted critics to his outstanding talent; references to the 'magic' of his mature watercolours were frequent. Combining innovative handling of the medium and cerebral subject matter, Turner secured the medium's elevation in status to one that was worthy for use by ambitious professional artists.

An onlooker afforded a rare glimpse of Turner at work described how he 'poured wet paint', then 'tore ... scratched ... scrubbed at [the paper] in a kind of frenzy' until, 'as if by magic', a watercolour came into focus.[1] While Turner could of course speedily dash off images with flair, the watercolours included in this section attest to a more protracted and meticulous process, though the results are no less spectacular. *Stangate Creek, on the River Medway* (no.120), for example, appears to reverberate with luminosity, an effect achieved by the painstaking application of pigment through fine dots and hatching, using a very fine brush made of just a single squirrel hair. *Norham Castle, on the River Tweed* (no.118), a subject the artist returned to repeatedly throughout his career (see pp.221–2), is thought to be one of the first works in which Turner applied colour prismatically, by superimposing different combinations of primary colours – red, yellow and blue – to make the secondary colours, orange, purple and green. Reflecting Turner's constant research into colour and light, this approach may have been informed by the theories of Scottish physicist Sir David Brewster (1781–1868), who Turner met during an 1818 trip to Edinburgh.[2]

In Turner's eyes, these finely wrought watercolours were waypoints in a process. Like most of the watercolours in this section, *Stangate Creek* and *Norham Castle* were painted to be reproduced as prints. When it came to their display, however, Turner's apparent preference was for watercolours to be close-framed in gilt surrounds, just like oil paintings.

While there were detractors, those who found his watercolours 'experimental and gaudy flimsies', there was a general astonishment and curiosity about Turner's techniques, particularly his way with colour.[3] 'No man has ever thrown such masses of colour upon paper', wrote one critic, while another mused, 'blended and sometimes delicately contrasted as [Turner's] colours are – the effects are exquisitely tender, but not without sufficient force, from a certain magic arrangement, a graphic secret of his own'.[4]

J.M.W. Turner *Norham Castle, on the River Tweed* (detail) c.1822–3 (p.148)

NO. 117 **J.M.W. Turner** *Crook of Lune, looking towards Hornby Castle* c.1816–18
Graphite, watercolour, bodycolour with scraping on wove paper, laid down on Japanese tissue, 29·1 × 42·8
The Courtauld, London (Samuel Courtauld Trust)

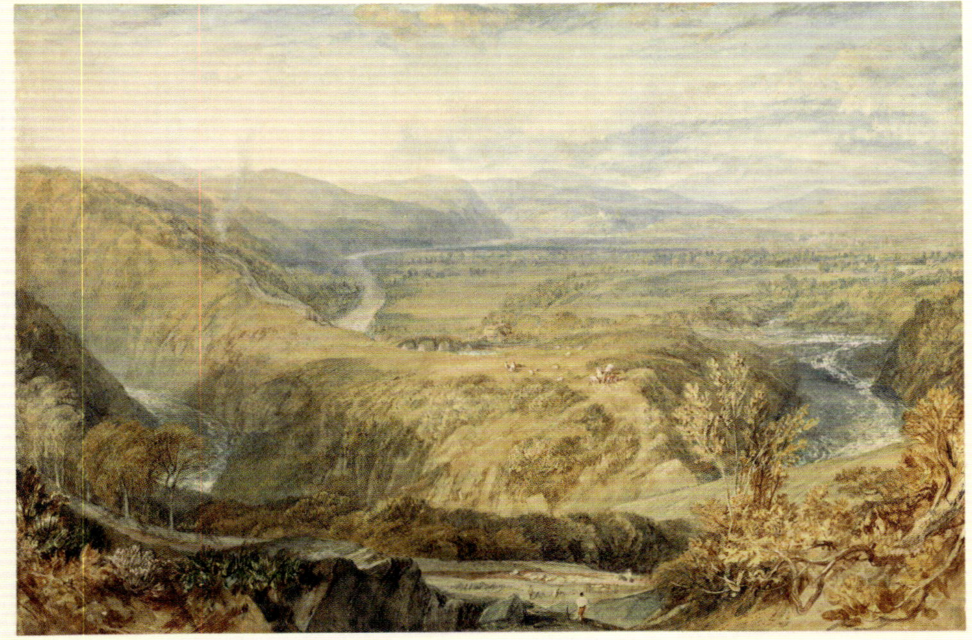

The wealth of detail in this watercolour, intended for reproduction as a print, demonstrates why Turner was so much in demand by publishers. The view overlooks the dramatic meander bend or 'crook' in the River Lune valley, four miles from Lancaster. Turner uses subtle gradations in tone to show the hills receding into the distance and amplifies the drama of the scene by steepening the river's banks. As well as the majesty of the natural landscape Turner shows us signs of human activity: Hornby Castle is a spec of white in the background, a fire smokes on the hillside to the left, while a brickworks in the centre and the quarry in the foreground (where a man holds a pick axe) tell of the extractive industries important to this area's economy. Turner worked all of this up from pencil sketches he made on his visit to the area in 1816.

NO. 118 **J.M.W. Turner** *Norham Castle, on the River Tweed* for *Rivers of England* c.1822–3
Watercolour on paper, 15·6 × 21·6
Tate. Accepted by the nation as part of the Turner Bequest 1856

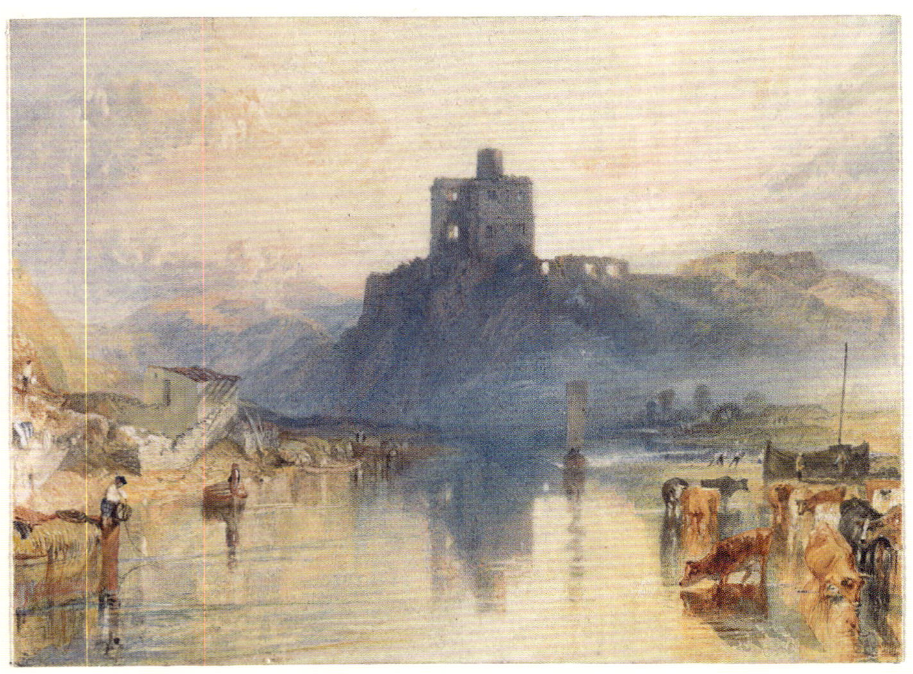

NO. 119 **J.M.W. Turner** *Folkestone from the Sea* c.1822–4
Watercolour and gouache on paper, 48·8 × 68·4
Tate. Accepted by the nation as part of the Turner Bequest 1856

It is not known why Turner stopped short of finishing this large, elaborate watercolour. One suggestion is that its subject – smuggling – might have been too contentious.

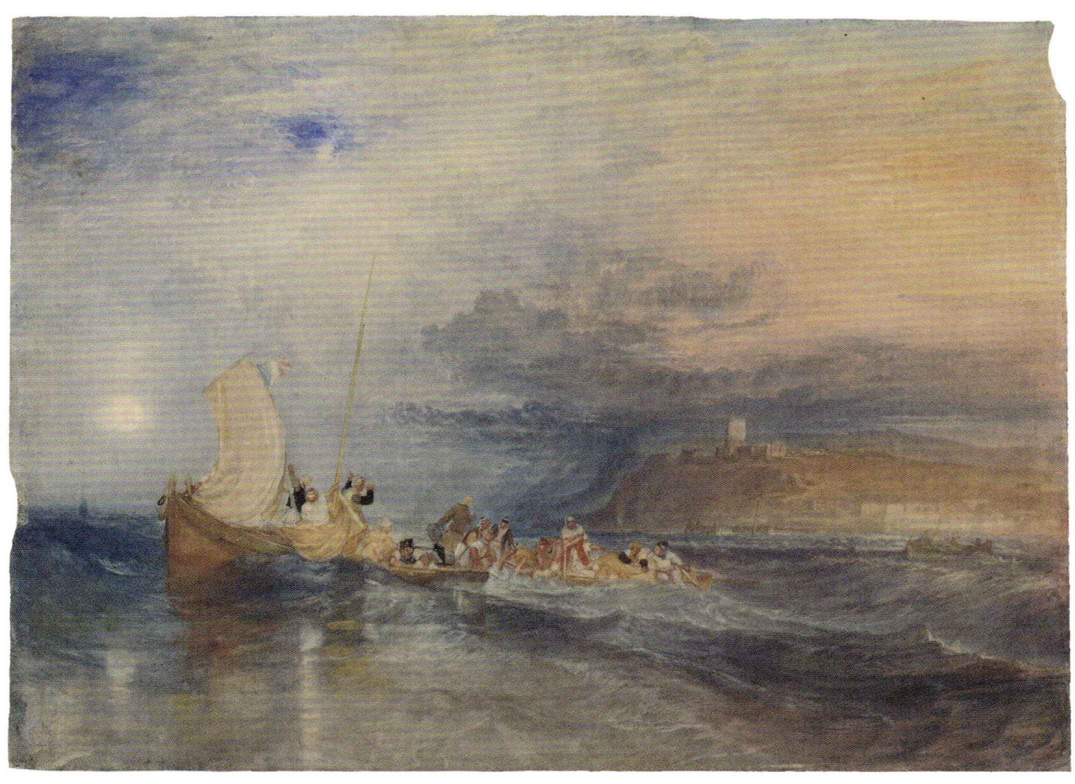

NO. 120 **J.M.W. Turner** *Stangate Creek, on the River Medway* for *Rivers of England* c.1823–4
Watercolour on paper, 16·2 × 24
Tate. Accepted by the nation as part of the Turner Bequest 1856

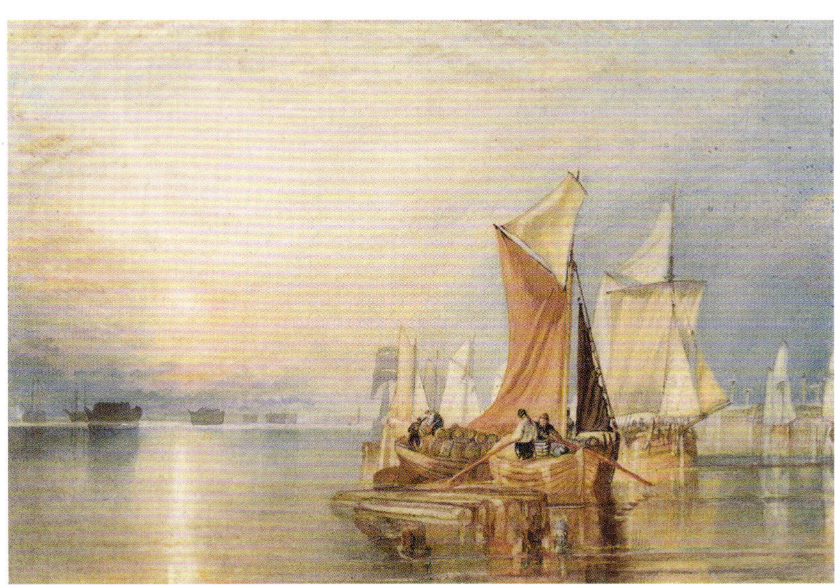

NO. 121 **J.M.W. Turner** *Brighthelmston, Sussex* for *Picturesque Views on the Southern Coast of England* c.1824
Pencil, pen and black ink and watercolour with scratching out on paper, 14·6 × 22·2
Brighton & Hove Museums

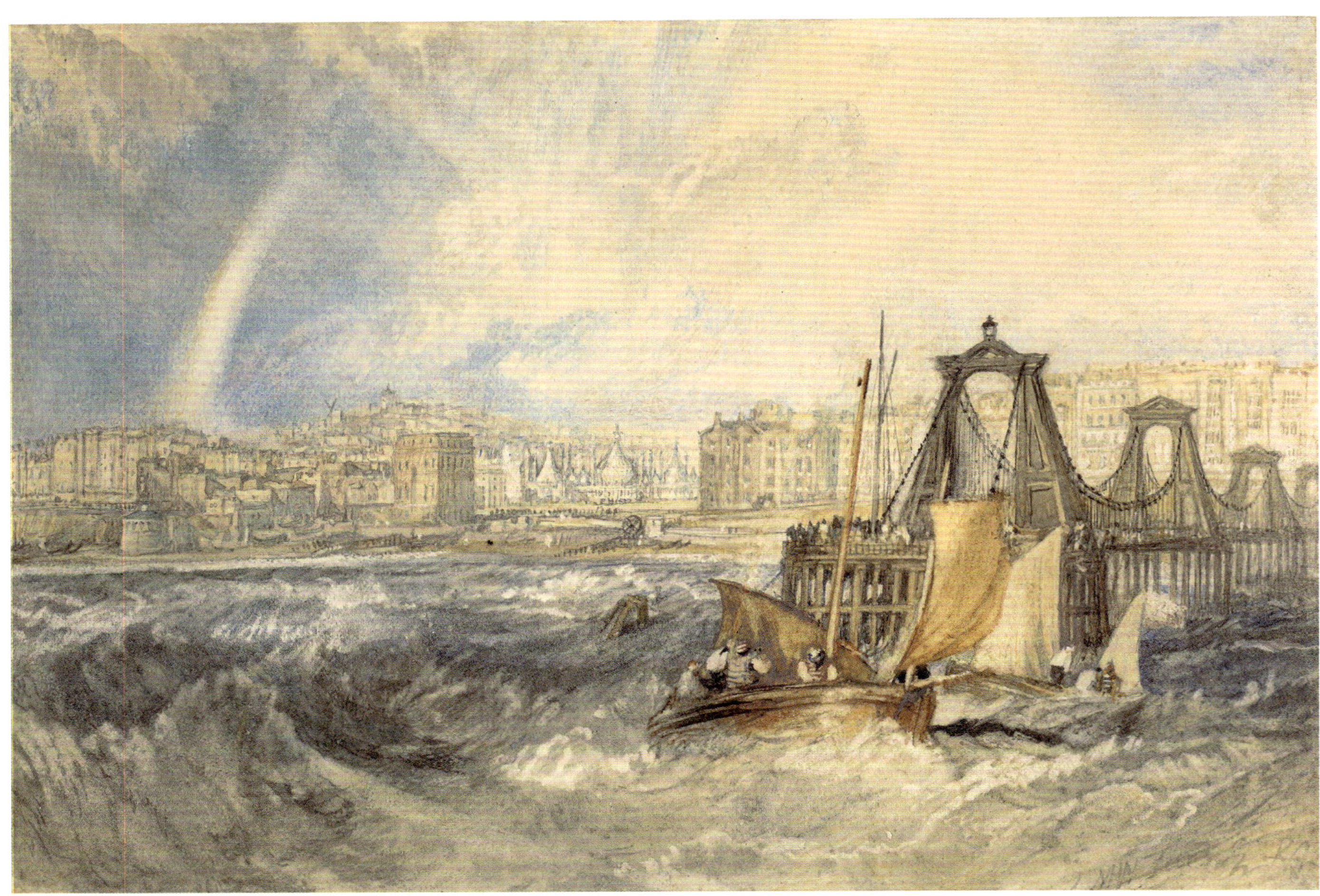

This dynamic image perfectly encapsulates the spirit of its subject. Brighthelmston (or Brighton, as it increasingly came to be known in this period), was a famously exciting place where old met new, and where high society holidayed in the hope of glimpsing the Prince Regent. Flouting topographical accuracy, Turner accords a central position to the Prince Regent's palace, recognisable from its onion domes. On the right we see the newly opened Chain Pier, a new symbol of Brighton's fashionable image. This engineering 'wonder' with neo-Egyptian architecture was built to dock the cross-Channel steamboat. Its customary crowds can be seen towards the end of the pier. Traditional boats are tossed around on the waves, as if close to colliding with the Chain Pier – perhaps a sign that while the contrast between old and new here could be aesthetically exhilarating it might also bring about social discord between the town's longstanding inhabitants and its seasonal visitors. The year Turner made this watercolour Constable was also in Brighton (see p.39).

NO. 122 **J.M.W. Turner** *Colchester, Essex* for *Picturesque Views in England and Wales* 1825–6
Graphite, watercolour, bodycolour, scraping on wove paper, now laid down on Japanese tissue, 28·7 × 40·7
The Courtauld, London (Samuel Courtauld Trust)

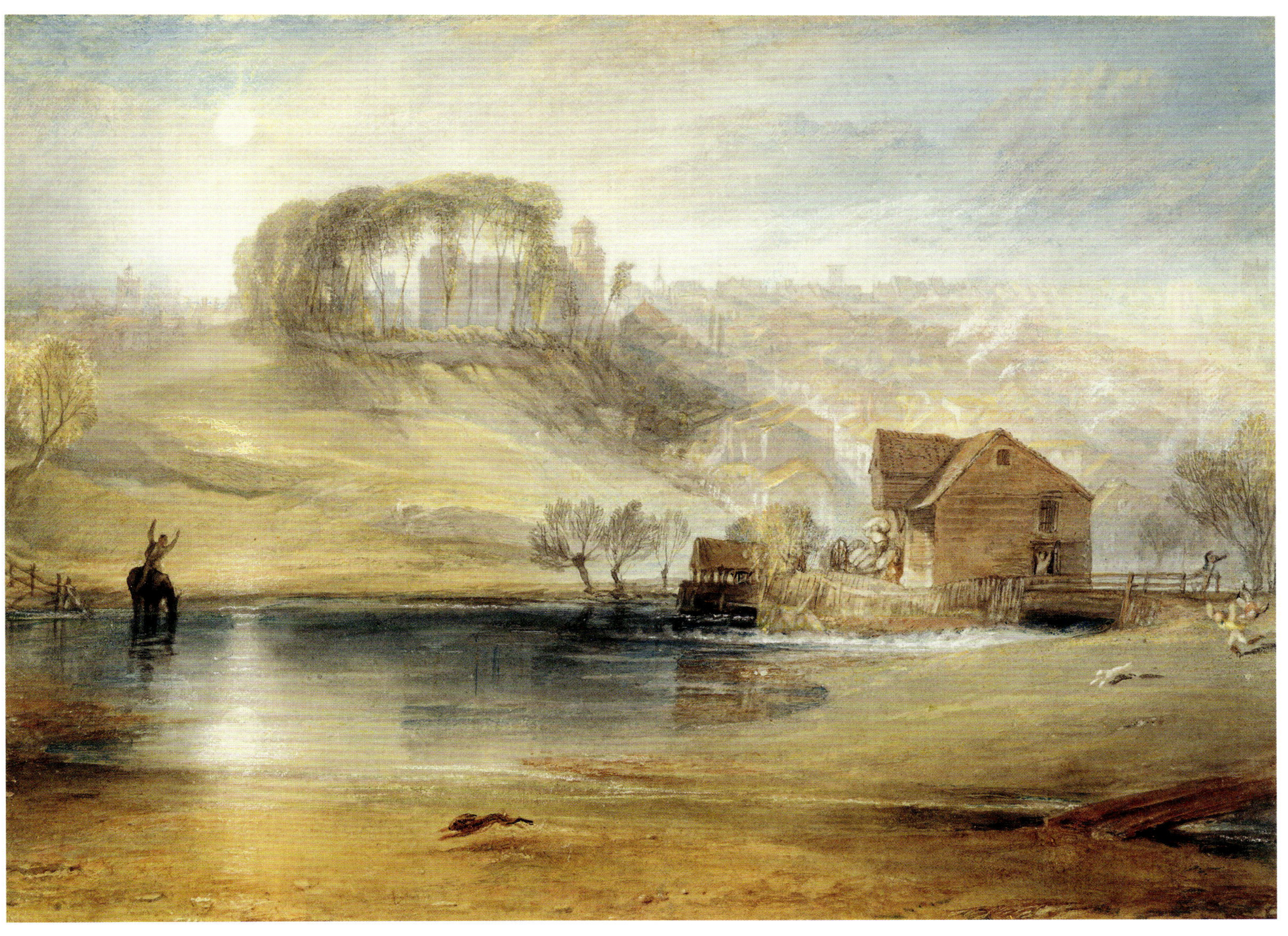

Exhilarating in atmosphere, composition and narrative, this is one of the finest watercolours Turner made for the print project, *Picturesque Views in England and Wales*, published between 1827 and 1838. A hare dashes across the foreground pursued by a white dog and three men, one of whom takes a tumble in the commotion. The figure on horseback appears to help scare away the hare. Turner's allusion here is to the notoriously punitive witch trials that took place in Essex in the 1600s – according to Nordic and British folklore witches could turn themselves into hares. It was in Essex that Elizabeth Lowys became the first person in Britain to be executed under a Witchcraft Act. She was imprisoned in Colchester Castle, which is glimpsed behind the clump of trees. Golden sunlight casts an appropriately mystical quality over the scene, its dominant yellow hue boldly cut through by the deep blue of the water. Despite its quality (Turner famously ensured his engravers met his high standards), *Picturesque Views* was a commercial failure, a victim of saturation in the landscape print market and competition from new, more cost-effective reproductive processes like steel engraving.

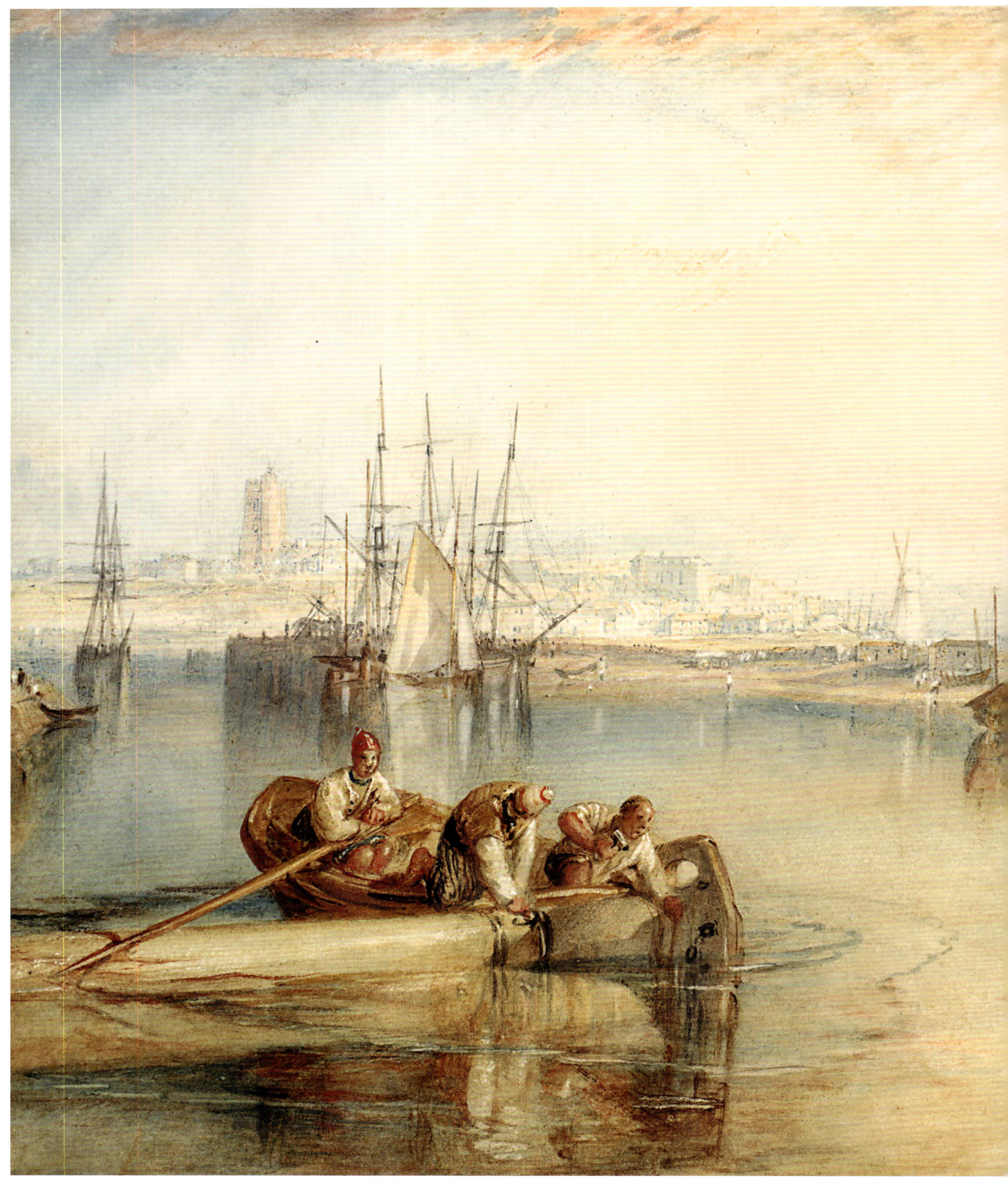

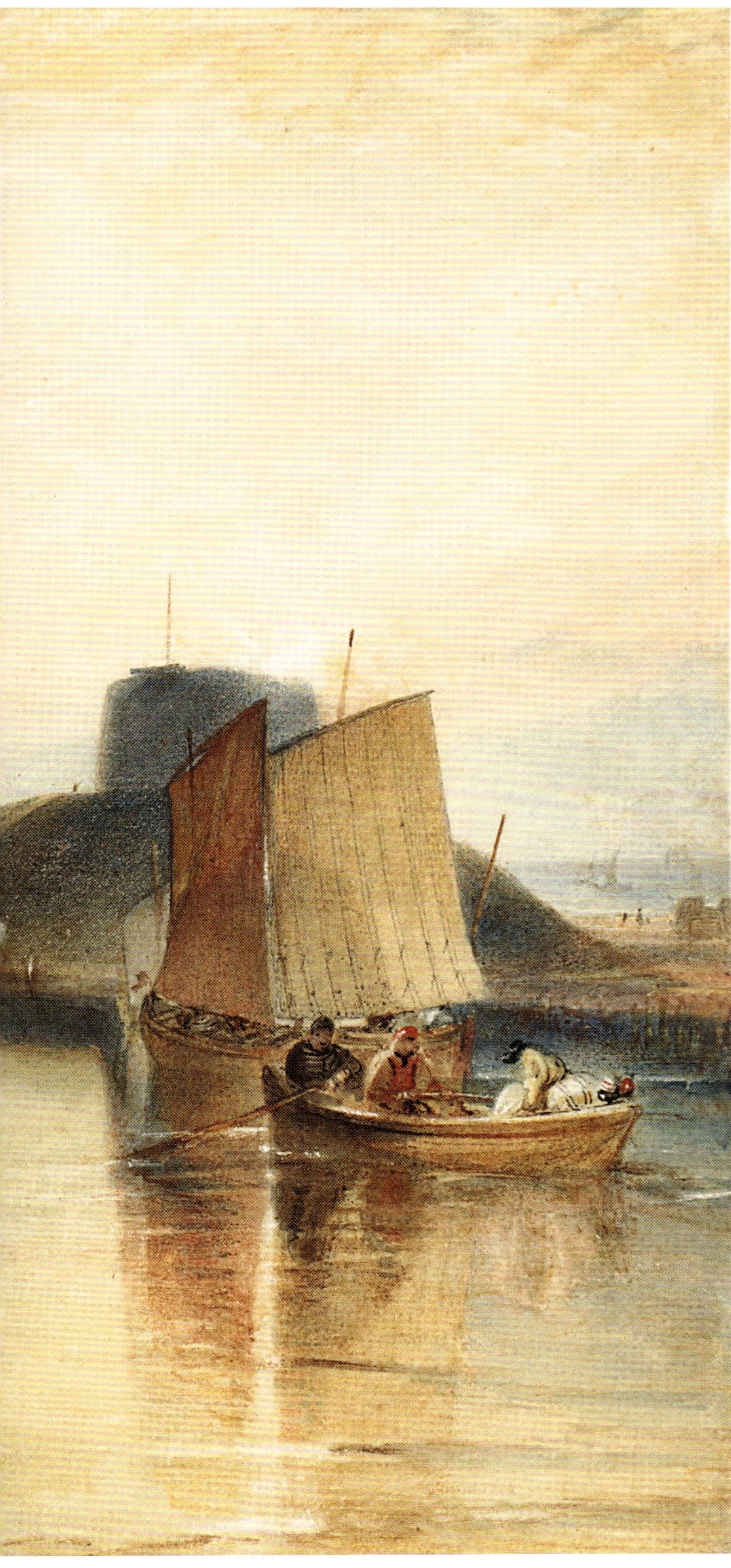

NO. 123 **J.M.W. Turner** *Aldborough, Suffolk* for *Picturesque Views in England and Wales* c.1826
Watercolour and gouache on paper, 28·3 × 40
Tate. Bequeathed by Beresford Rimington Heaton 1940

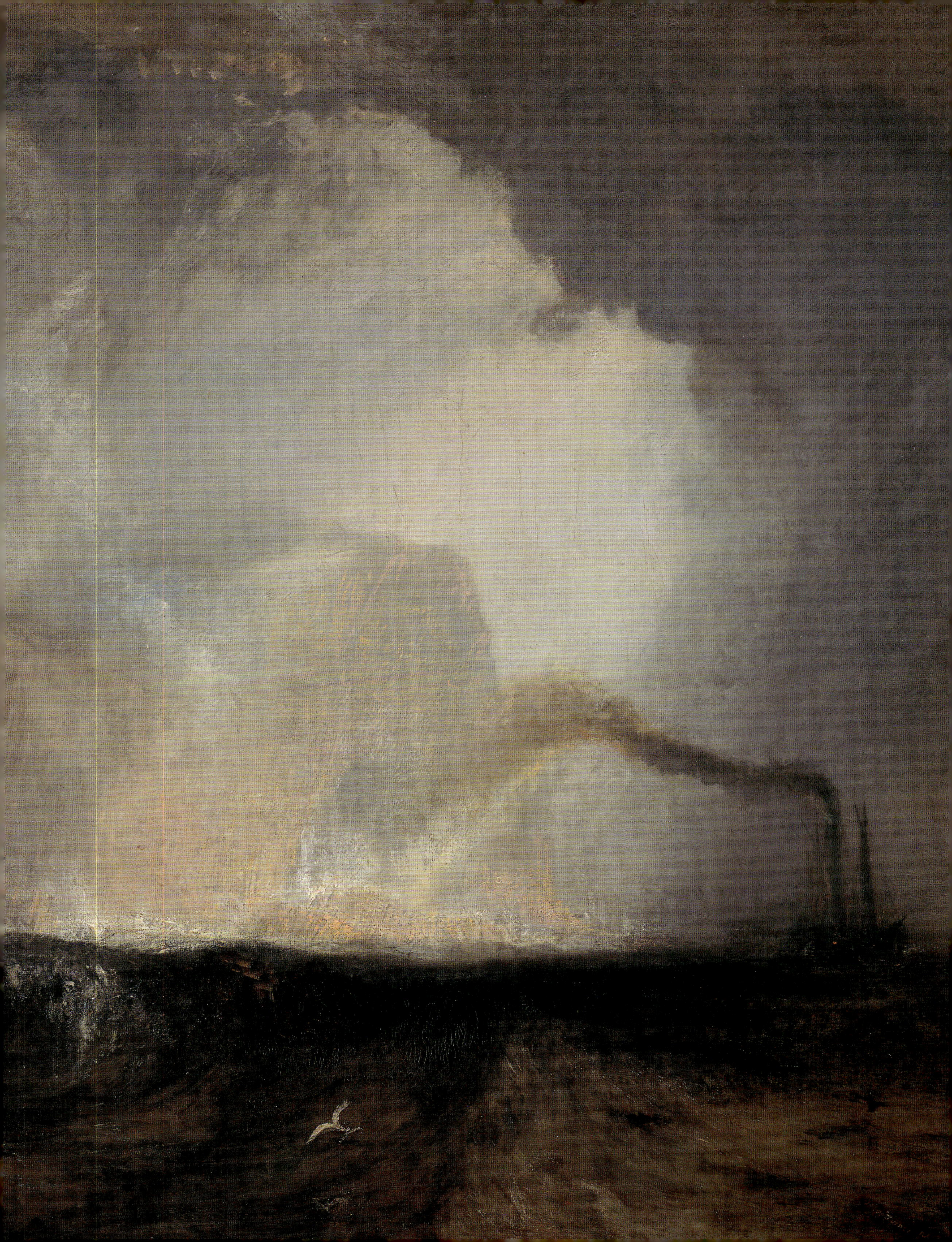

'FIRE AND WATER': THE ROYAL ACADEMY EXHIBITION

The Royal Academy's Annual Exhibition (forerunner of today's Summer Exhibition) was the stage on which the drama of artist rivalries and the making and breaking of reputations was set. Not only were its walls crammed with pictures of every genre hanging frame to frame, but the space itself was crowded with fashionable society who came to see but also to be seen. The exhibition was a mass shop window for exhibiting artists, their challenge being to find ways for their work to stand out from the crowd. In a lecture that Turner and Constable no doubt attended, the painter John Opie bemoaned that when it came to making works for exhibition in these conditions: 'He that talks loudest, not he that talks best, is surest of commanding attention.'[1]

At nearly two metres across, *The Fifth Plague of Egypt* (no.124) shows that Turner soon learned ways to command attention. Even bigger was *Dido Building Carthage: or the Rise of the Carthaginian Empire* (no.125). His eye-catching canvases were divisive, however. *Dido Building Carthage* was seen as 'transcendent' by one critic. More indicative of future alarm at Turner's growing predilection for intense colour was the judgement by Sir George Beaumont, Constable's mentor, of this work's colouring as 'violent' and 'not true to nature'.[2] Constable himself could appreciate the allure of Turner's work. Writing of the Royal Academy exhibition in 1828, he reported that: 'Turner has some golden visions – glorious and beautifull, but they are only visions – yet still they are art – & one could live with *such* pictures in the house.'[3]

Alongside demonstrations of his imaginative prowess in the realm of ancient history, Turner proved his credentials as a painter of contemporary life in works like *Staffa, Fingal's Cave*, the first of his major paintings to depict steam technology. Frequently controversial but always innovative, Turner's works rarely failed to get tongues wagging. In the 1810s, however, Constable was struggling to get noticed. Feedback that his paintings did not 'solicit attention' led to an important development, the making of large-scale paintings known as six-footers.[4] Scaling up paid off. The exhibition of *The White Horse* (no.127) saw him compared to Turner for the first time (as having 'none of the poetry of Nature like Mr Turner, but ... more of her portraiture').[5] The painting also led to his election as an Associate Member of the Royal Academy.

Both artists were affected by the politics of the exhibition. Turner quibbled over the placement of his work (see no.80), and only three of Constable's six large River Stour scenes made the Great Room, the Royal Academy's most prestigious space.[6] In 1830, a year after Constable had at last been made a full Academician, *Watermeadows at Salisbury* (no.133) was accidentally assessed by the exhibition's committee. They 'condemned' it as 'a poor thing', 'very green'.[7] Constable himself was a member of the committee that year and, perhaps out of embarrassment, had stayed quiet rather than defend his right as an Academician to have all his works shown.

It was said that artists hated being hung next to Turner, a fate 'as bad as being hung by an open window' because his paintings 'caught your eye the instant you entered the room'.[8] In 1831 Constable ran the gauntlet and hung his *Salisbury Cathedral from the Meadows* next to Turner's *Caligula's Palace and Bridge*, a juxtaposition labelled 'fire and water' by the critics (see pp.15–21). The following year one critic joked that Turner's work had been placed opposite Constable's to 'prevent the room from becoming damp'.[9] This was the year that Turner, who notoriously used the so-called Varnishing Days to alter his paintings in competition with others, modified *Helvoetsluys* (fig.41, p.187) with a red daub in response to Constable's *The Opening of Waterloo Bridge* (no.150). This act appeared to seal their rivalry when Constable retorted: '[Turner] has been here and fired a gun.'[10]

It is worth emphasising that London was not the only place to see Turner and Constable's work in their lifetimes. Collectors showed their works in exhibitions in Manchester and Birmingham, while Constable himself showed his *Salisbury Cathedral from the Meadows*, for example, in Birmingham (where he had regularly submitted work) and Worcester.[11] Internationally, Constable exhibited to great acclaim in Paris and Lille in the 1820s; Turner, meanwhile, gained little but notoriety when he showed a painting in Munich in 1843.[12]

J.M.W. Turner *Staffa, Fingal's Cave* (detail) exhibited 1832 (p.174)

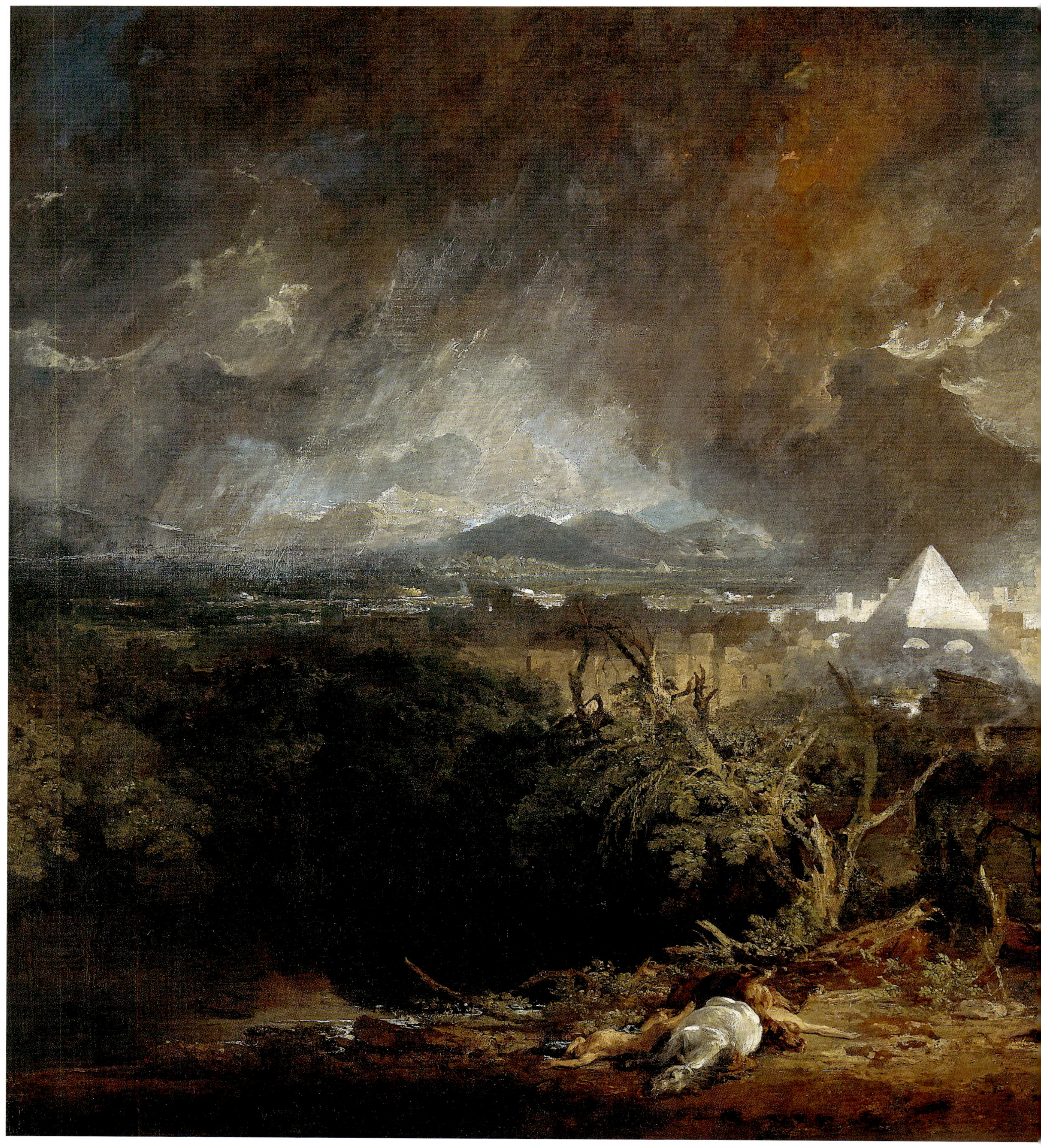

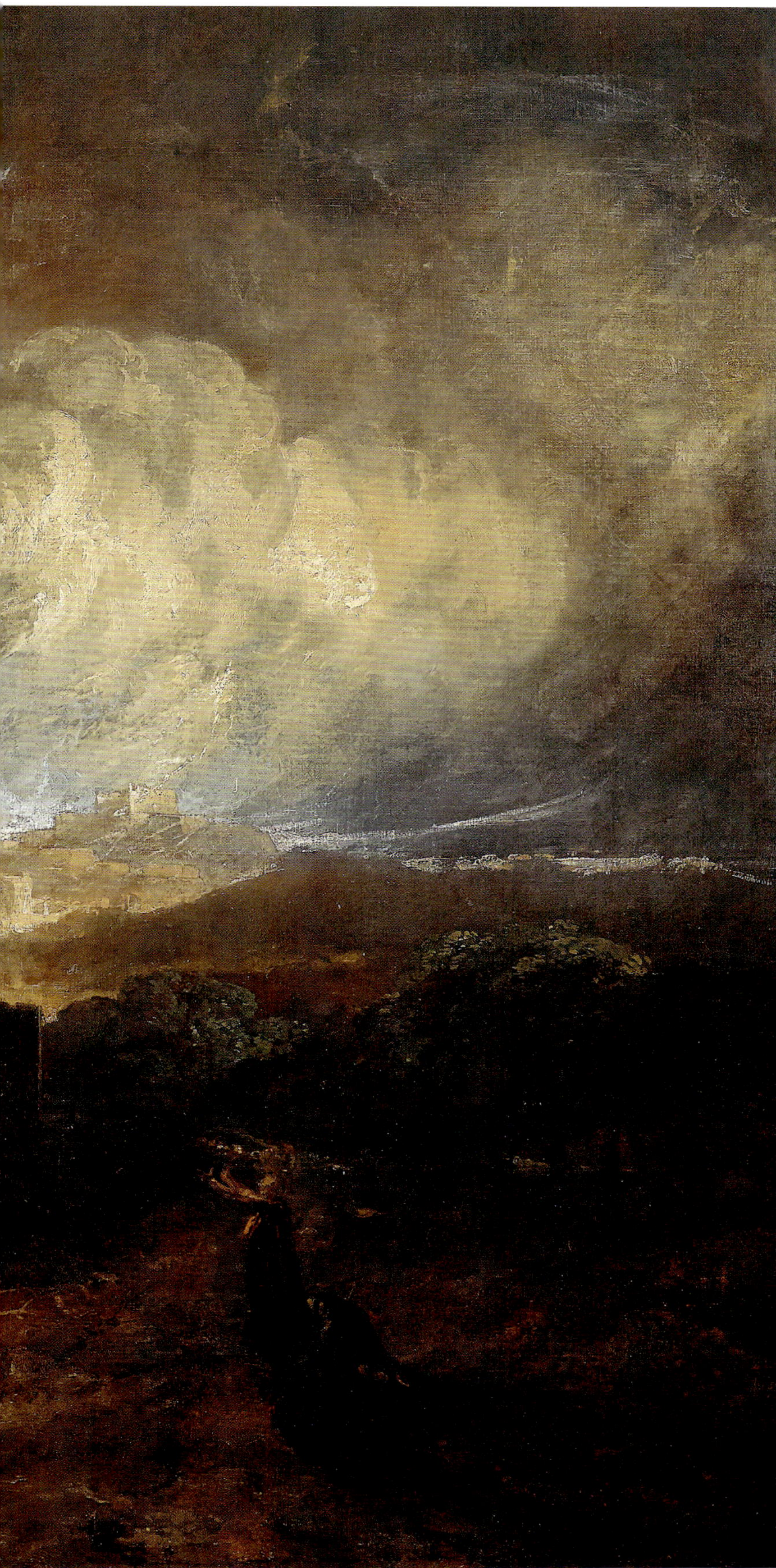

NO. 124 **J.M.W. Turner** *The Fifth Plague of Egypt* 1800
Oil paint on canvas, 121·9 × 182·8
Indianapolis Museum of Art at Newfields, Gift in memory of Evan F. Lilly, 55.24.

NO. 125 **J.M.W. Turner** *Dido building Carthage, or The Rise of the Carthaginian Empire* 1815
Oil paint on canvas, 155·5 × 230
The National Gallery, London. Turner Bequest, 1856

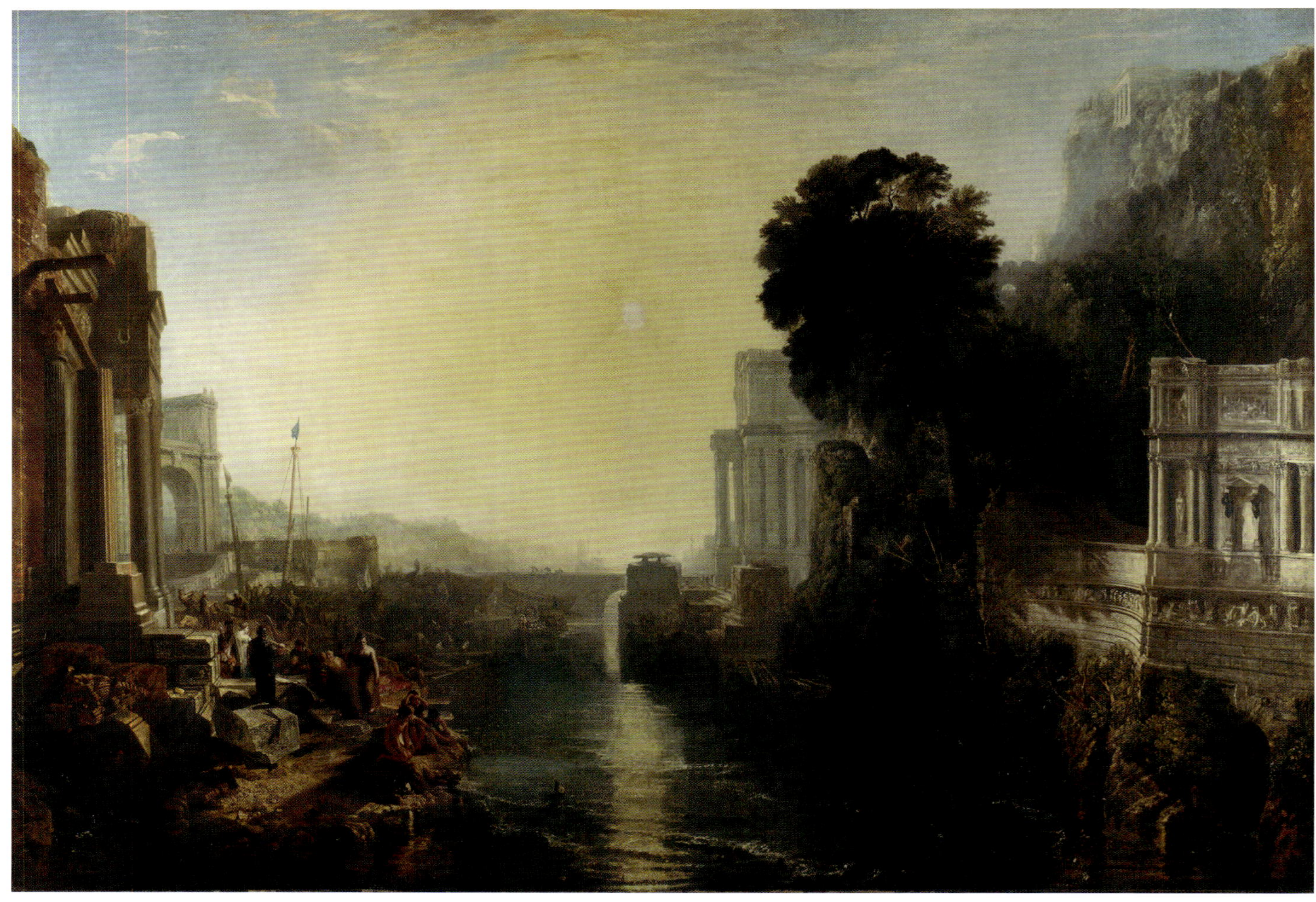

The classical subject matter of these paintings is discussed on pp.25–7 of this volume. Despite the timing of their exhibition (*Dido building Carthage* was shown just weeks before the Battle of Waterloo ended the Napoleonic Wars), critics made no comment about these paintings' contemporary relevance. Parallels were often drawn between warring factions Britain and France and ancient Rome and Carthage. Yet as much as Turner's statement on the rise and fall of Empire might be interpreted patriotically, as a rejoinder to defeated France, their theme was just as relevant to Britain. Indeed, Turner would go on to explore the human cost of war in paintings like *The Field of Waterloo* (Tate). The importance of this pair of paintings to Turner is signified by the first draft of his will, drawn up in 1829, in which he stated his wish was to see them hang alongside two paintings by Claude at the National Gallery. In the end, Turner swapped no.126 for *Sun Rising through Vapour* (National Gallery, London). Nevertheless, Turner was evidently keen to underline his reputation as the 'modern Claude' and claim a place for himself alongside his hero in the newly established National Gallery.

NO. 126 **J.M.W. Turner** *The Decline of the Carthaginian Empire* exhibited 1817
Oil paint on canvas, 170·2 × 238·8
Tate. Accepted by the nation as part of the Turner Bequest 1856

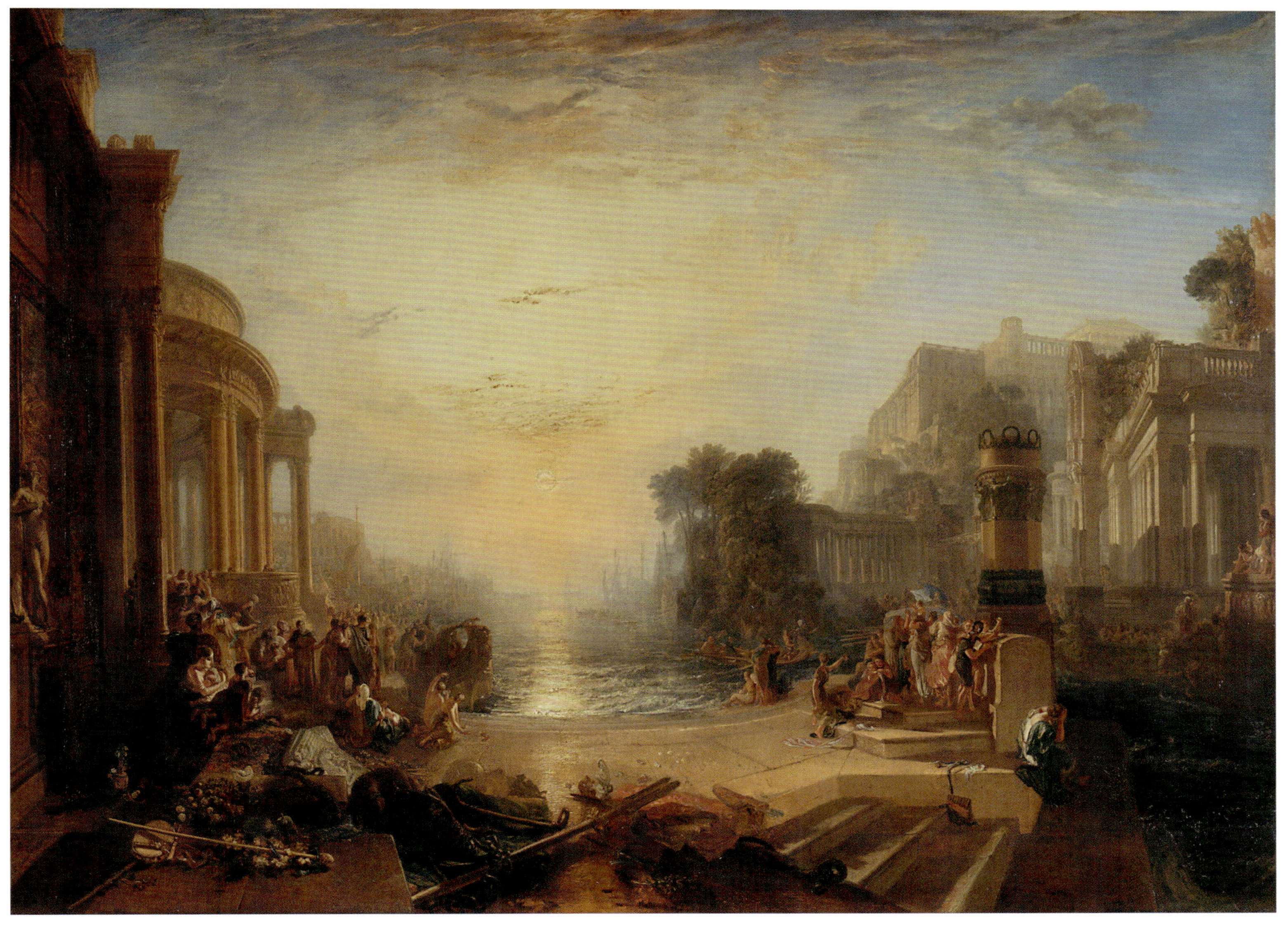

NO. 127 **John Constable** *The White Horse* exhibited 1819
Oil paint on canvas, 131·4 × 188·3
The Frick Collection, New York, Purchase, 1943

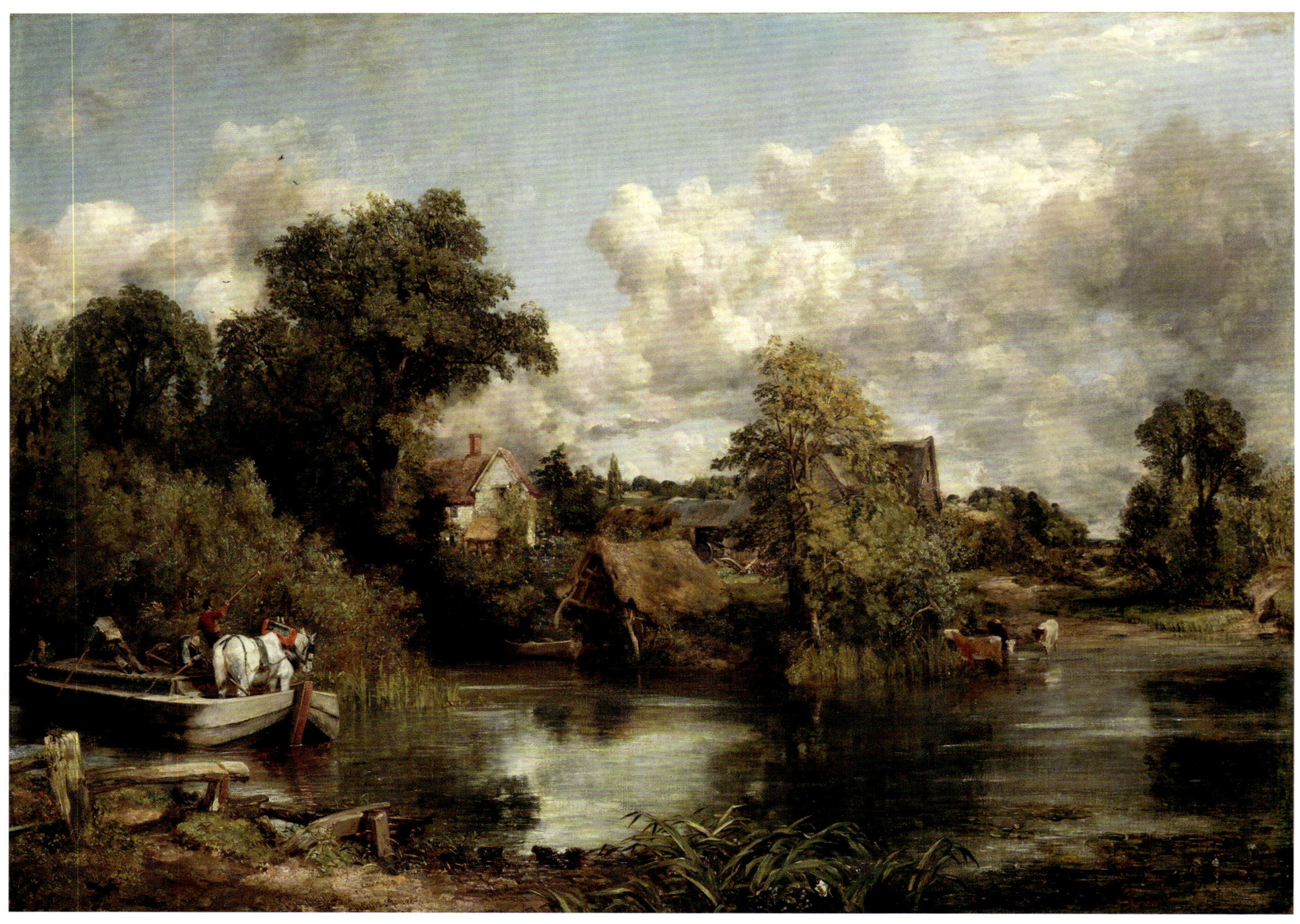

As the first painting on the grand 'six foot' scale that Constable had ever made, *The White Horse* represents a turning point in his career. This display of confidence and daring paid off and led to his election as an Associate Member of the Royal Academy (an accolade Turner had achieved some twenty years prior). Its making also marked a departure in Constable's process. It being impractical to paint a sketch of an equivalent large size outdoors, the full-size sketch for *The White Horse* (National Gallery of Art, Washington) was composed in the studio and based on an amalgamation of smaller sketches made at the scene. In 1894 the painting was exported to America after its acquisition by banker John Pierpont Morgan. See p.231 for painter Bridget Riley's recollection of seeing *The White Horse* in the Frick Collection on her first visit to New York in 1965.

NO. 128 **John Constable** *Stratford Mill* exhibited 1820
Oil paint on canvas, 127 × 182·9
The National Gallery, London. Presented to the National Gallery under the acceptance-in-lieu procedure, 1987

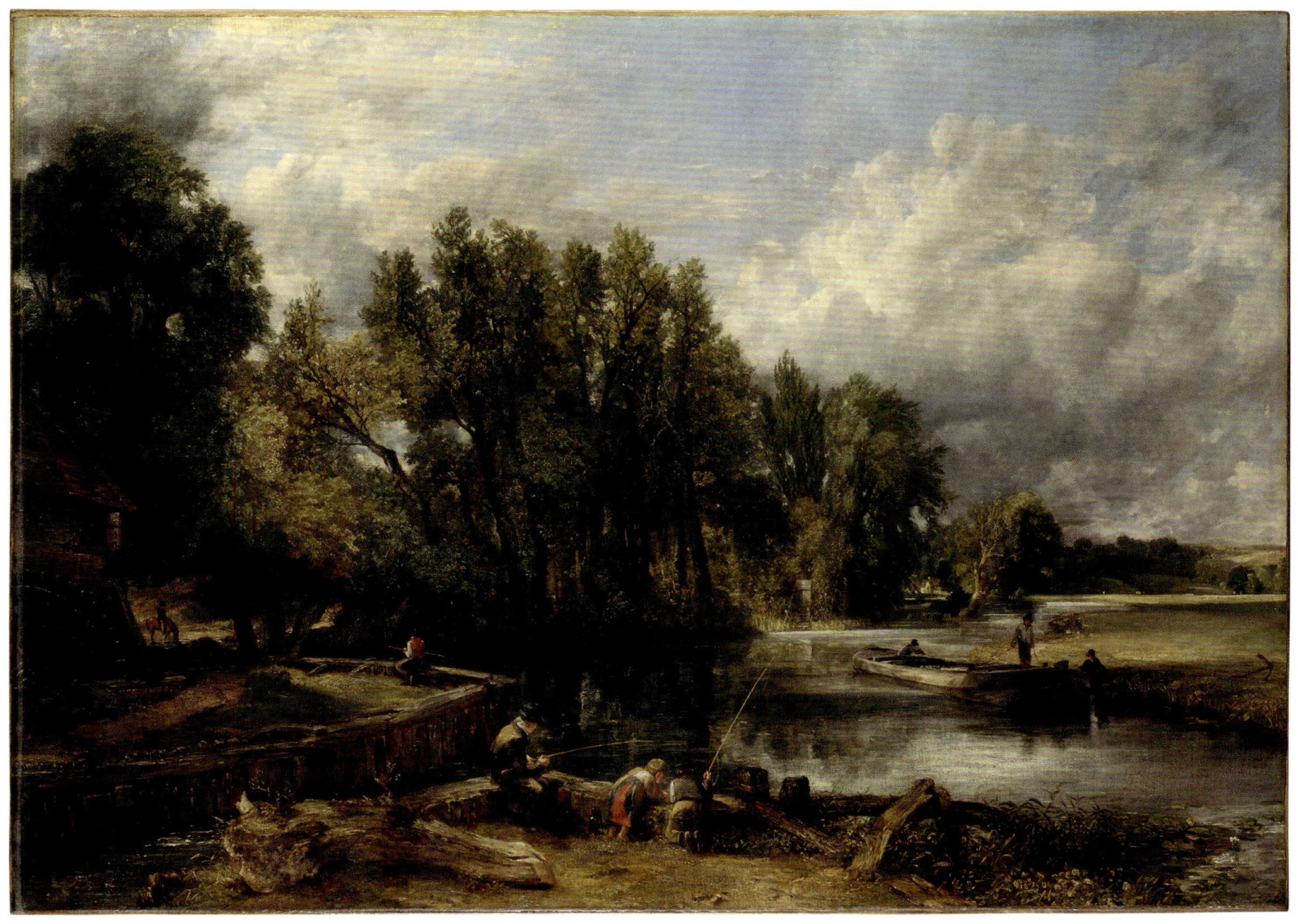

Constable was pleased with the art critics' reaction to this leisurely angling scene at Stratford Mill, a water-mill that powered a paper factory on the river Stour. Robert Hunt thought it had 'more exact look of nature than any picture we have seen by an Englishman' and that it was 'unequalled by very few of the boasted foreigners of former days, except in finishing' (*The Examiner*, 15 May 1820, p.316). Another wrote of its 'delicious freshness' (*The British Freeholder*, I, 1 July 1820, p.357). A year later, after the painting had sold, a less favourable reaction to the sky prompted Constable's statement on the importance of the sky as the "source of light' in nature' which 'governs everything', lamenting those who advised artists to consider the sky as a "White Sheet drawn behind the Objects" (Beckett, VI, pp.76–77).

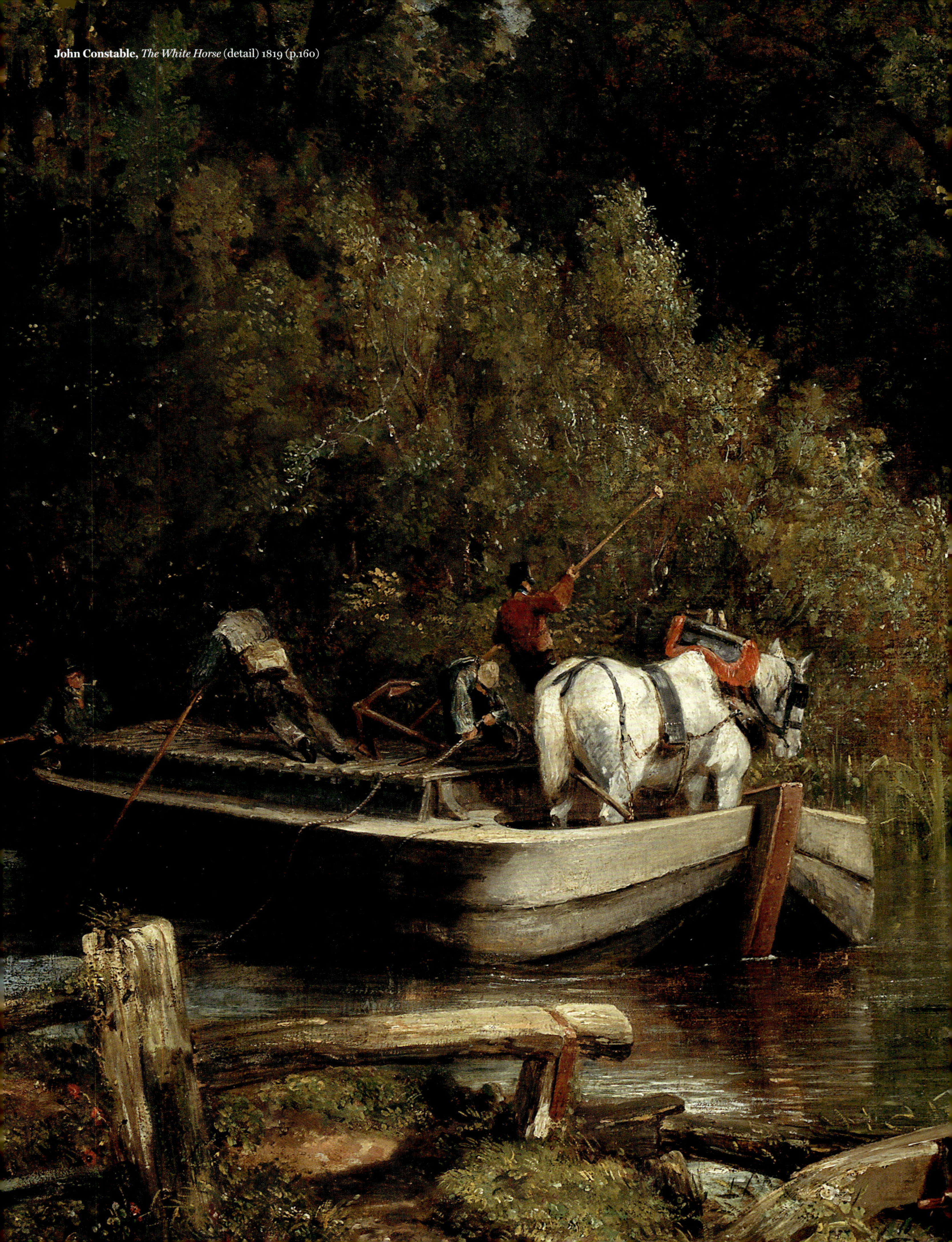

John Constable, *The White Horse* (detail) 1819 (p.160)

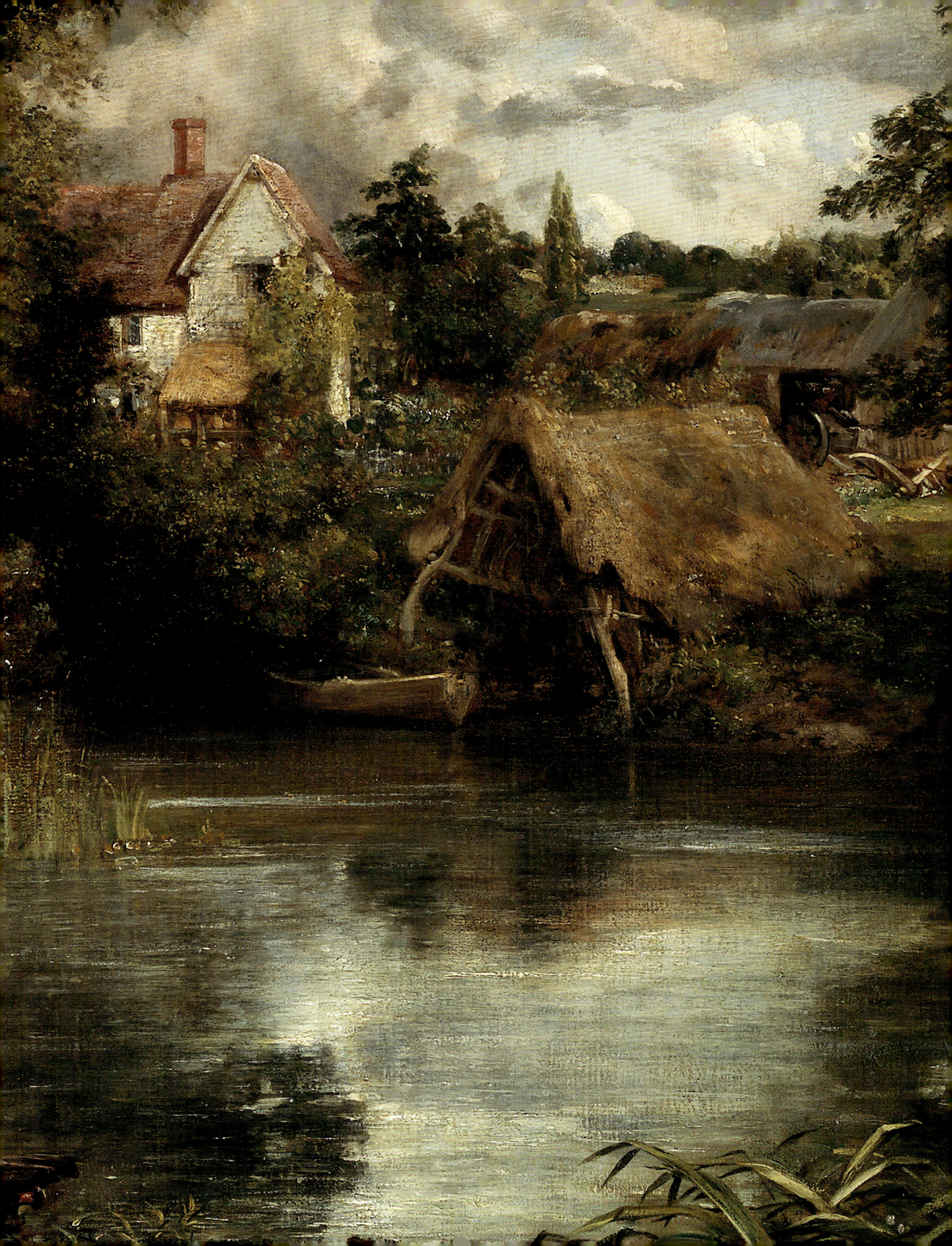

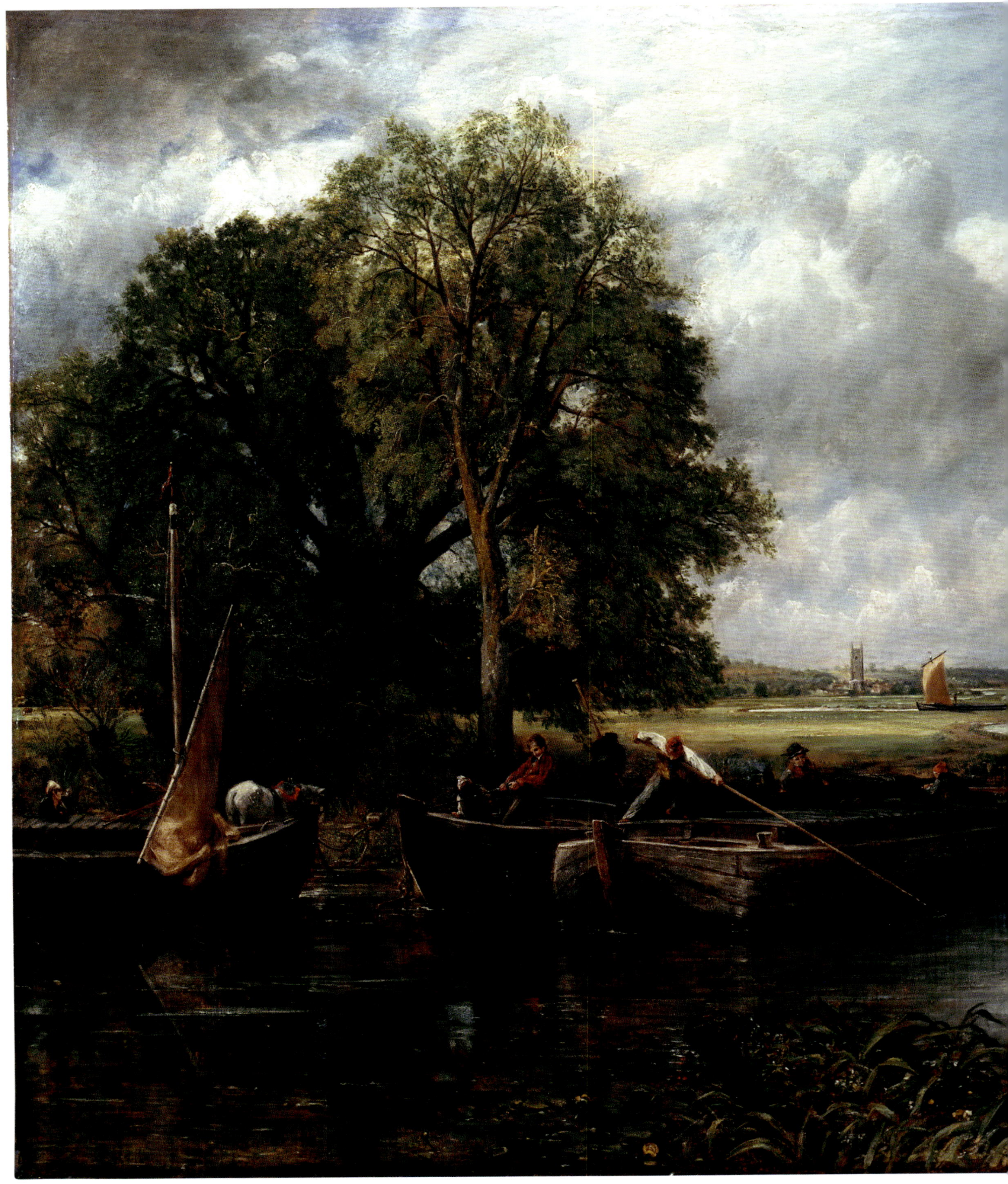

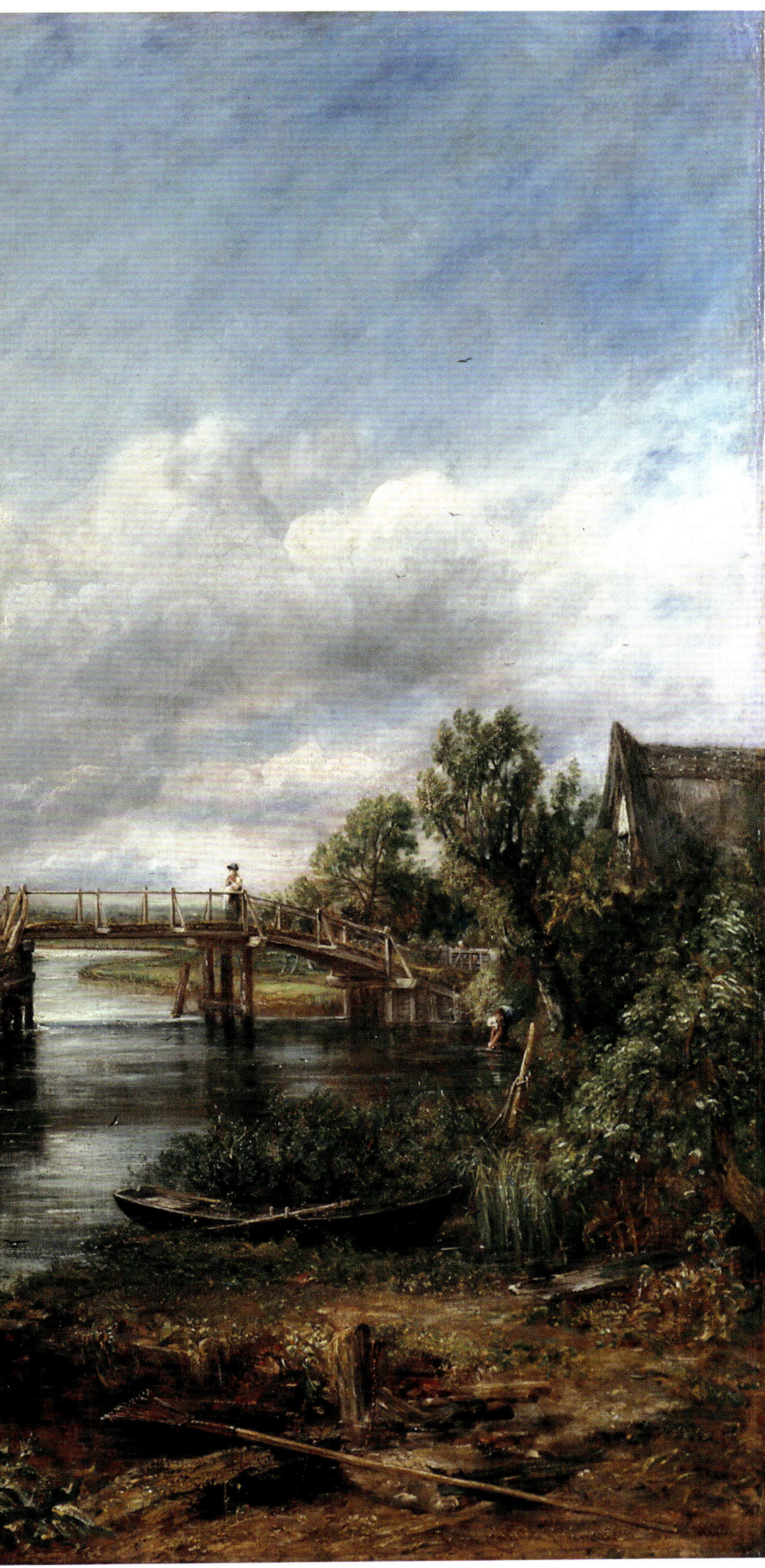

NO. 129 **John Constable** *View on the Stour near Dedham* exhibited 1822
Oil paint on canvas, 129·5 × 188
The Huntington Library, Art Collections, and Botanical Gardens

When Constable began painting his six-footers he and Maria were living with their young children in a rented house in Keppel Street, Bloomsbury. Although Constable had a painting room there, space was an issue and it appears that a window had to be taken out whenever one of his six-foot canvases had to leave the building (see Sarah Cove's research in Lyles, ed., *Great Landscapes*, p.55). In 1821 the family rented a home in Hampstead but Constable found the 'small shed in the garden' too small for painting six-footers and so rented a room at a glazier's shop in London (Beckett, VI, p.71). It was there that he worked on *View on the Stour near Dedham*. The physical distance between home and studio, however, caused him to worry that wherever he was he was either neglecting his family or this painting. In 1824 this work was exhibited with *The Hay Wain* at the Paris Salon, winning Constable the coveted gold medal there.

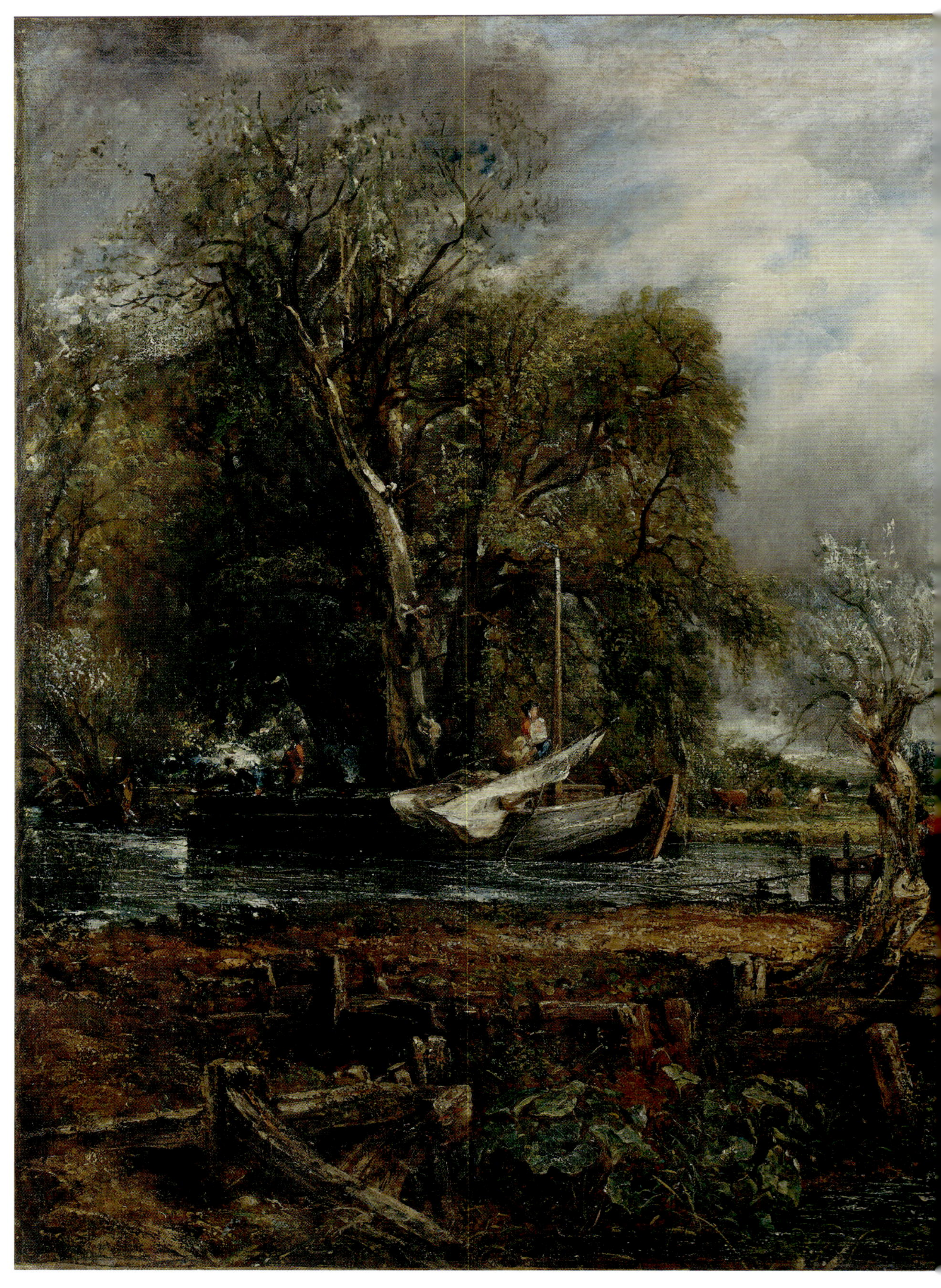

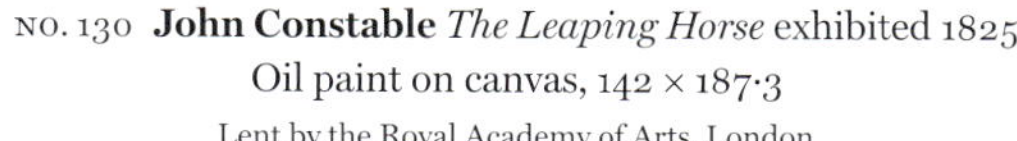

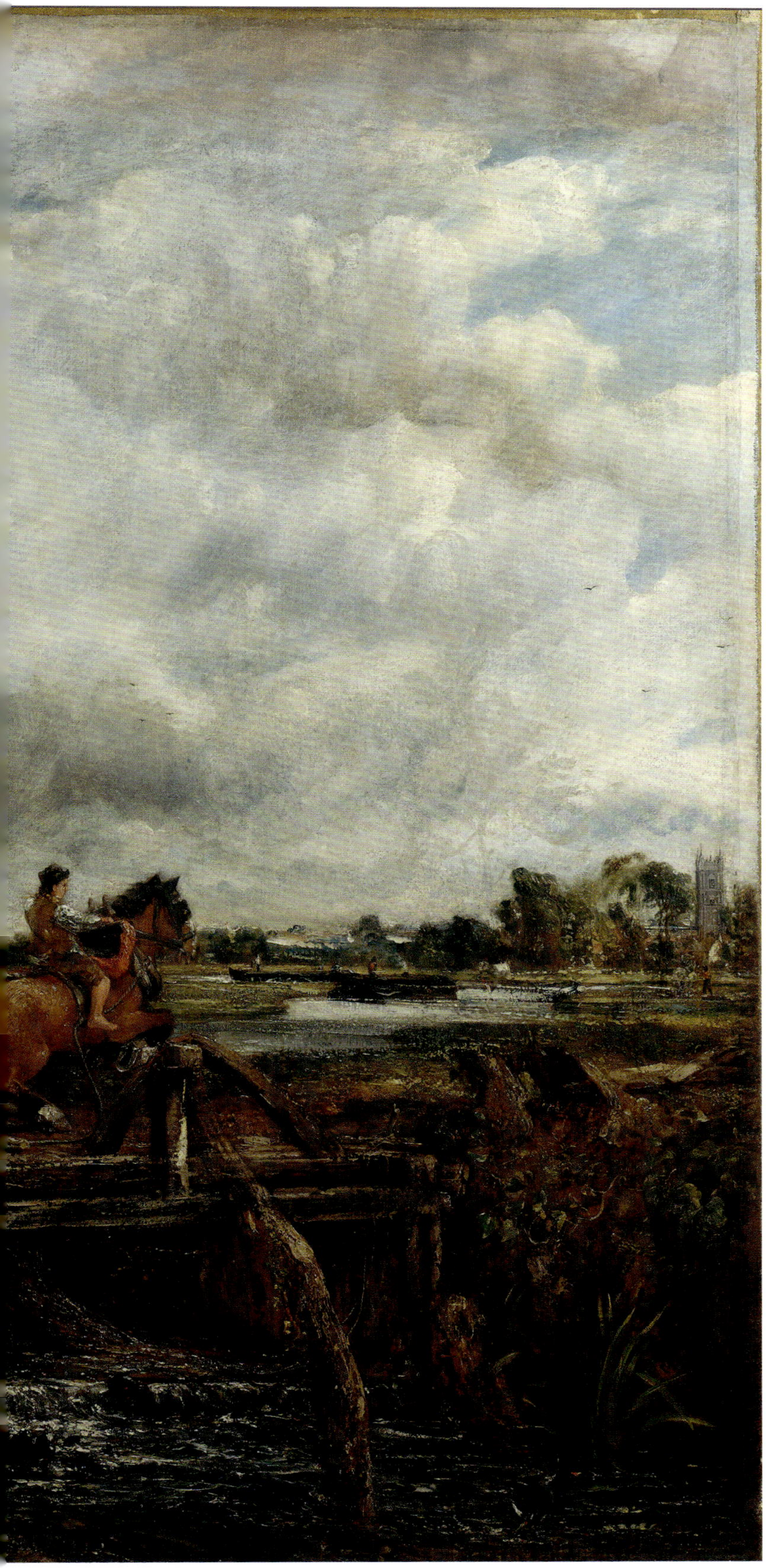

NO. 130 **John Constable** *The Leaping Horse* exhibited 1825
Oil paint on canvas, 142 × 187·3
Lent by the Royal Academy of Arts, London

This was the last in the sequence of large River Stour paintings that Constable exhibited between 1819 and 1825. It pictures what would have been a common but nonetheless impressive sight of one of the largest breeds of horse, a Suffolk Punch, leaping a barrier intended to stop cattle straying. The horse and its rider direct our attention to the spire of Dedham Church at the extreme right of the canvas. Thought to be the first instance of Constable deliberately distorting topography (a practice Turner had long been comfortable with), the church's inclusion underlines the importance of Christianity to Constable's world view. *The Leaping Horse* we see differs to that seen in 1825: not only did Constable modify the composition soon after exhibiting it but he also applied his paint differently, using larger brushes and a palette knife, foreshadowing the radical brushwork of paintings to follow.

NO. 131 **John Constable** *Sketch for 'Hadleigh Castle'* c.1828–9
Oil paint on canvas, 122·6 × 167·3
Tate. Purchased 1935

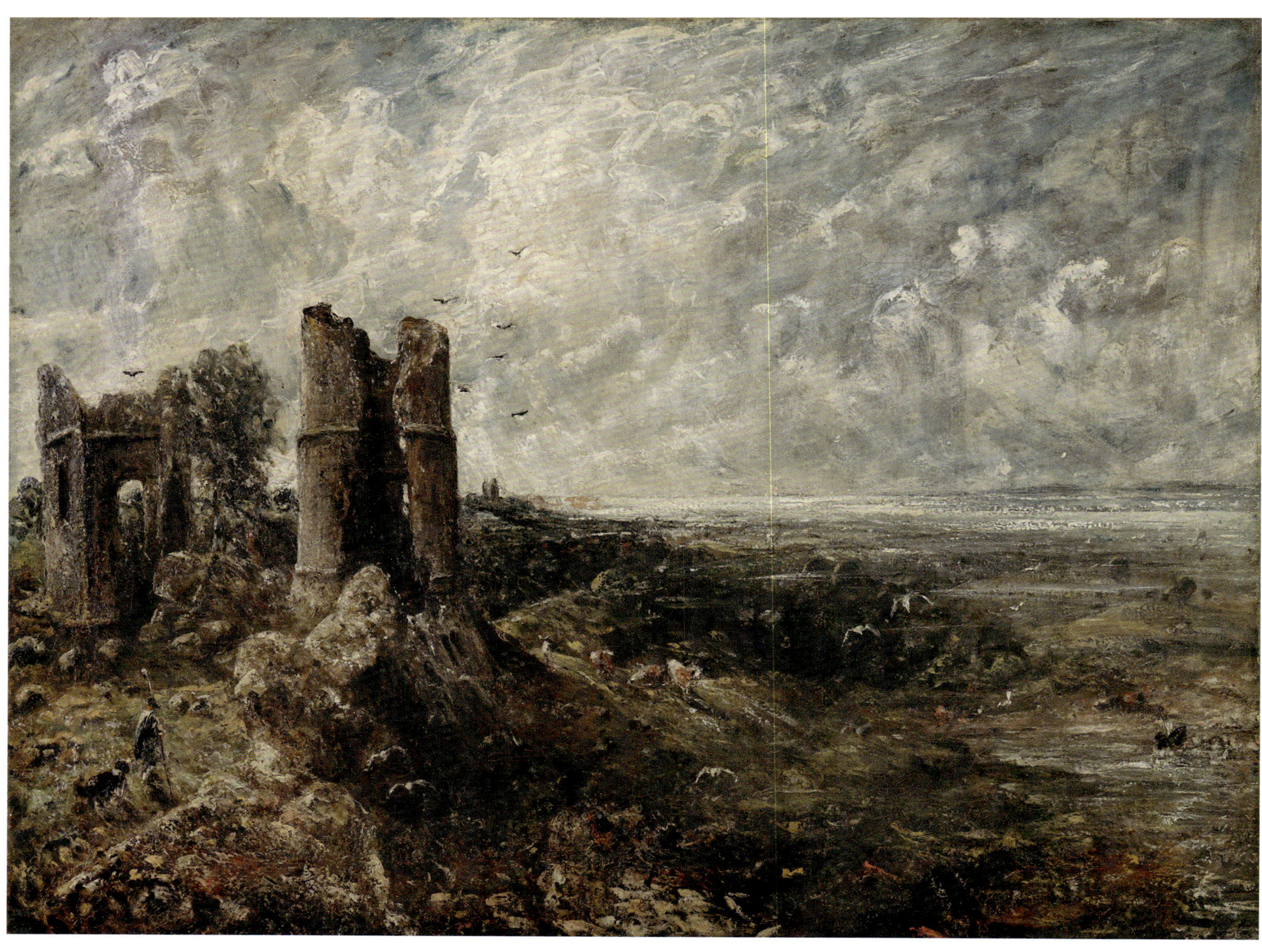

NO. 132 **John Constable** *Hadleigh Castle, The Mouth of the Thames – Morning after a Stormy Night* exhibited 1829
Oil paint on canvas, 121·9 × 164·5
Yale Center for British Art, Paul Mellon Collection

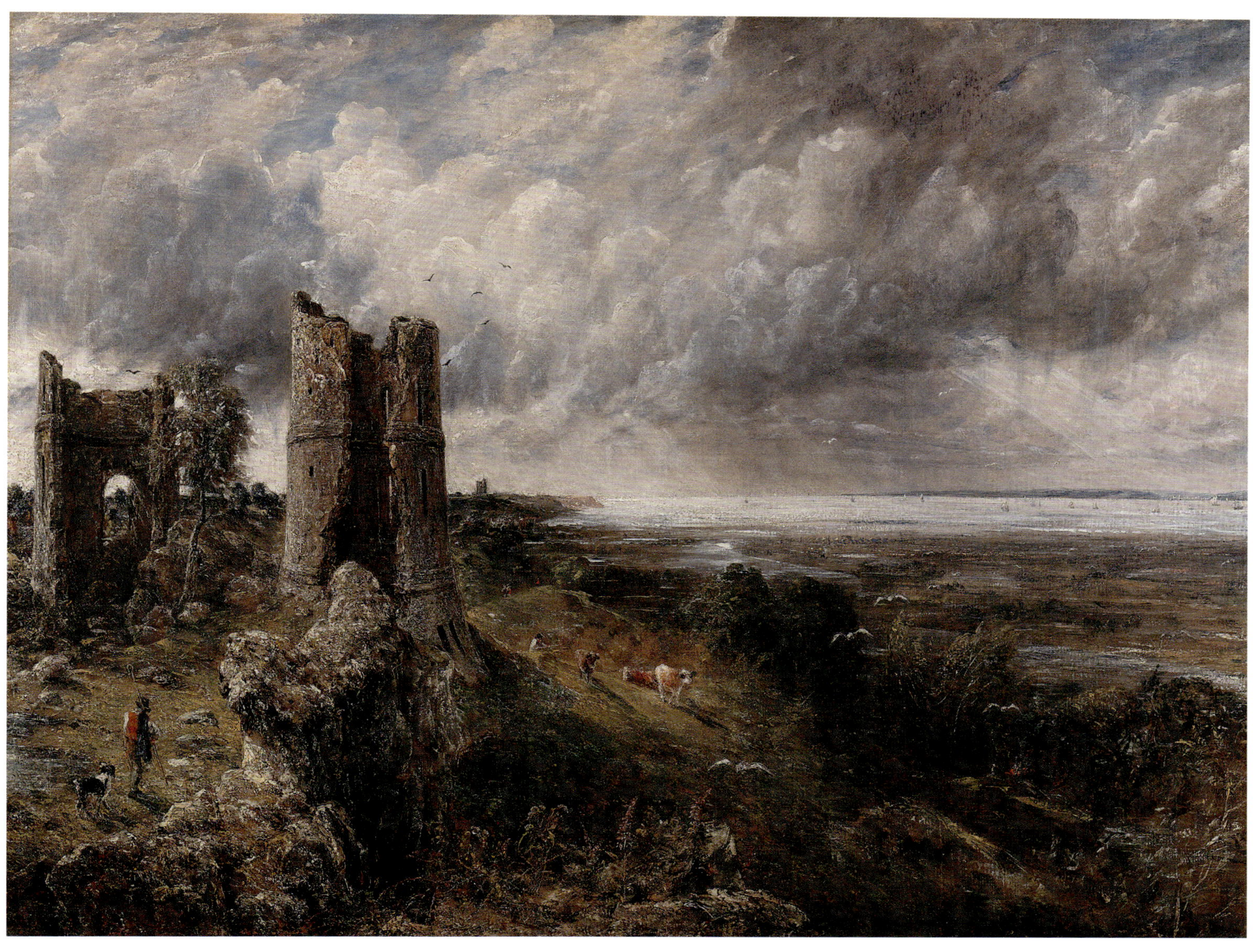

Sketch for Hadleigh Castle is celebrated for the palpable energy of its surface. Vigorous dashes and swirls characterise the sky; elsewhere the paint is thickly applied with a palette knife such that the surface appears sculpted. The composition has long been read as an allegory of life after the death of Constable's wife, Maria in 1828. He had had visited Hadleigh, Essex, in 1814, writing to Maria of its 'melancholy grandeur' (Beckett, II, p.127). The exhibited canvas (no.132) was the first major painting he showed after his long-awaited acceptance as a Member of the Royal Academy. It was accompanied by lines from James Thomson's 1727 poem, *The Seasons*, that included the phrase 'The desert joys / Wildly, through all his melancholy bounds / Rude ruins glitter'. The glitter of light was an effect Constable became particularly concerned with in his late works. While Turner is said to have commented sarcastically about Constable's use of white, the painting was well received on the whole.

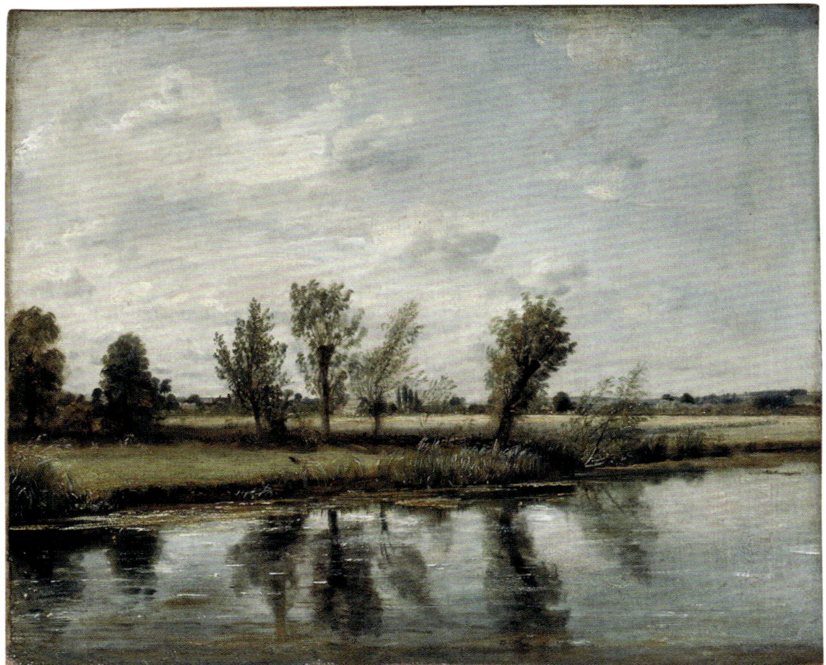

NO. 133 **John Constable** *Watermeadows at Salisbury* 1820
Oil paint on canvas, 45·7 × 55·3
Victoria and Albert Museum, London

NO. 134 **John Constable** *Letter from John Constable to John Smith*, 4 April 1831
18·7 × 23
Private Collection

friend Leslie tells me You have a very beautifull little "De Hooge" – pray let me know when You have the large Ruisdael – again "of the Church".
My large Church will leave me ~~tuesday next~~ tomorrow in the afternoon – if You or any of Your friends would ~~like~~ do me the favor to look in –
I hope You soon has something for the Exhibition –
Yours very truly
4 Apl 1831. John Constable

The recipient of this letter was frame-maker and gilder turned picture dealer, John Smith. His specialism was the Dutch and Flemish school, which Constable particularly admired. At the time of writing this letter Constable had churches on his mind. He writes: 'pray let me know when you have the large Ruisdael – again "of the Church." My large Church will leave me tomorrow'. Constable's 'large Church' was *Salisbury Cathedral from the Meadows* (no.135), the ambitious canvas he would exhibit at the 1831 Royal Academy exhibition. Only a month later he would purchase from Smith a 'magnificent church piece' by Emanuel de Witte, showing the interior of the Nieuwe Kerk, Amsterdam (Evans, *Making of a Master*, p.84). There appears to be no match in Smith's stock books for the 'large Ruisdael' featuring a church to which Constable refers to in his letter here, however, but as a well-connected expert in the sale of Dutch and Flemish works and an experienced framer, Smith was likely to receive many paintings into his shop for consultations, restoration or reframing. One candidate might be Ruisdael's *A Landscape with a Ruined Castle and a Church* (National Gallery, London) which Smith had sold in 1828; this was sold again in 1831 and by 1835 was owned by a client of Smith's. Yet perhaps Smith had indicated to Constable that a much more celebrated Ruisdael 'large church', *The Jewish Cemetery* of c.1654–55 (Detroit Institute of Arts), might arrive on his premises. This work had also been sold in 1828 and remained in London collections until the 1920s. Smith's thoughts on this important painting, as published in his 1835 catalogue raisonné of Dutch and Flemish painters, are reflected in a lecture Constable gave in 1836 (Evans, *Making of a Master*, p.163). Given the shared core compositional elements of church, rainbow, water and tree between *Salisbury Cathedral from the Meadows* and Ruisdael's *Jewish Cemetery* it is very possible that it was this painting Constable was keen to see at Smith's shop. Either way, however, this letter certifies the connection in Constable's mind between *Salisbury Cathedral* and a work by his celebrated antecedent Ruisdael.

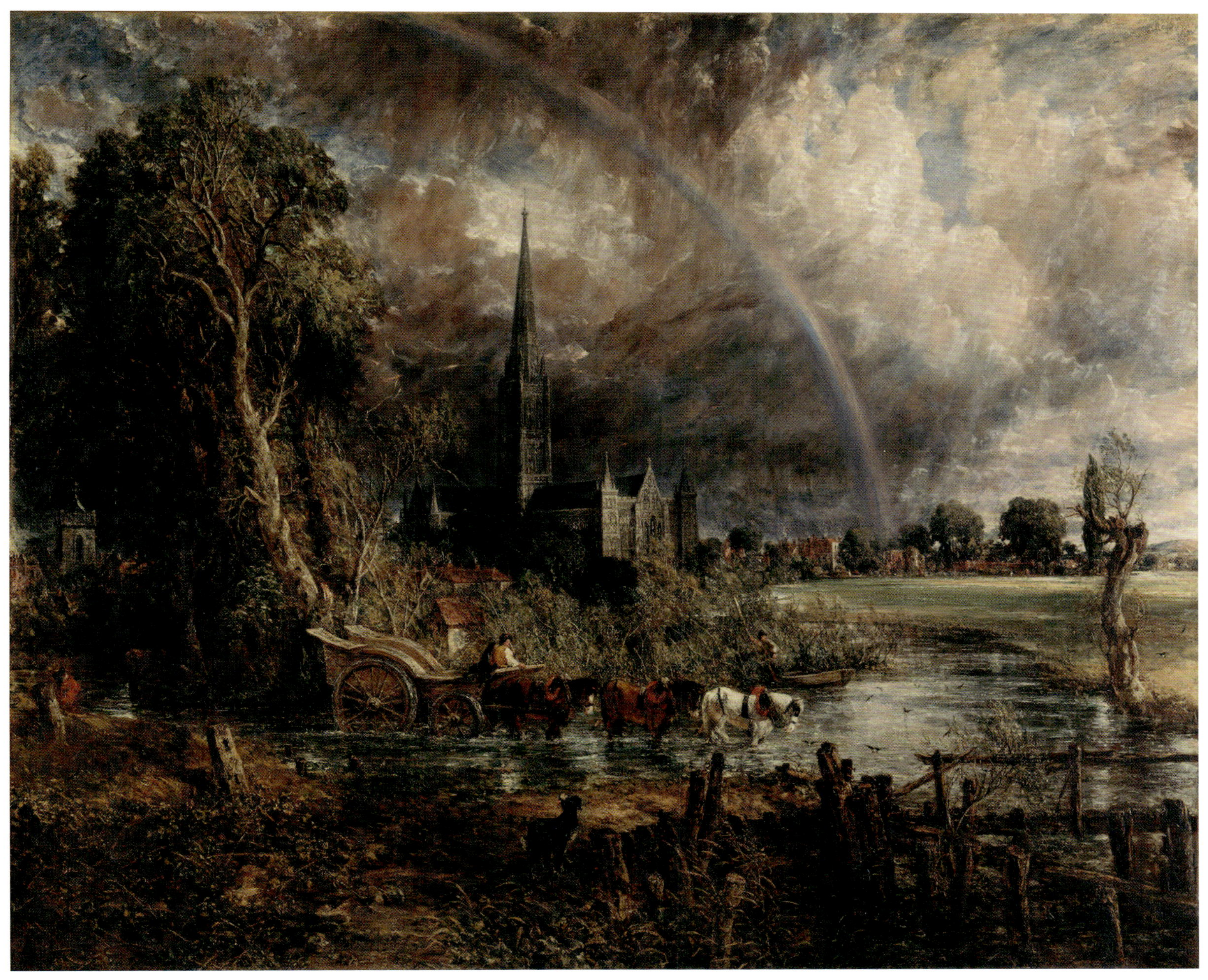

NO. 135 **John Constable** *Salisbury Cathedral from the Meadows* exhibited 1831
Oil paint on canvas, 153·7 × 192
Tate. Purchased by Tate with assistance from the National Lottery through the Heritage Lottery Fund, The Manton Foundation, Art Fund (with a contribution from the Wolfson Foundation) and Tate Members in partnership with Amgueddfa Cymru-National Museum Wales, Colchester and Ipswich Museums Service, National Galleries of Scotland, and The Salisbury Museum 2013

This painting is discussed in the essays on pp.15–22, pp.38–41 and on p.155.

NO. 136 **J.M.W. Turner** *Caligula's Palace and Bridge* exhibited 1831
Oil paint on canvas, 137·2 × 246·4
Tate. Accepted by the nation as part of the Turner Bequest 1856

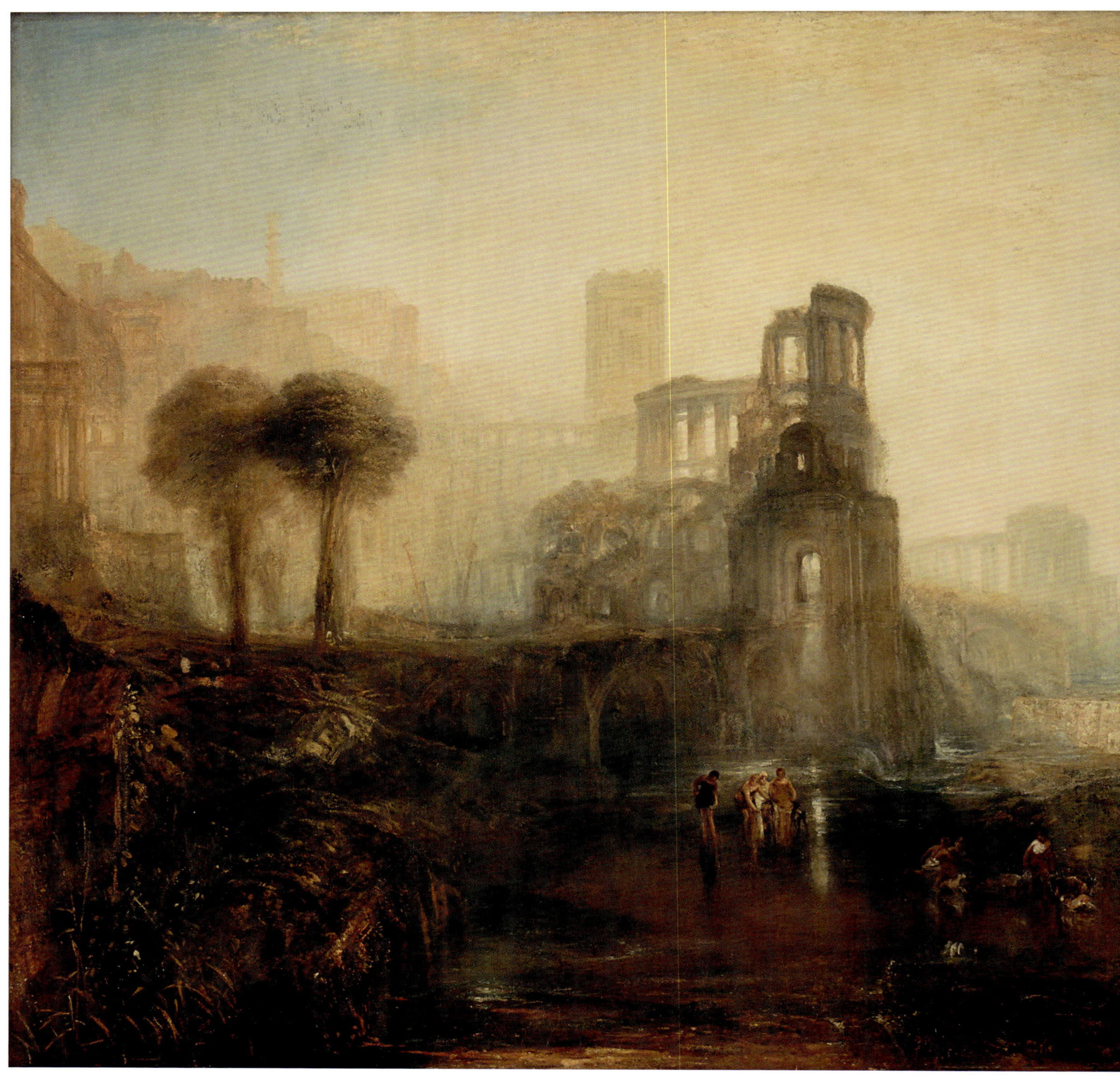

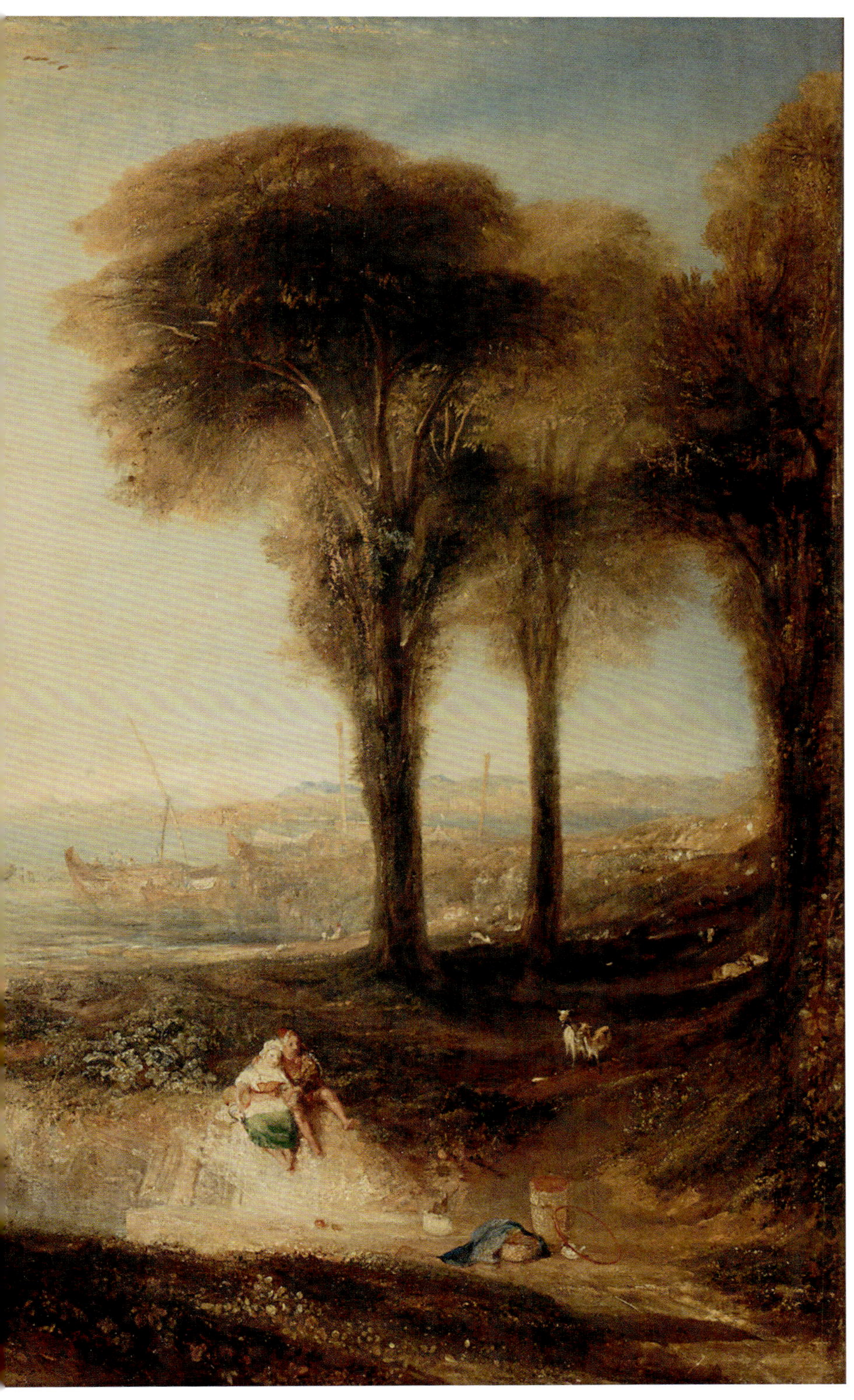

This painting is discussed in the essay on pp.15–22.

NO. 137 **J.M.W. Turner** *Staffa, Fingal's Cave* exhibited 1832
Oil paint on canvas, 90·8 × 121·3
Yale Center for British Art, Paul Mellon Collection

Since the late eighteenth century the Hebridean island of Staffa had been one of the most celebrated natural wonders of the British coast. Tourists sought out its gigantic basalt columns and wondrous caves. Turner journeyed there in late summer 1831 in search of sites related to Sir Walter Scott's poetry that he was to illustrate for a new edition of the poet's works. According to Turner's painting, visiting Staffa in the late summer of 1831 was a heady sublime experience, a perfect vehicle to explore the juxtaposition between humanity – represented by the steamboat – and nature's permanence and power. He later wrote a letter recalling the conditions he had experienced – 'the sun getting towards the horizon, burst through the raincloud, angry'. This account was written in a letter to the painting's first owner, New York lawyer James Lenox, whose acquisition of *Staffa* in 1845 made it the first of Turner's paintings to arrive in the United States. Turner was assisted in this sale by Constable's friend and posthumous biographer, the American painter Charles Robert Leslie. Constable himself had once written to Leslie, '[d]id you ever see a picture by Turner, and not wish to possess it?' (Beckett, II, p.312).

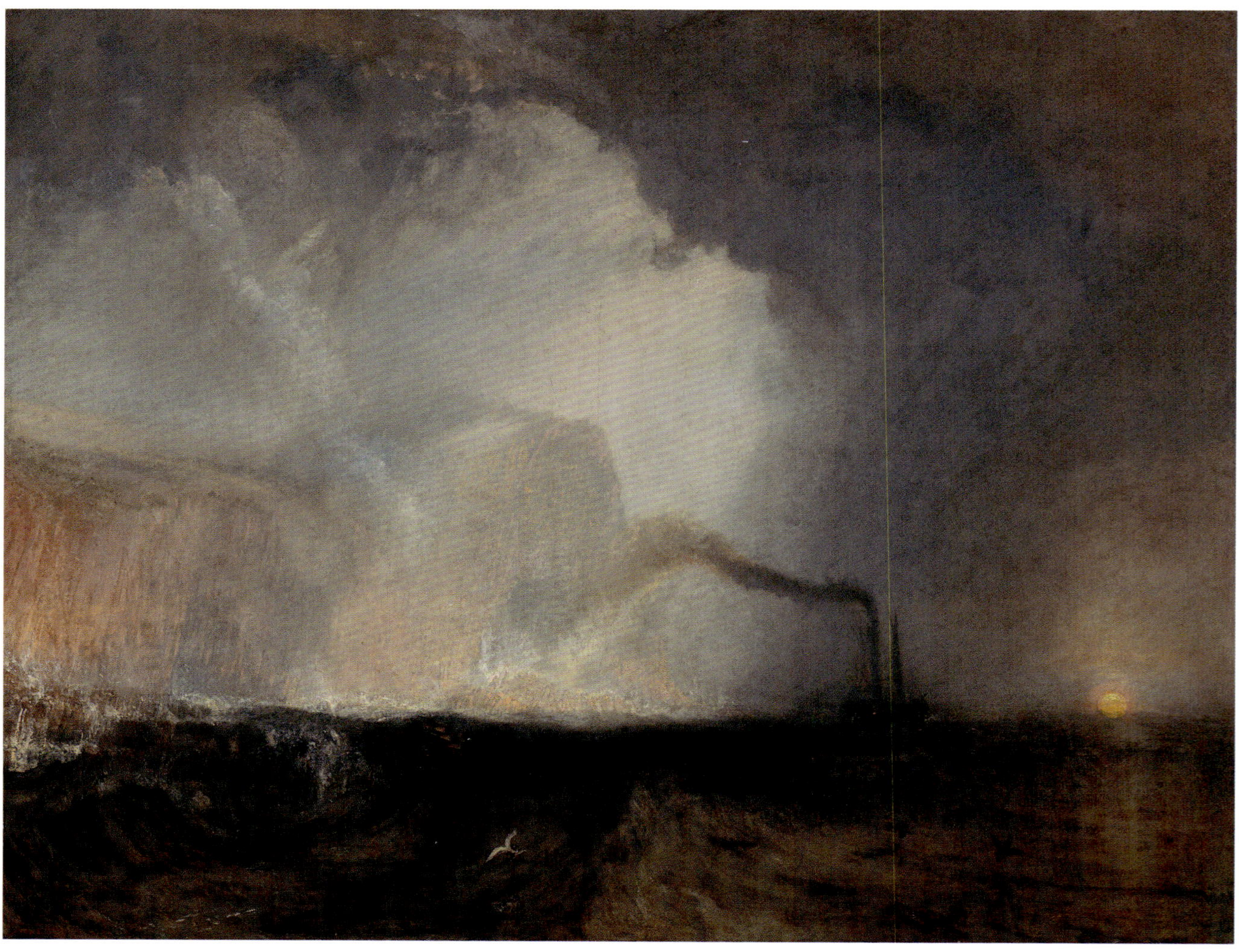

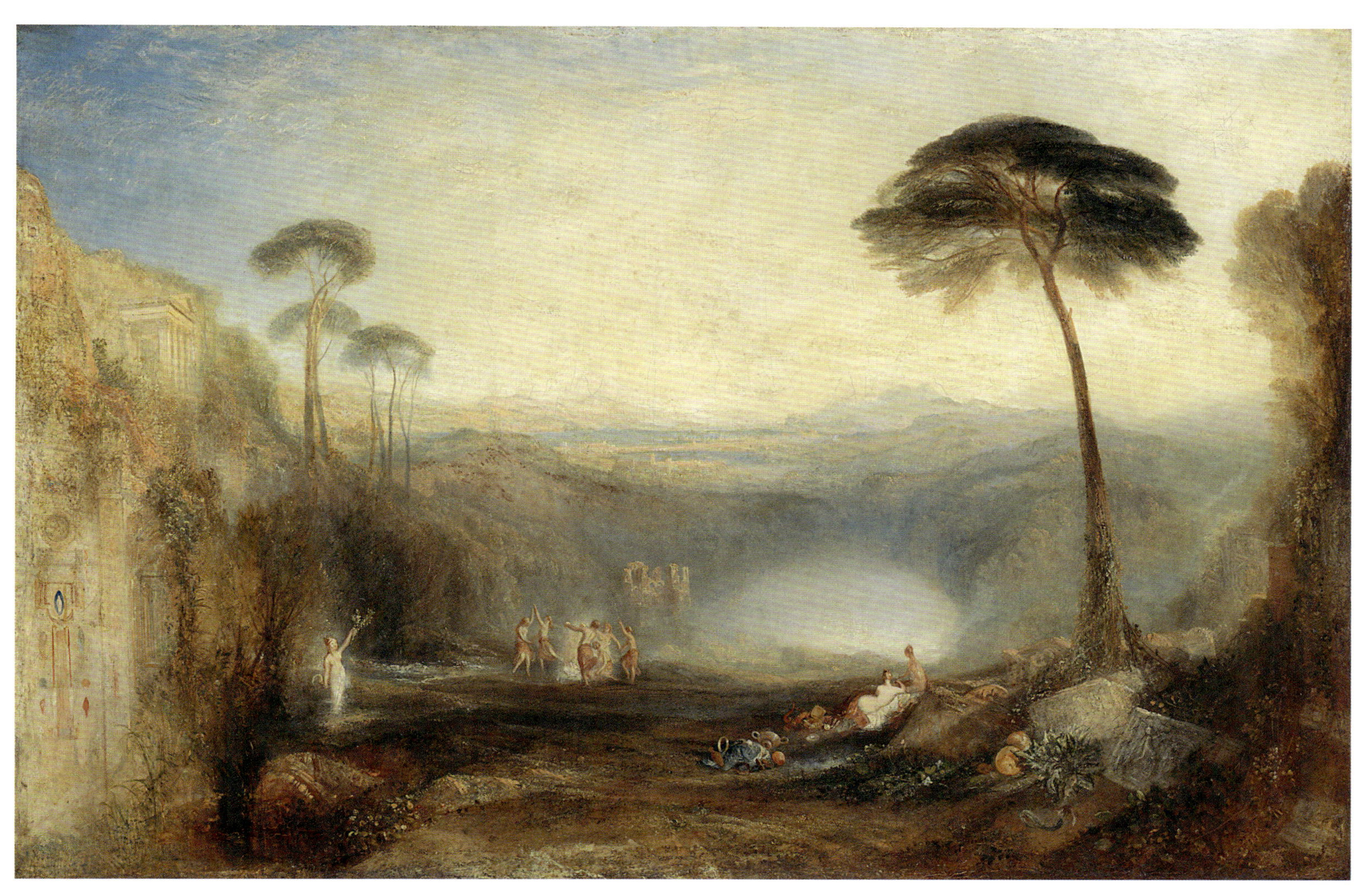

NO. 138 **J.M.W. Turner** *The Golden Bough* exhibited 1834
Oil paint on canvas, 104·1 × 163·8
Tate. Presented by Robert Vernon 1847

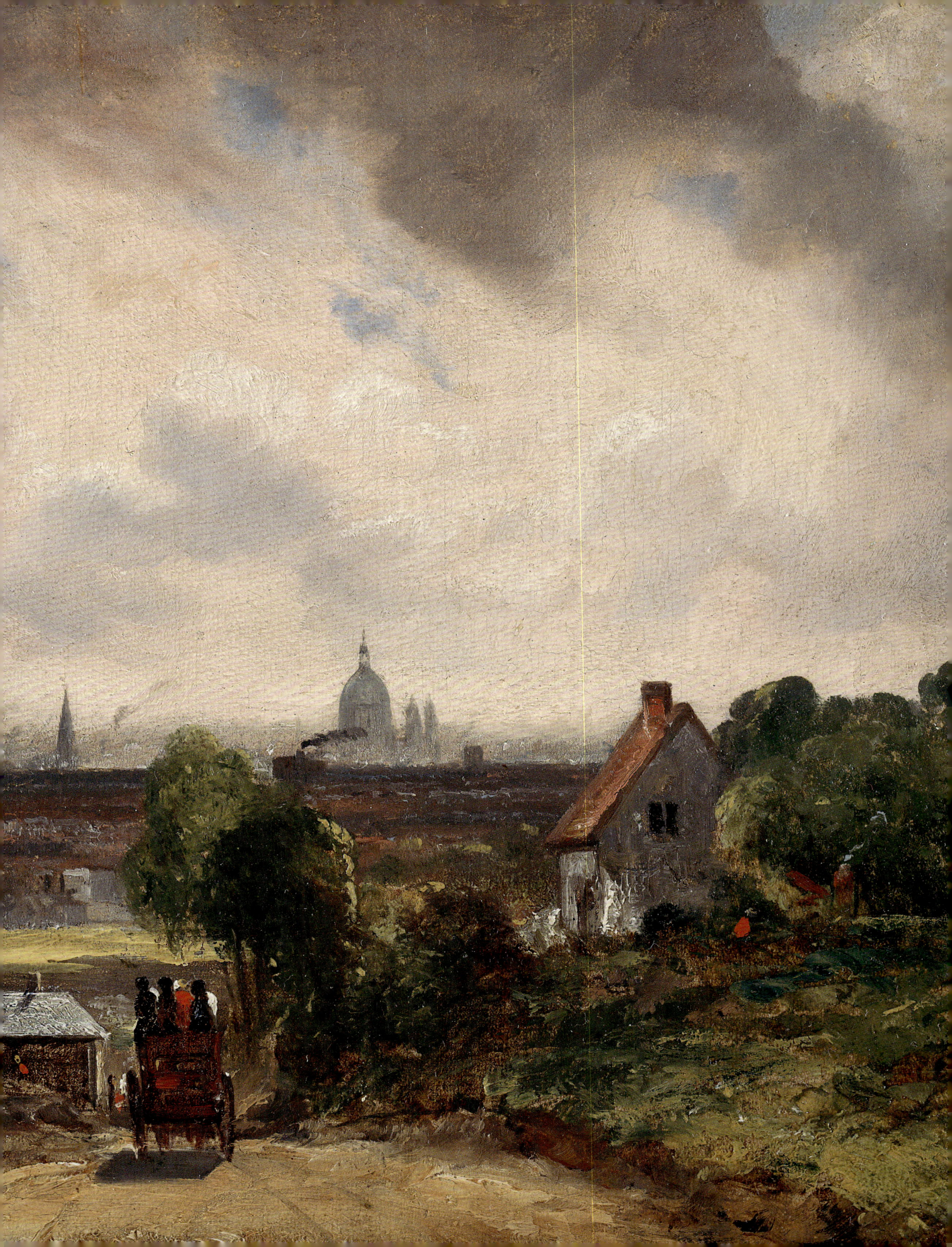

LATE CONSTABLE: BEYOND 'CONSTABLE COUNTRY'

The late 1820s ushered in much change for Constable. The death of his wife, Maria, in 1828 left him a widowed father to seven children, while his election as a Royal Academician in 1829 gained him a new professional footing (and a congratulatory visit from Turner). That same year he also began to encapsulate and disseminate his vision for landscape imagery in the mezzotint series *English Landscape Scenery* (see pp.48–9 and nos.177–8), a counterpart to Turner's earlier portfolio *Liber Studiorum* (nos.179–80).

Determined to prove his versatility and ambition, Constable varied the subjects of his six-footers. Sketches of the settings for *Chain Pier, Brighton* and *The Opening of Waterloo Bridge* show him tackling coastal storms, grand neoclassical architecture and, in common with his Stour subjects, paying close attention to working watercraft. Unusually, he seems to have skipped the step of making a full-scale sketch for his six-footer of Brighton. In his sketch for *Hadleigh Castle*, however, he deployed the palette knife to give the work a particularly agitated energy, which, along with his description of himself as akin to the lonely ruin depicted, has been interpreted as an expression of his grief (no.132).

Certainly, a new intensity is detectable in Constable's later work, his idiosyncrasies becoming ever more pronounced. He was compared to Turner, and, said one notoriously barbed reviewer, set on 'vulgar imitation' of 'Turner's freaks and follies'.[1] Most critics recognised Constable's uniqueness; indeed, one exasperated reviewer of *Waterloo Bridge*, seemingly lost for words, simply decried, 'Constable is Constable'.[2] More polite descriptions termed his works 'vigorous' and 'free and bold', but his detractors had a field day.[3] Advising of the need to 'keep your distance' from his paintings (so that their subject might come into focus), they fixated on his 'snow', his use of white highlights.[4] In *Salisbury Cathedral from the Meadows* (no.135) one critic saw 'glittering white speckly effects so offensive to the eye' and 'snow … melting away'.[5] While he had once been proud of his ability to conjure atmosphere so powerful that elder painter Henry Fuseli (1741–1825) had requested an umbrella to view his work, he was now aware that his bravura posed a danger to his quest for 'truth'.[6] When working on *Salisbury Cathedral*, he wrote:

> I have filled my head with certain notions of freshness – sparkle – brightness – till it has influenced my practice in no small degree, & is in fact taking the place of truth.[7]

Clearly, in the case of this painting at least, Constable's commitment to a bolder, more daring way of painting triumphed over his doubts.

Rainbows – signifying transience, mutability and hope – proliferate in Constable's late work. He was especially fond of a double rainbow, as seen in *Hampstead* and *Stonehenge* (nos. 173 and 172). The latter, along with *Old Sarum*, manifests Constable's increasing fascination for the mysterious world of the past as well as his adoption of watercolour in the 1830s. While repeated bouts of illness made watercolour a practical choice, his embracing of the medium sparked new creativity and, in illustration projects (a practice that continued to occupy Turner in the 1830s too), new avenues for his vision.[8]

John Constable *Sir Richard Steele's Cottage, Hampstead* (detail) 1831 (p.184)

NO. 139 **John Constable** *Brighton Beach* 12 June 1824
Oil paint on paper, 12 × 29·7
Victoria and Albert Museum, London. Given by Isabel Constable

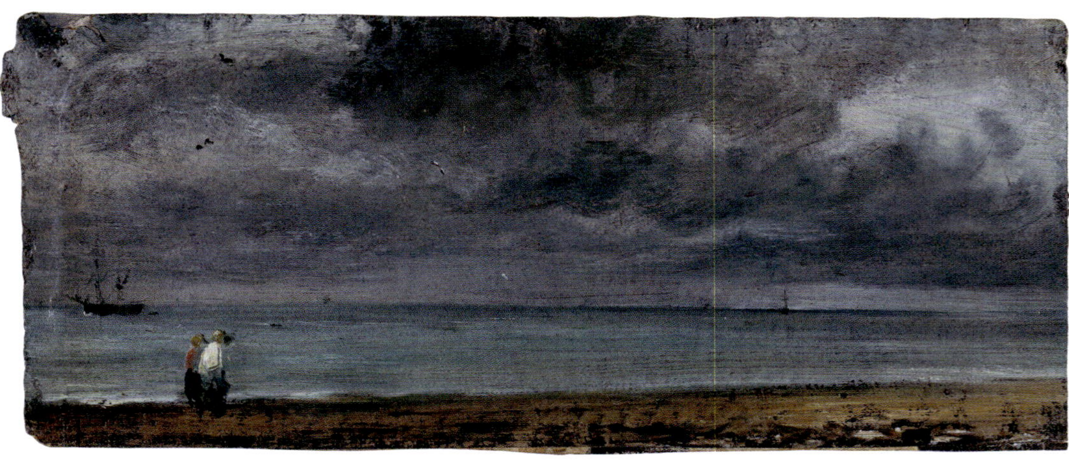

NO. 140 **John Constable** *Brighton Beach* 22 July 1824
Oil paint on paper, 16·5 × 30·4
Victoria and Albert Museum, London. Given by Isabel Constable

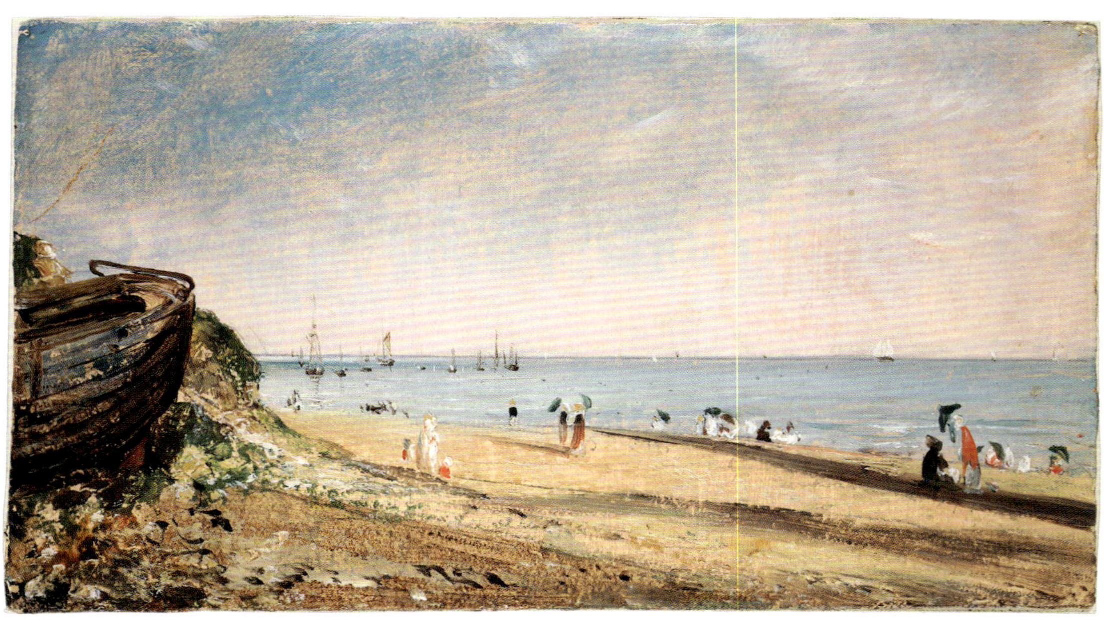

NO. 141 **John Constable** *A Windmill near Brighton* 1824
Oil paint on canvas, 20·3 × 25·1
Tate. Bequeathed by George Salting 1910

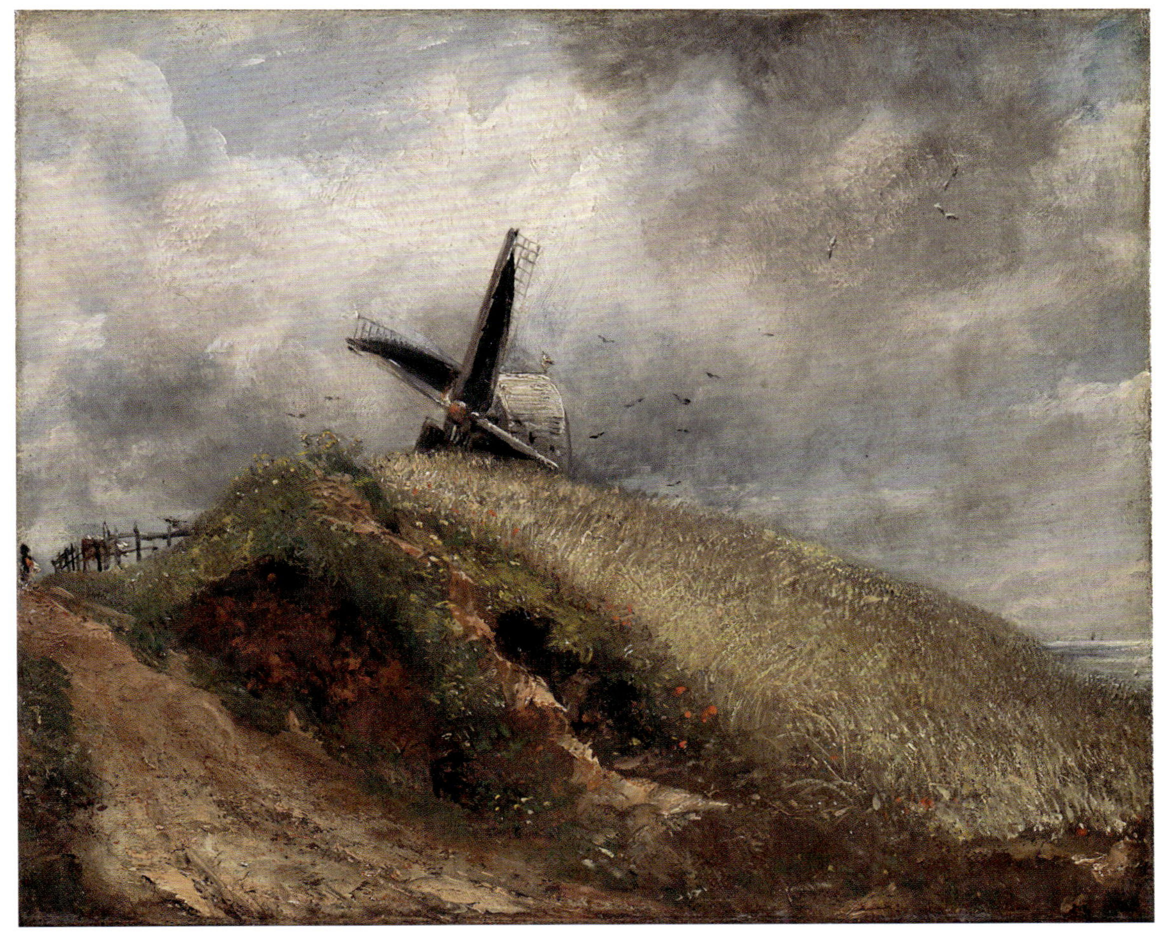

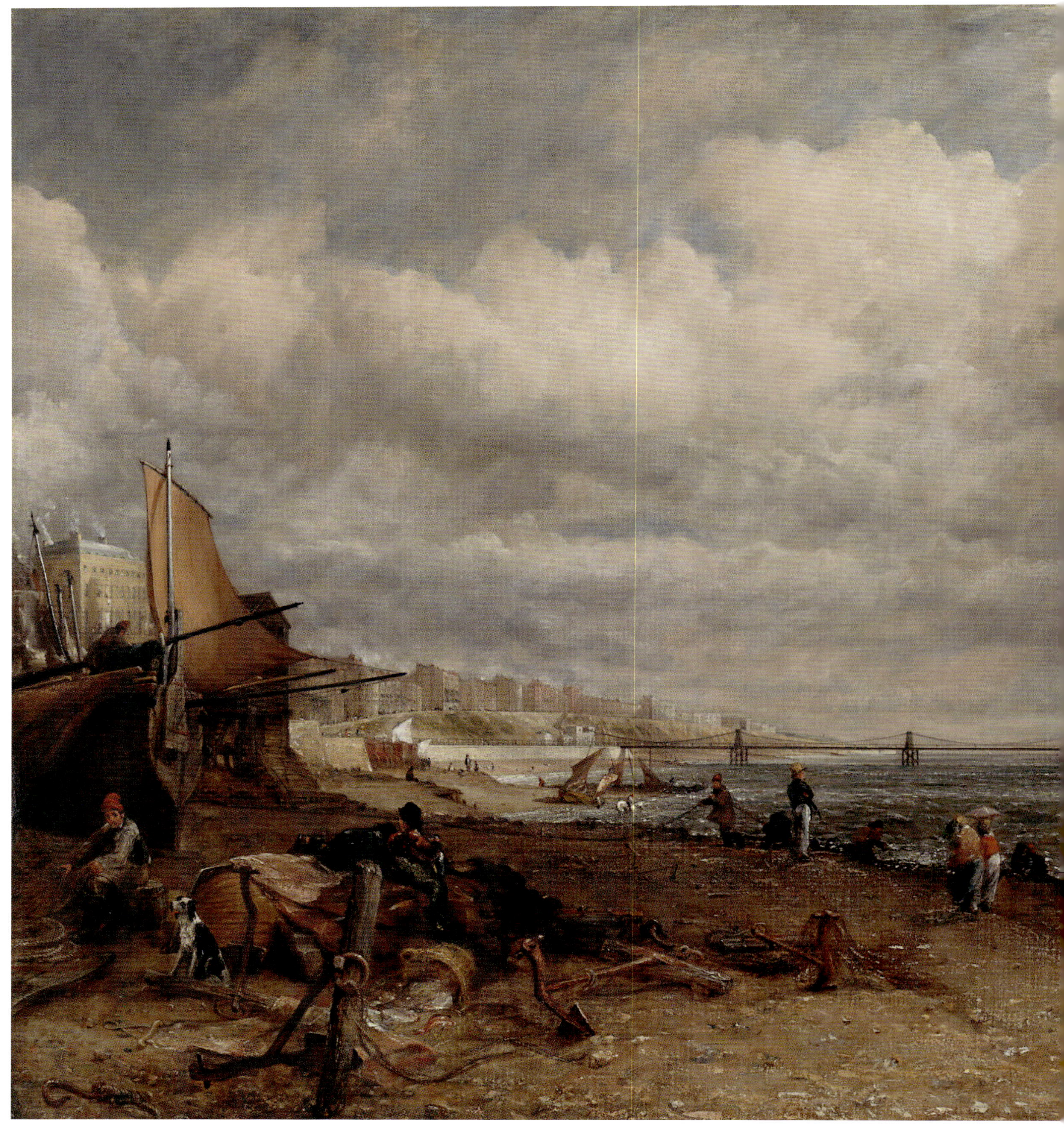

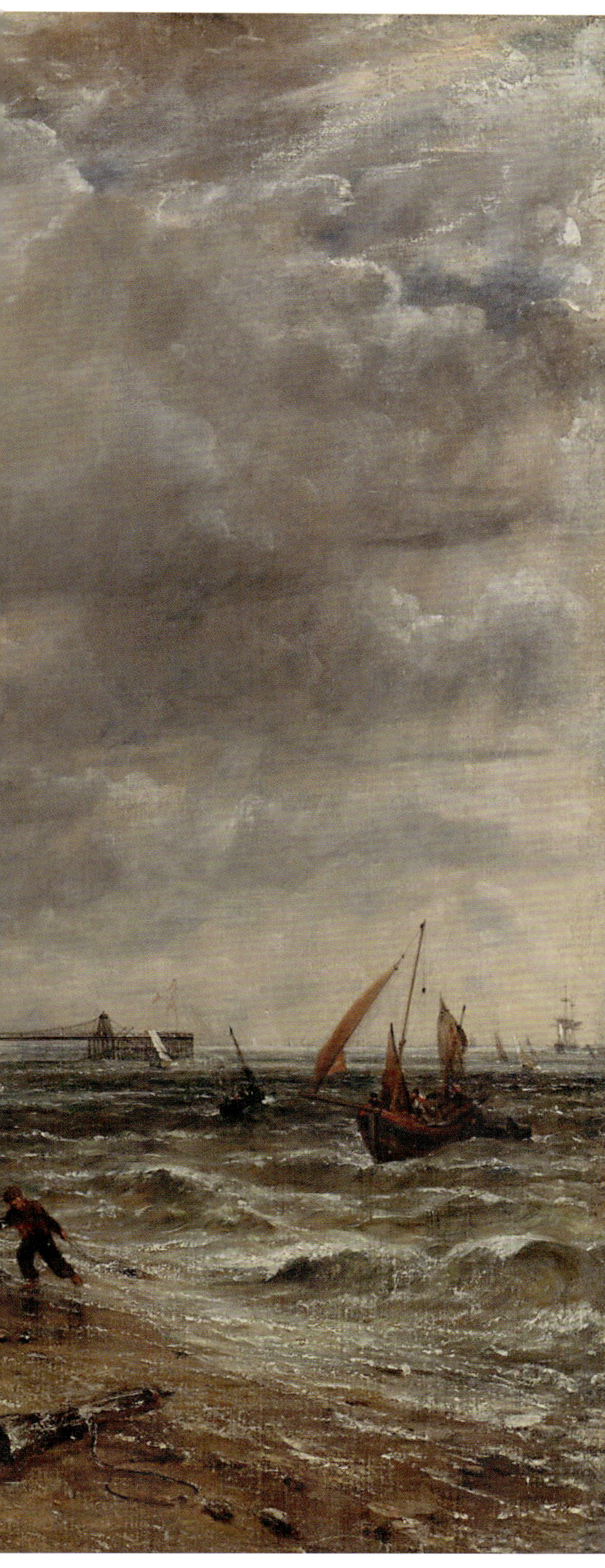

NO. 142 **John Constable** *Chain Pier, Brighton* exhibited 1827
Oil paint on canvas, 127 × 182·9
Tate. Purchased 1950

This painting is discussed on pp.38–9.

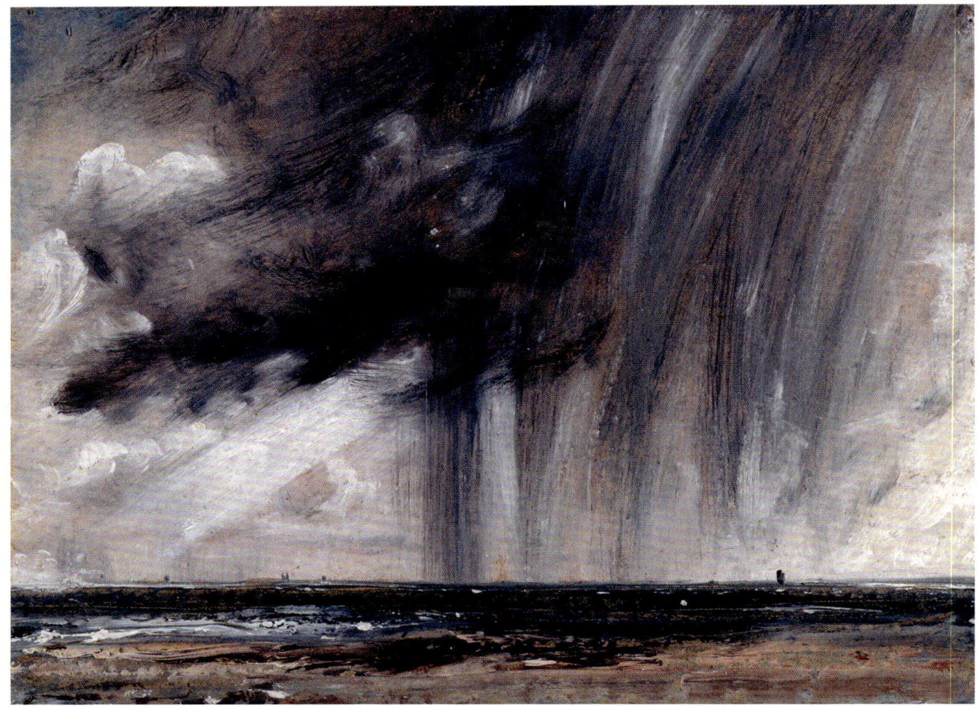

NO. 143 **John Constable** *Rainstorm over the Sea* 1824
Oil paint on paper laid on canvas, 23·5 × 32·6
Lent by the Royal Academy of Arts, London

NO. 144 **John Constable** *Seascape Study: Boat and Stormy Sky* 1828
Oil paint on paper laid on board, 18·5 × 15·5
Lent by the Royal Academy of Arts, London

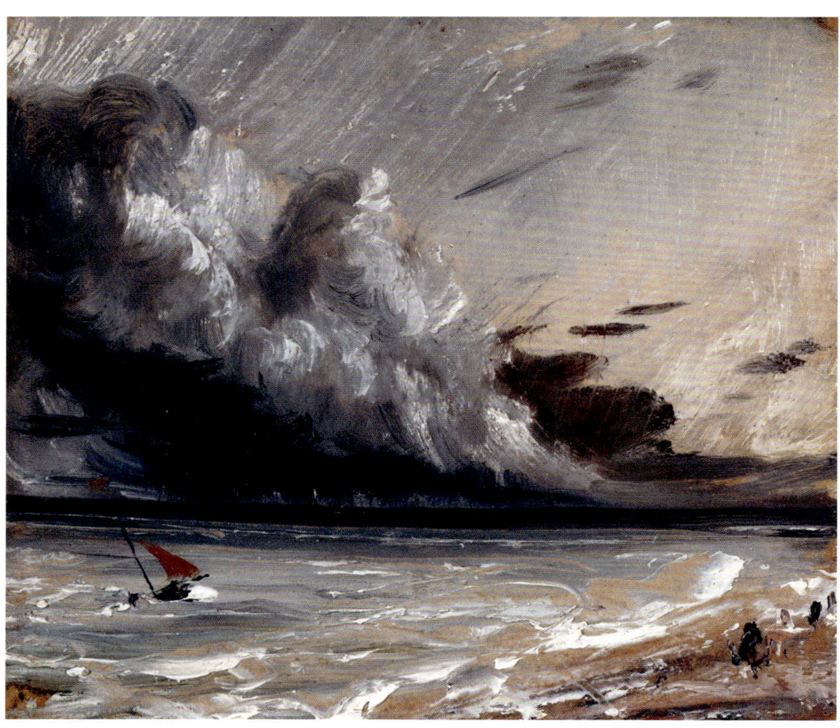

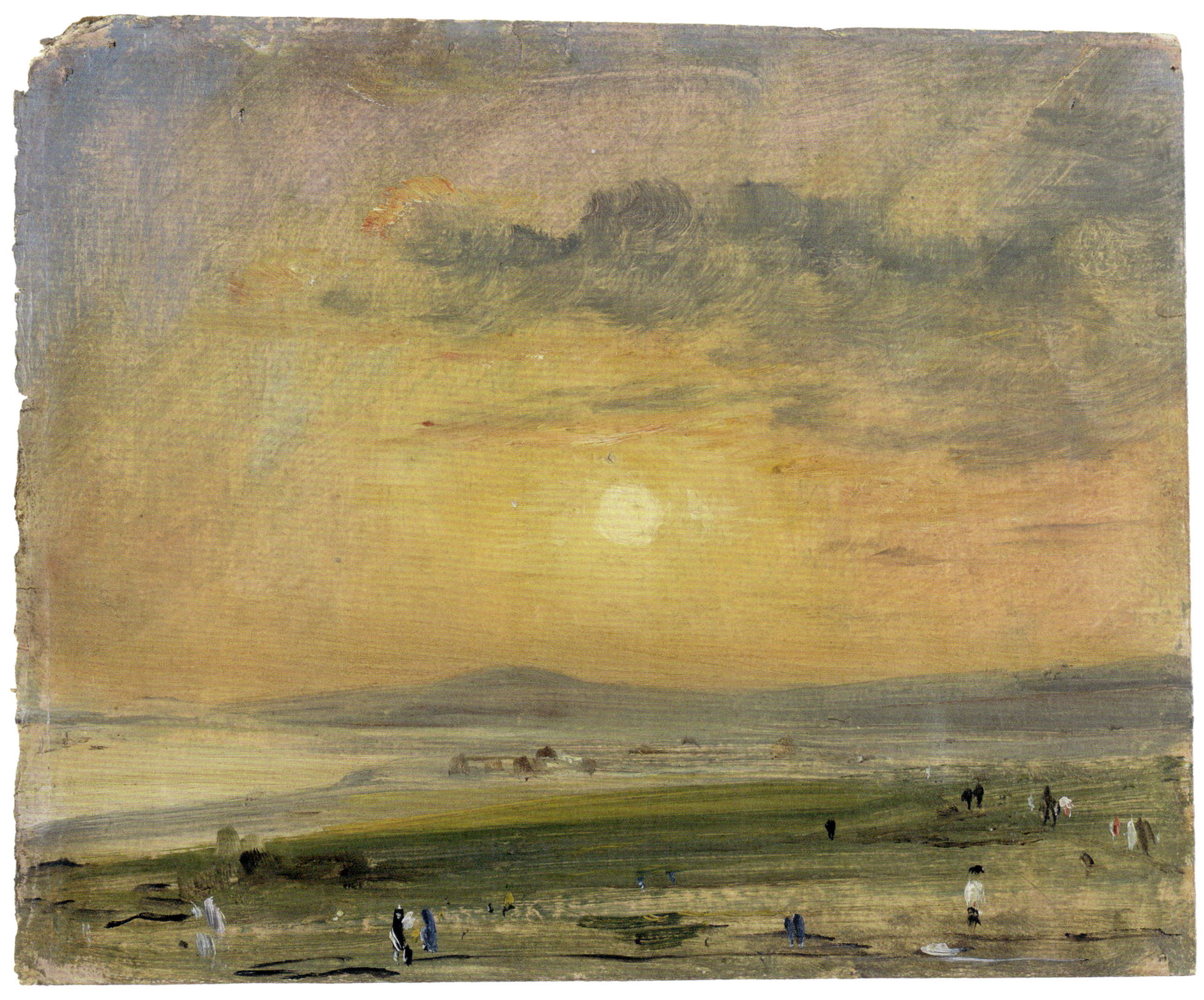

NO. 145 **John Constable** *Coast Scene at Brighton, Evening* 1828
Oil paint on paper, 20 × 24·8
Victoria and Albert Museum, London. Given by Isabel Constable

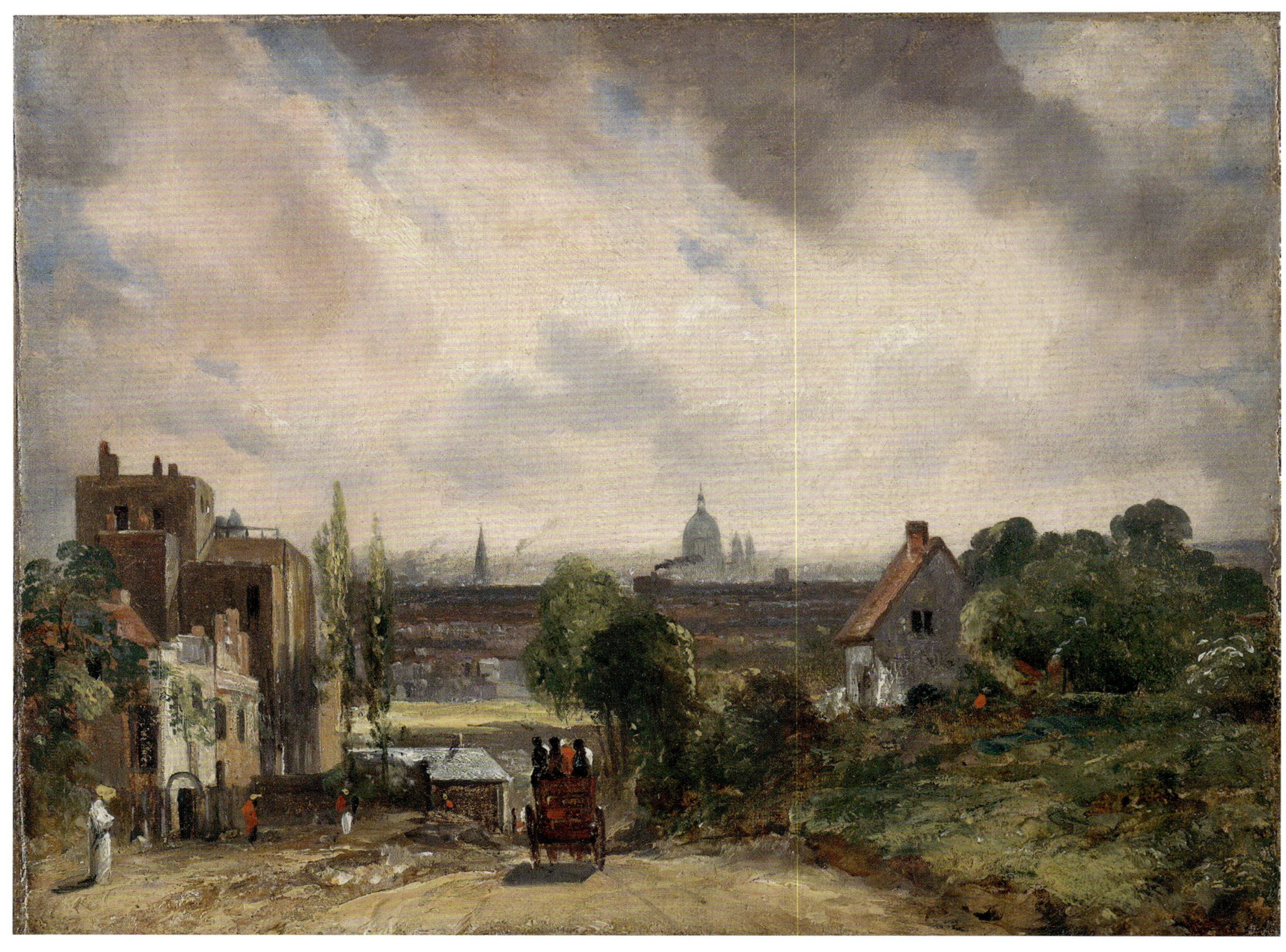

NO. 146 **John Constable** *Sir Richard Steele's Cottage, Hampstead* exhibited 1832
Oil paint on canvas, 21 × 28·6
Yale Center for British Art, Paul Mellon Collection

After Constable's move to Hampstead, the semi-rural suburb in which he could 'unite a town and country life' (Beckett, VI, p.228), he would come across this vista most mornings on his commute to his central London studio. The vantage point is Haverstock Hill, and the painting's title derives from the building on the right, the former home of eighteenth-century man of letters Sir Richard Steele. On the left is the Load of Hay Tavern, frequented by labourers from the surrounding hayfields. In the middle distance are Kentish Town and St Pancras and beyond the churches of the City of London. Most prominent is St Paul's Cathedral. Rising up before the cathedral is a black plume of smoke from a large bulky building, which Stephen Daniels has suggested is the Imperial Gasworks by the Regents Canal: a meeting of old and new.

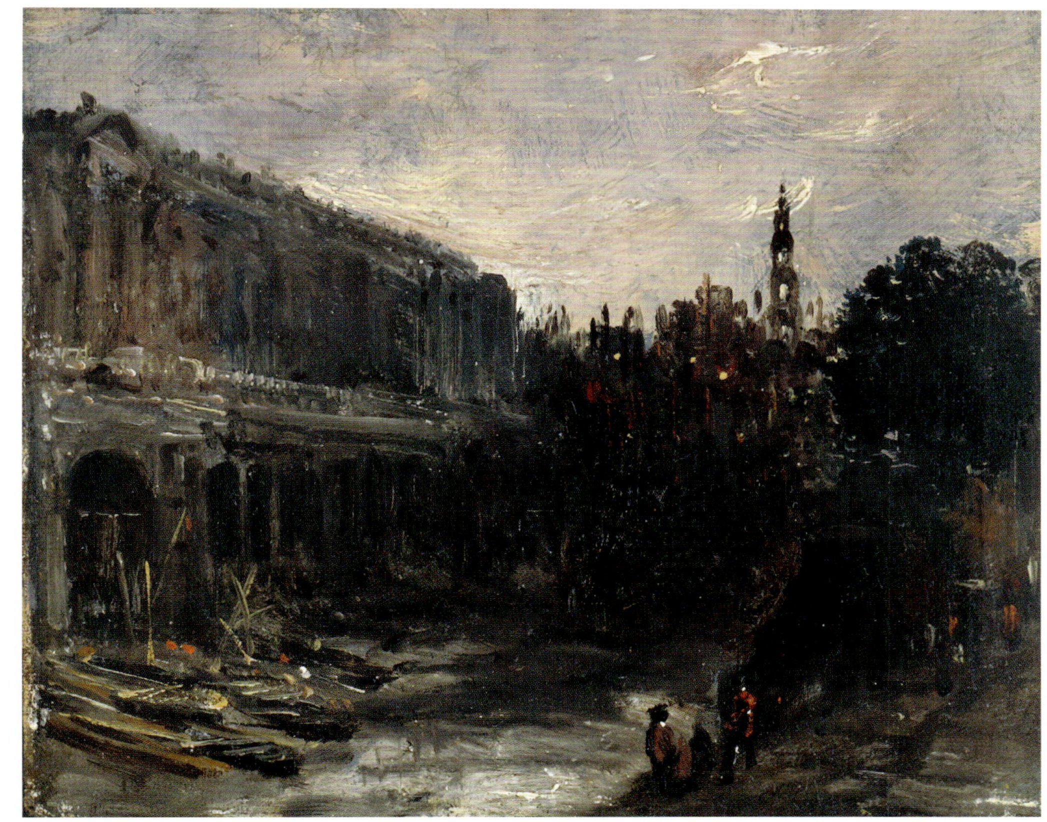

NO. 147 **John Constable** *Somerset House* 1819
Oil paint on paper laid on canvas, 20·3 × 25·4
Lent by the Royal Academy of Arts, London

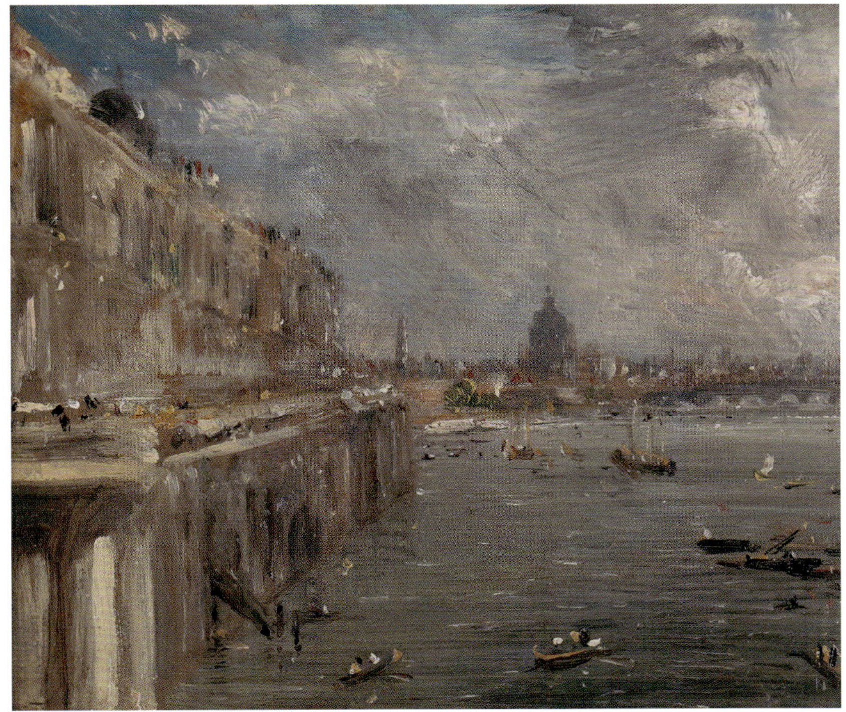

NO. 148 **John Constable** *Somerset House Terrace from Waterloo Bridge* c.1819
Oil paint on panel, 15·6 × 18·7
Yale Center for British Art, Paul Mellon Collection

NO. 149 **John Constable** *Waterloo Bridge from Whitehall Stairs* c.1819–20
Oil paint on canvas, 50 × 75
Daniel Katz Gallery, London

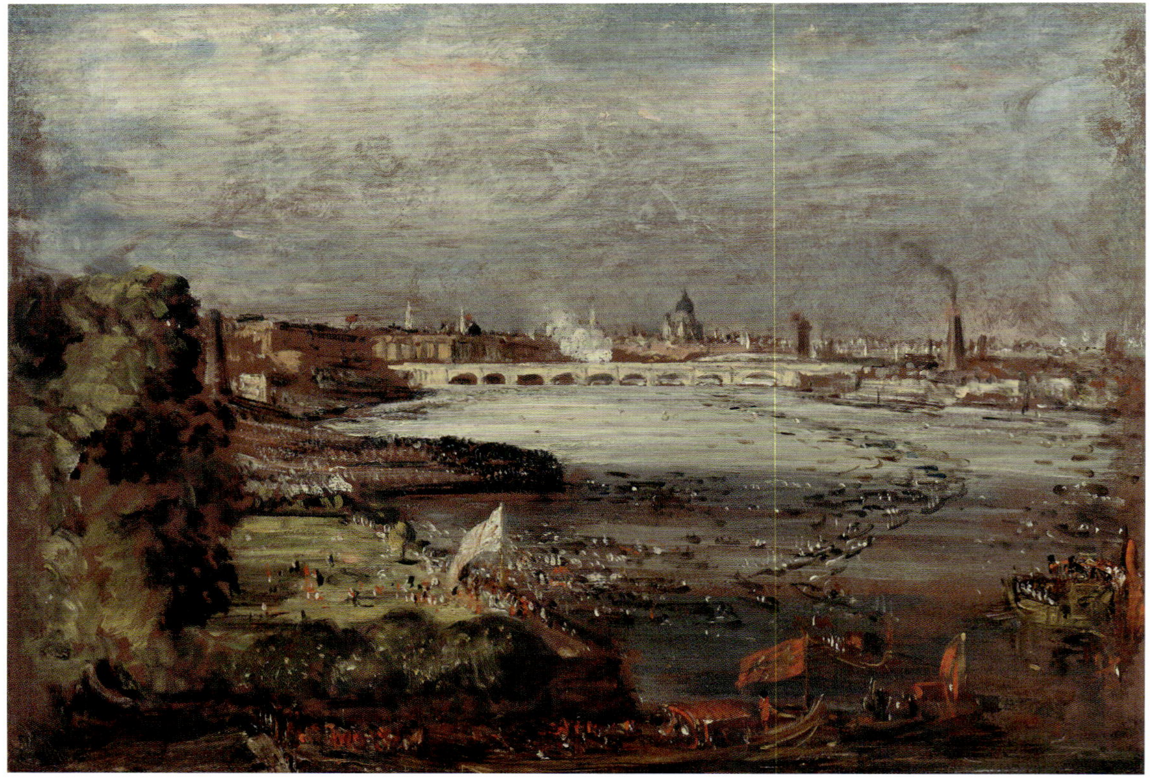

Last seen side-by-side in Constable's studio, this lively sketch and the resultant six-footer bookend Constable's tortuous thirteen-year relationship with this most recognisable central London vista (see pp.40–1). The sketch (no.149) was painted at a moment of buoyancy in Constable's career. Seeking out a new subject to keep up the momentum after his election as an Associate Member of the Royal Academy, he alighted on this scene. He shared his first attempt, likely to be no.149, with Joseph Farington (himself a painter of Thames views), only to find its aerial perspective criticised. Farington injured Constable's confidence in the composition once more a year later.

Constable oscillated between determination to show no.150 and despair that it was a 'blister' that had to be abandoned (Beckett, VI, p.207). Just before its exhibition in 1832 he wrote (aptly given its broken brushwork) of 'dashing away at the great London', adding, somewhat fatalistically, 'and why not? I may as well produce this abortion as another' (Beckett, IV, p.368). Despite referring to it as 'the devil' in 1833, he was still to be found 'brushing up' *Waterloo Bridge* in 1834 (Beckett, V, p.17). The composition bothered Turner enough, too, to have 'fired a gun' at the 1832 Royal Academy exhibition. He later began his own painting of this location (no.160).

NO. 150 **John Constable** *The Opening of Waterloo Bridge ('Whitehall Stairs, June 18th, 1817')* exhibited 1832
Oil paint on canvas, 130·8 × 218
Tate. Purchased with assistance from the National Heritage Memorial Fund, the Clore Foundation, the Art Fund, the Friends of the Tate Gallery and others 1987

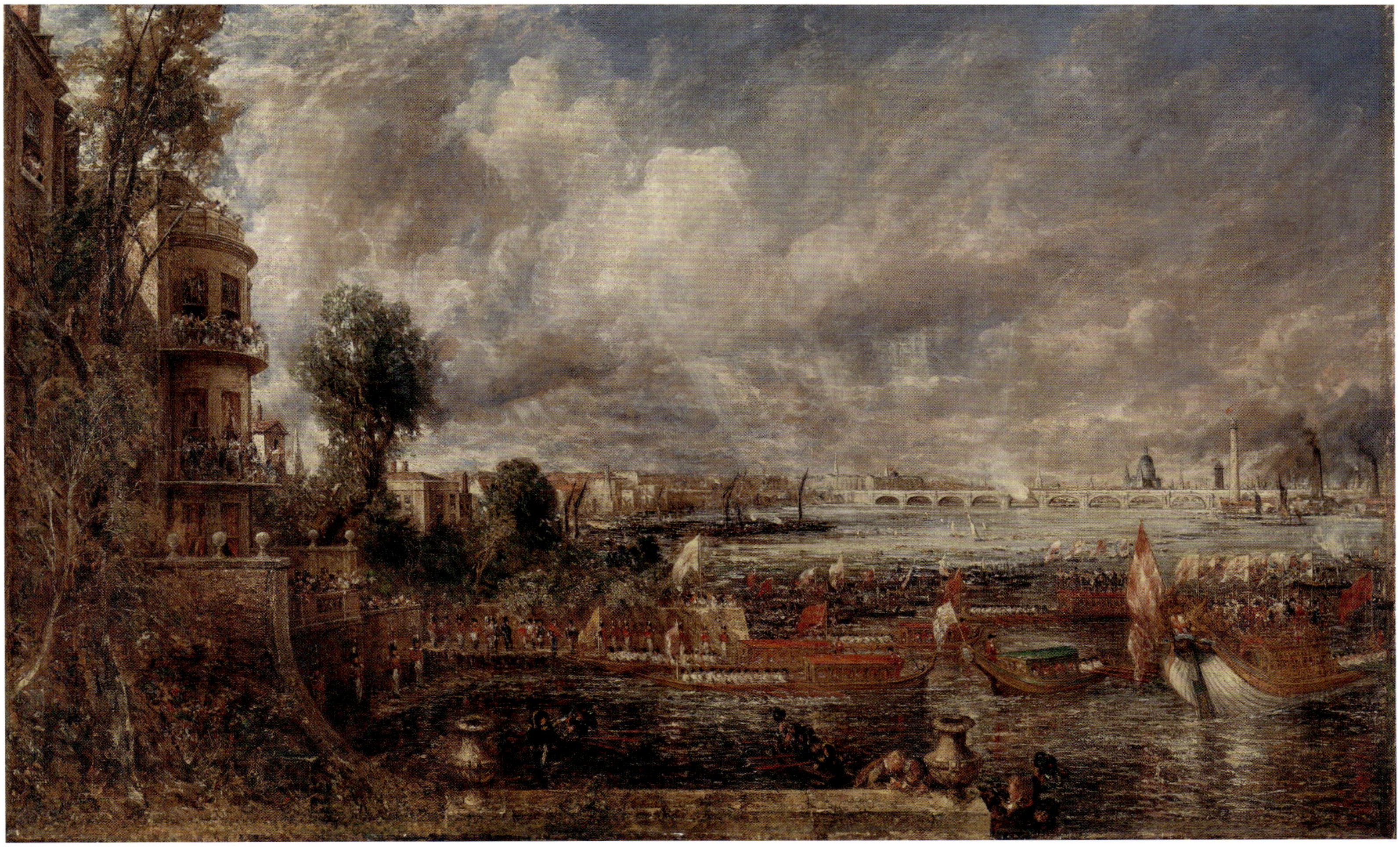

FIG. 41 **J.M.W. Turner** *Helvoetsluys ('Helvoetsluys; – the City of Utrecht, 64, going to sea')* exhibited 1832
Oil paint on canvas, 91·4 × 122
Tokyo Fuji Art Museum, Japan

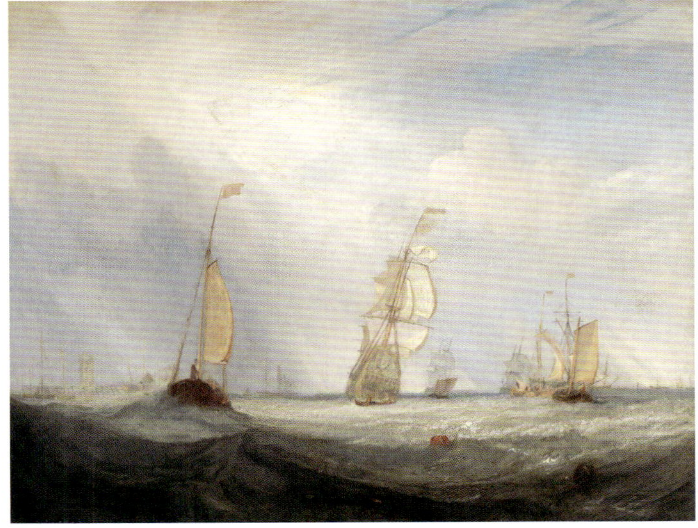

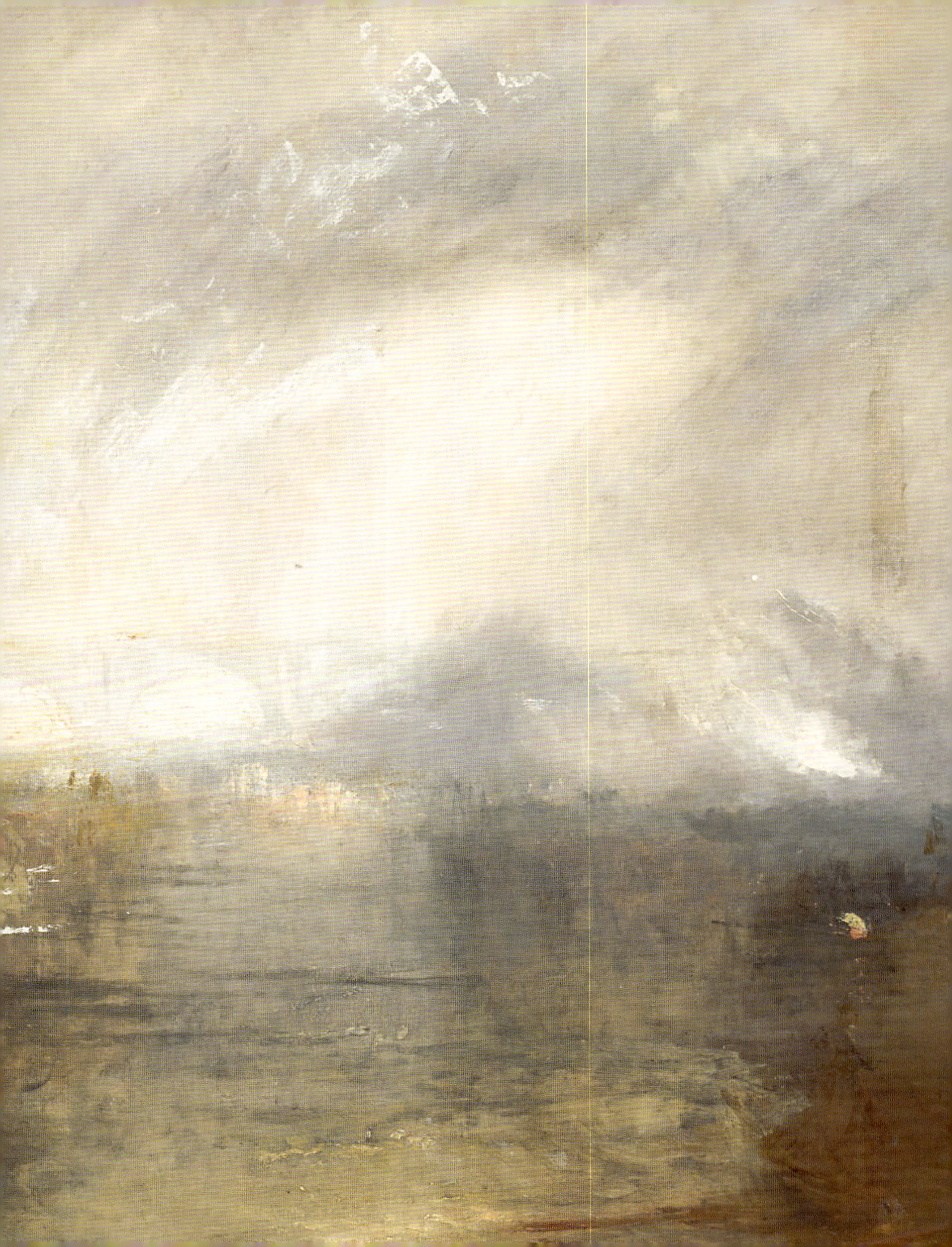

AIRY VISIONS: TURNER'S LATE WORK

In 1842 Turner made two extraordinary works that have become emblematic of the energy, experimentalism and boldness of his late work: the oil painting *Snow Storm – Steam-Boat off a Harbour's Mouth* and the watercolour *The Blue Rigi* (nos.166 and 158). Showing Turner's unmatched range and technical prowess, they point to the continuities and new initiatives that shaped the last fifteen years of his career. Both works extend the artist's lifelong exploration of nature's power, be that its terrifying force or awesome beauty. *Snow Storm* signposts Turner's enduring (and indeed, in this period, intensifying) fascination for the sea and modern technology but pushes representation of both to new affective heights. Resulting from Turner's rediscovery of the Alps (he began touring the area again from 1836), *The Blue Rigi* sees Turner scale new technical heights in the medium that launched his career. It belonged, however, to a new phase in which Turner did not exhibit watercolours, instead using an agent to show a select band of prospective clients draft versions of compositions the artist could then paint to order (such as no.157).

Turning sixty in 1835, he could very well have fallen back on his financial position and standing to fulfil contemporary expectations that one should slow down, but Turner did no such thing. He relentlessly pursued his vision with exceptional energy and vigour for some years to come. That year was marked by one of the most extensive and taxing of all his European sketching tours, and he continued to venture abroad until 1845. In late summer 1840 he was to be found in Venice for the last time. There, seemingly for his own pleasure, he made limpid, luminous watercolours of a place that had captivated him and spawned a significant body of work (nos.154–5).

Turner remained highly visible and engaged in the art world of the 1830s and 40s. While continuing to imagine the classical past, he made topical paintings of present-day issues. He painted a damning indictment of the transatlantic slave trade (fig.37, p.58), captured the catastrophic fire that destroyed the Houses of Parliament (no.162), and mused on the threat to traditional occupations posed by mechanisation (no.163). Maintaining his involvement with the print trade, he was commissioned by publishers to make watercolours of places he had not visited, such as the River Ganges and the Himalayas in India (nos.152–3).

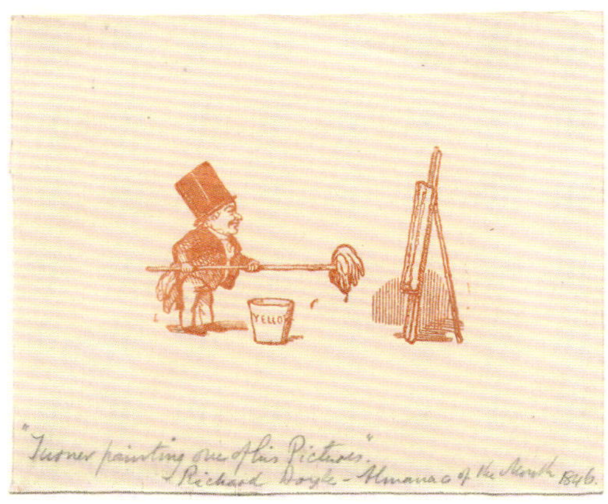

FIG. 42 J.M.W. Turner by Richard Doyle, 1846. Woodcut, 8·5 × 10·5 (paper size)
National Portrait Gallery, London. Acquired, 1973

In 1836 Constable commented on Turner's Royal Academy exhibits, which included *Juliet and her Nurse* (no.164): 'Turner has outdone himself – he seems to paint with tinted steam, so evanescent, and so airy.'[1] This eloquent description of his colleague's work came as journalistic criticism of Turner reached a new level of ferocity. For every sympathiser, there was an angry detractor. So while one might praise how Turner's colour 'dazzles the senses and storms the imagination', another would see 'extravagant colouring' or a 'flagrant abuse of his genius'.[2] Ridicule of his love of yellow, which since the 1820s had acquired him monikers like 'Yellow Dwarf', found visual form in a caricature of 1846 (fig.42). Some have perceived one of his most yellow paintings, *Ancient Italy – Ovid Banished from Rome* (no.165), as a veiled allegory on his own fate at the hands of critics.[3]

J.M.W. Turner *The Thames above Waterloo Bridge* (detail) c.1830–5 (p.196)

NO. 151 **J.M.W. Turner** *Dudley, Worcestershire* for *Picturesque Views in England and Wales* c.1832
Watercolour and bodycolour on paper, 29·3 × 43·2
National Museums Liverpool, Lady Lever Art Gallery

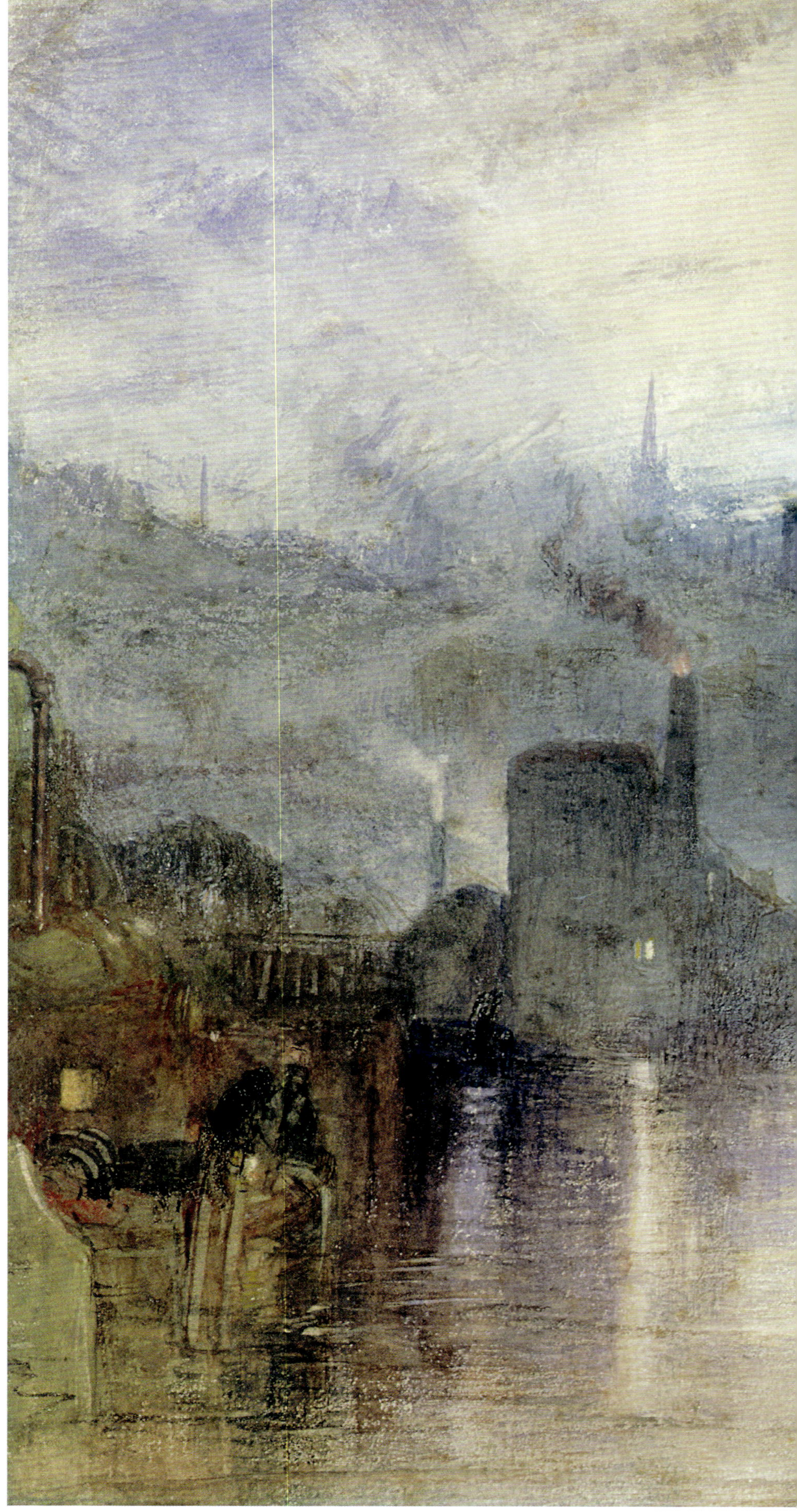

This powerful watercolour conveys the transformation wrought by the industrial revolution on the West Midlands town of Dudley, which Turner visited in 1830. In a composition that likely conflates two viewpoints (similar to the bending of topographical accuracy at Brighton, no.121), Turner presents a dramatic view down the canal – flanked by loaded barges, fiery furnaces, and smoking chimneys – to the town. Looming prominently above in a juxtaposition of old and new is the ruin of Dudley Castle. The watercolour's most arresting feature, however, is the thick veil of smoke. Rendered by Turner a Dudley landmark in itself, this haze is conjured by a combination of means – pigment applied with a drier brush, scrubbing away at the surface and thousands of stippled marks. This technical *tour de force* of a watercolour was engraved for the publishing project, *Picturesque Views in England and Wales*. More industrial sublime than strictly picturesque, perhaps, but Turner nevertheless demonstrates here, as in so many of his other late works, the beguiling pictorial potential of modern Britain, smog and all.

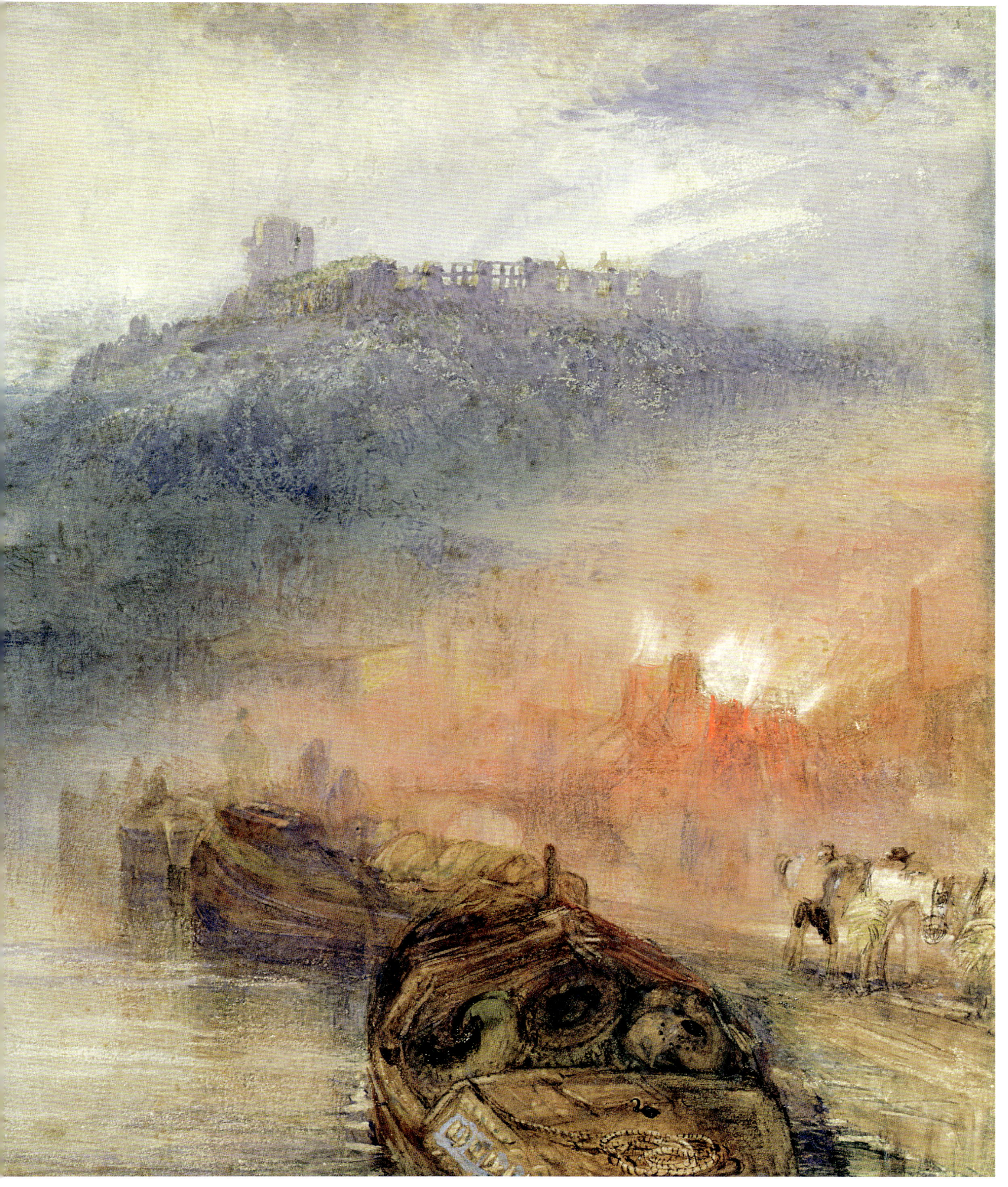

NO. 152 **J.M.W. Turner** *Mussooree and the Dhoon from Landour* 1835
Watercolour and gouache, over graphite, on off-white wove paper, edge mounted on cream wove card, 12·3 × 20·2
The Art Institute of Chicago, Gift of Dorothy Braude Edinburg to the Harry B. and Bessie K. Braude Memorial Collection, 2013.1039

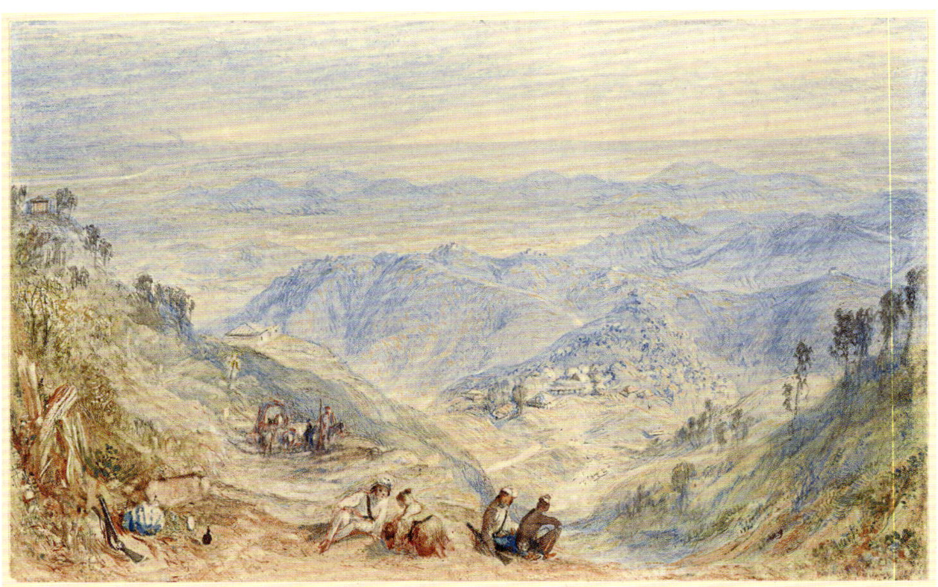

NO. 153 **J.M.W. Turner** *Rocks at Colgong (Kahalgaon) on the Ganges, Bihar, India* c.1835
Pencil and watercolour heightened with bodycolour and stopping out, 13·3 × 20·3
Taimur Hassan Collection

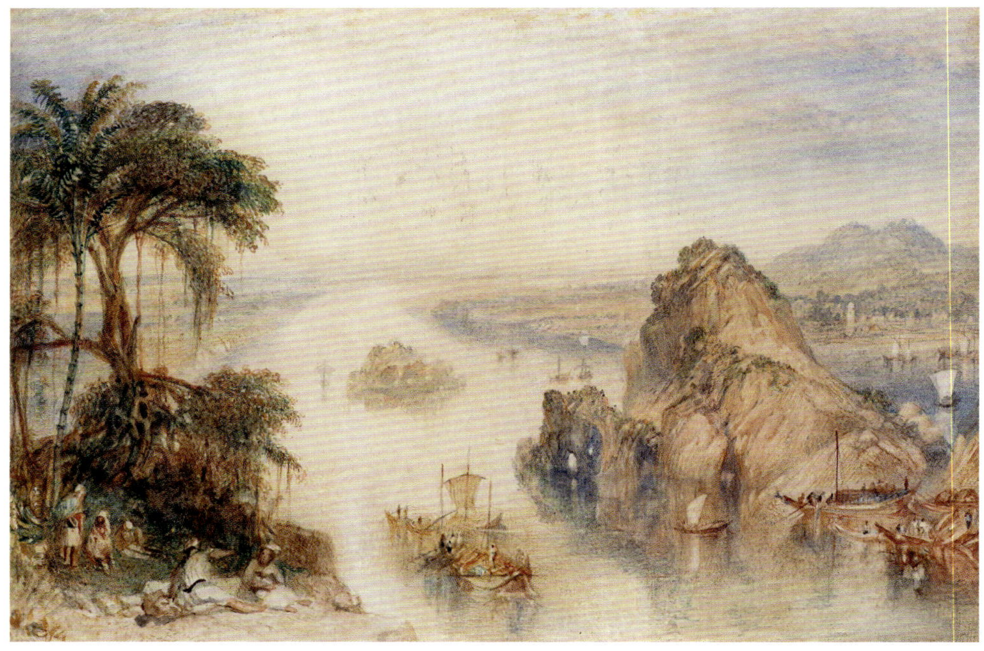

Despite never going to India Turner depicted it in several watercolours. Reflecting the growing British occupation of India, it was a frequent subject of imagery throughout his lifetime; indeed, Turner was friends with two of the most prominent producers of Indian landscape imagery, Thomas and William Daniell. Like the Indian battle scenes Turner painted around 1800 (see for example Tate, T04160), the present watercolour and *Mussooree and the Dhoon from Landour* (no.152) were based on images made by British military personnel, in this case the drawings of a young army officer, Lieutenant George Francis White (1808–1898). Turner's elaborations on White's drawing of Kahalgaon (known during British rule of India as Colgong) include the heightening of our vantage point over the Ganges, and the exaggeration of the height of the rocky island. He has included several river craft and figures and bathed the scene in a warm hazy light. Turner's elaboration of White's drawings were published in *Views in India, chiefly among the Himalaya Mountains taken during the tours in the direction of Mussooree, Simla, the sources of the Jumna and Ganges etc. in 1829, 31, 32* (Fisher, Son & Co, London and Paris, 1838).

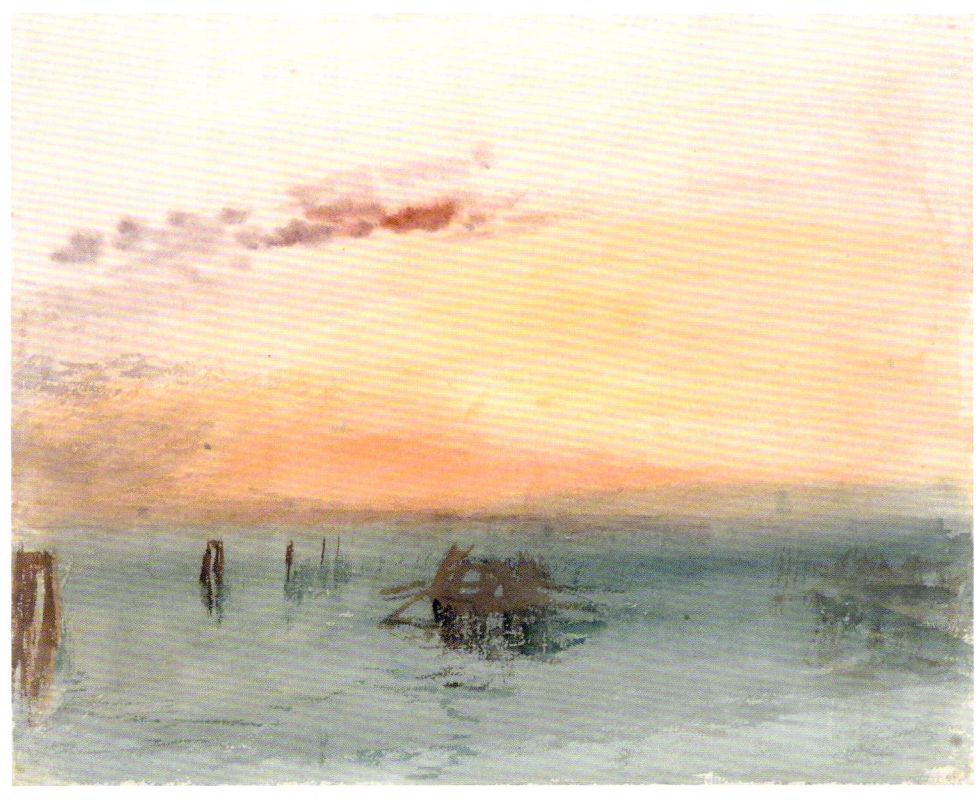

NO. 154 **J.M.W. Turner** *The Lagoon near Venice, at Sunset* 1840
Watercolour on paper, 24·4 × 30·4
Tate. Accepted by the nation as part of the Turner Bequest 1856

NO. 155 **J.M.W. Turner** *The Rooftops of Venice, with the Campanile of San Marco (St Mark's) and San Giorgio Maggiore, from the Hotel Europa Palazzo Giustinian) at Sunrise* 1840
Watercolour on paper, 19·8 × 28
Tate. Accepted by the nation as part of the Turner Bequest 1856

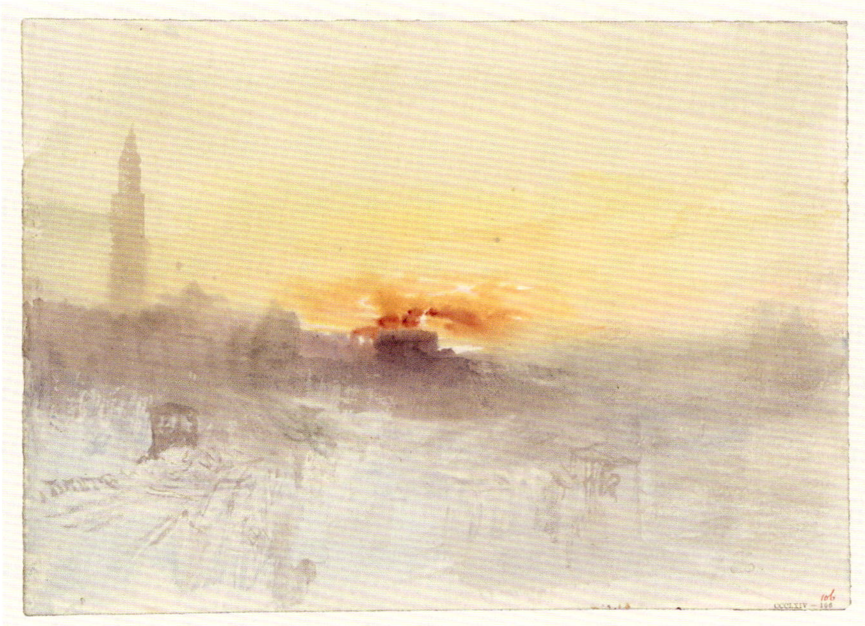

Like *The Lagoon near Venice, at Sunset* (no.154), this highly celebrated view of Venice at sunrise was made in 1840 on the last and longest of Turner's three visits to the 'City of Water'. Based on the identification of rooftop features amongst the pale grey marks in the foreground, it has been deduced that Turner painted this watercolour from a room high up in the Hotel Europa (Palazzo Giustinian), where he was staying. The campanile rises into the sky on the left and the dome of San Giorgio can be made out through the mist across the Bacino on the right. The real subject, however, is the brilliance of the morning sun rendered in molten dabs of yellow, orange and red watercolour applied and then left to bleed seamlessly into one another.

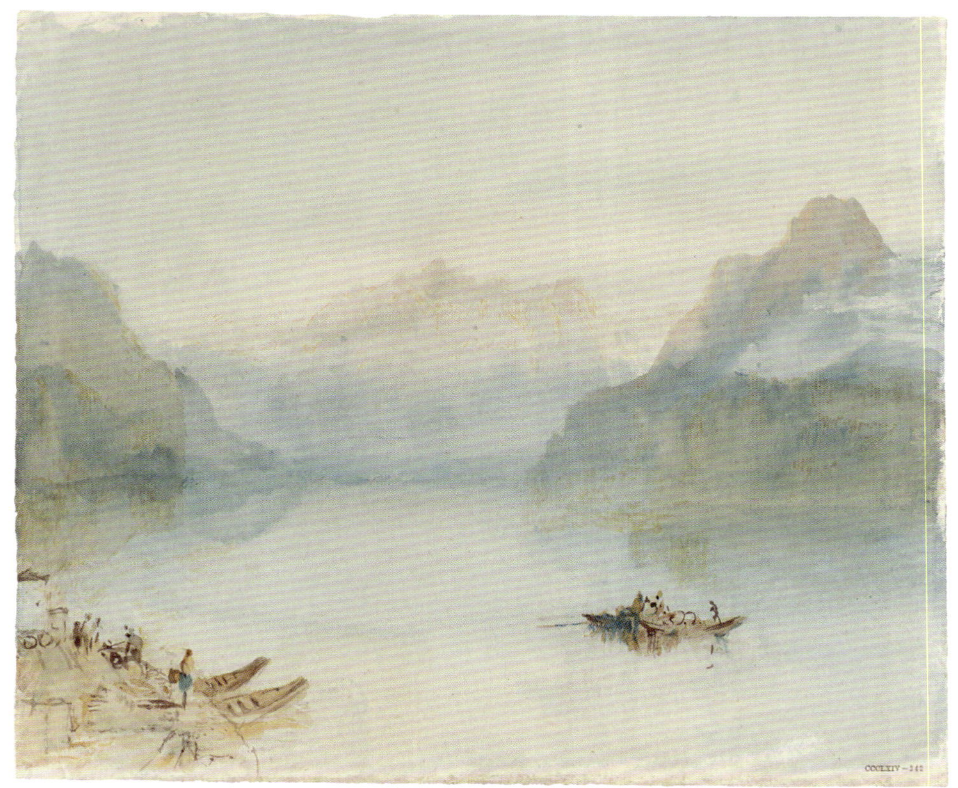

NO. 156 **J.M.W. Turner** *Lake Lucerne: The Bay of Uri, from Brunnen* c.1841–2
Watercolour on paper, 24·4 × 29·9
Tate. Accepted by the nation as part of the Turner Bequest 1856

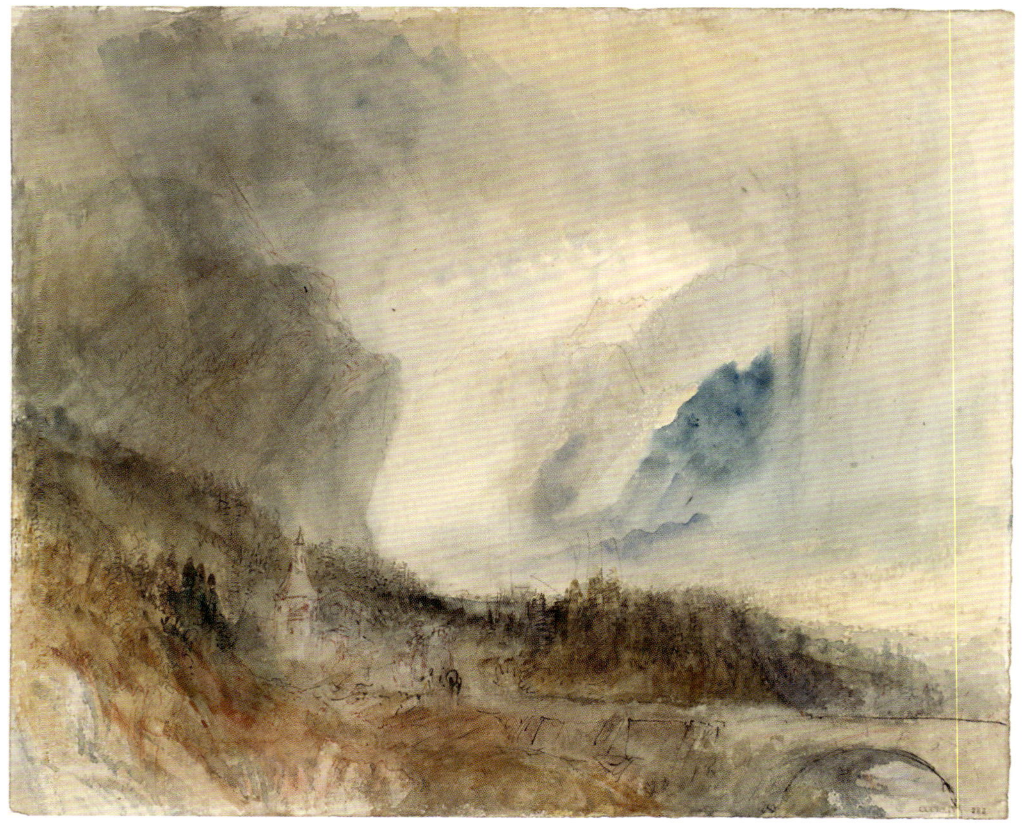

NO. 157 **J.M.W. Turner** *Storm in the St Gotthard Pass. The First Bridge above Altdorf: Sample Study* c.1844–5
Graphite, watercolour and pen on paper, 23·9 × 29·7
Tate. Accepted by the nation as part of the Turner Bequest 1856

NO. 158 **J.M.W. Turner** *The Blue Rigi, Sunrise* 1842
Watercolour on paper, 29·7 × 45
Tate. Purchased with assistance from the National Heritage Memorial Fund, the Art Fund (with a contribution from the Wolfson Foundation and including generous support from David and Susan Gradel, and from other members of the public through the Save the Blue Rigi appeal) Tate Members and other donors 2007

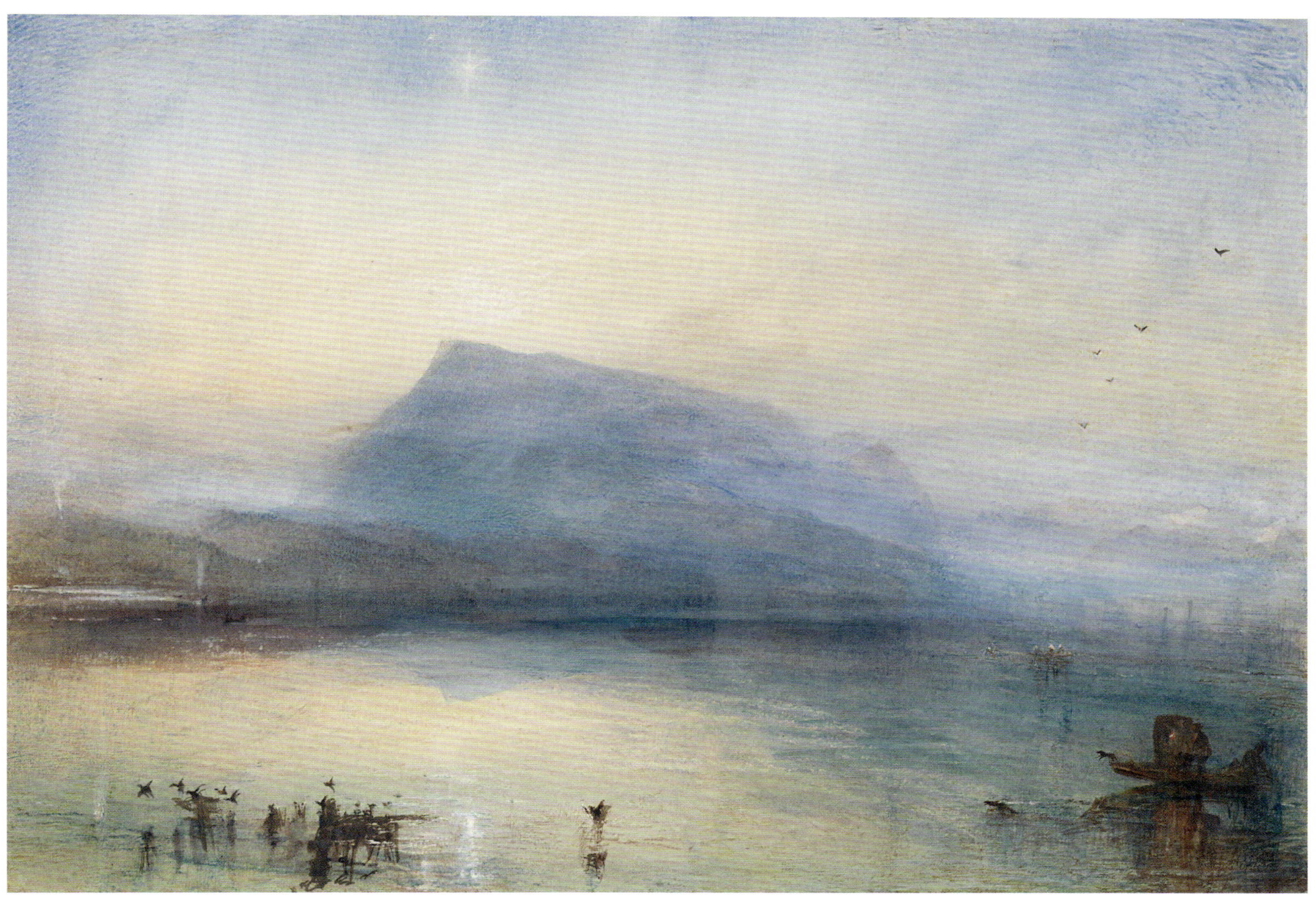

The Blue Rigi is amongst the most celebrated of Turner's works in watercolour. Turner had first pictured the famous mountain on Switzerland's Lake Lucerne, in 1802. Despite guidebooks enthusing about the panoramic views to be had from its summit, Turner never ascended the Rigi and was instead more interested in depicting its distinctive, isolated bulk beneath an array of skies. Robed in mist and silhouetted against the cool light of dawn, the majestic mountain emerges here from veils of transparent washes and an intricate tapestry of effects: paint has been dabbed away to create mist, while highlights on the lake and the morning star of Venus above have been scraped out, perhaps with the fingernail he was said to have kept long for this purpose. As much as we might revere it, *The Blue Rigi* was turned down by one potential purchaser on account of its radically different aesthetic to Turner's earlier watercolours. The artist was disappointed, too, by the sum his agent set for works like this, reportedly asking, 'Ain't they worth more?'

NO. 159 **Charles West Cope 1811–1890** *J.M.W. Turner* c.1828
Oil paint on card, 15·9 × 13
Lent by the National Portrait Gallery, London

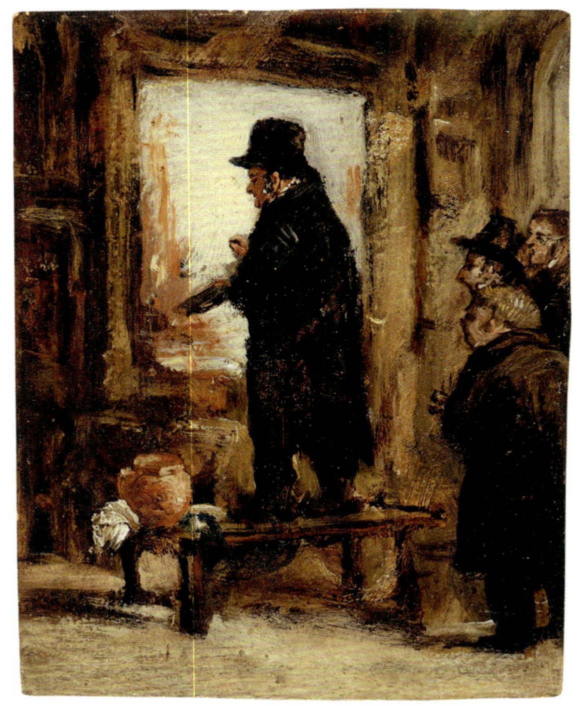

Turner is presented here in the guise by which he was often known in later life – as a 'magician' who used Varnishing Days (the days before exhibitions opened to the public) to finish his paintings or ensure they outshone his competitors'. This depiction also points to the complexities of Turner's public persona – despite being so secretive about his methods, he appears to have performed his stunts in front of an audience. He was observed working up his paintings into their finished form and applying the famous 'red blob' of 1832 (see pp.155 and 187). When the threat to curtail Varnishing Days arose, Turner reportedly said: 'Then you will do away with the only social meetings we have...on which we all come together in any easy unrestrained manner' (quoted in *Late Turner*, p.70). Turner's reaction reveals how much he valued those days as chance not just to size up competition but to enjoy a sense of camaraderie and collective achievement with his fellow Academicians.

NO. 160 **J.M.W. Turner** *The Thames above Waterloo Bridge* c.1830–5
Oil paint on canvas, 90·5 × 121
Tate. Accepted by the nation as part of the Turner Bequest 1856

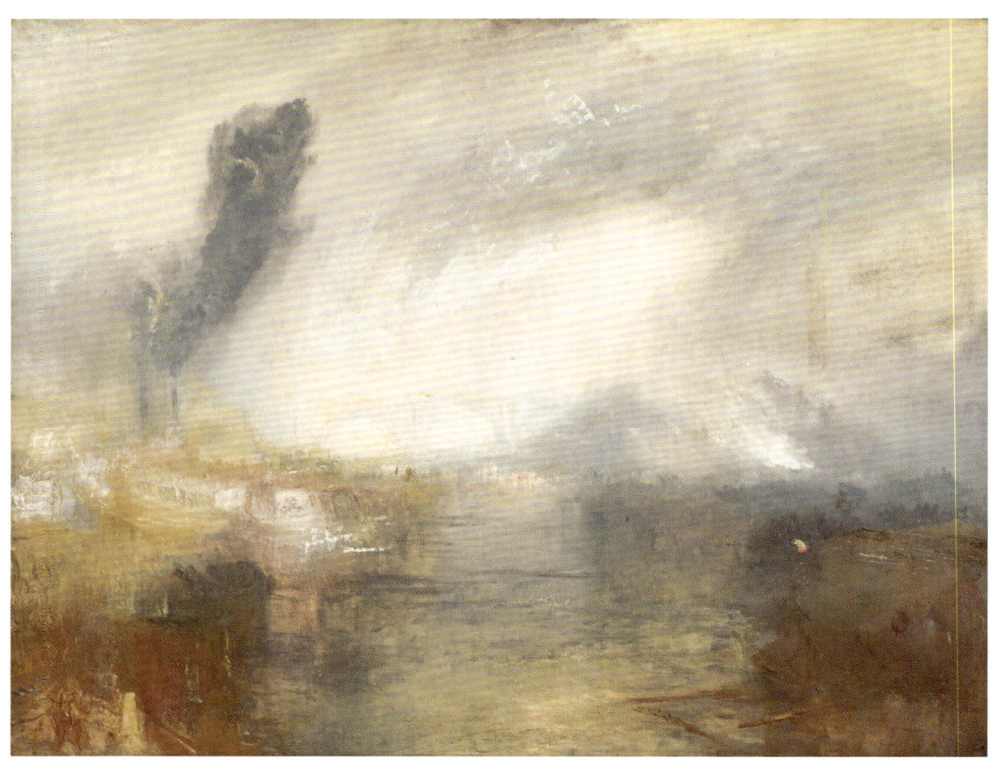

Turner may have had Constable's depiction of the same spot (no.150) in mind when he began this unfinished painting. Waterloo Bridge is barely discernible through the heavy atmosphere. This is surely Turner's point, for by the early 1830s the polluted environment of London was being hotly debated. Parliament discussed air pollution, operators of traditional barges complained about the dirt and disruption of the new steamboats and a cholera epidemic had swept the city in 1831–2. While industry does feature in Constable's painting its main subject was the 1817 opening of Waterloo Bridge; by 1832, when he exhibited it, this new landmark was old news. Indeed, in 1834 steamboat services began ferrying passengers from this very spot – Turner shows a large duel-funnelled steamer belching smoke. Perhaps Turner took up this view in order to expressly show what *really* characterised this vista in the 1830s – a disorientating cloud of fumes and a channel of churned up, filthy water.

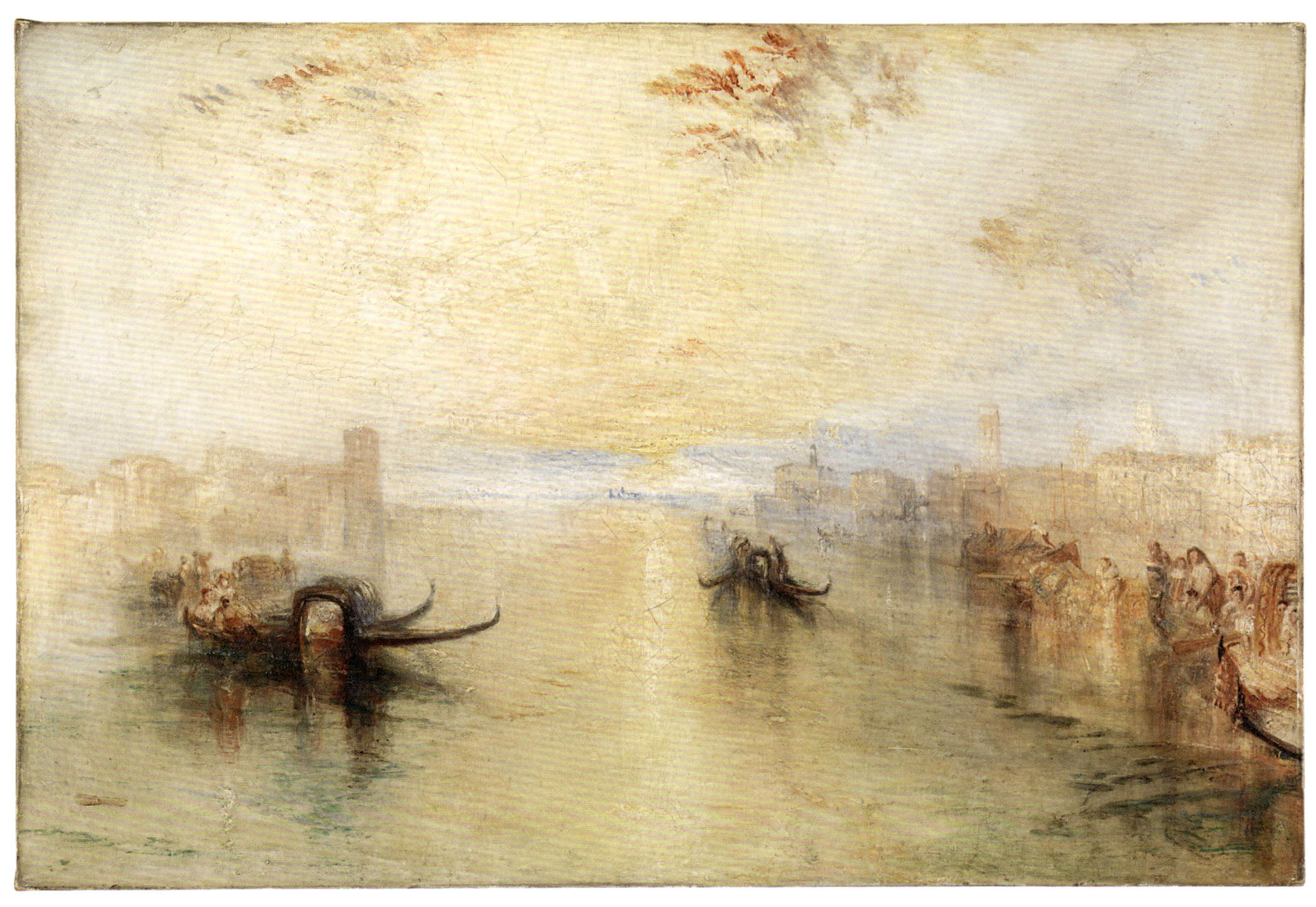

NO. 161 **J.M.W. Turner** *St Benedetto, Looking towards Fusina* exhibited 1843
Oil paint on canvas, 62·2 × 92·7
Tate. Accepted by the nation as part of the Turner Bequest 1856

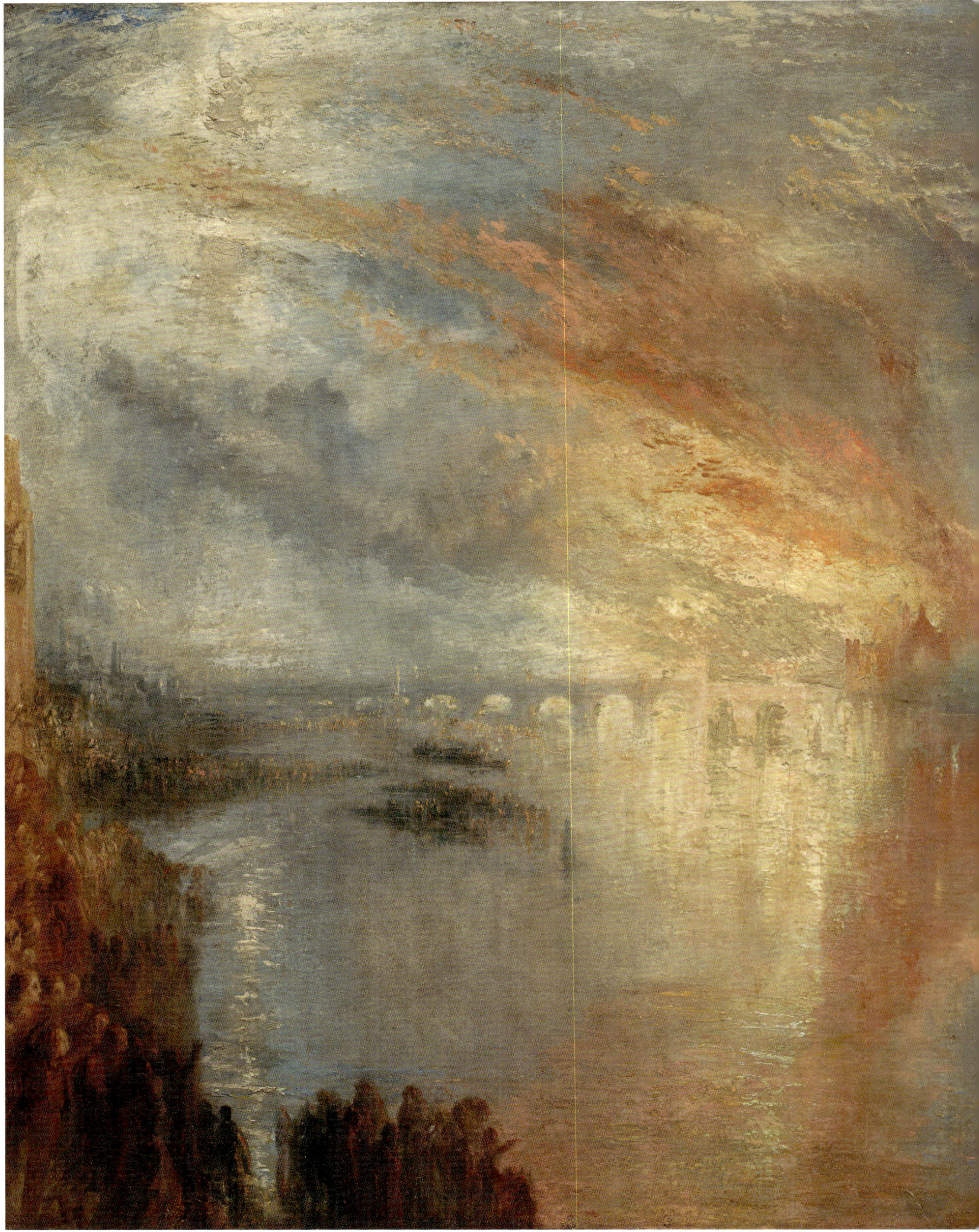

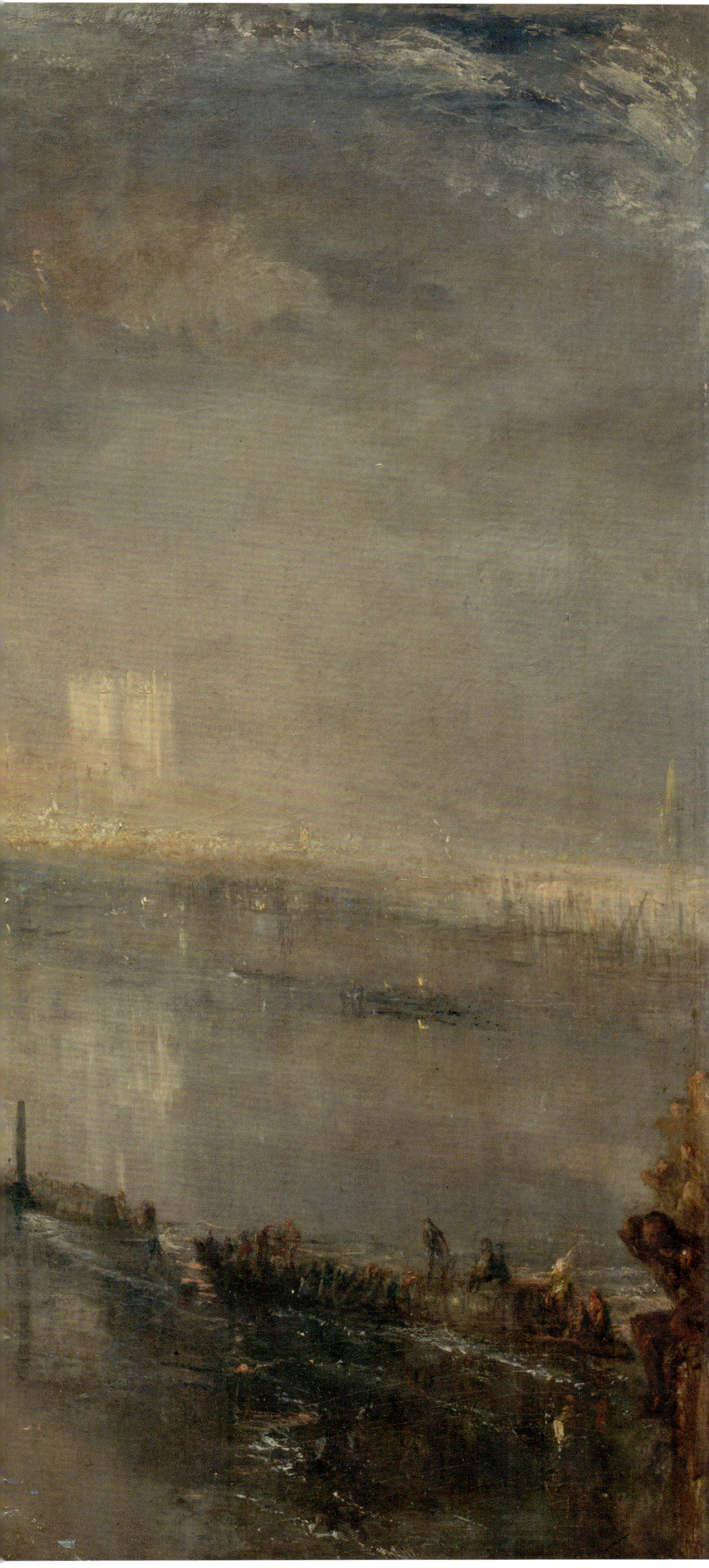

NO. 162 **J.M.W. Turner** *The Burning of the Houses of Lords and Commons, October 16, 1834* exhibited 1835
Oil paint on canvas, 92 × 123·2
The Cleveland Museum of Art, Bequest of John L. Severance 1942.647

The fire that destroyed the Houses of Parliament on the night of 16 October, 1834 was the perfect subject for Turner's brush. Since the start of his career Turner had painted all aspects of modern life, from the changes brought by industrialisation to momentous events such as this. Coming two years after the passing of the 1832 Representation of the People Act, which extended the right to vote to a greater number of people, the fire carried a powerful symbolism: it was as if the old order had self-combusted and a new political age was dawning. Turner clearly revelled in depicting the towering flames (which may well be exaggerated in height) and their reflection against the deep blue of night; indeed, he made another version of this spectacular subject (Philadelphia Museum of Art). The present version was last exhibited in London in 1883. In 2018 Birmingham Royal Ballet performed *Ignite*, a ballet inspired by this painting.

NO. 163 **J.M.W. Turner** *Keelmen Heaving in Coals by Moonlight* exhibited 1835
Oil paint on canvas, 92·3 × 122·8
National Gallery of Art, Washington, Widener Collection, 1942.9.86

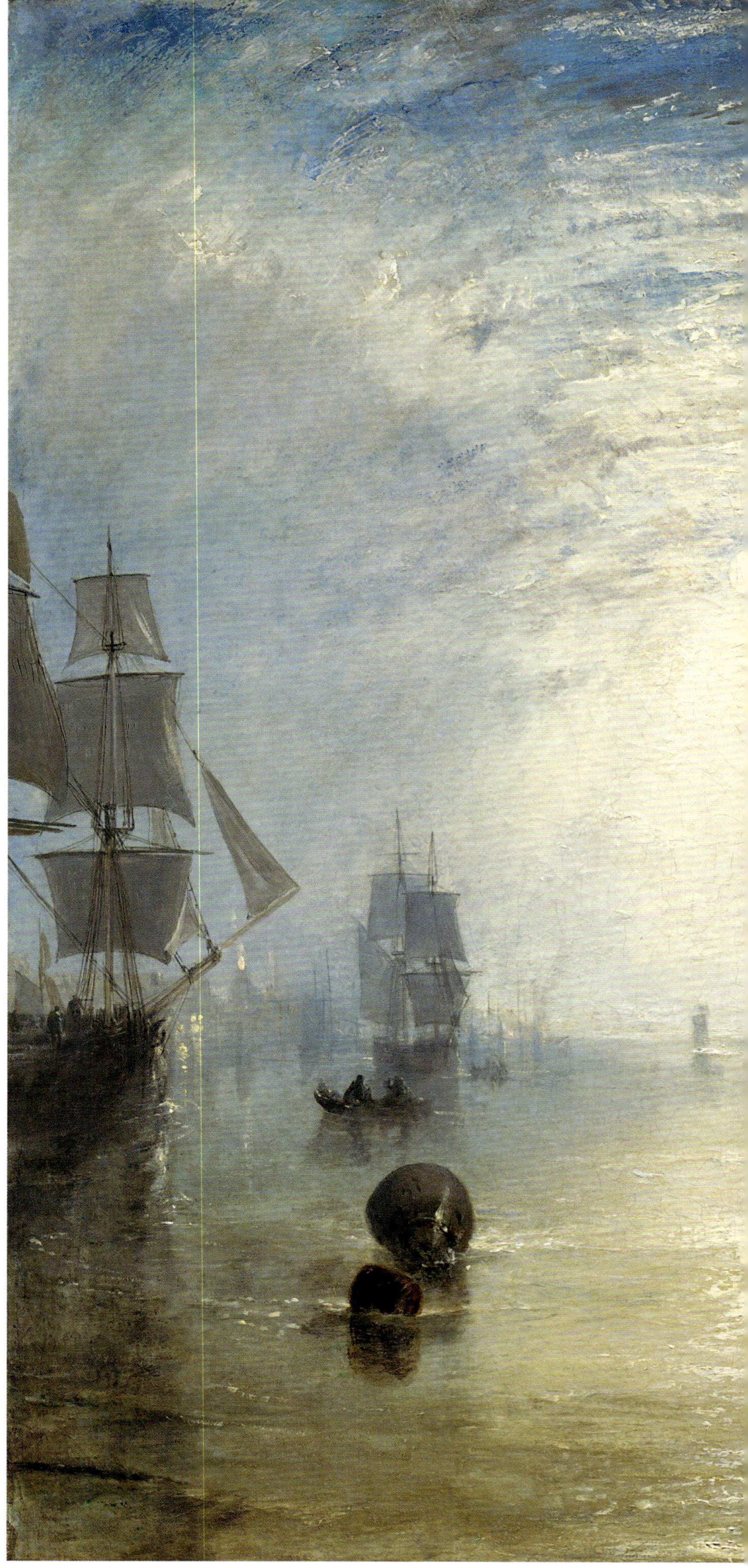

This is perhaps the most lyrical of all Turner's reflections on industry. Its setting is Shields, the port on the River Tyne near Newcastle in north-east England. The area was Britain's principle supplier of coal, and thus fuelled the nation's rapidly industrialising economy. On the right, men can be seen shovelling coal from barges known as keels into larger vessels for export around the country. Powerfully contrasting with the warm tones of firelight, the cool glow of the moon – its whiteness enhanced through juxtaposition with thick black smoke – is symbolic. While it indicates that industry never sleeps, in the same year that Turner completed *Keelmen* it was reported in the British press that the 'hardy, laborious keelmen' were being 'deprived of their ancient occupation… by means of new appliances', namely the newly constructed railways that soon negated the need for coal barges. *Keelmen* therefore demonstrates Turner's astute eye for a poignant narrative – illuminated by moonlight, the sun had already set on the keelmen's traditional occupation. This painting was commissioned by an industrialist, the Manchester cotton spinner Henry McConnel, as a pendant to his other Turner, of Venice, a pairing inviting comparison between the thriving state of industrial Britain's mercantile wealth and the downturn in fortunes of the once-dominant Venice.

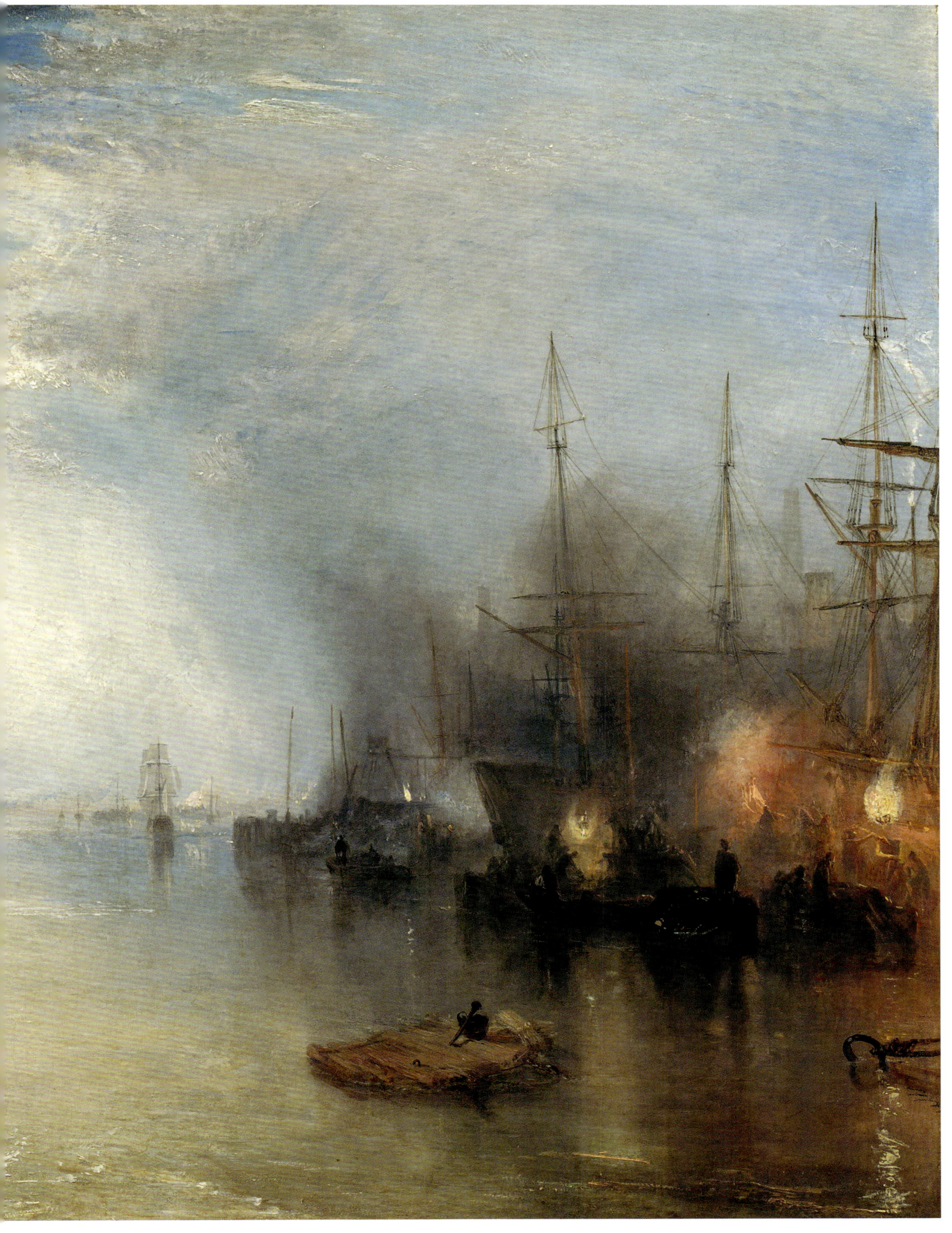

NO. 164 **J.M.W. Turner** *Juliet and Her Nurse* exhibited 1836
Oil paint on canvas, 88 × 121
Private Collection

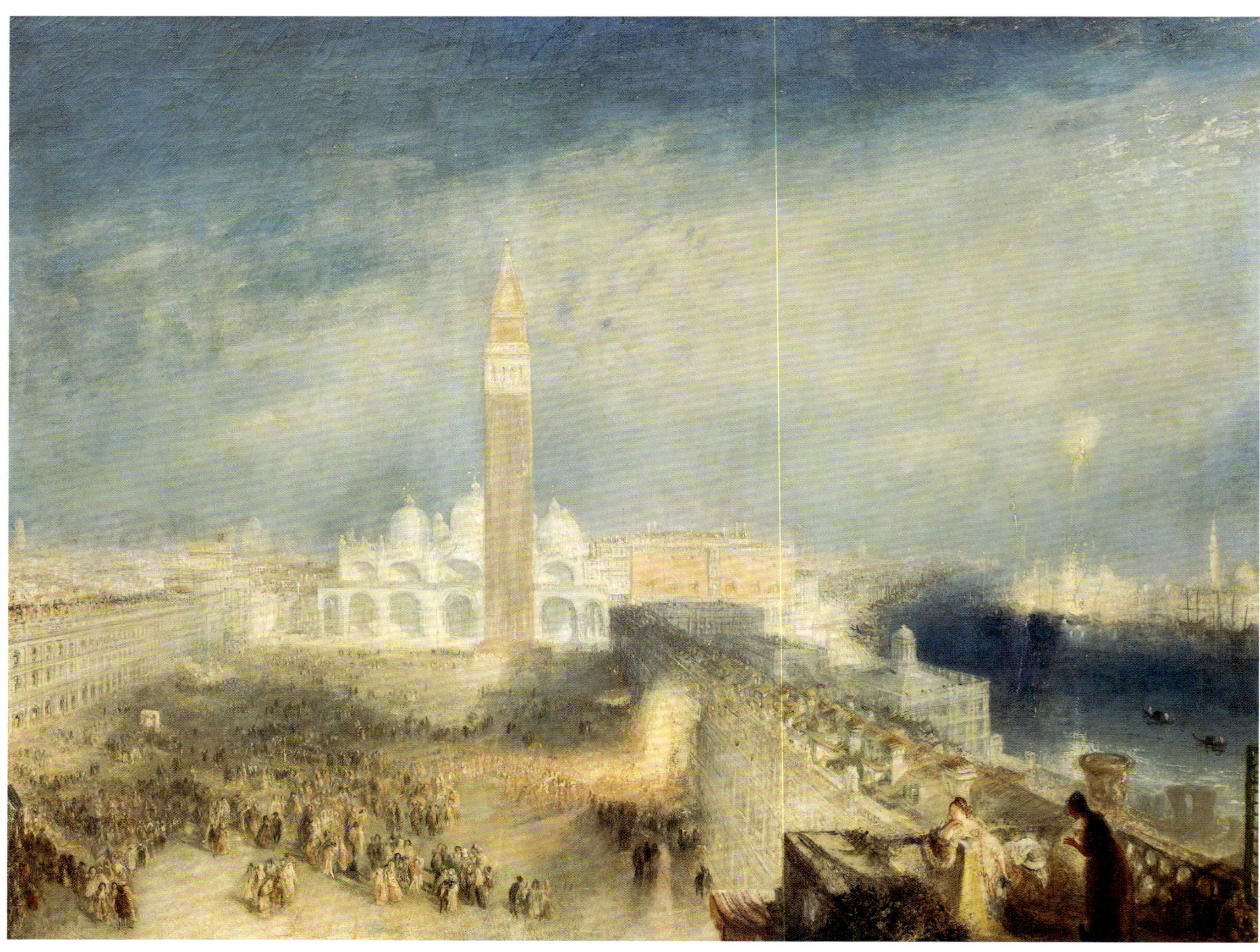

This painting lit the touchpaper of a new phase in Turner's reputation. An exceptionally caustic review describing it as a 'strange jumble...streaked blue and pink and thrown into a flour tub' (*Blackwood's Magazine*, October 1836) inspired a teenage John Ruskin to write to Turner, offering to publish a defence. Turner replied, 'I never move in these matters. They are of no import save mischief' (Gage, *Correspondence*, pp.160–61). Controversially, the picture places Shakespearean character Juliet (seen at lower right) in Venice, as opposed to Verona, *Romeo and Juliet*'s setting. Turner's Juliet has not only travelled to Venice, but also, seemingly, in time. From Punch and Judy in the Piazza to the possible glow of gas lighting (aside from the fire in the piazza), the scene has plenty of details to locate it in the 1830s (Warrell, *Turner and Venice*, pp.71, 73). Perhaps an allegory for modern-day romance in the so-called City of Love, Juliet's part in the painting is unclear. Nonetheless, *Juliet and Her Nurse* took on a life of its own as Ruskin's defence of it became the germ of his five-volume dissertation on Turner, *Modern Painters* (1843–60). Little did Turner know in 1836 that this painting and its young admirer would become so critical to his posthumous reputation.

NO. 165 **J.M.W. Turner** *Ancient Italy: Ovid banished from Rome* exhibited 1838
Oil paint on canvas, 94·6 × 125
Lent in honour of Richard Feigen by his children and grandchildren (in memoriam)

Seen through a dazzling yellow haze, a fantastical vision of Rome frames the white gold of the setting sun. The city's monuments are arranged in an impossible configuration: just to the left of the sun is the Arch of Constantine with the Aventine Hill rearing up behind it. Roman poet Ovid was banished from Rome in 8 AD; the figure grouping on the left, behind the chaos of what might be Ovid's ransacked belongings, appears to show his arrest. On the right two men push out a boat with a cage-like enclosure. Turner paired this work with *Modern Italy – the Pifferari* (Kelvingrove Art Gallery, Glasgow). Various suggestions as to their collective meaning have been made; *Ancient Italy* may signify the danger posed to the arts when creative freedom (symbolised by Ovid) is banished. Indeed, one critic resented Turner's creative licence here, citing the painting's 'supernatural' appearance and lamenting that 'talent, so mighty and poetical' was 'running riot into such frenzies' (*Athenaeum*, 12 May, p.347). Turner's high regard for the painting is evidenced by its status as one of a small number of works (including no.164) after which he issued stand-alone prints.

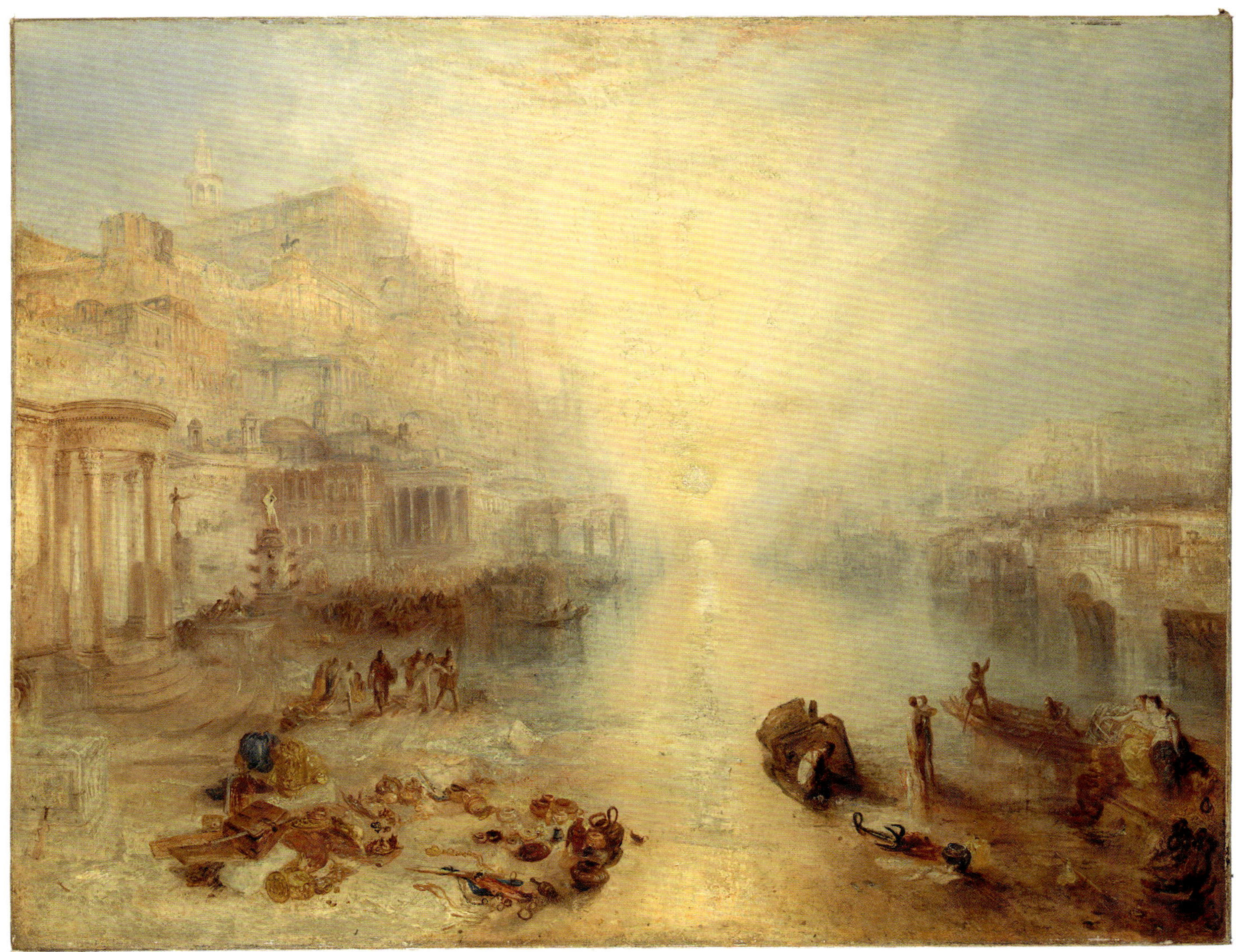

NO. 166 **J.M.W. Turner** *Snow Storm – Steam-Boat off a Harbour's Mouth making Signals in Shallow Water, and going by the Lead. The Author was in this Storm on the Night the Ariel left Harwich* exhibited 1842
Oil paint on canvas, 91·4 × 121·9
Tate. Accepted by the nation as part of the Turner Bequest 1856

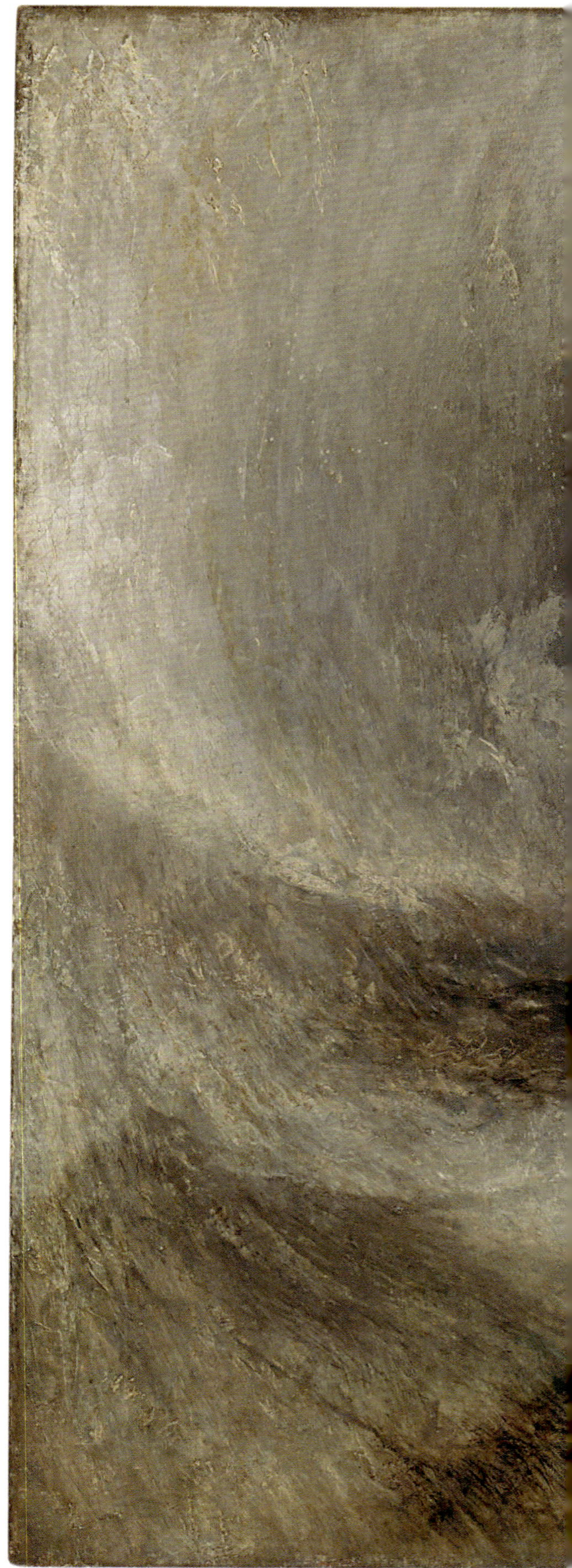

This is one of Turner's most daring paintings. In a battle between modern machine and nature, a steamboat faces a blizzard, its black fumes joining the whirling vortex of snow and sea. In a story that echoes one about eighteenth-century marine painter Claude-Joseph Vernet, Turner claimed he was lashed to the mast so that he could observe this storm. Neither this, nor his claim in the full title of the painting that the ship was the 'Ariel' can be proven, but Turner clearly wanted viewers to see this dizzying scene as an authentic record – just as Constable wished for his own work.

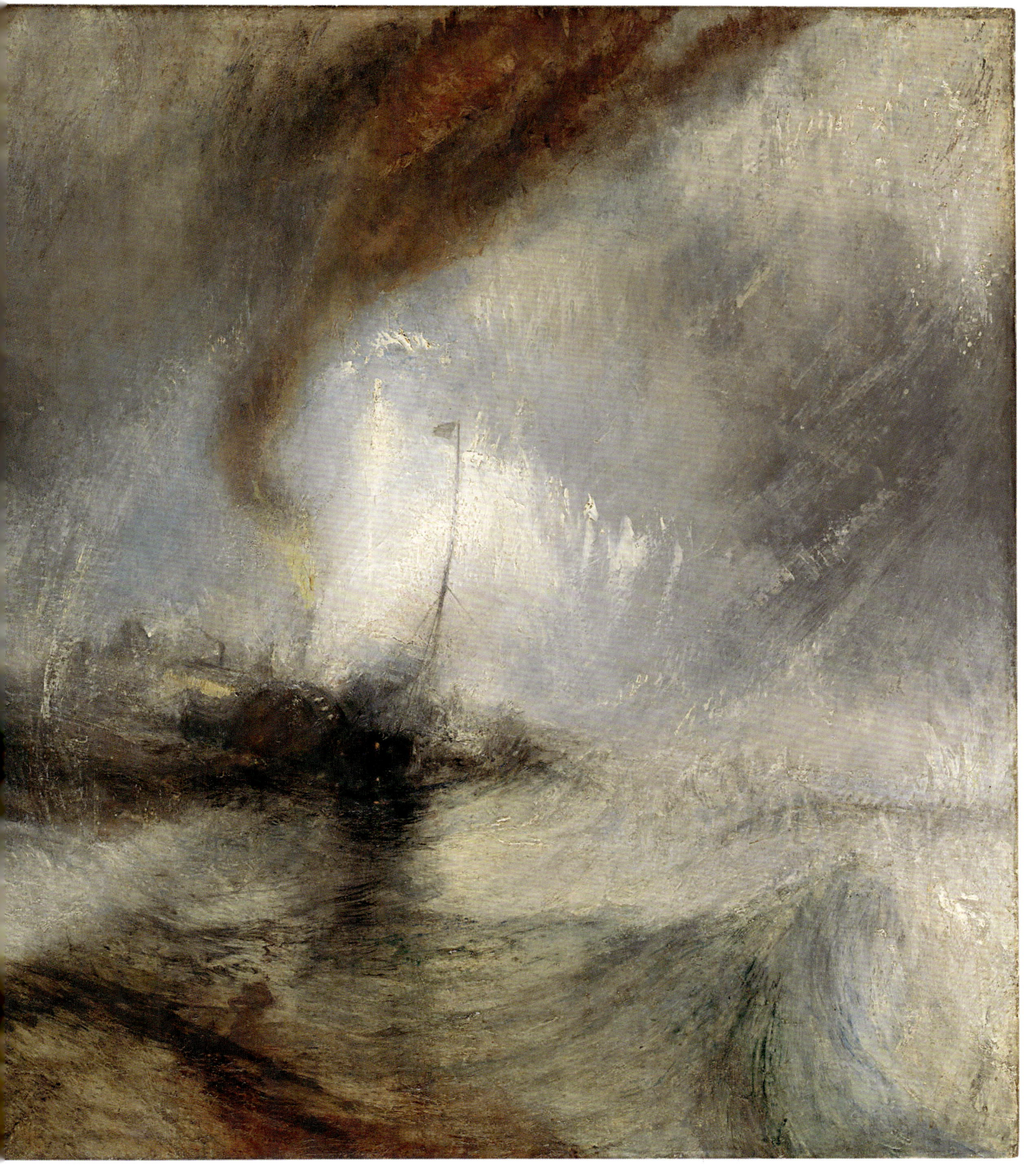

NO. 167 **J.M.W. Turner** *Light and Colour (Goethe's Theory) – the Morning after the Deluge – Moses Writing the Book of Genesis* exhibited 1843
Oil paint on canvas, 78·7 × 78·7
Tate. Accepted by the nation as part of the Turner Bequest 1856

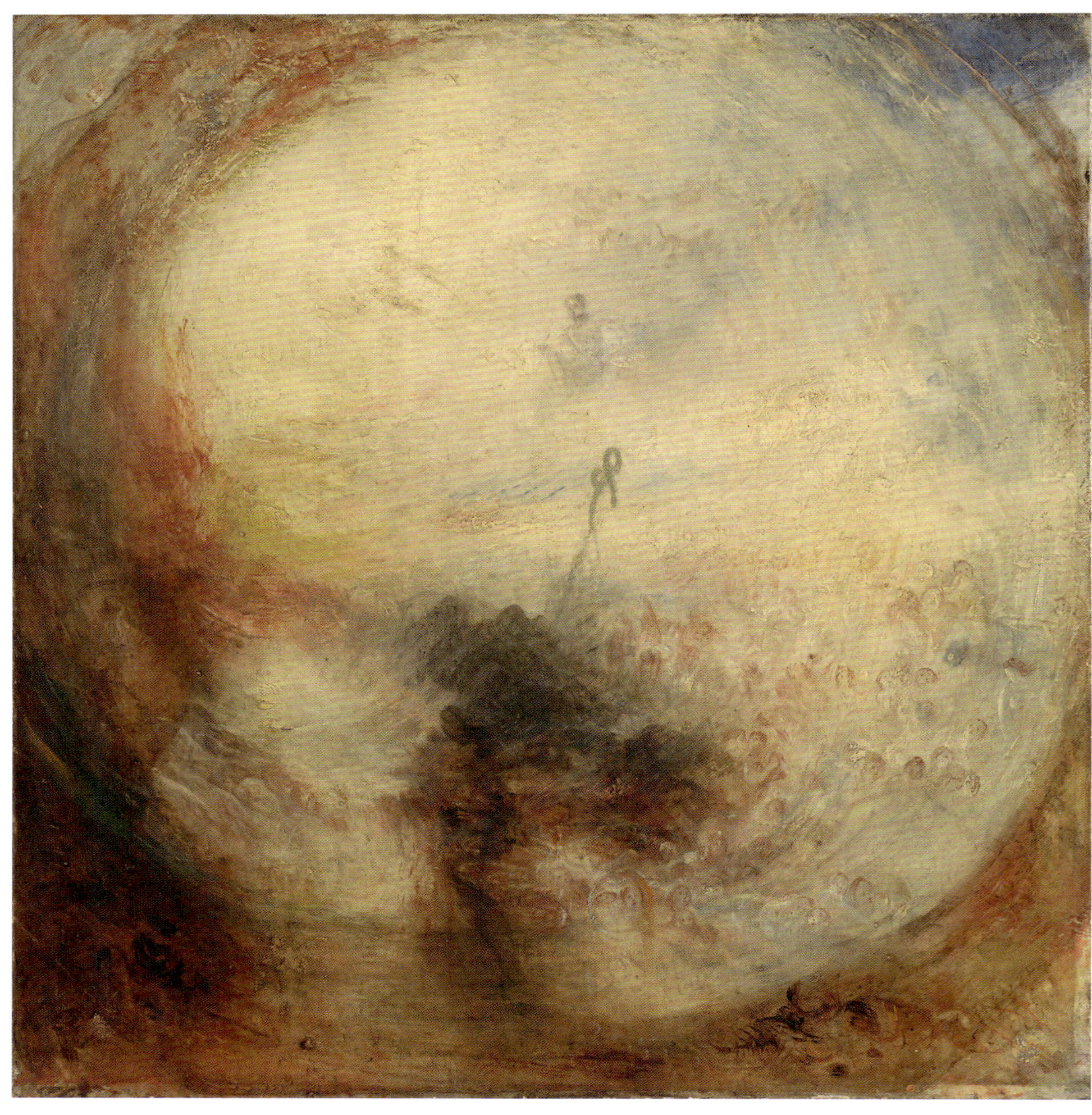

NO. 168 **J.M.W. Turner** *Shade and Darkness – the Evening of the Deluge* exhibited 1843
Oil paint on canvas, 78·7 × 78·1

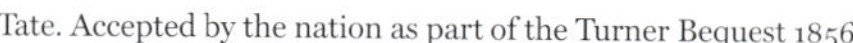

Tate. Accepted by the nation as part of the Turner Bequest 1856

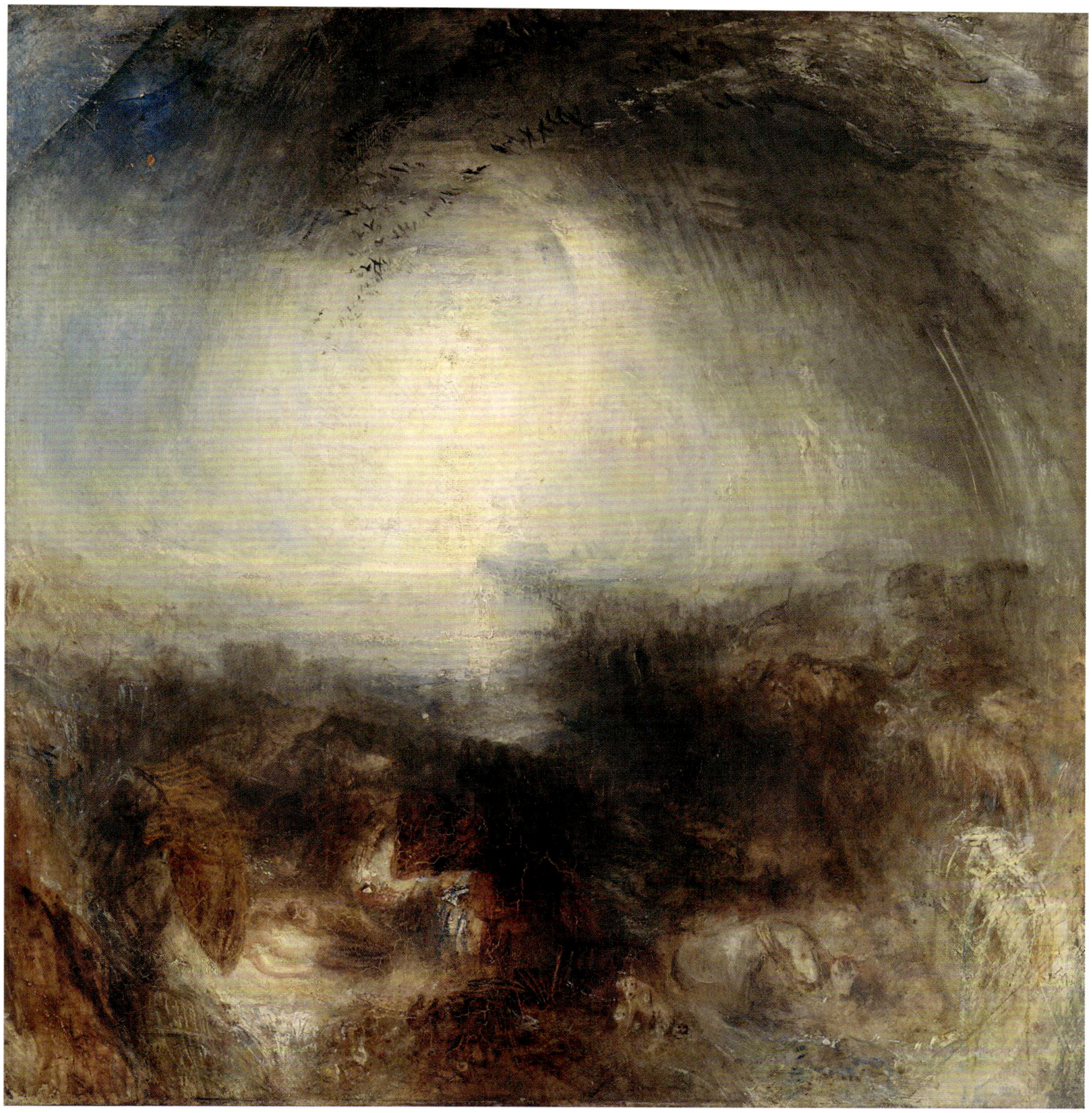

In 1840 Turner took to a new format, the square canvas. The description of this pair as 'octagon-shaped daubs' (*Spectator*, 13 May 1843) certifies that they were first shown with octagonal windows. Whatever final shape Turner gave their image, these square canvases produce an intense viewing experience. Emphatic vortexes characterise this pair: as much as our eye might seek rest, their whirlpools of paint pull our gaze into their spinning course. Combining Biblical imagery and colour theory, their meanings are as complex as their atmospheres are electrifying. Noah's ark is at the centre of no.168, with animals gathered in the foreground.

The figure in the sky of no.167 is Moses. Turner exhibited this painting with lines of his own poetry that described how the 'returning sun' '[e]xhaled earth's humid bubbles'. Instead of the rainbow mentioned in the Bible, Turner paints bubbles within what appears to be a giant bubble. Critics took him to task, questioning his theology and the 'prismatic chaos' of the pair (*Athenaeum*, 17 June 1843). Given Constable's passion for the rendering of light and shade it is tempting to wonder what he would have made of these paintings had he lived to see them.

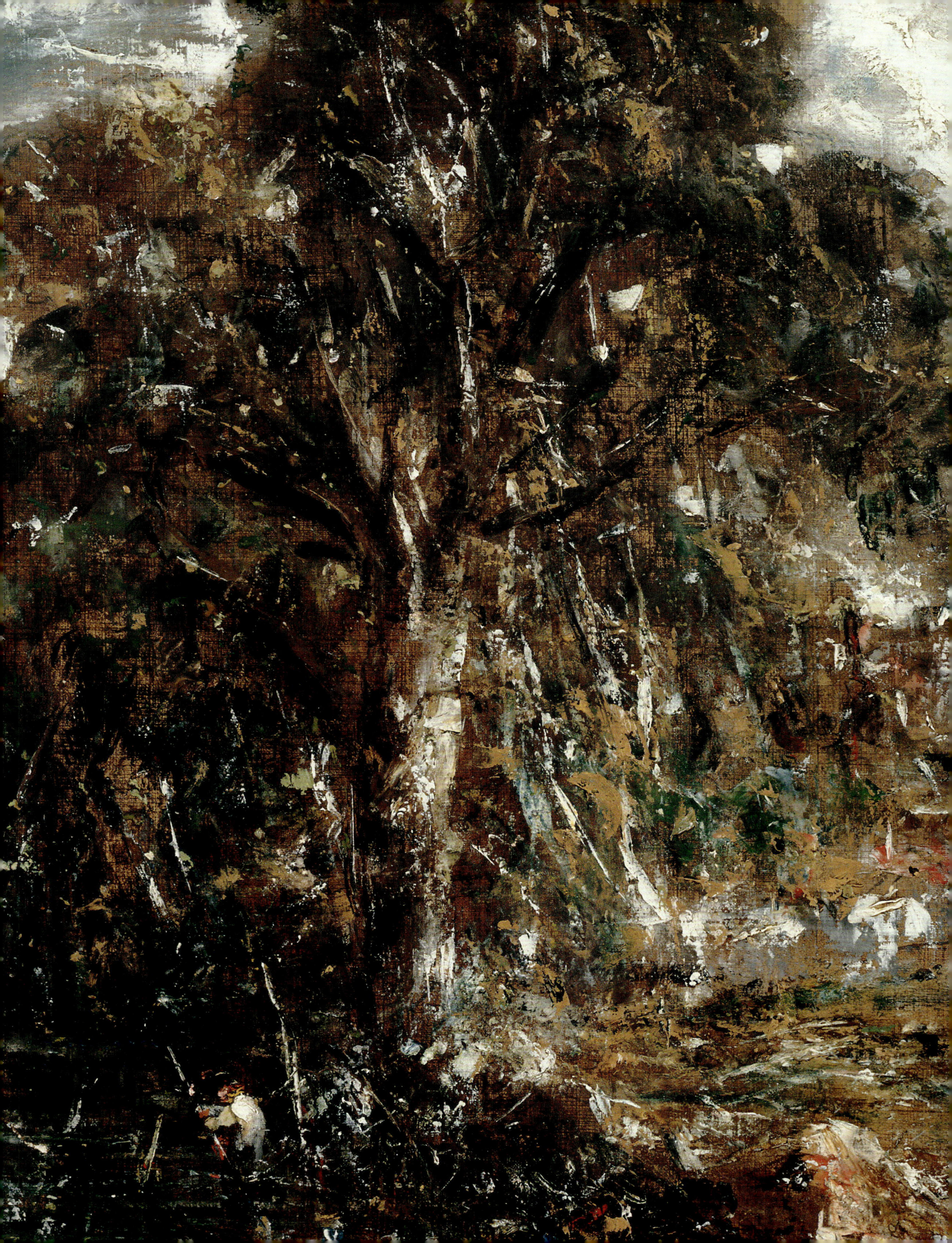

LANDSCAPE AND MEMORY

Constable died in 1837, aged sixty, and Turner in 1851, aged seventy-six. While of course neither could have foreseen the exact timing of their passing, especially in the case of Constable, who died suddenly, the last years of their lives bear many similarities.

Both remained intellectually and artistically active, though illness became a more frequent obstacle. Early in 1834 Constable reported being so ill that he had 'scarcely been able to do any one thing'.[1] His exhibits that year, all works on paper, included a drawing of a tree, possibly *Fir Trees at Hampstead* (no.169). Along with clouds, tree studies proliferated in Constable's studio, reflecting his love of them and desire to capture the particularities of different species.[2]

Constable's inclination to melancholy is reflected in the intense atmosphere of his late work. The warmer critical reception of his exhibits in 1835 led him to declare it 'the best year of my life – as to my being "liked"', but, still, he opined that the 'happy years are gone' (no.170). As much as he found solace in painting, reflecting that 'my canvas soothes me', the results are often far from soothing in mood: *On the River Stour* (no.174) reverberates with particularly restless energy.[3]

The year 1845 was a busy one for Turner. Having undertaken the role of acting President of the Royal Academy, by May he wrote, 'I have been so unwell that I was obliged to go away from Town to revival by a little change of fresh air'.[4] He turned to the sea for respite, boarding a boat to France where, on what would be his penultimate trip to the Continent, he made a series of meditative watercolours of sea and sky (no.183). After years of showing reworked canvases, in 1850 Turner exhibited four new works, a sequence that reflects his inclination to unfold a narrative across multiple canvases and which extended his lifelong fascination with classical mythology (no.184). In the Victorian art world, with the Pre-Raphaelites the talk of the town, these hazy renderings of now-unfashionable subjects were distinctly Turner's own. His age had been invoked in criticism of his work for decades already, but now 'it would seem as if Mr. Turner had possessed in youth all the dignity of age to exchange it in age for the effervescence of youth', as one critic wrote, continuing that it was still possible to 'trace through these eccentricities the hand of a great master and a matchless command over the materials of painting, careless of form and prodigal of light'.[5]

A significant parallel of the two artists' later years was their retrospective tendencies. Both looked back to their youth, painting landscape through the prism of memory to create new works out of old. This is emblematised by two enigmatic, unfinished paintings, Constable's *Stoke-by-Nayland* and Turner's *Norham Castle* (nos.176 and 181). Despite their apparent differences, these late works have much in common, reflecting their makers' preoccupation with the spirit of a place and with painting light. Based on compositions they had alighted on as young artists, they were significant enough to feature in their printed manifestos for landscape painting (nos.177–8 and 179–80). Constable issued a second edition of his *English Landscape Scenery* in 1833, a new subtitle explaining its purpose to 'Mark the Phenomena of the Chiar'Oscuro of Nature'. In a lecture given the year before he died, Constable spoke of chiaroscuro – the representation of light and shade – as the 'soul and medium of art'.[6] It was between these years that *Stoke-by-Nayland* was begun. Left unfinished, it thus became the makings of Constable's last painted essay on his life's pursuit, the depiction of light and shade in landscape. Perhaps with an eye on his own legacy as he turned seventy, in 1845 Turner was preparing a reprint of *Liber Studiorum*. It was probably then that the artist hatched the idea of painting *Norham Castle* and other *Liber* subjects afresh, recasting them to reflect the evolution of his vision for landscape (no.182). We will never know what Turner intended to do with this series or just how unfinished the works are. It is apt, however, that such a radiant canvas should be one of the last outputs of the artist of whom it was said that, in the moments before he died, 'the sun burst forth and shone directly on him with that brilliancy that he loved to gaze on'.[7]

John Constable *On the River Stour* (detail) c.1834–7 (p.215)

NO. 169 **John Constable** *Fir Trees at Hampstead* c.1833, ?exhibited 1834
Black lead on paper, 73·4 × 49·3
Trustees of the Cecil Higgins Art Gallery (The Higgins Bedford)

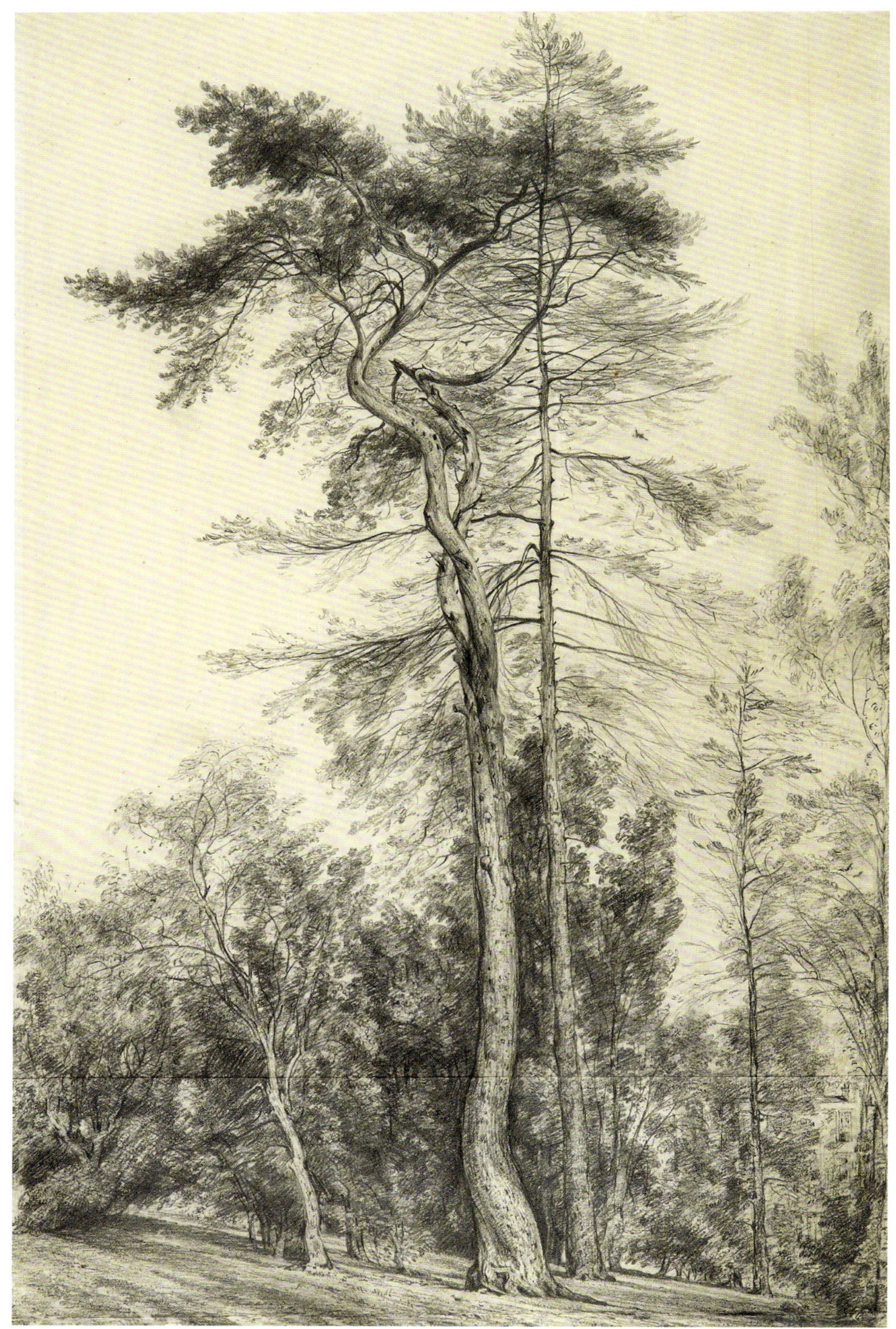

This has been described as one of the finest of Constable's late pencil studies of trees. He was clearly attracted to the contrasting forms of the two central firs – one which has grown straight, and another, more sinuous trunk that splits and twists around itself as it reaches up to the sky. Constable began this on a large sheet of paper; the 15cm strip of paper he added along the bottom of the drawing makes it even more imposing in size. This allowed him to continue the trunks down to the ground and show the trees in their context, including the buildings glimpsed through the branches at bottom right. He appears to have made these very detailed studies for his own benefit. In 1821, over ten years before this drawing was made, he quipped that he had made a particularly detailed drawing of 'ashes, elms & oak...which will be of quite as much service as if I had bought the feild [sic] and hedge row' (Beckett, VI, p.73).

NO. 170 *Letter from John Constable to Miss Mary Atkinson*, 14 May 1835
Ink on paper, 22·5 × 18·3
Private Collection

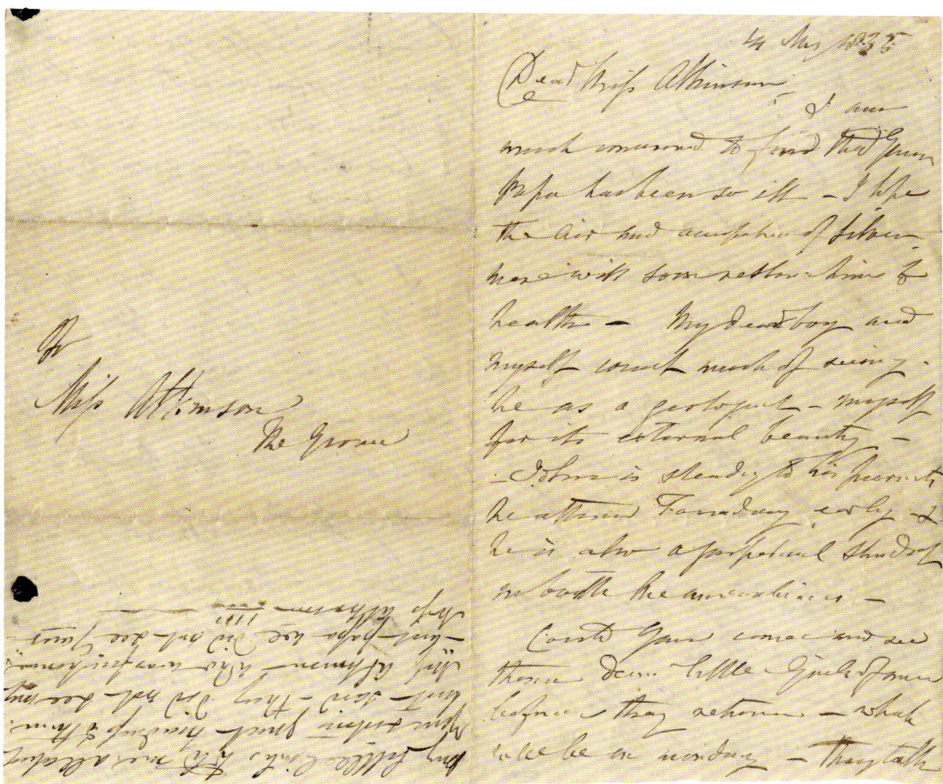

In this letter Constable describes 1835 as 'the best year of my life' 'with the exception of the days of my youth' in terms of the reception of his work. This was in spite of the critics' continued mention of his white highlights – 'my "hail and snow" at Midsummer'. Whereas once these remarks might have smarted more, perhaps now he could accept them as par for the course when breaking the mould. Poignantly, it conveys a moment of buoyancy and pride in a career which would be tragically cut short by his death two years later. It would seem from the traces of the letter's seal that Constable had continued to use black wax, signifying mourning, since the death of his wife Maria in 1828.

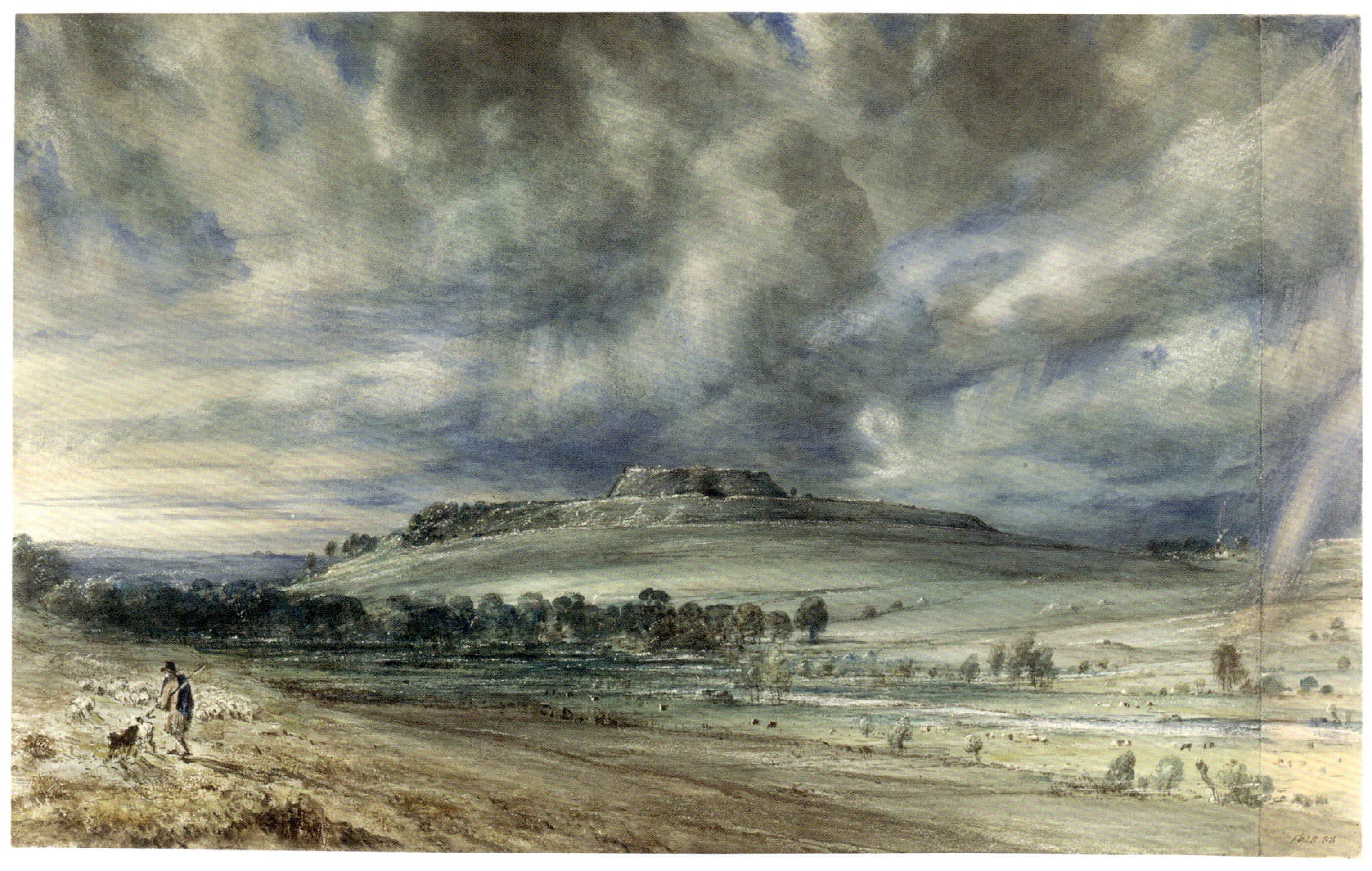

NO. 171 **John Constable** *Old Sarum* exhibited 1834
Watercolour on paper, 38 × 48·7
Victoria and Albert Museum, London. Bequeathed by Isabel Constable, daughter of the artist

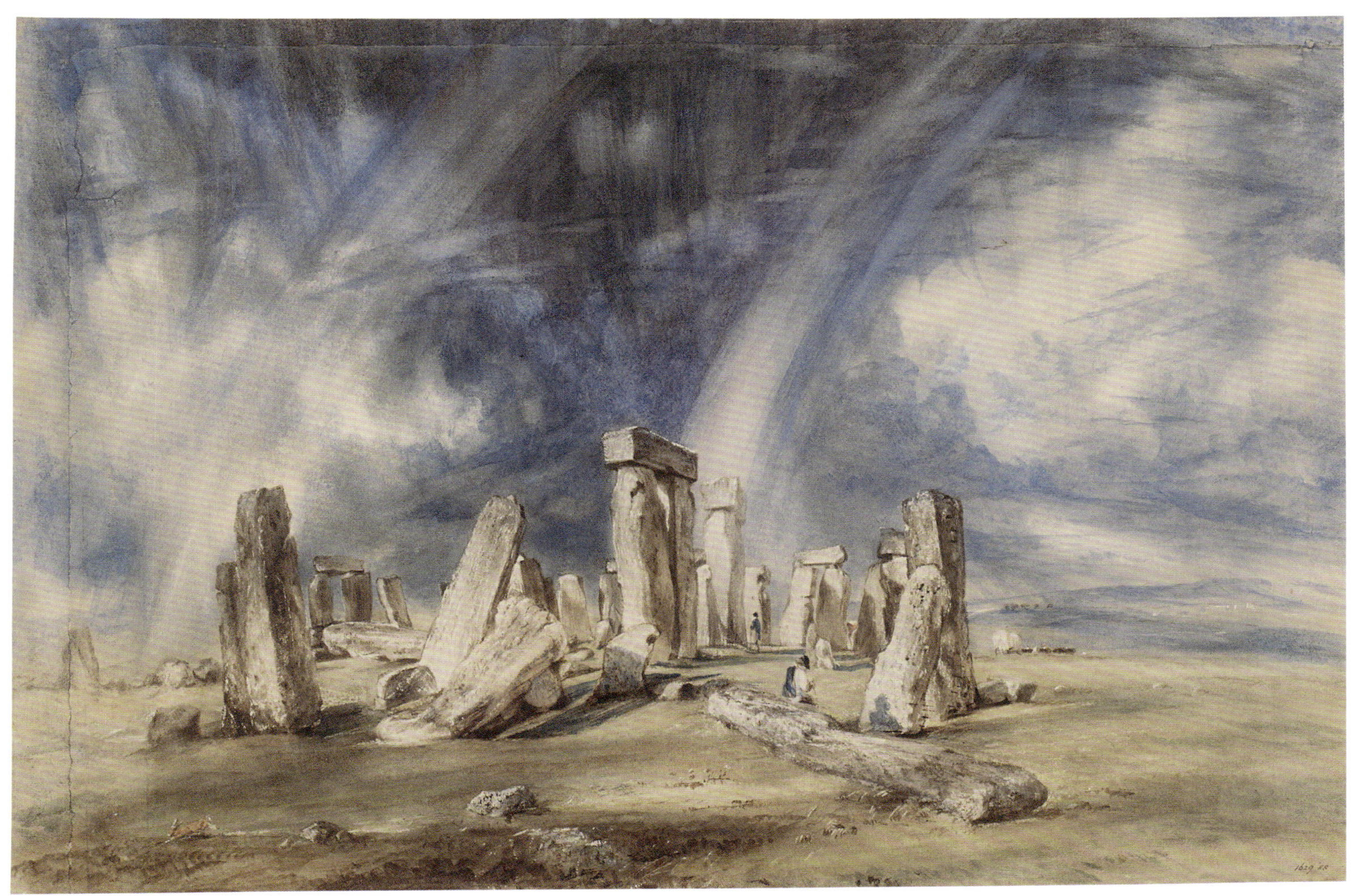

NO. 172 **John Constable** *Stonehenge* 1835, exhibited 1836
Watercolour on paper, 38·7 × 59·1
Victoria and Albert Museum, London

Representing the culmination of Constable's long association with their subjects and their locale, *Old Sarum* and *Stonehenge* are outstanding examples of his mature watercolour technique. Their expressive skies are reminiscent of those in his oil sketches; indeed the dragging and sweeping of deep purple pigment across the sky in *Stonehenge* radiates the same energy as *Rainstorm over the Sea* (no.143). Delicate highlights are created by scratching out to reveal gleaming white paper, such as on the mound of Old Sarum, the original site of Salisbury Cathedral.

Keen to avoid Stonehenge appearing like a '"stone quarry"', Constable wrote that any representation of the famous Neolithic earthwork would have to be a 'poetical one' (Beckett, V, p.85). Constable achieves this through his choice of angle, which foregrounds the most irregular, tilted and fallen stones, and through the spectacular double rainbow above. As the strip of paper added to the right of *Old Sarum* makes clear, Constable believed that this scene was not complete without a glimpse of his favoured atmospheric phenomena, the rainbow.

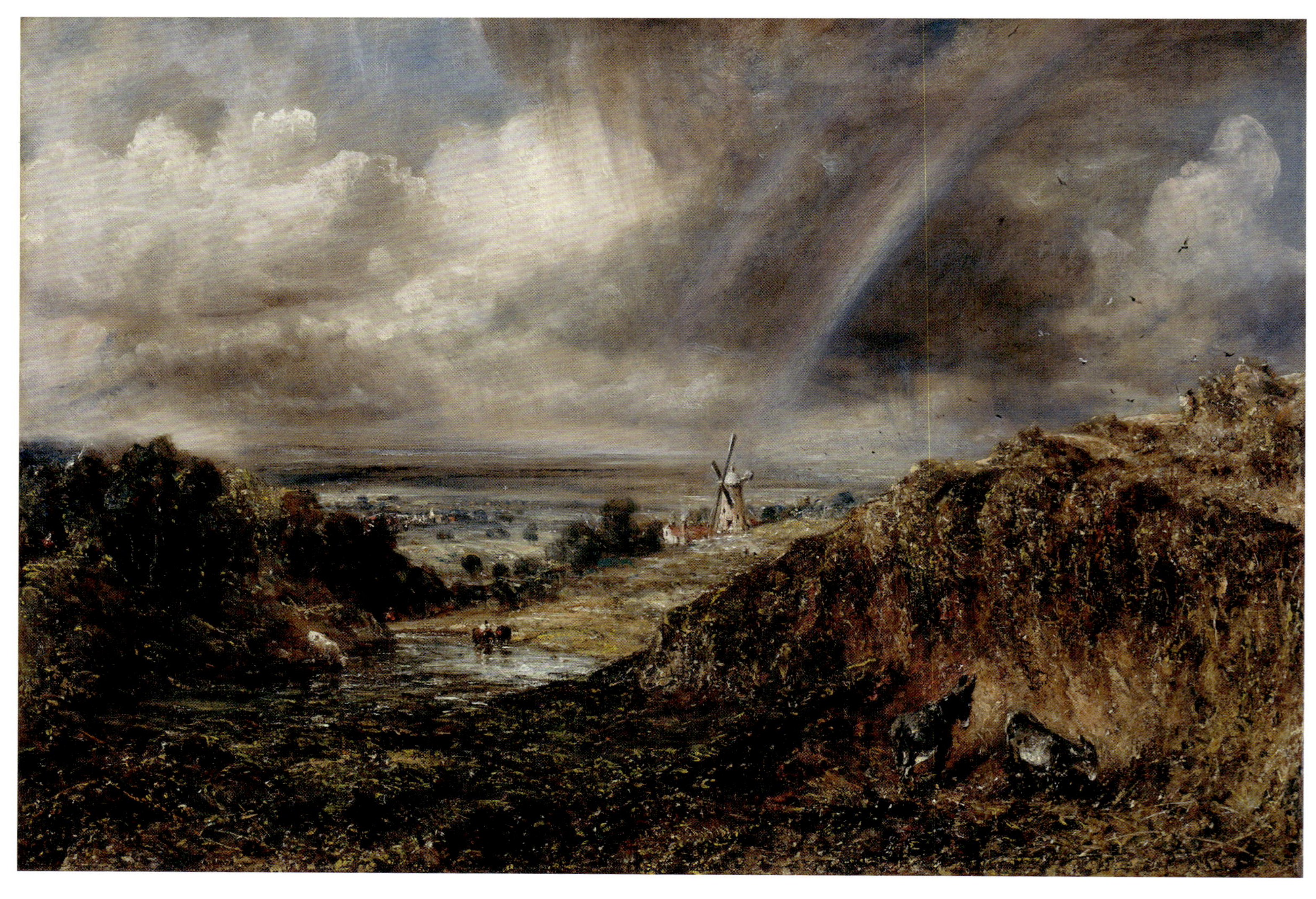

NO. 173 **John Constable** *Hampstead Heath with a Rainbow* 1836
Oil paint on canvas, 50·8 × 76·2
Tate. Bequeathed by Miss Isabel Constable as the gift of Maria Louisa, Isabel and Lionel Bicknell Constable 1888

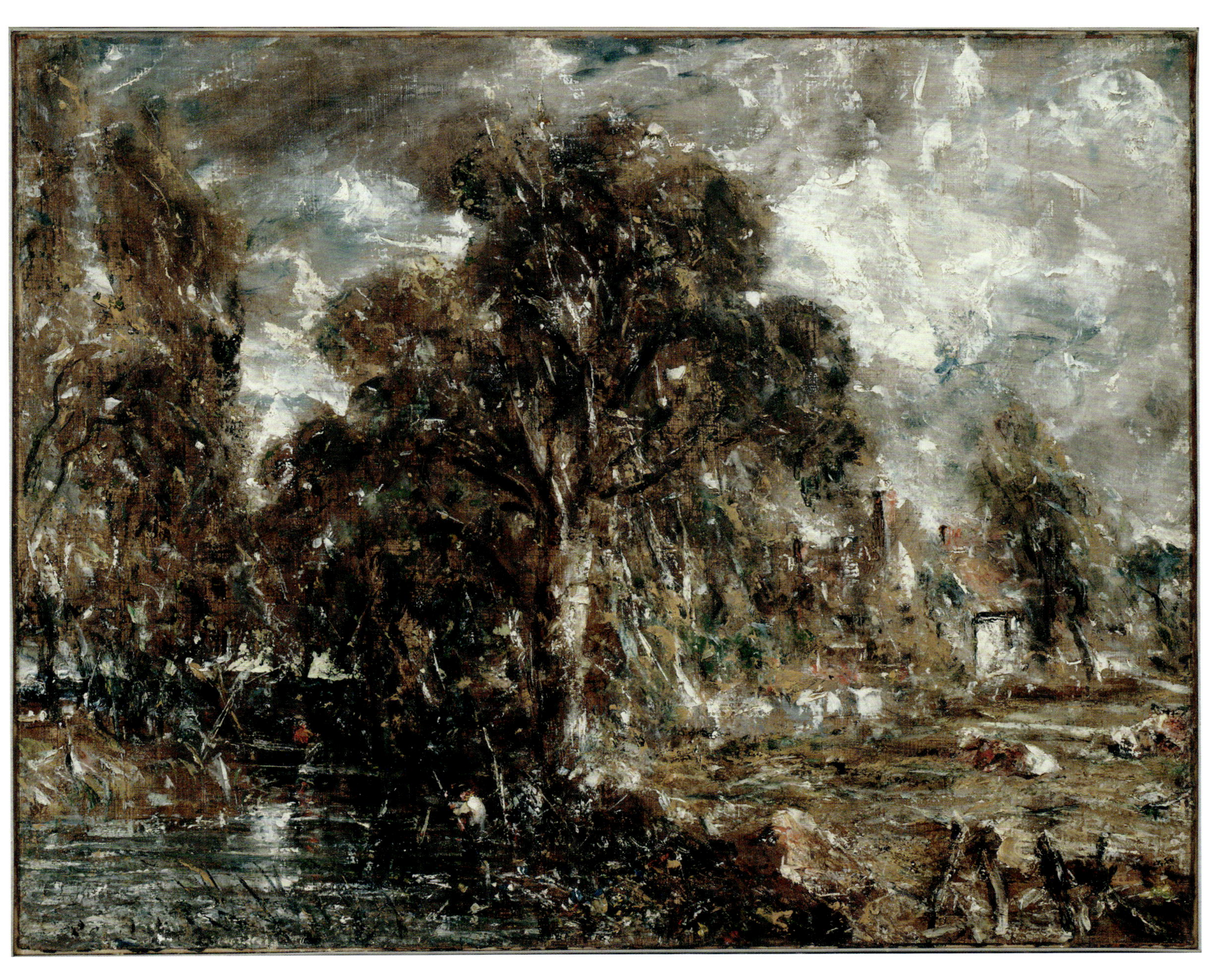

NO. 174 **John Constable** *On the River Stour* c.1834–7
Oil paint on canvas, 60·9 × 78·7
The Phillips Collection, Washington, D.C. Acquired 1925

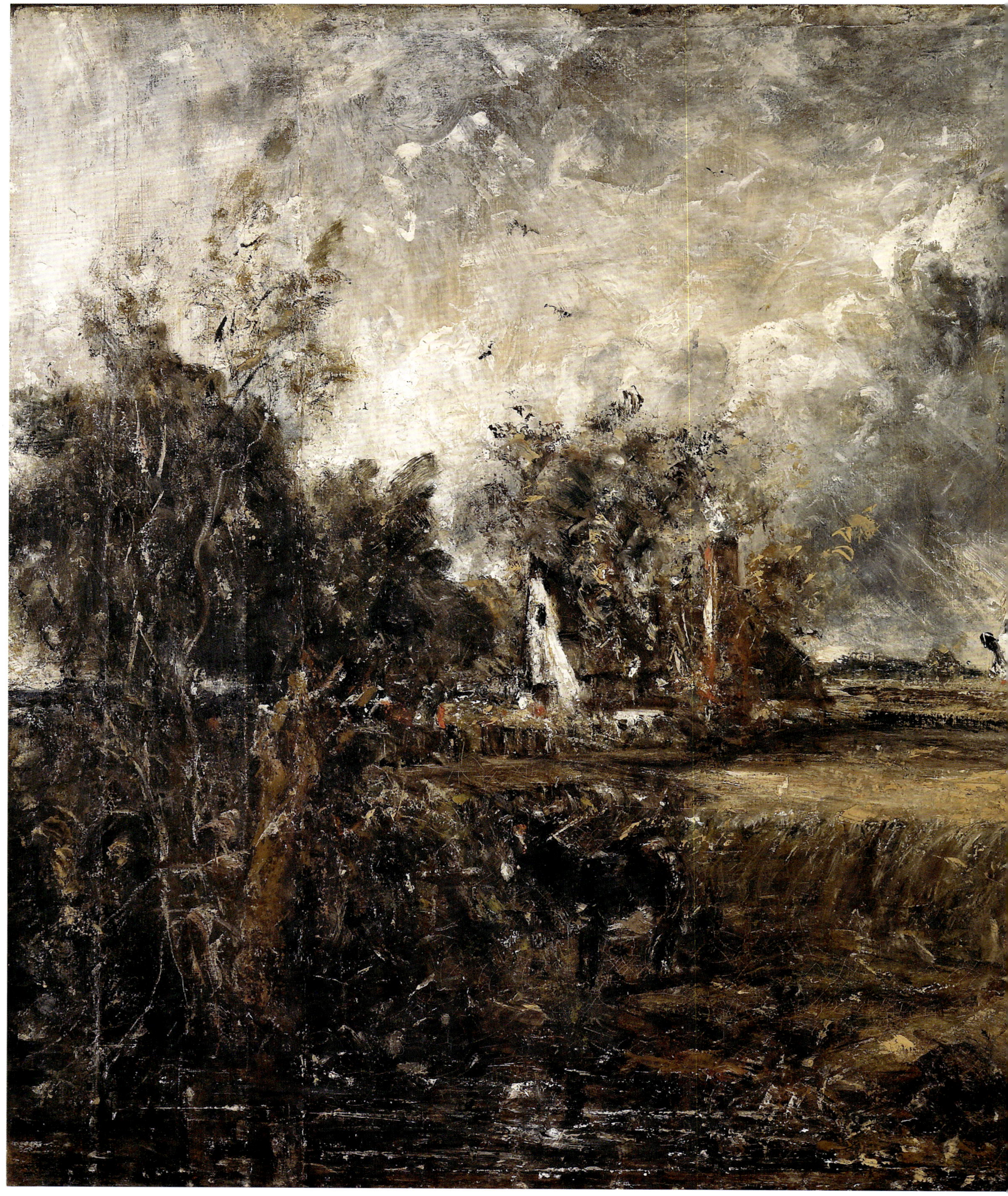

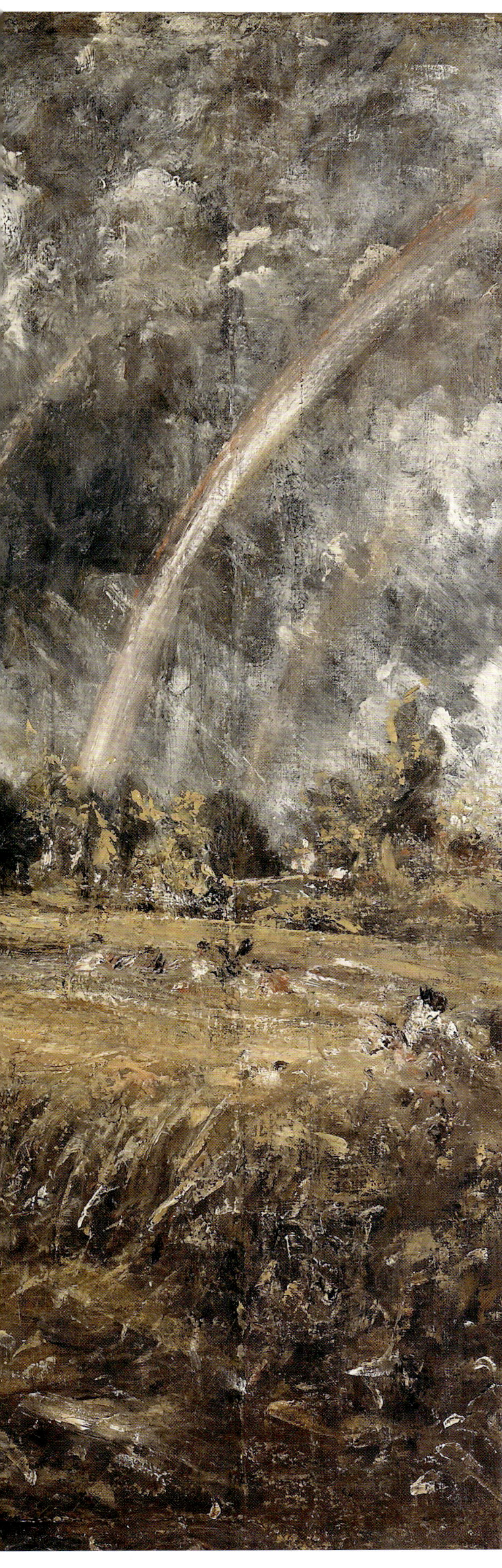

NO. 175 **John Constable** *A Cottage at East Bergholt* c.1836
Oil paint on canvas, 87·6 × 111·8
National Museums Liverpool, Lady Lever Art Gallery

NO. 176 **John Constable** *Stoke-by-Nayland* c.1835–7
Oil paint on canvas, 126 × 169
The Art Institute of Chicago, Mr. and Mrs. W. W. Kimball Collection, 1922.4453

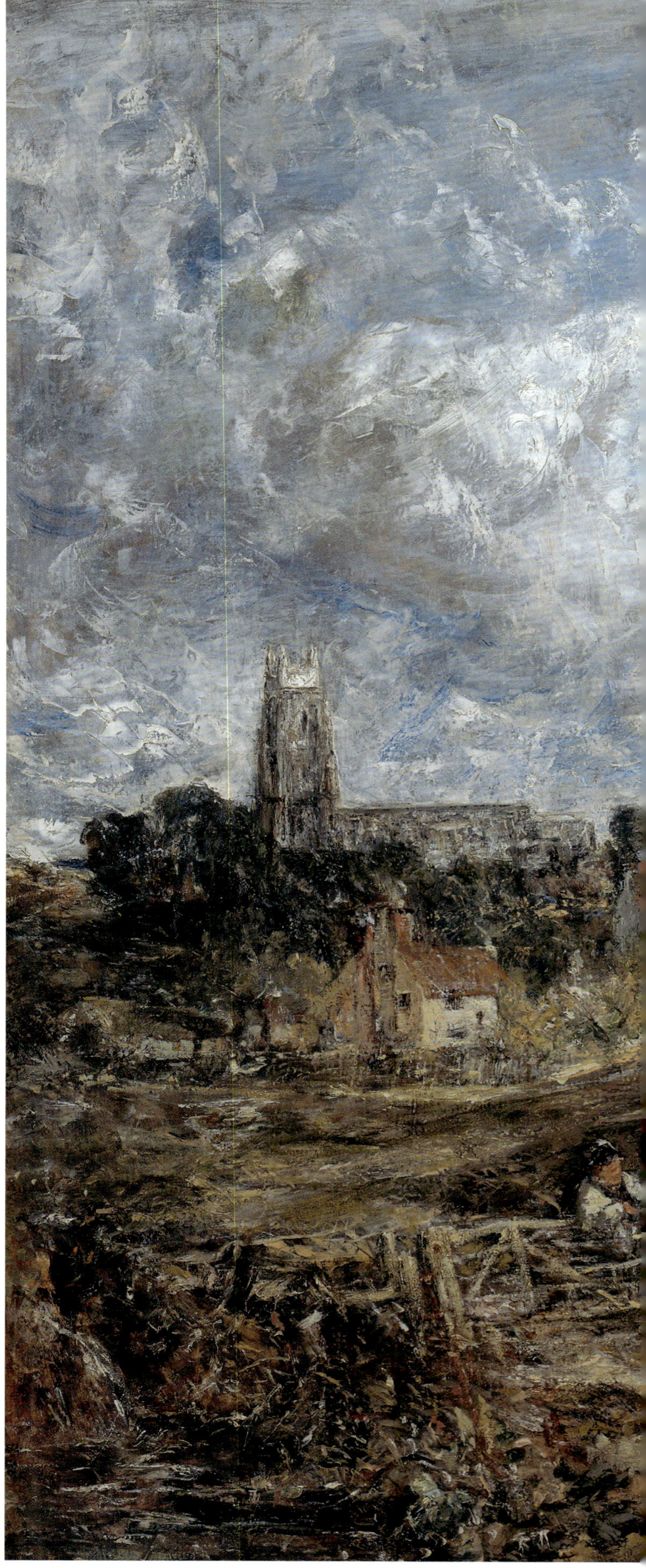

'What say you to a summer morning? July or August, at eight or nine o'clock, after a slight shower during the night', Constable asked a friend in 1835. Such a picture, he went on, would contain 'plough, cart, horse, gate, cows, donkey...all good paintable material for the foreground' and would be on a size of canvas 'sufficient to try one's strength, and keep one at full collar' (Beckett, V, p.44). Constable was describing *Stoke-by-Nayland*, the canvas that would become his last full-scale six-foot sketch. No equivalent finished painting exists, but the production of such may have been in Constable's mind before he died in March, 1837. Constable spent time in the Suffolk village of Stoke-by-Nayland in 1810. Returning to sketches he made then for the plate in *English Landscape Scenery* (no.178), he adjusted the position of houses around the soaring tower of St Mary's Church and, no doubt inspired by his work on the print, began evolving the composition further on this six-foot canvas. It is hard to believe that Constable would not have eventually added the rainbow seen in the print to this composition.

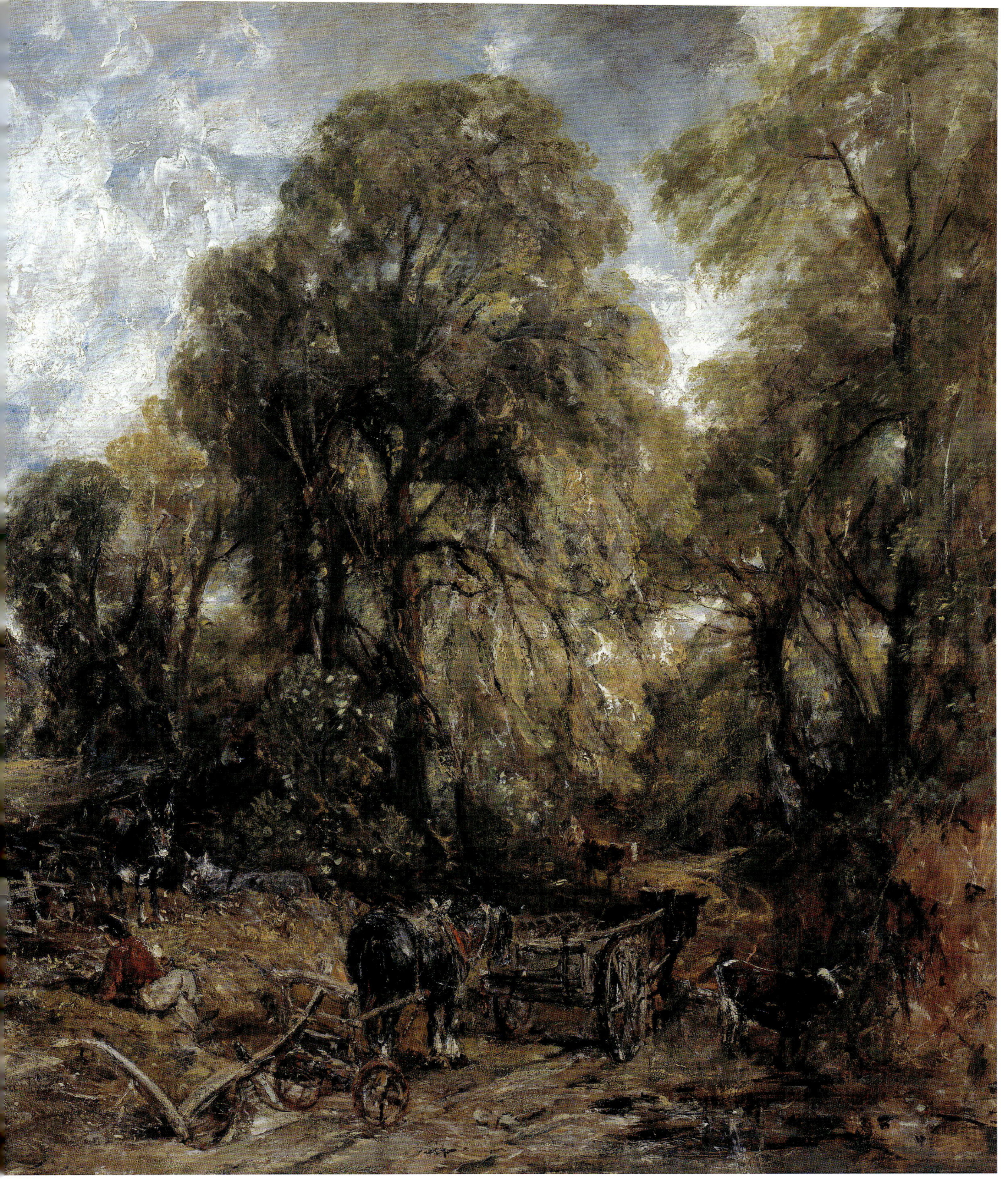

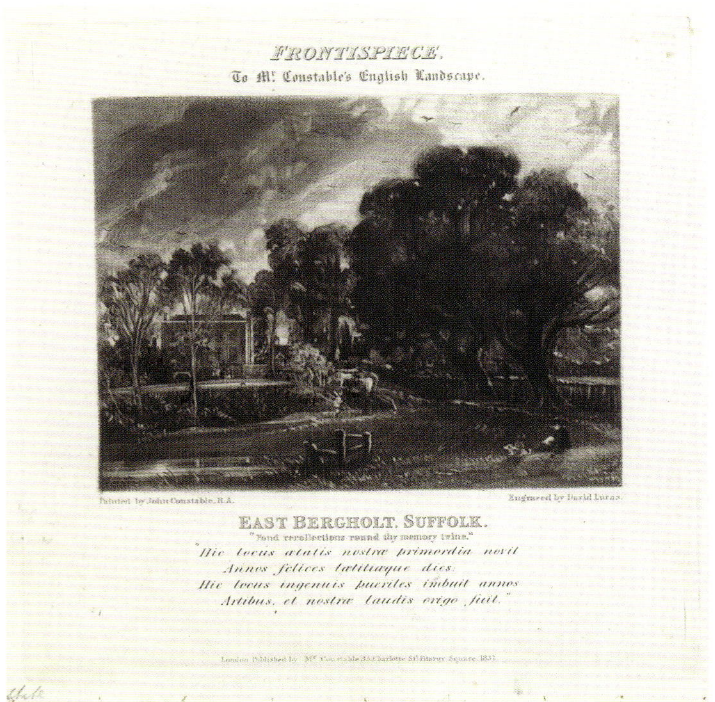

NO. 177 **David Lucas after John Constable** *Frontispiece: East Bergholt, Suffolk* published in *English Landscape Scenery* 1830–2
Mezzotint on paper, 13·9 × 18·7
Tate. Purchased 1985

NO. 178 **David Lucas after John Constable** *Stoke by Neyland, Suffolk* published in *English Landscape Scenery* 1830
Mezzotint on paper, 14·5 × 21·9
Tate. Purchased 1985

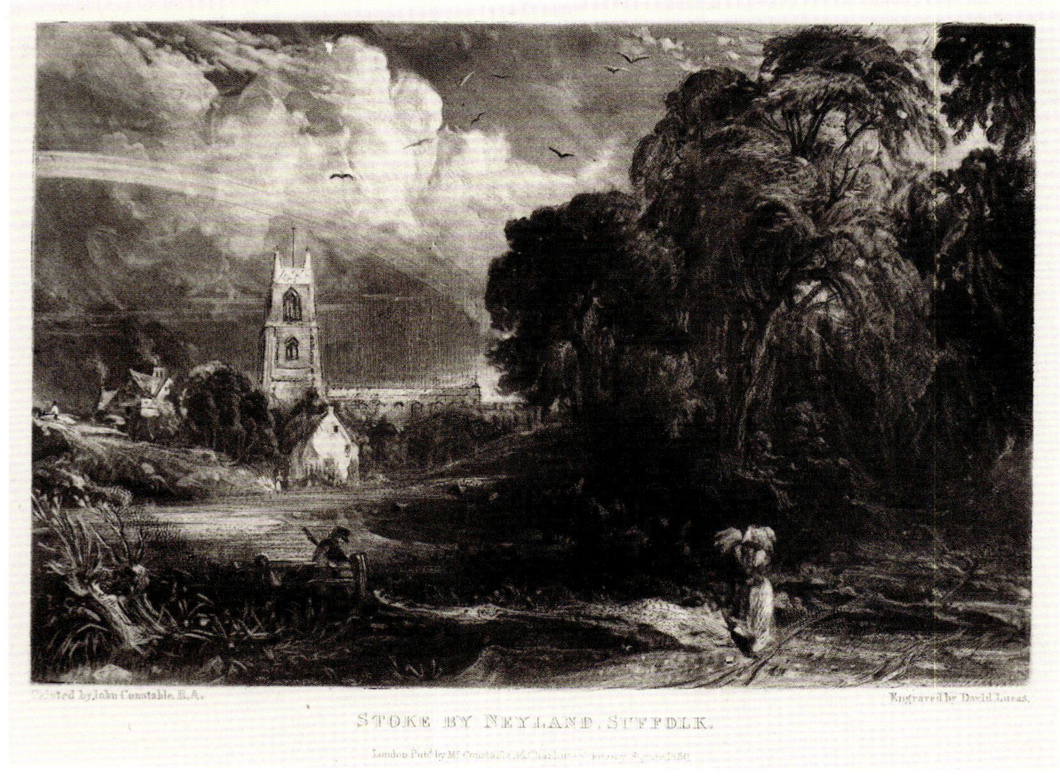

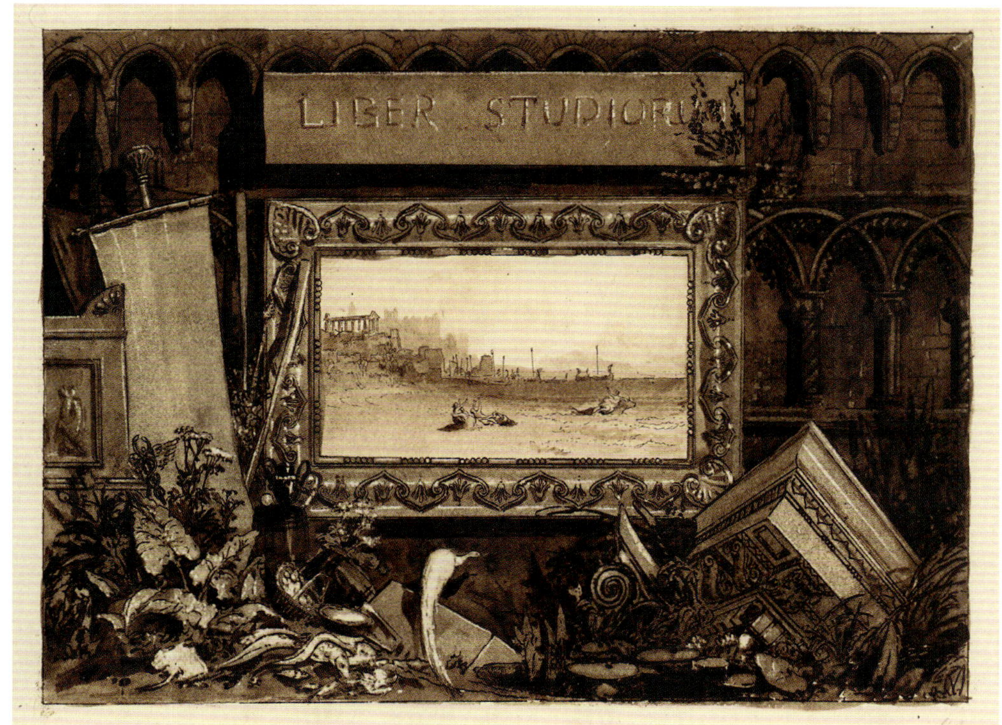

NO. 179 **J.C. Easling after J.M.W. Turner** *Frontispiece*, published in *Liber Studiorum* 1812
Etching and mezzotint on paper, 18·8 × 26·5
Tate. Presented by A. Acland Allen through the Art Fund 1925

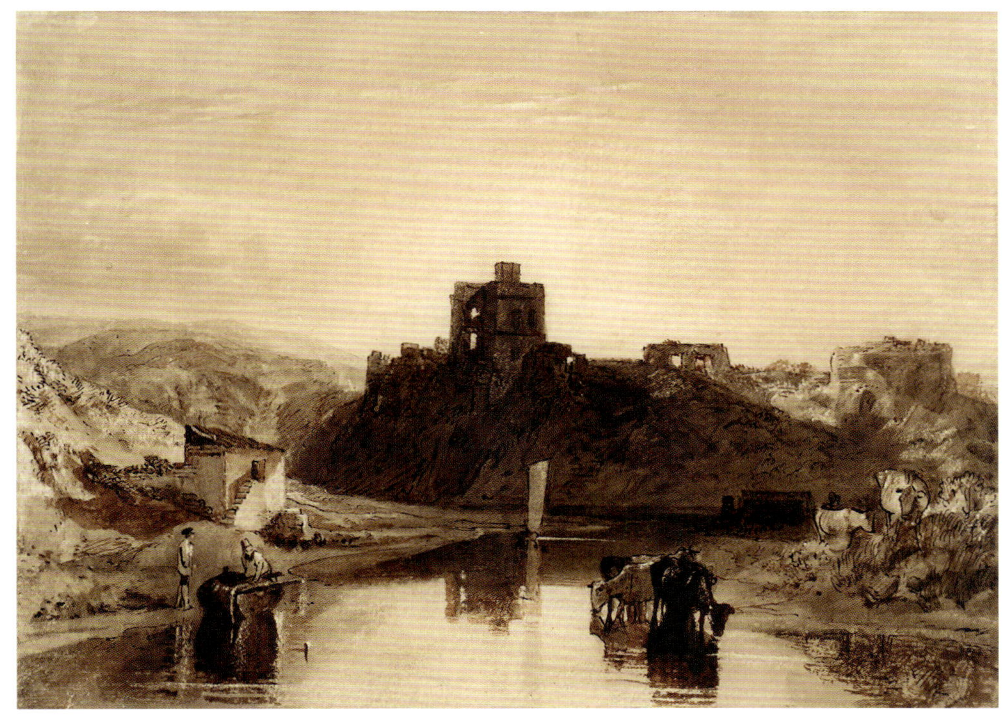

NO. 180 **J.M.W. Turner and Charles Turner** *Norham Castle on the Tweed*, published in *Liber Studiorum* c.1815
Engraver's proof
Etching and mezzotint printed in brown ink on cream laid paper, untrimmed, 17·6 × 26
Lent by the Royal Academy of Arts, London

NO. 181 **J.M.W. Turner** *Norham Castle, Sunrise* c.1845
Oil paint on canvas, 90·8 × 121·9
Tate. Accepted by the nation as part of the Turner Bequest 1856

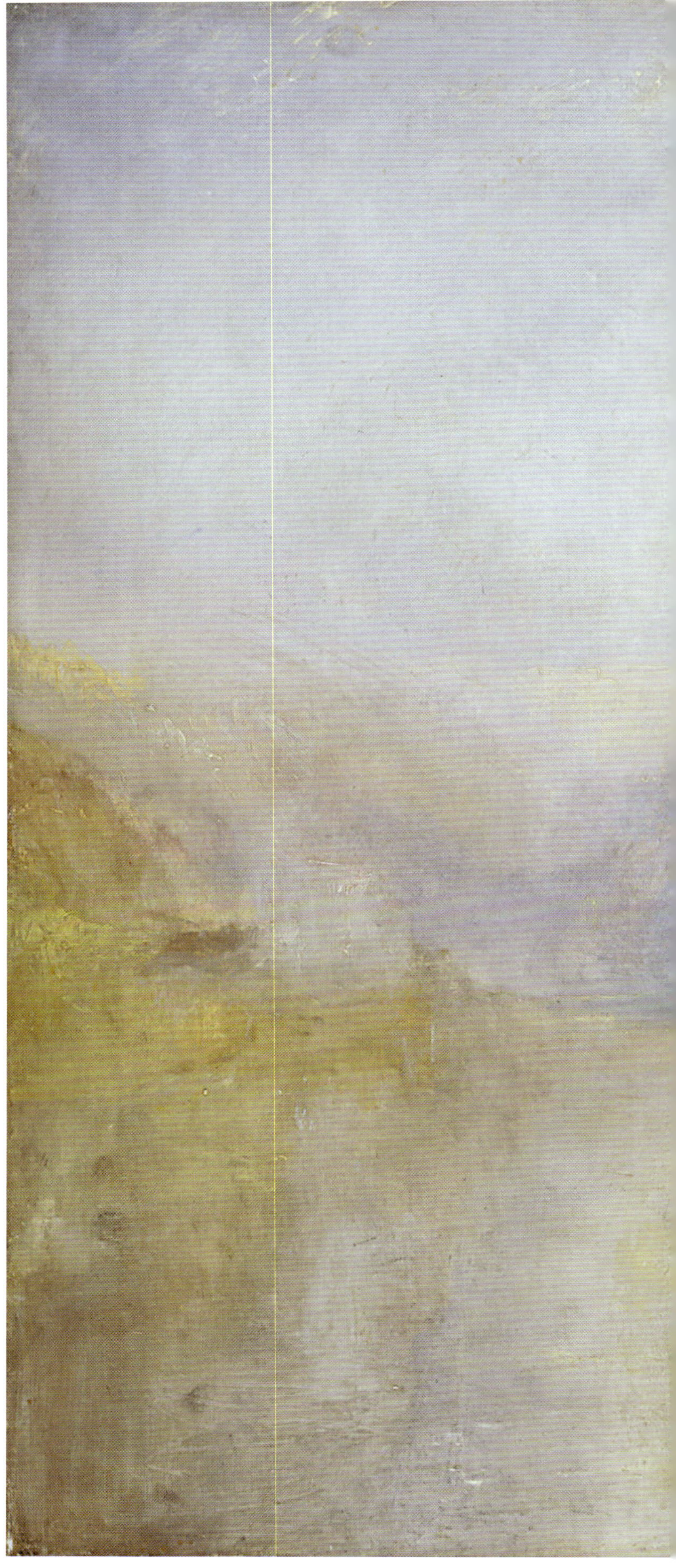

This enigmatic painting depicts one of Turner's favourite subjects. It belongs, like *Landscape with Walton Bridges* (no.182), to a series of luminous 1840s canvases based on the print series he began some forty years earlier, *Liber Studiorum* (1807–1819; see nos.179 and 180). The ruined bulk of Norham Castle, built as a key site in the defence of England from the Scots in the twelfth century, sits on the River Tweed in the north-eastern county of Northumberland. Having first encountered the castle in 1797 as a twenty-two-year-old, Turner depicted it multiple times, including a watercolour of c.1822–3 for the print series, *Rivers of England* and his earlier plate for his *Liber* (no.118). Visiting in 1831 he apparently bowed to the castle, doffing his hat to acknowledge the success an early picture of it brought him. Each time he depicted it he alighted on something new – a different mood, angle or foreground incident. In *Norham Castle, Sunrise* the scene is stripped back to the essence of the place, filtered through Turner's memory and imagination. His delight in his materials is obvious: painted with thin glazes of colour that in places trickle down the canvas in rivulets, Norham Castle seems to melt in the sun's rays. For all their scrutiny, the purpose and state of finish of the late *Liber Studiorum* paintings remain a mystery. Unlike *Mercury Sent to Admonish Aeneas* (no.184) they were not exhibited. Some appear to have passed to Turner's late-life companion, Mrs Sophia Booth, and then her son, Daniel Pound (son of her first husband). Their sale in the 1860s shows that these beguiling paintings – in which the power and daring of Turner's late vision are felt in full – were valued (by some, at least) half a century before his late work came to be fully appreciated.

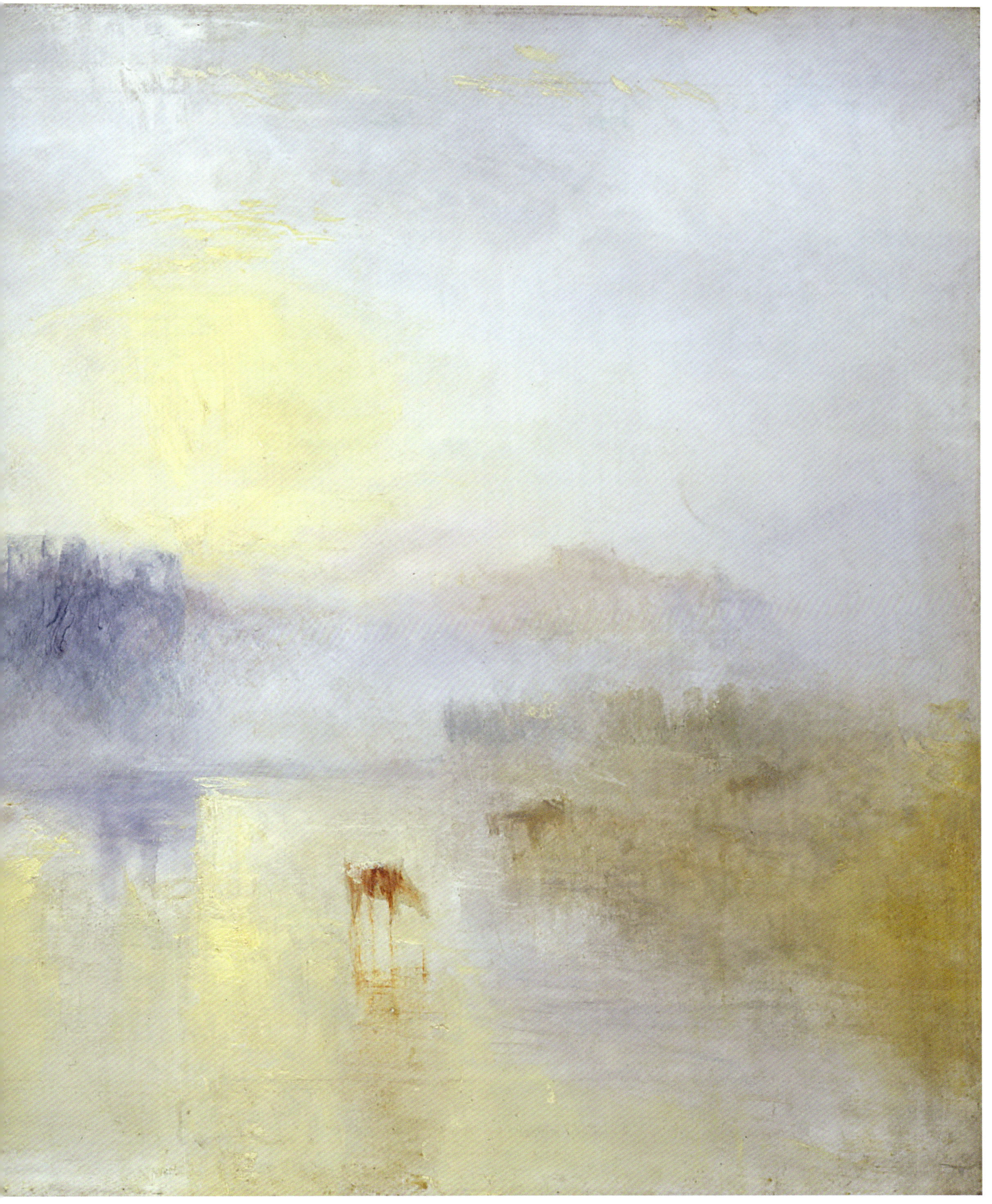

NO. 182 **J.M.W. Turner** *Landscape with Walton Bridges*, c.1840–50
Oil paint on canvas, 87·5 × 118
Private Collection

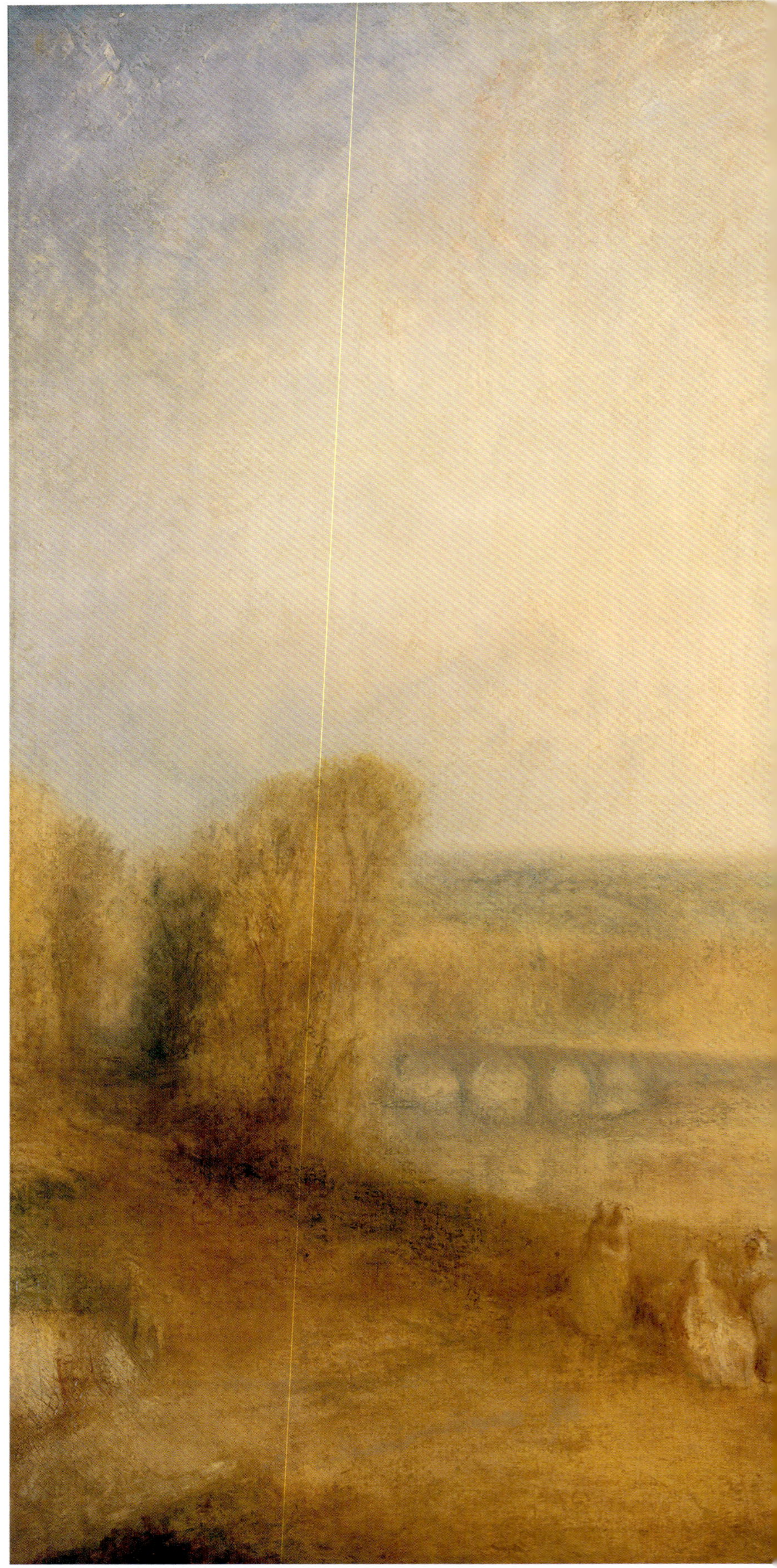

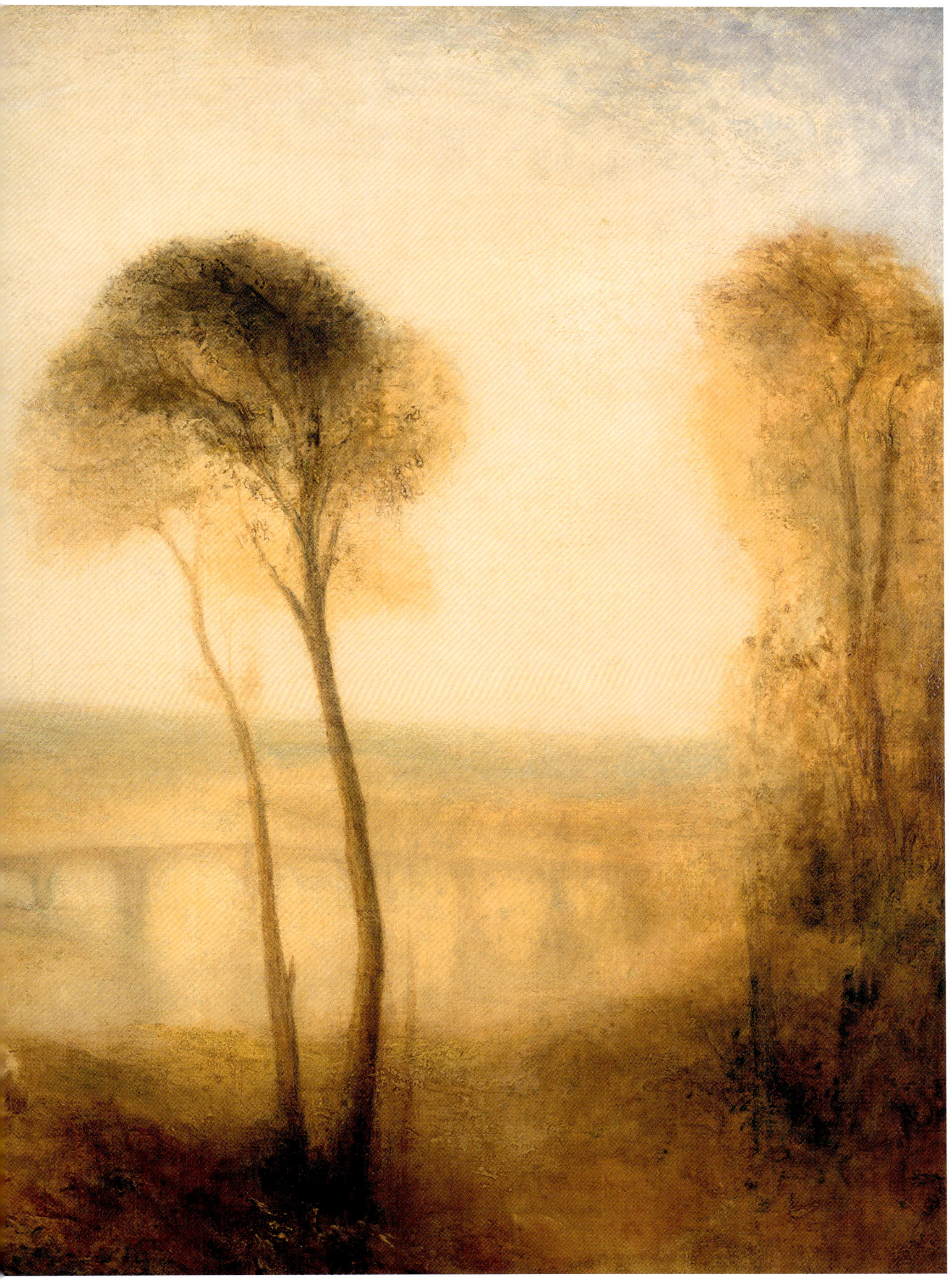

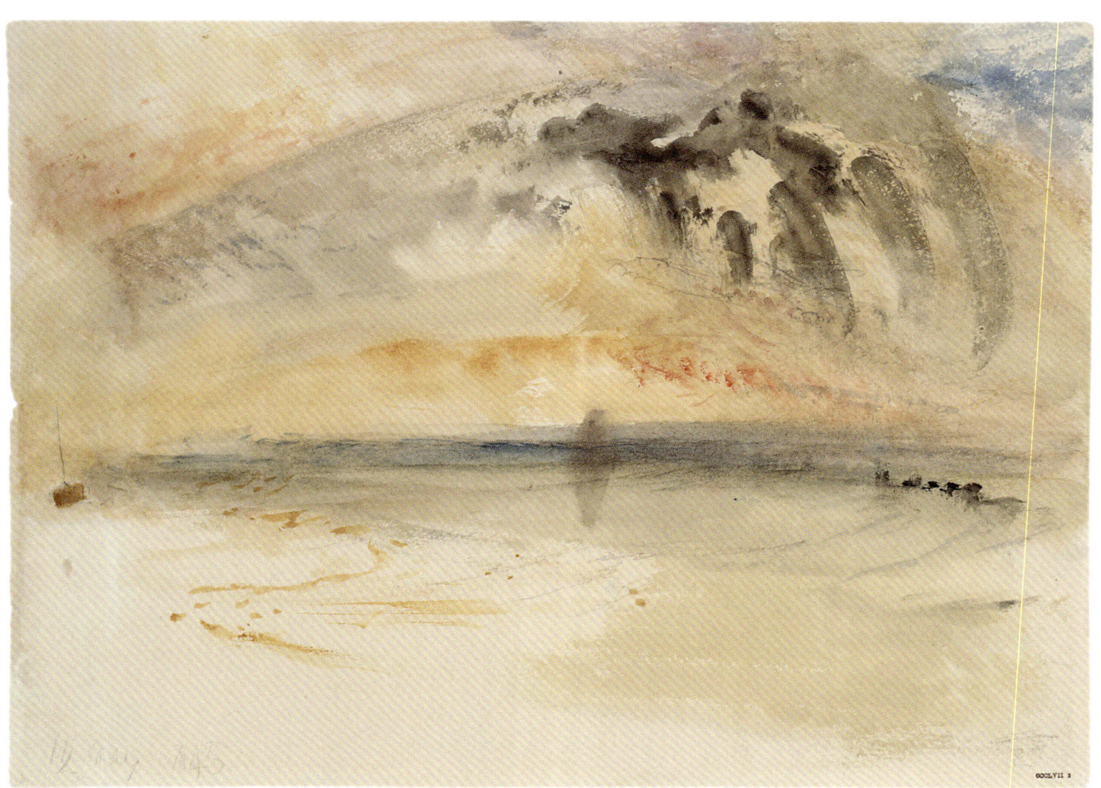

NO. 183 **J.M.W. Turner** *A Beach ?near the Tour de Croy, Wimereux* 1845
Graphite and watercolour on paper, 23·7 × 33·7
Tate. Accepted by the nation as part of the Turner Bequest 1856

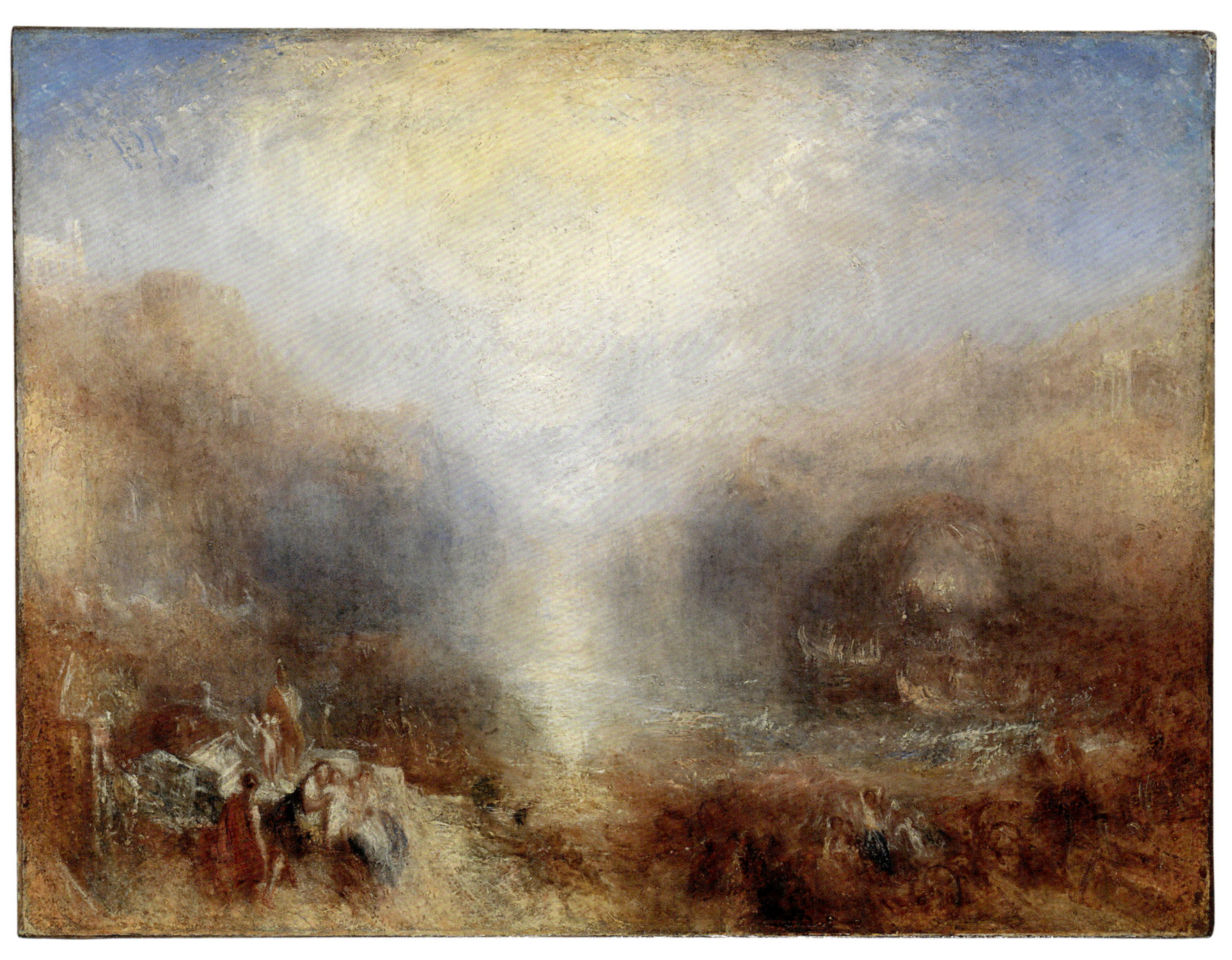

NO. 184 **J.M.W. Turner** *Mercury Sent to Admonish Aeneas* exhibited 1850
Oil paint on canvas, 90·2 × 120·6
Tate. Accepted by the nation as part of the Turner Bequest 1856

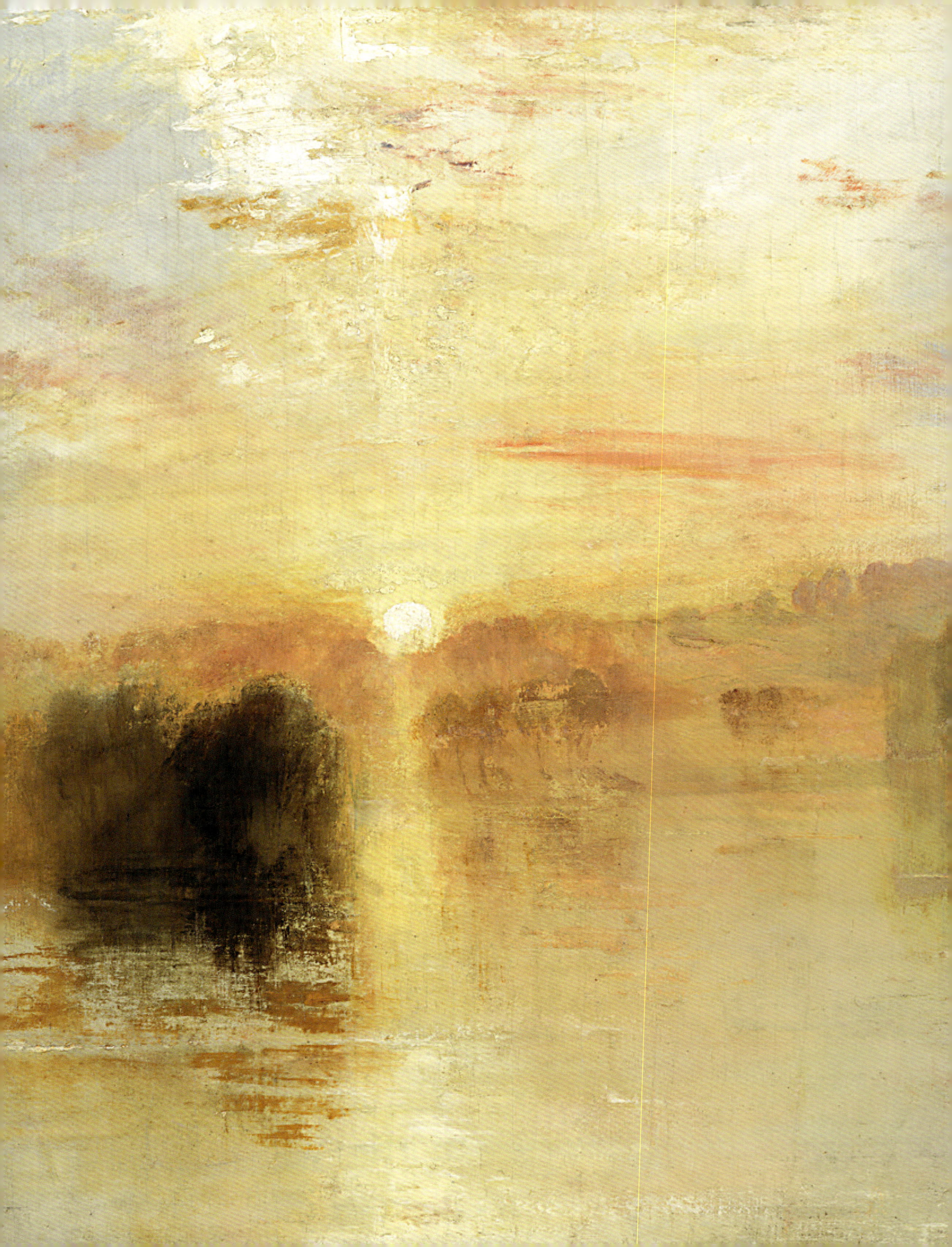

TURNER AND CONSTABLE'S LEGACY: ARTISTS TODAY

On 23 April 2025, the day that would have been Turner's 250th birthday, a poem by artist Tracey Emin (b.1963), 'For Turner', was projected onto the exterior of the Turner Contemporary building in Margate. Emin's 'love letter' to Turner and the site of its projection were a poignant reminder of the ever-evolving legacy of Turner and Constable and the creative dialogues they continue to spark across time.

Many artists have cited them as inspiration. Some might feel an affinity with one more than the other, like Lucian Freud (1922–2011), who had a deep understanding of Constable's work and spoke of finding it 'more moving than Turner['s]'.[1] Freud's friend Frank Auerbach (1931–2024) said that seeing Turner's *The Fighting Temeraire* (National Gallery, London) made him want to be an artist, but that while Constable came to hold more significance for him too, he believed they were both 'geniuses' and that '[p]ainters often come in couples, each helping to define the other'.[2]

When asked once whether he preferred Turner or Constable, David Hockney (b.1937) replied, 'What's the trick?'[3] Hockney has expressed his appreciation for both artists:

> It was only really when I began looking at landscape again that I got more interested in Turner and Constable. Their pictures are beautiful things, marvellously done.[4]

He has spoken of his understanding of Turner's approach to landscape as a 'spatial thrill' and animatedly of Constable's *Salisbury Cathedral from the Meadows* (no.135) as a 'juicy' and 'exciting' painting.[5]

Turner and Constable have inspired artists from across the world too. The work of American artist James Turrell (b.1943) extends Turner's quest to paint light by using light as a medium in immersive installations. Icelandic-Danish artist Olafur Eliasson (b.1967) has cited Turner's exploration of the sublime and his use of colour as a stimulus for his work and has described being 'gripped' by Constable's cloud studies as an art student.[6]

What follows here is a series of reflections on Turner and Constable by four artists – Frank Bowling (b.1934), Bridget Riley (b.1931), Emma Stibbon (b.1962) and George Shaw (b.1966) – invited to reflect on the role that Turner and Constable have played in their own artistic journeys.

J.M.W. Turner *The Lake, Petworth, Sunset; Sample Study* (detail) c.1827–8 (pp.98–9)

FRANK BOWLING

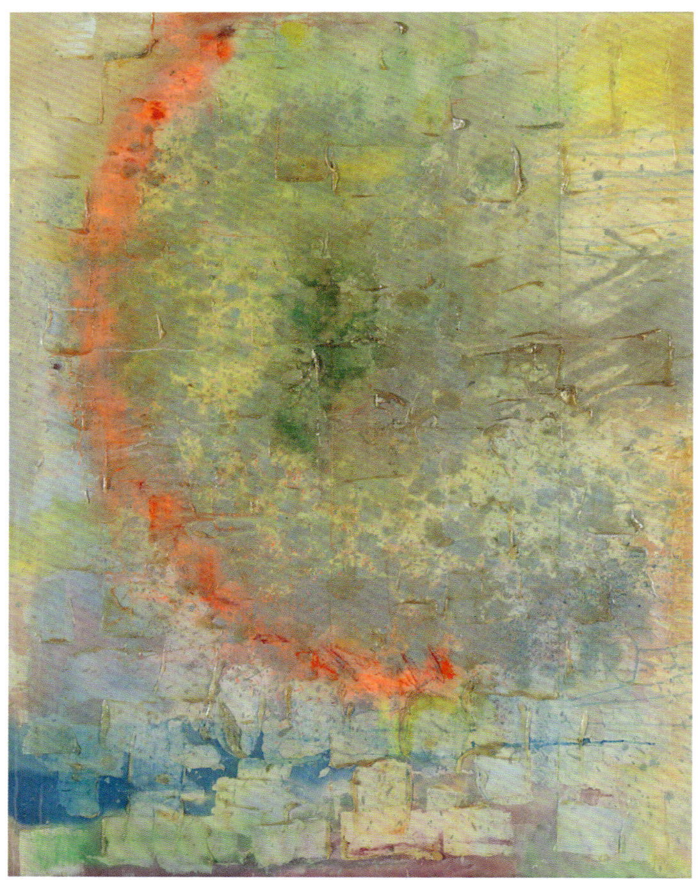

Frank Bowling *Sacha Jason Guyana Dreams* 1989
Acrylic paint and resin on canvas, 178 × 136
Tate. Purchased 2006

I tend to be the first to see the connection between Turner and the themes in my work; other people take much longer. I personally go and look at Turner all the time. I know if there's a Turner in a gallery, I want to look at it. There was something special about the way he went about things, and I clung to that. It's very convenient to be living where I do – I just walk around the corner, take a quick look and go back to my studio.

I used to go and look at Turner's work as a corrective, to sort of see if I've 'got this' – this way of hauling the paint or spreading the paint, one canvas next to the other, risking this and that. I was trying to find my own way of doing the same thing.

There's something you don't see when you're grasping for a way to make the marks make sense. The sort of abstraction that you get in Turner is instinctive. I can see the magic.

He used a brush rather more than a knife, but he used a knife as well. It is easier for me to go in with the knife, with the brush in the other hand. He was pulling and dragging the paint to perform – you can see the brush marks, him physically engaging. You can't help but see it and try it yourself. The turmoil of the beaten-up paint and colour in the work – that attracted me for a long time. It's what I'm into as well.

It's the most sound, freeing, aspect of the whole occupation, the freedom to put anything in there that you feel like. There's this tense feeling and excitement. You don't really want anyone else around. You feel your way by yourself. I think Turner felt it. His paintings come across as 'felt' – apart from just moulding the paint, kneading the paint back into that flat surface, it went through his body. He had a feeling for paint. Some people have it and some people don't.

Frank Bowling, excerpt from an interview with
Amy Concannon, 15 August 2024

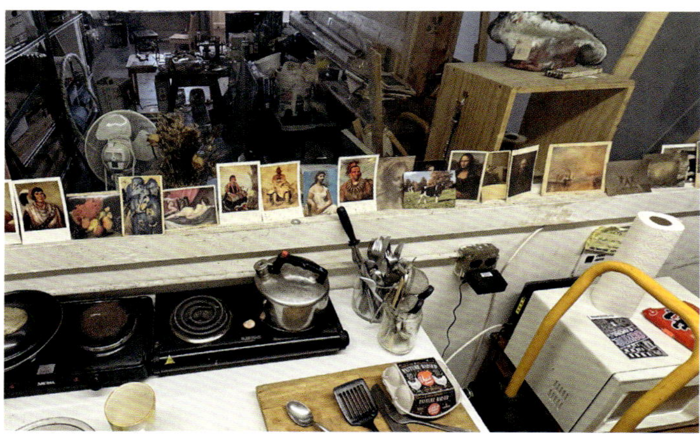

Still from Bowling Studio: Turner Postcard seen on the far right
(*The Fighting Temeraire*)

BRIDGET RILEY

Bridget Riley *Concerto I* 2024
Acrylic paint on canvas, 234·7 × 202·3
Tate. Presented by the artist 2025

Constable is one of my heroes and I admire him greatly. I first encountered his work when I was living in Cornwall during the Second World War. I had begun to enjoy looking at landscape through going on long walks and on my 13th birthday, I was given a large volume titled 'Masterpieces of British Painting'. I still have it. I loved its beautiful illustrations and the largest number of these showed paintings by Constable. Although they seemed remote from the Cornish coast, I found them so assured, so at ease and surprisingly familiar.

My interest in Constable grew as I developed my abstract painting. On my first trip to New York in 1965 I visited the Frick Collection of Old Master paintings and saw *The White Horse* (no.127). I was absolutely thrilled to discover it there. It is a striking, bold composition in which the white of the horse stands out in strong tonal contrast to the many shades of green around it. It is carried out with such conviction and mastery. Nothing escapes attention, from the beautifully clouded sky to the foliage and its reflection in the water. Gericault and Delacroix saw in Constable a new way forward for painting.

In 1992 I was interviewed by the art historian Ernst Gombrich who asked me what my views were on Constable's pronouncement that painting is a science. I said that I had always loved Constable, but that I couldn't quite agree that painting was a science or at least not what I understood by science. However, the science of Constable's time was closer to an enquiry into the laws of nature and, in this sense, Constable's paintings could be regarded as experiments in that science. Constable was discovering through measured and patient observation how to bring insights, understanding and love into painting. Studying atmospheric phenomena, as he did, and knowing exactly what gave rise to the formation of a particular cloud, for instance, set Constable free to respond in a fresh and informed way to nature. Through study he understood tone – 'chiaroscuro', a Renaissance term for light and shade. He paints clouds in shadow and clouds in bright light, and light bursting through openings in trees or between their leaves – these effects can only be achieved if they have been seen. Monet is right about 'the envelope of light' and I believe that Constable anticipates this in *his* use of light.

Constable's use of colour is exciting: broken colour applied by hundreds of separate brush strokes that have not been harmonised. He uses earthy tones alongside strong colours like viridian, blue, yellow and of course white – for the glitter of light – but no black. His paintings invite the eye to explore, to investigate these many tiny marks that bring a freshness and immediacy to the most familiar of open spaces.

Constable was an artist who felt deeply. This comes across in his paintings – they are fresh, lively and engaged. He was happiest when he was working, as am I.

Bridget Riley, February 2025

EMMA STIBBON

I feel a deep affinity with Turner and Constable in their commitment to working from nature. Living through a time of political upheaval, they both established landscape representation as a radical subject that took it far beyond a classical or idealised genre. Both artists were acutely aware of the transformation that was happening around them; for Turner, the impact of industrialisation with steam taking over from sail, and for Constable, the agricultural changes he could see with the enclosures act and mechanisation. As an artist working from landscape I feel their legacy, that it carries a moral obligation to show the changes happening in the world around us.

Working from landscape today has never been more pressing. My own commitment to represent the dynamic effects of snow and ice on landscape comes from a realisation that many glaciated sites are changing beyond recognition within my lifetime. While I'm drawing in my sketchbook, I want to root my work in that physical, visceral experience of being in a place, recording what I see. The challenges of working in the elements with the wind catching my paper or my watercolour and inks freezing somehow works its way into the drawing. Often when I am out working in the field, I have a sense of being a witness. I want to get down on the page the particularities of an iceberg or glacier front, to pay homage to something ephemeral and fleeting at that moment in time.

Turner's observations in his *St Gothard and Mont Blanc* sketchbook of 1802 (Tate) give scientists today an important record of the extent of Alpine glaciers in a time before photography. In his watercolours of the Mer de Glace, he has climbed up on to the ice and the glacier rears up in front, quite literally like a sea of ice (for example no.76 and D04615, Tate). Through this close encounter he draws us, the viewer, into the picture. We might feel overwhelmed by our encounter with what Turner shows us. His spare use of simple wet media on paper has a transformative power that affects me both physically and emotionally. Often improvising with his media and tools, such as using his fingers to move paint around on the page or scratching out with the end of his paintbrush, he gives us a visceral sense of the raw force of the weather and terrain. Drawing has the power to move us – we look at these watercolours with the added pathos that the Mer de Glace, the 'sea of ice', is now retreating. It is leaving a valley floor almost completely devoid of ice. Through Turner's mysterious alchemy of media and subject he makes us profoundly aware of what is at stake.

Emma Stibbon, May 2025

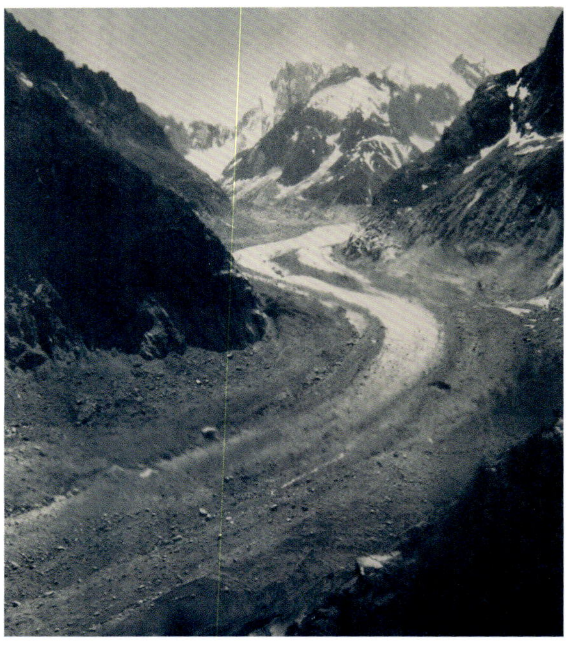

Emma Stibbon *Mer de Glace, Chamonix* 25 June 2018
Cyanotype, 39 × 36
Collection of the artist

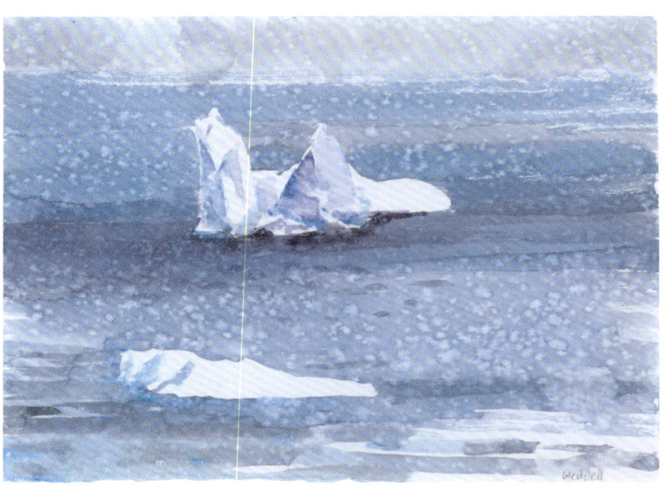

Emma Stibbon *Snow spotted bergs Weddell Sea* 2023
Watercolour with snow spots, 21 × 30
Collection of the artist

GEORGE SHAW

It was some time in the very early 1980s during a school trip that I sloped off to the V&A, and with a headful of The Jam and The Fall found by accident a room full of Constable studies. They seemed to me scraps of paintings, more like steamed and peeled patterned wallpaper, yet framed and oddly elevated. In their unpretentious presence I had obvious ideas that I could do that. Back home in the Midlands I trudged the flat landscape that bordered the estate, making drawings and watercolours in the bleak new year of fields and trees, a stream, a village church, the setting sun. In the milder weather I even took bits of hardboard and attempted oil and acrylic paintings. More of an escape artist then, perhaps.

> O'er grassy dale, and lowland scene
> Come see, come hear, the English Scheme.
> The lower-class, want brass, bad chests, scrounge fags.
> 'English Scene', The Fall, 1980

I've long felt that Constable brings the grander aspirations of art, *the Old Masters*, down to an earthier level. The compositions of other, more exotic lands, the unlikely stories of unworldly gods and interfering angels, are given over to more solid reliable matter: soil, trees, bricks and mortar, a familiar land. Even clouds in his paintings have a passing weight. In this way the far-fetched allegory forever glimpsed in the receding distance is, in Constable's hands, dragged forward into our everyday lives and our plod from one mediocrity to another. It is only in this confrontation with the reality of contemporary experience that any valuable insight can be gleaned, surely and unglamorously. Constable himself knew this, writing in 1832 that 'my limited and abstracted art is to be found under every hedge and in every lane, and therefore nobody thinks it worth picking up'.

On seeing one of Constable's drawings, William Blake is said to have told the painter that 'this is not drawing but inspiration', to which Constable replied, 'I never knew it before. I meant it for drawing.' This is all down-to-earth stuff. The subjects of art are the same subjects of life: our hefty presence on a gentle planet, one hour, one day turning into another, a journey from not being here or anywhere to suddenly being subject to gravity and then not being once again. Our lives are not fantasies or visions but the ruins we leave behind.

George Shaw, February 2025

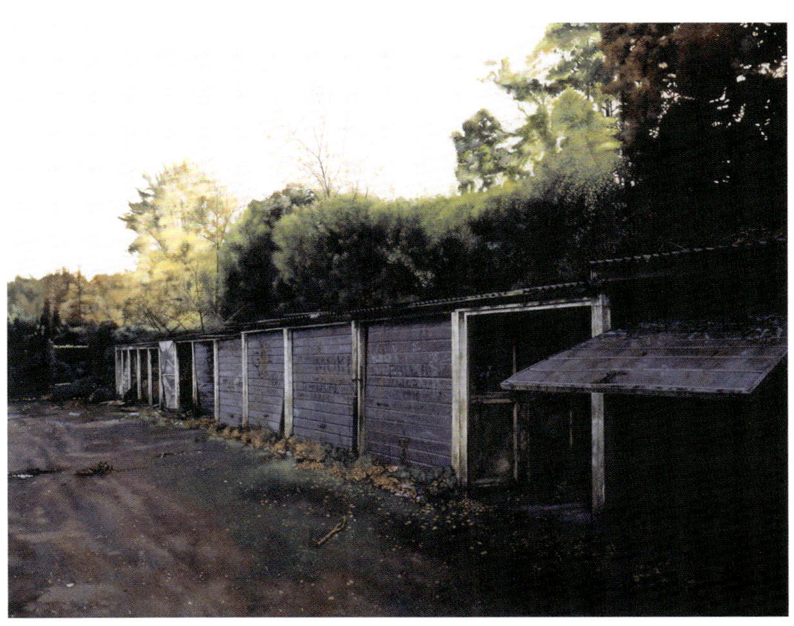

George Shaw *Scenes from the Passion: Late* 2002
Enamel paint on board 91·7 × 121·5
Tate. Presented by the Patrons of New Art Special Purchase Fund through the Tate Foundation 2003

NOTES

Turner and Constable: Rivals and Originals

1 Anonymous review, *Literary Gazette*, 14 May 1831, in Judy Crosby Ivy, *Constable and the Critics 1802–1837*, Woodbridge 1991, pp.150–1.
2 Ibid., and anonymous review, *Englishman's Magazine*, 1 June 1831, in Ivy 1991, p.153.
3 Robert Hunt, review for *The Examiner*, 27 June 1819, in Ivy 1991, p.82.
4 Anonymous review, *London Magazine*, June 1829, in Ivy 1991, p.135.
5 C.R. Leslie, *Autobiographical Recollections*, 2 vols, London 1860, vol.1, p.202.
6 The recent interest in exploring these relationships is evident in Stephan Wolohojian and Ashley Dunn, *Manet/Degas*, exh. cat., The Metropolitan Museum of Art, New York 2023.
7 Giorgio Vasari, *Lives of the Most Eminent Painters, Sculptors, and Architects* (1550). See Patricia Rubin, *Giorgio Vasari: Art and History*, New Haven and London 1995.
8 Obituary of James Tibbetts Willmore, ARA, *Art Journal*, 1 May 1863, p.88.
9 This account of Turner's life is notoriously fanciful. Walter Thornbury, *The Life of J.M.W. Turner, R.A. founded on Letters and Papers furnished by his Friends and Fellow Academicians*, rev. edn, London 1877, pp.222, 327.
10 John Constable to John Fisher, 23 January 1825, in R.B. Beckett (ed.), *John Constable's Correspondence*, 6 vols., Ipswich 1962–8, vol.6, p.191.
11 John Constable to David Lucas, 12 March 1831, in Beckett 1962–8, vol.4, p.344.
12 Anonymous review, *Athenaeum*, 20 May 1829, in Ivy 1991, p.134; another version appeared in the *London Magazine* the following month: 'that accursed bespotting with blanc d'argent, or white-wash splashing, as Mr. Turner will have it', *London Magazine*, June 1829, in Ivy 1991, p.135.
13 John Constable, letter to John Fisher, 4 July 1829, in Beckett 1962–8, vol.6, p.248.
14 Account of Essex miller John Crosier, cited in Michael Rosenthal, *Constable: The Painter and his Landscape*, New Haven and London 1983, p.8.
15 Nicola Moorby discusses recent examples of this, by the likes of Lucian Freud and others, in *Turner and Constable: Art, Life, Landscape*, New Haven and London 2005, pp.1–4, 268.
16 See Martin Myrone, *Making the Modern Artist: Culture, Class and Art-Educational Opportunity in Romantic Britain*, London 2020, pp.57, 80.
17 P.G. Hamerton, quoted in David Solkin, *Turner and the Masters*, exh. cat., Tate, London 2009, p.15.
18 For more detail, see Eric Shanes, *Young Mr. Turner*, London 2016.
19 For a discussion of these see Mark Evans, *The Making of a Master*, exh. cat., Victoria and Albert Museum, London 2014, pp.16–19.
20 In 1804 Constable had been 'much employed painting portraits as large as life' for a modest fee, but 'has time in the afternoons to cultivate Landscape painting', according to Joseph Farington, *The Diary of Joseph Farington*, eds. Kenneth Garlick, Angus Macintyre and Kathryn Cave, New Haven and London 1978–84, vol. 6, p.2340.
21 For analyses of Constable's work in relation to the social, economic and political climate of the time, see, for example, Andrew Hemingway, *Landscape Imagery and Urban Culture in early nineteenth-century Britain*, Cambridge 1992, and Michael Rosenthal, *Constable: The Painter and His Landscape*, New Haven and London 1983.
22 See Sarah Gould's text in this volume, pp.45–7.
23 Quoted in A.J. Finberg, *The Life of J.M.W. Turner, R.A.*, rev. edn, Oxford 1961, p.262.
24 See Anne Lyles and Michael Rosenthal, *Turner and Constable: Sketching from Nature*, London 2013.
25 Myrone 2020, p.60.
26 Ann Constable, letter to John Constable, 2 December 1807, in Beckett 1962–8, vol.1, p.22.
27 Letter from Turner to J. Hammersley, 4 December 1838, in John Gage (ed.), *The Collected Correspondence of J.M.W. Turner*, Oxford 1980, p.170.
28 This phrase was coined by Alice Rylance-Watson, 'Rivers Meuse and Moselle Sketchbook 1824', in David Blayney Brown and Matthew Imms (eds.), *J.M.W. Turner: Sketchbooks, Drawings and Watercolours*, Tate Research Publication, April 2015, www.tate.org.uk/art/research-publications/jmw-turner/rivers-meuse-and-moselle-sketchbook-r1174338, accessed 1 June 2025.
29 See Turner, 'Royal Academy Lectures', c.1807–38, British Library, London (Add MS 46151 A-BB), and Andrew Wilton, *Painting and Poetry*, London 1990.
30 Constable to Charles Boner, 22 April 1832, in Beckett 1960–8, vol.11, pp.156–7; see Felicity Myrone '"No Mercenary Views"? Constable's English Landscape', *Tate Papers*, no.33, 2020, www.tate.org.uk/research/tate-papers/33/no-mercenary-views-constable-english-landscape, accessed 8 June 2025.
31 See, for example, Trev Broughton's work on Constable's correspondence: 'Anxiety in Action: Letters of Advice between the Constables of East Bergholt in the Early Nineteenth Century', *Nineteenth-Century Studies*, no.26, 2017, pp.101–18.
32 See Gage 1980, pp.xxv–xxvi.
33 Constable, letter to Maria Bicknell, 30 June 1813, in Beckett (ed.), II, p.110.'
34 Myrone 2020, p.71.
35 For Constable's accent, see James Hamilton, *Constable: A Portrait*, London 2022, p.61; Constable to John Fisher, 6 December 1822, in 1962–8, vol.2, p.292.
36 See Joyce Townsend's text in this volume, pp.51–5.
37 Albeit the cart has been modified here to display the characteristics of a particular kind of vehicle, the bow-wagon, specific to the south-west region of England, as noted in Leslie Parris and Ian Fleming-Williams, *Constable*, exh. cat., Tate Gallery, London 1991, p.364. Another example of Constable painting the same dog into two paintings can be seen in *The Wheatfield* and *Stour Valley and Dedham Church* (nos.96 and 95).
38 Joshua Reynolds, *Discourses on Art*, VI, 1784, p.113.
39 Ian Warrell, "The Land of Bliss': Turner's Pursuit of the Light and Landscapes of Claude' in Warrell, ed., *Turner Inspired: In the Light of Claude*, exh. cat. National Gallery, London 2012, p.26; see also Kathleen Nicholson, 'Turner, Claude and the Essence of Landscape' in Solkin 2009, pp.57–72, and Evans 2014.
40 Constable, letter to John Fisher, 8 April 1826, Beckett 1962–8, vol.6, p.216; Turner to James Holworthy, 5 May 1826 in Gage 1980, p.100; E.T. Cook and Alexander Wedderburn (eds.), *The Works of John Ruskin*, 39 vols., London 1903–12, vol.13, p.477.
41 *Morning Post*, 2 June 1831, p.3.
42 See Kay Dian Kriz, *The Idea of the English Landscape Painter: Genius as Alibi in the Early Nineteenth Century*, New Haven and London 1997.
43 *The Athenaeum*, 2 June 1832, p.356; *The Athenaeum*, 27. December 1851, p.383.
44 For Turner's attitude on this, see Smiles, 'Introduction: Turner's Changing Reputation' in Karin Althaus, Nicholas Maniu and Matthias Mühling, (eds.), *Turner. Ein Lesebuch (Turner. A Reader)*, Munich 2023, p.19.
45 Constable borrows 'to one brief moment caught from fleeting time' from William Wordsworth here. John Constable, 'Letterpress to 'English Landscape'', in R.B. Beckett (ed.), *John Constable's Discourses*, Suffolk 1970, pp.9–10.
46 John Ruskin, 'Notes on the Turner Gallery at Marlborough House 1856–57' (5th edition, 1857), in Cook and Wedderburn 1903–12, vol.13, p.161.
47 Ibid., p.162.
48 The multiple meanings and context for this painting are explored in Timothy Wilcox, *Constable and Salisbury: The Soul of Landscape*, London 2011, and Amy Concannon, 'Urban Landscape in the Age of Reform: Salisbury, Bristol, Brighton, Lambeth, c.1820–1850', PhD thesis, University of Nottingham 2018, pp.57–93.
49 See Sam Smiles, *Turner and the Slave Trade*, New Haven and London (forthcoming, 2025).
50 See Amy Concannon, 'The Painting', in *Salisbury Cathedral from the Meadows* exhibited 1831 by John Constable, Tate Research Publication, 2017, https://www.tate.org.uk/research/in-focus/salisbury-cathedral-constable/the-painting, accessed 14 August 2025.
51 Constable, letter to John Chalon, 11 February 1829, Beckett 1960–8, vol.10, p.243.
52 Jacqueline Riding, '1832: Shot out of the Water?', *The Royal Academy Summer Exhibition: A Chronicle, 1769–2018*, https://chronicle250.com/1832, accessed 23 July 2025.
53 John Ruskin, *Notes on the Turner Gallery at Marlborough House 1856–7*, 2nd edition, London 1857, p.75.
54 John Ruskin, Appendix to 'Modern Painters III', in Cook and Wedderburn 1903–12, vol.5, p.423; for recent appraisals of Constable's legacy in Europe, see Nicholas Alfrey, 'John Constable and Paul Huet: Marsh and Flood', *Tate Papers*, no.33, 2020, www.tate.org.uk/research/tate-papers/33/john-constable-paul-huet-marsh-flood, accessed 30 April 2025, and Jenny Gaschke, '"Landscape not merely as seen but as experienced"': Constable and Europe', in Christine Riding (ed.), *Discover Constable and The Hay Wain*, exh. cat., National Gallery, London 2024, pp.52–61.
55 Cited in Sam Smiles, *The Turner Book* (Tate Essential Artists Series), London 2006, pp.155–6.
56 Monroe Wheeler, MoMA's Director of Exhibitions, quoted in Sam Smiles, *J.M.W. Turner: The Making of a Modern Painter*, Manchester 2007, p.202.
57 Norman Reid, memorandum, 20 August 1988, Tate Archive, TGA 881/30.
58 'D.S.M.', 'Art: The Winter Exhibition at Burlington House – I. English Masters', *The Spectator*, 9 January 1892, p.55; Roger Fry, *Reflections on British Painting*, London 1934, quoted in Ian Fleming-Williams and Leslie Parris, *The Discovery of Constable*, New York 1984, p.124.
59 Jonathan Jones, 'Late Turner at Tate Britain review', *Guardian*, 8 September 2014, www.theguardian.com/artanddesign/2014/sep/08/late-turner-tate-britain-review, accessed 23 July 2025.
60 Indeed, in the 1980s my parents were gifted a set of Cloverleaf Constable placemats, which were kept for 'best' and used only at Christmas. For analyses of Constable's work in relation to the social, economic and political climate of his time see, for example: Michael Rosenthal, *Constable: The Painter and His Landscape*, New Haven and London 1983; Ann Bermingham, *Landscape and Ideology: The English Rustic Tradition, 1740–1860*, New Haven and London 1989; Stephen Daniels, *Fields of Vision: Landscape Imagery and National Identity in England and the United States*, Cambridge 1992; Andrew Hemingway, *Landscape Imagery and Urban Culture in early nineteenth-century Britain*, Cambridge 1992. See Sarah Gould's text in this volume, pp.45–7.
61 See Mary McMahon, 'From 'dull replica' to 'national treasure': The Afterlife of 'The Hay Wain'', in Riding 2024, p.72.

Turner's Ancient Worlds: Myth and Reality

1 Martin Butlin and Evelyn Joll, *The Paintings of J.M.W. Turner*, revised edn, New Haven and London 1984, pp.273–5 nos.430–2.
2 *Aeneas and the Sibyl: Lake Avernus* c.1798, and a second version 1814–15, *Dido and Aeneas* 1815, *Dido Building Carthage* 1815, *Dido Directing the Equipment of the Fleet* 1828, *The Golden Bough* 1834.
3 Anthony Bailey, *Standing in the Sun: A Life of J.M.W. Turner*, London 2013, pp.22–3.
4 History painting was believed to be the most intellectual art form, as opposed to reproducing what could be taken from life. See Kay Dian Kriz, *The Idea of the English Landscape Painter: Genius as Alibi in the Early Nineteenth Century*, New Haven and London 1997, pp.9–32.
5 Philippa Simpson, 'Taking in the View: The Reception of Claude in Early Nineteenth-Century London', in Ian Warrell (ed.), *Turner Inspired: In the Light of Claude*, London 2012, pp.14–15.
6 Kathleen Nicholson, 'Turner, Claude and the Essence of Landscape', in David Solkin (ed.), *Turner and the Masters*, exh. cat., Tate, London 2009, pp.57–71.
7 David Solkin, 'Turner and the Masters: Gleaning to Excel', in Solkin 2009, p.13.
8 Butlin and Joll 1984, p.24 no.34. Turner would paint a second version of the composition in 1814–15, now in the collection of the Yale Center for British Art, New Haven.
9 Ibid., p.24 no.34.
10 Ibid., pp.135–6 no.226.
11 The city of Carthage would be largely destroyed in 146 BC, its citizens taken as prisoners of war, and became subsumed as a Roman province.
12 Gillian Forrester, 'Modern Histories: Turner's Chronicles of War, Peace and the Course of Empire', in *Turner's Modern and Ancient Ports: Passages Through Time*, New York 2017, pp.5–8.
13 Bailey 2013, p.154.
14 Butlin and Joll 1984, pp.139–40 no.230.
15 Quoted in Warrell 2012, p.43.
16 James Hamilton et al., *Turner and Italy*, Edinburgh 2009, pp.80–1.
17 For example, the only two other works in the Academy's Great Room were of classical scenes, compared to six works after Shakespeare. For the decline of classicism in painting in the nineteenth century, see Hugh Honour, *Neoclassicism*, Harmondsworth 1968, pp.187–90.
18 Anonymous review, *Literary Gazette*, 14 May 1831, quoted in Judy Cosby Ivy, *Constable and the Critics 1802–1837*, Woodbridge 1991, pp.150–1.
19 The paintings were not hung together in the 1850 Royal Academy Exhibition. Because of this, scholars have often sequenced the works by the order in which they appear in the catalogue. I have chosen to sequence them in the order the scenes appear

in the *Aeneid* and retellings of the Aeneas mythology.

'Worn-out boots': Turner and Travel

1 Lord Byron, letter to Thomas Moore, 31 August 1820, in Thomas Moore, *Life of Lord Byron*, vol.4, London 1854, p.336.
2 John Constable, letter to John Fisher, [May 1824], in R.B. Beckett (ed.), *John Constable's Correspondence*, vol.6, Ipswich 1968, p.161.
3 R.B. Beckett (ed.), *John Constable's Discourses*, Ipswich 1970, p.65. For further reading on Constable's attitude towards Dutch art, see Mark Evans, *John Constable: The Making of a Master*, London 2014, pp.112–15 and 155–62.
4 John Constable, letter to John Fisher, 9 May 1823, in Beckett vol.6, p.117.
5 John Constable, letter to John Fisher, 26 August 1827, in ibid., p.231.
6 This term and other bird or flying related metaphors can be found throughout Turner's correspondence, as early as 1809 and as late as 1847. See, for example, John Gage (ed.), *Collected Correspondence of J.M.W. Turner*, Oxford 1980, pp.34, 67, 103, 119, 143, 174, 231.
7 For more extensive discussions regarding the link between Turner's sketchbooks and his travels, see Andrew Wilton, *Turner as Draughtsman*, Aldershot and Burlington, VT, 2006, pp.71–8; Nicola Moorby, 'An Italian Treasury: Turner's Sketchbooks', in James Hamilton, *Turner and Italy*, Edinburgh 2009; Ian Warrell, *Turner's Sketchbooks*, London 2014, pp.7–17. For a more in-depth comparison of Turner's sketchbook practice with Constable's, see Nicola Moorby, *Turner and Constable: Art, Life, Landscape*, New Haven and London 2025, pp.86–90.
8 Mrs Uwins, *A Memoir of Thomas Uwins, R.A.*, vol.2, London 1858, p.240, quoted in Cecila Powell, *Turner in the South: Rome, Naples, Florence*, New Haven and London 1987, p.19.
9 Turner Bequest, CLXXVI, 86, D14651: 'Venice to Ancona' sketchbook, 1819. See Matthew Imms, '*Inscriptions by Turner ?and Others: Italian Words and Phrases and English Equivalents* 1819 by Joseph Mallord William Turner', catalogue entry, March 2017, in David Blayney Brown and Matthew Imms (eds.), *J.M.W. Turner: Sketchbooks, Drawings and Watercolours*, Tate Research Publication, July 2017, https://www.tate.org.uk/art/research-publications/jmw-turner/joseph-mallord-william-turner-inscriptions-by-turner-and-others-italian-words-and-phrases-r1186387, accessed 2 April 2025.
10 J.M.W. Turner, letter to F.H. Fawkes, 28 December 1844, in Gage 1908, p.203.

Turner and his Eco-critics: Tracing Environmental Concerns in the Artist's Work

1 Martin Butlin and Evelyn Joll, *The Paintings of J.M.W. Turner*, rev. edn, New Haven and London 1984, p.69, no.97.
2 Tom Taylor (ed.), *Life of Benjamin Robert Haydon*, vol.1, New York 1859, p.52.
3 Lord Byron, *Don Juan*, Canto 10, London 1819.
4 David Blayney Brown, 'Atmospheres', in David Blayney Brown et al., *Turner's Modern World*, London 2020, p.170.
5 The exhibition *A World of Care: Turner and the Environment* (Turner's House, Twickenham, 2024) included examples of such subjects.
6 John Ruskin, in E.T. Cook and A. Wedderburn (eds.), *The Works of Ruskin. Vol. XIII*, London 1904, p.435.
7 Suzanne Fagence Cooper and Richard Johns (eds.), *Ruskin, Turner & the Storm Cloud*, London 2019, p.17 n.4, and essays by Robert Macfarlane, Emma Stibbon, Joanna Haigh, Caroline Ascott and others.
8 Sarah Gould, 'The Ecological Turn(er)', *J.M.W. Turner: State of the Field Symposium*, Yale Center for British Art, New Haven CT, 22–23 Sept. 2023.
9 Blayney Brown and Sam Smiles, 'Introduction' in Blayney Brown et al., *Turner's Modern World*, p.18, and Sarah Gould, 'The Polluted Textures of J.M.W. Turner's Late Works', *Victorian Network*, vol.10, 2021, https://doi.org/10.5283/vn.117, accessed 15 June 2024.
10 Frédéric Ogée, '"To be broken up": Turner, English Landscape, and the Anthropo(s)cenic', *State of the Field Symposium*, 2023.
11 Ibid. See also Frédéric Ogée, '"A New and Unforeseen Creation": Turner, English Landscape, and the Anthropo(s)cene', in Charlotte Gould and Sophie Mesplède (eds.), *British Art and the Environment*, London and New York 2021, pp.166–81.
12 John Constable, letter to George Constable, 12 May 1836, in R.B. Beckett (ed.), *John Constable's Correspondence*, vol.5, Ipswich 1967, pp.32–3. Useful overviews are Jonathan Ribner, 'The Poetics of Pollution', in Katharine Lochnan and Ian Warrell, *Turner, Whistler, Monet: Impressionist Visions*, London 2004, pp.51–63, and Jonathan Hill, *Weather Architecture*, Abingdon 2012, pp.168–70.
13 William H. Rodner, 'Humanity and Nature in the Steamboat Paintings of J.M.W. Turner', *Albion: A Quarterly Journal Concerned with British Studies*, vol.18, no.3, Autumn 1986, pp.455–74.
14 Michel Serres, 'Turner Translates Carnot', in Michel Serres, *Hermes: Literature, Science, Philosophy*, ed. Josué V. Harari and David F. Bell, Baltimore 1982, pp.54–62, and Michel Serres, 'Science and the Humanities: The Case of Turner', *SubStance*, vol.26, no.2, 1997, p.7; James Nisbet, 'Environmental Abstraction and the Polluted Image', *American Art*, vol.31, no.1, Spring 2017, pp.114–31, p.117; Gould 2021. See also Antonio Somaini, 'The Atmospheric Screen: Turner, Hazlitt, Ruskin', in Craig Buckley, Rüdiger Campe and Francesco Casetti (eds.), *Screen Genealogies: From Optical Device to Environmental Medium*, Amsterdam 2019, pp.159–86; Martin A. Danahay, 'A Matter out of Place: The Politics of Pollution in Ruskin and Turner', *CLIO*, vol.21, no.1, Fall 1991, pp.61–77; and Carmen Casaliggi, '"Indistinctness is my forte": Turner, Ruskin, and the Climate of Art', in Shun-Liang Chao and John Michael Corrigan (eds.), *Romantic Legacies: Transnational and Transdisciplinary Contexts*, New York 2019, pp.233–48.
15 C.S. Zerefos et al., 'Further evidence of important environmental information content in red-to-green ratios as depicted in paintings by great masters', *Atmospheric Chemistry and Physics*, vol.14, 2014, pp.2987–3015, and Anna Lea Albright and Peter Huybers, 'Paintings by Turner and Monet depict trends in 19th century air pollution', *PNAS*, vol.120, no.6, 2023, https://doi.org/10.1073/pnas.2219118120, accessed 15 June 2025.
16 David Trotter, *Cooking with Mud: The Idea of Mess in Nineteenth-Century Art and Fiction*, Oxford 2000, pp.35, 43.
17 David Stacey, 'Images of Industry: Material Sources in British Art c.1800', *British Art Journal*, vol.11, no.1, Spring 2010, pp.62–8.
18 James Hamilton, *Turner and the Scientists*, London 1998, p.54.
19 Malcom Ferdinand, *Decolonial Ecology: Thinking from the Caribbean World*, trans. Anthony Paul Smith, Medford, MA, and Cambridge 2022 (originally published in French in 2019).
20 I am grateful to Caterina Franciosi for sharing unpublished material from her PhD thesis, 'Latent Light: Energy and Nineteenth-Century British Art', Yale University (forthcoming).
21 Tobah Aukland-Peck, 'Turner's Pencil: Graphite Landscapes and Extractive Industry', *State of the Field Symposium*, 2023.
22 Amy Concannon, 'Whalers, Burning, Blubber: Material, Marks and Meaning in Turner's Whalers Sketchbook', *Turner and the Whale Symposium*, Hull Maritime Museum, organised by the University of York, 28 Oct. 2017. See also Jason Edwards, 'Turner's Dark Veganism', University of York, https://wayback.archive-it.org/19637/20250115104015/https://hoaportal.york.ac.uk/hoaportal/turnerwhaleEssay.jsp?id=305, accessed 15 June 2024.
23 Nathan Hensley, 'J.M.W. Turner's Burning World' (talk), Georgetown University Global Engagement, https://global.georgetown.edu/events/j-m-w-turner-s-burning-world, accessed 15 June 2025. See also Hill 2012, pp.171–4.
24 Tate declared a climate emergency in 2019: https://www.tate.org.uk/press/press-releases/tate-directors-declare-climate-emergency. Environmental actions inspired by themes in Turner's works are offered in the free guide accompanying the exhibition *A World of Care*: https://bit.ly/WorldofCareGuide, accessed 15 June 2025.

Early Impressions of Constable Country

1 'Warehouses and shipping on the Orwell at Ipswich', 5 October 1803, Victoria & Albert Museum, London, inv.no.626-1888.
2 George Frost to John Constable, (n.d., ?c.1807), in R.B. Beckett (ed.), *John Constable's Correspondence*, 6 vols., Ipswich 1962–8, vol.2, pp.36–9.
3 Emma Roodhouse and Caleb Howgego, *Creating Constable*, Colchester 2021, p.43. Constable had first come across Frost's name in 1797 when researching Gainsborough's time in Ipswich for artist and printmaker, John Thomas Smith. Letter, Constable to J.T. Smith, 7 May 1797, in Beckett 1962–8, vol.6, pp.11–12.
4 Lucy Hurlock to Constable, Dedham, 9 April 1800, in Beckett 1960–8, vol.2, p.19.
5 There were the Taylors at Dedham, the Masons and the Strutts in Colchester, and the Dysarts at Helmingham.
6 On 25 February 1799 Constable called on Farington in London: 'Mr J Constable of Ipswich calld'; Leslie Parris, Conal Shields and Ian Fleming-Williams (eds.), *John Constable, Further Documents and Correspondence with a Tribute to R.B. Beckett by Norman Scarfe*, Ipswich and London 1975, p.129.
7 John Constable to John Dunthorne Snr, 29 May 1802, in Beckett 1960–8, vol.2, p.32.
8 John Constable, 'Old Windmill, East Bergholt', two fragments of wood, 1792. Colchester City Council collection, inv.no.COLEM 136A.
9 John Constable to John Dunthorne Snr, Spring 1800, in Beckett 1960–8, vol.2, p.24.
10 Maria Bicknell to John Constable, 3 February 1816, ibid., p.172.
11 There are two other church commissions: *Christ Blessing the Children* 1805 at St Michael's church, Brantham, and *The Ascension* 1821 at the church of St Michael, Manningtree.
12 Ann Constable to John Constable, 8 May 1810, in Beckett 1960–8, vol.1, p.43.
13 Leslie Parris, Conal Shields and Ian Fleming-Williams (eds.), *John Constable, Further Documents and Correspondence with a Tribute to R.B. Beckett by Norman Scarfe*, Ipswich and London 1975, p.227.
14 Turner sketchbooks D40801 (1806–8) and D40571 (1805), Tate.
15 Beckett 1960–8, vol.1, p.128.
16 'In the coach yesterday coming from Suffolk, were two gentlemen and myself all strangers to each other. In passing through the valley about Dedham, one of them remarked to me – on saying it was beautiful – "Yes Sir – this is Constable's country!" I then told him who I was lest he should spoil it.' John Constable to David Lucas, 14 November 1832, in Beckett 1960–8, vol.4, p.387.
17 Roodhouse and Howgego 2021, p.8.

'Nothing Here for the Painter'? Constable's Urban Landscapes

1 John Constable to Maria Bicknell, 12 November 1814, in R.B. Beckett (ed.), *John Constable's Correspondence*, 6 vols., Ipswich 1962–8, vol.2, p.136.
2 Brighton's population increasing from around 7,000 to around 46,000 between 1801 and 1841. Peter Clark (ed.), *The Cambridge Urban History of Britain, vol.2, 1540–1840*, Cambridge 2000, p.64.
3 Richard Russell, *A Dissertation Concerning the Use of Sea Water in the Diseases of the Glands*, London 1752.
4 For more on Turner and Constable in Brighton, see Ian Warrell, 'In Pursuit of Originality in Brighton,' and 'Taking on the Chain Pier – and Turner' in Shân Lancaster (ed.), *Constable and Brighton: 'Something Out of Nothing'*, London 2017, pp.43–69.
5 John Constable, Letterpress for 'A Sea-Beach – Brighton', in *English Landscape Scenery*, in Andrew Wilton, *Constable's 'English Landscape Scenery'*, London 1979, p.42.
6 Letterpress for 'A Sea-Beach – Brighton', in Wilton 1979, p.42.
7 Leslie Parris, Conal Shields and Ian Fleming-Williams (eds.), *John Constable, Further Documents and Correspondence with a Tribute to R.B. Beckett by Norman Scarfe*, Ipswich and London 1975, p.20.
8 Robert Southey, *Letters from England by Don Manuel Alvarez Espriella. Translated from the Spanish*, London 1807, pp.51–2; John Britton, *The Beauties of Wiltshire, Displayed in Statistical, Historical, and Descriptive Sketches: Interspersed with Anecdotes of the Arts*, vol.1, London 1801, p.43.
9 John Constable to John Britton, 2 February 1834, in Beckett 1962–8, vol.4, p.386.
10 Amy Concannon, 'The Painting', in Salisbury Cathedral from the Meadows exhibited 1831 by John Constable, Tate Research Publication, 2017, https://www.tate.org.uk/research/in-focus/salisbury-cathedral-constable/the-painting, accessed 14 August 2025.
11 *Gentleman's Magazine*, vol.97, part 1, March 1827, p.528.
12 Amy Concannon, 'Urban Landscape in the Age of Reform: Salisbury, Bristol, Brighton, Lambeth, c.1820–1850', PhD thesis, University of Nottingham 2018, pp.244–246.

The Organ of Sentiment

1 John Constable, 'Lectures on Landscape' (1836), in R.B. Beckett (ed.), *John Constable's Discourses*, Ipswich, 1970, p.64.
2 C.R. Leslie, *Memoirs of the Life of John Constable, Esq. R.A., Composed Chiefly of his Letters*, 2nd edn, London 1845, pp.4–5.
3 Constable 1836 (1970), p.64.
4 For more, see John E. Thornes, John *Constable's Skies: A Fusion of Art and Science*, Edgbaston 1999; Edward Morris, *Constable's Clouds: Paintings and Cloud Studies* by John Constable, Edinburgh 2009; Mark Evans, *Constable's Skies*, London and New York 2018.
5 R.B. Beckett, letter to Louis Hawes, 29 March 1965, quoted in Louis Hawes, 'Constable's Sky Sketches', *Journal of the Warburg and Courtauld Institutes*, vol.32, 1969, p.358.
6 Constable, letterpress accompanying Spring, from *English Landscape Scenery*, in Beckett 1970, p.14.
7 Constable to John Fisher, 23 October 1821, in R.B. Beckett (ed.), *John Constable's Correspondence*, vol.6, Ipswich 1968, p.77.
8 Constable 1836 (1970), p.69.
9 [Gilbert White], *The Natural History and Antiquities of Selborne, in the County of Southhampton*, London, 1789.
10 Richard Hamblyn, *The Invention of Clouds: How an Amateur Meteorologist Forged the Language of the Skies*, New York 2002.
11 Kurt Badt, John Constable's Clouds, London 1950.
12 Jan Golinski, *British Weather and the Climate of Enlightenment*, Chicago 2007; and Katharine Anderson, *Predicting the Weather: Victorians and the Science of Meteorology*, Chicago 2005.
13 For more, see Nicholas Robbins, 'John Constable, Luke Howard, and the Aesthetics of Climate', *The Art Bulletin*, vol.103, no.2, 2021, pp.50–76.
14 Nikolaus Pevsner, *The Englishness of English Art*, New York 1956, p.18.
15 Mary Favret, *War at a Distance: Romanticism and the Making of Modern Wartime*, Princeton 2010; Richard Taws, *Time Machines: Telegraphic Images in Nineteenth-Century France*, Cambridge MA 2025.

More Matter with Less Art': Constable's Textural Aesthetic

1 John Constable, letter to John Dunthorne, 29 May 1802, in R.B. Beckett (ed.), *John Constable's Correspondence*, vol.2, Ipswich 1964, pp.31–2.
2 Elie Faure, *History of Art: Modern Art*, trans. Walter Pach, London 1924, p.278 (originally published in French in 1919–21).
3 The art historian Matthias Krüger has identified the mid- to late nineteenth century as a pivotal era in which the material relief of painting ignited a vibrant art-critical discourse in France, as against academic art. Matthias Krüger, *Das Relief der Farbe: pastose Malerei in der französischen Kunstkritik 1850–1890*, Munich 2007, p.14.
4 Nicola Suthor uses the term 'bravura' as a descriptor of both brushwork and artistic character of the style that emerged in sixteenth-century Venice and spread throughout Europe during the seventeenth century. Nicola Suthor, *Bravura: Virtuosity and Ambition in Early Modern European Painting*, Princeton 2021.
5 Philip Edwards (ed.), *Hamlet, Prince of Denmark* (The New Cambridge Shakespeare), Cambridge 1985, p.123 (Act 2, Scene 2, line 95).
6 Typical of this type of gibe, we can quote the *Athenaeum*'s review of *Snow Storm – Steam-Boat off a Harbour's Mouth* 1842: 'This gentleman has, on former occasions, chosen to paint with cream, or chocolate, yolk of egg, or currant jelly – here he uses his whole array of kitchen stuff'; *The Athenaeum*, 14 May 1842. Similarly, in *John Bull*, 'MR TURNER, indeed, goes further, for he curries the rivers, and the bridges, and the boats upon the rivers, and the ladies and gentlemen in the boats'; *John Bull*, 27 May 1827, p.165.
7 *The Times*, 8 May 1832, quoted in Judy Crosby Ivy, *Constable and the Critics, 1802–1837*, Woodbridge 1991, p.159. Edward Dubois, *Observer*, 27 May 1832; *Morning Post*, 5 May 1832, in Ivy 1991, p.15. *The Athenaeum*, 7 May 1828, p.439, in Ivy 1991, p.46. Charles M. Westmacott, *Descriptive and Critical Catalogue to the Exhibition of the Royal* Academy, London 1823, p.13, in Ivy 1991, pp.102–3.
8 Ibid., p.102.
9 Henry Fuseli, 9 May 1823, in (ed.), *John Constable's Correspondence*, vol.6, Ipswich 1968, p.116.
10 Mark Hallett, '1825: Fresh', in Mark Hallett, Sarah Victoria Turner and Jessica Feather (eds.), *The Royal Academy Summer Exhibition: A Chronicle, 1769–2018*, London 2018.
11 For example, *Morning Herald*, 7 May 1830, p.5, in Ivy 1991, p.139.
12 'The Technology of Enchantment and the Enchantment of Technology', in Alfred Gell, *The Art of Anthropology: Essays and Diagrams*, ed. Eric Hirsch, London 1999, pp.159–86.
13 About *Salisbury Cathedral*: *The Times*, 6 May 1831, p.4, cited in Ivy 1991, p.150. See also, among others, *Morning Post*, 5 May 1832, cited in Ivy 1991, p.158; *Bell's Weekly Messenger*, 24 June 1832, p.201, cited in Ivy 1991, p.163.
14 Nicholas Robbins, 'John Constable, Luke Howard, and the Aesthetics of Climate', *The Art Bulletin*, vol.103, no.2, 2021, pp.50–76, p.65.
15 For further analysis, see Robbins 2021.
16 Sarah Cove, 'The Painting Techniques of Constable's "Six-Footers"', in Anne Lyles, *The Great Landscapes*, London 2006, p.65.
17 Jennifer L. Roberts, 'Things: Material Turn, Transnational Turn', *American Art*, vol.31, no.2, 2017, pp.64–9.
18 Joshua Reynolds, '*Discourse XIV*, 10 December 1788', in Robert R. Wark (ed.), *Discourses on Art, 1769–1790*, New Haven and London 1997, pp.257–8.
19 The term 'School of London' was invented by the artist and group member R.B. Kitaj to loosely describe the group of artists comprising Michael Andrews, Frank Auerbach, Leon Kossoff, Francis Bacon, Lucian Freud and David Hockney, to cite the most illustrious. Their works were grouped in the controversial 1976 Hayward Gallery exhibition *The Human Clay*, organised by Kitaj.

'Ut Umbra sic Vita': Life is but a Shadow

1 This piece takes ideas from my forthcoming thesis for a Collaborative Doctoral Partnership (CDP) supported by the V&A and the University of Sussex and generously funded by the AHRC.
2 John Constable, Introduction to the second edition of *English Landscape*, 1833.
3 Letter from John Constable to David Lucas, 12 March 1831, in R.B. Beckett (ed.), *John Constable's Correspondence*, Ipswich 1962–8, vol.4, p.344.
4 Andrew Wilton, *Constable's 'English Landscape Scenery'*, London 1979, p.12; Felicity Myrone, '"No Mercenary Views"? Constable's *English Landscape*', *Tate Papers*, no.33 (2020), https://www.tate.org.uk/research/tate-papers/33/no-mercenary-views-constable-english-landscape, accessed 28 Aug. 2025; Katharine Martin, forthcoming.
5 Judy Crosby Ivy, 'Reading Mezzotints: Mr Constable's *English Landscape*', *Journal of the Printing Historical Society*, no.25 (1996), pp.51–2; Susan Owens, *Spirit of Place*, London 2020, p.189.
6 Wilton 1979, p.13; Leslie Parris, *The 'English Landscape' Prints of John Constable & David Lucas*, London 1986; Leslie Parris and Ian Fleming-Williams, 'The English landscape mezzotints', in *Constable*, London 1996, p.319; Stephen Calloway, 'Canon: "the Chiar'oscuro of Nature"', in Mark Evans, *John Constable: The Making of a Master*, London 2014, pp.182–207; Antony Griffiths, *The Print Before Photography*, London 2016, p.255.
7 Constable's adoption of the spelling 'Stoke-by-Neyland' on the plate might be explained by Frederic Shoberl's adoption of the same spelling in *The Beauties of England and Wales; or, Delineations, topographical, historical, and descriptive, of each county*, London 1813, vol.14, p.143, a copy of which Constable owned.
8 This is the first time that this proof has been published and forms part of my CDP research project.
9 Instalment with blue wrapper for the second edition of *Various Subjects of Landscape, Characteristic of English Scenery, Principally Intended to Display the Phenomena of the Chiar'oscuro of Nature*, 1833. V&A E.1100:4/1-2016 to E.1100:4/4-2016.
10 Constable to Lucas, 4 December 1831, 28 February 1832, 5 May 1832 and 26 February 1830, in Beckett 1962–8, vol.4, pp.360, 367, 373, 325.
11 Constable to Lucas, 16 December 1834, in ibid., pp.416.
12 *Athenaeum*, 26 June 1830, p.396; Judy Crosby Ivy, *Constable and the Critics, 1802–1837*, Woodbridge 1991, p.143; Myrone 2020.

Turner and Constable: Colour

1 Joyce H. Townsend, *How Turner Painted: Materials and Techniques*, London and New York 2019, pp.108–19.
2 William James Russell and William de Wiveleslie Abney, *Report on the Action of Light on Watercolours*, London 1888.
3 For their analysis, see Joyce H. Townsend, 'The Materials of J.M.W. Turner: Pigments', *Studies in Conservation*, vol. 38, 1993, pp.231–54. Some had been investigated earlier; see Norman W. Hanson, 'Some Painting Materials of J.M.W. Turner', *Studies in Conservation*, vol.1, 1952–4, pp.162–73.
4 Hanson (1952–4) used up all the residues on the bottle tops, leaving none for later analysis that would have given more information.
5 For this and other paintings, see analysis reports by Joyce Townsend in the respective Tate conservation records.
6 Tony Smibert and Joyce Townsend, *Tate Watercolour Manual*, London 2014. Tony Smibert, *Turner's Apprentice: A Watercolour Masterclass*, London and New York 2020.
7 Sarah Cove, 'Constable's Oil Painting Materials and Techniques', in Leslie Parris and Ian Fleming-Williams, *Constable*, exh. cat., Tate Gallery, London 1991, pp.493–529.
8 Author of *Chromatography; or, a Treatise on Colours and Pigments, and of their Powers in Painting*, London 1835, which would be edited and reprinted posthumously for most of the nineteenth century.
9 Martin Wyld and Ashok Roy, 'A Technical Examination of the Painting', in Judy Egerton, *Turner: The Fighting Temeraire*, exh. cat., National Gallery, London 1995, pp.121–3.

Constable and Turner Remade

1 Ellen Owens (civil servant), in Colin Painter, *At Home with Constable's Cornfield*, London 1996, p.38.
2 Painter 1996, p.7.
3 Richard Cork, 'A horse and cart among our souvenirs', *The Times*, 8 June 1991.
4 See, for example, John Barrell, *The Dark Side of the Landscape: The Rural Poor in English Painting 1730–1840*, Cambridge 1980; and Michael Rosenthal, *Constable: The Painter and his Landscape*, New Haven and London 1983. The most detailed analysis of Constable's shifting reputation in the twentieth century is offered by Stephen Daniels, 'John Constable and the Making of Constable Country', in his *Fields of Vision: Landscape Imagery and National Identity in England and the United States*, Princeton NJ 1993, pp.200–42.
5 See, for example, Chris Blackhurst, 'Constable's greatest painting a "contested landscape"? They'll be cancelling it next ...', *Independent*, 25 July 2024; 'National Gallery refuses to make its collection woke and instead celebrates Europe's painters', *Sunday Telegraph*, 11 May 2025.
6 Sam Johnson-Schlee, *Living Rooms*, London 2022, pp.28–30.
7 Susan Heathcote (secretary), quoted in Painter 1996, p.24.
8 Kennard's work belongs to a long history of remaking *The Hay Wain*, sometimes legal, sometimes not. For an overview of the painting's colourful afterlife, see 'Mary McMahon "dull replica" to "national treasure": The Afterlife of *The Hay Wain*', and other essays, in Christine Riding (ed.), *Discover Constable and The Hay Wain*, London 2024.
9 John Ruskin, 'Modern Painters', in E.T. Cook and Alexander Wedderburn (eds.), *The Works of John Ruskin*, 39 vols, London 1903–12, vol.3, pp.571–3.
10 For the most recent and thoroughgoing analysis of the *Slave Ship* in its historical context, see Sam Smiles, *Turner and the Slave Trade*, New Haven and London 2025. Other key works in the large historiography of the painting include John McCoubrey, 'Turner's "Slave Ship": Abolition, Ruskin, and Reception', *Word and Image*, vol.14, no.4 (Oct.–Dec. 1998), pp.319–53; Leo Costello, *J.M.W. Turner and the Subject of History*, Farnham 2012; and Kay Dian Kriz, 'Turner's Slavers, Race, and the Ridiculous Human Fragment' in Theresa Kelley and Jill H. Casid (eds.), *Visuality's Romantic Genealogies* (December 2014), https://www.romantic-circles.org/praxis/visualities/kriz, accessed 28 Aug. 2025.
11 Catalogue entry for *Slave Ship (Slavers Throwing Overboard the Dead and Dying, Typhoon Coming On)*, Museum of Fine Arts, Boston, https://collections.mfa.org/objects/31102, accessed 28 Aug. 2025.
12 David Dabydeen, *Turner: New & Selected Poems*, London 1994, p.x.
13 The Otolith Group, *Hydra Decapita*, https://otolithgroup.org/work/hydra-decapita, accessed 28 Aug. 2025.
14 The Middle Passage refers to the forced journey from West Africa to the Americas during the transatlantic slave trade. Between 1500 and 1866, more than 12 million enslaved Africans were transported in this way. Of those, around 2 million died during the voyage.
15 Perry's installation in London developed from and incorporated an earlier work, *Wet and Wavy Looks – Typhoon coming on for a Three Monitor Workstation* (2016). See *Sondra Perry: Typhoon Coming On*, Serpentine Galleries, https://www.serpentinegalleries.org/whats-on/sondra-perry-typhoon-coming-on, accessed 28 Aug. 2025.
16 Kara Walker, '"I'm an Unreliable Narrator": *Fons Americanus*' (2019),

Tate, https://www.tate.org.uk/art/artists/kara-walker-2674/kara-walkers-fons-americanus, accessed 28 Aug. 2025.
17 An incomplete list of contemporary artists who have engaged with the *Slave Ship* includes Frank Bowling, Ellen Gallagher, playwright Winsome Pinnock, poet Claudia Rankine, and rapper and singer Lupe Fiasco, whose 2018 album *Drogas Wave* opens with lines from Turner's fragmentary poem 'Fallacies of Hope' that accompanied the painting when it was exhibited at the Royal Academy in 1840.

Diploma Works

1 Turner in fact offered two paintings, but *Dolbadern Castle* was unanimously chosen by the Council. See Shanes, *Young Mr. Turner*, p.224.
2 See David Solkin and Philippa Simpson, 'Turner and the North', in David Solkin, *Turner and the Masters*, London 2009, pp.162–3.
3 Barry Venning, *Turner*, London 2003, pp.51–2.
4 *The Lock 1824*, oil on canvas, 121 × 140 cm, private collection.
5 See Anne Lyles, 'Truth to Painting: Constable's Late Work', in Anne Lyles (ed.), *Late Constable*, exh. cat., Royal Academy of Arts, London 2022, pp.31–2.
6 Constable, letter to John Fisher, 23 October 1821, in Beckett 1962–8, vol.6, p.77.
7 Ibid., p.78.
8 John Constable to John Fisher, 29 August 1824, in Beckett 1962–8, vol. 6, p.172.

Foundations

1 See Stephen Hebron, Conal Shields and Timothy Wilcox, *The Solitude of Mountains: Constable and the Lake District*, exh. cat., Wordsworth Trust, Grasmere 2006.

Behind Closed Doors: Turner's studio

1 One of the most fanciful biographers of Turner, Walter Thornbury, claimed there were as many as seven cats roving Turner's studio, as quoted in 'J.M.W. Turner, R.A.', *Blackwood's Edinburgh Magazine*, January 1862, p.30. There are cat-paw prints found on several sheets in the Turner Bequest at Tate, including the versos of D17049, D16972 (Turner's diagrams for his lectures as Professor of Perspective at the Royal Academy), D08959 and D08960.
2 William Leighton Leitch, 'The Early History of Turner's Yorkshire Drawings', *Athenaeum*, no.3480, 7 July 1894, p.327.
3 David Solkin, *Turner and the Masters*, London 2009, p.191.
4 For a discussion of Turner and Constable's studio spaces, see Rhian Addison McCreanor, 'Indoor Spaces for Outdoor Minds: Landscape Artists' Studios in London, 1780–1850', PhD thesis, University of York 2023.
5 The painting with damage indicating use as a cat flap is *Fishing upon the Blythe-Sand, Tide Setting In* (Tate, N00496).

In the Outdoors: Constable and the oil Sketch

1 John Constable to John Dunthorne Snr, 29 May 1802, in R.B. Beckett (ed.), *John Constable's Correspondence*, 6 vols., Ipswich 1962–8, vol.2, pp.31–2.
2 John Constable to John Fisher, 5 January 1825, in ibid., vol.6, p.189.
3 One critic (*The Sun*, 21 May 1806) noted the 'coarseness' of Turner's *The Fall of the Rhine at Schaffhausen* 1806 (Boston Museum of Fine Arts), remarking that it gave the effect of having been painted with 'sand and chalk'.
4 Robert Hunt in *The Examiner*, 7 June 1812, p.363.
5 *London Chronicle*, 11–12 June 1812, p.567.

'No small wonder': Turner in Italy and the Alps

1 Turner added a description of his landing at Calais to a sketchbook drawing (Tate, D04960).
2 Quoted in Barry Venning, 'Turner's Annotated Books: Opie's "Lectures on Painting" and Shee's "Elements of Art"' (part 2), *Turner Studies*, vol.2, no.2 (Winter 1983), p.45.

Fields and Skies: new phases in Constable's search for 'truth'

1 John Constable to Maria Bicknell, 27 August 1815, in R.B. Beckett (ed.), *John Constable's Correspondence*, 6 vols., Ipswich 1962–8, vol.2, p.149.
2 Constable looked at John Julius Angerstein's Claudes, including *A Seaport* (National Gallery, London, NG5). See Leslie Parris and Ian Fleming-Williams, *Constable*, exh. cat., Tate Gallery, London 1991, p.155.
3 Robert Hunt in *The Examiner*, 28 May 1815, p.351.

Magic Arrangements: Turner's watercolours

1 E.M. Fawkes, quoted in Andrew Wilton, 'An Authoritative Lesson in Art', in Cecilia Powell (ed.), *Paths to Fame: Turner Watercolours from the Courtauld*, exh. cat., Wordsworth Trust, Grasmere 2008, pp.5–6.
2 Ian Warrell, *Turner: The Fourth Decade. Watercolours, 1820–30*, London 1991, p.31.
3 *British Freeholder*, 1819, pp.436–7, quoted in Ian Warrell, '"The wonder-working artist": Contemporary Reponses to Turner's Exhibited and Engraved Watercolours', in Eric Shanes (ed.), *Turner: The Great Watercolours*, exh. cat., Royal Academy of Arts, London 2000, p.38.
4 Robert Hunt in *The Examiner*, no.780, 5 January 1823.

'Fire and water': The Royal Academy Exhibition

1 Opie's Lectures on Painting, 1805–9, quoted in Kay Dian Kriz, *The Idea of the English Landscape Painter: Genius as Alibi in the Early Nineteenth Century*, New Haven and London 1997, p.39.
2 *St James's Chronicle*, 11–13 May 1815; Beaumont's comments are recorded in Joseph Farington, *The Diary of Joseph Farington*, eds. Kenneth Garlick, Angus Macintyre and Kathryn Cave, New Haven and London 1978–84, vol.13, pp.4, 637–8, quoted in David Solkin, *Turner and the Masters*, London 2009, p.24.
3 Constable to John Fisher, 11 June 1828, in R.B. Beckett (ed.), *John Constable's Correspondence*, 6 vols., Ipswich 1962–8, vol.6, p.236.
4 John Fisher to John Constable, 13 November 1812, in ibid., p.18.
5 *The Examiner*, 27 June 1819, p.413.
6 They were *Stratford Mill* (no.128), *View on the Stour near Dedham* (no.129) and *The Lock* (private collection), as detailed in Anne Lyles, 'Soliciting Attention: Constable, the Royal Academy and the Critics', in Anne Lyles (ed.), *Constable: The Great Landscapes*, exh. cat., Tate, London 2006, p.37.
7 An account of this occasion is given in Ian Fleming-Williams, Leslie Parris and Conal Shields, *Constable: Paintings, Watercolours and Drawings*, exh. cat., Tate Gallery, London 1976, pp.158–60.
8 This remark comes from George Dunlop Leslie, the son of artist Charles Robert Leslie, who was a friend of Constable's; Solkin 2009, p.186.
9 *Literary Gazette*, 19 May 1832, p.314.
10 C.R. Leslie, *Autobiographical Recollections*, 2 vols, London 1860, vol.1, pp.202–3.
11 See Amy Concannon, 'The Painting', in Amy Concannon (ed.), *Salisbury Cathedral from the Meadows Exhibited 1831 by John Constable*, Tate Research Publication, 2017, https://www.tate.org.uk/research/in-focus/salisbury-cathedral-constable/the-painting, accessed 10 June 2025.
12 See David Blayney Brown, 'The Opening of the Walhalla', in David Blayney Brown, Amy Concannon and Sam Smiles (eds.), *Late Turner: Painting Set Free*, exh. cat., Tate, London 2014, p.160.

Late Constable: beyond 'Constable Country'

1 Edward Dubois in the *Observer*, 29 May 1831.
2 *Athenaeum*, 2 June 1832, p.356.
3 *London Magazine*, vol.3, 3rd ser., June 1829, p.604; *Athenaeum*, 27 May 1829, p.331.
4 Edward Dubois in the *Observer*, 27 May 1832.
5 *Library of the Fine Arts*, 1 June 1831, p.421.
6 Constable himself recounted Fuseli's remark to John Fisher in a letter of 9 May 1823, in R.B. Beckett (ed.), *John Constable's Correspondence*, 6 vols., Ipswich 1962–8, vol.6, p.116.
7 Constable to Fisher, 24 May 1830, in ibid., vol.6, p.258.
8 See Matthew Hargraves, 'Majestic Darkness: Constable's Late Drawings', in Anne Lyles (ed.), *Late Constable*, exh. cat., Royal Academy of Arts, London 2021, pp.53–63.

Airy visions: Turner's late work

1 John Constable to George Constable, 12 May 1836, in R.B. Beckett (ed.), *John Constable's Correspondence*, 6 vols., Ipswich 1962–8, vol.5, pp.32–3.
2 *Morning Post*, 25 May 1836, quoted in Martin Butlin and Evelyn Joll, *The Paintings of J.M.W. Turner*, rev. edn, New Haven and London 1984, p.217; *Athenaeum*, 14 May 1836, quoted in ibid., p.219; *Athenaeum*, 17 June 1843, quoted in ibid., p.253.
3 See David Blayney Brown, '"Poetical" or "Preposterous"? History Painting', in David Blayney Brown, Amy Concannon and Sam Smiles (eds.), *Late Turner: Painting Set Free*, exh. cat., Tate, London 2014, p.125.

Landscape and Memory

1 Constable to C.R. Leslie, 20 January 1834, in R.B. Beckett (ed.), *John Constable's Correspondence*, 6 vols., Ipswich 1962–8, vol.3, p.246.
2 On Constable's trees, see Charles Watkins, 'Landscape Management', in Amy Concannon (ed.), *Salisbury Cathedral from the Meadows Exhibited 1831 by John Constable*, Tate Research Publication, 2017, https://www.tate.org.uk/research/in-focus/salisbury-cathedral-constable/landscape-management, accessed 14 June 2025.
3 Constable to C.R. Leslie, December 1834, in Beckett 1962–8, vol.3, pp.122–2.
4 Turner to John James Ruskin, 15 May 1845, in John Gage (ed.), *The Collected Correspondence of J.M.W. Turner*, Oxford 1980, pp.206–7.
5 *The Times*, 4 May 1850.
6 John Constable, 'The Establishment of Landscape,' second lecture, Royal Institution (2 June 1836), in R.B. Beckett (ed.), *John Constable's Discourses*, Ipswich 1970, p.60.
7 As reported by Dr William Bartlett to Ruskin in a letter of 1857, quoted in Alexander J. Finberg, *The Life of J.M.W. Turner, R.A.*, rev. edn, Oxford 1961, p.438.

Turner and Constable's Legacy: Artists Today

1 William Feaver (ed.), *Lucian Freud on John Constable*, London 2003, p.38.
2 'Frank Auerbach: Constable, Turner and me', *Guardian*, 21 September 2014, https://www.theguardian.com/artanddesign/2014/sep/21/frank-auerbach-constable-turner-and-me-interview, accessed 25 February 2025.
3 'Are You A Turner or Constable Man?', outtake from Bruno Wollheim's film *David Hockney: A Bigger Picture*, https://www.youtube.com/watch?v=mMNpqLk9CjM&t=13s, accessed 25 February 2025.
4 'David Hockney in conversation with David Blayney Brown', in Simon Grant (ed.), *Hockney on Turner Watercolours*, London 2007, p.18.
5 Ibid., pp.29, 30; 'Are You A Turner or Constable Man?'.
6 Olafur Eliasson, 'Reality is Ephemeral: Turner Colour Experiments', *Tate Etc.*, no.32 (Autumn 2014), https://www.tate.org.uk/tate-etc/issue-32-autumn-2014/reality-ephemeral, accessed 25 February 2025.

TURNER

Pre-1780

–

23 April 1775 – widely accepted date of birth of Joseph Mallord William Turner in Maiden Lane, Covent Garden, London. Son of William Turner, barber and wig-maker, and Mary (née Marshall).

1780–1789

–

Following the death of his little sister in 1783, Turner is intermittently sent away from London: to his uncle's in Brentford, Middlesex (1785); and to Margate (1786), where he attends Coleman's school and makes his earliest surviving drawings and watercolours.

His father encourages his talent, displaying his watercolours to customers in his barber shop. Early training includes working in an architect's office and studying with artist Thomas Malton the younger.

1789 – age fourteen, he is admitted to the Royal Academy Schools.

1790–1799

–

While still a student Turner becomes a regular exhibitor at the annual Royal Academy Exhibition (he exhibits his first watercolour in 1790 and his first oil in 1793, nos.4 and 7). He is also awarded the 'Greater Silver Palett' by the Royal Society of Arts for best 'landscape drawing after nature'.

From 1791 he begins his lifelong habit of sketching tours: early destinations include the West Country, Wales, the Midlands and the Isle of Wight. In 1794 he receives his first commission, to produce topographical watercolours for engraving in the Copper-Plate Magazine.

Around this time he starts evening visits to the 'Academy' of Dr Thomas Monro, copying watercolours and socialising with other artists, including Thomas Girtin.

By the end of the decade he is both financially and professionally successful. His earnings are considerable (clients include William Beckford, Lord Yarborough and the Earl of Essex) and he is well-off enough to move to new professional premises in Marylebone.

In 1799, age twenty-four, he is elected an Associate of the Royal Academy (ARA). Self-Portrait probably dates from this time (no.16).

1800–1809

–

To safeguard his professional reputation Turner keeps his private life a secret, including his relationship with a widow, Sarah Danby, and the birth of a daughter, Evelina Danby, in 1801. Meanwhile, having been mentally unwell for a number of years his mother is permanently committed to the Bethlem public asylum where she dies in 1804.

Turner's upward career trajectory continues with ambitious exhibition oils executed in the style of the European Old Masters and grand sublime landscapes inspired by his recent travels to Wales and Scotland, and then in 1802, his first trip abroad to France and the Swiss Alps.

In 1802, he becomes the youngest ever Royal Academician, aged twenty-seven.

CONSTABLE

Pre-1780

–

11 June 1776 – birth of John Constable at East Bergholt House, East Bergholt, Suffolk. Son of Golding Constable, mill owner and grain merchant, and Ann (née Watts).

1780–1789

–

Constable grows up in East Bergholt with five siblings. Age seven he is sent to school in Lavenham but is very unhappy and is brought home to attend nearby Dedham Grammar School. He later acknowledges the happy and secure nature of his 'careless boyhood'.

1790–1799

–

Begins working for his father, training to take over the Constable milling and grain exportation business. Carves a windmill into the timbers of the mill in which he is working (no.18).

In his spare time he paints in the countryside around East Bergholt with a local friend, John Dunthorne and he also undertakes a sketching tour of Norfolk (1794).

His interest in art is encouraged by an introduction to Sir George Beaumont, a connoisseur and collector whose art collection includes paintings by Claude Lorrain.

Following a business trip to Edmonton, north London, Constable is further inspired by meeting artists, John Thomas Smith and John Cranch.

By the end of the decade, his younger brother, Abram, takes his place in the family business, freeing him up to pursue a career as an artist.

1799 – he moves to London and is admitted into the Royal Academy Schools, age twenty-three.

1800–1809

–

Constable progresses swiftly through the RA Schools and in 1802 exhibits his first painting at the annual Exhibition.

Still financially supported by his father he only occasionally makes money from painting, mostly through portrait commissions for family acquaintances. He is determined, however, to specialise in landscape.

He undertakes sketching tours of the Peak District and Derbyshire (1801), the Kentish coast on board an East Indiaman (1803), and the Lake District (1806), where he experiments with watercolour. Royal Academy exhibits through the decade include several Lake District landscapes and a watercolour of the Battle of Trafalgar, though these receive little public notice.

In 1804 he opens 'Turner's Gallery', an autonomous commercial display space on the corner of Harley Street and Queen Anne Street West, where he holds annual exhibitions of his work. Many of the exhibits are Thames paintings inspired by residential sojourns in Isleworth (1805) and Hammersmith.

1806 after seeing the Victory in the Thames Estuary he exhibits a large painting, *The Battle of Trafalgar*.

Other notable achievements during this decade include the first engraving after one of his works (*The Shipwreck* 1805), the launching of the seminal landscape print publication, the *Liber Studiorum*, and being appointed the Royal Academy's Professor of Perspective.

By the end of the decade his prominent client base includes important collectors, Walter Fawkes of Farnley Hall in Yorkshire, and the 3rd Earl of Egremont of Petworth House in Sussex.

–

A second daughter, Georgiana, is born, though Turner's involvement as a father seems to be very limited. At some point during the next few years his relationship with Sarah Danby appears to end.

From 1812 he designs and builds Sandycombe Lodge in Twickenham, a country retreat and retirement home for his father.

His energies are focused on diverse work projects including further instalments of the *Liber Studiorum*, and the preparation of a course of perspective lectures.

Visits to Walter Fawkes in Yorkshire inspire well-received oils, *Snow Storm, Hannibal Crossing the Alps* (1812) and *Frosty Morning* (1813), a painting which Constable's friend, John Fisher jokes 'beats' *Landscape: Boys Fishing* at exhibition that year.

Other notable exhibits include classically themed paintings on the story of Dido and Aeneas (no.125) and *The Field of Waterloo* (1818).

Watercolour commissions for private patrons and for topographical engraving projects prompt extensive travelling within Britain including tours of the West Country for *Picturesque Views on the Southern Coast of England*, published from 1814.

Following the Battle of Waterloo in 1815, he is able to resume travel on the Continent, starting with tours of Germany and the Low Countries (1817), and a six-month expedition through Italy (1819).

In 1819 he is the undisputed star of an exhibition of watercolours held at Fawkes's London home – the first time a large number of his watercolours had been seen publicly for several years.

After exhibiting a very large oil painting *England: Richmond Hill on the Prince Regent's Birthday*, it fails to attract royal patronage and remains unsold in his studio.

1810 – 1819

He regularly visits East Bergholt and Suffolk, where he pursues outdoor oil sketching for the purpose of achieving what he calls 'natural painture'. His father buys him copyhold of a small property in the village which he uses as a studio.

In 1809, during a trip to East Bergholt, he falls in love with Maria Bicknell, the granddaughter of the local reverend. Faced with family objections to their match, they are forced into a long-term, long-distance engagement that causes them both much heartache.

–

His 1810 painting, *The Church Porch, East Bergholt*, marks the beginning of a new focus upon Suffolk for exhibition oil paintings, a theme which will dominate the next two decades.

Forbidden from seeing Maria, his courtship of her continues by letter. The enforced separation causes him much anxiety and unhappiness, at times impacting his ability to work. During this time, he regularly returns to sketch in East Bergholt where the pursuit of 'natural peinture' inspires him to paint exhibition pictures out-of-doors.

He also visits Salisbury where he meets John Fisher, the nephew of his patron, the bishop. The two will be lifelong friends and correspondents.

–

28 June 1813 – he meets Turner for the first time at a Royal Academy dinner. Describes him as having a 'wonderful range of mind'. His practice of outdoor oil sketching evolves to include painting exhibitable works in the open air.

After the death of his parents (his mother in 1815 and his father in 1816), his inheritance enables him to marry Maria, irrespective of her family's disapproval. The painting *Flatford Mill – Scene on a Navigable River* 1817 (no.102) marks this transition point. It is the last and largest picture executed mainly on the spot. Going forward Constable's exhibition landscapes become London-based studio productions.

–

He later describes the five years after his marriage as the 'happiest and most interesting' of his life, both from a personal and professional perspective. Having set up home in London, the Constables start a family (a son, John Charles, is born at the end of 1817 and a daughter, Minna, in 1819).

In 1819, he exhibits his first River Stour 'six-footer', *The White Horse*, which is critically well-received (including, for the first time, direct comparison to Turner). After almost a decade of unsuccessful attempts, he is elected as an Associate of the Royal Academy.

In subject and appearance Turner's paintings begin to reflect the experiences of his European travels. The dominant use of yellow in particular becomes a recurring criticism amongst the art press.

From 1822–4 he works on his only royal commission, *The Battle of Trafalgar, 21 October 1805* (National Maritime Museum) for St James's Palace. His interpretation of the theme is heavily censured and rather than retain it for the Royal Collection George IV eventually gifts it to the Naval Hospital, Greenwich.

Travels in Britain and Europe continue to feed into multiple different topographical series, including the *Rivers of England* and *Picturesque Views in England and Wales*. In 1824 he explores Sussex, including Brighton (coinciding with the first year the Constable family are in town).

His print commissions also now include a number of literary projects, including book illustrations for Samuel Rogers, Lord Byron and others.

Trips to France provide material for *Wanderings by the Loire and Wanderings by the Seine* (engraved and published during the 1830s). Other expeditions include a tour of the Meuse and Mosel rivers (1824); the Netherlands (1825); and a second tour of Italy (1828), during which time he exhibits a group of Italian oils in Rome to a largely negative local reception.

1827 and 1828 Turner is at Petworth House fulfilling a commission for site-specific paintings to be installed in the Carved Room. One of the subjects is *The Chain Pier, Brighton*, which depicts (perhaps deliberately) the opposite viewpoint to Constable's 1827 exhibit.

1826 Turner sells Sandycombe Lodge and moves his father back to London. William Turner senior dies in September 1829.

1829 Turner makes his first will including early ideas for a bequest to the nation. In the ensuing years this document will be repeatedly revised and changed.

Turner continues to exhibit landscape oils dominated by European subjects and history. Continental tours during this decade include France (1832, 1837 and 1838), Germany, Austria and Venice (1833), Denmark, Germany and Bohemia (1835), the Val d'Aosta and the Alps (1836), and Belgium, Luxembourg and Germany (1839).

British travels meanwhile are driven by further work for the print market including the *England and Wales* series and illustrations for several publications by Sir Walter Scott. He also starts regularly visiting Margate and eventually forms a relationship with his landlady, Sophia Booth.

1834 Turner witnesses the destruction by fire of the Houses of Parliament (as does Constable) and the following year exhibits two oils on the subject. By now he is routinely criticised by the press for the 'heat' and 'fire' of his pictures, often with reference to the 'freshness' and 'water' associated with Constable.

Reviews of Turner's 1836 exhibits, including *Juliet and her Nurse*, are particularly abusive, inspiring a seventeen-year-old John Ruskin to write his first defence of the artist. Constable describes him as painting with 'tinted steam, so evanescent and so airy'.

Turner is part of the council committee tasked with moving the Royal Academy to Trafalgar Square in 1837. He also serves on the hanging committee that posthumously exhibits Constable's *Arundel Mill and Castle*.

In 1838 the battleship Temeraire is tugged to a breaker's yard on the Thames in Rotherhithe. The following year, Turner exhibits *The Fighting Temeraire* to widespread acclaim.

1820 – 1829

By repeatedly painting and exhibiting River Stour 'six-footers', Constable establishes a landscape specialism of his own, securing a reputation as a painter of fresh English countryside. However, despite his growing fame he is still not selling many landscapes and his annual bids to become a Royal Academician continue to be unsuccessful.

The Constable family continues to grow in number (Charley, born 1821; Isabel, born 1824; Emily, born 1825; Alfie, born 1826, and Lionel, born 1828). Prompted by concerns for the health of his wife and children Constable rents a series of second homes in Hampstead. From here in 1821 and 1822 he undertakes an extensive course of what he calls 'skying' – outdoor oil sketches of clouds and atmospheric effects.

In 1822 Constable moves to 35 Charlotte Street, a bigger property in central London which includes a large painting room. In due course he also constructs a gallery showroom for visitors to view his paintings.

In 1824 Constable sends paintings to be exhibited at the French Salon in the Louvre. They are very well received, particularly *The Hay Wain*, leading to increased sales and exposure of his work in France. He is awarded a Gold Medal inscribed 'Peintre de Paysage' ('Painter of Landscape').

Suffering from consumption (tuberculosis), Maria Constable's health declines. From 1824 she and the children regularly stay in Brighton for the benefits of the sea air, with Constable travelling back and forth from London. Inspired by the resort he paints studies of the sea and sky, and in 1827 exhibits his first marine 'six-footer', *Chain Pier, Brighton*.

Constable purchases 6 Well Walk, Hampstead, as a permanent home. It is here in November 1828 that his wife finally succumbs to her illness and dies. Constable mourns her for the rest of his life and is now left as a single father to seven young children.

Not long after, in February 1829 Constable is finally elected a Royal Academician. Turner calls to congratulate him.

1830 – 1839

The early years of the decade are a difficult time for Constable as he struggles with bereavement and illness, and with balancing home and work life.

His creative output is dominated by *English Landscape Scenery* (1830–2), a collaboration with printmaker, David Lucas, to produce mezzotints after Constable's work. The project causes him much anxiety and is a commercial failure. The resulting prints, however, fulfil a new exploration of the qualities of chiaroscuro in nature.

His painting meanwhile heads in new directions, characterised by a more monumental and symbolic treatment of landscape. He also returns to watercolour as a medium for exhibition (the first time since 1806). Criticism of his work centres on his visible white brushstrokes, often described as 'snow', but he is also praised for his freshness and natural colouring.

The Valley Farm 1835 is sold directly off the easel to prominent British collector, Robert Vernon.

New duties at the Academy are an added pressure. In 1830 he is publicly criticised in the press for curatorial decisions while hanging the Great Room for the Exhibition. The following year he splits up a pairing of works by Turner with his own *Salisbury Cathedral from the Meadows*, a move which is later characterised by David Roberts as a competitive abuse of power. There is extensive comparison of his paintings with Turner's, centring on the elemental differences between them as 'fire' and 'water'.

During the early 1840s Turner undertakes annual visits to Switzerland until prevented from doing so by his health. His last European expeditions are two short trips to the north coast of France in 1845.

He begins to employ an agent, Thomas Griffith, to market and sell his works, particularly his watercolours which are routinely bought by a loyal group of collectors including John Ruskin.

Exhibited oil paintings are now widely noted for their esoteric subjects, unorthodox formats and hazy 'unfinished' appearance. Dominant themes during this decade include multiple paintings of Venice and subjects taken from modern life such as *Snow Storm – steam boat off a harbour's mouth* (1842) and *Rain, Steam and Speed: The Great Western Railway* (1844). As an intellectual vindication of Turner's style Ruskin publishes the first volume of *Modern Painters* (1843).

Notwithstanding his reputation for radical experimentation Turner is by now a respected figure in the art world. In 1845 he is made acting President of the Royal Academy.

By 1846 he is secretly co-habiting with Mrs Booth in a riverside house she has bought in Chelsea.

He continues painting, particularly European landscapes and a revisitation of scenes from the *Liber Studiorum*. However, with his health in decline he now employs a studio assistant, Francis Sherrell, and exhibits fewer new works.

1848 is the first Royal Academy Exhibition without a Turner exhibit since 1824.

In 1850 he exhibits for the last time at the Royal Academy (a related cycle of four works on the theme of Dido and Aeneas, no.184). The following year he attends as a visitor only.

After months of ill health, he dies in Chelsea on 19 December 1851, age seventy-six and is buried in St Paul's Cathedral.

1856 Court of Chancery ruling on Turner's will leads to the acceptance by the nation of the Turner Bequest.

1861 Walter Thornbury publishes the first biography of Turner.

1840–1849

1850 onwards

In 1832 he exhibits *The Opening of Waterloo Bridge*, a large painting first conceived around fifteen years earlier. In reaction to this work Turner adds a blob of red pigment to his adjacent exhibit, *Helvoetsluys*, and Constable reportedly describes the other artist as having 'fired a gun'. Charles Robert Leslie's later anecdote about this moment adds fuel to the idea that the two painters were rivals.

1833–6 he delivers a series of lectures at various venues on the history of landscape. In 1836 his last exhibit at the Royal Academy's old premises at Somerset House is *Cenotaph to the Memory of Sir Joshua Reynolds*, a symbolic work about the academic status of landscape painting.

A new friend, George Constable, prompts an interest in the scenery of Sussex, especially Arundel. He is still working upon a painting, *Arundel Mill and Castle*, when he suddenly becomes unwell and dies during the early hours of 1 April 1837, age sixty. He is buried in Hampstead.

Arundel Mill is posthumously exhibited in the Royal Academy's new premises within the National Gallery. *The Cornfield* is purchased by subscription and presented to the nation.

1843 Charles Robert Leslie publishes his influential biography of the artist, *Memoirs of the Life of John Constable* (second edition 1845).

At least three of Constable's children become exhibitors at the Royal Academy. The most successful of these is the youngest, Lionel, whose work is sometimes mistaken for his father's.

In 1888, Constable's sole surviving child, Isabel, gifts a significant body of works to the nation. These include many oil sketches, leading to a new appreciation of Constable's art.

LIST OF EXHIBITED WORKS

Arranged first by artist and then by chronological order.

John Constable (1776–1837)

Signed carving of a windmill on two pieces of wood 1792
Wood
12·4 × 8·5 & 9·5 × 17
On loan from Colchester Borough Council: Colchester and Ipswich Museum Service

Helmingham Dell 1800
Inscribed, bottom right, 'July 23 1800 | Afternoon'
Graphite and wash on paper
53·7 × 66·5
Private Collection

The Valley of the Stour, with Langham Church in the Distance 1800
Watercolour and pen on paper
34·6 × 53·3
Victoria and Albert Museum

A Mill on the Banks of the River Stour 1802
Black chalk, charcoal and traces of red chalk on paper
25·8 × 39·7
Victoria and Albert Museum. Given by Isabel Constable, daughter of the artist

Dedham Vale from the Coombs 1802
Oil paint on canvas
43·5 × 34·4
Victoria and Albert Museum. Given by Isabel Constable

John Constable c.1799–1804
Pencil and black chalk heightened with white and red chalk
24·8 × 19·4
Lent by the National Portrait Gallery, London

Folly Bridge, Borrowdale 1806
Graphite on paper
28 × 48
Private Collection

Leatheswater (Thirlmere) 1806
Pencil and grey wash on paper
34·3 × 38·7
Victoria and Albert Museum. Given by Isabel Constable, daughter of the artist

Saddleback and part of Skiddaw 1806
Inscribed, verso, '21 Sep. 1806 Stormy Day – noon'
Pencil and watercolour on paper
7·6 × 29·5
Victoria and Albert Museum. Given by Isabel Constable, daughter of the artist

View along the River Brathay towards Skelwith Bridge 1806
Inscribed, lower left, '7 [?] Sepr. 1806'
Graphite on paper
25 × 37·8
Private Collection

View of Bowfell (Cumbria) and the Langdale Pikes from near Harry Place September 1806
Watercolour and graphite on buff wove paper
16·5 × 30·5
Philadelphia Museum of Art: Purchased with funds contributed by Boies Penrose, 1930-39-59

Bow Fell, Cumberland 1807
Oil paint on canvas
20·4 × 25·4
Clark Art Institute, Williamstown, Massachusetts, USA, gift of the Manton Art Foundation in memory of Sir Edwin and Lady Manton

The River Stour at Sunset, Looking Towards Dedham; (verso, not exhibited) *Golding Constable's House, East Bergholt* 1809–10
Oil paint on paper
25 × 19·5
Private Collection

View of Dedham from the Lane Leading from East Bergholt Church to Flatford c.1809–10
Oil on paper laid on canvas
23·9 × 30·2
Victoria and Albert Museum. Given by Isabel Constable

Dedham Vale 1810
Oil paint on canvas
12·7 × 21·5
Private Collection

Edge of a Heath by Moonlight 1810
Oil paint on canvas
15 × 25·7
Private Collection

Flatford Mill from the Lock 1810
Oil paint on beige paper mounted on canvas
19 × 24·1
Clark Art Institute, Williamstown, Massachusetts, USA, gift of the Manton Art Foundation in memory of Sir Edwin and Lady Manton

The Mill Stream c.1810
Oil paint on board
21 × 29·2
Tate. Bequeathed by Henry Vaughan 1900. N01816

The Stour 1810
Inscribed, top right, '27. Sepr. 1810'
Oil paint on canvas
23·8 × 23·5
John G. Johnson Collection, 1917, cat. 857

View toward the Rectory, East Bergholt 1810
Inscribed, vertically at top right edge, '30 Sep | 1810 | E.Bergholt | Common'
Oil paint on canvas on panel
15·6 × 24·8
John G. Johnson Collection, 1917, cat. 856

A sketch of East Bergholt from East Bergholt House 1811
Inscribed, upper left, '10 August 1811'
Oil paint on canvas
12·5 × 19·3
Private Collection

Flatford Mill from the Lock exhibited 1812
Oil paint on canvas
66 × 92·7
Private Collection

The Valley of the Stour at Sunset 1812
Inscribed, reverse, '31. Octr 1812'
Oil paint on canvas
11·8 × 28
Private Collection

The Mill Stream c.1810–14
Oil paint on canvas
71·1 × 91·5
On loan from Ipswich Borough Council: Colchester and Ipswich Museum Service

Barge-building, and *Drawings of Boat Builders* from the *1814 Sketchbook* July to October 1814
Graphite on paper in bound leather sketchbook
79 × 108
Victoria and Albert Museum. Given by Isabel Constable, daughter of the artist

Scene of Flatford Mill 1814
Oil paint on canvas
34·3 × 40·6
Private Collection

Flailing Turnip Heads, East Bergholt 1812–15
Oil paint on canvas
35·6 × 44·5
Clark Art Institute, Williamstown, Massachusetts, USA, gift of the Manton Art Foundation in memory of Sir Edwin and Lady Manton

Willy Lott's House seen over the Stour by moonlight and *Two Drawings on One Page: two cows; Stratford Hall and Stratford St Mary Church 1813–1815*, from John Constable's sketchbook 1813–15
Graphite on paper in bound sketchbook
8·9 × 12·1
Victoria and Albert Museum. Given by Isabel Constable, daughter of the artist

Boat Building near Flatford Mill 1815
Oil paint on canvas
50·8 × 61·6
Victoria and Albert Museum. Given by John Sheepshanks, 1857

Stour Valley and Dedham Church c.1815
Oil paint on canvas
55·6 × 77·8
Museum of Fine Arts, Boston. Warren Collection–William Wilkins Warren Fund

Path Towards Stratford St Mary 1816
Oil paint on paper laid on canvas
26·7 × 19·1
Private Collection

Study for 'Flatford Mill' c.1816
Pencil tracing
25·5 × 31·2
Tate. Purchased 1988. T05493

The Wheatfield exhibited 1816
Oil paint on canvas
54·6 × 78·1
Clark Art Institute, Williamstown, Massachusetts, USA, gift of the Manton Art Foundation in memory of Sir Edwin and Lady Manton

Willy Lott's House 1816
Oil paint on paper laid on canvas
19·4 × 23·8
On loan from Ipswich Borough Council: Colchester and Ipswich Museum Service

East Bergholt Church, from the south west 1815–17
Graphite on wove paper
31·8 × 24
The Courtauld, London (Samuel Courtauld Trust)

Flatford Mill ('Scene on a Navigable River') exhibited 1817
Oil paint on canvas
101·6 × 127
Tate. Bequeathed by Miss Isabel Constable as the gift of Maria Louisa, Isabel and Lionel Bicknell Constable 1888. N01273

A Cornfield c.1817
Oil paint on canvas
61·3 × 51
Tate. Accepted by HM Government in lieu of inheritance tax and allocated to Tate 2004. T11862

Dedham Lock and Mill ?exhibited 1818
Oil paint on canvas
70 × 90·5
Private Collection

Somerset House c.1819
Oil paint on paper laid on canvas
20·3 × 25·4
Lent by the Royal Academy of Arts, London

Somerset House Terrace from Waterloo Bridge c.1819
Oil paint on panel
15·6 × 18·7
Yale Center for British Art, Paul Mellon Collection

The White Horse exhibited 1819
Oil paint on canvas
131·4 × 188·3
The Frick Collection, New York, Purchase, 1943

The Opening of Waterloo Bridge, seen from Whitehall Stairs, London, 18 June 1817 c.1819–20
Oil paint on canvas
50 × 75
Daniel Katz Gallery, London

A Vivid Sunset 1820
Oil paint on paper laid on panel
8·9 × 17·3
Private Collection

Stratford Mill exhibited 1820
Oil paint on canvas
127 × 182·9
The National Gallery, London. Presented to the National Gallery under the acceptance-in-lieu procedure, 1987

Watermeadows at Salisbury 1820
Oil paint on canvas
45·7 × 55·3
Victoria and Albert Museum. Given by John Sheepshanks, 1857

A Study of High Clouds 1821
Oil paint on paper
24·1 × 29·2
Private Collection

Cloud Study, Hampstead, Tree at Right 11 September 1821
Oil paint on paper laid on board, red ground
24·1 × 29·9
Lent by the Royal Academy of Arts, London

Cloud Study 10 September 1821
Oil paint on paper laid on board
25·5 × 30
Private Collection

Cloud Study 1821
Oil paint on paper laid on board
24·8 × 30·2
Yale Center for British Art, Paul Mellon Collection

Cloud Study 1821
Oil paint on paper laid on panel
21·3 × 29·2
Yale Center for British Art, Paul Mellon Collection

Cloud Study 1821–2
Oil paint on board
11 × 16
Private Collection

Study of Clouds over a Landscape 1821–2
Oil paint on laminate cardboard mounted on canvas
24·4 × 29·5
Clark Art Institute, Williamstown, Massachusetts, USA, gift of the Manton Art Foundation in memory of Sir Edwin and Lady Manton

Cloud Study 1822
Oil paint on paper
19·8 × 32
Private Collection

Cloud Study 1822
Oil paint on paper on board
47·6 × 57·5
Tate. Presented anonymously 1952. N06065

Cloud Study 1822
Oil paint on two superimposed sheets of wove paper laid down on a third sheet
30·5 × 49
The Courtauld, London (Samuel Courtauld Trust)

Study of Clouds 30 September 1822
Oil paint on paper
48 × 59
The Ashmolean Museum, University of Oxford. Presented by Sir E. Farquhar Buzzard, Bt, 1933·

View on the Stour near Dedham exhibited 1822
Oil paint on canvas
129·5 × 188
The Huntington Library, Art Museum, and Botanical Gardens

Salisbury Cathedral from the Bishop's Grounds exhibited 1823
Oil paint on canvas
87·6 × 111·8
Victoria and Albert Museum. Given by John Sheepshanks, 1857

A Windmill near Brighton 1824
Oil paint on canvas
20·3 × 25·1
Tate. Bequeathed by George Salting 1910. N02657

Brighton Beach 12 June 1824
Oil paint on paper
12 × 29·7
Victoria and Albert Museum. Given by Isabel Constable

Brighton Beach 22 July 1824
Oil paint on paper
16·5 × 30·4
Victoria and Albert Museum. Given by Isabel Constable

The Leaping Horse exhibited 1825
Oil paint on canvas
142 × 187·3
Lent by the Royal Academy of Arts, London

A Boat Passing a Lock 1826 exhibited 1829
Oil paint on canvas
101·6 × 127
Lent by the Royal Academy of Arts, London

Chain Pier, Brighton exhibited 1827
Oil paint on canvas
127 × 182·9
Tate. Purchased 1950. N05957

Rainstorm over the Sea c.1824–28
Oil paint on paper laid on canvas
23·5 × 32·6
Lent by the Royal Academy of Arts, London

Coast Scene at Brighton, Evening 1828
Oil paint on paper
20 × 24·8
Victoria and Albert Museum. Given by Isabel Constable

Seascape Study: Boat and Stormy Sky 23 July 1828
Oil paint on paper laid on board
18·5 × 15·5
Lent by the Royal Academy of Arts, London

Dedham Vale exhibited 1828
Oil paint on canvas
144·5 × 122
National Galleries of Scotland. Purchased with the aid of The Cowan Smith Bequest and Art Fund,1944

Sketch for 'Hadleigh Castle' c.1828–9
Oil paint on canvas
122·6 × 167·3
Tate. Purchased 1935. N04810

Hadleigh Castle, The Mouth of the Thames – Morning after a Stormy Night exhibited 1829
Oil paint on canvas
121·9 × 164·5
Yale Center for British Art, Paul Mellon Collection

Letter, John Constable to John Smith, framers and dealers of 137 New Bond Street 4 April 1831
Ink on paper
18·7 × 23
Private Collection

Salisbury Cathedral from the Meadows exhibited 1831
Oil paint on canvas
153·7 × 192
Tate. Purchased by Tate with assistance from the National Lottery through the Heritage Lottery Fund, The Manton Foundation, Art Fund (with a contribution from the Wolfson Foundation) and Tate Members in partnership with Amgueddfa Cymru–National Museum Wales, Colchester and Ipswich Museums Service, National Galleries of Scotland, and The Salisbury Museum 2013. T13896

Sir Richard Steele's Cottage, Hampstead exhibited 1832
Oil paint on canvas
21 × 28·6
Yale Center for British Art, Paul Mellon Collection

The Opening of Waterloo Bridge ('Whitehall Stairs, June 18th, 1817') exhibited 1832
Oil paint on canvas
130·8 × 218
Tate. Purchased with assistance from the National Heritage Memorial Fund, the Clore Foundation, the Art Fund, the Friends of the Tate Gallery and others 1987. T04904

Fir Trees at Hampstead c.1833 ?exhibited 1834
Black lead on paper
73·4 × 58·2
Trustees of the Cecil Higgins Art Gallery (The Higgins Bedford)

Old Sarum exhibited 1834
Watercolour on paper
38 × 48·7
Victoria and Albert Museum. Bequeathed by Isabel Constable, daughter of the artist

Letter, John Constable to Miss Mary Atkinson 14 May 1835
Ink on paper
22·5 × 18·3
Private Collection

Stonehenge 1835 exhibited 1836
Watercolour on paper
38·7 × 59·1
Victoria and Albert Museum. Bequeathed by Isabel Constable, daughter of the artist

A Cottage at East Bergholt c.1836
Oil paint on canvas
87·5 × 112
National Museums Liverpool, Lady Lever Art Gallery

Hampstead Heath with a Rainbow 1836
Oil paint on canvas
50·8 × 76·2
Tate. Bequeathed by Miss Isabel Constable as the gift of Maria Louisa, Isabel and Lionel Bicknell Constable 1888. N01275

On the River Stour c.1834–7
Oil paint on canvas
60·9 × 78·7
The Phillips Collection, Washington, D.C. Acquired 1925

Stoke-by-Nayland c.1835–7
Oil paint on canvas
126 × 169
The Art Institute of Chicago, Mr. and Mrs. W. W. Kimball Collection,1922·4453

John Constable's Paint Box
Wood paint box with metal components containing hair and wood brushes, metal palette knives, a Cumberland lead pencil, a double-ended metal pencil holder (porte-crayon), glass phials of powdered pigments and dried paint, Royal Academy lecture entry tickets made of ivory, brick, lapiz lazuli
23 × 30 × 4·5
On loan from the Constable Family courtesy of Gainsborough's House

John Constable's Sketching Chair c.1800–15
Wood, cane and brass
34 × 35 × 65
On loan from the Constable Family courtesy of Gainsborough's House

Wooden palette belonging to John Constable with oil paint and mixed media
Paint on wood
40·5 × 24·5
Presented to the National Gallery in 1887 by Isabel Constable, transferred to Tate Gallery in 1953. TGA/8135/6

David Lucas after John Constable
Stoke by Neyland, Suffolk published in *English Landscape Scenery* 1830
Mezzotint on paper
14·5 × 21·9
Tate. Purchased 1985. T04040

David Lucas after John Constable
Frontispiece: East Bergholt, Suffolk published in *English Landscape Scenery* 1830–2
Mezzotint on paper
13·9 × 18·7
Tate. Purchased 1985. T03985

Joseph Mallord William Turner (1775–1851)

J.M.W. Turner c.1790
Miniature, watercolour on paper
9·5 × 7
Lent by the National Portrait Gallery, London

View of the Archbishop's Palace, Lambeth 1790
Watercolour on paper
26·7 × 38·1
Indianapolis Museum of Art at Newfields, Gift in memory of Dr. and Mrs. Hugo O. Pantzer by their children, 72·166

Travellers Passing a Ruined Abbey in Squally Weather c.1791
Watercolour on paper
18·5 × 26
Private Collection

The Rising Squall, Hot Wells, from St Vincent's Rock, Bristol exhibited 1793
Oil paint on canvas
59·8 × 74
Private Collection

(?) Thomas Girtin and J.M.W. Turner after John Robert Cozens
Tivoli, Villa of Maecenas 1794–7
Graphite and watercolour on paper
49·5 × 32·4
The Huntington Library, Art Museum, and Botanical Gardens. Gilbert Davis Collection

A Transparency: A Moss-Covered Cottage and Shed, with a Man Smoking and a Lantern 1794–5
Gouache, graphite and watercolour on paper
33·1 × 23·5
Tate. Accepted by the nation as part of the Turner Bequest 1856. D00693

A Transparency: A Moss-Covered Cottage and Shed, with a Man Smoking and a Lantern 1794–5
Watercolour on paper
33·1 × 23·5
Tate. Accepted by the nation as part of the Turner Bequest 1856. D40335

London: York House Water-Gate, Westminster, with York Buildings Waterworks 1794–5
Graphite and watercolour on paper
29·8 × 41·9
Tate. Accepted by the nation as part of the Turner Bequest 1856. D00684

Fishermen at Sea exhibited 1796
Oil paint on canvas
91·4 × 122·2
Tate. Purchased 1972. T01585

Sunset over a River from the *Wilson* sketchbook 1796–7
Gouache, graphite and watercolour on paper
Each page 11·3 × 9·3
Tate. Accepted by the nation as part of the Turner Bequest 1856. D01141, D01142

View across Derwentwater towards Skiddaw from Grange Fell from the *Tweed and Lakes* sketchbook 1797
Graphite on paper
27·4 × 37
Tate. Accepted by the nation as part of the Turner Bequest 1856. D01079

Buttermere Lake, with Part of Cromackwater, Cumberland, a Shower exhibited 1798
Oil paint on canvas
88·9 × 119·4
Tate. Accepted by the nation as part of the Turner Bequest 1856. N00460

Cader Idris: A Stream among Rocks near the Summit from the *Hereford Court* sketchbook 1798
Graphite on paper
22·9 × 33·2
Tate. Accepted by the nation as part of the Turner Bequest 1856. D01324

Morning amongst the Coniston Fells, Cumberland exhibited 1798
Oil paint on canvas
122·9 × 89·9
Tate. Accepted by the nation as part of the Turner Bequest 1856. N00461

Self-Portrait c.1799
Oil paint on canvas
74·3 × 58·4
Tate. Accepted by the nation as part of the Turner Bequest 1856. N00458

Dolbadern Castle, North Wales exhibited 1800
Oil paint on canvas
119·4 × 90·2
Lent by the Royal Academy of Arts, London

The Fifth Plague of Egypt exhibited 1800
Oil paint on canvas
129·9 × 182·9
Indianapolis Museum of Art at Newfields, Gift in memory of Evan F. Lilly, 55·24

Commentary on Titian's 'Entombment of the Dead Christ' (Inscription by Turner) and *The Entombment of the Dead Christ, after Titian* from the *Studies in the Louvre* sketchbook 1802
Graphite on paper
Each page 12·8 × 11·4
Tate. Accepted by the nation as part of the Turner Bequest 1856. D04314, D04315

Group of Peasants from the *Swiss Figures* sketchbook 1802
Graphite and watercolour on paper
Each page 19·8 × 16·3
Tate. Accepted by the nation as part of the Turner Bequest 1856. D04814, D04816

South view of Salisbury Cathedral from the Cloisters 1802
Watercolour on paper
89·8 × 72·5
Victoria and Albert Museum

The Source of the Arveyron below the Glacier du Bois and Mer de Glace 1802
Graphite, watercolour and gouache on paper
31·3 × 46·8
Tate. Accepted by the nation as part of the Turner Bequest 1856. D04613

The Passage of Mount St Gothard from the centre of Teufels Broch (Devil's Bridge) 1804
Watercolour with scraping out on paper
101 × 68
Abbot Hall, Kendal (Lakeland Arts Trust)

The Thames near Isleworth with a Double Rainbow from the *Hesperides* sketchbook 1805
Pen and ink on paper
17·1 × 26·2
Tate. Accepted by the nation as part of the Turner Bequest 1856. D05837

Sunset on the River 1805
Oil paint on mahogany veneer mounted onto wooden panel
15·6 × 18·7
Tate. Accepted by the nation as part of the Turner Bequest 1856. N02311

St Catherine's Hill, Guildford c.1807
Oil paint on mahogany veneer
36·5 × 73·7
Tate. Accepted by the nation as part of the Turner Bequest 1856. N02676

The Thames near Windsor c.1807
Oil paint on mahogany veneer mounted onto board
18·7 × 26
Tate. Accepted by the nation as part of the Turner Bequest 1856. N02305

Tree Tops and Sky, Guildford Castle, Evening c.1807
Oil paint on mahogany veneer
27·6 × 73·7
Tate. Accepted by the nation as part of the Turner Bequest 1856. N02309

Designs for Sandycombe Lodge, Twickenham from the *Sandycombe and Yorkshire* sketchbook c.1809–11
Pen and ink and graphite on paper
12·6 × 20·1
Tate. Accepted by the nation as part of the Turner Bequest 1856. D08966

The Ivy Bridge, on the River Erme at Ivybridge and *Printed Page of Coltman's 'British Itinerary'* from the *Devonshire Coast* sketchbook 1811
Graphite on paper and engraving on paper
Each page 11·7 × 7·5
Tate. Accepted by the nation as part of the Turner Bequest 1856. D08655, D08656

J.M.W. Turner and J.C. Easling
Frontispiece, published in *Liber Studiorum* 1812
Etching and mezzotint on paper
18·8 × 26·5
Tate. Presented by A. Acland Allen through the Art Fund 1925. A00912

Charles Turner after J.M.W. Turner
Norham Castle on the Tweed, (from 'Liber Studiorum', London, ([1807–19], Part XII, [pl. 57], engraver's proof, annotated by the artist) c.1815
Etching and mezzotint printed in brown ink on cream laid paper, untrimmed
17·6 × 26
Lent by the Royal Academy of Arts, London

Snow Storm: Hannibal and his Army Crossing the Alps exhibited 1812
Oil paint on canvas
146 × 237·5
Tate. Accepted by the nation as part of the Turner Bequest 1856. N00490

Study for a Picture, Possibly Related to 'Crossing the Brook' from the *Woodcock Shooting* sketchbook c.1812–13
Ink on paper
17·8 × 11
Tate. Accepted by the nation as part of the Turner Bequest 1856. D09122

Inscription by Turner: Notes from Nicholson's 'Dictionary of Practical and Theoretical Chemistry' from the *Chemistry and Apuleia* sketchbook c.1813
Graphite on paper
Each page 8·8 × 11·3
Tate. Accepted by the nation as part of the Turner Bequest 1856. D09964, D09965

Lake Avernus: Aeneas and the Cumaean Sibyl 1814
Oil paint on canvas
71·8 × 97·2
Yale Center for British Art, Paul Mellon Collection

Crossing the Brook exhibited 1815
Oil paint on canvas
193 × 165·1
Tate. Accepted by the nation as part of the Turner Bequest 1856. N00497

Dido building Carthage, or The Rise of the Carthaginian Empire exhibited 1815
Oil paint on canvas
155·5 × 230
The National Gallery, London, Turner Bequest, 1856

Crook of Lune, looking towards Hornby Castle 1816
Graphite, watercolour, bodycolour with scraping on wove paper, laid down on Japanese tissue
29·1 × 42·8
The Courtauld, London (Samuel Courtauld Trust)

Study for 'Landscape: Composition of Tivoli' c.1817
Graphite and watercolour on paper
66·7 × 100·6
Tate. Accepted by the nation as part of the Turner Bequest 1856. D17191

The Decline of the Carthaginian Empire exhibited 1817
Oil paint on canvas
170·2 × 238·8
Tate. Accepted by the nation as part of the Turner Bequest 1856. N00499

St Peter's and the Vatican from the Gardens of the Villa Barberini, Rome 1819
Gouache, graphite and watercolour on paper
23·1 × 37
Tate. Accepted by the nation as part of the Turner Bequest 1856. D16347

The Colosseum, Rome, from the West 1819
Gouache, graphite and watercolour on paper
22·9 × 36·8
Tate. Accepted by the nation as part of the Turner Bequest 1856. D16364

The Forum, Rome, Looking South-East Towards the Arch of Titus and *The Forum, Rome from the Temple of Saturn, Looking towards the Palatine* from the *Albano, Nemi, Rome* sketchbook 1819
Graphite on paper
Each page 11·3 × 18·9
Tate. Accepted by the nation as part of the Turner Bequest 1856. D15423, D15422

The Grand Canal, Venice, with the Entrance to the Cannaregio Canal beside the Church of San Geremia; Gondolas near a Low Bridge and *The Grand Canal, Venice, with the Entrance to the Cannaregio Canal beside the Church of San Geremia* from the *Milan to Venice* sketchbook 1819
Graphite on paper
Each page 11·2 × 18·5
Tate. Accepted by the nation as part of the Turner Bequest 1856. D14482, D14483

The So-Called Temple of Minerva Medica, Rome, at Sunset 1819
Gouache on paper
23 × 3·68
Tate. Accepted by the nation as part of the Turner Bequest 1856. D16362

Twelve Copies of Engravings after John 'Warwick' Smith from 'Select Views in Italy' and *Two Landscapes; one with Ducks and Swans* from the *Italian Guide Book* sketchbook c.1819
Graphite on paper
Each page 15·5 × 9·9
Tate. Accepted by the nation as part of the Turner Bequest 1856. D13969, D13970

Venice: San Giorgio Maggiore – Early Morning 1819
Watercolour on paper
22·3 × 28·7
Tate. Accepted by the nation as part of the Turner Bequest 1856. D15254

Vesuvius and the Sorrentine Peninsula from Via Posillipo 1819
Graphite and watercolour on paper
25·3 × 40·3
Tate. Accepted by the nation as part of the Turner Bequest 1856. D16106

View of the Forum, Rome, with a Rainbow 1819
Graphite, watercolour and gouache on paper
23 × 36·7
Tate. Accepted by the nation as part of the Turner Bequest 1856. D16375

Norham Castle, on the River Tweed for *Rivers of England* c.1822–3
Watercolour on paper
15·6 × 21·6
Tate. Accepted by the nation as part of the Turner Bequest 1856. D18148

The Bay of Baiae, with Apollo and the Sibyl exhibited 1823
Oil paint on canvas
145·4 × 237·5
Tate. Accepted by the nation as part of the Turner Bequest 1856. N00505

Folkestone from the Sea c.1822–4
Watercolour and gouache on paper
48·8 × 68·4
Tate. Accepted by the nation as part of the Turner Bequest 1856. D18158

A Church Spire Reflected in Water, with Storm Clouds from the *Old London Bridge* sketchbook c.1823–4
Ink wash on paper
9·8 × 16·2
Tate. Accepted by the nation as part of the Turner Bequest 1856. D17888

Stangate Creek, on the River Medway for *Rivers of England* c.1823–4
Watercolour on paper
16·2 × 24
Tate. Accepted by the nation as part of the Turner Bequest 1856. D18134

Brighthelmston, Sussex for *Picturesque Views on the Southern Coast of England* c.1824
Pencil, pen and black ink and watercolour with scratching out on paper
14·6 × 22·2
Brighton & Hove Museums

Sketch Map of the Meuse between Mouzon and Sedan; List of Distances between Northern French and Belgian Towns and *Sketch Map of the Meuse between Verdun and Mouzon; Other Notes and Sketches* from the *Rivers Meuse and Moselle* sketchbook 1824
Graphite and ink on paper
Each page 11·8 × 7·8
Tate. Accepted by the nation as part of the Turner Bequest 1856. D19552, D40727

Figures under Umbrellas in a Punt on a River, with a Rainbow from the *Thames* sketchbook c.1825
Watercolour on paper
Each page 11·4 × 18·8
Tate. Accepted by the nation as part of the Turner Bequest 1856. D18626

Shields Lighthouse c.1823–6
Watercolour on paper
23·4 × 28·3
Tate. Accepted by the nation as part of the Turner Bequest 1856. D25431

Colchester, Essex for *Picturesque Views in England and Wales* 1825–6
Graphite, watercolour, bodycolour, scraping on wove paper, now laid down on Japanese tissue
28·7 × 40·7
The Courtauld, London (Samuel Courtauld Trust)

Aldborough, Suffolk for *Picturesque Views in England and Wales* c.1826
Watercolour and gouache on paper
28·3 × 40
Tate. Bequeathed by Beresford Rimington Heaton 1940. N05236

The Lake, Petworth, Sunset; Sample Study c.1827–8
Oil paint on canvas
66 × 142·2
Tate. Accepted by the nation as part of the Turner Bequest 1856. N02701

The Sun Rising over Water c.1825–30
Watercolour on paper
33·4 × 47·2
Tate. Accepted by the nation as part of the Turner Bequest 1856. D25186

The Scarlet Sunset: A French Town on a River c.1830
Watercolour and gouache on paper
13·4 × 18·9
Tate. Accepted by the nation as part of the Turner Bequest 1856. D24666

Saint-Germain-en-Laye c.1829–31
Watercolour on paper
35·3 × 50·8
Tate. Accepted by the nation as part of the Turner Bequest 1856. D40520

Caligula's Palace and Bridge exhibited 1831
Oil paint on canvas
137·2 × 246·4
Tate. Accepted by the nation as part of the Turner Bequest 1856. N00512

Dudley, Worcestershire for *Picturesque Views in England and Wales* c.1832
Watercolour and bodycolour on paper
29·3 × 43·2
National Museums Liverpool, Lady Lever Art Gallery

Sail Boats and *Sail Boats; Margate, Kent* from the *Gravesend and Margate* sketchbook c.1832
Graphite on paper
Each page 20·6 × 8·6
Tate. Accepted by the nation as part of the Turner Bequest 1856. D27290, D27291

Staffa, Fingal's Cave exhibited 1832
Oil paint on canvas
90·8 × 121·3
Yale Center for British Art, Paul Mellon Collection

The Golden Bough exhibited 1834
Oil paint on canvas
104·1 × 163·8
Tate. Presented by Robert Vernon 1847. N00371

The Thames above Waterloo Bridge c.1830–5
Oil paint on canvas
90·5 × 121
Tate. Accepted by the nation as part of the Turner Bequest 1856. N01992

Stettin: View across the Oder to St James's and St John's Churches and the Castle and *Dresden: View on the Bank of the Elbe near the Brühl Terrace, Looking Downstream to the Bridge, with Trees in Background; English and German Phrases* from the *Copenhagen to Dresden* sketchbook 1835
Graphite on paper
Each page 8·9 × 16·2
Tate. Accepted by the nation as part of the Turner Bequest 1856. D31024, D31093

Keelmen Heaving in Coals by Moonlight exhibited 1835
Oil paint on canvas
92·3 × 122·8
National Gallery of Art, Washington, Widener Collection, 1942·9·86

Mussooree and the Dhoon from Landour 1835
Watercolour and gouache, over graphite, on off-white wove paper, edge mounted on cream wove card
12·3 × 20·2
The Art Institute of Chicago, Gift of Dorothy Braude Edinburg to the Harry B. and Bessie K. Braude Memorial Collection, 2013·1039

Rocks at Colgong (Kahalgaon) on the Ganges, Bihar, India c.1835
Pencil and watercolour heightened with bodycolour and stopping out on paper
13·3 × 20·3
Taimur Hassan Collection

The Burning of the Houses of Lords and Commons, October 16, 1834 exhibited 1835
Oil paint on canvas
92 × 123·2
The Cleveland Museum of Art, Bequest of John L. Severance 1942·647

Juliet and her Nurse exhibited 1836
Oil paint on canvas
99·2 × 123
Private Collection

The West Front of the Cathedral at Reims and *Three Sketches: The Porte de Mars, Reims; Mountains ?on the Col du Bonhomme; and Church and Mountains at Contamines above St Gervais on the Route to the Col du Bonhomme* from the *Val d'Aosta* sketchbook 1836
Graphite on paper
Each page 11·3 × 19
Tate. Accepted by the nation as part of the Turner Bequest 1856. D29163, D29164

Ancient Italy: Ovid banished from Rome exhibited 1838
Oil paint on canvas
94·6 × 125
Lent in honour of Richard Feigen by his children and grandchildren (in memoriam)

The Lagoon near Venice, at Sunset 1840
Watercolour on paper
24·4 × 30·4
Tate. Accepted by the nation as part of the Turner Bequest 1856. D32162

The Rooftops of Venice, with the Campanile of San Marco (St Mark's) and San Giorgio Maggiore, from the Hotel Europa Palazzo Giustinian) at Sunrise 1840
Watercolour on paper
19·8 × 28
Tate. Accepted by the nation as part of the Turner Bequest 1856. D35949

Snow Storm – Steam-Boat off a Harbour's Mouth exhibited 1842
Oil paint on canvas
91·4 × 121·9
Tate. Accepted by the nation as part of the Turner Bequest 1856. N00530

The Blue Rigi, Sunrise 1842
Watercolour on paper
29·7 × 45
Tate. Purchased with assistance from the National Heritage Memorial Fund, the Art Fund (with a contribution from the Wolfson Foundation and including generous support from David and Susan Gradel, and from other members of the public through the Save the Blue Rigi appeal) Tate Members and other donors 2007. T12336

Lake Lucerne: The Bay of Uri, from Brunnen c.1841–2
Watercolour on paper
24·4 × 29·9
Tate. Accepted by the nation as part of the Turner Bequest 1856. D36202

Light and Colour (Goethe's Theory) – the Morning after the Deluge – Moses Writing the Book of Genesis exhibited 1843
Oil paint on canvas
78·7 × 78·7
Tate. Accepted by the nation as part of the Turner Bequest 1856. N00532

Shade and Darkness – the Evening of the Deluge exhibited 1843
Oil paint on canvas
78·7 × 78·1
Tate. Accepted by the nation as part of the Turner Bequest 1856. N00531

St Benedetto, Looking towards Fusina exhibited 1843
Oil paint on canvas
62·2 × 92·7
Tate. Accepted by the nation as part of the Turner Bequest 1856. N00534

Storm in the St Gotthard Pass. The First Bridge above Altdorf: Sample Study c.1844–5
Graphite, watercolour and pen on paper
23·9 × 29·7
Tate. Accepted by the nation as part of the Turner Bequest 1856. D36135

A Beach ?near the Tour de Croy, Wimereux 1845
Graphite and watercolour on paper
23·7 × 33·7
Tate. Accepted by the nation as part of the Turner Bequest 1856. D35387

Landscape with Walton Bridges c.1840–50
Oil paint on canvas
87·5 × 118
Private Collection

Norham Castle, Sunrise c.1845
Oil paint on canvas
90·8 × 121·9
Tate. Accepted by the nation as part of the Turner Bequest 1856. N01981

Mercury Sent to Admonish Aeneas exhibited 1850
Oil paint on canvas
90·2 × 120·6
Tate. Accepted by the nation as part of the Turner Bequest 1856. N00553

Six Paint Brushes of various sizes belonging to J.M.W. Turner 1800–51
Wood and animal hair
33 (longest brush)
Private Collection

Leather bound travelling watercolour case belonging to J.M.W. Turner 1800–51
10 × 11·1 × 7
Private Collection

Metal paintbox belonging to J.M.W. Turner n.d.
8·9 × 33·8 × 23·6
Metal
Tate Archive, TGA 7315/6

Fishing rod belonging to Turner, made up of five sections, cased n.d.
27·2 × 89 × 7·2
Lent by the Royal Academy of Arts, London

Case Containing Two Pairs of Turner's Spectacles, his Watercolour Palette and Two Palette Knives
Wood, glass, paint and metal
3·5 × 35·5 × 29·2
Lent by the Ashmolean Museum, Oxford

Other artists

Charles West Cope (1811–1890)
J.M.W. Turner c.1828
Oil paint on card
15·9 × 13
Lent by the National Portrait Gallery, London

Ramsay Richard Reinagle (1775–1862)
John Constable c.1799
Oil paint on canvas
76·2 × 63·8
Lent by the National Portrait Gallery, London

IMAGE CREDITS

All images are © Tate unless otherwise stated below:

Abbot Hall, Kendal (Lakeland Arts Trust) NO. 77
Courtesy of the Art Institute of Chicago NO. 176
The Art Institute of Chicago/Art Resource, NY/Scala, Florence NO. 152
Courtesy of the artist PAGE 232 (both)
© Ashmolean Museum, University of Oxford NOS. 34, 113
Douglas Atfield NOS. 59, 60
Birmingham Museums Trust FIG. 13
© 2025 Museum of Fine Arts, Boston FIG. 37 NO. 95
Courtesy of Frank Bowling's Studio. Photo: Spencer Richards PAGE 230 (bottom)
Bridgeman Images NO. 182
Christie's Images/Bridgeman Images FIG. 23
Courtesy of Clark Art Institute. clarkart.edu FIG. 32 NOS. 28, 70, 71, 96, 105
Courtesy of the Cleveland Museum of Art BACK COVER (paperback), FRONT COVER (hardback), NO. 162
Colchester and Ipswich Museums Service: Colchester Borough Council Collection NO. 18
Colchester and Ipswich Museums Service: Ipswich Borough Council Collection FIGS. 18,19, 25 NOS. 74, 75
© The Courtauld/Bridgeman Images NOS. 97, 115, 117, 122
Michael Cullen, Toronto NOS. 23, 27, 64, 68, 101
© 2018 Mike Din, courtesy Serpentine FIG. 38
© The Frick Collection, New York BACK COVER (hardback), FRONT COVER (paperback), NO. 127
© Future Publishing/The Week FIG. 7
© Courtesy of the Huntington Art Museum, San Marino, California NOS. 9, 129
Courtesy of the Indianapolis Museum of Art at Newfields NOS. 4, 124
© National Museums Liverpool/Bridgeman Images NOS. 151, 175
© The National Gallery, London. All Rights Reserved FIGS. 1, 2, 11, 17, 35, 40 NOS. 125, 128
Courtesy of The Metropolitan Museum of Art, New York FIG. 28
© The Metropolitan Museum of Art/Art Resource/Scala, Florence NO. 165
© National Portrait Gallery, London FIG. 42 NOS. 3, 17, 22, 159
© National Trust Images/Tate/Andrew Dunkley and Marcus Leith FIG. 10
Courtesy of the Philadelphia Museum of Art NOS. 24, 63, 66
The Phillips Collection, Washington, D.C. NO. 174
Justin Piperger NO. 153
Michael Pollard NOS. 35, 36
Prudence Cuming Associates Ltd. NO. 149 PAGE 231
Robson90/Alamy FIG. 8
© Royal Academy of Arts, London NO. 147
© Royal Academy of Arts, London. Photo: John Hammond NOS. 107, 143, 144, 180
© Royal Academy of Arts, London. Photo: Prudence Cuming Associates Ltd. NOS. 1, 2, 37, 130
© Royal Collection Enterprises Limited 2025 | Royal Collection Trust FIG. 20
Royal Pavilion & Museums, Brighton & Hove NO. 121
With kind permission of Salisbury Museum FIG. 22
National Galleries of Scotland. Photo: Antonia Reeve NO. 32
© Sotheby's NO. 7
Tokyo Fuji Art Museum/Bridgeman Images FIG. 41
© The Trustees of the British Museum FIGS. 3, 14
Trustees of the Cecil Higgins Art Gallery (The Higgins Bedford) NO. 169
© Victoria and Albert Museum, London FIGS. 5, 26, 27 NOS. 6, 20, 21, 25, 26, 31, 62, 92, 93, 93, 116, 133, 139, 140, 145, 171, 172
Courtesy of National Gallery of Art, Washington FIG. 39 NO. 163
Courtesy of Yale Center for British Art NOS. 81, 109, 111, 132, 137, 146, 148

COPYRIGHT CREDITS

© 2025 Frank Bowling. All Rights Reserved, DACS PAGE 230 (top)
© 2025 Peter Kennard. All Rights Reserved, DACS FIG. 36
© Sondra Perry FIG. 38
© Bridget Riley 2025. All Rights Reserved PAGE 231
© George Shaw, courtesy of Anthony Wilkinson Gallery, London PAGE 233
© Emma Stibbon PAGE 232 (both)

The publishers have made every effort to trace the copyright holders of the works illustrated and apologise for any omissions or errors that may have been made.

SELECT BIBLIOGRAPHY

Both Turner and Constable are served by vast bodies of literature; writing on Turner is particularly extensive. This bibliography points towards a range of resources with an emphasis on more recent literature. Online research publications have proliferated; the catalogue of sketches, drawings and watercolours in the Turner Bequest is entirely online, for example. It is referenced below.

Turner

Karin Althaus, Nicholas Maniu, and Matthias Mühling (eds.), *Turner. Ein Lesebuch / Turner. A Reader*, exh. cat., Lenbachhaus 2024.

Anthony Bailey, *Standing in the Sun: A Life of J.M.W. Turner*, London 2013.

David Blayney Brown and Matthew Imms (eds.), *J.M.W. Turner: Sketchbooks, Drawings and Watercolours, Tate Research Publication*, 2012–2025. https://www.tate.org.uk/art/research-publications/jmw-turner/search-the-catalogue-r1176978

David Blayney Brown, Amy Concannon and Sam Smiles (eds.), *Late Turner: Painting Set Free*, exh. cat., Tate Britain, London 2014.

David Blayney Brown, Amy Concannon, Sam Smiles et. al. (eds.), *Turner's Modern World*, exh. cat., Tate Britain, London 2020.

Martin Butlin and Evelyn Joll, *The Paintings of J.M.W. Turner*, rev. edn, New Haven and London 1984.

Leo Costello, *J.M.W. Turner and the Subject of History*, Farnham 2012.

Suzanne Fagence Cooper and Richard Johns (eds.), *Ruskin, Turner and the storm cloud*, exh. cat. York Art Gallery and Abbot Hall Art Gallery, Kendal, London 2019.

Gillian Forrester, *Turner's 'Drawing Book': The Liber Studiorum*, London 1996.

John Gage (ed.), *The Collected Correspondence of J.M.W. Turner*, Oxford 1980.

Susan Grace Galassi, Ian Warrell and Joanna Sheers Seidenstein, *Turner's Modern and Ancient Ports: Passages Through Time* exh.cat., Frick Collection, New York, New Haven and London 2017.

Joyce H. Townsend, *Turner's Painting Techniques*, exh. cat., Tate Gallery, London 1993.

James Hamilton (ed.), *Turner and Italy*, exh. cat., National Gallery of Scotland, Edinburgh 2009.

Luke Herrmann, *Turner Prints: The Engraved Work of J.M.W. Turner*, Oxford 1990.

Imogen Holmes-Roe (ed.), *Turner In Light and Shade*, exh. cat., The Whitworth, Manchester 2025.

Evelyn Joll, Martin Butlin and Luke Herrmann (eds.), 2001, *The Oxford Companion to J.M.W. Turner*, Oxford 2001.

Andrew Loukes, *Artists Series: JMW Turner*, London 2024.

Kathleen Nicholson, *Turner's Classical Landscapes: Myth and Meaning*, Princton 1990.

Cecilia Powell, ed., *Turner Society News*, magazine of the Turner Society. Contents of issues published since 2000 can be seen at https://www.turnersociety.com/magazine/

Christine Riding and Richard Johns, *Turner and the Sea*, exh. cat., National Maritime Museum, London 2013.

Eric Shanes, *J.M.W. Turner: The Great Watercolours*, exh. cat., Royal Academy of Arts, London 2000.

Eric Shanes, *Young Mr Turner*, New Haven and London 2016.

Sam Smiles, *J.M.W. Turner: The Making of a Modern Artist*, Manchester 2007.

Sam Smiles, *The Late Works of J.M.W. Turner: The Artist and his Critics*, New Haven and London 2020.

Sam Smiles, *Turner and the Slave Trade*, New Haven and London, 2025.

Sam Smiles, *The Turner Book*, London and New York 2006.

David Solkin (ed.), *Turner and the Masters*, exh. cat., Tate Britain, London 2009.

Ian Warrell, with contributions by Gillian Forrester, *Turner*, New Haven and London, 2025.

Ian Warrell, *Turner's Sketchbooks*, London 2017.

Andrew Wilton, *Turner in his Time*, London 1987.

Constable

R.B. Beckett (ed.), *John Constable's Correspondence*, 6 vols., Ipswich 1962–8.

Jonathan Clarkson, *Constable*, London 2010.

Amy Concannon, 'Urban Landscape in the Age of Reform: Salisbury, Bristol, Brighton, Lambeth, c.1820–1850', unpublished PhD thesis, University of Nottingham 2018.

Amy Concannon (ed.), *In Focus: Salisbury Cathedral from the Meadows*, Tate Research, 2017, https://www.tate.org.uk/research/in-focus/salisbury-cathedral-constable

Judy Crosby Ivy, *Constable and the Critics 1802–1837*, Woodbridge 1991.

Mark Evans, *John Constable: Oil Sketches from the V&A*, London 2011.

Mark Evans, Stephen Calloway and Susan Owens, *John Constable – The Making of a Master*, exh. cat., Victoria and Albert Museum, London 2014.

Mark Evans, *Constable's Skies: Paintings and Sketches*, London 2018.

Ian Fleming-Williams, *Constable and His Drawings*, London 1990.

Gillian Forrester, *Artists Series: John Constable*, London 2024

Stephen Hebron, Conal Shields and Timothy Wilcox, *The Solitude of Mountains: Constable and the Lake District*, exh. cat., The Wordsworth Trust, Grasmere 2006.

David Hill, *Constable's English Landscape Scenery*, London 1985.

Charles Robert Leslie, *Memoirs of the Life of John Constable*, 1845; ed. J. Mayne, London 1951.

Anne Lyles (ed.), *Constable: The Great Landscapes*, exh. cat., Tate Britain, London 2006.

Anne Lyles and Matthew Hargraves (eds.), *Late Constable*, exh. cat., Royal Academy of Arts 2021

Felicity Myrone, '"No Mercenary Views"? Constable's English Landscape', *Tate Papers* 33, 2020. https://www.tate.org.uk/research/tate-papers/33/no-mercenary-views-constable-english-landscape

Leslie Parris and Ian Fleming-Williams, with Sarah Cove, *Constable*, exh. cat, Tate Gallery, London 1991.

Graham Reynolds, *The Later Paintings and Drawings of John Constable*, 2 vols, New Haven and London 1984.

Graham Reynolds, *The Early Paintings and Drawings of John Constable*, 2 vols, New Haven and London 1996.

Christine Riding (ed.), *Discover Constable and The Hay Wain*, exh. cat., National Gallery, London 2024.

Bridget Riley, 'On Works by Constable and Delacroix', in *Bridget Riley: Perceptual Abstraction*, digital exh. cat., New Haven: Yale Center for British Art 2022 https://bridget-riley.publications.britishart.yale.edu/c-and-d/

Emma Roodhouse and Caleb Howgego, *Creating Constable*, exh. cat., Colchester and Ipswich Museum Service 2021.

Michael Rosenthal, *Constable: The Painter and his Landscape*, New Haven and London 1983.

Michael Rosenthal, *Constable*, London 1987.

Charles S. Rhyne, *John Constable. Toward A Complete Chronology*, 1991 https://www.reed.edu/art/rhyne/papers/jc_chronology.pdf

Conal Shields et al., *John Constable*, exh. cat., Teylers Museum, Haarlem 2020–1.

John Thornes, *John Constable's Skies: A Fusion of Art and Science*, Birmingham 1999.

Iris Wien, 'The Opaque Nature of John Constable's Naturalism', in *Canadian Art Review*, 41, no.2 (2016), pp.44–61.

Iris Wien, 'Constable and the Dynamics of Vision', *Tate Papers* 33, 2020. https://www.tate.org.uk/research/tate-papers/33/constable-dynamics-vision

Turner and Constable

David Blayney Brown, "Fire and Water": Turner and Constable at the Royal Academy, 1831", *Tate Papers* 33, 2020. https://www.tate.org.uk/research/tate-papers/33/fire-water-turner-constable-royal-academy

Ronald Paulson, *Literary Landscape: Turner and Constable*, New Haven and London 1982.

Maurice Davies and Annette Wickham, *"He Has Been Here and Fired a Gun": Turner, Constable and the Royal Academy* London, 2019.

Nicola Moorby, *Turner and Constable: Art, Life and Landscape*, New Haven and London 2025.

Michael Rosenthal and Anne Lyles, *Turner & Constable: Sketching from Nature*, London 2013.

Contextual Literature

John Barrell, *The Dark Side of the Landscape: the rural poor in English painting 1730–1840*, Cambridge 1983.

Ann Bermingham, *Landscape and Ideology: The English Rustic Tradition, 1740–1860*, New Haven and London 1989.

David Blayney Brown, *Romanticism*, London 2001.

Stephen Daniels, *Fields of Vision: Landscape Imagery and National Identity in England and the United States*, Cambridge 1992.

Mark Hallett, Sarah Victoria Turner and Jessica Feather (eds.), *The Royal Academy of Arts Summer Exhibition: A Chronicle, 1769–2018*, Paul Mellon Centre for Studies in British Art, London 2018. https://chronicle250.com/

James Hamilton, *A Strange Business: Making Art and Money in Nineteenth-Century Britain*, London 2014.

Andrew Hemingway, *Landscape Imagery and Urban Culture in early nineteenth-century Britain*, Cambridge 1992.

Nigel Llewellyn and Christine Riding (eds.), The Art of the Sublime, Tate Research Publication, January 2013, https://www.tate.org.uk/art/research-publications/the-sublime/christine-riding-and-nigel-llewellyn-british-art-and-the-sublime-r1109418

Martin Myrone, *Making the Modern Artist: Culture, Class and Art-Educational Opportunity in Romantic Britain*, London 2020.

Patrick Noon, David Blayney Brown, Christine Riding et al., *Constable to Delacroix: British Art and the French Romantics 1820–1840*, exh. cat., Tate Britain, London 2003.

Susan Owens, *Spirit of Place: Artists, Writers and the British Landscape*, London 2020.

David Solkin (ed.), *Art on the Line: The Royal Academy Exhibitions at Somerset House 1780–1836*, exh. cat., Courtauld Institute of Art, London 2001.

David Solkin, *Art in Britain 1660–1815*, New Haven and London 2015.

INDEX

Page numbers in *italic* type refer to reproduction.

R

S

T

SUPPORTING TATE

Tate relies on the generosity of supporters – individuals, foundations, companies and public sector sources – to enable us to deliver our programme of activities, both on and off our gallery sites. This support is essential for Tate to acquire works of art for the collection, run education, outreach and exhibition programmes, care for the collection in storage and enable art to be displayed, both digitally and physically, inside and outside Tate.

Donations, no matter the size, are gratefully received, either to support particular areas of interest, or to contribute to general activity costs. Please contact us at:

Development Office
Tate
Millbank
London SW1P 4RG
T: +44 (0) 20 7887 8945
www.tate.org.uk/join-support

Corporate Partnerships
Corporate Partners support world-renowned programmes – ranging from exhibitions, performances, and annual artist commissions to education, research, conservation, digital innovation, sustainability initiatives and more. These partnerships are truly collaborative, enabling brand alignment, creative campaigns, engaging events, and unique opportunities that connect businesses, employees, and audiences with the arts.

Corporate Membership
Corporate Membership offers companies opportunities for corporate entertaining and the chance for a wide variety of employee benefits. These include special private views, special access to paying exhibitions, out-of-hours visits and tours and invitations to events.

Legacies
Leaving a gift in your Will allows Tate to confidently plan for the future. Legacy gifts of all sizes have and will continue to have a transformative impact in celebrating how art is made and seen around the world today and caring for the national collection.

All legacy gifts are free of inheritance tax and can take the form of a residual share of an estate, a specific cash sum, or an item of property such as a work of art. Letting us know of your intentions allows us to thank you for your future gift now and to invite you to join The 1897 Circle, a group of supporters who have pledged future gifts to Tate.

Offers in lieu of tax
Donate a work of art or cultural artefact of outstanding importance to a public collection and settle your Inheritance Tax or Estate Duty liabilities. It can be made a condition of the offer that the work of art is allocated to Tate.

Tate Members
Tate Members enjoy unlimited free admission throughout the year to all exhibitions at Tate, as well as several other benefits such as exclusive use of our Members' Rooms and a free annual subscription to Tate Etc. Members support a range of programmes and projects in our galleries in London, Liverpool and St Ives

Tate Patrons
Tate Patrons share a passion for art and are committed to supporting Tate on an annual basis. Patrons help enable the acquisition of works across Tate's broad collecting remit and the staging of major exhibitions in the galleries. They also give their support to vital conservation, learning and research projects. The scheme provides a forum for Patrons to share their interest in art and meet curators, artists and one another through a regular programme of events.

Charity Details
The Tate Gallery is an exempt charity; the Museums & Galleries Act 1992 added the Tate Gallery to the list of exempt charities defined in the 1960 Charities Act. Tate Foundation, an independent charity that supports the work of Tate, is a registered charity (number 1085314).

Tate Americas Foundation
Tate Americas Foundation is an independent charity based in New York that supports the work of Tate in the United Kingdom. It receives full tax-exempt status from the IRS under section 501(c)(3) allowing United States taxpayers to receive tax deductions on gifts towards annual membership programmes, exhibitions, learning and capital projects.

https://tateamericas.org/

This information is correct as of the beginning of July 2025

Tate Britain Donors to the Centenary Development Campaign
The Annenberg Foundation
The Asprey Family Charitable Foundation
Ron Beller and Jennifer Moses
Alex and Angela Bernstein
The Charlotte Bonham-Carter Charitable Trust
Lauren and Mark Booth
Ivor Braka
The CHK Charitable Trust
The Clore Duffield Foundation
Sadie Coles
Giles and Sonia Coode-Adams
Alan Cristea
Thomas Dane
The D'Oyly Carte Charitable Trust
Sir Harry and Lady Djanogly
The Dulverton Trust
Maurice and Janet Dwek
Friends of the Tate Gallery
Bob and Kate Gavron
Sir Paul Getty, KBE
Alan Gibbs
Mr and Mrs Edward Gilhuly
Helyn and Ralph Goldenberg
Nicholas and Judith Goodison
Richard and Odile Grogan
Pehr and Christina Gyllenhammar
The National Lottery Heritage Fund
Jay Jopling
Mr and Mrs Karpidas
Howard and Lynda Karshan
Peter and Maria Kellner
Madeleine Kleinwort
Brian and Lesley Knox
The Kresge Foundation
Catherine and Pierre Lagrange
Mr and Mrs Ulf G Linden
Ruth and Stuart Lipton
Anders and Ulla Ljungh
Lloyds TSB Foundation for England and Wales
David and Pauline Mann-Vogelpoel
Sir Edwin and Lady Manton
Nick and Annette Mason
Viviane and James Mayor
Anthony and Deirdre Montagu
Sir Peter and Lady Osborne
Maureen Paley
William A Palmer
Mr Frederik Paulsen
The Pet Shop Boys
The P F Charitable Trust
The Polizzi Charitable Trust
John and Jill Ritblat
Barrie and Emmanuel Roman
Lord and Lady Sainsbury of Preston Candover
Mrs Coral Samuel, CBE
David and Sophie Shalit
Mr and Mrs Sven Skarendahl
Pauline Denyer-Smith and Paul Smith
Mr and Mrs Nicholas Stanley
The Jack Steinberg Foundation
Charlotte Stevenson
Tate Gallery Centenary Gala
Carter and Mary Thacher
Mr and Mrs John L Thornton
The Trusthouse Charitable Foundation
David and Emma Verey
Dinah Verey
Clodagh and Leslie Waddington
Gordon D Watson
Mr and Mrs Anthony Weldon
The Duke of Westminster, OBE TD DL
Sam Whitbread
Mr and Mrs Stephen Wilberding
Michael S Wilson
The Wolfson Foundation
and those who wish to remain anonymous

Donors to The Tate Britain Millbank Project
Alan Cristea Gallery
The Deborah Loeb Brice Foundation
Clore Duffield Foundation
Sir Harry and Lady Djanogly
The Gatsby Charitable Foundation
J Paul Getty Jr Charitable Trust
The National Lottery Heritage Fund
The Hiscox Foundation
James and Clare Kirkman
The Linbury Trust and The Monument Trust
The Manton Foundation
The Mayor Gallery
Ronald and Rita McAulay
Simon and Midge Palley
PF Charitable Trust
The Porter Foundation
The Dr Mortimer and Theresa Sackler Foundation
Mrs Coral Samuel, CBE
Jake and Hélène Marie Shafran
Tate Members
The Taylor Family Foundation
Sir David and Lady Verey
Sir Siegmund Warburg's Voluntary Settlement
Garfield Weston Foundation
The Wolfson Foundation
and those who wish to remain anonymous

Tate Britain and Tate Modern Benefactors and Major Donors

A4 Arts Foundation
Abakanowicz Arts and Culture Charitable Foundation
Ab-Anbar Gallery
Walid Abu-Suud
acb Galéria, Budapest
Shane Akeroyd
Shane Akeroyd Acquisition Fund for British Art
AKO Foundation
Princess Alia Al-Senussi
Jim Amberson
The Ampersand Foundation
Gregory Annenberg Weingarten, GRoW @ Annenberg
The Anson Charitable Trust
Antenna Space
Art Fund
Art Mentor Foundation Lucerne
Artangel
ARTIST ROOMS Foundation with funds provided by Agnes Gund
Arts and Humanities Research Council
Arts Council England
ARTscapades
Asymmetry
Celia and Edward Atkin, CBE
Mr Bishoy Azmy and Mrs Mary Habib
Abigail and Joseph Baratta
Rosa Barba
James Bartos
Perihan Bassatne
Beckett-Fonden
Corinne Bellow Charity
Allison Berg
The David Bermant Foundation
Blavatnik Family Foundation
Anna Boghiguian
The Charlotte Bonham-Carter Charitable Trust
Charles Booth-Clibborn
Sophie Bowness
Bowness Family Foundation
Ivor Braka, in honour of Maria Balshaw
The William Brake Foundation
Deborah Loeb Brice Foundation
British Council
Britton Family Foundation
Rory and Elizabeth Brooks Foundation
The John Browne Charitable Trust
Victoria Bruhn
The Bukhman Foundation
Beatrice Bulgari | In Between Art Film
The Estate of Andrew Burt
John Bute
Andrew Cameron, AM and Cathy Cameron
Carlos/Ishikawa
The Estate of Lady Caro (Sheila Girling)
The Estate of Sylvia Carter
John Caudwell, London
Richard Chang
Lisa Kim and Eunu Chun
Clore Duffield Foundation
Cockayne Grants for the Arts, a Donor Advised Fund, held at The Prism Charitable Trust
Contemporary Art Society
Michael Corman and Kevin Fink
The Cosman Keller Art and Music Trust
Jill Cowan
Crankstart Foundation
Creative Australia
Stefan Cross KC (Hon)
Tang Da Wu
Danish Arts Foundation
Dimitris Daskalopoulos
Harry and Lana David
Tara Davies
The Estate of Professor Martyn Davis
François-Xavier and Natasha de Mallmann
Tiqui Atencio Demirdjian and Ago Demirdjian
Department for Culture, Media and Sports
The Destina Foundation
Dr Alan Diamond, OBE
Harry A Dickinson
The Dinan Family Foundation
D'Lan Contemporary
Peter Doig, in honour of Sir Nicholas Serota
Joe and Marie Donnelly
Joe and Marie Donnelly Acquisition Fund
Yan Du
The Peter Dubens Family Foundation
The Easton Foundation
Lonti Ebers
Maryam and Edward Eisler
Ibrahim El-Salahi through Vigo Gallery
Endeavor
European Commission
An Jo Fermon
Margaret and Richard Finch
The Finnis Scott Foundation
Wendy Fisher
Wendy Fisher and the Kirsh Foundation
Lt Commander Paul Fletcher
Ford Foundation
Eric and Louise Franck
Helen Frankenthaler Foundation
Freelands Foundation
Amanda and Glenn Fuhrman
Fuhrman Family Foundation
Gagosian
Larry Gagosian
Yufeng (Andy) Gao and Peter Wei
Mala Gaonkar
Gates Foundation
Heloisa Genish
Raghida Ghandour Al Rahim
Carole Gibbons
The Hon HMT Gibson's Charity Trust
Peter Gidal
Gauri Gill
Gillian Jason Gallery
Golden Bottle Trust
Nicholas and Judith Goodison's Charitable Settlement
Lydia and Manfred Gorvy
Nicholas Leonidas Goulandris
The Granville-Grossman Bequest
Grenfell Foundation
David and Louise Grob
Lorin Gu
Wang Guangyi
The Estate of Ron Gulley
Agnes Gund
Anthony and Sandra Gutman
Guy and Alexandra Halamish
Paul Hamlyn Foundation
Kemal Has and Tala Cingillioglu
Hauser & Wirth
Esther and Fritz Heer Zacek
The Drue Heinz Charitable Trust
The Estate of Barbara Hepworth
Charles Hett
Galerie Max Hetzler
Damien Hirst
David Hockney
Stanley and Valery Jacqueline Honeyman
Alexandra Howell
Huo Family Foundation
Yasuharu Ishikawa, Japanese Friends of Tate
Ivor Braka Limited
Pamela J Joyner and Alfred J Giuffrida
Elizabeth and William Kahane
Kahng Foundation
Rasheed Kamel
Judi Kaufman and Arthur Rubin
KD Collection
Mike Kelley Foundation for the Arts
Peter and Maria Kellner
Ellsworth Kelly and Jack Shear, in honor of Sir Nicholas Serota
Dr Martin Kenig
Balraj Khanna
Henrik Kielland, Hartfield Foundation
David Killick
Charles and Jean Kim
Jack Kirkland
The Klimt Charitable Trust
Ministry of Culture, Sports and Tourism of Korea, Korea Arts Management Service, and the grant program Fund for Korean Art Abroad
Korean Cultural Centre UK
Josef Koudelka
Gladys Krieble Delmas Foundation
Peter Kulloi
Andreas Kurtz and Ulrike Kurtz
Lachaise Foundation
The Lagrange Family
Kourosh Larizadeh and Luis Pardo
The Leche Trust
Mr Edward Lee
Edward Lee in memory of Agnès Lee
Dana and Gregory Lee
Kyungsoon Lee and Jungwoo Shon
Miyoung Lee and Neil Simpkins
Wendy Lee
Lefevre Fine Art Ltd. and the Corcoran Family
Robert Lehman Foundation
Lehmann Maupin, New York, Seoul, and London
The Christian Levett Collection
Ruben Levi
Marjorie and Michael Levine
Lévy Gorvy
Ken Li
The Linbury Trust
James Lindon
Dina Liu
Loewe
Andrew and Amanda Love
Sarah Lucas
Peter Lukeš
LUMA Foundation
Asbjorn Lunde Foundation, Inc.
The Lunder Foundation
Lyndsey Ingram Ltd
The Peter Magnone Foundation
The Estate of Sir Edwin Manton
The Manton Foundation
Massimo Marcucci
Steve Martin and Anne Stringfield
Theodore Matoff
Lord McAlpine of West Green
Paul Mellon Centre for Studies in British Art
Mellon Foundation
Joel Meyerowitz
Elizabeth Miller
Victoria Miro
Fondazione Mohsen Vaziri Moghaddam
Mondriaan Fund
Henry Moore Foundation
Simon Mordant AO and Catriona Mordant AM
Hariklia Moundreas
MTArt Agency
Oscar Murillo
The Murray Family
National Heritage Memorial Fund
The National Lottery Heritage Fund
Mark Nelson
New Carlsberg Foundation
Simon Nixon and family
Christl Novakovic
Fondation Opale
Open Hand
Oranges and Sardines Foundation
Barbro Osher Pro Suecia Foundation
Gretel Packer, AM
Midge and Simon Palley
Irene Panagopoulos
Véronique Parke
Jorge M. and Darlene Pérez
Catherine Petitgas
Estate of Rosemary Ann Phelps
Estate of Murray Ashley Pickering
Pilgrim Trust
Anna Plowden Trust and The Clothworkers' Foundation
The Polish Cultural Institute in London
Donald Porteous
Professor Richard Portes, CBE, FBA
Portrait Fund
David W Posnett, OBE
Mr Gilberto and Mrs Daniela Pozzi
PPOW Gallery
Jacqueline Pruskin
Michael Rakowitz
Julia and Hans Rausing
Alice Rawsthorn
Rennie Collection, Vancouver
András Réti
The Bridget Riley Art Foundation
Danny and Manizeh Rimer
Valeria Rodnyansky
Su Rogers
The Rokos Family
Barrie and Emmanuel Roman
Roman Family Collection
The Estate of William George Roper
Rosenberg Memorial Fund
Rothschild Foundation
Roland Rudd
Sadie Coles HQ
The Estate of Simon Sainsbury
Gillian and Simon Salama-Caro
The Estate of Martin T Salmon
Rajeeb and Nadia Samdani
Sammlung Hoffmann Gbr
Fanny Sanín Legacy Project
Charlotte Santo Domingo
Bjorn Saven, CBE
Peter Saville, CBE
Clare Scherrer
The Estate of Barbara Schofield
Marnie Schreiber
The Bern Schwartz Family Foundation
Selma Selman
Rose and Alfredo Setubal
Jake and Hélène Marie Shafran
Eleanor and Francis Shen
Simon Sicko
The Estate of Gurminder Sikand
Sikkema Jenkins & Co.
Veronica Slater
Matthew Slotover and Emily King
The Estate of David Smith
Wendy Smith
Southwark Council
The Estate of Unity Spencer
Sprüth Magers
Norah and Norman Stone Collection (Tate Americas Foundation)
Mercedes and Ian Stoutzker, CBE
STPI – Creative Workshop & Gallery, Singapore
John J Studzinski, CBE
Maria and Malek Sukkar
Mitra Tabrizian
Tabula Rasa Gallery
Tamares Real Estate Holdings Inc. in collaboration with the Zabludowicz Collection
Faisal Tamer
Lorraine Tarabay
Tate 1897 Circle
Tate Africa Acquisitions Committee
Tate Americas Foundation
Tate Asia Pacific Acquisitions Committee
Tate Central and Eastern Europe Plus Acquisitions Committee
Tate European Collection Circle
Tate International Council

Tate Latin American Acquisitions Committee
Tate Members
Tate Middle East North Africa Acquisitions Committee
Tate North American Acquisitions Committee
Tate Patrons
Tate Photography Acquisitions Committee
Tate South Asia Acquisitions Committee
Ellen and Bill Taubman on behalf of the A. Alfred Taubman Foundation
Tavolozza Foundation
Ralph Tawil
Ryan Taylor
Teiger Foundation
Terra Foundation for American Art
The Nicholas Themans Trust
The Estate of Michael Thurman
Barry Townsley, CBE
Teresa Tsai
Luc Tuymans
The Tymure Collection
The Uggla Family Foundation
UK Research & Innovation
Yoonjung and Edouard Ullmo
Vadehra Art Gallery
The Family of Maryn Varbanov
David and Emma Verey Charitable Trust
Paulo Vieira
Marie-Louise von Motesiczky Charitable Trust
Amanda and John Waldron
Margaret Wang
The Andy Warhol Foundation for the Visual Arts
Westminster City Council
White Cube
Michael and Jane Wilson, CBE
Joan Winchell
Marcin and Izabela Wiszniewski
Laurie Wolfert
The Lord Leonard and Lady Estelle Wolfson Foundation
Yang Won Sun Foundation
Terry Wu
Zhang Xiaogang
Cherry Jing Xu
Cherry Xu / CHERUBY
Salle Yoo and Jeff Gray
Hee Yoon
The Estate of Tony Young
The Zabludowicz Collection
Mr Zahid and Ms Binladin
Qiao Zhibing, in honour of Gregor Muir
and those who wish to remain anonymous

Platinum Patrons
Eric Abraham and Sigrid Rausing
Walid Abu-Suud
Mr Shane Akeroyd
Celia and Edward Atkin, CBE
Mr Bishoy Azmy and Mrs Mary Habib
The Hon Ms A Bagri
Alex Beard
Beecroft Charitable Trust
John Booth
Rory and Elizabeth Brooks
The John Browne Charitable Trust
Karen Cawthorn Argenio
XiaoMeng Cheng
Beth and Michele Colocci
Ms Miel de Botton
Pascale Decaux
Sophie Diedrichs
Sima Ganwani Ved
David Herro
Mr Yan Huo
Mr Phillip Hylander (Chair) and Ms Ellie Harrison-Read
Judy Idriss
Natascha Jakobs-Linssen
François Jourdain and Verity Soper-Jourdain
Peter Kellner
Ms Matilda Liu
Mr M J Margulies
Svetlana Marich
Suling Mead
Omenaa Mensah
Mary Moore
Batia and Idan Ofer
Simon Palley
Alexander V Petalas
Jan-Christoph Peters
Mr Gilberto and Mrs Daniela Pozzi
Frances Reynolds
Sybil Robson Orr
Jake and Hélène Marie Shafran
Andrée Shore
Grey Skipwith
Maria and Malek Sukkar
Aizel Trudel
Michael and Jane Wilson, CBE
Lady Wolfson of Marylebone
Mr Mingfang Yu
Jessica Zirinis
and those who wish to remain anonymous

Gold Patrons
Ms Mila Askarova
Lars Bane
Mica Bowman
Angela Choon
David Corbell
Harry G David
Émilie De Pauw
Valentina Drouin
Edwin Fox Foundation
Amanda Gowing
Alexander Green
Olga Grishina
Jennifer Klein
Judith Licht
Bobby Molavi
Asta Paulauskaite
Mathew Prichard
Valerie Rademacher
Almine Ruiz-Picasso
Michael Sacher
Tatiana Salomon
Lord Snowdon
Jennifer N C Stahl
Kimberly Stallvik
Matthew Steinmetz
Yuko Takano
Tobias van Gils
Manuela and Iwan Wirth
Chizuko Yashiro
and those who wish to remain anonymous

Silver Patrons
Cameron Amiri
The Anson Charitable Trust
Toby and Kate Anstruther
Hannah Armstrong
James Arnell
Aspect Charitable Trust
Peter Barham
Mrs Jane Barker
Oliver Barker
Victoria Barnsley, OBE
Jim Bartos
Mr Richard Bazzaz
Ms Anne Berthoud
Madeleine Bessborough
Sara Blonstein
David Blood and Beth Bisso
Harry and Fabiana Bond
Caroline Boseley
Viscountess Bridgeman
Basia Briggs
Laura and William Burlington
Michael Burrell
Mrs Marlene Burston
Mrs Aisha Cahn
Mark Capelle
Timothy and Elizabeth Capon
Liza Cawthorn
Roger Cazalet
Lord and Lady Charles Cecil
Shuqi Chen
Claudia Cheng
David Cheng
Dr Peter Chocian
John F Clappier
Frank Cohen
Mrs Jane Collins
Terrence Collis
Mr and Mrs Oliver Colman
Giles and Sonia Coode-Adams
Pilar Corrias
Tommaso Corvi-Mora
Kathleen Crook and James Penturn
Averil Curci
Sir Howard Davies
Robert Deans
Anne Chantal Defay Sheridan
Mr Damon and The Hon Mrs de Laszlo
Pier-Luigi del Renzio
Mr Robert Devereux
Mira Dimitrova
Lord and Lady Egremont
Jake Elsley
John Erle-Drax
Paul Ettlinger
Stuart and Margaret Evans
Leonie Fallstrom
Ernest Fasanya
Mr and Mrs Laurent Ganem
Mala Gaonkar
Thibault Geffrin
Elena Geuna
Hugh Gibson
Davide and Azzurra Giordano
Mr Mark Glatman
Ms Emily Goldner and Mr Michael Humphries
Kate Gordon
Dimitri Goulandris
Martyn Gregory
Richard and Odile Grogan
Professor John Gruzelier
Jill Hackel Zarzycki
Mark Harris
The Heller Family
Drew Hess
Soo Hitchin
Muriel Hoffner
James Holland-Hibbert
Lady Hollick, OBE
Holtermann Fine Art
Jeff Horne
Ben Houston
Lucca Hue-Williams
Mr Haydn John
Mike Jones
Jay Jopling
Mrs Brenda Josephs
Tracey Josephs
Andrew Kalman
Dr Martin Kenig
Mr and Mrs Simon Keswick
Dr Rahma Khazam
Neha Khosla
Mrs Mae Khouri
Gerald Kidd
David Killick
David P Korn
Kowitz Trust
Mr and Mrs Herbert Kretzmer
Norman Leinster
John Lellouche
Tali Levy Morley
Yimeng Lin
Mr Gilbert Lloyd
Mrs Elizabeth Louis
Alison Loyd
Eykyn Maclean
Nadia Mahmud
Ayesha Mahomed
Yuanyuan and Alan Malek
Audrey Mandela
Marsh Christian Trust
Mazzoleni Art
Professor Rob Melville
Melissa Merryweather
Shahid Miah
Maloles Mira costa Antignac
Victoria Miro
Mrs William Morrison
Ms Deborah Norton
Reine and Boris Okuliar
Julian Opie
Pilar Ordovás
Luz Maria Osorio
Leslie Osterling
Gulsah Ozturk
Maureen Paley
Sir Michael Palin
Mrs Kathrine Palmer
Anthea Peers
Frederique Pierre-Pierre
Mary Pollock
Professor Richard Portes, CBE, FBA
Augusta Prado
Susan Prevezer, QC
Mr and Mrs Ryan Prince
Chelsea Purvis
Emily Quesada
Ivetta Rabinovich
Adriana Citlali Ramirez-Perez
Irith Rappaport
Frankie Rossi
Mr David V Rouch
Mr Charles Roxburgh
Mr Alex Sainsbury and Ms Elinor Jansz
Mrs Cara Schulze
Melissa Sesana
The Hon Richard Sharp
Sadie Sherman
James Shoreland
Shakthi Shrima
Neville Shulman, CBE
Oliwia Siem
Tammy Smulders
Violeta Sofia
Louise Spence
Brunhild Stelter
Mr James Swartz
The Sylvie Fleming Collection
Elaine Thomas
Ian Tollett
Misa Toshinari
Karen Townshend
Mr Philippos Tsangrides
Ceyda Ulasan
Celine Valligny
Christian von Sanden
Andreas Vourecas-Petalas
Audrey Wallrock
Linda Waterhouse
Offer Waterman
Miss Cheyenne Westphal
Professor Sarah Whatmore
Mr Douglas Woolf
Adam Wurr
Phoebe and Arthur Yates
Clara Zevi
and those who wish to remain anonymous

Young Patrons
Elizabeth Abati
Nubia Abdellatif
Khaled Abu-Suud
Omar Abu-Suud
Tarek Abu-Suud
Nadine Adams
Maia Adelia
Estelle Akeroyd Hunt
Tasneem Aliewi
HRH Princess Alia Al-Senussi
Marc Anani-Isaac (Co-Chair, Young Patrons Ambassador Group)

Mihai Anca
Aurore E Ankarcrona Hennessey
Gulru Arvas
Miss Olivia Aubry
Menel Baran
Nico Barawid
Isabel Bardawil
Yulia Barinskaya
Katrina Beechey
Eleni Beveratou
Dr Maya Beyhan
Benedetta Buitoni
Matthew Charlton
Ariel Chen
Tatiana Cheneviere
Vicky Cheng
Maria Chitu
Nowk Choe
Tatiana Clarke
Caroline Cole
Thamara Corm
Stephanie Courmont
Bella M Coxon
Huguette Craggs
Douglas Cuadrado
Helena Czernecka
Eduardo Da Costa Catoquessa
Robert Dalmeida
Henry Danowski
Countess Charlotte de la Rochefoucauld
Michele Di Robilant
Sophie Dickson
Claudia Diers
Eleanor Dilloway
Ioana Dobrin
Indira Dyussebayeva
Christina Eberli
Lara Eckes-Chantré
Alexandra Economou
Jennifer Ellis
Kate Fensterstock
Jane and Richard Found
Sylvain Fresia
Brian Fu
Ayo Gabriel
Mr Andreas Gegner
Stefano Giulietti
Pierre-Antoine Godefroy
Javier Godino de Frutos
Elissa Goldstone
Frederick Gordts
Andrea Grigsby
Laura Grinberga
Kitty Hadaway
Patrick Hennessey
Max Edouard Friedrich Hetzler
Elise Huff
Lola Hylander
Faye Jiang
Daniel Jones
Soyeon Jung
Jasmine Kailey
Miss Meruyert Kaliyeva
Melih Kaplan
Helen Kempthorne
Joe Kennedy
Ms Chloe Kinsman
Daria Kocherova
Daria Kravchenko
Alma Kuntermann
Lamb Gallery
Giulia Lecchini
Alexander Lewis (Co-Chair, Young Patrons Ambassador Group)
Samuel Lewis
Alexandra Lindsay
Phoebe Liu
Tasmin Love
Alica Maclean
Giulia Magnani
Ms Sonia Mak
Mr Jean-David Malat
Fiorenzo Manganiello
Mary McNicholas
Stefan Miesner
Laura Moses
Tilak Nathwani
Jingxiu Niu
Ikenna Obiekwe
Sheena Ohnemus
Cuppy Otedola
Periklis Panagopoulos
Pietro Pantalani
Divya Pathak
Alonso Peña Alfaro
Christopher Pullen
Miss Yasmine Rahimzadeh
Briana Redzeposki
Alexander Santema
Sinclair Schäfer
Simonetta Scheidt
Sneha Shah
Wei Shi
Joshua Silver
Louise Simpson
Amar Singh
Mandeep Singh
Nancy Singh
Zoe Karafylakis Sperling
Ilgin Surel
Molly Susman
Valeria Szabó Facchin
Evangeline Tawil
Ryan Taylor
Lorna Tiller
Mr Giancarlo Trinca
Dr Dimitrios Tsivrikos
Nicholas Walker
Hanna Wentz
Thomas Williams
Fergus Wiltshire
Benedict Winkler
Edward Worthy
HRH Princess Eugenie of York
Brian Jia Qing Yue
Tiffany Zhang
Marcelo Osvaldo Zimmler
Alexandra Zirinis
Lukas M Zueger-Knecht
and those who wish to remain anonymous

International Council Members
Aigboje Aig-Imoukhuede
Abdelmonem Bin Eisa Alserkal
Mrs Anita Belgiorno-Nettis, AM
Nicolas Berggruen
Jo and Tom Bloxham
Pontus Bonnier
Paloma Botín O'Shea
Mr William Bowness, AO
Ivor Braka
The Deborah Loeb Brice Foundation
Rory and Elizabeth Brooks
Andrew Cameron, AM
Christina Chandris
Pierre Chen, Yageo Foundation, Taiwan
Evan Chow
Mr Euisun Chung and Mrs Geesun Chung
Mr Dimitris Daskalopoulos, OBE
Ms Miel de Botton
Tiqui Atencio Demirdjian and Ago Demirdjian
Robert and Renée Drake
Mrs Olga Dreesmann
Füsun and Faruk Eczacibasi
Désiré Feuerle and Sara Puig
Kathrine Fredriksen
Fuhrman Family Foundation
Hideaki Fukutake, Chairman of Fukutake Foundation
The Gaudio Family Foundation
Mrs Yassmin Ghandehari
Lydia and Manfred Gorvy
Bianca and Noam Gottesman
Mimi and Peter Haas Fund
Mrs Susan Hayden
Ms Ydessa Hendeles
Ms Katrin Henkel
Marlene Hess and James D Zirin
Ms Maja Hoffmann
Sangita Jindal
Dakis and Lietta Joannou
Simon Johnson
HRH Princess Firyal of Jordan
Maya Junger
Pamela Kramlich
Andreas Kurtz (Co-Vice Chair) and Ulrike Kurtz
Ms Catherine Lagrange
Mr Pierre Lagrange
Edward Lee
Seo Hyun Lee
Jacqueline and Marc Leland
Christian Levett
Elizabeth Lewin
Li Lin
Ms Dina Liu
Aarti Lohia
Andrew J Love
Suling Mead
Naomi Milgrom, AC
Audrey and David Mirvish, Toronto
Professor Cav. Simon Mordant, AO (Co-Vice Chair) and Catriona Mordant, AM
Mrs Yoshiko Mori
Gael Neeson
Dr Mark Nelson
Hélène Nguyen-Ban
Mr and Mrs Takeo Obayashi
Mr and Mrs Eyal Ofer
Andrea and José Olympio Pereira
Hideyuki Osawa
Ms Gretel Packer, AM
Midge Palley, OBE
Irene Panagopoulos
Véronique Parke
Yana and Stephen Peel
Catherine Petitgas
Ana Pinho
Lekha Poddar
Miss Dee Poon
Smita Prabhakar
Ms Miuccia Prada and Mr Patrizio Bertelli
Patrizia Sandretto Re Rebaudengo and Agostino Re Rebaudengo
Frances Reynolds
Michael Ringier
Erica Roberts
Sybil Robson Orr and Matthew Orr
Ms Hanneli M Rupert
E. Melisa Sabanci Tapan
Rajeeb and Nadia Samdani
Alejandro Santo Domingo
Tarana and Tarun Sawhney
Czaee Shah
Dasha Shenkman, OBE
Jon and Kimberly Shirley
Poonam Bhagat Shroff
Uli and Rita Sigg
John J Studzinski, CBE
Maria and Malek Sukkar
Ed Tang
Lorraine Tarabay
Dr Andreas Teoh
Richard and Maggie Tsai
Rachel Verghis
Paulo A W Vieira (Chair)
Mercedes Vilardell
Robert and Felicity Waley-Cohen
Diana Widmaier Picasso
Christen and Derek Wilson
Mrs Sylvie Winckler
The Hon Dame Janet Wolfson de Botton, DBE
Poju Zabludowicz and Anita Zabludowicz, OBE
and those who wish to remain anonymous

Africa Acquisitions Committee
Kola Aina
John Basnage de Beauval
The Beachum Charitable Fund
Mrs Kavita Chellaram
Vikram S Chellaram
Harry G David
Lana de Beer David (Co-Chair)
Reem El Roubi
Farah Fakhri
Amanda Gowing
Kent Kelley
Samallie Kiyingi
Caro Macdonald
Dale Mathias
Omenaa Mensah
Valentina Mintah & Kwame Mintah
Wissam and Hiba Nesr Art Foundation
Charlotte L Newman
Obinna Onyeagoro, Jr.
Emile Stipp
Jorge Fernández Vidal
Mercedes Vilardell
Mr Hasnaine Yavarhoussen
and those who wish to remain anonymous

Asia-Pacific Acquisitions Committee
Shane Akeroyd
Jim Amberson
Director of Arario Museum
Arndt Foundation, Matthias Arndt
Mrs Victoria Bruhn
Lito and Kim Camacho
Mrs Marisa Chearavanont
Jonathan Cheung
Punn Chirakiti
Lawrence Chu
Yan Du
Lonti Ebers
Mrs Yassmin Ghandehari
Nathaniel P Gunawan
Esther Heer-Zacek
Philippa Hornby
Shareen Khattar Harrison (Co-Chair)
Ms Ellie Lai
Alan Lau (Co-Chair)
Wendy Lee
Alexander Lewis
Ms Dina Liu
M Art Foundation, WU Meng
Yoonwhe Leo Moon & Young Ran Yun
Francis and Eleanor Shen
Kazunari Shirai
Raksha Sriram
Arif Suherman
Mr Patrick Sun
Timothy Roy Tan
Rudy Tseng
Janice S Y Wang
Margaret M Wang
Cherry Xu
Lingnan Xu
Yang Bin
Jenny Yeh
Dayea Yeon
Dan Yu
ZHI Foundation
Fernando Zobel de Ayala
and those who wish to remain anonymous

Central and Eastern Europe Plus Acquisitions Committee
Árpád Balázs and Andrea Dénes
Francise Hsin-Wen Chang
Artur Dela
Anna Filipowicz
Gabriela Gantenbein
Jan Hammer (Co-Chair)
Patrick Hessel
Erki Kilu
Kasia Kulczyk
Peter Kulloi
Vita Liberte

Peter Lukeš
Danica and Eduard Maták
Luba Michailova
Christl Novakovic
Linda Péter
Florin Pogonaru
Donald Porteous
The Pudil Family Foundation
Ivana (Co-Chair) & Martin Ridler
Valeria Rodnyansky
Robert Runták
Ovidiu Şandor
Simon Sicko
The Terziev Family
Attila G Vizi
The Vujičić Collection
Mr Jānis Zuzāns
and those who wish to remain anonymous

Latin American Acquisitions Committee
Monica and Robert Aguirre
María Amalia León
Giselle Araoz and Mirko Stiglich
Juan Ball
Viviana Barberi
Celia Birbragher
Countess Nicole Brachetti Peretti
Estrellita Brodsky
Teresa A Bulgheroni
Simone Coscarelli Parma
HSH the Prince Pierre d'Arenberg
Tiqui Atencio Demirdjian
Isabela Mosconi Katchuian Galvao
Heloisa Genish (Co-Chair)
Jonathan Grad
Barbara Hemmerle Gollust
Julian Iragorri
Marjorie and Michael Levine
José Luis Lorenzo
Denise and Felipe Nahas Mattar
Susan McDonald
Gabriela Mendoza
Lisa Miller
Alexandra Mollof
Veronica Nutting
Mario Pacheco
William Palley
Silvia Paz-Illobre
Jorge and Darlene Pérez
Catherine Petitgas
Claudio Federico Porcel
Thibault Poutrel
Paulina Rider Wilhelmsen
Erica Roberts (Co-Chair)
Alin Ryan Lobo
Fernanda Vilela
and those who wish to remain anonymous

Middle East North Africa Acquisitions Committee
Nassib Abou-Khalil
Dr Hana Abu-Hassan
Walid Abu-Suud
H.E. Huda Alkhamis-Kanoo, Founder of the Abu Dhabi Music & Arts Foundation
Nora Hamza Alkholi
HRH Princess Alia Al-Senussi
Abdelmonem Bin Eisa Alserkal
Marwan T Assaf
Perihan Bassatne
Mrs Elisabeth Bauchet-Bouhlal
Nissreen Darawish
Maryam Eisler
Ola Al Dajani and Hisham El-Khazindar
Dr Farhad Farjam
Hossein and Dalia Fateh
Ranya Ghandour
Raghida Ghandour Al Rahim
Mareva Grabowski
Mary Habib and Bishoy Azmy
Yasser Hashem
Judy Idriss
Fady Jameel
Rasheed Kamel
Mr Elie Khouri
Maha Kutay
Faisal Mahmood
Shabin and Nadir Mohamed
Hashem Montasser
Maria (Co-Chair) and Malek Sukkar
Faisal Tamer (Co-Chair)
Mr Zahid and Ms Binladin
Roxane Zand
and those who wish to remain anonymous

North American Acquisitions Committee
Abigail Baratta (Co-Chair)
Dr Eraka Bath
Allison Berg
Tyson Boudreaux
Alla Broeksmit
Rachel Carr Goulding
Lewis Cheng
Dillon Cohen
Michael Corman and Kevin Fink
Marcia Dunn
Lisa Garrison
Joshua Greenberg
Samer Hamade
Jennifer Hawks Djawadi
Craig Hollingworth
David Israel
Peter Kahng
Patricia Kaneb Kelly
Christian Keesee
Charles Kim
Ekaterina Klim
Dana and Greg Lee
Marc J Lee and Armando Abounce
Miyoung Lee
Marjorie and Michael Levine
James Lindon
Matt McClure
Samantha McManus
Gregory R Miller
Sami Mnaymneh
Shabin and Nadir Mohamed
Yana Peel
Holly Peterson
Laura Roberson Fisch
Stephanie Robinson
Leo Rogath
Susan Sawyers
Ralph Segreti and Richard Follows
Ayesha Selden
Francis and Eleanor Shen
Kimberly and Jon Shirley
Ann Tang Chiu
Amelie von Wedel
George Wells (Co-Chair)
Christen Wilson and Derek Wilson
Debi Wisch
and those who wish to remain anonymous

Photography Acquisitions Committee
Ryan Allen
Nicholas Barker
Cynthia Lewis Beck
Pierre Brahm
Elizabeth (Co-Chair) and Rory Brooks
Lisa and Mark Caputo
Lucy and Andrew Darwin
Sophie Diedrichs
David Fitzsimons
Natascha Jakobs-Linssen
Elizabeth and William Kahane
Jack Kirkland (Co-Chair)
Nathalie Lambert-Besseddik and Cyril Besseddik
Suling Mead
Nicholas Stanley
Maria and Malek Sukkar
Tia Tanna
Michael and Jane Wilson, CBE
and those who wish to remain anonymous

South Asia Acquisitions Committee
Dr Arani and Mrs Shumita Bose
Surabhi K Chaudhary, Unnati Foundation
Krishna Choudhary
Akshay Chudasama
Jai Danani
Taimur Hassan
Blanca Hirani
Shruti Hora
Dr Amin Jaffer
Neha and Sumedh Jaiswal
Sonam Kapoor Ahuja
Deepanjana Klein
Simran Kotak and Vir Kotak
Ms Aarti Lohia
Hiroo and Haresh Motwani
Moklasur Rahman Pinto
Alka and Amit Ruia
Isheta Salgaocar
Nadia Samdani, MBE
Rajeeb Samdani (Co-Chair)
Sally Eugenia Schwartz
Minal Vazirani (Co-Chair)
Damian Vesey
Manuela and Iwan Wirth
and those who wish to remain anonymous

The 1897 Circle
Lynn Allan
Maureen Bampton
Ms Anne Berthoud
The Estate of Marilyn Bild
James Birch
David and Deborah Botten
Geoff Bradbury
Charles Brett
Eloise and Francis Charlton
Alex Davids
Sally Davies
Jonathan Davis
Sean Dissington
Ronnie Duncan
Ian Fletcher
Mr and Mrs R.N. and M.C. Fry
Richard Hamilton
L.A. Hynes
John Iddon
The Estate of Brian and Pauline John
Vanessa Koster-Goodliffe
Isa Levy
Miss Vikki Louise-Fabian
Tony Miller
Sonya Newell-Smith
Miss Susan Novell and Mr Graham Smith
Martin Owen
Ruth Rattenbury
Simon Reynolds
Dianne Roberts
Ann M Smith
Alan Sprince
Deborah Stern
Jennifer Toynbee-Holmes
Audrey Wallrock
Rosie Watts
The Estate of Professor Brian Whitton
Kay and Dyson Wilkes
Simon Casimir Wilson
The Estate of Andrew Woodd
The Estate of Mr and Mrs Zilberberg
and those who wish to remain anonymous

European Collection Circle
Mandy Cawthorn Argenio
Trustees of the Gaudio Family Foundation (UK) Limited
Nicholas Leonidas Goulandris
Maya Junger
Edward Lee (Chair)
Monica Reitan
Danny Rimer, OBE
Stichting Hartwig Foundation
and those who wish to remain anonymous

Tate Britain and Tate Modern Corporate Partners
Access Holdings Plc
Anthropic
Arcis Capital
Audio Gold
Bank of America
Bloomberg
Bottega Veneta
Burberry
Chanel
Coronation Group Ltd
Deutsche Bank UK
EY
Gucci
Handpicked Wines
House Of Arras
Hyundai Motor Company
La Caixa
Little Greene
Lockton
Louis Vuitton
Minirig
The National Gallery of Australia & Wesfarmers Arts
PJT Partners
PPL
Sotheby's
Sony Music Entertainment Japan
SWATCH
Uniqlo
Van Cleef & Arpels
White & Case LLP
and those who wish to remain anonymous

Tate Britain and Tate Modern Corporate Members
Aspen Insurance Group
Clifford Chance LLP
Dalkia
Dentsu UK Limited
DLA Piper UK LLP
FGS Global (UK) Limited
Heidrick & Struggles UK Ltd
JATO Dynamics Ltd
Korea Tourism Organization
Lygon Group
Maples and Calder
Morgan Stanley UK Limited
Slaughter and May
STATE STREET BANK AND TRUST- London Branch
Tata Consultancy Services Limited
T. Rowe Price
and those who wish to remain anonymous

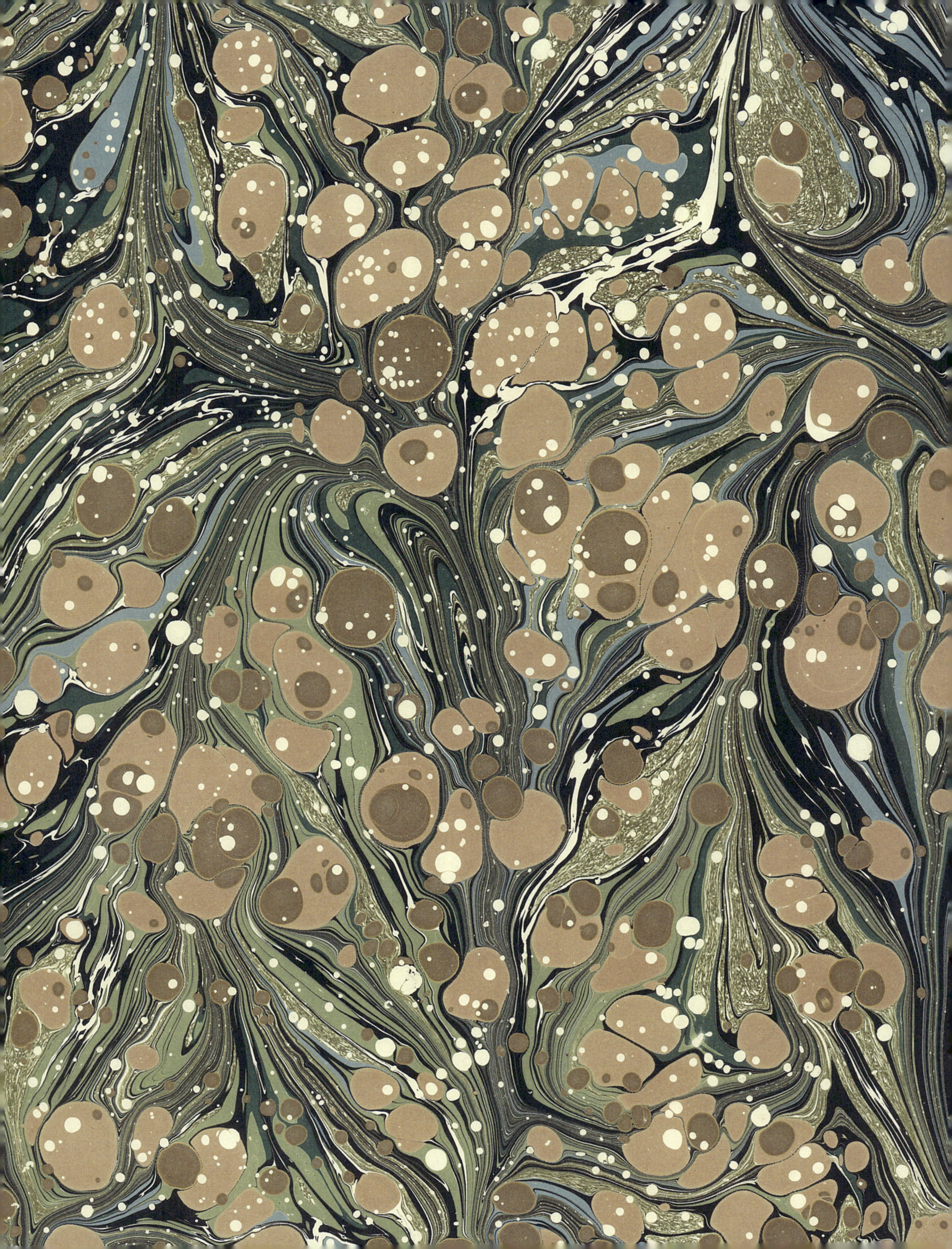

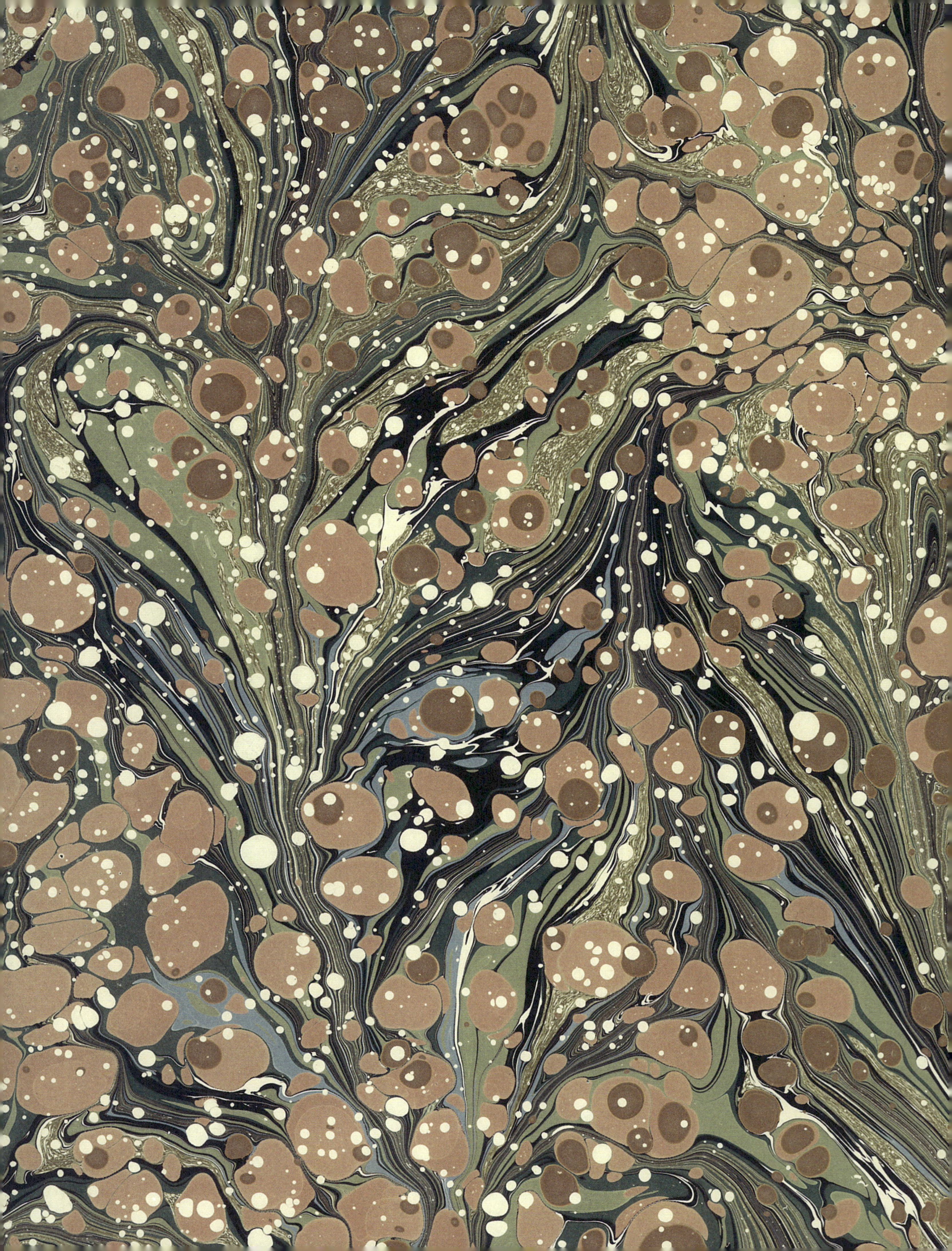